Lecture Notes in Computer Science 5614

Commenced Publication in 1973
Founding and Former Series Editors:
Gerhard Goos, Juris Hartmanis, and Jan van Leeuwen

T0189412

Constantine Stephanidis (Ed.)

Universal Access in Human-Computer Interaction

Addressing Diversity

5th International Conference, UAHCI 2009
Held as Part of HCI International 2009
San Diego, CA, USA, July 19-24, 2009
Proceedings, Part I

 Springer

Volume Editor

Constantine Stephanidis
Foundation for Research and Technology - Hellas
Institute of Computer Science
N. Plastira 100, Vassilika Vouton
70013, Heraklion, Crete, Greece
and
University of Crete
Department of Computer Science
Crete, Greece
E-mail: cs@ics.forth.gr

CR Subject Classification (1998): H.5, I.3, I.2.10, I.4, I.5

LNCS Sublibrary: SL 2 – Programming and Software Engineering

ISSN   0302-9743

springer.com

© Springer-Verlag Berlin Heidelberg 2009

Typesetting: Camera-ready by author, data conversion by Scientific Publishing Services, Chennai, India
Printed on acid-free paper   SPIN: 12704774   06/3180   5 4 3 2 1 0

Foreword

The 13th International Conference on Human–Computer Interaction, HCI International 2009, was held in San Diego, California, USA, July 19–24, 2009, jointly with the Symposium on Human Interface (Japan) 2009, the 8th International Conference on Engineering Psychology and Cognitive Ergonomics, the 5th International Conference on Universal Access in Human–Computer Interaction, the Third International Conference on Virtual and Mixed Reality, the Third International Conference on Internationalization, Design and Global Development, the Third International Conference on Online Communities and Social Computing, the 5th International Conference on Augmented Cognition, the Second International Conference on Digital Human Modeling, and the First International Conference on Human Centered Design.

A total of 4,348 individuals from academia, research institutes, industry and governmental agencies from 73 countries submitted contributions, and 1,397 papers that were judged to be of high scientific quality were included in the program. These papers address the latest research and development efforts and highlight the human aspects of the design and use of computing systems. The papers accepted for presentation thoroughly cover the entire field of human–computer interaction, addressing major advances in knowledge and effective use of computers in a variety of application areas.

This volume, edited by Constantine Stephanidis, contains papers in the thematic area of Universal Access in Human–Computer Interaction, addressing the following major topics:

- Interaction and Support for People with Sensory Impairments
- Older Users and Technology
- Interaction and Support for People with Cognitive Impairments
- Design Knowledge and Approaches for Accessibility and Universal Access

The remaining volumes of the HCI International 2009 proceedings are:

- Volume 1, LNCS 5610, Human–Computer Interaction—New Trends (Part I), edited by Julie A. Jacko
- Volume 2, LNCS 5611, Human–Computer Interaction—Novel Interaction Methods and Techniques (Part II), edited by Julie A. Jacko
- Volume 3, LNCS 5612, Human–Computer Interaction—Ambient, Ubiquitous and Intelligent Interaction (Part III), edited by Julie A. Jacko
- Volume 4, LNCS 5613, Human–Computer Interaction—Interacting in Various Application Domains (Part IV), edited by Julie A. Jacko
- Volume 6, LNCS 5615, Universal Access in Human–Computer Interaction—Intelligent and Ubiquitous Interaction Environments (Part II), edited by Constantine Stephanidis

- Volume 7, LNCS 5616, Universal Access in Human–Computer Interaction—Applications and Services (Part III), edited by Constantine Stephanidis
- Volume 8, LNCS 5617, Human Interface and the Management of Information—Designing Information Environments (Part I), edited by Michael J. Smith and Gavriel Salvendy
- Volume 9, LNCS 5618, Human Interface and the Management of Information—Information and Interaction (Part II), edited by Gavriel Salvendy and Michael J. Smith
- Volume 10, LNCS 5619, Human Centered Design, edited by Masaaki Kurosu
- Volume 11, LNCS 5620, Digital Human Modeling, edited by Vincent G. Duffy
- Volume 12, LNCS 5621, Online Communities and Social Computing, edited by A. Ant Ozok and Panayiotis Zaphiris
- Volume 13, LNCS 5622, Virtual and Mixed Reality, edited by Randall Shumaker
- Volume 14, LNCS 5623, Internationalization, Design and Global Development, edited by Nuray Aykin
- Volume 15, LNCS 5624, Ergonomics and Health Aspects of Work with Computers, edited by Ben-Tzion Karsh
- Volume 16, LNAI 5638, The Foundations of Augmented Cognition: Neuroergonomics and Operational Neuroscience, edited by Dylan Schmorrow, Ivy Estabrooke and Marc Grootjen
- Volume 17, LNAI 5639, Engineering Psychology and Cognitive Ergonomics, edited by Don Harris

I would like to thank the Program Chairs and the members of the Program Boards of all thematic areas, listed below, for their contribution to the highest scientific quality and the overall success of HCI International 2009.

Ergonomics and Health Aspects of Work with Computers

Program Chair: Ben-Tzion Karsh

Arne Aarås, Norway
Pascale Carayon, USA
Barbara G.F. Cohen, USA
Wolfgang Fricsdorf, Germany
John Gosbee, USA
Martin Helander, Singapore
Ed Israelski, USA
Waldemar Karwowski, USA
Peter Kern, Germany
Danuta Koradecka, Poland
Kari Lindström, Finland

Holger Luczak, Germany
Aura C. Matias, Philippines
Kyung (Ken) Park, Korea
Michelle M. Robertson, USA
Michelle L. Rogers, USA
Steven L. Sauter, USA
Dominique L. Scapin, France
Naomi Swanson, USA
Peter Vink, The Netherlands
John Wilson, UK
Teresa Zayas-Cabán, USA

Human Interface and the Management of Information

Program Chair: Michael J. Smith

Gunilla Bradley, Sweden
Hans-Jörg Bullinger, Germany
Alan Chan, Hong Kong
Klaus-Peter Fähnrich, Germany
Michitaka Hirose, Japan
Jhilmil Jain, USA
Yasufumi Kume, Japan
Mark Lehto, USA
Fiona Fui-Hoon Nah, USA
Shogo Nishida, Japan
Robert Proctor, USA
Youngho Rhee, Korea

Anxo Cereijo Roibás, UK
Katsunori Shimohara, Japan
Dieter Spath, Germany
Tsutomu Tabe, Japan
Alvaro D. Taveira, USA
Kim-Phuong L. Vu, USA
Tomio Watanabe, Japan
Sakae Yamamoto, Japan
Hidekazu Yoshikawa, Japan
Li Zheng, P.R. China
Bernhard Zimolong, Germany

Human–Computer Interaction

Program Chair: Julie A. Jacko

Sebastiano Bagnara, Italy
Sherry Y. Chen, UK
Marvin J. Dainoff, USA
Jianming Dong, USA
John Eklund, Australia
Xiaowen Fang, USA
Ayse Gurses, USA
Vicki L. Hanson, UK
Sheue-Ling Hwang, Taiwan
Wonil Hwang, Korea
Yong Gu Ji, Korea
Steven Landry, USA

Gitte Lindgaard, Canada
Chen Ling, USA
Yan Liu, USA
Chang S. Nam, USA
Celestine A. Ntuen, USA
Philippe Palanque, France
P.L. Patrick Rau, P.R. China
Ling Rothrock, USA
Guangfeng Song, USA
Steffen Staab, Germany
Wan Chul Yoon, Korea
Wenli Zhu, P.R. China

Engineering Psychology and Cognitive Ergonomics

Program Chair: Don Harris

Guy A. Boy, USA
John Huddlestone, UK
Kenji Itoh, Japan
Hung-Sying Jing, Taiwan
Ron Laughery, USA
Wen-Chin Li, Taiwan
James T. Luxhøj, USA

Nicolas Marmaras, Greece
Sundaram Narayanan, USA
Mark A. Neerincx, The Netherlands
Jan M. Noyes, UK
Kjell Ohlsson, Sweden
Axel Schulte, Germany
Sarah C. Sharples, UK

Neville A. Stanton, UK
Xianghong Sun, P.R. China
Andrew Thatcher, South Africa

Matthew J.W. Thomas, Australia
Mark Young, UK

Universal Access in Human–Computer Interaction

Program Chair: Constantine Stephanidis

Julio Abascal, Spain
Ray Adams, UK
Elisabeth André, Germany
Margherita Antona, Greece
Chieko Asakawa, Japan
Christian Bühler, Germany
Noelle Carbonell, France
Jerzy Charytonowicz, Poland
Pier Luigi Emiliani, Italy
Michael Fairhurst, UK
Dimitris Grammenos, Greece
Andreas Holzinger, Austria
Arthur I. Karshmer, USA
Simeon Keates, Denmark
Georgios Kouroupetroglou, Greece
Sri Kurniawan, USA

Patrick M. Langdon, UK
Seongil Lee, Korea
Zhengjie Liu, P.R. China
Klaus Miesenberger, Austria
Helen Petrie, UK
Michael Pieper, Germany
Anthony Savidis, Greece
Andrew Sears, USA
Christian Stary, Austria
Hirotada Ueda, Japan
Jean Vanderdonckt, Belgium
Gregg C. Vanderheiden, USA
Gerhard Weber, Germany
Harald Weber, Germany
Toshiki Yamaoka, Japan
Panayiotis Zaphiris, UK

Virtual and Mixed Reality

Program Chair: Randall Shumaker

Pat Banerjee, USA
Mark Billinghurst, New Zealand
Charles E. Hughes, USA
David Kaber, USA
Hirokazu Kato, Japan
Robert S. Kennedy, USA
Young J. Kim, Korea
Ben Lawson, USA

Gordon M. Mair, UK
Miguel A. Otaduy, Switzerland
David Pratt, UK
Albert "Skip" Rizzo, USA
Lawrence Rosenblum, USA
Dieter Schmalstieg, Austria
Dylan Schmorrow, USA
Mark Wiederhold, USA

Internationalization, Design and Global Development

Program Chair: Nuray Aykin

Michael L. Best, USA
Ram Bishu, USA
Alan Chan, Hong Kong
Andy M. Dearden, UK

Susan M. Dray, USA
Vanessa Evers, The Netherlands
Paul Fu, USA
Emilie Gould, USA

Sung H. Han, Korea
Veikko Ikonen, Finland
Esin Kiris, USA
Masaaki Kurosu, Japan
Apala Lahiri Chavan, USA
James R. Lewis, USA
Ann Light, UK
James J.W. Lin, USA
Rungtai Lin, Taiwan
Zhengjie Liu, P.R. China
Aaron Marcus, USA
Allen E. Milewski, USA

Elizabeth D. Mynatt, USA
Oguzhan Ozcan, Turkey
Girish Prabhu, India
Kerstin Röse, Germany
Eunice Ratna Sari, Indonesia
Supriya Singh, Australia
Christian Sturm, Spain
Adi Tedjasaputra, Singapore
Kentaro Toyama, India
Alvin W. Yeo, Malaysia
Chen Zhao, P.R. China
Wei Zhou, P.R. China

Online Communities and Social Computing

Program Chairs: A. Ant Ozok, Panayiotis Zaphiris

Chadia N. Abras, USA
Chee Siang Ang, UK
Amy Bruckman, USA
Peter Day, UK
Fiorella De Cindio, Italy
Michael Gurstein, Canada
Tom Horan, USA
Anita Komlodi, USA
Piet A.M. Kommers, The Netherlands
Jonathan Lazar, USA
Stefanie Lindstaedt, Austria

Gabriele Meiselwitz, USA
Hideyuki Nakanishi, Japan
Anthony F. Norcio, USA
Jennifer Preece, USA
Elaine M. Raybourn, USA
Douglas Schuler, USA
Gilson Schwartz, Brazil
Sergei Stafeev, Russia
Charalambos Vrasidas, Cyprus
Cheng-Yen Wang, Taiwan

Augmented Cognition

Program Chair: Dylan D. Schmorrow

Andy Bellenkes, USA
Andrew Belyavin, UK
Joseph Cohn, USA
Martha E. Crosby, USA
Tjerk de Greef, The Netherlands
Blair Dickson, UK
Traci Downs, USA
Julie Drexler, USA
Ivy Estabrooke, USA
Cali Fidopiastis, USA
Chris Forsythe, USA
Wai Tat Fu, USA
Henry Girolamo, USA

Marc Grootjen, The Netherlands
Taro Kanno, Japan
Wilhelm E. Kincses, Germany
David Kobus, USA
Santosh Mathan, USA
Rob Matthews, Australia
Dennis McBride, USA
Robert McCann, USA
Jeff Morrison, USA
Eric Muth, USA
Mark A. Neerincx, The Netherlands
Denise Nicholson, USA
Glenn Osga, USA

Dennis Proffitt, USA
Leah Reeves, USA
Mike Russo, USA
Kay Stanney, USA
Roy Stripling, USA
Mike Swetnam, USA
Rob Taylor, UK

Maria L.Thomas, USA
Peter-Paul van Maanen, The Netherlands
Karl van Orden, USA
Roman Vilimek, Germany
Glenn Wilson, USA
Thorsten Zander, Germany

Digital Human Modeling

Program Chair: Vincent G. Duffy

Karim Abdel-Malek, USA
Thomas J. Armstrong, USA
Norm Badler, USA
Kathryn Cormican, Ireland
Afzal Godil, USA
Ravindra Goonetilleke, Hong Kong
Anand Gramopadhye, USA
Sung H. Han, Korea
Lars Hanson, Sweden
Pheng Ann Heng, Hong Kong
Tianzi Jiang, P.R. China

Kang Li, USA
Zhizhong Li, P.R. China
Timo J. Määttä, Finland
Woojin Park, USA
Matthew Parkinson, USA
Jim Potvin, Canada
Rajesh Subramanian, USA
Xuguang Wang, France
John F. Wiechel, USA
Jingzhou (James) Yang, USA
Xiu-gan Yuan, P.R. China

Human Centered Design

Program Chair: Masaaki Kurosu

Gerhard Fischer, USA
Tom Gross, Germany
Naotake Hirasawa, Japan
Yasuhiro Horibe, Japan
Minna Isomursu, Finland
Mitsuhiko Karashima, Japan
Tadashi Kobayashi, Japan

Kun-Pyo Lee, Korea
Loïc Martínez-Normand, Spain
Dominique L. Scapin, France
Haruhiko Urokohara, Japan
Gerrit C. van der Veer, The Netherlands
Kazuhiko Yamazaki, Japan

In addition to the members of the Program Boards above, I also wish to thank the following volunteer external reviewers: Gavin Lew from the USA, Daniel Su from the UK, and Ilia Adami, Ioannis Basdekis, Yannis Georgalis, Panagiotis Karampelas, Iosif Klironomos, Alexandros Mourouzis, and Stavroula Ntoa from Greece.

This conference could not have been possible without the continuous support and advice of the Conference Scientific Advisor, Prof. Gavriel Salvendy, as well as the dedicated work and outstanding efforts of the Communications Chair and Editor of HCI International News, Abbas Moallem.

I would also like to thank for their contribution toward the organization of the HCI International 2009 conference the members of the Human–Computer Interaction Laboratory of ICS-FORTH, and in particular Margherita Antona, George Paparoulis, Maria Pitsoulaki, Stavroula Ntoa, and Maria Bouhli.

Constantine Stephanidis

HCI International 2011

The 14th International Conference on Human–Computer Interaction, HCI International 2011, will be held jointly with the affiliated conferences in the summer of 2011. It will cover a broad spectrum of themes related to human–computer interaction, including theoretical issues, methods, tools, processes and case studies in HCI design, as well as novel interaction techniques, interfaces and applications. The proceedings will be published by Springer. More information about the topics, as well as the venue and dates of the conference, will be announced through the HCI International Conference series website: http://www.hci-international.org/

General Chair
Professor Constantine Stephanidis
University of Crete and ICS-FORTH
Heraklion, Crete, Greece
Email: cs@ics.forth.gr

Table of Contents

Part II: Older Users and Technology

Part III: Interaction and Support for People with Cognitive Impairments

Part IV: Design Knowledge and Approaches for Accessibility and Universal Access

Part I

Interaction and Support for People with Sensory Impairments

Technology Support for Analyzing User Interactions to Create User-Centered Interactions

Dirk Burkhardt, Kawa Nazemi, Nadeem Bhatti, and Christoph Hornung

Fraunhofer Institute for Computer Graphics Research (IGD), Fraunhoferstrasse 5,
64283 Darmstadt, Germany
{Dirk.Burkhardt,Kawa.Nazemi,Nadeem.Bhatti,
Christoph.Hornung}@igd.fraunhofer.de

Abstract. Alternative interaction devices become more important in the communication between users and computers. Parallel graphical User Interfaces underlay a continuous development and research. But today does no adequate connection exist between these both aspects. So if a developer wants to provide an alternative access over more intuitive interaction devices, he has to implement this interaction-possibility on his own by regarding the users perception. A better way to avoid this time-consuming development-process is presented in this paper. This method can easy implement by a developer and users get the possibility to interact on intuitive way.

Keywords: User-Centered Interactions, Human-Computer-Interaction, gesture recognition.

1 Introduction

Alternative interaction devices get nowadays more importance in the communication between human and computer. Different game pad developer established such interaction devices with a more intuitive way of usage. One of the most common devices is the WiiMote from Nintendo. The benefit of such devices is the support and orientation on humans' behavior and acting. Nintendo Wii's success is an indicator for the trend and the necessity of such devices. The low cost controller play a key role for its mass circulation.

Another trend is the research and development of Graphical User Interfaces (GUI). Innovative GUIs visualize information, for example by using semantic technologies on the web and, herewith, reduce the cognitive overload of the processes for users, which require gathering information.

In the last years, both processes, the research on graphical visualizations as well as the research in alternative interaction techniques, have underlain a rapidly development. But, nevertheless, up to now there exists no adequate connection between them. One of the goals of this paper is to develop a method for using alternative and more intuitive interaction-devices e.g. the WiiMote in web-based graphical visualization. Within the range of this development, there are further aspects, which have to be regarded. Intuitive use is a subjective perception of a person [1], so the user's perceptions must flow into the development-process. But the considering of the users individual perception is time-consuming, which the most developers cannot or does not want to offer.

C. Stephanidis (Ed.): Universal Access in HCI, Part I, HCII 2009, LNCS 5614, pp. 3–12, 2009.
© Springer-Verlag Berlin Heidelberg 2009

In this paper a technique will be presented, how these problems can easily be solved. The technique allows developers to use alternative controllers on an easy way and provide them an easy to use and easy to implement programming interface, so that they can pre-configure it for the use in web-applications. To realize a user-centered design, the concept will orientate on the Process Model of User-Centered Software Design Process [1]. Later a user is able to extend the pre-configured interface by his personal perceptive actions, if it is necessary. For evaluation issues the system is developed for Nintendo's Wii.

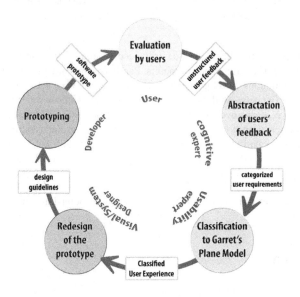

Fig. 1. Process Model of User-Centered Software Design [1]

2 Related Work

Concerning adaptive user interfaces there exist several approaches. The most common research there is focused on gesture recognition techniques or the specific implementation of such techniques on new input device. Less weighted are surrounding aspects like culture specific interactions or the support from developers of user-centered applications. The relation between a cultural background and how it influences the execution of a gesture is described in [2]. Rehm et al. concentrate on the districting of the properties power, speed and spatial extend with which they classify the different cultures. During a recognition-process these properties will help to identify a gesture. By the use of low-level gestures e.g. a movement to the right sight such influences can neglect, because the shape and at the end a gesture for specific common instructions within applications is similar.

2.1 WiiMote-Based Recognition Systems

In our prototypical implementation Wii-Controller is used. Two most prominent libraries Wiinput [3] and WiiGee [4] exist for Wii-Controller to realize a gesture-recognition. Both of them are not able to be used within web-applications and cannot be configured individually for or by the user and they do not support a developer by implementing an alternative interaction controller. But, from a recognition point of view, they provide a similar functionality.

The first is Wiinput, which is developed by Polak M. [3] and implements a type of instance-base learning. Wiinput is primary designed for games and is trained only once by the developers. Users have no possibility to commit their perception. Another problem is the recognition-process and when the gesture recognition should be started. In the existing version a button on the controller must be released to start the recognition.

The second recognition program is WiiGee, which is developed by Popinga B. [4] and is one of the most powerful programs for recognizing gestures with the WiiMote. It uses an implementation of a Hidden-Markov-Model and achieves well recognition results. The recognition-process also has to be initialized over the release of a button. WiiGee is designed for small programs but not for usage on web-applications. There is a way to teach the system, but it is not possible to let a user commit his perception of intuitive gesture. Only a developer can train the system by his own understanding of rational gestures. In later times it is hard to extend the system with additional gesture-executions by a developer, too.

2.2 Methods and Techniques for Recognizing Gestures

For gesture-recognition at all, a well-working method for gesture-recognition is necessary to provide a useful interface to a user to interact in an intuitive way. Many approaches were developed in the last years, to realize a accurate gesture recognition on the one hand and fast recognition on the other hand, so that an interface will be intuitively usable. The most common methods, which are described in LaViola et al. [5], can be divided into 3 classes:

1. Feature Extraction, Statistics and Models
2. Learning Algorithms
3. Miscellaneous Techniques

To the first class belong all methods, which are working on the base of mathematical concepts like models, statistics or indirectly by the extractions of special mathematical features. The most used methods of this category are Template Matching, Dynamic Time Warping, Feature Extraction and Active Shape Model.

Template Matching and Active Shape are working on a similar way. To identify a gesture with Template Matching, the data will be compared with a template that borders the specific gesture properties. When using the Active Shape Model, a shape is given, which will scale down up to the gesture will fits best and, if the difference is in a certain range, the gesture is recognized.

Dynamic Time Warping has a pool of known gesture-graphs. To identify a performed gesture the data-graph will be compared with the known gesture-graphs. The searched gesture is that with the smallest Euclidean distance between the gesture and data-graph.

Feature Extraction works by finding significant information within the gestures, like speed, duration or acceleration. A performed gesture will be indicated, if the extracted information is similar to one of known gestures.

Table 1. List of common methods for Feature Extraction, Statistics and Models

Method	Vision	Glove	Accuracy	Previous Work	Implementation complexity
Template Matching	Yes	Yes	High	Extensive	Simple
Active Shape Model	Yes	No	Low	Minimal	Simple
Dynamic Time Warping	No	Yes	High	Moderate	Moderate
Feature Extraction	No	Yes	High	Moderate	Moderate

The second class Learning Algorithms contains methods that are getting better accuracies after they have learned more interaction information. So it is common that gestures will be taught as many times as possible to the system, to attain well recognition results. Common methods are Neuronal Networks, Markov Models and Instance-Based Learning. Often they are computational intensive during their recognition or learning phase, so that high performance computers are required.

Neural Networks emulate the functionality of a human brain with its neurons and the links between them. In comparison to Markov Models, a re-training is necessary if a new gesture is learned. Markov Models are working with probabilistic models, often a kind of Hidden Markov Models is used where the probabilistic model is encapsulated as a separate hidden part.

Instance-Based Learning is different from neutral networks and Markov models. While the latter ones store the information after they are assimilated, in instance-based learning the information is saved uncalculatedly, so that the uncompressed information has to be compared with the data of a performed gesture, which has to recognized.

Table 2. List of common methods for Learning Algorithms

Method	Vision	Glove	Accuracy	Previous Work	Implementation complexity
Neuronal Networks	Yes	Yes	High	Extensive	Extensive
Markov Models	Yes	Yes	High	Extensive	Moderate
Instance-Based Learning	Yes	Yes	High	Minimal	Simple

Some special kinds for gesture recognition are summarized in the third class, Miscellaneous Techniques. These techniques have very different rudiments in comparison to the previously called methods. Common examples are The Linguistic Approach and Appearance-Based Motion Analysis.

By the Linguistic Approach, gestures are mapped to a grammar, which specifies a series of token and production rules. Humans are able to recognize actions from images with very low resolution and with little or almost no information about the three-dimensional structure of a scene. The Appearance-Based Motion Analysis is based on these facts.

Table 3. List of common methods for Miscellaneous Techniques

Method	Vision	Glove	Accuracy	Previous Work	Implementation complexity
Linguistic Approach	Yes	Yes	Moderate	Minimal	Simple
Appearance-Based Motion Analysis	Yes	Yes	High	Minimal	Simple

3   WiiMote as a Representative Intuitive Interaction Device

The Nintendo Wii game-console came on the market in 2006. Within a short time it had an amazing success which can be read from the selling chart (Fig. 2). In the year 2008 the Wii console broke as first game console the border of 10 million sales within one year [6].

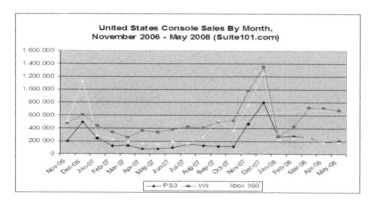

Fig. 2. Console Sales of the 3 most common Game Consoles, by Month, since the Wii's release in November 2006 [7]

The Wii profits at most by his new innovative input-controller, the WiiMote. This controller is a good example for the above-mentioned development process of alternative interaction-devices.

The WiiMote is designed from the shape, use and feel like a TV-Remote [8]. So the first of 3 ways of using this controller is like a Remote over the Buttons. The second way is by using the Infrared-Sensors, so that it can be used as pointing-device – equal to a classical pointer. But the most popular way especially in Wii-Games is the functionality of the accelerators. With these accelerators the WiiMote is able to know its location and the movements within a 3D-room. This way it is suitable for an interaction with gestures. The accelerators generally have sensors for all 3 directions (X, Y, Z-Axis) and, additionally, can calculate the rotation around these 3 axis. With this possibility this controller can defined as an input device with a six degree of freedom.

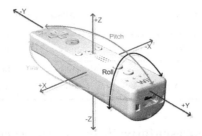

Fig. 3. The Wii Remote as three dimensional input device and the 6 degree of freedom realized by the integrated accelerators. With these accelerators this controller is suitable as controller to perform gestures.

4   Concept of a Technique to Realize User-Centred Interaction

To create a User-Centred interface, the user´s needs have to be regarded, for that fact the key-concept during the implementation was the Process Model of User-Centred Software Design (Fig. 1).

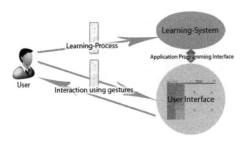

Fig. 4. Process of learning interactions: The Learning Process will realized within the Learning-Tool and interaction works with an integrated API, that uses the learned functions for recognizing the gestures

The goal of our technique is to realize gesture-recognition witch works on an abstract level, so that it can later also be used with other controllers than the WiiMote. Another aspect is the configuration of the interface. So of course the developer must define the required commands that, later on, will be linked with the several gestures. As a consequence thereof the developer must be able to define default-gestures. But later on, a user must also get the possibility to permit the own perceptions of intuitive gestures for the several commands.

These facts make it essential to divide the problem in 2 elements. The first is the Learning-Process with which a developer and a user can set gestures on an easy way. The second element is the recognition application programming interface (API) that provides an easy to implement interface to an existing application. This API uses the learned function from the Learning-Process.

4.1 The Learning-Process

To support developers by using alternative intuitive devices the focus does not lie on the recognition, even although it is relevant. So we decided to use an implementation of Template Matching method, which is useful for a high accuracy during the gesture recognition in real-time on the one hand and because of the missing of a big probabilistic model like by Markov Models it can be implemented without difficulties on the other hand.

Because of the autonomous handling in storing and analysing of defined gestures in Template Matching, gestures can generally be added, dropped and edited without risking a bad accuracy. Typical use-cases for the adding of gestures are the learning of new commands or the perception of new gestures for already existing commands.

Another advantage is, that it can easily be adapted to other interaction devices which work with accelerators like a modern mobile phone (e.g. Apple's iPhone) etc. Alternative devices need only an equal interface to the sensors-information.

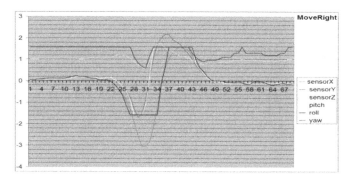

Fig. 5. Example graph of the accelerators of the WiiMote during a performed gesture (a side-move to the right)

To provide an easy way of teaching new gestures, the "WiiGesture Learning" tool (see below) generates the templates autonomously. This happened after the demonstration of a gesture to the system with the WiiMote, after that the calculation-process starts and generates a template. The template consists of equal properties that can find within the repetitions. As property the turning points of the different functions of the sensors are defined. After generating the template-functions, they will be saved in a configuration file, so that they can be published with API-using application.

The screenshot (Fig. 6) shows the elements of the Learning-Tool "WiiGesture-Learning". On the left-top side the status of the WiiMote will be shown. On the top a graph by three physically accelerated and the functions by representing the rotation around these axis. The bar-chart and the list on the right hand side represent the extracted properties of a performed gesture. The text-field on the left side is for saving new gestures and list underneath shows the actual known gestures.

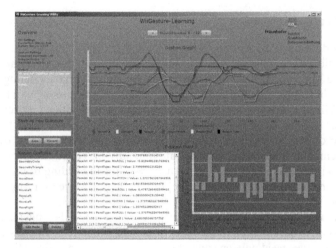

Fig. 6. Screenshot of the Learning-Tool "WiiGesture-Learning"

4.2 The Gesture-Interaction-Process

By the use of an alternative interaction-device an application has to integrate the "Gesture-API". The API interprets performed gestures to commands and provides them to the application. Herewith, the developer has to specify the needed commands only. The rest of the work is overtaken by the API, which will load the configuration file on startup and read the previously learned template-functions. After that all performed gestures over the WiiMote will be compared with the templates to recognize gestures.

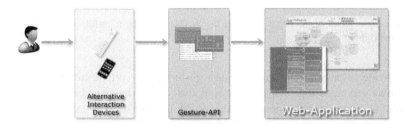

Fig. 7. Concept of the Gesture-Interaction-Process by using Gesture-API within a Web-Application

5   Evaluation

For the evaluation purpose, the participants used a preconfigured system by a developer. So the commands are defined and also a small set of possible gestures for the commands. After that the users have to activate 16 commands in a special to observed order. The average results of the users are shown in Fig. 8 in the category of "Predefined System".

After this step, the users train the system with gestures, which fit with the individual personal perception of intuitive gestures for existing commands. Then the users have to activate the same 16 commands in the same observed order. The average results are presented in Fig 8 in the category "User-customized System".

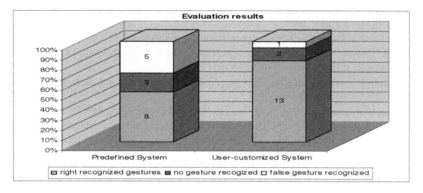

Fig. 8. Evaluation results of users before and after customizing the system with own intuitive perceptions

The recognition-results become better, after the system was extended by the personal perception of the users. The error rate of not or false detected gestures fell down from nearly 50% to less than 20%.

To evaluate the easy integration in existing web-application to support developers, the API was included in some existing applications to provide the possibility to interact via gestures. Only a small number of additional source-code was necessary, so it was no big deal for the developers. One of the applications is the seMap-Visualization [9] that provides a new form for presenting semantic information.

6 Conclusion and Discussion

In this paper a technique was shown, how developers can be supported by providing programs that allow the easier use of alternative interaction-devices and how personal perception of intuitive metaphors of users can be used. The Evaluation proved the described technique and shows that also better recognition-results can be achieved, if users get the possibility to commit there perception of intuitive gestures. In later works the developed tools can be extended, so that both elements are combined in only one API. A further learning after that is possible during the normal interaction.

The innovative point of this paper is the support of developers, where they are now able to provide an intuitive interface to the users which can also customized by users to permit their own perception for intuitive gestures. Furthermore the technique is encapsulated in an Application Programming Interface, so that the integration in existing applications takes only less time.

References

1. Nazemi, K., Hornung, C.: Intuitive Authoring on Web: a User-Centered Software Design Approach. In: Proceedings of World Conference on Educational Multimedia, Hypermedia and Telecommunications 2008, pp. 1440–1448. AACE, Vienna (2008)
2. Poppinga, B.: Beschleunigungsbasierte 3D-Gestenerkennung mit dem Wii-Controller, Universität Oldenburg (2007)
3. Polak, M.: Entwicklung einer Gestenerkennung auf Basis des Beschleunigungssensors in der Wii Remote, Diplom-Thesis, Fachhochschule Köln – Campus Gummersbach: Fakultät für Informatik und Ingenieurwissenschaften (2008)
4. Poppinga, B.: Beschleunigungsbasierte 3D-Gestenerkennung mit dem Wii-Controller, Universität Oldenburg (2007)
5. LaViola Jr., Joseph J.: A Survey of Hand Posture and Gesture Recognition Techniques and Technology, Brown University: Department of Computer Science, Providence (1999)
6. Nintendo: Wii & Nintendo DS Set New Industry Records (2009), http://www.nintendo.com/whatsnew/detail/3vrEIL4gq33i0RmNbYJ9i97j65EwSpVI
7. Jonathan Coley: Video Game Console Sales and Top-Selling Video Games (2008), http://videoonlinegames.suite101.com/article.cfm/may_2008_video_game_sales_charts
8. Iwata, Satoru: Iwata Asks: Wii Remote, Part 1-3 (2006), http://wii.nintendo-europe.com/164.html
9. Nazemi, K., Breyer, M., Hornung, C.: SeMap: A Concept for the Visualization of Semantics as Maps In: HCI-International (2009)
10. Keogh, E.J., Pazzani, M.J.: Derivative Dynamic Time Warping. In: Proc. of the 1st SIAM Int. Conf. on Data Mining (2001)
11. Ekman, P., Friesen, W.V.: The repertoire of nonverbal behavior: categories, origins, usage and coding. Semiotica 1 (1969)
12. Grudin, J.: Utility and Usability: Research Issues and Development Contexts. Interacting with Computers 4(2), 209–217 (1992)
13. Hassenzahl, M., Sandweg, N.: From mental effort to perceived usability: transforming experiences into summary assessments. In: CHI 2004: CHI 2004 extended abstracts on Human factors in computing systems. ACM, New York (2004)
14. Kendon, A.: Current Issues in the Study of Gesture. In: Nespolous, J.L., Perron, P., Lecours, A.R. (Hrsg.) Laurence Erlbaum Associates (Veranst.): The Biological Foundations of Gestures: Motor and Semiotic Aspects, Hillsdale, London, pp. 23–48 (1986)
15. Myers, B.A., Rosson, M.B.: Survey on user interface programming. In: CHI 1992: Proceedings of the SIGCHI conference on Human factors in computing systems, pp. 195–202. ACM, New York (1992)
16. Pavlovi'c, V.I., Sharma, R., Huang, T.S.: Visual Interpretation of Hand Gestures for Human-Computer Interaction: A Review. IEEE Transactions on Pattern Analysis and Machine Intelligence 19, 677–695 (1997)
17. Watanabe, T., Lee, C.-W., Tsukamoto, A., Yachida, M.: Real-Time Gesture Recognition Using Maskable Template Model. In: ICMCS, pp. 341–348 (1996)

User-Centred Design and Literacy Tools for the Deaf

Tania di Mascio[1] and Rosella Gennari[2]

[1] University of L'Aquila, Monteluco di Roio, L'Aquila, I-64100, Italy
`tania@ing.univaq.it`
[2] Free University of Bozen-Bolzano, via della Mostra 4, Bolzano, 39100, Italy
`gennari@inf.unibz.it`

Abstract. The need of literacy intervention and of tools for deaf people is largely documented in the literature of deaf studies. This paper aims at eliciting the interests of HCI researchers and practitioners alike on the creation of more intelligent web tools for the literacy of deaf people. Our paper overviews several e-tools for the literacy of the deaf, and it assesses them according to the user centred design methodology. It concludes with a proposal, namely, a first set of guidelines for designing usable e-tools for deaf people, and calls for a debate on the need of a deaf user centred design.

1 Introduction

The reading delay of deaf people is largely documented, e.g., see [15, 17, 18]. However, their literacy in a verbal language (VL) is varied and can depend on several factors [12]. Recent research in information technology has concentrated on the creation of e-tools for sign languages (SLs), notably, e-dictionaries [2]—roughly speaking, an SL is a gestural-visual language with signs as lexical units, whereas a VL is an oral-auditive language with words as lexical units. Information technologists seem to be paying less attention to the development of e-tools for improving deaf people's literacy in VLs (simply *literacy*, onwards). However, the latter is also a critical issue, as substantiated by linguists and psychologists working in deaf studies, crucial for the integration of deaf people into the hearing society.

When it comes to designing for people with disabilities, the popular terms are "adaptive" and "assistive". To the best of our knowledge, nowadays there are no standard usability guidelines specific for designing and developing web tools usable by deaf people.

Our paper describes several e-tools for the literacy of the deaf, reviewing them according to the user centred design methodology (UCDM) [3, 20]. Why the UCDM? Deaf users have unique and highly variable characteristics, which depend on several factors, such as the degree of deafness, different language instruction methods as well as the level of socio-cultural integration; classifying deaf users as well-known user types is difficult.

The UCDM can be helpful in this respect; it places the users at the centre of the design process; a web tool becomes then truly accessible by deaf users if it is usable by them, being designed and evaluated iteratively with deaf users. Moreover, the UCDM foresees multidisciplinary competences, and a literacy e-tool for the deaf usually

C. Stephanidis (Ed.): Universal Access in HCI, Part I, HCII 2009, LNCS 5614, pp. 13–20, 2009.
© Springer-Verlag Berlin Heidelberg 2009

require them, for instance, the e-tool may demand the competencies of linguists that are expert of deaf studies. This paper also serves to substantiate such claims.

Supported by the findings of deaf studies, our own experience and the review of e-tools for the deaf, we conclude this paper with a challenge: building on the UCDM, we advance a first set of guidelines for designing usable literacy e-tools for deaf people.

2   A Review of Literacy E-Tools for the Deaf

This section reviews some e-tools for the deaf, selected because they are web tools, or they include artificial intelligence techniques or technologies, or they adopt user design methodologies. An orthogonal and equally relevant criterion for our selection is that the review should cover diverse literacy aspects, ranging from word knowledge to global reasoning on texts. Table 1 offers a bird-eye view of the tools, and it assesses whether the tools are meant for children or adults.

2.1   Description of the Tools

CornerStones is a tool for teachers of early primary-school children who are deaf, or have visual learning capabilities and literacy problems; see [11, 4].

LODE is a web tool for children who are novice readers, primarily deaf children. It tackles the global comprehension of written stories, by stimulating children to correlate events of the stories through apt exercises. The exercises are created and resolved in real time by means of a constraint programming system; see [8, 10].

SMILE is not an application for improving the literacy of deaf children, instead, it helps them learn mathematics and science concepts; see [1, 16]. SMILE is mentioned here because it adopts the UCDM.

The primary goal of ICICLE is to employ natural language processing and generation to tutor deaf students on their written English; see [14, 9]. At the time of writing, an ICICLE prototype was not available, hence we could not test it.

MAS (Making Access Succeed for deaf and disabled students) was a project for improving the reading comprehension of deaf signers; see [7, 13]. SIMICODE 2002 (SIMICODE) is a web tool developed within MAS. The tool is made up of thirty hypertexts related to ten themes; a human tutor is necessary for the feedback.

Finally, we analyse some e-dictionaries for deaf people; there is quite a literature on e-dictionaries for SL, which impels us to include them in our review although they are not, strictly speaking, e-tools for the literacy in a VL [2]. Here, we confine our analysis to three case studies, chosen because: they are bimodal dictionaries, that is, dictionary from a SL to the VL of the same country and vice-versa; they are for the web, or adopt a user centred design, or are intelligent.

MM-DASL (Multimedia Dictionary of American SL) was conceived by Sherman Wilcox and William Stokoe in 1980; see [19]. Albeit it was not a web dictionary (at the time of the creation of MM-DASL, the web was not an option), it was a pioneering work in the world of e-dictionaries, and its interface is intelligent.

Woordenboek is a web bilingual dictionary for Flemish SL (VGT); see [21]. Users search for a sign by selecting its sign components. However, users are not expertly guided through the definition of the sign (i.e., there is no artificial intelligence in the tool), thus users can easily specify a gesture that corresponds to no VGT sign, or a sign that does not occur in the dictionary database.

The creation of a web dictionary for Italian SL (Lingua Italiana dei Segni, LIS) is part of the e-LIS project, which commenced at the end of 2004, see [5, 6]. The e-LIS dictionary from LIS to verbal Italian is based on a sign ontology which constraints and guides the users in composing their sign.

2.2   The Tools and the UCDM

Table 1 summarises the main features of the reviewed e-tools. SMILE, LODE, e-LIS explicitly refer to the UCDM; the remaining e-tools do not seem to mention the UCDM or other methodologies with the user at the centre of the design process.

Table 1. Reviewed literacy e-tools for the deaf

Tool	For the web	Use of Artificial Intelligence	For adults	For children	Use of UCDM
CornerStones	No	No	No	Yes	No
LODE	Yes	Yes (constrain programming)	No	Yes	Yes
SMILE	No	No	No	Yes	Yes
ICICLE	No	Yes (natural language processing)	Yes	No	No
MAS	Yes	No	Yes	No	No
MM-DASL	No	Yes (database technologies)	Yes	Yes	No
Woordenboek	Yes	No	Yes	Yes	No
e-LIS	Yes	Yes (OWL + query tool)	Yes	Yes	Yes

However, by analysing the literature, we can find aspects of the tools that pertain to the UCDM, namely, the context of use, the user requirements, if there is a prototype and its evaluation. The results of our analysis are summarised in Table 2.

The context of use is the primary context for which the tool is developed; home indicates any environment in which the user feels at ease. For instance, the context of use of SMILE is the virtual world. The user requirements are not necessarily those of the end user; they are usually the requirements that characterise the end user according to the designers, that is, they coincide with the usability goals of the tool.

As Table 1 shows, not all the tools have a prototype yet; sometimes, the existing prototypes are still in the initial stage of development, and it is unclear whether they underwent any evaluation. This likely depends on the intrinsic difficulties of developing tools for not clearly defined users, and calls for a set of guidelines that can help designers in developing literacy e-tools usable by the deaf.

Table 2. Reviewed literacy e-tools and the UCDM

Tool	Context of use	User requirements	Design—latest product	Evaluation
CornerStones	Primary school	VL literacy	Web demo	Yes
LODE	Home or primary school	VL literacy	Web demo	Yes
SMILE	Virtual world	Science literacy	Downloadable	Yes
ICICLE	Home	VL literacy	Unavailable	Unclear
MAS	Home	VL literacy	Unavailable	Yes
MM-DASL	Home	SL literacy	Discontinued	Unclear
Woordenboek	Home	SL literacy	Web prototype	Unclear
e-LIS	Home	SL literacy	Web prototype	Yes

3 Towards a Deaf User Centred Design

3.1 Know Your Users

Deaf studies are mainly authored by psychologists, linguists and educators, and not by usability experts. User centred designers should include such studies and interview experts of deaf studies, in particular for establishing the context of use and the user requirements of their tools for the deaf. Albeit the reviewed e-tools for the deaf do not explicitly mention the UCDM, their designers implicitly follow it whenever they consult and collaborate with experts of deaf studies.

Designers may have problems in communicating directly with deaf users, as these may prefer their SL or simply tend to distrust unfamiliar people. Therefore the designers may require the assistance of interpreters or, more in general, intermediaries that deaf users are familiar with, for instance, the parents or a teacher of a deaf child.

In designing and evaluating a web tool for the deaf, control groups of hearing people can also be of assistance or even necessary; in this setting, control groups are formed by hearing people with a profile similar to the intended deaf users' profile.

This is all in accordance with the UCDM, which foresees the presence of different users, besides the end-users, in the development process. Table 3 classifies the users that we believe are necessary in the UCD of a web tool for the deaf, in line with the literature of deaf studies and our review of e-tools for the deaf.

However, ours is a coarse-grained classification. The assistance of experts of deaf studies and intermediaries is highly recommended for fine-tuning the classification for the specific e-tool under development, and its specific users. Therefore, in the remainder of this paper, we advance a first set of guidelines for developing a deaf user centred design methodology.

3.2 UCDM Guidelines

Given the types of users that we summarised in Table 3, the iterative process for designing the e-tool can start. First, the context of use is analysed, then the user requirements are established. A first prototype is designed and evaluated. The results of the evaluations are checked against the user requirements, which can be refined, and the iteration may restart. In the remainder, we provide a concrete guide to each step of the iteration and highlight some User Evaluation Methodologies (UEMs) that designers could employ.

Table 3. Types of users

User types	Description
End users	The deaf people for which the tool is developed
Usability experts	HCI experts
Deaf study experts	HCI experts
Intermediaries	People who are familiar with the end users, e.g., the parents of a deaf child
Control users	Hearing people with a profile similar to that of the end users

3.3 Context of Use

The design team should analyse the state of the art, mainly through the literature of deaf studies and ad-hoc inquiries with experts of deaf studies. These and intermediaries are also essential for refining the classification of the tool's end users. For instance, let us consider LODE, a literacy tool for children; the experts of deaf studies may help in focusing the range of application of the tool, as well as in understanding whether it makes sense to classify deaf children according to their language education, e.g., oral or bimodal, or whether the children's age is a more relevant factor.

Such experts and intermediaries can also assist in choosing the best context for evaluating or using the tool. Again, let us reconsider the case of LODE as example; experts and intermediaries may suggest whether the child's home is more apt than a school lab for testing or using the tool.

> Suggested UEM's in this stage of development are: inquiries with experts of deaf studies.

3.4 Definition and Analysis of the User Requirements

In order to establish the user requirements, designers should consult with experts of deaf studies and HCI. Experts in deaf studies help in setting on firmer grounds the requirements, e.g., if the tool is meant for correcting a specific type of grammatical errors, like ICICLE, then the experts could confirm whether the tool's end users commit such type of errors, or that the type of feedback of the tool is indeed useful.

Then the designers should assess the requirements with the end users, with the assistance of intermediaries. The assessment can be done via structured inquiries, or observational evaluations. These evaluations should be organised right at this stage of the project, even with small groups of end users given the difficulty in recruiting deaf users for tests, and possibly with a control group; controlled evaluations will assess whether there are significant differences between the two types of users. For instance, let us reconsider a web tool for improving the grammatical production of deaf signers. In the analysis of user requirements, the observation and comparison of a group of deaf users and a group of hearing users working with the tool can serve to ascertain a significant difference between the grammatical productions of the two groups, and which grammatical interventions may be more suited to the former group of users.

One should also consider that deaf people, and deaf signers in particular are often organised in networks; a positive experience within the network can spread rapidly and elicit more deaf uses to participate in future evaluations of the tool. Moreover, such tests will also serve to assess the most comfortable environment for the users, the best test timing, hardware equipment etc.

With deaf signers, the assistance of an SL interpreter is highly desirable during the tests; similarly, deaf children may need the assistance of a person they trust and that can work as intermediary. To this end, the evaluators should gather information on the participants with questionnaires, prior to the observational evaluations; in this manner, the evaluators can assess if the their deaf participants need interpreters, their first language (VL or SL), their level of acquaintance with computers, …

> Suggested UEM's in this stage of development are: inquiries with experts of HCI and experts of deaf studies; inquiries, observational evaluations and controlled evaluations with even a small group of deaf users and a control group.

3.5 Design and Evaluation

The designers should produce several prototypes, even paper and pencil drawings. We detail such steps in the remainder of this paper.

Specific features of the first prototype should be evaluated with experts of deaf studies and HCI. As soon as possible, the subsequent prototypes should be evaluated with even a small number of the intended end users and a control group, observed while interacting with the tool; the results should be then compared with controlled evaluations. For instance, let us reconsider the case of a literacy tool such as LODE, which aims at stimulating children to globally reason on written stories. Generally at around the age of 8, children are novice readers, they start reasoning globally on a story and deducing logical relations among episodes of the story—all critical steps for developing an expert literacy. The usability of a mature prototype of LODE is thus tested with deaf children and a control group composed of hearing novice readers, that is, 7–8 year old children.

As the design cycle progresses, the evaluators should recruit a significant number of deaf users and observe them while they are interacting with the tool. It may be easier to have a number of these evaluations of the same prototype with few users.

In general, designers should consult with experts along the whole design process: experts of deaf studies help to ensure that the prototypes meet the end-user requirements; experts of HCI serve to ensure that the prototypes fulfil the usability goals. Intermediaries should assist designers along the observational evaluations. They can also help in structuring the inquiries for gathering information prior as well as post evaluations.

> Suggested UEM's in this stage of development are: expert-based evaluations with usability experts; observational evaluations and inquiries with experts of deaf studies; observational evaluations and inquiries with deaf users; observational evaluations and inquiries with control groups; controlled evaluations.

4   Conclusions

Our review of literacy e-tools for deaf people showed that there are several e-tools for the deaf that cover diverse aspects of literacy, e.g., in-depth context-based knowledge of words, global reasoning on stories, grammatical aspects of text production.

According to our review, some e-tools lack or do not have a clear evaluation. This is very likely due to the absence of assessed guidelines for developing e-tools for deaf people, usable by deaf people, with deaf users at the centre of the design process.

Thereby this paper advances a first set of such guidelines, based on the UCDM; they emerge from our own experience in developing web tools for deaf people, the multidisciplinary findings of deaf studies, the analysis of the literature and of several literacy e-tools for the deaf.

The guidelines aim to ease the design of new tools for the deaf, to improve the development of existing tools and, more ambitiously, to open a debate within HCI on the creation of a deaf user centred design. We hope that more HCI researchers and practitioners, elicited to work on e-tools for the deaf, will assess the guidelines, and contribute to the debate.

References

1. Adamo-Villani, N., Wright, K.: SMILE: an Immersive Learning Game for Deaf and Hearing Children. In: SIGGRAPH 2007, San Diego, USA, August 2007. ACM, New York (2007)
2. Branson, J., Miller, D.: Research Methods for Studying the Language of the Signing Deaf. In: Horneberger, N., Corson, P. (eds.) Encyclopedia of Language and Education (1997)
3. Chadia, A., Maloney-Krichmar, D., Pree, J.: User-Centered Design. In: Bainbridge, W. (ed.) Encyclopedia of Human-Computer Interaction, pp. 763–778. Berkshire (2004)
4. CornerStones Working Group, http://ncam.wgbh.org/cornerstones/cornerstones.html (retrieved December 23, 2008)
5. Di Mascio, T., Gennari, R.: An Intelligent Visual Dictionary for Italian Sign Language. Journal of Web Engineering 7(4) (2007)
6. e-LIS Working Group, http://elis.eurac.edu/diz/ (retrieved January 2, 2009)
7. Ferrer, A., Romero, R., Martìnez, M., Asensi, M., Andreu, A.: Improving Reading Skills in Adult Deaf People: The Spanish MAS Module
8. Gennari, R., Mich, O.: Constraint-based Temporal Reasoning for E-learning with LODE. In: Bessière, C. (ed.) CP 2007. LNCS, vol. 4741, pp. 90–104. Springer, Heidelberg (2007)
9. ICICLE Working Group, http://www.eecis.udel.edu/research/icicle/ (retrieved December 23, 2008)
10. LODE, working group (2008), http://www.inf.unibz.it/lode (retrieved January 14, 2009)
11. Loeterman, M., Paul, P., Donahue, S.: Reading and Deaf Children. Reading Online 6(5) (2008)
12. Marschark, M., Spencer, P.: Oxford Handbook of Deaf Studies, Language and Education. Oxford University Press, Oxford (2003)
13. MAS Working Group (2002), http://acceso.uv.es/mas/index.html (retrieved January 2, 2009)
14. Michaud, L.N., McCoy, K.F.: Capturing the Evolution of Grammatical Knowledge in a CALL System for Deaf Learners of English. International Journal of Artificial Intelligence in Education (IJAIED) 16(1), 65–97 (2006)
15. Schirmer, B., Williams, C.: Approaches to Teaching Reading. In: Marschark, M., Spencer, P. (eds.) Handbook of Deaf Studies, Language and Education. Oxford University Press, Oxford (2003)
16. SMILE Working Group, http://www2.tech.purdue.edu/cg/i3/SMILE/ (retrieved December 23, 2008)
17. Traxler, C.B.: The Stanford Achievement Test, 9th Edition: National Norming and Performance Standards for Deaf and Hard-of-hearing Students. Journal of Deaf Studies and Deaf Education 5, 337–348 (2000)
18. Wauters, L.N., van Bon, W.H.J., Tellings, A.E.J.M.: Reading Comprehension of Dutch Deaf Children. Reading and Writing 19, 49–76 (2006)
19. Wilcox, S.: The Multimedia Dictionary of American Sign Language: Learning Lessons about Language, Technology and Business. Sign Languages Studies iii(4), 379–392 (2003)
20. Woodson, W.: Human Factors Design Handbook. McGraw-Hill Education, New York (1981)
21. Woordenboek Working Group, http://gebaren.ugent.be/visueelzoeken.php (retrieved January 2, 2009)

Sign Language Recognition, Generation, and Modelling: A Research Effort with Applications in Deaf Communication

Eleni Efthimiou[1], Stavroula-Evita Fotinea[1], Christian Vogler[1], Thomas Hanke[2], John Glauert[3], Richard Bowden[4], Annelies Braffort[5], Christophe Collet[6], Petros Maragos[7], and Jérémie Segouat[8]

[1] Institute for Language and Speech Processing
{eleni_e,evita,cvogler}@ilsp.gr
[2] Universität Hamburg
thomas.hanke@sign-lang.uni-hamburg.de
[3] University of East Anglia
J.Glauert@uea.ac.uk
[4] University of Surrey
R.Bowden@surrey.ac.uk
[5] LIMSI/CNRS
annelies.braffort@limsi.fr
[6] Université Paul Sabatier
collet@irit.fr
[7] National Technical University of Athens
maragos@cs.ntua.gr
[8] WebSourd
jeremie.segouat@websourd.org

Abstract. Sign language and Web 2.0 applications are currently incompatible, because of the lack of anonymisation and easy editing of online sign language contributions. This paper describes Dicta-Sign, a project aimed at developing the technologies required for making sign language-based Web contributions possible, by providing an integrated framework for sign language recognition, animation, and language modelling. It targets four different European sign languages: Greek, British, German, and French. Expected outcomes are three showcase applications for a search-by-example sign language dictionary, a sign language-to-sign language translator, and a sign language-based Wiki.

Keywords: Sign Language, Deaf communication, HCI, Web accessibility.

1 Introduction

The development of Web 2.0 technologies has made the WWW a place where people constantly interact with another, by posting information (e.g. blogs, discussion forums), modifying and enhancing other people's contributions (e.g. Wikipedia), and sharing information (e.g., Facebook, social news sites). The choice of human-computer interface plays a critical role in these activities.

C. Stephanidis (Ed.): Universal Access in HCI, Part I, HCII 2009, LNCS 5614, pp. 21–30, 2009.

Today's predominant human-computer interface is relatively manageable for most Deaf people, despite lingering accessibility problems. The use of a language foreign to them is restricted to single words or short phrases. The graphical user interface, however, puts severe limitations on the complexity of the human-computer communication, and therefore it is expected that in many contexts the interface will shift to spoken human language interaction.

Obviously, with such a shift, a far better command of the interface language is required than with graphical environments. Most Deaf people would, therefore, be excluded from this future form of human-computer communication, unless the computer is also able to communicate in sign language. Moreover, they already are largely excluded from interpersonal communication among themselves on the Web, given the current lack of support for applications for sign language-to-sign language, but also spoken-to-sign language, and sign-to-spoken language.

Sign language videos, their current popularity notwithstanding, are not a viable alternative to text, for two reasons: First, they are not anonymous – individuals making contributions can be recognized from the video and therefore excludes those who wish their identity to remain secret. Second, people cannot easily edit and add to a video that someone else has produced, so a Wikipedia-like web site in sign language is currently not possible.

In order to make the Web 2.0 fully accessible to Deaf people, sign language contributions must be displayed by an animated avatar, which addresses both anonymisation and easy editing. The remainder of the paper describes the Dicta-Sign project, the overarching goal of which is to lay the groundwork for Web 2.0-style contributions in signed languages.

2 The Dicta-Sign Project

Dicta-Sign (http://www.dictasign.eu) is a three-year consortium research project that involves the Institute for Language and Speech Processing, the University of Hamburg, the University of East Anglia, the University of Surrey, LIMSI/CNRS, the Université Paul Sabatier, the National Technical University of Athens, and WebSourd. It aims to improve the state of web-based communication for Deaf people by allowing the use of sign language in various human-computer interaction scenarios. It will research and develop recognition and synthesis engines for signed languages at a level of detail necessary for recognizing and generating authentic signing.

In this context, Dicta-Sign aims at developing several technologies demonstrated via a sign language-aware Web 2.0, combining work from the fields of sign language recognition, sign language animation via avatars, sign language linguistics, and machine translation, with the goal of allowing Deaf users to make, edit, and review avatar-based sign language contributions online, similar to the way people nowadays make text-based contributions on the Web.

Dicta-Sign supports four European sign languages: Greek. British, German, and French Sign Language. Users make their contributions via webcams. These are recognized by the sign language recognition component (Section 3) and converted into a linguistically informed internal representation which is used to animate the contribution with an avatar (Section 4), and to translate it into the other respective three sign languages (Section 5).

Dicta-Sign differs from previous work in that it aims to integrate tightly recognition, animation, and machine translation. All these components are informed by appropriate linguistic models from the ground up, including phonology, grammar, and nonmanual features. A key aspect of the Dicta-Sign project is the creation of parallel corpora in the four above-mentioned different signed languages with detailed annotations. These not only greatly aid the development of language models for both recognition and animation, but also allow for the direct alignment of equivalent utterances across the four languages, which is useful for creating machine translation algorithms in a sign language-to-sign language translator (Sections 5 and 6).

The project will work closely with the Deaf communities in the countries of the project partners throughout its lifecycle to ensure that its goals are met, and to evaluate user acceptance. A major part of this evaluation consists of three showcase applications that highlight how the various aspects of the system work together (Section 6).

We now cover the three major components of the system —recognition, animation, and linguistic resources— in detail.

3 Sign Language Recognition

Despite intensive research efforts, the current state of the art in sign language recognition leaves much to be desired. Problems include a lack of robustness, particularly when low-resolution webcams are used, and difficulties with incorporating results from linguistic research into recognition systems. Moreover, because signed languages exhibit inherently parallel phenomena, the fusion of information from multiple modalities, such as the hands and the face, is of paramount importance. To date, however, relatively little research exists on this problem [1].

Fig. 1. Signer-independent visual tracking and feature extraction

3.1 Visual Tracking and Feature Extraction

The features that serve as input to the recognition system comprise a mix of measurements obtained by statistical methods, and geometrical characterisations of the signer's body parts, as shown in Figure 1. In the example shown in this figure, the face is roughly located via the Viola-Jones face detector [2], which then gives rise to a skin color model, which in turn is used to locate the signer's face and hands with a greater degree of precision. Based on these initial estimates, object-oriented morphological filtering extracts the silhouette of the face and the hands [3, 4].

In order to make the feature extraction process robust even when the image comes from commodity webcams, the computer vision algorithms need to operate on multiple scales. Moreover, the basic feature extraction processes need to be combined with statistical and learning-based methods, such as active appearance models for facial expression tracking [5, 6].

3.2 Continuous Sign Language Recognition

Hidden Markov model (HMM)-based approaches are the most popular approach to continuous sign language recognition, partly due to their great success in speech recognition [7, 8]. At the same time, there are important differences between speech and sign language recognition; foremost among them is the fact that sign language is inherently multimodal: both hands move in parallel, while the face and body exhibit grammatical and prosodic information [9]. Hence, sign language recognition must deal with the problem of fusing multiple channels of information.

Product and parallel HMMs have been suggested in the past as a possible solution to the problem [10, 8]; however, both approaches have the drawback that they require assigning weights that reflect the relative importance of each modality. Choosing these weights statically, as has been done in previous work, is ultimately unsatisfactory, because the reliability of the information in each channel can change dynamically, due to noise, the context in which the signs are executed, and the signing style of the particular person. A robust dynamic weighting scheme must, therefore, be chosen, so as to evaluate the amount of information that each modality carries, and to maximize their discriminative abilities.

To ensure user acceptance, the recognition system must be able to work in a signer-independent way. To this end, it employs well-known HMM adaptation methods from the speech recognition. Even so, given the current state of the art in sign language recognition, one cannot expect the system to recognize the full range of expressiveness in signed languages. We deal with this limitation in two ways: First, the prototype application is domain-specific, with a restricted vocabulary of no more than 1500 signs. Second, the system employs a dictation-style interface (hence the name "Dicta-Sign"), where the user is presented with the closest-matching alternatives if a sign is not recognized reliably.

The output of the recognition component is converted into a linguistically informed representation that is used by the synthesis and language modelling components, respectively.

4 Synthesis and Animation

Speech technology has exploited properties of phonological composition of words with respect to spoken languages, so as to develop speech synthesis tools for unrestricted text input. In the case of sign languages, a similar approach is being experimented with, with the goal of generating signs (word level linguistic units of sign languages) with an avatar not by mere video recording, but rather by the composition of sign phonology components (Figure 2) [11, 12].

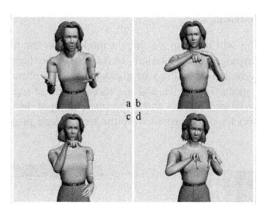

Fig. 2. The signing avatar

Sign language synthesis is heavily dependent on the natural language knowledge that is coded in a lexicon of annotated signs, and a set of rules that allows structuring of core grammar phenomena, making extensive use of feature properties and structuring options. This is necessary in order to guarantee the linguistic adequacy of the signing performed. In the Dicta-Sign project, the annotated parallel corpora provide the basis for these rules (see also Section 5.3), which encompass manual and non-manual features, as well as the role of placement of signs in space [13].

The internal representation of sign language phrases is realized via SiGML [14], a Signing Gesture Markup Language to support sign language-based HCI, as well as sign generation. The SiGML notation allows sign language sequences to be defined in a form suitable for execution by a virtual human, or avatar, on a computer screen. The most important technical influence on the SiGML definition is HamNoSys, the Hamburg Notation System [15], a well-established transcription system for sign languages. The SiGML notation incorporates the HamNoSys phonetic model, and hence SiGML can represent signing expressed in any sign language.

One of the most difficult problems in sign synthesis is converting a linguistic description of the signed utterance into a smooth animation via inverse kinematics, with proper positioning of the hands in contact with the body, and generating realistic prosodic features, such as appropriate visual stress. To this end, the sign language corpus, as described in the next section, does not only encompass phonetic and grammatical information, but also prosodic information. Together with the features derived from the visual tracking and recognition component, this allows for greatly increased realism in the animations.

5 Sign Language Linguistic Resources

In the following, we describe the linguistic resources that contribute to all the other components of the Dicta-Sign project. They can broadly be divided into language modelling, support for annotation tools, and the collection of parallel sign language corpora.

5.1 Linguistic Modelling

Linguistic modelling will develop a coherent model from the phonetic up to the semantic level of language representation, envisaged to be language-independent in
most aspects. This modelling will cover a broad range of phenomena, including the
use of the signing space (Figure 3), and the coordination of manual with nonmanual
features, such as facial expressions and eye gaze. The input data for the development
of the linguistic model will be provided by the lemmatized project corpora (see also
Section 5.3).

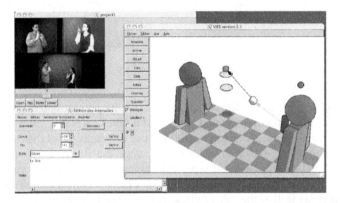

Fig. 3. Editor used to model the signing space

Whereas the first sign language grammar models developed in previous projects
(ViSiCAST [12] and SYNENNOESE [16]) were mainly dedicated to generation
purposes, Dicta-Sign aims to extend modelling capabilities toward a common representation of sign language grammar and the lexicon —or alternatively two coherent
representations— to accommodate both sign language recognition and synthesis.
Overall, this represents a major advance over previous work, since language modelling has been largely neglected particularly in the recognition field.

5.2 Annotation Tools

Most mainstream annotation tools, such as ELAN and Anvil, are geared toward the
processing of spoken languages. As such, they lack some features that would facilitate
the processing of signed languages. These include a graphical representation of sign
language utterances, and special input methods for sign language notation systems
(e.g., HamNoSys [15]). Although some tools exist for specifically processing signed
languages, such as iLex, none of these tools currently provide any kind of automated
tagging, so the annotation process is completely manual.

An experimental version of the AnCoLin annotation system allows some image
processing tasks to be initiated from within the annotation environment and to compare the results with the original video [17,18]. It also connects to a 3D model of the
signing space, but still lacks a coherent integration into the annotation workflow.

It is expected that one of the major outcomes of the Dicta-Sign project will be greatly improved annotation tools, with image processing and recognition integrated into the annotation workflow. Their long term utility can be judged by the uptake by other sign language researchers.

5.3 Sign Language Corpora and Translation

An electronic corpus is of the utmost importance for the creation of electronic resources (grammars and dictionaries) for any natural language. For multi-lingual research and applications, parallel corpora are basic elements, as in the case of translation-memory applications and pattern-matching approaches to machine translation. Furthermore, a substantial corpus is needed to drive automatic recognition and generation, so as to obtain sufficient data for training and language representation.

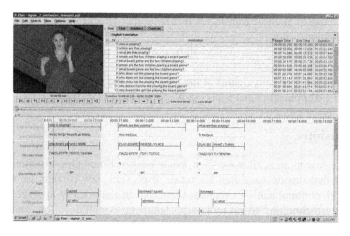

Fig. 4. Annotation of existing Greek Sign Language corpus with ELAN

The quality and availability of sign language corpora has improved greatly in the past few years [19, 20], where, among others, high-quality corpora exist for Greek, American, and German sign language (Figure 4). Yet, to date, multi-lingual sign language research has been hampered by the lack of sufficiently large parallel sign language corpora. One of the most important goals of Dicta-Sign is to collect the world's first large parallel corpus of domain-specific utterances across four signed languages (Greek, British, German, and French), with a minimum of three hours of signing in each language, and a minimum vocabulary of 1500 signs.

This corpus will be fully annotated, showcase best practices for sign language annotations, and be made available to the public. It is expected that the availability of this corpus will significantly boost the productivity of sign language researchers, especially those who are interested in comparing and contrasting multiple languages. In addition, the utterances in the respective four languages can be aligned automatically, thus opening the door for implementing shallow machine translation techniques [21,22], similar to state-of-the-art techniques for spoken languages (see also the showcase application in Section 6).

6 Application Domains

Dicta-Sign is an ambitious project that aims to integrate recognition, synthesis and linguistic modelling on a hitherto unseen scale. One of its key metrics of success is acceptance by the respective Deaf communities in the participating countries. To this end, three proof-of-concept prototypes will be implemented and evaluated within Dicta-Sign.

First, a search-by-example system will integrate sign recognition for isolated signs with interfaces for searching an existing lexical database. Aside from the obvious utility to sign language learners, this prototype will also showcase the technology behind the dictation characteristics of the user interface, where multiple alternatives are presented if a sign cannot be recognized reliably.

Second, a sign language-to-sign language translation prototype will pioneer a controlled-vocabulary sign language-to-sign language translation on the basis of the parallel language resources developed within the project. It will be the first project of its kind to make use of shallow translation technologies. This prototype will also serve as the project demonstrator.

Third, a sign language-based Wiki will be developed, providing the same service as a traditional Wiki but using sign language. This prototype will specifically showcase the integration of all major components of the project. At the same time, it will also demonstrate a Web 2.0 application that is accessible to the Deaf from the beginning to end.

7 Conclusions

Today, just a few months after the "European Year of Equal Opportunities for All," it is important that drastic measures are taken to prevent new barriers from arising, as new forms of communication establish their role in the society at large. Dicta-Sign will be a key technology to promote sign language communication, and to provide Web 2.0 services and other HCI technologies to Deaf sign language users, an important linguistic minority in Europe so far excluded from these new developments.

As the field of sign language technology is still very young, it is beyond the scope of a three-year project to catch up completely with mainstream language technology, and to deliver end-user products. Nevertheless, Dicta-Sign is poised to advance significantly the enabling technologies by a multidisciplinary approach, and to come close enough to let designers of future natural language systems fully take sign languages into account.

Acknowledgements. The research leading to these results has received funding from the European Community's Seventh Framework Programme (FP7/2007-2013) under grant agreement n° 231135.

References

1. Ong, A.C.W., Ranganath, S.: Automatic Sign Language Analysis: A Survey and the Future beyond Lexical Meaning. IEEE Trans. PAMI 27(6), 873–891 (2005)
2. Viola, P., Jones, M.J.: Robust real-time face detection. Int. J. Comput. Vision 57(2), 137–154 (2004)

3. Maragos, P.: Morphological Filtering for Image Enhancement and Detection. In: Bovik, A.C. (ed.) The Image and Video Processing Handbook, 2nd edn., pp. 135–156. Elsevier Acad. Press, Amsterdam (2005)
4. Sofou, A., Maragos, P.: Generalized Flooding and Multicue PDE-based Image Segmentation. IEEE Transactions on Image Processing 17(3), 364–376 (2008)
5. Cootes, T.F., Edwards, G.J., Taylor, C.J.: Active Appearance Models. IEEE Trans. PAMI 23(6), 681–685 (2001)
6. Papandreou, G., Maragos, P.: Multigrid Geometric Active Contour Models. IEEE Trans. Image Processing 16(1), 229–240 (2007)
7. Starner, T., Weaver, J., Pentland, A.: Real-Time American Sign Language Recognition Using Desk and Wearable Computer-Based Video. IEEE Trans. Pattern Analysis and Machine Intelligence 20(12), 1371–1375 (1998)
8. Vogler, C., Metaxas, D.: A Framework for Recognizing the Simultaneous Aspect of ASL. CVIU 81, 358–384 (2001)
9. Neidle, C., Kegl, J., MacLaughlin, D., Bahan, B., Lee, R.G.: The Syntax of American Sign Language: Functional Categories and Hierarchical Structure. MIT Press, Cambridge (2000)
10. Gravier, G., Potamianos, G., Neti, C.: Asynchrony modeling for audiovisual speech recognition. In: Proc. Human Language Technology Conference, San Diego, California (March 2002)
11. Fotinea, S.-E., Efthimiou, E., Karpouzis, K., Caridakis, G., Glauert, J. (eds.): A Knowledge-based Sign Synthesis Architecture. Emerging Technologies for Deaf Accessibility in the Information Society: Editorial. Journal of Universal Access in the Information Society 6(4), 405–418 (special issue, 2008)
12. Marshall, I., Sáfár, E.: Grammar Development for Sign Language Avatar-Based Synthesis. In: Proceedings HCII 2005, 11th International Conference on Human Computer Interaction (CD-ROM), Las Vegas, USA (July 2005)
13. Braffort, A., Bossard, B., Segouat, J., et al.: Modélisation des relations spatiales en langue des signes française. In: TALS 2005, atelier de TALN 2005 (2005)
14. Elliott, R., Glauert, J.R.W., Kennaway, J.R., Marshall, I.: Development of Language Processing Support for the Visicast Project. In: ASSETS 2000 4th International ACM SIGCAPH Conference on Assistive Technologies, Washington, DC, USA (2000)
15. Hanke, T.: HamNoSys - representing sign language data in language resources and language processing contexts. In: Streiter, O., Vettori, C. (eds.) LREC 2004, Workshop proceedings: Representation and processing of sign languages, pp. 1–6. ELRA, Paris (2004)
16. Efthimiou, E., Sapountzaki, G., Karpouzis, K., Fotinea, S.-E.: Developing an e-Learning Platform for the Greek Sign Language. In: Miesenberger, K., Klaus, J., Zagler, W.L., Burger, D. (eds.) ICCHP 2004. LNCS, vol. 3118, pp. 1107–1113. Springer, Heidelberg (2004)
17. Braffort, A., Choisier, A., Collet, C., et al.: Toward an annotation software for video of Sign Language, including image processing tools and signing space modelling. In: LREC 2004 (2004)
18. Gianni, F., Collet, C., Dalle, P.: Robust tracking for processing of videos of communication's gestures. In: International Workshop on Gesture in Human-Computer Interaction and Simulation (GW 2007), Lisbon, Portugal (May 2007)
19. Efthimiou, E., Fotinea, S.-E.: GSLC: Creation and Annotation of a Greek Sign Language Corpus for HCI. In: Stephanidis, C. (ed.) HCI 2007. LNCS, vol. 4554, pp. 657–666. Springer, Heidelberg (2007)

20. Neidle, C., Sclaroff, S.: Data collected at the National Center for Sign Language and Gesture Resources, Boston University (2002),
    `http://www.bu.edu/asllrp/ncslgr.html`
21. Koehn, P., Och, F.J., Marcu, D.: Statistical Phrase-Based Translation. In: Proceedings of the Human Language Technology Conference 2003 (HLT-NAACL 2003), Edmonton, Canada (May 2003)
22. Diab, M., Finch, S.: A Statistical Word-Level Translation Model for Comparable Corpora. In: Proceedings of the Conference on Content-Based Multimedia Information Access, RIAO 2000, Paris, France, April 12-14 (2000)

Improving Static Print Design Readability Using Mobile Reading Filters

Jackson Feijó Filho and Wilson Prata

Nokia Technology Institute, Community Group,
Av. Torquato Tapajós km 12, Manaus,
Amazonas Brazil
{Jackson Feijó Filho,Wilson Prata}@indt.org.br

Abstract. This work proposes the use of mobile computer cameras as an alternative assistive technology for people who do not read easily. It attempts to explore mobile camera software options to improve readability, making use of well known reading filters concepts. A proof of concept of this work is demonstrated by the implementation and demonstration of a mobile application prototype that applies various real-time filters to the viewfinder.

Keywords: Readability, mobility, visual impairments, accessibility.

1 Introduction

Either due to visual impairments or contextual adversities, many people may find difficulties to read or to recognize general symbols. These situations exclude cognitive impairments (neurodiversity), and can be supported by a number of assistive technologies driven by regulations or best practices documents [1]. They cover a wide range of recommendations for making design content more accessible. They apply to design pieces to be seen through digital media or prints. Digital design count on advanced image processing solutions, available on desktop PCs, notebooks, handhelds, mobile phones and basically anything with an digital display, in order to make the reading process more accessible, when rendering the content. However, print design – books, posters, signs - has much less assistive solutions to count on, due to its static nature.

2 The Problem Space

Image processing techniques can be easily applied to digital content when manipulated by the end user, in order to make it more accessible. However, static print design represent a different scenario, where no dynamic assistive technology can stand between the eye of the reader and the reading object. Therefore, all recommendations from regulations or best practices documents should be applied prior to publish. After that, the design piece is subject to contextual adversities such as low light or color light, poor-quality print, or visual impairments.

C. Stephanidis (Ed.): Universal Access in HCI, Part I, HCII 2009, LNCS 5614, pp. 31–37, 2009.
© Springer-Verlag Berlin Heidelberg 2009

3 Mobile Reading Filters

As we watch the transition of the mobile phones to mobile computers, many fronts of interaction research arise. Mobiles (phones) are smoothly changing the way people interact with computers. The philosophy behind Personal Computers is getting even more personal. Not only as a data processing unit, mobile computers gather mobility and a wide variety of connectivity options. In addition, a growing list of sensoring options (cameras, microphones, touch screens, accelerometers, etc) enriches the user's perception of the environment. Therefore, phones are becoming empowered to be seen as a potential assistive technology, for many different disabilities.

The phone cameras have been used as assistive technology for the visually impaired on prior works, as in [10]. This work presents a camera phone-based currency reader that can identify the value of U.S. paper currency.

The cameras embedded to mobile phones have many configurations options that involve known readability improvement concepts such as brightness, contrast, gamma, hue, sharpness, saturation, focus range, zoom factor, etc.

4 Use Cases

As a general classification structure, the WCAG 2.0 [1] Principle 1: "Perceivable - Information and user interface components must be presentable to users in ways they can perceive" and its sub-item, Guideline 1.4 "Distinguishable - Make it easier for users to see and hear content including separating foreground from background" will be considered. It states general recommendations on how to make design content more accessible, from the readability point of view.

The following criteria of the guideline 1.4 will be used (the missing items are audio related):

- 1.4.1 Use of Color [2] – Apply filters that will affect the colors: negative and saturation.
- 1.4.3 Contrast (Minimum) [3] – Apply filters that will affect the contrast: contrast and exposure compensation.
- 1.4.4 Resize text [4] – Apply filters that will magnify the image.
- 1.4.5 Images of Text [5] – This item is related to using text over images of text. In printed media, there is no such distinguishment. Therefore, this item does not apply to the use of filters.
- 1.4.6 Contrast (Enhanced) [6] – will be treated the same as 1.4.3.
- 1.4.8 Visual Presentation [7] – this item is related to alignment and layout, properties that cannot be changed in printed media. Therefore, this item does not apply to the use of filters.
- 1.4.9 Images of Text (No Exception) [8] - will be treated the same as 1.4.5.

Example use cases will be taken from the everyday life and will be related to the intersection between the criteria mentioned above and the mobile filters. The application is installed on the mobile and runs on the background of the operating system and it can be brought to foreground by the touch of a button or by the selection of an icon on the menu.

The following filters can be applied in order to adjust the reading perception according to the criteria: Magnify, (Color) Saturation, (Color) Negative, Contrast, Exposure compensation.

4.1 Medicine Facts Label – First Reading Use Case

This is a situation where the information to be read is critical and it is typically displayed with dark font and light background, providing maximum contrast. However,

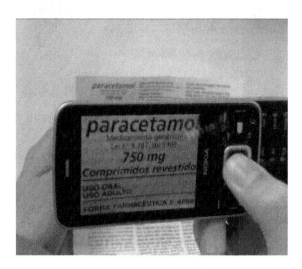

Fig. 1. Applying magnification only

Fig. 2. Applying magnification and contrast

Fig. 3. Applying magnification, contrast and negative

the font size is generally too small due to essential information to be printed in small areas, e.g., nutritional facts in food packages, electronic devices manuals, buying receipts, etc.

4.2 Boarding Pass–Second Reading Use Case

This is a situation where the information to be read is printed in a background that is watermarked, causing an overall low contrast. This situation can be easily identified in design pieces where the information (text) is not highly prioritized, e.g., institutional folders, technical magazines, etc.

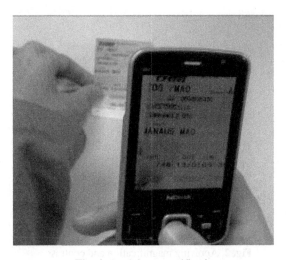

Fig. 4. Applying magnification

Fig. 5. Applying magnification and contrast

Fig. 6. Applying magnification, contrast and negative

4.3   Magazine Advertisement–Third Reading Use Case

This is a situation where the graphic composition has a strong esthetical appeal, hindering readability and causing communication noise. This situation can also be identified in careless color compositions or design pieces poorly planned.

Fig. 7. Applying magnification

Fig. 8. Applying magnification and contrast

Fig. 9. Applying magnification, contrast and negative

5 Results

This work was motivated by the improvement of reading conditions by the development of an application the uses the mobile camera to apply real-time filters to the viewfinder [9]. The experiments were conducted according to everyday life reading situations. The selection of the use cases were driven by the variations of foreground and background compositions. Each use case represented a different combination of contrast, saturation, font sizes and colors, background design, etc. Specific sets of filters were applied to each use cases, in order to improve readability.

The application is based on well known mobile camera filters, providing an easy to use interface for reading static print media through the mobile camera viewfinder.

References

1. W3C - Web Content Accessibility Guidelines 2.0,
   http://www.w3.org/TR/WCAG20/
2. http://www.w3.org/TR/2008/WD-UNDERSTANDING-WCAG20-
   20080430/visual-audio-contrast-without-color
3. http://www.w3.org/TR/2008/WD-UNDERSTANDING-WCAG20-
   20080430/visual-audio-contrast-contrast.html
4. http://www.w3.org/TR/2008/WD-UNDERSTANDING-WCAG20-
   20080430/visual-audio-contrast-scale.html
5. http://www.w3.org/TR/2008/WD-UNDERSTANDING-WCAG20-
   20080430/visual-audio-contrast-text-presentation.html
6. http://www.w3.org/TR/2008/WD-UNDERSTANDING-WCAG20-
   20080430/visual-audio-contrast7.html
7. http://www.w3.org/TR/2008/WD-UNDERSTANDING-WCAG20-
   20080430/visual-audio-contrast-visual-presentation.html
8. http://www.w3.org/TR/2008/WD-UNDERSTANDING-WCAG20-
   20080430/visual-audio-contrast-text-images.html
9. http://en.wikipedia.org/wiki/Viewfinder
10. Liu, X.: A Camera Phone Based Currency Reader for the Visually Impaired. In: 10th international ACM SIGACCESS conference on Computers and accessibility, pp. 305–306. ACM, New York (2008)

ICT Services for Every Citizen:
The Challenge of Gaps in User Knowledge

Kristin Skeide Fuglerud

Norsk Regnesentral, Gaustadalléen 23, P.O. Box 114, Blindern, NO-0314 Oslo, Norway
kristin.skeide.fuglerud@nr.no

Abstract. Many services in our society are digitalized. Being able to access and use information and communication products and services (ICTs) has become a prerequisite for independent living and to fully be able to take part in society. Therefore, ICTs should be designed in such a way that they are usable and accessible to all citizens. Experiences and results from four case studies involving diverse user groups are discussed in this paper. The focuses of the studies were usability and accessibility of ICTs intended to be used by "anyone." When looking across user interaction observations of these mainstream ICTs, the challenge of gaps in user knowledge were striking. The challenge of defining a basic level of usable and accessible ICT features is also discussed.

Keywords: universal usability, e-Inclusion, universal design, gaps in user knowledge, accessibility, user diversity, elderly, visually impaired.

1 Introduction

In today's society, we encounter information and communication-based services (ICT services) everywhere. Services in important areas such as government, education, health, culture, travel, commerce and others are increasingly digitalized. Being able to access and use ICT services has become a precondition for independent living and to be able to take part fully in society. Therefore, ICT services should be designed in such a way that they are usable and accessible to all citizens.

In order to reach the goal of producing products and services that are accessible and usable for all, it is necessary to focus on the variety of users and usage contexts. Detailed knowledge about how the wide diversity of users with diverse needs affects the use of ICTs is needed.

Four case studies involving diverse user groups will be presented and discussed in this paper. The focuses of the studies were usability and accessibility of mainstream ICTs. When looking across user interaction observations of these mainstream ICTs, the gaps in user skills and knowledge were striking. This leads to a discussion of how to deal with this, and whether it is possible to define a basic level of usable and accessible ICT features that developers of mainstream ICT services can build upon.

2 Related Work

Several design approaches that encompass the goal of designing products and services that are accessible and usable for all have emerged within the ICT-communities since

C. Stephanidis (Ed.): Universal Access in HCI, Part I, HCII 2009, LNCS 5614, pp. 38–47, 2009.
© Springer-Verlag Berlin Heidelberg 2009

the mid-1980s; see [1-4]. The overall goal of these approaches is to enable the widest possible range of users to benefit from ICTs.

In an article entitled Universal Usability, Shneiderman outlines a research agenda for making ICT services available to every citizen [3]. Three main challenges in attaining universal usability are highlighted: technology variety, user diversity and gaps in user knowledge. This paper will focus on the last two challenges, i.e., the challenge of user diversity and gaps in user knowledge. User diversity is about accommodating users with different age, gender, disability, skills, literacy and culture. Common ways to deal with this challenge are to let the user customize elements of the interface, such as font sizes, contrasts, mouse click speed and key combinations, language and so on, and to follow accessibility guidelines and standards such as W3C/WAI [5] and ISO/TS 16071:2003[6].

Another challenge is that even if accessibility guidelines are applied, great variations in the applications are often observed. Thus, users who move from one ICT service to another face the need to learn new ways and conventions even for functions they have mastered well in one service. The challenge of gaps in user knowledge is somewhat related and is about how to bridge the gap between what users know and what they need to know. Common ways of dealing with this challenge is different types of user training and teaching, the use of standard terminology, metaphors and different types of online help. Layered interfaces and scaffolding are also proposed to meet the challenge of gaps in user knowledge [7, 8].

There is much ongoing work to define the ICT skills needed for doing basic ICT tasks in the information society. Several different certification programs exist, such as e-skills passport [9] and e-citizen computer skills certification [10]. A myriad of ICT skills assessment tools and teaching programs also exist [11].

3 Four Case Studies

The four case studies are based on four projects. In each project, users have been studied while performing tasks with mainstream ICT. For convenience, the projects are numbered from P1 to P4 in this article.

P1: ICT for an inclusive working life (15 participants): The main goal of this project was to identify possible ICT barriers for workers in practical occupations when they were required to make use of a new ICT product. Employees were studied while performing tasks with a software tool for control and management of invoicing and an e-learning course for in-house security training [12]. Participants were recruited through the human resources department of two large enterprises using the software tools to be studied. The participants had low education and little previous ICT experience. Participants were from 30–61 years old.

P2: DIADEM (22 participants): Elderly and people with cognitive difficulties were studied while using two different electronic forms: a travel reimbursement form and an application form for a safety alarm. Participants were recruited among patients with cognitive impairments after brain injuries at a rehabilitation hospital (33–47 years old), from the organization seniornett.no, promoting ICT use by the elderly

(65–75 years old), and among two groups of relatively low educated workers (cleaners and workers serving food to hospital patients) at a hospital (57–65 years old).

P3: UNIMOD (four participants): Users at an employment training program were studied while filling out an electronic job application form. Some of the participants had low ICT competence and some of the participants had cognitive challenges (participants were in their twenties).

P4: ICT barriers for the visually impaired (28 participants): Visually impaired users were observed while using different ICT products and services, among them also the safety alarm form used in P2 and the job application form in P3. The intention was to give a broad overview of the situation for visually impaired and the participants varied widely with regard to age, sex, education, ICT-experience and job experience. The participants were from 17–60 years old [13].

Table 1. Overview of the four case studies

Project no	Project name (project period).	Case ICT: task	Target groups	No of participants
P1	IKT-arbeidsliv (2005). Eng: "ICT for an inclusive working life".	- Software related to purchasing and invoicing. - E-learning security course.	People with - low education - low ICT skills	15
P2	DIADEM (2006-2009). Delivering Inclusive Access for Disabled or Elderly members of the community.	- Electronic forms: travel reimbursement and safety alarm.	People with - cognitive difficulties - elderly (65+)	22
P3	UNIMOD (2007-2009). Universal design in multimodal interfaces.	- Electronic form: job application.	People with - low education - cognitive difficulties	5
P4	Synshemmedes IKT-barrierer (2007). Eng: "ICT barriers for visually impaired".	- Electronic forms: safety alarm and job application.	- Visually impaired (17 – 60 years)	28

3.1 Similarities and Differences of the Tasks Across the Studies

The following tasks were studied:

- Controlling an invoice by looking at scanned orders and documentation (P1).
- Going through a security course by using a web-based e-learning application (P1).
- Filling out an electronic form for travel reimbursement based on provided travel scenario and dummy information (travel plan and receipts) (P2).

- Filling out and submitting a job application form based on provided dummy information (P3 and P4).
- Filling out and submitting an application for a safety alarm to the local authorities. Dummy information was provided (P2 and P4).

The first task was based on a stand-alone software application; the other tasks were web based. Two of the forms, the safety alarm application and the job application had very similar layout as they were designed by the same provider. These two forms also followed user interface guidelines for Norwegian governmental forms on the Internet [14]. Forms following these guidelines were used in three of the projects (P2, P3 and P4). This provided a good basis for making comparisons on the performance across different user groups: the elderly, people with cognitive difficulties and the visually impaired.

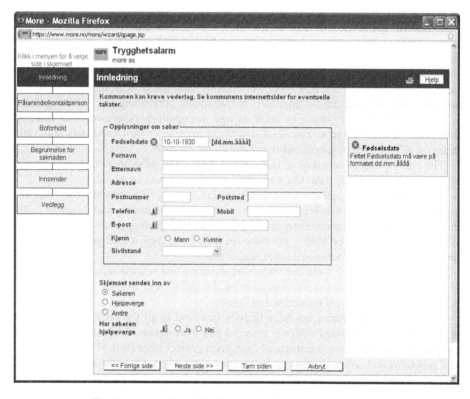

Fig. 1. A screenshot of the first page of the safety alarm form

3.2 User Diversity in the Four Studies

All the studies were qualitative and the users were recruited through different channels as indicated in the project descriptions above. Although there were several young participants in P4, most of the participants were middle aged and elderly. The ICT skills varied widely. It was a prerequisite in all the four projects that all participants should have some previous experience using a PC. In general, the participants had little formal ICT training. The actual ICT skills varied greatly within each project and across the projects. Most participants had no problems in opening web pages and sending e-messages. Also, there were some participants with very high ICT skills, especially in P4. Other background variables also varied across the projects. Some participants were in education (P4), had low education level (P1, P2, P3 and P4), had high education level (P2 and P4), were young (17–25 years) (P3 and P4), were elderly (65+) (P2 and P4), had cognitive challenges related to concentration, orientation, memory or reading/writing (P2 and P3), were visually impaired (P4), were in an employment training program (P3), were employed (P1, P2 and P4) and were retired or unemployed (P2, P3 and P4).

3.3 Research Design and Data Collection

A qualitative approach was used in all four projects, and the overall procedure was fairly similar across the projects: notes on background variables, a short, semi-structured interview on the participant's experience and attitudes on use of ICTs and then solving a practical ICT task. In each project an interview guide and concrete ICT tasks were developed. The ICT tasks were mainly web based, with the exception of a task in a software program for document management, purchasing and invoicing (P1).

Some background information such as age, occupation, experience and training was noted in each project. The semi-structured interviews on experiences and attitudes on ICTs varied in length and detail across the projects.

The participants were asked to think aloud during the subsequent task-solving activity. For the electronic form tasks, dummy information was provided.

The whole session, including the interview and task-solving session were voice recorded. During the task-solving phase, the researcher took notes on all types of difficulties, obstacles and misinterpretations. Sometimes the participants would get stuck. If they seemed not to be able to continue on their own, they would get tips from the researcher on how to continue. This was also noted.

Notes and recordings were used when transcribing and summarizing each user session. A fairly detailed set of minutes from each session were written, although not all parts of each session were transcribed in detail.

The author of this paper has been heavily involved in all the projects. In order to refresh and be familiarized with the material and to compare observations across the studies, the minutes from the sessions from each project were re-read. Notes on special problems and issues that seemed important were taken. From these problems and issues, themes were formed and the notes were coded (with color) according to the different themes.

4 Data Analysis

Many of the participants in all projects encountered problems while solving their task. While going through the material, the difficulties that seemed to be related to the same type of ICT-feature or functionality were grouped. We tried to see whether there were special patterns, similarities or differences between the problems experienced by the elderly, people with cognitive challenges and the visually impaired. It turned out that many participants across these three groups had problems with many of the same features. Especially, many participants across the groups had problems with navigation and overview. The reason for the problems seemed to vary. Several of the visually impaired had more e-skills than participants from the other groups, and their problems were to a much greater extent related to inaccessible design. Many of the difficulties of the other groups seemed to be correlated to lack of ICT experience. The participants with the least ICT experience appeared to feel that the task was overwhelming. Here are some examples of common features or functionality that caused difficulties in the studies:

Need for scrolling up and down the pages: Several of the participants did not know how to, or did not think of the possibility of, scrolling down the page. This led to problems with progressing both for the e-learning application and the forms, because the "next" button often was placed "below" the screen, requiring the user to scroll down in order to find it.

Navigation: Both in the e-learning course and in the electronic forms, many users had problems in understanding how to navigate from page to page. In both cases, a list of page headers was presented to the left of the screen (see Fig. 1.) It was possible to navigate between the pages by clicking on the page headers. The users that had problems with this feature and the scrolling feature would have serious problems in knowing how to proceed.

Precise use of mouse: All participants had used a PC before and they knew basic operation of the mouse. The electronic forms could be operated without a mouse, so in general this did not cause trouble for the visually impaired. For the other groups, especially the elderly, it was a common problem that the clickable area of selectable items on the screen was too small. An example was difficulties when trying to tick off a radio button. When clicking and nothing happened because they didn't hit the right area, they became doubtful about how to handle the item. This could lead to the conclusion that they were not supposed to click on the item anyway.

Formatting and special characters: Many difficulties were related to a combination of strict formatting requirements, incomprehensible information about the required format and the need for entering special characters. For example, a time field required the user to separate hours and minutes with a colon (e.g., 12:30). First, many of the users didn't understand the need for entering a correct separating character. Second, entering a colon required pressing both the *shift key* and the *period key* at the same time. Several participants did not know how to do this. Similar problems occurred when entering dates. This caused problems for very many participants across the studies. An example of a typical error when entering date of birth (Fødselsdato) is shown in Fig. 1.

Switch between windows and close windows: Sometimes new windows were opened, typically with help information. Some participants did not know how to get rid of the help information, i.e., close the help window, and in some cases, when the new help window covered the whole screen the user got lost.

Upload a file: Two of the forms, the safety alarm and the job application, suggested that the user should upload documents as attachments to the form. The concept of uploading a file was not known to the majority of the participants and caused confusion. There were instructions on how to do this, but in general they were not able to understand the instructions and most participants failed in this part of the task.

Open and close file catalogs: Many of the participants were not familiar with the concept of a file catalog and the way to open and collapse such catalogs by pressing the plus or minus buttons. This caused problems when uploading a file. It also caused problems in navigating through the content in the e-learning course, because the content was presented in a file catalog structure, with main headers and sub headers.

Use of drop-down lists: Several of the participants had problems in operating drop-down lists. Some participants had problems in hitting the right choice because their hand movements were not precise enough. Some participants had problems with opening the drop-down lists as well. They did not react to the little arrow indicating a list. They became confused because they thought they should enter information into the field.

Find and make use of help facilities: In general, the users did not use any of the existing help resources. In all three of the forms, there was a help button at the top of the screen, to the right. This was hardly ever used. In addition, there were small icons marked with an "i" indicating more information placed in connection to many of the fields in the forms. Even when stuck or confused the participants hardly ever made use of this information button. After the session, they were asked whether they had considered this opportunity. Most participants said that they did not think of it or notice it. The visually impaired users had large problems in localizing the help features. For the participants using a magnifier, the problem was that the help information tended to fall outside the screen and too far from where the problem occurred on the screen. The design of the help features turned out to be inaccessible for the blind participants using a screen reader or text-to-speech software. There was no meaningful text connected to the information icon, and there were no direct links to the error information showing up to the right when an error occurred.

To summarize, many of the participants were not familiar with one or more of the features or functionalities listed above. In general, the participants had little formal training, and their knowledge seemed to be quite arbitrary. This affected their task-solving performance and many got stuck and could not complete the task on their own. Even when stuck or in trouble, many users did not try to find or use the help facilities. An overall impression is that lack of basic ICT skills seems to be a more severe obstacle to task completion than having an impairment, except when the feature were totally inaccessible. This was the case both for the visually impaired and also for people with cognitive impairments. Participants with solid previous ICT-experience and a cognitive impairment due to brain injury (P2) or other cognitive difficulties (P3) performed considerably better than the workers with little ICT experience (P2). It seemed to be the case that those users that needed help the most were least inclined to use the help facilities. Other studies also show that users often do not use help functions very effectively or even ignore them totally [15, 16].

5   Discussion

The question is how we may overcome the problems of users that are not able to use such features and functionalities as listed above. Many would think of these features as quite basic ICT features. A combination of several strategies is probably needed and here are some main possibilities:

1. Make the features more accessible and easier to use, in other words strive for universal design.
2. Change the help resources so that more users utilize them.
3. Change the design in order to avoid "difficult" or complicated features.
4. Personalize and adapt the user interface to each particular user.
5. Define a basic set of universally designed ICT features and train citizens to use them.

Even though there is an increased focus on usability and accessibility, there seems to be a huge potential in improving the usability and accessibility of many applications. For example, many of the problems caused by strict formatting requirements could probably be avoided by better design and possibly by more robust and intelligent field content validation. Better designs of drop-down lists are also suggested, for example to provide a default text such as "Nothing selected" rather than blank.

As stated above, users seem to be reluctant to utilize help functionality. A second strategy might be to improve online help features to be more attractive, usable and accessible. Examples of recent advice and approaches are to provide more examples [16, 17], live help systems [18], embedded user assistance [19], animated talking assistants [20] and just in time learning through short instructional videos [21]. The UNIMOD project (P3) has developed prototype instructional videos or so-called screen casts and is investigating accessibility issues related to this.

Another possibility would be to avoid some of the features causing problems, such as the need for entering special characters and the need for scrolling. However, the user's ability to solve the ICT tasks will be dependent on many factors, such as (dis)ability, previous experience, training and culture. It is not obvious that it is possible, for each "difficult" feature, to come up with alternative designs that would be usable and accessible to all. Layered interfaces and scaffolding are suggested to meet the challenge of gaps in user knowledge [7, 8, 22]. But it is pointed out that these approaches need to be extended with frameworks and methods to define the basic layer [8] and to prioritize functionality for scaffolds [7].

A related strategy to avoid difficult features would be to personalize and adapt the user interface to the particular user. This is the goal of the ongoing DIADEM project (P2). The DIADEM technology monitors the ability of the user to interact with electronic forms and dynamically offers assistance and personalization of the interface. The target groups are the elderly and people with cognitive challenges. One interesting feature of the DIADEM system is that it can transform electronic forms from different providers to one common look and feel, thus reducing the user's need to learn new ways and conventions all the time. In order for this approach to succeed, it is vital that the adapted design is easy to use for the particular user, and that the support features are able to analyze the situation accurately and give meaningful and helpful advice.

One of the seven principles of universal design, as defined by the Center for Universal Design [1] is that the design is easy to understand, regardless of the user's experience, knowledge, language skills or current concentration level. Many seem to interpret this to mean that the design should be usable without previous ICT experience and training. The question is whether this is achievable in reality. What seems to be lacking is a set of basic ICT-features that developers of mainstream services can build upon, a set of features that are usable and accessible and that they can assume that the users would be able to understand or handle. Especially it seems to be important to put people in a position so that they can make use of help and learning facilities, so that they can more easily solve problems and extend their skills. The above-mentioned approaches, such as help systems, layered interfaces, etc., could build upon such basic features.

The studies have highlighted the importance of having some basic ICT-skills in order to use mainstream ICT services. For many people, the most effective way of achieving the required level of skills would probably be to go through some kind of systematic ICT training program. The various initiatives on developing e-skills and e-literacy frameworks are trying to define what skills are needed to take part in the information society. It would probably be beneficial for developers and the HCI community to look to this work and vice versa. A closer co-operation will possibly result in an increasing overlap and alignment between what training the citizen gets and what type of skills and competencies are needed to use common mainstream ICT services.

6   Conclusion

This paper has reported four field studies of diverse users using mainstream ICTs. In each study, there were mismatches between the ICT skills required to be able to use the case application and the participants' ICT skills and knowledge. This lack of what we may call basic ICT skills would hinder task completion for many of the participants.

The studies shed light on the variances of user skill and knowledge. All the case applications made use of ICT features that some of the participants did not understand and manage to use. Examples are navigation, entering dates, using drop-down lists and make use of help features. The case applications made use of different subsets of features, and the participants knew yet other subsets of features.

Different strategies to close the gap between what users know and what users need to know in order to fully take part in the information society have been discussed. These strategies are universal design, improved help facilities, avoiding difficult features, personalization and adaptation. Finally the emergence of a common basic set of universally designed ICT features, that application developers can build upon and citizens can be trained to use, are called for. Advancements in all these areas are required in order to lower the threshold to the information society.

Acknowledgments. This work built upon four projects: UNIMOD, IKT-arbeidsliv, Synshemmedes IKT barrierer and DIADEM. The first three projects have been partly funded by the Norwegian research council and the DIADEM project is supported by the European Commissions' 6th Framework program. The paper is partly funded by the UNIMOD project and the DIADEM project. Special thanks to all the end user participants the project co-workers and colleagues.

References

1. Center for Universal Design, http://www.design.ncsu.edu/cud/
2. Design for All (DfA),
   http://ec.europa.eu/information_society/policy/
   accessibility/deploy/dfa/index_en.htm
3. Shneiderman, B.: Universal usability. Commun. ACM 43, 84–91 (2000)
4. Stephanidis, C., Savidis, A.: Universal Access in the Information Society: Methods, Tools, and Interaction Technologies. Universal Access in the Information Society 1, 40–55 (2001)
5. Web Accessibility Initiative (WAI), http://www.w3.org/WAI/
6. ISO/TS 16071: Ergonomics of human-system interaction – Guidance on accessibility for human-computer interfaces. Technical specification. International Organisation for Standardisation. ISO, Switzerland (2003)
7. Lee, A.: Scaffolding visually cluttered web pages to facilitate accessibility. In: Proceedings of the working conference on advanced visual interfaces. ACM, Gallipoli (2004)
8. Shneiderman, B.: Promoting universal usability with multi-layer interface design. In: CUU 2003. ACM, Vancouver (2003)
9. e-skills Passport, http://www.e-skills.com/e-skills-UK-in-work/e-skillspassport/1863
10. e-citizen, http://www.ecdl.ie/homepage.aspx
11. ICT Digital Literacy Skills Assessment, http://www.ictliteracy.info/ICT-Assessment.htm
12. Fuglerud, K.S.: IKT for et inkluderende arbeidsliv (Eng: ICT for an inclusive working life). Report number: 1009. Norwegian Computing Center, Oslo, 28 (2005)
13. Fuglerud, K.S., Solheim, I.: Synshemmedes IKT-barrierer (Eng: ICT-barriers for the visually impaired). Report number: 1016. Norwegian Computing Center, Oslo, 91 (2008)
14. ELMER, Simplification of public forms, http://www.elmer.no/english/
15. Aleven, V., Stahl, E., Schworm, S., Fischer, F., Wallace, R.: Help Seeking and Help Design in Interactive Learning Environments. Review of Educational Research 73, 277–320 (2003)
16. Novick, D.G., Ward, K.: Why don't people read the manual? In: SIGDOC 2006. ACM, Myrtle Beach (2006)
17. Moallem, A.: Usability of Software Online Documentation: A User Study. In: HCI International 2003, vol. 1, pp. 549–553 (2003)
18. Aberg, J., Shahmehri, N., Maciuszek, D.: User modelling for live help systems: initial results. In: EC 2001. ACM, Tampa (2001)
19. Matthew, E.: Embedded user assistance: the future for software help? Interactions 14, 30–31 (2007)
20. Foglia, P., Giuntoli, F., Prete, C.A., Zanda, M.: Assisting e-government users with animated talking faces. Interactions 14, 24–26 (2007)
21. Baecker, R.: Showing instead of telling. In: SIGDOC 2002. ACM, Toronto (2002)
22. Baecker, R., Booth, K., Jovicic, S., McGrenere, J., Moore, G.: Reducing the gap between what users know and what they need to know. In: CUU 2000. ACM, Arlington (2000)

Transmission of Acoustic Information of Percussion Instruments through Tactile Sensation Using Air-Jet Stimulation for Hearing Impaired Person

Tomokazu Furuya[1], Yuki Yanagisawa[1], Takahiro Tamesue[2], and Kazunori Itoh[2]

[1] Graduate School of Science and Technology, Shinshu University,
4-17-1 Wakasato, Nagano-shi, Nagano 380-8553, Japan
tomo_f@cd5.so-net.ne.jp, t08a568@shinshu-u.ac.jp
[2] Faculty of Engineering, Shinshu University,
4-17-1 Wakasato, Nagano-shi, Nagano 380-8553, Japan
{tamesue,itoh}@cs.shinshu-u.ac.jp

Abstract. We are trying to transfer acoustic information to hearing impaired persons through tactile sensation using air-jet stimuli. We focused on psychological tonal impressions given when hearing various sounds, and examined whether these impressions could be given by air-jet stimuli. In order to replace percussion sounds with air-jets, we connected the acoustic characteristics to the parameters of the air-jet stimuli. Relationships between the acoustic characteristics of percussion instruments and the physical characteristics of air-jets have been found by analysis of psychological impressions given when hearing percussion instrument sounds and perceiving air-jet stimuli. As a result, transmitting musical information was possible.

Keywords: Acoustic information, Percussion sound, Tactile sensation, Air-jet stimulation, Hearing impaired person, Psychological impression.

1 Introduction

People can enjoy listening to music whenever and wherever thanks to the spread of portable music players. However, hearing impaired persons may have little or no access to them, because it is difficult for them to enjoy listening to music. It is necessary to develop a new interface device so they can enjoy listening to music. Accordingly, we are trying to transfer acoustic information to hearing impaired persons using tactile stimuli.

Vibratory stimuli or electric stimuli were used for transmitting rhythm in previous work[1], [2], [3], [4]. We thought that the transmission of timbre and melody were important, and focused on psychological tonal impressions given when hearing music. Transmission of the impressions was tried by tactile stimuli. An air-jet was used for the tactile stimuli. Air-jet stimuli evoke various tactile impressions such as powerfulness and weakness, sharpness and dullness, warmth and coldness, which are similar to psychological impressions induced by natural phenomena such as hurricanes and gentle winds, gusts and constant winds, warm breezes and cold winds. It was thought that

C. Stephanidis (Ed.): Universal Access in HCI, Part I, HCII 2009, LNCS 5614, pp. 48–57, 2009.

an impression similar to the tonal impression can be given by air-jet stimuli. Furthermore, it is possible to control the flow volume, injection time and temperature of an air-jet by a compact lightweight actuator. Air-jets are applied also in the field of virtual reality[5], [6].

In order to examine the transmission of music information by air-jet stimuli, we did a basic experiment[7]. As a result, the minimum perceptible interval is 65ms, the minimum perceptible flow volume is 4L/min, and the minimum perceptible differential flow volume is 1L/min. It was confirmed that air-jet stimuli are able to transmit rhythm and strength.

In this paper, we examined the psychological impressions of instrument sounds, and examined whether similar impressions were given by air-jet stimuli. It is difficult to examine the psychological impressions of musical instruments such as pianos and violins because these musical instruments have a lot of sounds. Thus, percussion instruments which have no musical scale were examined. Air-jets with various flow volumes, injection times, nozzle diameters and temperatures were used to examine psychological tactile impressions. As a result, transmitting psychological impressions similar to impressions given when hearing percussion instrument sounds by air-jet stimuli was possible.

2 Basic Concept and Procedure

We explain the basic concept and procedure of this research in this chapter. Fig. 1 shows the basic concept and procedure of this research. There are six steps in the procedure as numbered in Fig. 1. The procedure is shown as follows.

1. Psychological impressions given when hearing various percussion instruments are evaluated by adjective pairs. Principal factors on tonal impression are extracted by factor analysis.
2. The acoustic characteristics of the percussion instruments such as intensity and frequency are analyzed, and acoustic characteristics that influence factors are examined.
3. Psychological impressions of air-jet stimuli as well as tonal impressions of percussion instruments are evaluated by adjective pairs, and principal factors for tactile stimuli are extracted by factor analysis.
4. The physical characteristics of the air-jet, such as flow volume and temperature that influence factors are analyzed.
5. Each factor is related by a common adjective.
6. Common adjective scales to represent both tonal impression and tactile impression are estimated. Acoustic information from percussions is converted into control signals for the air-jet actuator.

A psychological tactile impression similar to that given when hearing a percussion sound can be given using an air-jet stimulus by the above-mentioned procedure.

For example, a powerful factor was extracted when a percussion instrument was heard (1). The acoustic characteristic that influenced this factor was the intensity (2). At this moment, a quantity factor was extracted when perceiving the air-jet stimulus (3).

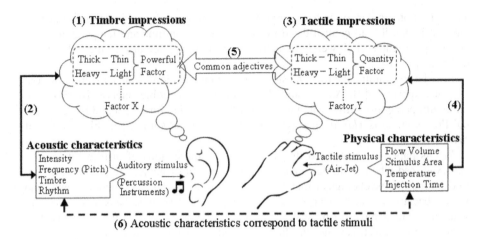

Fig. 1. Basic concept of this research

This factor is related to the flow volume (4). If common adjective pairs are included in both factors, the powerful factor and the quantity factor are similar impressions, and it is possible to relate them (5). In consequence, the intensity corresponds to the flow volume (6), and the air-jet stimulus can give an impression similar to the tonal impression.

3   Relationships between Psychological Impressions of Timbre and Acoustic Characteristics of Percussions

The psychological impression given when hearing a percussion sound was evaluated using the semantic differential (SD) method, and the factors of the psychological impression were investigated.

3.1   Psychology Evaluation Experiment of Percussion Instruments

In this study, 47 percussion instruments, which have been defined as such by the general musical instruments digital interface (MIDI), were classified and 22 percussion instruments were selected from them to be used for the psychological evaluation [8]. Table 1 shows the selected percussion instruments.

As for the adjective pairs used for the psychological evaluation, the eight adjective pairs that were in both the list of 40 Japanese adjective pairs used for the psychological evaluation of music and the list of 20 Japanese adjective pairs used to evaluate materials were selected [9], [10]. In Table 2, the selected adjective pairs are expressed in both English and Japanese [11].

In this study, 20 healthy persons (20–24 years old) were used as the subjects. The subjects wore a headphone in a soundproof chamber, and they heard the percussion sounds shown in Table 1 projected at comfortable volumes. They were asked to grade the sounds on a seven level scale (from –3 to +3) in terms of the eight adjective pairs shown in Table 2.

Table 1. Percussion instruments

Classification	Note No.	Instrument
Wooden Idiophone	73	Short Guiro
	75	Claves
	77	Low Wood Block
Metallic Idiophone	42	Closed Hi-hat
	46	Open Hi-hat
	49	Crash Cymbal 1
	53	Ride Bell
	56	Cowbell
	68	Low Agogo
	81	Open Triangle
Other Idiophone	69	Cabasa
	70	Maracas
	39	Hand Clap
	58	Vibra-slap
Membranophone	36	Bass Drum 1
	38	Acoustic Snare
	47	Low-Mid Tom
	54	Tambourine
	61	Low Bongo
	66	Low Timbale
	64	Low Conga
	79	Open Cuica

Table 2. Adjective pairs

No.	Adjective pair		
1	Thick (Atsuminoaru)	–	Thin (Usupperana)
2	Sharp (Surudoi)	–	Blunt (Nibui)
3	Heavy (Omoi)	–	Light (Karui)
4	Hard (Katai)	–	Soft (Yawarakai)
5	Cold (Tsumetai)	–	Warm (Atatakaminoaru)
6	Pointy (Togetogeshii)	–	Round (Maruminoaru)
7	Dry (Kawaita)	–	Wet (Uruoinoaru)
8	Rough (Arai)	–	Smooth (Kimenokomakai)

The levels obtained for each percussion sound were averaged, and the standard deviation was calculated. The results obtained using three typical percussion instruments (Low Wood Block, Crash Cymbal 1, and Bass Drum 1) are shown in Fig. 2. For example, for the adjective pair "sharp–blunt", the values shown in this figure are represented as follows: 0, neither of them; −1, rather sharp; −2, considerably sharp; −3, very sharp; +1, rather blunt; +2, considerably blunt; and +3, very blunt. The Low Wood Block type of wooden idiophone was evaluated highly in terms of light and smooth. Crash Cymbal 1 type of metal idiophone was evaluated highly in terms of pointy and dry. Bass Drum 1 type of membranophone was highly evaluated in terms of thick, heavy, and rough; this result was contrary to that of the Low Wood Block. As shown in Fig. 2, the evaluations changed significantly according to the type of percussion instrument.

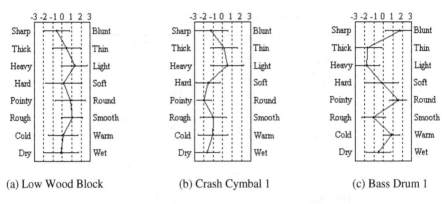

(a) Low Wood Block   (b) Crash Cymbal 1   (c) Bass Drum 1

Fig. 2. The result of the psychological evaluation of percussion instruments

Factor analysis was performed on the data obtained from the psychological evaluation using the principal factor method and varimax rotation, and consequently, two factors (Factors 1 and 2) were extracted. Table 3 shows the factor loading of each. Previous studies have demonstrated that the image of each tone was determined by its powerful, metallic, and aesthetic factors. When the above was taken into consideration, Factors 1 and 2 could be interpreted as powerful and metallic factors, respectively. The reasons why only two factors were extracted were possibly that the number of adjective pairs was insufficient and the subjects hardly received any aesthetic impressions due to the very short sounds of the percussion instruments. In addition, since the difference in the factor loading was small between cold and warm and between rough and smooth, these adjective pairs were not used in the factor analysis.

Table 3. Factor loading for timbre impression of percussion

No.	Adjective Pair			Factor1	Factor2
1	Thick (Atsuminoaru)	–	Thin (Usupperana)	-0.656	-0.216
3	Heavy (Omoi)	–	Light (Karui)	-0.639	-0.040
2	Sharp (Surudoi)	–	Blunt (Nibui)	0.521	0.157
6	Pointy (Togetogeshii)	–	Round (Maruminoaru)	0.281	0.729
4	Hard (Katai)	–	Soft (Yawarakai)	0.090	0.535
7	Dry (Kawaita)	–	Wet (Uruoinoaru)	0.025	0.513
5	Cold (Tsumetai)	–	Warm (Atatakaminoaru)	0.421	0.453
8	Rough (Arai)	–	Smooth (Kimenokomakai)	0.471	-0.428

3.2 Acoustic Characteristics of Percussive Instruments

Among the adjective pairs used for the psychological evaluation, those with high factor loadings were considered to represent the factors of the psychological impression. As shown in Table 3, the adjective pair representing the powerful factor is "thick–thin," and that representing the metallic factor is "pointy–round." Then, the relationship between the evaluation results of these adjective pairs and the physical quantities of percussion sounds was investigated. The frequency of the sound pressure waveform was analyzed as a physical quantity, and the frequency with the largest power was obtained. Fig. 3 shows the results. As shown in this figure, the feeling of powerful represented by thick increased as the frequency with the largest power decreased. Moreover, the impression of pointy increased as the frequency with the largest power increased.

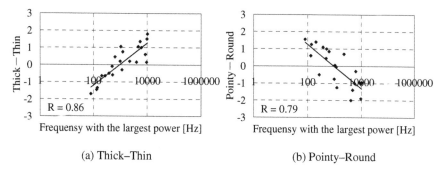

(a) Thick–Thin   (b) Pointy–Round

Fig. 3. Relationship between the evaluation result and acoustic characteristics

4   Relationships between Psychological Impressions of Tactile Sensation and Physical Characteristics of Air-Jet Stimuli

The psychological impression given when perceiving an air-jet stimulus was evaluated using parameters and factors involving tactile stimuli were also investigated.

4.1   Psychological Evaluation Experiment of Air-Jet Stimuli

The device shown in Fig.4 was used for the psychological evaluation of air-jet stimuli. The device consists of an air-jet compressor, a PIC microcomputer, an electromagnetic valve, a flow volume sensor, a heater, a nozzle. We can control the nozzle diameter, flow volume, injection time and temperature of the air-jet.

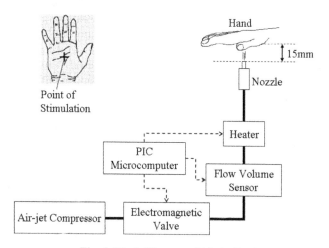

Fig. 4. Block Diagram of Air-jet Device

Each subject evaluated the 16 air-jet stimuli shown in Table 4 and graded them on a seven level scale in terms of the eight adjective pairs shown in Table 2. The distance between the palm and the nozzle is 15mm, and the center of palm was stimulated. The subjects were 8 healthy persons (21–32 years old).

Table 4. Parameters of Air-jet stimulations

No.	Nozzle diameter (mm)	Flow Volume (L/min)	Injection Time (ms)	Temperature (C)
1	0.5	5.9	940	11
2	0.5	5.9	62	11
3	0.5	3.1	62	11
4	0.5	3.1	940	11
5	1.5	4.7	940	28
6	1.5	4.7	62	28
7	1.5	9,5	62	28
8	1.5	9.5	940	28
9	0.5	5.9	940	28
10	0.5	5.9	62	28
11	0.5	3.1	62	28
12	0.5	3.1	940	28
13	1.5	4.7	940	11
14	1.5	4.7	62	11
15	1.5	9,5	62	11
16	1.5	9.5	940	11

The psychological evaluation results obtained by the air-jet stimuli with various parameters were averaged and the standard deviation was calculated. Fig. 5 shows some typical results. In this figure, No. 3 is an air-jet stimulus with a combination of the parameters' minimum values, and the evaluation results indicate the impressions of thin, light, and cold. No. 8 is an air-jet stimulus with a combination of the parameters' maximum values, and the evaluation results indicate the impressions of thick and warm; this result was contrary to that of No. 3. Therefore, it was demonstrated that when the parameters of an air-jet stimulus changed, the impressions received by the subjects also changed. No. 11 is an air-jet stimulus with parameters in which only the temperature differed from that of No. 3. Since the temperature was high in No. 11, the evaluation level of warm was expected to be high, similar to the results of No. 8. However, that level was almost equivalent to the mean value. Therefore, the impression was considered to change not only because of one parameter but also as a combination of multiple parameters.

Factor analysis was performed on the data obtained from the psychological evaluation using the principal factor method and varimax rotation, and, consequently, two factors (Factors 1 and 2) were extracted. Table 5 shows the factor loading of each. Since Factor 1 was related to the adjective pairs of "pointy–round" and "hard–soft," this factor could be interpreted as representing the feelings of quality. Since Factor 2 was related to the adjective pairs of "thick–thin" and "heavy–light," this factor could be interpreted to represent the feelings of quantity. Therefore, Factors 1 and 2 were defined as quality and quantity factors, respectively. In addition, since the difference in the factor loading was small between cold and warm, this adjective pair was not used in the factor analysis.

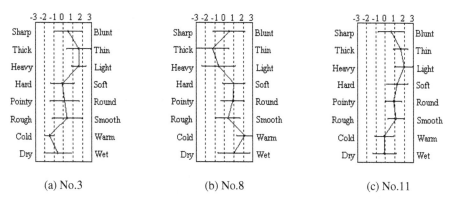

(a) No.3   (b) No.8   (c) No.11

Fig. 5. The result of psychology evaluation of air-jet stimuli

Table 5. Factor loading matrix for tactile impression by air-jet stimulations

No.	Adjective Pair			Factor1	Factor2
6	Pointy (Togetogeshii)	–	Round (Maruminoaru)	0.909	0.022
4	Hard (Katai)	–	Soft (Yawarakai)	0.834	0.125
2	Sharp (Surudoi)	–	Blunt (Nibui)	0.738	0.155
7	Dry (Kawaita)	–	Wet (Uruoinoaru)	0.468	-0.007
8	Rough (Arai)	–	Smooth (Kimenokomakai)	0.450	0.190
1	Thick (Atsuminoaru)	–	Thin (Usupperana)	0.030	0.896
3	Heavy (Omoi)	–	Light (Karui)	0.236	0.777
5	Cold (Tsumetai)	–	Warm (Atatakaminoaru)	0.347	-0.271

4.2   Physical Characteristics of Air-Jet Stimuli

The adjective pair with the highest factor loading was selected as the representative of each factor. As shown in Table 5, the adjective pair representing the quality factor was "pointy–round," and the one representing the quantity factor was "thick–thin." Fig. 6 shows the relationship between the evaluation results of each adjective pair and the parameters of the air-jet stimuli. As shown in this figure, the feelings of quantity and quality increased as the nozzle diameter increased; here, the feeling of quality was expressed as pointy.

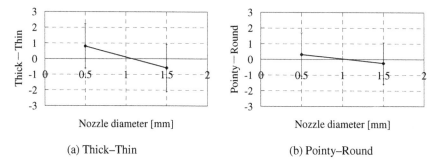

Nozzle diameter [mm]   Nozzle diameter [mm]

(a) Thick–Thin   (b) Pointy–Round

Fig. 6. Relationship between the evaluation result and physical characteristics of air-jet stimuli

5 Correlation between the Acoustic Features and the Parameters Used for the Air-Jet Stimuli

The impressions received by percussion sounds were compared with those received by air-jet stimuli. The adjective pair "thick–thin" had the highest factor loading among the adjective pairs related to the powerful factor of a percussion sound. Also, this adjective pair had the highest factor loading among the adjective pairs related to the quantity factor of an air-jet stimulus. Moreover, the adjective pair "pointy–round" had the highest factor loading among the adjective pairs related to the metallic factor of a percussion sound and also had the highest factor loading among the adjective pairs related to the quality factor of an air-jet stimulus. Therefore, it can be said that the powerful factor corresponds to the quantity factor, and the metallic factor corresponds to the quality factor.

The frequency with the largest power of the percussion sound was correlated to the evaluation result of the adjective pair "thick–thin." Moreover, the nozzle diameter used for the air-jet stimuli was also correlated to the adjective pair "thick–thin." Since sounds with a low frequency have the impression of thickness, if the impression of thickness is desirable, the nozzle diameter should be enlarged. By enlarging the nozzle's diameter, an impression similar to that given when a percussion sound was heard can be given by an air-jet stimulus. However, the impression changes according to a combination of multiple parameters, and the interaction between these parameters must be taken into consideration.

6 Conclusion

In this study, adjective pairs to evaluate tones and the tactile sense were selected. By using the selected adjective pairs, psychological evaluations and factor analyses were performed. Moreover, the principal factor of the impression when hearing a percussion sound and that of the impression when receiving an air-jet stimulus were analyzed. Consequently, it was demonstrated that powerful and metallic factors are related to percussion sounds, and quality and quantity factors are related to air-jet stimuli. Moreover, since the correlation between the acoustic features and the parameters used for air-jet stimuli were observed, the physical quantities of a percussion sound could be replaced by the parameters used for an air-jet stimulus. Therefore, an impression similar to that given when a percussion sound was heard can be given by an air-jet stimulus.

In a basic experiment, the rhythm and intensity of a sound were demonstrated to be transmitted. In this study, the different impressions due to different percussion sounds were demonstrated to be given by air-jet stimuli. Therefore, transmission of musical information was possible. In the future, by using MIDI sound sources, we will actually apply air-jet stimuli to the hearing-impaired and investigate the transmission of this musical information.

References

1. Miura, S., Sugimoto, M.: T-RHYTHM: A System for Supporting Rhythm Learning by Using Tactile Devices. In: Proceedings of the IEEE International Workshop on Wireless and Mobile Technologies in Education, pp. 264–268 (2005)
2. Kawashima M.: Transcutaneous Electrical Rhythm Stimulator for Hearing Impaired People, Technical report of IEICE ET2003-83, pp.1–4 (2004) (in Japanese)
3. Schurmann, M., Caetano, G., Hlushchuk, Y., Jousmaki, V., Hari, R.: Touch activates human auditory cortex. NeuroImage 30, 1325–1331 (2006)
4. Gunther, E., Davenport, G., O'Modhrain, S.: Cutaneous Grooves: Composing for the Sense of Touch. In: Proceedings of the 2002 International Conference on New Interfaces for Musical Expression - NIME 2002, pp. 37–42 (2002)
5. Suzuki, Y., Kobayashi, M.: Air Jet Driven Force Feedback in Virtual Reality. IEEE Computer Graphics and Applications, 44–47 (2005)
6. Amemiya, K., Tnaka, Y.: Portable Tactile Feedback Interface Using Air Jet. In: Proceedings of 9th International Conference on Artificial Reality and Tele-Existence (ICAT 1999), pp. 115–122 (1999)
7. Furuya, T., Itoh, K.: Basic study for transmission of music information through tactile sensation using air-jet stimulation for Hearing Impaired Person. In: SOBIM 2006 Society of Biomechanisms, Japan, pp. 115–118 (2006) (in Japanese)
8. Fletcher, N.H., Rossing, T.D.: The Physics of Musical Instruments, 2nd edn. Part V Percussion Instrument, pp. 581–707. Springer, Heidelberg (1998)
9. Kitamura, O., Ni-i, S.-i., Kuriyama, J., Masuda, N.: The factor analytical research on tone color for the youth of today - in the case of monophonic sound. Transactions on Technical Committee of Psychological and Physiological Acoustics, Acoustical Society of Japan, H-51–H-11 (1978) (in Japanese)
10. Yoshida, M.: Dimensions of tactual impressions. Memoirs of the Japan weman's university 13, 47–68 (1963) (in Japanese)
11. Namba, S., Kuwano, S., Hashimoto, T., Berglund, B., Da Rui, Z., Schick, A., Hoege, H., Florentine, M.: Verbal expression of emotional impression of sound: A cross-cultural study. Journal of Acoustical Society of Japan (E) 12(1), 19–29 (1991)

Enabling People – Creating Inclusive Human-Computer Interactions

Rama Gheerawo and Yanki Lee

Helen Hamlyn Centre, Royal College of Art, Kensington Gore,
London, SW7 2EU, UK
rama.gheerawo@rca.ac.uk, yan-ki.lee@rca.ac.uk

Abstract. Inclusive design has traditionally dealt with physical design and differences in age and ability. However, as information technology becomes more pervasive, the new barriers to inclusivity are increasingly digital. Centring design around people can increase competitiveness and value, especially in fast-moving technology markets, but technology-specific, people-centred strategies need to be developed that build on existing inclusive design processes and go beyond the 'technology-push needs-pull' approach to accommodate the social complexity that surrounds the everyday use of technology. This paper focuses on the challenges of implementing inclusive design in an technology context, illustrating this with examples drawn from the Royal College of Art Helen Hamlyn Centre (HHC). It outlines work done with students within an educational context and projects completed by design graduates working with industry. The case studies aim to demonstrate an approach that brings together the user's voice and the designer's creativity to enable a more inclusive approach.

Keywords: Inclusive design, technology, people-centred.

1   Introduction

Digital technologies are a growing and increasingly important part of the consumer experience, influencing every area of design from product design to service design. The rapid growth in the number of handheld devices is representative of the significance of this technology and the aspirational value that it can hold for consumers. However, the majority of inclusive design focus has been on the built environment or the design of physical objects and artifacts with an emphasis on accessibility and capability. The Seven Principles of Universal Design from North Carolina State University which have influenced much inclusive design practice are typically aimed at products and environments. Adapting and evolving current inclusive design methods and thinking to create more people-centred, digital technologies that are desirable and fulfill user aspiration becomes a key challenge.

Technology, as used in this paper, refers to information technology (IT), in particular those that provide communications, information and entertainment. These areas of IT are becoming less bespoke, more convergent and more pervasive in both personal and professional lives [1]. They represent the richest area for inclusive design research and the most potential to influence student designers and commercial partners.

C. Stephanidis (Ed.): Universal Access in HCI, Part I, HCII 2009, LNCS 5614, pp. 58–67, 2009.
© Springer-Verlag Berlin Heidelberg 2009

1.1 Getting Older and Being Disabled

By 2020, close to half the adult population of Europe will be over 50 [2], and one third of the inhabitants of the United States will be over 55 [3]. Population ageing is a real and demonstrable phenomenon and will result in a body of older consumers who will demand more from technology and be less accepting of its shortcomings. In particular, the baby boomers who are becoming pensioners will want to continue to use IT into later life to maintain their social circle and support their communication needs [4]. They will demand active participation within society, and want to live independent, vibrant lifestyles that are different from the institutionalised thinking that has been prevalent for most of the last century [5].

The physical results of getting older involve multiple, minor impairments affecting eyesight, hearing, dexterity, mobility and memory [6]. IT that is hard use, or difficult to access will not satisfy the needs of older people and this has significant implications for design that is mismatched to functional ability [7]. However, design for older people should go beyond physical requirements to also address personal aspiration and emotional connection, something that people continue to value as they get older [8].

This is very much aligned to the thinking contained within inclusive design, defined as comprehensive, integrated design that encompasses consumers of diverse age and capability in a wide range of contexts [9]. Designs should be 'age inclusive' rather than 'age exclusive' as no older customer will want to buy an IT product or service that singles them out as an age group. They are consumers with contemporary expectations who control significant amounts of disposable income and are valuable participants in the economy.

1.2 Technology Push, User Pull

Technology is often associated with rapid technical development and cutting edge innovation in a digital or silicon context and this has resulted in affordable devices and products. However, these are not always designed to account for variance in age and ability. Involving users throughout the development of IT-based consumer products and services is generally not prevalent in the commercial environment beyond the traditional focus group set-up that is used to validate or test a new idea or prototype once it gets close to market. Involving users in more creative ways further upstream in the design development process is rarer. This perceived separation and tension between technology and its users is widely described as 'technology-push, user-pull'.

The terms 'push' and 'pull' originated in logistics and supply chain management [10], but have become widely used in business and marketing. They take on special meaning in an IT context as they articulate the difference between an approach where the technology drives the ideation process or where the market demands it. The latter has historically been referred to as 'user pull', 'needs pull' or 'demands pull'. In the 1960's, strategists realized that 'demand pull' would effectively support programmes biased towards a 'technology push' [11]. In the mid-70's, 'demand pull' grew in visibility to be seen as an equal route towards innovation [12] whilst a decade later, researchers into the stimuli of the innovation process reported that the number of innovations stimulated by 'need pull' substantially exceeded those stimulated by 'technology push' [13]. In critical areas of design such as medical equipment, empirical studies concluded that 'understanding user need' was a discriminating factor between commercially successful industrial product and process innovations, and those that failed [14].

The 1990's saw technology developing rapidly as well as the industrial innovation process which was driving this change. An integrated model of industrial innovation grew from the simple linear 'technology push' and 'need pull' models of the 1960s and early 1970s and the 'coupling model' of the late 1970s and early 1980s [15]. Fourth and Fifth Generation models of innovation responded to an increasing pace and the multi-layered nature of technology processes. Innovation in this sector was no longer sequential – it became parallel and even complex [16].

1.3 Complexity and Community

The need to include complexity when designing IT solutions can be further understood by trying to define what 'user pull' means in the context of the relationship between technology and society [17]. People are complex and their relationship to a technological device or service has this complexity as a background. People do not buy a technology device – they buy an artifact to support their lifestyle and if this technology fails to engage and support them on multiple levels and provide perceived benefit to their life, it becomes less useful. 'User pull' in today's context can carry the implication of needing to understand the intricate and complex nature of human beings and their lifestyles. Designers working in IT have the challenge of engaging with this context, projecting user needs into the future and appropriating technologies that support their aspirations. The methods and learning afforded by an inclusive design approach can provide one way of balancing 'technology push' with 'user pull', and promote an understanding as to what 'pulls' or attracts users to a particular type of technology in today's context.

Some aspects of IT have a history of collaborating with people. Software designers have tended to include users throughout the design and development process seeing active participation as a way of iteratively moving towards design solutions. Since 1970, Cooperative Design has involved designers and users as equals in the design of IT products and devices [18]. Co-design is prevalent in architecture and business but is also used when designing information systems and mobile phone development [19]. Working with communities can establish focus not just on commercial products but also new understanding of technology's use [20]. This becomes important in moving the designer's view beyond the artifact or the technology and onto the rich area of designing to support communication, lifestyle and information exchange for the users.

2 Method

The Helen Hamlyn Centre (HHC) based at the Royal College of Art (RCA) in London focuses on people-centred design and innovation. Its multi-disciplinary team of designers, engineers, architects, anthropologists and communication experts undertake practical research and projects to advance an approach to design within the RCA that is people-centred and socially inclusive. The research looks at developing the practice and theory of inclusive design and working with older and disabled people has remained a central activity over the last ten years.

The HHC works with a range of external business, academic, government and voluntary sector partners. Its programmes engage with four design communities: students, new graduates, professional designers and academics. The case studies described in this paper draw on two of these programmes. The first looks at work completed with RCA Masters students and the second outlines projects with industry carried out by new RCA design graduates.

2.1 Working with People

An important part of HHC practice is to involve users within the design process so that projects have social relevance and value for the end user. Students and new graduates are encouraged to work with people in their own space to empathise with their lifestyles and understand their context as nothing can replace this type of direct contact [21]. This is especially important when a young designer is tasked with designing for a person who might be more than 50 years older than them. The designers are schooled in a range of research techniques including questionnaires, expert consultation, user diaries, interviews, observation 'in situ', testing with prototypes, and research 'kits' that can be left with people to gather responses without the designer being present.

Users are selected carefully to challenge the scope of the project and are involved from the outset to provide initial inspiration and insights rather than just acting as 'test subjects' to validate the designers own thoughts at the end of the process. People are seen individually or in small groups to encourage a richer exchange of information and opinion, which in turn, can become a powerful instigation for creating new design insights and inspiration. Working in this manner allows designer and user to act as equals, an important factor in maintaining 'user push' over 'technology pull' and in understanding the complexity of the particular context that the resultant IT designs will have to function in for the user.

3   Case Study 1

The 'Design for Our Future Selves' (DFOFS) awards programme is a three-term programme for all Masters students in their final year at the RCA. The programme is divided into three stages: Define, Develop and Delivery. In the first stage, students from different art and design disciplines submit their own design proposals that aim to address some aspect of social change. Fifty to sixty students are then shortlisted and invited to join the develop stage, where groups of users, with different disabilities, ages and occupations, will challenge the design briefs and encourage the students to stretch the creative envelope in unanticipated ways. Finally, in the delivery stage, twenty-five to thirty students are selected to present to an international panel of judges who look carefully at how they have transferred the user research data into creative design solutions. The programme ends with an awards ceremony at the end of the academic year for selected, winning designs.

3.1 YuType

The project started with the student defining a social issue to investigate as part of their final year work on the RCA Industrial Design Engineering Masters degree. Computer technology can improve the quality of life and promote independence for older people. However, the primary point of interface, the keyboard, presents some difficulties. Touch-typing is a relatively underused technique, with 79 per cent of keyboard users, a disproportionate number of these being older, adopting a two-fingered approach (or 'hunt and peck') to typing. This requires users to locate keys by sight, shift their gaze to the screen to check for errors then return their attention to the keyboard to continue as shown in Fig. 1. Not only is this approach slow and less accurate, it also provokes repetitive head movements, sometimes aggravating neck muscles, and puts unnecessary strain on the overused digits. Although these issues affect users of all ages, the negative effects of repetitive strain, muscle ache and joint immobility can be over-emphasized in an older age group.

Fig. 1. User research with older people revealed a range of neck movement when typing

A variety of existing systems such as single-handed keyboards and instructional software were evaluated with the need of older users in mind. A series of ideas were then generated to address the main issues identified and these were further evaluated with older people. The most successful of these ideas was then refined and a working prototype was constructed. This prototype was taken to one of the users who had been involved in the project from the beginning in order to validate and optimise its effectiveness and to receive further feedback. This improved the aesthetics and allowed the designer to test the results in the complexities of a 'real' situation.

Users were involved throughout the project. This started with an online survey to gauge opinion and gather early data and was followed by home visits to a number of different computer users over the age of 55 in order to develop the hypothesis and see the daily difficulties that people have with IT devices. Informal interviews were initially conducted to develop an overview of daily computing habits, aspirations and perceived difficulties. Observation and filming was carried out with a specific user who fitted the strict test criteria of this project. This person was a daily computer user who had tried to learn touch-typing but was unsuccessful, and had subsequently adopted the two-fingered approach. They had arthritis and stiffness in the neck, which became aggravated during computer usage. This individual was selected as the lead user for the project as they had the most challenging condition.

The result was a device that allows the typist to see what they have typed without having to shift constantly their glance from the keyboard area to the screen. It has the potential to reduce neck movement and strain whilst increasing typing speed and accuracy. The device is a small LCD high contrast screen, which connects directly to the computer and displays the most recently typed text within the users' immediate field of vision. It can be repositioned to suit different people and does not require any set-up procedure or software to use (see Fig. 2).

Fig. 2. The final design attached to the keyboard

4   Case Study 2

The HHC's Research Associates (RA) Programme demonstrates a process in which academia can work with business to transfer design knowledge, capability and understanding, allowing companies to use inclusive design as an organisational asset to invent, create and improve. It works by taking new RCA graduates from a range of design disciplines and partnering them with an industry organisation. Throughout the year, they draw on the creativity of the RCA whilst developing user-centred design skills through the Helen Hamlyn Centre network. Each yearlong project addresses an area of interest for the partner organisation, where an inclusive design approach can be practically implemented within a 'real world' business context. As well as realising the design concepts and exemplars, each designer produces an extensive report cataloguing the research process and results typically including an assessment of potential business impact.

The programme maintains a core interest in working with IT companies to improve their consumer offer and work with older or disabled communities. Between 1999 and 2009 the HHC has undertaken over 100 projects with 75 companies including many from the technology sector. The Research Associates Programme operates on an annual basis, running from October to October. Each year ends with a symposium and exhibition launch event for research partners and collaborators. Around 300 people attend the symposium, and there are more than 1000 visitors to the exhibition.

4.1 TwoTone Phone

The project was partnered with UK telecoms company and service provider BT with a focus on developing creative new ways to connect the over-60s to the communication benefits of broadband. Two new graduates from the RCA department of Industrial Design Engineering were employed to conduct this work. The resulting designs had to enable non terminal-based access to the Internet and explore more ambient and pervasive methods of information handling. BT was looking for marketable products that addressed a future of five years from the project start date in 2006.

More than 14 million people in the UK can be termed 'digitally excluded' and the majority of these are older people. Some have never had access to a computer and many are never likely to. Many older people cannot justify the costs of buying a computer or the complications of learning to use one. This means that they cannot access services and communications that are becoming increasingly dependent on the Internet whether it is shopping for the best deals, communicating to a dispersed family network or obtaining impartial healthcare advice. The project aimed to bring the older user into the foreground and push the technology into the background. The focus was on promoting independent living and choice instead of simply providing another hard-wired, telecare solutions.

Fig. 3. Four of the six users interviewed

The research consisted of two phases. The first selected six lead users aged over 60 and interviewed them in their homes (see Fig. 3). This group represented a mix in terms of age, gender, physical proximity to their family, living alone or with a partner, and urban and rural location. The interviews were video-recorded and consisted of an informal, but guided discussion within which a holistic impression of the participant's lifestyle and their attitude towards technology could be discovered. The topics discussed aimed to cover the complexity and diversity of each user's life and topics included attitudes to technology, lifestyle, healthcare, social networks, organization of personal information and communications. The key aim of this was to assemble a series of insights that the designers could relate to, and make reference to throughout the design process to inform the decision making from the point of view of the users.

The second phase addressed the difficulty in exploring the potential of broadband with a group of people who have minimal grasp of the internet and are therefore unable to fully understand the technical jargon associated with IT devices and services.

Six tester design concepts that visualised different ways in which the internet could be accessed without using a standard computer terminal were developed so that users could visualise potential benefits and react to new ideas. These concepts ranged from a 'piggy bank' that displays credit or debit card information to a simplified keyboard that groups keys alphabetically and into logical clusters. Visuals depicting these imaginary concepts were taken to the interviews with the existing group of six older people and used to provoke reaction. Feedback was gathered on the participants' understanding of each concept, the relevance of the concept to their lifestyle, the way in which the product functions and the aesthetic quality of each.

The interviews were run during the early stages of the design process allowing the designers to respond to early feedback and evolve the concepts in between visits. This approach meant that designs were directly challenged by the users from the briefing stage, allowing the creative process to move unhindered into spaces that the designers had not previously considered. This research highlighted a number of issues in terms of who the outcomes should be aimed at and what technology should be used. In its latter stages, the project focused on the over-70s for whom cost is especially important, as is ergonomics of use such as tactility of buttons and easy-to-read displays. This group wanted any new devices to build on familiar interfaces and any benefits to be self-evident.

Fig. 4. The final design showing the black internet 'face' when docked and the white landline 'face' in use

The main design outcome of the study, the TwoTone Phone, addresses these issues. It is effectively two phones in one unit. The white face acts as a normal, cordless house phone but the black face is a Voice Over Internet Protocol (VoIP) phone that utilises existing VoIP services to allow calls to be made over a broadband connection (see Fig. 4). Turning over the phone activates its different modes: the VoIP mode does not have a screen but simply has six large buttons on which users can write the names of their contacts. The buttons turn orange if the person is online and flash when that person calls, with the added benefit of indicating who is available to chat.

Whilst designed with the older person in mind, the concept is also aimed at the mainstream market. Users can connect the phone to their television in order to make video calls and the base unit also acts as a wireless router. Although the TwoTone Phone has a large number of functions, these are presented in a way that does not intimidate or confuse. The user can choose the level of functionality and adapt the phone to suit their needs. For digitally excluded older people, it provides a simple way to communicate freely, using previously unattainable broadband services.

5 Conclusion and Discussion

The work described has provided RCA students and new graduates with the tools to see IT designs in the broader scope of social context, and interaction with user groups as a way of successfully achieving that. This was done in a way that did not present inclusive design practice as a token practice or special process. Instead, it was used as a vehicle for rethinking and reinvigorating the creative process, to understand the complexity of 'user need' and 'user pull' and put it before the binary approach of 'technology pull', allowing the designers to create IT solutions that meet user aspiration whilst remaining grounded in the context of everyday life.

People acquire technology for the purpose of supporting their lifestyle and because of this they need shades of communication from the design that is appropriate to their need and easily understood. Using binary language or technical jargon alienates rather than empowers the older user. Involving people upstream challenges designers throughout the design process and means that user insights can be used for inspiration and help to define key directions rather than just passively validating a designer's own thoughts towards the end of the project. This is especially important for the fast-moving IT sector where new software, devices and typologies are developed at a rapid pace. Small groups of carefully selected users can help to orientate work at critical developmental stages, providing early inspiration for designers and saving time and cost for manufacturers and makers.

Designers have to look for the convergent points where 'technology push' meets 'user pull' and where users' needs can be met by technological progress. Technology should not fight the user and the user should not have to significantly adapt their learnings and lifestyle in order to access technology. Designers need to develop clever and interesting ways to engage older users as equals within IT research and build on existing inclusive design methodologies to create new ways to talk about digital technology to an analogue-minded audience.

References

1. Woods, M.: Design in a Digital World. In: Inclusive Design – Design for the Whole Population, vol. 34, pp. 576–581. Springer, London (2003)
2. Coleman, R.: A Demographic Overview of the Ageing of First World Populations. Applied Ergonomics 24(1), 5–8 (1993)
3. Mueller, J.: Universal Products in the US. In: Inclusive Design – Design for the Whole Population, vol. 19, pp. 318–335. Springer, London (2003)
4. Newell, A.: The Future for ICT. In: Inclusive Design – Design for the Whole Population, vol. 19, pp. 566–575. Springer, London (2003)
5. Coleman, R., Harrow, D.: A Car for All – Mobility for All. In: Paper presented at the Institute of Mechanical Engineers. Design Age Publications, London (1997), http://www.hhrc.rca.ac.uk/resources/publications/CarforAll/carforall1.html (retrieved December 5, 2008)

6. Haigh, R.: The Ageing Process: A Challenge for Design. Applied Ergonomics 24(1), 9–14 (1993)
7. Laslett, P.: Design Slippage over Life Course. In: Studies in Health Technology and Infomatics, pp. 84–92. IOS Press, Amsterdam (1998)
8. Audit Commission: Fully Equipped: The Provision of Equipment to Older or Disabled People by the NHS and Social Services in England and Wales. The Audit Commission. London (2000)
9. British Standards Institute: BS 7000-6; Design management systems. Managing inclusive design. Guide, UK (2005)
10. Hinkelman, E., Putzi, S.: Dictionary of International Trade - Handbook of the Global Trade Community. World Trade Press (2005)
11. Roberts, R., Gadberry, H.: Study of A Contractors Capabilities Center And The Technology Transfer Process. Technology Utilization Division, Office of Technology Utilization, National Aeronautics and Space Administration, Washington (1968)
12. Lewis, J.D.: Technology Incentive Programs. Science 189(4208), 1066–1067 (1975)
13. Voss, C.A.: Technology Push and Need Pull: A New Perspective. R&D Management 14(3), 147–151 (1984)
14. Shaw, B.: The Role of the Interaction between the User and the Manufacturer in Medical Equipment Innovation. R&D Management 15(4), 283–292 (1985)
15. Rothwell, R.: Successful industrial innovation: critical factors for the 1990s. R&D Management 22(3), 221–240 (1992)
16. Rothwell, R.: Towards the Fifth-generation Innovation Process. International Marketing Review 11(1), 7–31 (1994)
17. MacKenzie, D., Wajcman, J. (eds.): The Social Shaping of Technology, 2nd edn. Open University Press, Buckingham (1998)
18. Greenbaum, J., Kyng, M. (eds.): Design At Work - Cooperative design of Computer Systems. Lawrence Erlbaum, Mahwah (1991)
19. Balarin, F., Di Giusto, P., Jurecska, A., Passerone, C., Sentovich, E., Tabbara, B., Chiodo, M., Hsieh, H., Lavagno, L., Sangiovanni-Vincentelli, A., Suzuki, K.: Hardware-software Co-design of Embedded Systems: The Polis Approach. In: Springer International Series in Engineering and Computer Science (1997)
20. Hofmeester, K., de Charon de Saint Germain, E. (eds.): Probing for Inspiration. Presence – New Media for Older People, pp. 2–26. Netherlands Design Institute (1995)
21. Warbuton, N.: Everyday Inclusive Design. Inclusive Design – Design for the Whole Population 15(254), 250–269 (2003)

A Multimodal Board Game System Interface Using Finger Input for Visually Impaired Computer Users

Yusuke Hamaguchi[1], Daisuke Nagasaka[2], Takahiro Tamesue[2],
Kazunori Itoh[2], Michio Shimizu[3], Masahiko Sugimoto[1,4],
Masami Hashimoto[2], and Mizue Kayama[2]

[1] Graduate School of Science and Technology, Shinshu University, 4-17-1 Wakasato
Nagano-shi, Nagano 380-8553 Japan
t07a690@shinshu-u.ac.jp
[2] Faculty of Engineering, Shinshu University, 4-17-1 Wakasato
Nagano-shi, Nagano 380-8553 Japan
t055064@shinshu-u.ac.jp,
{tamesue,itoh,hasimoto,kayama}@cs.shinshu-u.ac.jp
[3] Nagano-ken College, 8-49-7 Miwa
Nagano-shi, Nagano 380-8525 Japan
michio@nagano-kentan.ac.jp
[4] Takushoku University Hokkaido College, 4558 Memu
Fukagawa-shi, Hokkaido 074-8585 Japan
sugimoto@takushoku-hc.ac.jp

Abstract. In this paper, we developed a new board game system on a PC that feels like a real board game. The main improvements of this system are the tactile guide, the finger input interface, and an output method using vibrating stimuli. These improvements allow players to grasp the layout better than previous systems. We evaluate the system using the Othello game. As the result, we see that visually impaired persons can play the Othello game.

Keywords: visually impaired person, tactile guide, speech guide, auditory display, vibrating stimulus.

1 Introduction

Recently, in order to improve the quality of life for visually impaired persons, various communication systems using the personal computer (PC) are studied [1], [2]. As the related study, there are many things that use the hearing and tactile senses like a screen reader [3] and tactile display [4]. Games are one of the communication methods used. Board games are fun not only for sighted persons but also for visually impaired persons. There are two kinds of board games for people with visual impairment: real board games and computer games [5], [6]. The former often use tactile sense, the latter often use hearing. Many board games use an 8 x 8 layout, so we need to grasp the layout of the board. The layout of real boards can be recognized by touching. In contrast, the advantages of computer games are that we can play the game through the Internet and can play against a computer opponent.

C. Stephanidis (Ed.): Universal Access in HCI, Part I, HCII 2009, LNCS 5614, pp. 68–77, 2009.
© Springer-Verlag Berlin Heidelberg 2009

We already reported a board game system for Mini-Go [7]. In this system, the board layout is difficult to grasp because a pen is used as the input device. To improve on this system, we developed a new computer board game system that makes it easier to understand the layout of a game board.

As board games, there is Checkers, Chess, and Othello. In this study, this system uses the Othello game. The Othello game is also known as Reversi [8], and has the advantage that the algorithm of the game is easy. Also, many people play Othello.

We describe a multimodal interface of our system and evaluate playing Othello games using this system.

2 Components of the Board Game System

When we play the Othello game, it is necessary to grasp the layout of the board, planning a strategy of game and putting a piece. So, it is important how to support these movements using our system.

We need to know some information such as the color and arrangement of the piece, the position where we can put a piece, victory or defeat of a game, start and end of game. In these we define the information about position as positional information. Also, we define other information that is necessary for the game as semantic information. In this system, positional information is obtained by touching the board, semantic information about color of a piece is obtained from a vibrating stimulus, and other positional and semantic information is obtained by hearing.

The block diagram of the board game system is shown in Fig.1. This system contains input-output units. The input units are a tactile guide and an input interface attached to a finger. On the other hand, the output units are an auditory display, a speech guide, and vibrating stimuli. The Othello game is played on an 8 x 8 matrix. Therefore, we use a tactile guide which has 8 x 8 = 64 holes with a diameter of about 1 cm to fit the size of a finger. The size of the guide is about 13 cm long and wide and it is fixed to the surface of the tablet. The layout of the board and the input position can be recognized by touching the tactile guide. The input position is converted into auditory information, which is then output through the headphones using a sound (auditory display). Also, a speech guide tells you the positions with a female voice. Furthermore, vibrating motors are attached to several fingers to give the user information about the layout.

The components and transmitted information of the interfaces is shown in Table.1. These are explained below.

Table 1. Components and transmitted information of interface

	Interface	Sense	Positional information	Semantic information
Input	Tactile guide	Tactile sense	O	–
	Input with finger		O	–
Output	Vibrating stimulus	Tactile sense	–	O
	Speech guide	Auditory sense	O	O
	Auditory display		O	–

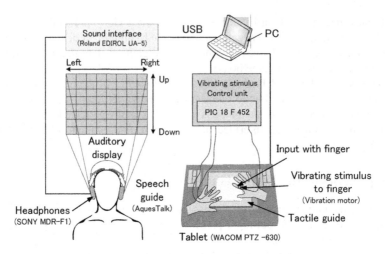

Fig. 1. Block diagram of the board game system

2.1 Tablet and Tactile Guide

In this system, we want to know the layout of the board by touching. Therefore, we introduce a tablet interface from which we can obtain absolute coordinates. Also, we assume the guide (the tactile guide) gives information equivalent to the layout of a board on the tablet. Then, we select the WACOM PTZ-630 tablet, because it has an input area of 203.2mm x 152.4mm, it is an electromagnetic induction type and it detect inputs up to approximately 15mm from the surface.

We cut and create the tactile guide, which is made from an acrylic board, with a machine tool. The thickness of the board is 4mm because the tablet can recognize touches trough an acrylic board with this thickness. Fig.2 shows the layout of the tactile guide for the Othello game. Tactile guide has pointing holes in an 8 x 8 array in order to correspond to the layout of a real board.

The center of the tactile guide is called the center point. The second positional hole in each diagonal direction from the center points an index hole. The index holes show the middle of each direction from the center point. The center point and the index hole have a protuberance in the shape of a cone. Also, taper processing is carried out to the edge of the positional hole and the index hole in order to enable a smooth scan with fingers. On the extension of up and down, left and right of the center point, the four center guides is prepared so that the center of the tactile guide is known. Function holes (Fn holes) are prepared outside of the matrix in order to carry out all setting of the game on the tablet. The eight Fn holes are for future expansion and the top right one has function telling a game mode.

The specification of the tactile guide which described above is shown in Table.2. The various parameters are decided by the psychophysical experiment that evaluated the size and height which is easy to recognize when playing the game for an adult. The top-left pointing hole is the origin (A1). Also, the row and column address of the

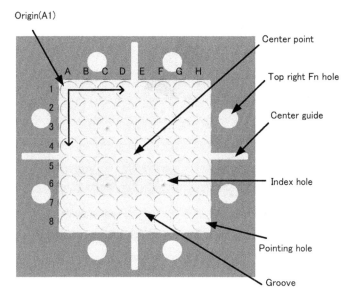

Fig. 2. Layout of tactile guide for the Othello game

Table 2. Main specification of tactile guide

Name	Number	Diameter, width (mm)	Depth (mm)
Fn hole	8	10.5	1.20
Pointing hole	60	9.0	2.50
Index hole	4	10.0	2.50
Center guide	4	3.5	1.25

pointing holes indicate alphabet and numerical number as a coordinate, respectively. In addition, the specifications of the guide such as size and shape and the number of pointing holes can be changed according to a use.

2.2 Finger Input Interface

The input unit attached to a finger is the interface which uses tactile sense, and is made using parts of the mouse that comes with the tablet. An illustration of the instruments which are attached to a finger is shown Fig.3. Because the tablet can detect touches from a height of approximately 15mm, the pointing coil is attached to the first joint of the index finger like a ring. Also, we equip the middle of the second joint and the third joint with button A and B corresponding to the left and the right button of a mouse in the direction of the thumb. The pointing coil is used to let the tablet know buttons and the position of the index finger. Moreover, we can use buttons to determine commands.

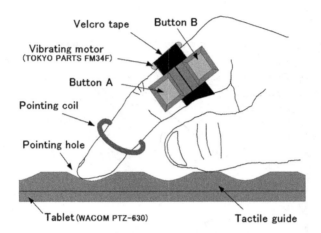

Fig. 3. The appearance of the instruments which attached to a finger

2.3 Vibrating Stimulus

We use a small vibrating motor in order not to disturb input movement. The vibration motor (coin type coreless vibration motor FM34F) is fixed on the index finger of right, the index finger of left, and the ring finger of left as shown in Fig.1. The motor provides the semantic information, such as the point where you can put a virtual piece, white or black. These stimuli are transmitted from the PC to the microprocessor via USB. After the microprocessor (Microchip PIC18F452), which is a vibrating stimulus control unit, processes the information using the Othello game, the information is outputted by carrying out 70 ms operation of about 200Hz vibration that minimize an adaptation effect and maximize sensitivity.

2.4 Speech Guide

A game mode announcement, position coordinates, and choice of various commands are output through the headphones using synthesized speech. The female voice of the AquesTalk is chosen as the synthesized speech for its availability and clear voice. The speech guide has two varieties. Information of game progress such as start or end of game is automatically output, while information of the color of the piece or the coordinates is output on demand by clicking the button A.

2.5 Auditory Display

As an assist of the positional information of the tactile guide, an auditory display is also provided. It is 150 ms white noise convoluted with the HRTFs corresponding to each position of the tactile guide. The sound of each direction corresponding to the tactile guide is generated using the median plane HRTFs obtained by the measurement using a dummy head (KOKEN SAMRAI) and sound source 50 cm distant, and ITD (Interaural Time Difference) and also ILD (Interaural Level Difference) shown in Table.3 below.

Table 3. The direction of sound images vs pointing holes on the tactile guide

			Horizontal (degrees)							
			Left							Right
			−60	−43	−26	−9	9	26	43	60
	Up	60	A1	B1	C1	D1	E1	F1	G1	H1
		43	A2	B2	C2	D2	E2	F2	G2	H2
Vertical (degrees)		26	A3	B3	C3	D3	E3	F3	G3	H3
		9	A4	B4	C4	D4	E4	F4	G4	H4
		−9	A5	B5	C5	D5	E5	F5	G5	H5
		−26	A6	B6	C6	D6	E6	F6	G6	H6
		−43	A7	B7	C7	D7	E7	F7	G7	H7
	Down	−60	A8	B8	C8	D8	E8	F8	G8	H8

3 Evaluation of the Positional Information

It is important to put a piece quickly and accurately on the board when we play the Othello game, so we evaluated effectiveness of the positional information about the tactile guide, the speech guide, and the auditory display.

3.1 Method of the Experiment

Five ordinary persons in their 20's are chosen as the subjects. Subjects wear an eye mask to be a blind artificially. Subjects move their finger toward the target position by voice from the top right Fn hole as the start position and click the button B. The time they spent and the moving process is observed. The 20 coordinates out of 64 points are chosen evenly. We measured 5 times on each condition.

The conditions are as follows: using each interface separately, using two interfaces combined, and using all interfaces at the same time. Also we measured using tactile guide exclusively without an eye mask for comparison.

3.2 Result of the Experiment

The results of experiments are shown as Fig.4, Fig.5. Fig.4 indicates the average time of all subjects per trial. Fig.5 indicates average wrong times per trial. According to Fig.4, it is faster to use the tactile guide, the speech guide, and the auditory display in that order. The variance of the result of the auditory display is great. The time is almost constant except for the condition of the auditory display. Therefore, it is faster when using the tactile guide or the speech guide. Combining interfaces results in a time close to that of sighted condition.

Fig.5 indicates there is little error except the condition of the auditory display. Particularly, there is no error in the condition of the speech guide as well as sighted. Therefore, the accuracy improves when using the speech guide and the tactile guide.

As a result, we find out that subjects can input the target position by using every interface. In addition, all subjects can input the target faster and more accurately by using the tactile guide and the speech guide. Therefore, the tactile guide and the speech guide are useful interfaces to play the board game. Also, it is unnecessary to practice using the interface because the average time is almost constant except the condition of the auditory display.

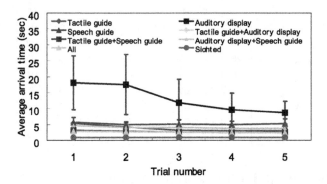

Fig. 4. Comparison of the average arrival time

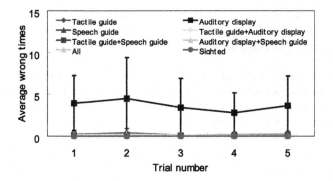

Fig. 5. Comparison of the average wrong times

4 Evaluation of the Game

We considered playing the Othello game using our system. For the game to proceed not only positional information but also semantic information is necessary. Then we carry out the evaluation which focuses attention on the time to place a piece. The situation of the Othello game is shown in Fig.6.

4.1 Method of the Experiment

In the experiments, three subjects play the Othello game on the computer. Also, subjects wear an eye mask. At that time, the behaviors of subjects and the time to put a piece are observed. The procedure of the Othello game is shown bellow.

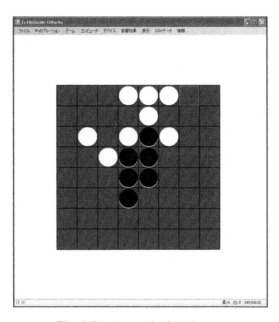

Fig. 6. Situation to the Othello game

First, you can select from the black player or the white player to start the game. If you select the black player, the speech guide tells you that you are the first move, and the game starts. Then, you must put a piece on a place on the board that has at least one straight (horizontal, vertical, or diagonal) occupied line between the new place and another black piece with one or more contiguous white piece. After placing the piece, you can turn over all white pieces lying on a straight line between the new piece and any anchoring preoccupied black piece. This operation is controlled by the PC. Next is the white player's turn. The white player is a computer and this player operates under the same rule as the black player. Players take alternate turns. If one player cannot make a valid move, the turn passes back to the other player. When neither player can move, the game ends. The player with the most pieces on the board at the end of the game wins.

We measured 5 times for each condition. The conditions are as follows: using our system, using our system without an eye mask, using the Othello board for the blind. When using our system, the computer has three techniques shown below [9].

Level 1: Check the board from top to bottom, for a place to put a piece.
Level 2: Check the four corners, and does the same as Level 1 when the four corners cannot be used.
Level 3: Check the four corners. If the four corners cannot be used put a piece on a place that does not allow your opponent to put a place on a corner.

4.2 Result of the Experiment

The result of subject A is shown as Fig.7. Each condition shown in Fig.7 wins the game. The horizontal axis and the vertical axis of Fig.7 indicate the number of moves and the input time of putting a piece.

As the result, all subjects can play the Othello game by using this system. It shows that the input time of the level 1 is shorter than the Othello board for the blind on the whole. When use the Othello board, we grasp the layout on the board at first, put the piece after planning the strategy. However, our system instantly indicates a place where a piece can be placed by the vibrating stimulus. It is thought that this time difference occurs because of this stimulus.

We compare the difference of the level in our system next. It is generally thought that a strategy becomes difficult with the rise of the level. Moreover, it is remind to expect the situation on the board next turn and do not put at the corner. Especially, the result that wins the level 3 is said that we put a piece after having considered the strategy. Therefore, we see that visually impaired persons can play the Othello game.

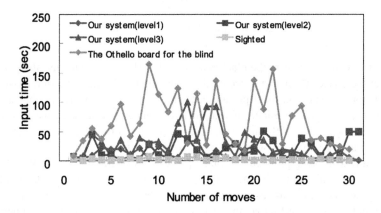

Fig. 7. The time of putting a piece

5 Conclusion

In order to develop a useful interface using the auditory and tactile feedback for visually impaired persons, we perform experiments by using a board game. To obtain positional information, a tactile guide and a speech guide are useful interfaces to play the board game. In the evaluation of the game, we found that our system allows visually impaired computer users to play the Othello game.

In the future, we will make a co-operative system and a system that can get closer to the level of play of Othello by a sighted person. Moreover, we will apply this system to other board games such as the Mini-Go and the Checkers game.

References

1. Kaczmirek, L., Wolff, K.G.: Survey Design for Visually Impaired and Blind People. In: Proceedings of UAHCI 2007, Part Held as Part of HCII 2007, pp. 374–381 (2007)
2. Sharma, R., Pavolovic, V.I., Huang, T.S.: Toward Multimodal Human-Computer Interface. Proceedings of the IEEE 86(5), 853–869 (1998)
3. Mukherjee, S., Ramakrishnan, I.V., Kifer, M.: Semantic Bookmarking for Non-Visual Web Access. In: ASSETS 2004, USA, October 2004, pp. 185–192 (2004)
4. Ng, J.Y.C., Man, J.C.F., Fels, S., Dumont, G., Ansermino, M.: An Evaluation of a Vibro-Tactile Display Prototype for Physiological Monitoring. Anesthesia Analgesia 101, 1719–1724 (2005)
5. http://www.afb.org/Section.asp?SectionID=40&TopicID=219&DocumentID=2241 (2009/2/23 accessed)
6. Grammenos, D., Savidis, A., Stephanidis, C.: UA-Chess: A Universally Accessible Board Game. In: Proceesdings of UAHCI 2005, vol. 7 (2005)
7. Shimizu, M., Sugimoto, M., Itoh, K.: Interface of Online Mini-Go-Game with Pen Input Guide for the Blind. In: Proceedings of UAHCI 2007, Part Held as Part of HCII 2007, pp. 806–812 (2007)
8. http://en.wikipedia.org/wiki/Reversi (2009/2/23 accessed)
9. http://homepage1.nifty.com/rucio/main/dotnet/shokyu/standard52.htm (2009/2/23 accessed in Japanese)

Applying Human-Centered Design to Rehabilitation Device

Lan-Ling Huang and Dengchuan Cai

National Yunlin University of Science and Technology, Graduate School of Design,
123 University Road, Section 3, Douliu, Yunlin 64002, Taiwan, R.O.C.
{g9630806,caidc}@yuntech.edu.tw

Abstract. The current study investigated the patients' problems and needs during therapy process. The investigation results were transferred to the product requirements of the rehabilitation device. The features of the new rehabilitation device included the following: 1) a webcam that can provide patients to communicate with his/her families or doctors during the therapy process, 2) a visual display that provides patients the function to see their posture and is able to correct their actions immediately, 3) physiological data such as movement angle, strength, and exercise time which were provided for diagnosis application for the doctors and their families, and 4) the main operational was designed to be adjustable for different individuals including its height, angle, and direction. The current design obtained positive evaluation preliminary by the occupational therapists. The procedure, methods and design of this study can be used as a reference for rehabilitation product design.

Keywords: upper extremities, rehabilitation therapy, product design.

1 Introduction

The aging population has become a world-wide phenomenon. Health care for the aging has been a popular issue. With aging, the physical condition degenerates and diseasing become more possible. According to the analytical report [4], cerebrovascular disease has become one of the top three causes of death in America. In Taiwan, cerebrovascular diseases also occupied the third cause of death for the year of 2007 [2]. On the other hand, it is still a main cause contributing to stroke.

Upper-extremity motor deficit is one of the main symptoms for stroke patients [3]. About 85% of stroke patients have upper-extremity function impairment at the beginning stage of stroke, and about 40% of patients still are with the function impairment at the final stage of stroke [6]. Some common upper-extremity symptoms of stroke patients are feeble muscle strength, unnatural synergies, and deficit in coordination within the joints etc [5]. In order to recover the function for daily life, rehabilitation therapy is needed for stroke patients.

The six most frequently used products in hospitals in Taiwan for stroke patients are listed below. 1) Arm/ hand skate: the main movement direction is horizontal from left to right and reversed. 2) Climbing board and bar: the main movement direction is vertical from bottom to top and reversed. 3) Resistive pinch exerciser: the main

C. Stephanidis (Ed.): Universal Access in HCI, Part I, HCII 2009, LNCS 5614, pp. 78–85, 2009.
© Springer-Verlag Berlin Heidelberg 2009

movement direction is vertical from bottom to top and reversed. 4) Vertical ring tree: the main movement direction is vertical from bottom to top and reversed. 5) Single curved shoulder arc: the main movement direction is horizontal from left to right and reversed. 6) Incline board: the main movement direction is vertical from bottom to top combining with horizontal from rear to the front and reversed [9].

The study results [9] showed that 1) the main movement directions of the above six pieces of equipment can be summarized as: horizontal from left to the right and reversed, vertical from bottom to top and reversed, horizontal from rear to front and reversed, and small arc movements, 2) most of the equipment was old and outdated.

In many cases, using an unaffected extremity to promote the affected extremity for restoring its lost movement ability has been conducted and proved in many studies [1] [7]. The theory for using an upper extremity on the unaffected side of the body to facilitate the other extremity on the affected side to recover its original movement ability for the stroke patients has been proposed and verified in various experiments and products.

According to the above theory, using the unaffected muscles to facilitate the affected muscle in the same extremity to recover its lost movement ability was proposed

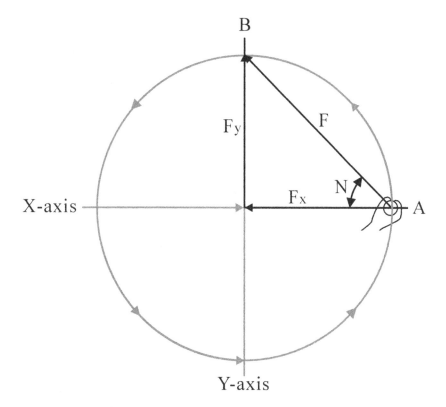

Fig. 1. Illustration for using unaffected muscle to facilitate the affected muscle

by the study. The idea is that supposing the affected muscle lost its movement ability along Y-axis direction and the unaffected muscle is still able to move along X-axis direction. Let the patients move their arms along a circular route, the unaffected muscle exercises a force F to move the arm from point A to point B witch made an angle of N between line AB and X-axis, then the affected muscle will be provided a component force Fy (F sin(N)) along Y-axis and the hand being forced to move to point B (Fig. 1). Therefore, the affected muscle will be trained by the component force Fy and will be facilitated in its movement ability along the Y-axis direction. When the circular movement continued, the movement ability of the affective muscles will be drilled and progressed continuously. The rehabilitation therapy theory was then applied to design an integrated rehabilitation product for the upper extremities.

2 Methods

The main methods in the study included a field observation and interview, a literature review for understanding state of the art of the rehabilitation products in Taiwan, a systematic design process, and applying a rehabilitation therapy theory and using a concept on human-centered design.

The field observation and interview were used to survey the patients' problems and needs during their therapy process. The results of the field observation and interview as well as the results of literature review were then transferred to the product requirements of the rehabilitation devices. During the design processes, serial design activities such as brainstorming, ides sketch, and 3D model making were used and a rehabilitation therapy theory (using unaffected muscle to facilitate affected muscle for restoring its lost function) and a human-centered design concept were applied into product requirements to design an integrate rehabilitation equipment.

3 Field Observation and Interview

3.1 Subjects

There were 10 patients served as participants interviewed in the study. The patients mean age was 66.2 years (SD=28.1 years). All of them patients were hemiplegia and treated with occupational therapy at the rehabilitation center of National Cheng Kung University Hospital DouLiu Branch. The recovery stages for arms of the patients are at stages 3 to 4. Patients at stage 4, their upper extremities and fingers have few functions and are able to bend. Besides the patients, we also investigated 3 therapists being employed in this hospital.

3.2 Interview Contents

The main interview contents included individual information, the needs of the patients during their therapy process and the requirements of the rehabilitation devices for the therapists which are described below:

1. The individual information include age and recovery stages for arms.
2. The needs of the patients included the following questions: a) are your psychologically feeling lonely during the therapy process? b) do you need family or friends to accompany you during the therapy process? c) what things do you want to have when you do the same and repetitive therapy movement ? d) do you want to know your rehabilitation progress every time when you finish the daily therapy process?
3. The needs of the therapists included the following questions: a) do you have any problems or needs for using the rehabilitation devices? And 2) what functions does the rehabilitation device should provide?

3.3 Procedures

First, the researchers described the study purpose to the therapists. The therapists selected suitable patients for the interview. We asked the patients if they were willing to participate. Then the researchers observed their activites during rehabilitation process. After observing the therapy process, we asked the interview questions to the patients and recorded their answers. The field observation and interview spent a week, 8 hours a day for the investigation.

3.4 Results

The investigation results indicated the following: 1) the patients usually had a sense of loneliness and helplessness during the therapy process and hoped their families or friends could be around them. 2) The patients felt uninteresting toward the rehabilitation devices and the repetitive activities. They hoped it could allow for them to chat with their family or friends, listen music or watch TV, etc. 3) The patients and therapists all preferred the product could record and display their rehabilitation performance and record physiological data for every patient. The data could be a good evaluative reference of the patient's recovery state by the therapists. 4) The rehabilitation devices should provide an adjustable function and fit to Taiwanese anthropometric data. 5) It should provide the functions of recording the movement state of the subject's body postures and the whole therapy process. As a result, the therapists can control the patient's posture easily.

4 Design Processes

According to the research results, the needs of the patients and therapists during the therapy process, the design objectives were formulated below.

4.1 Design Objectives

The design objectives included 1) the users were limited to the third to fourth level stroke patients. Patients' upper extremity at the fourth level his/her upper extremity and fingers have few functions and are able to bend, 2) the product needed to have a video and audio functions, 3) the movements should include flexion and extension, abduction and adduction, upward and downward and rotation, 4) product should provide adjustable resistance and operational conditions, and 5) should provide a function to record rehabilitation data for patients.

4.2 Design Features

According to these design objectives, we used a systematic design process which was then followed to create the rehabilitation product. The main sizes of the parts of the product were designed to fit the body dimension measurements of Taiwanese. The range of rotation radius was designed with the arm length for those from 18-64 years. The lower limit was 525mm adopting the 5th percentile of arm dimensions of 64-years-old Taiwanese females and the upper limit was 685mm adopting the 95th percentile of arm dimensions of 20-years-old Taiwanese males [8].

The product design features are as follows: 1) The rotation bar has three segments. Each segment was 250mm which is a half hand length of a female. Therefore the adjustable range was 250-750mm (Fig. 2). This allows the subject to adjust it to fit their arm length. The product was also designed with a scale for showing the length (Fig. 3). 2) The product was set on a floor and could be operated along crown, sagittal, or transverse planes for rehabilitation (Fig. 4-7). 3) A brake mechanism was designed on the rotation shaft providing adjustable friction forces for different levels of rehabilitations (Fig. 8). 4) The handle was designed to fit the hand style and size of the Taiwanese (Fig. 9). 5) The height of the operated column and the display could be adjustable. This allows subject to adjust to fit their operating posture (sitting or standing) (Fig. 10). 6) The produce has video and conversation functions in the computer and includes a microphone on the operation column. It can provide the subject conversation with family or friends during their therapy process (Fig. 11). 7) The back of the product has a space to put a computer (Fig. 12). 8) The display is provided to show the rehabilitation data and video picture. It also has a camera that can track the movements of the subject and record the whole therapy process. The therapists can realize the patient's posture easily through the recording process and correct their posture immediately (Fig. 12). This design was evaluated by three occupational therapists and got a high evaluation.

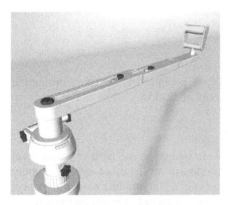
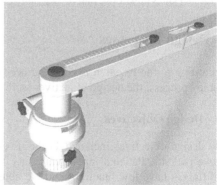

Fig. 2. Adjustable rotation radius   **Fig. 3.** Totation scale on joint

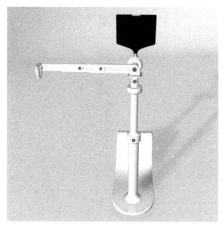

Fig. 4. Rotated on crown plane

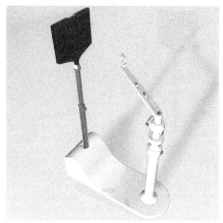

Fig. 5. Rotated on transverse plane

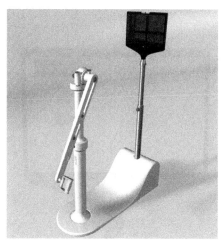

Fig. 6. Rotated on sagittal plane

Fig. 7. Rotated on any plane

Fig. 8. A brake mechanism

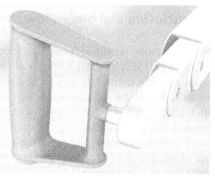

Fig. 9. Handle

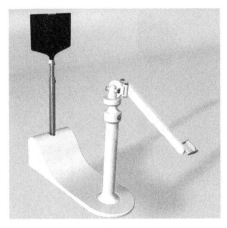

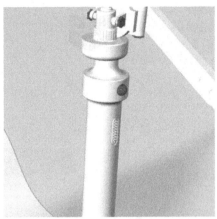

Fig. 10. The heightj of the operated column could be adjustable

Fig. 11. Microphone on the operated column

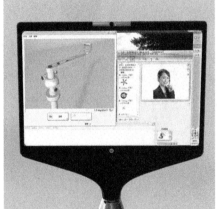

Fig. 12. Space for computer

Fig. 13. Display

5   Conclusion and Suggestions

The investigation results indicated the following: 1) the patients usually had a sense of loneliness and helplessness during the therapy process and hoped their families or friends could be around them. 2) The patients felt uninteresting toward the rehabilitation devices and the repetitive activities. They hoped it could allow for them to chat with family or friends, listen music or watch TV, etc. 3) The patients and therapists all preferred the product could record and display their rehabilitation performance and record physiological data for every patient. The data could be a good evaluative reference of the patient's recovery state by the therapists. 4) The rehabilitation devices should provide an adjustable function and fit to Taiwanese anthropometric data. 5) It should provide the function of recording the movement state of the subject's body postures and the whole therapy process. As a result, the therapists can realize the patient's posture easily. The results were then transferred to the product requirements for rehabilitation device. Through a serial design processes, the product was then proposed. The design features included: 1) a webcam that can provide patients to communicate with his/her families or doctors during the therapy process, 2) a visual display that provides patients the function to see their posture and is able to correct their actions immediately, 3) physiological data such as movement angle, strength, and exercise time which can be used to communicate with their families and doctors, and 4) an operational bar that is adjustable for different individuals including its height and operating direction. The current design obtained positive evaluation preliminary by the occupation therapists. The procedure, methods and design of this study could be used as a reference for rehabilitation product design.

References

1. Cunningham, C.L., Stoykov, M.E.: Bilaterial facilitation of motor control in chronic hemiplegia. Acta Psychological 110(2), 321–337 (2002)
2. Department of Health, Executive Yuan in Taiwan, http://www.doh.gov.tw
3. Gowland, C., DeBruln, H., Basmajian, J.V., Piews, N., Burcea, I.: Agonist and antagonist activity during voluntary upper-limb movement in patients with stroke. Physical Therapy 72, 624–633 (1992)
4. Kung, H.C., Hoyert, D.L., Xu, J., Murphy, S.L.: Deaths: Final Data for 2005. National Vital Statistics Reports 56(10), 5 (2008)
5. Levin, M.F., Michaelsen, S.M., Cirstea, C.M., Roby-Brami, A.: Use of the trunk for reaching targets placed within and beyond the reach in adult hemiparesis. Experimental Brain Research 143, 171–180 (2002)
6. McCrea, P.H., Eng, J.J., Hodgson, A.J.: Biomechanics of reachin: clinical implications for individuals with acquired brain injury. Disability and Rehabilitation 24, 534–541 (2002)
7. Mudie, M.H., Matyas, T.A.: Can simultaneous bilateral movement involve the undamaged hemisphere in reconstruction of neural networks damaged by stroke? Disability Rehabilitation 22, 23–37 (2000)
8. Wang, M.J., Wang, M.Y., Lin, Y.C.: Anthropometric Data Book of the Chinese People in Taiwan, Ergonomics Society of Taiwan, Hsinchu, Taiwan (2002)
9. Huang, L., Cai, D.: Product design for hand rehabilitation, Project Report, National Yunlin University, Yunlin, Taiwan (2008)

Implications of Participatory Design for a Wearable Near and Far Environment Awareness System (NaFEAS) for Users with Severe Visual Impairments

Si-Jung Kim[1], Tonya Smith-Jackson[1], Katherine Carroll[2], Minyoung Suh[2], and Na Mi[1]

[1] Virginia Tech, Industrial and Systems Engineering,
250 Durham Hall, Blacksburg, VA 24061 USA
{hikim,smithjack,na8}vt.edu
[2] North Carolina State University, College of Textiles,
Box 8301, Raleigh, NC 27695 USA
{katecarroll,msuh2}ncsu.edu

Abstract. This paper presents experiences from a study that included five users with Severe Visual Impairments (SVIs), fashion designers, and human factors engineers. We used participatory design (PD) to develop a wayfinding and object-recognition system. The PD study consisted of three sessions and was designed to include actual users in the design process. The primary goal of the PD was to validate the system concept and to determine the attributes of system interaction. Two of the three sessions are discussed here. We obtained several insights from a technological perspective, textile and apparel perspective, and user interface design perspective. Among the results identified, users with SVIs preferred to wear assistive technology unless that was not distracting to the participant or those that came into contact with the participant. Auditory feedback was chosen as a primary modality in user interface design, and we realized that constructing a good pool of PD members is essential to transform actual users' needs and requirements into the design process.

Keywords: participatory design, usability, inclusive design, user interface, assistive technology, wearable technology, severe visual impairment.

1 Introduction

Individuals with Severe Visual Impairments (SVIs) are legally blind and have a visual acuity of 20/200 in each eye or worse that cannot be overcome with corrective lenses. Although individuals with SVIs maintain or develop very effective compensatory sensory-perceptual capabilities, they may still be challenged by tasks that require object recognition and wayfinding. Some SVIs can navigate independently in familiar places such as home since they have an internal map of the layout based upon a spatial mental model developed from past experience. However, independent wayfinding may be challenge unfamiliar places. To overcome these challenges, there are assistive technologies to support independent wayfinding tasks based on GPS (Global Positioning System), Wi-Fi (Wireless Fidelity), RFID (Radio Frequency Identification) or

C. Stephanidis (Ed.): Universal Access in HCI, Part I, HCII 2009, LNCS 5614, pp. 86–95, 2009.

infrared technology [1, 2]. However, people with SVIs often experience frustration when they use assistive technologies, including some that are designed to be assistive [3]. The problems and frustrations associated with the use of advanced assistive technologies impose an urgency to develop a more inclusive interaction paradigm derived from human ecologies and contexts of use. This approach is known as situated design [4]. Coincidentally, the definition of usability given by ISO 9241-11 emphasizes the need to design with an understanding of the context of use, which includes users' experiences in ecologies of information (stimuli) reflecting cultural, social, and physical experiences.

This paper presents several lessons learned from two participatory designs (PD) [5, 6] sessions involving five consultants with SVIs who served as members of our participatory design team (PD members). The goal of this effort is to determine whether a garment-based wearable environment awareness system called Near and Far Environment Awareness System (NaFEAS) [7] is effective, efficient, and acceptable to users with SVIs. Here, we defined the near environment as being between 18 inches and 4 feet (48 inches) from the user. The far environment was considered to be the space that was greater than 4 feet from the user. This paper also discusses how we planned each participatory design meeting and the activities that we used to engage the team.

The presentation of this paper has four sections. In the Background section, we describe background related to PD. The Participatory Design for NaFEAS section describes our PD for a wearable environment awareness system. In this section, we describe the construction of the PD team, the objective of the 1st and 2nd PD, and procedures of each PD. The results of the 1st and 2nd PD are described at the end of each subsection. The Discussion section is devoted to describe facts (that) made our PD success, and the Conclusion and Future Works section makes a conclusion with future works.

2 Background

The participatory design (PD) [5] is a collection of user-centered design methods geared to ascertain user needs and validate concepts by bringing actual users to a design process and to discuss the assessment, design, and development of technological or organizational systems. It is used in many disciplines as a means of creating environments that are more responsive and appropriate to their inhabitants and to users' cultural, emotional, spiritual and practical needs. PD can be used information architecture, where tacit knowledge is elicited to capture user's needs [8]. For example, professionals in the field of architecture and urban design enhance the quality of design work with citizen involvement [9]. In software development, PD plays an important role in building up the method of scenario-based usability engineering. To solve design problems, PD uses the collective knowledge of stakeholders rather than the individual creativity of designers.

The primary reason for using PD in many disciplines is that reflecting actual users' opinion is crucial in designing systems or products. Therefore, PD is more focused on the design process rather than a design output. PD is also an extension of user-centered design. User-centered design does not automatically imply the involvement of users on the design team. PD is a type of user-centered design that is based on the philosophy of empowering representative users to be intimately involved in the design effort. Beck [10] stated that isolated technology developments are no longer probable in well-defined communities of work since we use technology anytime and anywhere even when on the move. This gives us an important fact that the new design paradigm to develop new technology should be a partnership consisting of actual users along with researchers and developers. Another reason that we should consider PD is that the underlying hardware of our systems is advancing at a dramatic rate paralleled by our ever-shifting environment. However, the capabilities of the human user remain the same. Therefore, bringing the actual users into the design process and considering their characteristics are essential to assess the concept and functionality for them to integrate the emerging technologies.

PD was used in the assistive technology area of designing a wheelchair convoy system. [11]. Wu et al [12] conducted PD with people with anterograde amnesia who had difficulty storing new memories. Using PD, they analyzed their cognitive deficit unrelated to memory and designed a tool called a Personal Digital Assistants (PDA). Similar to this research, PD was used in a study about adapting and combining traditional design methods to design assistive technology especially for people with cognitive disabilities and their family caregivers [13]. To support individuals with aphasia, a handheld hybrid desktop system was developed using PD [14]. In this research, PD was employed to include speech-language pathologists into the design process as proxies to target population. PD has been utilized to explore the accessibility of the World Wide Web for individuals with SVIs especially those with novice computer users [15]. The motivation of this PD method was to ascertain alternative modes of feedback mechanisms through auditory and tactile interactions, page as a screen reader, reading the content on a screen aloud for SVIs is required to undergo extensive training. Recently, distributed PD [16] has emerged because of ubiquitous infrastructures that make our interactions seamless. We use computing technology along with wireless networks to send and receive information anywhere or anytime. Distributed PD is a design approach and philosophy that supports the direct participation of actual users and other possible stakeholders in design work and its analysis. The reason is that the possible stakeholders would like to create environments that are more responsive and appropriate while the majority of design teams are distributed to join the PD. As a result, distributed PD also aims to facilitate understanding between people from different backgrounds by giving them an opportunity to engage their background in the design process.

3   Participatory Design for NaFEAS

Near and Far Environment Awareness System (NaFEAS) is a garment-based wayfinding system consisting of wireless devices embedded in a garment. It is used to support people with SVIs in wayfinding and navigation with a goal of ensuring that these tasks can occur independently while receiving appropriate near and far environmental information. The primary reason that we use a PD method in designing NaFEAS is to bring users with SVIs into the design process and as proxies for target populations. SVI participation is necessary to integrate the needs and capabilities of actual users, and thus finally to remove any bias caused by developers or researchers.

The main objective of our PD is to ascertain primary design factors, features and guidelines of NaFEAS and to analyze the fundamental interaction process of people with SVIs in wayfinding tasks.

Table 1 shows our PD consisting of three sessions, and the results reported here came from the first two PDs. Five participants called consultants with SVIs participated in this study to serve as members of our participatory design team (PD members). A total of 10 research members consisting of Human Factors, Textile and Apparel and Human Computer Interaction participated in this study. Each PD session was limited to one and half hours and focused on understanding and finding fundamental interaction factors of people with SVIs in wayfinding tasks. Each session was recorded using audio and video devices and transcribed for further analysis. As seen in table 1, the first PD session was designed to discuss the overall concept of wearable NaFEAS and to validate its concept. The rest of the two PD sessions were designed to discuss user feedback modalities and to give experience to the consultants with SVIs about the low fidelity of NaFEAS components and discuss their insights.

Table 1. The outline of the three design meetings

	1st PD	2nd PD	3rd PD
Purpose	NaFEAS concept Evaluation	Interaction analysis (near environment awareness)	Interaction analysis (far environment awareness and user feedback modality)
Team Composition	5 consultants with SVIs. 10 research members	5 consultants with SVIs along with 10 research members	5 consultants with SVIs with 10 research members
Study Type	Discussion	Experience and discussion	Experience and discussion
Task	Open-ended question	Finding objects' name and purpose	Finding/ understanding tactile feedback for direction
Duration	1.5 hours	1.5 hours	1.5 hours
Data Collection	Audio/video	Audio/video	Audio/video
Status	Conducted	Conducted	Scheduled

3.1 PD Member Recruitment and Team Composition

The PD team consisted of two groups: consultants and research group. The consultants group consisted of five individuals with SVIs and they joined our study from the Roanoke Alliance for the Visually Enabled (RAVE) supporting SVIs in the Roanoke Valley, Virginia. The research group consisted of 10 members that were divided into three teams according to their unique goals and interests. The three teams' configurations were Human Factors (4 people) with focus on analyzing SVIs' interaction process, Human Computer Interaction (4 people) with focus on designing user interfaces, and Textile and Apparel (2 people) with focus on designing functional garments. The reason for including the three teams as a research group was to analyze the mental model and interaction process of people with SVIs in terms of cognitive science, user interfaces and wearable platforms and thus provided them with an unbiased wearable assistive technology. Another reason that we constructed the three teams within the research group was to reflect different insights coming from each unique discipline to the design process of NaFEAS. Table 2 below shows the final PD team composition.

Table 2. PD team composition

Group	Team	Members	Role
Consultants with SVIs	Consultants with SVIs	5	Analyze the concept and features of NaFEAS
Research group	Human Factors	4	Analyze cognitive factors
	Human Computer Interaction	4	Analyze user interactions and feedback modalities
	Textile and Apparel	2	Analyze wearable design options
Total		15	

3.2 The 1st PD

• Objective: the primary goal of the first PD was to discuss the overall concept of NaFEAS and validate it. Three objectives were established listed below.

1. Inviting individuals with SVIs as consultants into NaFEAS design meetings as long as possible in the design process of the overall system.
2. Interacting directly with the consultants with SVIs to discuss and validate the concept of NaFEAS.
3. Engaging the consultants with SVIs to control design decision.

• Procedure: Once we obtained the informed consent form on the site of RAVE, we introduced the purpose of the first study and read an anecdotal scenario of NaFEAS. A part of the anecdotal scenario is listed below.

> *...... Now imagine a system that can detect and give you feedback on where you are going, what is around and in front of you by using something on your body and/or a mobile device you can carry in your pocket or your hands. This is the goal of Portable Awareness Clothing (PAC), which is the name we are giving to a system that will help individuals with severe visual impairments to walk around spaces independently and be able to get information about obstacles such as buildings, people, trees, etc. ...... This system will also learn, so that everything you encounter or tell it to mark or store will be stored in a database. The next time you encounter that object, the system will recognize it.*

After the scenario, we asked the consultants with SVIs several open-ended questions to evaluate the scenario and to ascertain how they imagine the system. Some of the questions that we asked were: How would you imagine this system to operate? If this system needs to go with you wherever you go on your body, what's the best way to make this happen? How do you expect this system should look?

• Lessons: We obtained a few design implications. First, the consultants with SVIs did not want the system to replace their canes. Second, the consultants with SVIs primarily wanted a wearable system unless it is noticeable and would be a distraction to her or himself or to others. This implied that they were concerned with their appearance and to be seen as ordinary people while wearing NaFEAS. One PD member suggested an attachable device such as a wrist band or fanny pack, and this implied that they do not want any additional devices that dominated their body. This means that the consultants with SVIs wanted to have the freedom to remove assistive technology from their body when it was not in use. Third, the function to turn the entire system on and off was desired to secure users from being disturbed unnecessarily by technology. Fourth, most research team members were surprised that finding a trash can in a room was the most difficult task that the consultants with SVIS confronted in their daily living. From a technological perspective, they wanted precise near environment information such as where items in a room are. They remembered unique landmarks in a room to find specific items in their homes and to navigate independently.

3.3 The 2nd PD

• Objective: The second PD was aimed at demonstrating a low fidelity NaFEAS near environment awareness component to the consultants with SVIs and then discussing their experience. It was to validate and determine the attributes of interactions of NaFEAS. Below are two objectives established in the second PD.

1. Giving a technological experience to the consultants with SVIs
2. Discussing their experience and analyzing the attributes of interactions of NaFEAS

To demonstrate the near environment awareness of NaFEAS, four objects: a bottle of cold medicine (syrup), an allergy relief medicine (tablet), a blue shirt (checkered) and a pink shirt (unicolor) were selected and they were tagged by RFID tags. The four objects and the RFID tags are shown in Fig. 1.

Fig. 1. Four objects used in the 2nd PD. An allergy relief (tablet) and a bottle of cold medicine (syrup) (left), a blue shirt (checker) and a pink shirt (unicolor) (middle), RFID tag samples embedded in the four objects (right).

• Procedure: We introduced the objective of the second PD that was a technological experience for the consultants with SVIs. The technological experience consisted of two experience sessions described in table 3. As shown in the table, all the consultants with SVIs have attempted to recognize the four objects twice: without NaFEAS and with NaFEAS. This gives them a technological experience at the onset and then an opportunity to discuss the experience of the NaFEAS technology. The rationale for this approach is that we prepared two similar box type medicines and two articles of clothing in order to add difficulty to the tests. We also would like to better understand how the consultants with SVIs recognize medicine and clothing that are very important to their health and their appearance.

Table 3. NaFEAS technological experience

	Four Objects			
	Cold Medicine	Allergy Relief	Blue Shirt	Pink Shirt
Without NaFEAS	Experience Session 1 (the all consultants with SVIs)			
With NaFEAS	Experience Session 2 (the all consultants with SVIs)			

In the first experience session, each PD member was asked to recognize the four objects by themselves without any technological help as shown in Fig. 2 (left) and then the team discussed their experience. After the first session, the second experience session followed with the same procedure except that a RFID based object awareness system was used as shown in Fig. 2 (middle). A RFID reader was attached to the lower arm close to the wrist as shown in Fig. 2 (right). In the second session of experience, the consultants with SVIs were assisted by the technology as they were trying to recognize the four objects. The consultants with SVIs received a headset in order to receive only audio information from the objects. As in the first experience session, discussion followed the experience.

Fig. 2. Snapshots of NaFEAS technological component experience. Object recognition without NaFEAS (left), Object recognition with NaFEAS (middle), A RFID reader mounted close to the wrist (right).

• Lessons: The second PD was also successful as it gave the team many insights from a technological and a garment design perspective. The first lesson was when the consultants with SVIs use NaFEAS how to organize information. For instance, which information is most beneficial and how to convey the information effectively? Actually, the consultants with SVIs most like to know about the dosage of the two medicines. They were also interested in knowing the color of the clothing. They commented that expiration date and cooking instructions are also important for them. We realized that NaFEAS should provide them with appropriate information depending on the specific item. Another lesson that we obtained was how to physically attach the component of NaFEAS technology to users with SVIs. An arm band was not sufficient to attach a RFID reader on a lower arm and this led us to speculation about a pocket that can be closed after inserting the RFID reader. Velcro or a magnetic button was preferred for stability and ease of use. Since we are in preliminary stages of testing the feasibility of NaFEAS, further investigation will follow as to the feasibility of embedding the receiver into the woven structure of a garment.

4 Discussion

A PD approach with the consultants with SVIs allowed us to refine the efficient design of NaFEAS, even though the 3rd PD has yet to be completed. The PD has shown itself to be a viable solution to the research members in the design process of NaFEAS. In this section, we discuss a few things that made our PD successful.

First, one should consider a design boundary in a PD. We wanted to cover not only issues regarding the concept or features of NaFEAS, but also how the technological components benefit users with SVIs or how the system will be utilized in the real world. We wanted the consultants with SVIs to have the ability to decide what should or could be done and what trade-offs need to be made.

Second, PD team composition is a key to draw the needs and requirements of actual users. From the two PDs, we conclude that a group composition is very important to lead successful PD. Including actual users who can act as proxies to the target population are crucial for team success. Other members are also important to analyze the results of PD. Since we are dealing with a wearable assistive technology for SVIs, we have included experts in Textile and Apparel, Human Factors, and Human Computer Interactions. As a result, we realized that constructing a PD team that is relevant to the study and proxies to interact directly with users are crucial in PD.

Third, how to engage actual users into a PD is also an important factor. If the actual users are not fully engaged in the PD, there will be no insights that will be gained for future design processes. In our study, we configured our PD from discussing the concept of NaFEAS to experiencing the low fidelity of NaFEAS technological component in order to engage them to NaFEAS. We discussed the concept of NaFEAS in the first PD and assessed the efficacy of the NaFEAS technological component in the second PD. In fact, the technological experience session in the second PD helped the consultants with SVIs understand the concept of NaFEAS better as they realized how the system worked and how to properly use it.

Finally, questions or discussion topics are foundations of PD as improvements can be made based on them. We have met a few times so that each team can and validate questionnaires, and also to lead and finish each PD within the limited time. We recommend in order to obtaining polished research questions, we should administer iterative design meetings, among the configured teams.

5 Conclusion and Future Work

This paper reflects on two sessions of conducting intensive PD with five individuals with Severe Visual Impairments (SVIs) for Near and Far Awareness Environment System (NaFEAS), which is a wearable assistive technology in wayfinding tasks. We discussed the activities and ways to engage the actual users and how we used a combination of sources to influence the needs analysis phase. We also reflect on several lessons obtained from the first and second PD. It is to make NaFEAS the result of collaboration of a designer's detailed understanding of the needs of users with SVIs and his or her in-depth understanding and thereby lends itself to contextual design. All studies will be used to develop a prototype of NaFEAS which will be reviewed and iteratively designed before being evaluated by about 24 evaluation participants with SVIs in a formative evaluation.

Acknowledgments. We are grateful to the five consultants with SVIs for sharing their time and valuable feedbacks. We thank the Roanoke Alliance for the Visually Enabled (RAVE) for their support and thank the four Senior Design Team members in Industrial and Systems Engineering at Virginia Tech. This project was funded by the National Science Foundation and the State Council for Higher Education of Virginia.

References

1. Hub, A., Hartter, T., Ertl, T.: Interactive tracking of movable objects for the blind on the basis of environment models and perception-oriented object recognition methods. In: ACM SIGACCESS Conference on Assistive Technologies, Portland, Oregon, USA, pp. 111–118 (2006)
2. Willis, S., Helal, S.: RFID information grid for blind navigation and wayfinding. In: 9th IEEE International Symposium on Wearable Computers, pp. 34–37 (2005)
3. Smith-Jackson, T., Williges, R.: User-centered design of tele-support systems. Assistive Technology 13, 144–169 (2001)
4. Lueg, C., Pfeifer, R.: Cognition, situatedness, and situated design Second International Conference on Cognitive Technology. Humanizing the Information Age 124-135 (1997)
5. Schuler, D., Namioka, A.: Participatory Design: Principles and Practices. Lawrence Erlbaum Associates, Hillsdale (1993)
6. Muller, M.J.: PICTIVE - An exploration in participatory design. SIGCHI conference on Human factors in computing systems, New Orleans, Louisiana, United States, pp. 225–231 (1991)
7. Smith-Jackson, T., Carroll, K., Quek, F.: Embodied Interaction Paradigm for Users with Severe Visual Impairments (Research Grant Proposal). National Science Foundation (2008)
8. Sanders, E.B.N.: Postdesign and Participatory Culture. In: The Proceedings of Useful and Critical: The Position of Research in Design, Tuusula, Finland, pp. 9–11 (1999)
9. Crewe, K.: The quality of participatory design. Journal of the American Planning Association 6, 437–455 (2001)
10. Beck, E.: P for Political - Participation is Not Enough. Scandinavian Journal of Information Systems 14, 77–92 (2002)

11. Sharma, V., Simpson, R.C., LoPresti, E.F., Mostowy, C., Olson, J., Puhlman, J., Hayashi, S., Cooper, R.A., Konarski, E., Kerley, B.: Participatory design in the development of the wheelchair convoy system. Journal of NeuroEngineering and Rehabilitation 2 (2008)
12. Wu, M., Richards, B., Baecker, R.: Participatory design with individuals who have amnesia. In: Proceedings of the eighth conference on Participatory design: Artful integration: interweaving media, materials and practices, Toronto, Ontario, Canada, vol. 1, pp. 214–223 (2004)
13. Dawe, M.: Design Methods to Engage Individuals with Cognitive Disabilities and their Families. In: Position paper in CHI 2007, San Jose, CA, USA (2007)
14. Boyd-Graber, J., Nikolova, S., Moffatt, K., Kin, K., Lee, J., Mackey, L., Tremaine, M., Klawe, M.: Participatory design with proxies: developing a desktop-PDA system to support people with aphasia. In: The Proceedings of ACM CHI 2006, pp. 151–160. ACM Press, New York (2006)
15. Mak, T., Gillis, D.: Adapting participatory design for the blind: audible access to the world wide web. In: The 5th Annual Human Factors Engineering Inter-University Workshop, University of Waterloo, Waterloo, Canada (2004)
16. Farshchian, B.A., Divitini, M.: Using Email and WWW in a Distributed Participatory Design Project. ACM SIGGROUP Bulletin 20, 10–15 (1999)

Design of an Assistance System for Elderly Based on Analyses of Needs and Acceptance

Stefan Lutherdt[1], Carsten Stiller[2], Katrin Lienert[3], Sabine Spittel[3], Fred Roß[2], Christoph Ament[2], and Hartmut Witte[1]

[1] Ilmenau University of Technology, Dept. of Biomechatronics
[2] Ilmenau University of Technology, Dept. of Systems Analysis
PF 10 05 65, 98684 Ilmenau, Germany
[3] AWO Alten-, Jugend- und Sozialhilfe gGmbH
Pfeiffersgasse 12, 99084 Erfurt, Germany
{stefan.lutherdt,carsten.stiller}@tu-ilmenau.de,
lienert@awo-thueringen.de,sabine.spittel@awo-thueringen.de,
{fred.ross,christoph.ament,hartmut.witte}@tu-ilmenau.de

Abstract. The changing demography requires new kinds of support for elderly people. The project WEITBLICK aims to give seniors assistance to gather information about several services and their providers, relaying the access to such services and offer them in an individualized manner. To determine the requirements of elderly users a broad analysis will be performed in four stages. To fulfill the aims of the project the system has two principles incorporated: the service relay can be triggered by the users' former activities or by the users actively themselves. The base for both is a database with user and service profiles.

Keywords: assistance system for elderly, requirement analyses, user and service profiles, changing demography, information gathering, individualization.

1 Introduction and Motivation

Besides normal but individual changes (in a medical-statistic meaning) dissociations of physical and cognitive abilities become more important relatively and absolutely because of demographic shifts and an increasing life expectancy. Highly mobile Dementia patients as well as mobility handicapped with normal mental and social abilities surrounded by young people are going to be not the exception but the accustomed way in everyday life. The growing need of assistance in daily-life executions and activities is an extra-risk which is no longer securable by the national insurances but belongs more and more to general, not assurable life risks. At one hand this will be boosted by an increase of spatial and social mobility with the linked breakup of classic families as the former generation-overall structure of solidarity. At the other hand women's part in our society changes towards working women, which are no longer all-time available service providers for their families. This situation will get more complicated by the increase of single-person households. The percentage of single households has changed f. e. in Thuringia[1] from 25% in 1991 to 38% in 2006. Further

---

[1] Thuringia: a German Federal State with about 2.3 million inhabitants.

C. Stephanidis (Ed.): Universal Access in HCI, Part I, HCII 2009, LNCS 5614, pp. 96–105, 2009.
© Springer-Verlag Berlin Heidelberg 2009

38% of persons from these households were older than 64 years. (Data from Thuringian State Office for Statistics, given from AWO).

By now it is an across-social consensus that changing demography of our society as mentioned above also causes new requirements on support for elderly people. This group will grow more and more like is to be seen in fig. 1. It is expected that in 2020 the German population will consists more from people over 60 years than all other in working age.

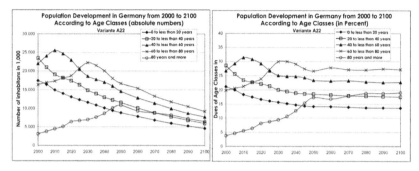

Fig. 1. Population development in Germany until 2100 according to age classes [acc. to 1]

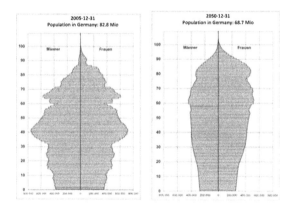

Fig. 2. Population development in Germany until the year 2050 (population pyramids according to [1])

This above-mentioned fact already has an effect today in health- and custodial care areas. So the number of long-term care facilities in Thuringia has increased by 6% (693 absolute) between December 2005 and December 2007 and the number of ambulant custodial services by 3.3% [2]. During the same time the number of patients has ascended to 72,213, which is an increase of 7.7% [3].

Additional to this rise of the absolute numbers the (future) seniors will be more active and mobile and have a higher level of technical affinity (and experiences) than seniors today. This also causes new requirements for assistance systems to organize their daily life.

2 Aim and Core of the Desired System

Employees in social care services are more and more confronted with off-topic tasks. But as they work in rigid organizational structures (because of the assignment of tasks of these care services) they cannot react flexible to day-to-day accumulating wishes of their patients: The coordination of services coming from outside does not belong to the duties of the care personnel. But there is an insufficiency for people with mobile deficits or discrepancies between cognitive and physical mobility, which enormously complicates the self-determined organization of the daily life. Even meetings with like-minded people become to an exception because of the lack of adequate communicational facilities. The left hand side of fig. 3 shows the situation described above schematically.

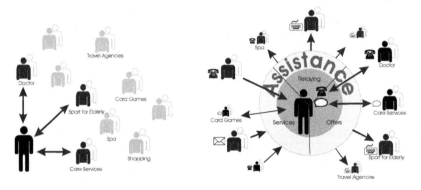

Fig. 3. Organization of daily life without (left) assistance and with the newly assistance system for elder people (right) (according to [4])

To design an assistance system with the focus on these organizational issues like shown at the right hand side of fig. 3, a consortium was founded by partners from science, economy and eldercare. This consortium with the funding by the German ministry of education and research (BMBF) has the ambitious aim to create, design and prototype an interactive assistance system for seniors with several grades of autonomy, activity and mobility. This system will be both integrating and individualizable. With the system described here deficits in support of elderly should be overcome to realize a better access to necessary information, attendances and to other elderly with the same interests and similar conditions. This access is an essential component to a self–determined arrangement of daily-life routines. At the same time the system is able to compensate mobility deficits by an individualized planning as well as to optimize the custodial services. With the deployment of the system it is possible for elderly people to extend the residence in their own domesticity. Furthermore the system brings benefit to the eldercare service provider.

The core of the system is its capability to adapt to personal preferences and psycho-physical conditions of users. Thereby questions of age-correlated perceptual and mobility constrictions play a decisive role as well as the eligible interest of the elder, their relatives and the operating company on safety aspects. Therefore components for personal monitoring and tracking on an individual settable level and components for data and communication security are integral system elements.

The main and most important element of the system will be a broad but complementary communication structure linked with a dynamically self-adapting knowledge base. By this general structure it is possible to request services well adjusted to the needs, to coordinate the supply chain of services and to integrate (new) users into the system. The kind of services, which are integrable and relizable within this assistance system is not limited. But during the first stage the main focus lies on care and custodial services and spa added by social activities.

3 Technical Components and Principles

To fulfill this complex needs it is necessary to design the system as much adoptable to the user as possible. Therefore the aim is to create a platform capable of dealing with a wide selection of handling concepts, preferable concepts already known to the users. Possible devices to interact with the system include stationary systems as TV/set-top box-combinations or personal computers as well as mobile systems like PDAs, mobile phones and specially designed easy to use front-ends. The deficit of lacking information caused by the missing ability to interact with modern technical devices can also be addressed if the "interface" to the system is represented by the social interaction with a care giving person. All these diverse ways of accessing the system require a flexible communication infrastructure as described in [5].

Information deficits as described above can lead to decreasing social contacts and loneliness. To remedy those deficits an "Assistance Module" is implemented for the system. It is used to relay services to users who otherwise possibly would not know about these services. For that purpose two basic principles of gathering information from the system had been described in [6]:

— A user initiated service relay starts with a query to the system, which is then augmented by information from a user profile, including interests and abilities. A recommender system is used to match this query with service profiles to select one or more possible services. If necessary additional information, i.e. about availability of services at a certain timeslot, can be added after an enquiry to the service provider and as a last step the recommended services are shown to the user. (See fig. 4a)
— An event initiated service relay (shown in fig. 4b) might be triggered by previous actions of the user, i.e. to recommend a transport service to a previously booked opera concert, or to inform users about new services entered in the system. In contrast to the former procedure in this case the recommendation process is used to predict how services match to users. If the event does not specify the services appropriate service profiles have to be found in the first step. These service profiles are then matched with the user profiles and the according interests and abilities of the user. Here again the event itself can specify the user or a range of users can be chosen by the system.

Further development within the project will include a "Monitoring Module" to assist users with different deficits. One application is the monitoring of spatial boundaries for Dementia patients. An individualizable route planning and navigation algorithm developed in a previous project (see [7] for details) will be integrated into this module to provide personalized navigation for each user.

Both modules described here will be implemented to give an example how further functionality can be added to the system. To open the system to other system providers to add their existing services and functionality standardized interfaces are used. Thereby it's possible to support and augment existing services from care and recreational domains but also to offers the opportunity to create new services not realizable or existing before.

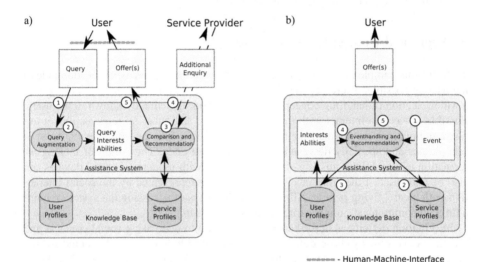

Fig. 4. Offer relaying in the WEITBLICK assistance system [6]. a) user initiated relaying, b) event initiated relaying.

4 Strategies to Fulfill the Users Needs and Expectations

As shown in previous research projects (e.g. TAS – a tourist assistance system for handicapped, see [8, 9, 10, 11]) it is necessary and beneficial for the outcome to involve potential future users into the development process at a very early stage. This maxim of usability engineering has also to be incorporated into the design and development of assistance systems. Because of the lack of time during such projects on one hand and in most cases also a lack of an adequate number of available test persons to execute multiple cycles of design iterations, a widely linear design process should be performed. But the wanted information has to been gathered to reach the design goals anyhow. To bridge this gap two main strategies will be applied:

1. Shifting the complexity from the commonly cyclic executed design items toward the analysis and determination of the user's requirements at the beginning of the whole process, especially to an extensive study of their needs and tasks.

2. To avoid that the system will be created only from a very technical point of view it is necessary to involve experts from social and health services into the design process. Their task is to supervise all stages of the development process and to compare consistently the results with the user terms.

5   Execution of the User Requirement Analysis

5.1   Common Analysis and Questions

It is obvious that the first task to solve is to bring all relevant information about services and activities they can use to the seniors. But the group of these so-called "seniors" is highly heterogeneous. This leads to a large variety of interests and abilities and beyond that to a different grade of acceptance of technical equipments and the use of it [12, 13].

The requirements of elder people and their use, acceptance and approach to technologies were well and often analyzed in a number of studies like project *Sentha* from the TU Berlin [14]. Norbey [15] analyzed the use of home entertainment technologies by seniors of different age classes partly in the same area in which the project WEITBLICK will be executed (see [18]). But in this project the focus does not lay on technologies of home entertainment, and otherwise the results of these studies are not unlimited representative for the project aims. Another interesting system called SOPHIA (see (http://www.sophia-tv.de/) does not cover the area of WEITBLICK because it has the focus on emergency tasks.

Because of this lack of information and the general strategy of this project (see chapter 4) a broad requirement analysis was planned and already partially performed. The base of all examinations is the two modules of WEITBLICK: the assistance module and the monitoring module. For both of these modules the acceptance and the needs have to be determined. To simplify the inauguration process of the test persons into the special problems of the system design three model scenarios were defined:

— Scenario "HOME" contains typical, every-day actions in home environments of self-dependent living seniors including basic outdoor activities like shopping, hairdresser, hobbies, cultural events and basic care services (home assistances)
— Scenario "MOBILE" contains typical and every-day actions around assisted living and home for aged with all their particularities under inclusion of hobbies, walking, visits of relatives and care services (home assistance)
— Scenario "ACTIVE" covers activities like day trips, (short-time) holidays, leisure-time activities and so on including the use of the previously developed tourist assistance system (TAS, see [10])

5.2   Executing of Requirement Analysis

Based on a review of literature, congresses and other projects as well as first contacts with the addressed users some initial hypotheses were formed to start the analyze process. These first hypotheses where that the users are strong affected by their actual living condition and their biography, esp. their profession and their social status (esp. family structures). Another wide influence is expected from age and existing handicaps or diseases. The acceptance of and interest in new technological items is expected to be very poor and to depend on the (visible and perceptible) benefit for the elderly users.

The starting point for examinations was the usually executed analyses during the usability engineering in other technical areas like software development (see Section 4). The whole process was parted into four stages (qualitative and quantitative parts):

— Initial expert interview (structured interview with about ten experts)
— Pretest with a set of questions given by the expert interview (five to ten potential users by a guide-lined interview)
— Focus group (about ten persons covering all of the three scenarios)
— Interrogation in form of individual or small group interviews (at least ten of each scenario, altogether 30-40 persons) for quantitative analyses

For the finished guideline-based expert interviews twelve persons were recruited from all domains involved around the future system. Those were relatives of long-term care patients, employees and executives of these long-term facilities, staff of information centers and personnel of ambulant services.

The focus group will be oriented at facilitation guidelines for focus groups by Krueger [16]. Special considerations for those focus groups with elderly like suggested by Barrett and Kirk [17] should be following in achievement of the analyzed interviews. The usefulness of focus groups for this user clientele was already demonstrated amongst others by Demiris et al. [18]

6 First Results

So far the expert interviews and first pretest interviews (currently not analyzed) were executed. During the expert interviews 550 minutes of data were gathered. All interviews were transcribed; the data were extracted, counted and analyzed according to Grounded Theory [19].

The first analyzes confirm some results from Friesdorf and Heine [14], who state that elder people are not generally reluctant to new technologies. This is shown amongst others by the high rate of used electronic devices used for gathering information (57.1% of all nominations) and of the existing electronic devices (20 nominations, amongst these five times telephone, mobile phone and PC three times each). Of course this is influenced by the fact that everyone has a TV set and is using it heavily. But only 21.4% named the TV as the main information source, but the same rate named the Internet (both three times). The most important way to get information about services and special activities is word-of-mouth-recommendation (50% of all interviewees) and different kinds of print media (which was named 24 times by the 14 interrogated). The most named in this category were "Gathering information by daily press and local newspapers" by eight interviewees and "Notices or placards"[2] by six interviewees. This shows the strong local affected answers because these media are only accessible in a small surrounding around the area where the interviewees live

---

[2] These notices principally could hang everywhere, but a control question had shown that the interviewees meant notices within the care facilities and assisted living houses.

and work. It appears that the most influence to the seniors by word-of-mouth-recommendation have the care service employees (71.4% of nominations) and other seniors (28.6%). Nobody named the family in this item.

Another interrogation item was possibly missing offers for the seniors. Here the experts were not in complete agreement. At least five of them said that there are no offers missing, the remaining distributed the nominations to care and supervision offers (four interviewees), to engagement offers for the seniors (eight nominations) and subsidiary assistance offers (nine nominations). A special focus was laid by three of the interviewees on periodic recurring offers regardless of which kind.

The estimation of the attendees concerning possible problems in everyday life of seniors brought out two emphases: problems with missing health and various kinds of diseases (14 times) and problems with simple everyday activities (like shopping, cooking and so on, 17 times). Third place of nominations reached missing mobility (nine times).

Very important for the further design work were the information about design details of the new system as well as its user interface components. Eleven times the attendees estimated that the system should have or use a (large) display, maybe with touch functionality. Of course they want a simple use (six times), easy understanding and handling (six and three times). Other items with more than two nominations were: handy or light-weight, big and easy to find, accessible and everywhere usable, always with support function.

The kind of information gathering depends on the kind of living facility. Individual ways like print media or electronic devices will be used by self-determined living seniors in their own domesticity or in assisted living facilities. Word-of-mouth-recommendations, notices and placards will be more used by residents of long-term care facilities.

The decreasing mobility caused by several diseases and age-related problems leads to transport problems to and away from offers outside the residence and finally to miss an appointment or activity offer.

All of the answers (and therewith the whole design process) are remodeled by the age and the personal biography of seniors. These items will be a good first indicator for a classification in combining with abilities or existing handicaps to choose the right user interface and kind and amount of wanting information.

7   Conclusions for Further Work

From the data of the expert interviews some hypotheses and operation guidance for the further work can be extracted. At first it is indispensable to explain in detail the meaning and benefit of an assistance system in that area of life - as well for the employees in custodial services as for the seniors as the first addressed use group. Activity offers outside of the facilities are as far as possible irrelevant, the same applies for cultural and sport offers. Here is a lack in retrieving information about such offers as well in the integration into the daily life routines. That boosts the project because it is one aim to fill this existing gap with an assistance system for all involved.

With the extracted results and hypotheses the focus groups and user interviews will now be executed to get more information about interests, missing offers, the kind of a possible use of the system as well as of the offers. These interviews will be analyzed quantitatively and qualitatively to get the initial data to form the database and its query algorithms. Also from these data some basic design decisions will be derived, especially about the used front-end and user interface(s).

Acknowledgement. This paper emerged from a project funded by the German Federal Ministry of Education and Research (BMBF) under the support code 01FC08029 named "WEITBLICK". The authors would like to thank all the involved members of staff of the Ilmenau University of Technology from the Depts. of Communicational nets and Audiovisual Technology and the partners from outside the University: the AWO Alten-, Jugend- und Sozialhilfe gGmbH, Falcom Wireless Communications GmbH in Langewiesen and KDS Services GmbH & Co. KG, Erfurt.

References

1. Birg, H.: Die demographische Zeitenwende - Der Bevölkerungsrückgang in Deutschland und Europa. C.H. Beck, München (in German). Data and images (2003), http://www.herwig-birg.de/downloads/simrechnung/
2. Thuringian State Office for Statistics. Press Release 366: 389 Ambulant Custodial Services and 304 Stationary Long-term Care Facilities at the End of 2007 in Thuringia. Actual Index of Ambulant and Stationary Long-term Care Facilities in Thuringia Released (in German) (2008), http://www.tls.thueringen.de/
3. Thuringian State Office for Statistics. Press Release 367: More than Every 32nd Thuringian Was in Need of Care at the End of 2007 (in German) (2008), http://www.tls.thueringen.de/
4. WEITBLICK Knowledge Based Technologies and Services Adjusted to the Needs of Seniors by Individualized Care Concepts. Grant Application of Ilmenau University of Technology to the German Ministry of Education and Research (BMBF), Support Code 01FC08029. (in German) (2008), http://foerderportal.bund.de/foekat/jsp/
5. Renhak, K., Stiller, C., Schade, H.P., Seitz, J., Schön, E., Roß, F., Ament, C., Hildebrandt, H., Oswald, M.: WEITBLICK – Wissensbasierte Technologien und bedarfsgerechte Leistungen für Senioren durch individualisierte Care-Konzepte. In: Proc. of Usability Day VII 2009, Dornbirn, Austria (2009)
6. Stiller, C., Roß, F., Ament, C., Renhak, K., Seitz, J., Schön, E., Schade, H.P., Hildebrandt, H., Oswald, M.: WEITBLICK – Infrastruktur für eine bedarfsgerechte Dienstleistungsvermittlung. In: 2. Deutscher AAL-Kongress 2009, Berlin, Germany (2009)
7. Stiller, C., Roß, F., Karimanzira, D., Rost, R., Stein, M.: A Framework for Individualized Route Planning and Navigation for Pedestrian Users. In: Proc. of 51st IWK 2006, Ilmenau (2006)
8. Lutherdt, S., Fröber, U., Witte, H., Kurtz, P., Wernstedt, J.: Development of assistance systems for user groups with specific handicaps – a challenge for the ergonomic design process. In: Proc. XIX ISOES 2005, Las Vegas (2005)
9. Fröber, U., Lutherdt, S., Stiller, C., Roß, F., Witte, H., Kurtz, P.: The design of a tourist assistance system for several handicapped and elderly. In: Proc. of IEA 2006 - 16th World Congress on Ergonomics. Elsevier Ltd., Amsterdam (2006)

10. Lutherdt, S., Witte, H.: TAS – Touristisches Assistenzsystem für Urlaubs-, Freizeit- und Bildungsaktivitäten – Ein InnoRegio-Projekt der TU Ilmenau. In: Leidner, R., Neumann, P., Rebstock, M. (eds.) Von Barrierefreiheit zum Design für Alle – Erfahrungen aus Forschung und Praxis, AG Angewandte Geographie Münster e.V. Heft 38. Münster (2007)

11. Roß, F., Lutherdt, S.: Abschlussbericht TAS - Touristisches AssistenzSystem für barrierefreien Zugang zu Urlaubs-, Freizeit- und Bildungsaktivitäten Förderkennzeichen 03I2808. Technische Universität Ilmenau (2006)

12. McCreadie, C., Tinker, A.: The acceptability of assistive technology to older people. Ageing and Society 25, 91–110 (2005)

13. Hensel, B.K., Demiris, G., Courtney, K.L.: Defining Obtrusiveness in Home Telehealth Technologies: A Conceptual Framework. Journal of the American Medical Informatics Association 13(4), 428–431 (2006)

14. Friesdorf, W., Heine, A.: Sentha – seniorengerechte Technik im häuslichen Alltag. Ein Forschungsbericht mit integriertem Roman. Springer, Berlin (2006)

15. Norbey, M.: Die Erwartungen älterer Menschen an Geräte der Unterhaltungselektronik – Ergebnisse einer explorativen Studie. Diskussionsbeiträge, Inst. für Medien- und Kommunikationswissenschaft, TU Ilmenau, Ilmenau (2007)

16. Krueger, R.A., Casey, M.A.: Focus groups: A practical guide for applied research, 3rd edn. Sage Publications, Thousand Oaks (2000)

17. Barrett, J., Kirk, S.: Running focus groups with elderly and disabled elderly participants. Appl. Ergon. 31, 621–629 (2000)

18. Demiris, G., Hensel, B.K., Skubic, M., Rantz, M.: Senior residents' perceived need of and preferences for "smart home" sensor technologies. International Journal of Technology Assessment in Health Care 24(1), 120–124 (2008)

19. Flick, U., von Kardorff, E., Steinke, I. (eds.): Qualitative Forschung. Ein Handbuch. 4. Auflage, pp. 32-42. Rowohlt Hamburg (2005)

Educational Sound Symbols for the Visually Impaired

Steve Mannheimer, Mexhid Ferati, Davide Bolchini, and Mathew Palakal

Indiana University School of Informatics
535 West Michigan Street, Indianapolis, Indiana 46202
{smannhei,mferati,dbolchin,mpalakal}@iupui.edu

Abstract. Acoustic-based computer interactivity offers great potential [1], particularly with blind and visually impaired users [2]. At Indiana University's School of Informatics at IUPUI, we have developed an innovative educational approach relying on "audemes," short, nonverbal sound symbols made up of 2-5 individual sounds lasting 3-7 seconds - like expanded "earcons"[3] - to encode and prompt memory. To illustrate: An audeme for "American Civil War" includes a 3-second snippet of the song *Dixie* partially overlapped by a snippet of *Battle Hymn of the Republic*, followed by battle sounds, together lasting 5 seconds. Our focus on non-verbal sound explores the mnemonic impact of metaphoric rather than literal signification. Working for a year with BVI students, we found audemes improved encoding and long-term memory of verbal educational content, even after five months, and engaged the students in stimulating ways.

Keywords: Audeme, sound, acoustic, interface, accessibility, blind and visually impaired, cognition, long-term memory, education.

1 Introduction

For most people the visual sense dominates the day-to-day perception of the world. The recent proliferation of visual or screen-based technologies has reinforced that domination, and elevated language over non-verbal sounds that in some contexts may be considered irrelevant or, worse, interference [18] or at best a mixed blessing [19]. This exacerbates the educational challenges to blind and visually impaired (BVI) students. "Screen-reader" or text-to-speech (T2S) applications are restrictively linear and affectively empty, making long T2S translations hard to remember. Not enough research has leveraged the common ability to instantly remember non-verbal sounds such as old song melodies or the voice of a long-lost friend, as well as the innate ability to identify a wide range of natural and machine-based sounds. The affective, cognitive and mnemonic power of non-verbal sound has been an indispensible element in the entertainment media for nearly a century, but has generally taken a back seat to language-based approaches in information technologies and educational settings.

Our research explores the efficacy of non-symmetrical paradigms of acoustic interactivity, and the utility of non-verbal sound as the output process from computers. In some contexts non-verbal sound offers a superior means to achieve cognitive goals dependent on memory and the semantic construction of meaning.

C. Stephanidis (Ed.): Universal Access in HCI, Part I, HCII 2009, LNCS 5614, pp. 106–115, 2009.
© Springer-Verlag Berlin Heidelberg 2009

The preliminary hypothesis of our research is that short non-speech acoustic symbols, which we have called audemes (to suggest an auditory morpheme, lexeme and/or phoneme) can substitute for visual/textual labels/icons to improve computer-mediated access to educational material for BVI users. An audeme is a combination of raw sounds crafted into a brief audio track, generally in the 3-7 second range, used to signify a specific theme and to prompt memory of an associated body of verbal content. Audemes may combine 1) iconic sounds made by natural and/or manufactured things (e.g. surf and seagulls, cash registers); 2) abstract sounds manufactured by computers (e.g. buzzes, blips, etc.); 3) music; and 4) occasional snippets of language gleaned from songs or well-known cultural sources (e.g. President Kennedy's "Ask not what your country can do for you..."). The semiotic structure of an audeme is shown in Fig. 1.

Working over a year with students and staff of the Indiana School for the Blind and Visually Impaired (ISBVI) we determined that audemes work best when combining 2-5 separate sounds. Our 20 ISBVI student collaborators could identify most iconic sounds available from commercial sound effects libraries, sometimes after only 2-3 seconds. This allowed researchers to construct relatively complex sequenced and/or layered audemes (see Fig. 1). For example, an audeme of key jangles + car engine revving = driving trip + shore sounds = trip to the beach. More complexly, an audeme signifying the American Civil War contains short snippets of Dixie and Battle Hymn of the Republic, staggered and conflicting musically for two seconds, followed by the sound of rifle and cannon fire, all combined in 5-second audeme.

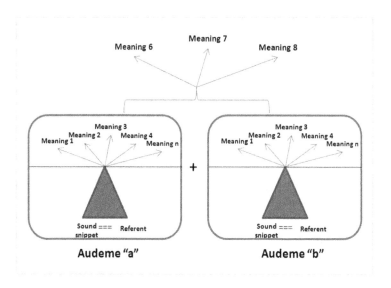

Fig. 1. Semiotic structure of an audeme. For example, audeme "a" (key jangle) references "keys," but which meaning of "keys?" Adding audeme "b" (car engine revving) directs that meaning toward the process of driving, thus suggesting "trip." The process of constructing meaning is expandable: Adding an audeme "c" (sea gulls and surf) steers the meaning toward "trip to the beach" or "vacation."

In audeme design we utilized a mix of sound types but avoided speech as much as possible. This decision enabled us to explore whether symbolic or metaphoric associations of audeme-to-content were stronger than literal associations (simply using a verbal title for content). It also allowed our collaborators a more engaged and creative participation in constructing audeme meanings. Constructions were often debated because common sounds (e.g. the jangle of keys) can suggest different meanings depending on the contexts most familiar to users (access to home; a car; locks and security; even "the key" to a problem) and thus required more sounds to direct the meaning (e.g. jangle + typing = computer security). We also observed the strong impact of affect and "aesthetic" quality in audemes. Users preferred audemes and audeme sequences that were ingeniously interpreted to connect to target themes. This indicated the strong value of play in itself and for meaning construction, expressed both as self-satisfaction or in competition with others.

Audemes are more complex and contextually variable than graphic symbols, and are perhaps more comparable to signs in American Sign Language (ASL), in which users create new signs for new ideas in the world (e.g. the sign for "credit card" is SIGNATURE-RECTANGULAR; "tranquilizer" is signed as PILL-QUIET) [22]. We found it useful at times to think of our growing dictionary of audemes like a deck of cards, with each card clearly capable of fulfilling different roles depending on the individual dynamics of any "hand" in any game being played. Because audemes exhibit a natural semantic flexibility, and due to our subjects' preference for playful engagement with audemes, we chose to develop an infrastructure and interface that could be "played" like a game or "played with" like a deck of cards or a musical instrument that allows either improvisation, set pieces or hybrids with either autotelic or pre-defined goals. This strategy parallels the practice of Web-surfing and other types of information exploration or discovery used in education.

2 Related Work

Foundational work in psychoacoustics [1] raised questions about how speech and non-speech stimuli proceeded from short-term memory to long-term memory. With the advent of the personal computer in the 1980s, exploratory work in the use of acoustic cues for graphic interfaces was performed by researchers such as W. Gaver [9], S. Brewster [4], M, Blattner et al [3], A. Edwards [7] and others. This helped promote work with sound-based interfaces, including speech-based, for BVI people, or in "eyes free" situations such as driving [7], [16]. One conceptual debate in this arena concerned the relative value of speech vs. non-speech sound cues to supplement graphic-textual displays. Smither suggested that synthetic speech is generally less memorable than natural speech [15] and Brewster agrees [4]. Anecdotal testimony from the BVI community supports this.

Further debate concerns the relative value of abstract sound (beeps, blips, et al.) vs. natural sounds (also called metaphoric or iconic) referring to a topic (e.g., the sound of rain to signify rain, a weather report or meteorology). Gaver [9] suggested that iconic sounds are more memorable cues for content, both more long-lasting in memory and better able to conjure a range or depth of content associations. Conversy [5] suggested abstract or synthesized sounds can signify concepts such as speed or waves.

As suggested by Back and Des [1], popular media strongly influence how we expect the natural world to sound. As we know from movies "...thunder must crack, boom, or roll, and seagulls must utter high lonesome cries or harsh squawks..." [10] Our ISBVI subjects easily identified natural or mechanical sounds that they would only have experienced via entertainment media (e.g. tiger growls or machine-gun fire). A judicious mix of sound types may be best. In their workshop, Frohlich and Pucher [8] state, "Some pioneering projects have presented promising design ideas and informal usability evaluations of auditory systems, in which a systematic integration of sound and speech played a significant role."

Studies strongly suggest that sound can be a powerful prompt for memory [13]. In some performed with BVI students [6] their performance was superior to that of sighted students, perhaps due to a relative lack of acoustic acuity in sighted children [12]. Other researchers created games that enhanced children's short-term memory [11]. Previous work on earcons or other sound symbols has focused on short-term associations with relatively simple content or meanings, and has not, to our knowledge, explored their long-term potential to encode and cue relatively large amounts of thematically complex material. Our study helps fill this gap.

To address broad concerns that audemes might work primarily as mnemonic cues simply because they were unusual stimuli associated with content, or would function no better or worse than verbal cues, we conducted a series of simple tests. In previously published work [23], we determined that 1) memory for random numbers presented with audemes was 14.88% stronger than memory for random number presented with spoken words; 2) that audemes with thematic or metaphoric connection to verbal content (e.g., footsteps in snow + gunfire = The Cold War) were 67.82% more effective as memory cues than audemes with no thematic relation to their texts (e.g. mechanical buzz + snippet of classical music = National Grange); 3) that audemes with positive affect (explained as good, happy, positive, I like it, etc.) improved recall in 67.86% of the cases while audemes with negative affect (bad, unhappy, I don't like it) improved memory in 32.14% of the test cases.

3 Methods

3.1 Experimental Environment

Audemes. Audemes are very short sounds tracks that may include natural, mechanical, musical or abstract sounds. Verbal cues also may be included as song lyrics or thematic quotations. In our work, audeme design was a dialogic process between researchers and students. For the three initial memory tests we created audemes for "Radio," for "Slavery" and for "US Constitution." Researchers also created three essays of approximately 500 words each from accepted content from Web-based sources. The "Radio" audeme was the sound of a radio dial being twisted through different stations with static in between. The "Slavery" audeme combined an opening short passage of a choir singing "Swing Low, Sweet Chariot" punctuated at the end by a whip crack. The "US Constitution" audeme combined the sound of a gavel (symbolizing courts and legal processes), the sound of quill pen writing and the opening bars of *Star Spangled Banner*. The audemes were constructed using Soundtrack Pro software, to be heard through inexpensive speakers.

Participants. For this study we conducted weekly sessions with approximately 20 students of the Indiana School for the Blind and Visually Impaired (ISBVI), working in ISBVI classrooms with an ISBVI faculty monitor. Students ages ranged from 9 to 17 years old. Eleven of them were completely blind, and the others were partially blind. Because of occasional other commitments, the number of participants fluctuated from 15-20. For their recruitment, consent of the school and their parents was granted. They were recruited with IBSVI guidance and volunteered to participate.

3.2 Experiment 1

The same experimental format was followed for the initial memory tests of 3 audeme-essay combinations. Students were divided into three groups in a careful single-stage sampling to evenly distribute students by age, learning abilities, and level of visual impairment. Group I (named IU) was the control group, while Group II (named Notre Dame) and Group III (Purdue) were the experimental groups. A pretest was conducted with all groups to establish a baseline of their previous knowledge of the essay content. The pretest contained 10 questions derived from the essay and these were printed in Braille or large-print. All three groups took the same test. After the pretest Group I was moved to a separate classroom; Groups II and III remained together to hear the essay read aloud. In its room, Group I (the control group) listened to the essay without audemes. Group II and III listened to the same essay with the single relevant audeme played between each paragraph, approximately 8-10 times for each essay. Two weeks after each initial session, we conducted a posttest with all 3 groups. The test contained the questions from the pretest, but in randomized order. Additionally, we added 3 more questions as statistical noise. The posttest was the same for the 3 groups, except that Group I and II took the posttest without hearing the audeme, while the Group III heard the audeme played before and after each of the questions. In short,

- Group I was not exposed to the audeme, allowing researchers to track how well students remember the essay as speech after two weeks.
- Group II was exposed to audeme when hearing the essay but not when taking the posttest, allowing researchers to track how well the audemes enhanced the encoding of the spoken essay.
- Group III was exposed to the audeme when hearing the lecture and also when taking the posttest, allowing us to track how well the audemes enhanced encoding and recall of the essay.

The results of the tests in Fig. 2 strongly indicated that exposure to the audemes increased encoding and recollection of the essay information. For "Radio," Group III showed a 52% increase in knowledge of the content included in the test (from 4.2 correct answers to 6.4), factored against the pre-knowledge. For the "US Constitution" essay, Group III showed a 65% increase (from 3.3 correct answers in the pre-test to 5.50 correct answers in the post-test). For "Slavery," Group III showed an 80% increase (from 3.75 correct answers in the pre-test to 6.75 correct answers in the post-test). Group II showed a 38% increase in knowledge for "Radio" (from 4.2 to

5.80 correct answers); and a 16% increase for "US Constitution" (from 5.16 to 6.00 correct answers) and a 12% increase for "Slavery" (6.25 to 7.00). The Group I, the control group, demonstrated a 47% increase in knowledge for "Radio" (3.40 to 5.00), then a 3.6% *decrease* in knowledge for "US Constitution" (4.67 to 4.50); and a 20% increase for "Slavery" (5.00 to 6.00) (Table 1).

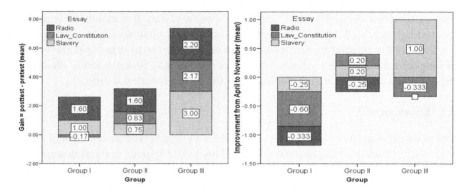

Fig. 2. Posttest results for all three essays   **Fig. 3.** Cumulative test results after 5 months

Table 1. Results for all groups

Essay	Radio			US Constitution			Slavery		
Group	I	II	III	I	II	III	I	II	III
Count(#students)	5	5	5	6	6	6	4	4	4
Mean(difference)	1.6	1.6	2.2	-0.17	0.83	2.17	1	0.75	3
% Improvement	47	38	52	-3.6	16	65	20	12	80

Table 2. Anova

Gain

	Sum of Squares	df	Mean Square	F	Sig.
Between Groups	60.023	2	30.011	7.641	.001
Within Groups	329.931	84	3.928		
Total	389.954	86			

Data Analysis. The statistical analysis of the data began by computing the difference between the pretest and posttest scores for each participant. Afterwards, we analyzed those differences in a One-Way ANOVA. This difference was called Gain.

$$\text{Gain} = \text{posttest} - \text{pretest} \qquad (1)$$

The *p*-value is .001 ($p<.05$), which means that there is significant difference in the level of improvement among the three groups.

3.3 Experiment 2

Five months later we re-tested the students on all three essays. We reshuffled the order of the questions and multiple-choice answers. Results are shown in Fig. 3. The average result for the Group I (heard no audemes) showed a -7.2% change (decrease) in long-term memory of the essays; the average score for Group II (heard audemes during encoding five months prior but not during this test) improved .78% and the average score for Group III (heard audemes during encoding five months prior and for this testing) increased 3.8%. Although mindful of the limitations of our small sample size, we are encouraged by the apparent power of audemes to help resist the erosion of long-term memory. We believe the increased recall may be attributed to the encoding of correct answers given to students after the earlier round of testing.

3.4 Experiment 3

The practical goal of our work is a user interface by which BVI students could access a complex database of educational content. This would require navigating sequences or sets of audemes, or the use of very long (VL) audemes incorporated many sounds in tracks over 15 seconds. We debated whether this navigation worked best as a hierarchy or as a semantic web. Through this debate, as well as discussions with our subjects and a series of experiments, we ultimately concluded that audemes worked best as semantically flexible signifiers or acoustic landmarks in an autotelic exploration, more akin to a semantic web. Our observations based on subject testimony: 1) ISBVI students enjoyed the challenge of interpreting or constructing narratives to explain arbitrary sequences of 2, 3, 4, 5, 6, 7 and even 8 audemes; 2) sequences of 3 or 5 audemes were easier for them to narrate; 3) even-numbered sequences did not readily resolve into narrative structures; 4) sequences of more than 6 audemes were generally too difficult to coherently narrate. 5) With very little practice, some of the students could generate interpretations, sometimes amazingly sensible, for any arbitrary sequence of 3-5 audemes. More research should help clarify these results.

In related tests, we explored how our subjects judged similarities between, on the one hand, core sets of 6 audemes (called C for Charlie, D for David and E for Edward) and, on the other, new sets recombined from these cores. We determined the following factors were most powerful in determining the perception of similarity between core sets and new: 1) Majority: Subjects linked new sets to cores 69.85% of the time when a majority of new set audemes came from that core. 2) Core-first position: Of all positions in core sets, first audemes (C1, D1, E1) had the greatest "genetic" impact for establishing resemblance with new sets. 3) New-last position: Of all positions in new sets, last audemes had the strongest genetic influence on resemblance with core sets; 4) Core-Consecutiveness: Audeme "chunks" (e.g., core chunk C3-4-5 in new set D5-C3-4-5-E4-2), did not demonstrate appreciable genetic impact in establishing resemblance to core sets. We also tested very long (VL) audemes (18 seconds), vs. standard versions (6 seconds) abbreviated from the VLs. Using the established three groups (IU, Notre Dame and Purdue) we performed two versions of this experiment to test 1) changes in recall when encoding with VL audemes but testing with standard versions; and 2) changes in recall when encoding with standard audemes but testing with VL. The results indicated that IU, the group that encoded with VL audemes then tested with the abbreviated standards, and next encoded with standard then tested with VL, scored lowest. While Purdue and Notre Dame, which heard either VL-then-VL or standard-then-standard scored clearly higher. This suggests that consistency in audeme exposure maximizes, or inconsistency interferes with, recall of associated content.

3.5 Experiment 4

Researchers tested the subjects' sense of the virtual or intuited location for audemes on a rectangular field. This experiment followed and hoped to build upon the very interesting work of the Sonic Mapper [20], in which sounds of common objects were shown to "cluster" by referenced category. Anecdotal testimony from our IBSVI collaborators confirmed the general idea that location is a critical element in their auditory perception, and that the same sound issuing from different locations can carry different meanings. Location is also an important factor in ASL, in which a sign made, for instance, near the signer's chin has a different meaning than the same sign made away from the head.   On a more abstract level, we hoped to explore how BVI people positioned acoustic symbols in a virtual or metaphoric framework or space. This question has roots in the ancient art of memory, which relied on an imagined architectural framework or "memory palace" in which ideas were placed [21]. More recent analyses of the correlation of space and ideation comes from Julian Jaynes, who argued that the consciousness of any idea occupied a virtual space, and that thinking involved positioning ideas as if they were visible objects with distinct locations. A senior ISBVI senior technology staff suggested that blind people rely instead on metaphoric acoustic spaces. We hoped our experiment might suggest what such a space might be. We played 20 previously unheard audemes and asked subjects to intuitively locate each with a crayon mark on a separate piece of graph paper. All audemes were played without stereo effects, and avoided specific references to spatial realms of the experienced world (no airplanes or bird calls). No group discussion was allowed. This experiment failed to demonstrate any consensus or statistically significant clustering for any single audeme or general type of audeme. Further experiments will be needed to provide better data and clearer concepts.

4 Discussion and Conclusion

From our experiments and interviews with our subject-collaborators we have determined that audemes increase memory for associated text and may contribute to very long-term retention of that textual information. We also determined that audemes can be remembered in sets and that its "set memory" can become part of the overall semantic identity and mnemonic power of any single audeme. Other factors that increase the mnemonic power of audemes include metaphoric connection between audeme and content, and positive affect. Because the same constituent sound or audeme can be interpreted differently depending on any established context or adjacent audemes, mnemonic success was also influenced by the users' abilities to creatively and playfully interpret audemes. We believe these factors can be applied to the design and implementation of an acoustic interface combining audemes and associated content through a touch-screen monitor to serve the educational goals of BVI students. Further, we believe this total platform will work best through a variable set of game-like processes and protocols to provide a fun and flexible learning environment for the students. Our immediate goal is to integrate this interface/platform into the pedagogy of the ISBVI. Our larger goal is to offer the audeme dictionary, games and overall concept to the larger BVI community via the Web. We hope this community will help guide the expansion and application of the platform in ways we may not have anticipated.

Moreover, we believe that these results also can be practically applied to a broad range of mainstream applications including 1) the development of sound-based interfaces and content symbols for Web searches and Website translation; 2) for handheld devices with limited screen space; or 3) uses in "eyes free" contexts such as driving. In a larger sense, we believe this work points toward a new understanding of the potential of auditory cognition, with much territory still to explore. This territory includes ideas about the semantic flexibility of acoustic stimuli, the construction of meaning from the combination and context of several stimuli, and the role of metaphoric and/or semantic association in this semiotic and signification process.

Acknowledgment. This work was supported by a grant from the Nina Mason Pulliam Charitable Trust. Researches thank the students and the staff of Indiana School for the Blind and Visually Impaired.

References

1. Back, M., Des, D.: Micro-Narratives in Sound Design: Context, Character, and Caricature in Waveform Manipulation. In: ICAD (1996)
2. Baddeley, A.: Short-term memory for word sequences as a function of acoustic, semantic and formal similarity. Quarterly Journal of Experimental Psychology 18, 362–365 (1996)
3. Blattner, M.M., Sumikawa, D.A., Greenberg, R.M.: Earcons and Icons: Their structure and common design principles. Human-Computer Interaction 4, 11–44 (1989)
4. Brewster, S.A.: Providing a Structured Method for Integrating Non-Speech Audio into Human-Computer Interfaces. PhD thesis, University of York (1994)
5. Conversy, S.: Ad-hoc synthesis of auditory icons. In: ICAD (1998)
6. Doucet, M.-E., Guillemot, J.-P., Lassonde, M., Gagne, J.-P., Leclerc, C., Lepore, F.: Blind subjects process auditory spectral cues more efficiently than sighted individuals. Springer, Heidelberg (2004)
7. Edwards, A.N.D.: Modelling Blind Users' Interactions with an Auditory Computer Interface. International Journal of Man-Machine Studies (1989)
8. Frohlich, P., Pucher, M.: Combining Speech and Sound in the User Interface. In: ICAD 2005 (2005)
9. Gaver, W.W.: The SonicFinder: An Interface That Uses Auditory Icons. Human-Computer Interaction 4(1), 67–94 (1989)
10. Mynatt, E.D.: Designing with auditory icons: how well do we identify auditory cues? In: Proceedings of the 2nd International Conference on Auditory Display (1994)
11. Sanchez, J., Flores, H.: AudioMath: blind children learning mathematics through audio. In: Proceedings of Fifth Conf. Disability, Virtual Reality & Assoc. Tech., Oxford, UK (2004)
12. Sanchez, J., Jorquera, L.: Interactive virtual environments for blind children: usability and cognition. Department of Computer Science, University of Chile (2001)

13. Sanchez, J., Flores, H.: Memory enhancement through Audio. Department of Computer Science, Chile (2004)
14. Scavone, G.P., Lakatos, S., Harbke, C.: The Sonic Mapper: An Interactive Program For Obtaining Similarity Ratings With Auditory Stimuli. In: Proceedings of the 2002 International Conference on Auditory Display, Kyoto, Japan (2002)
15. Smither, J.A.: Short term memory demands in processing synthetic speech by old and young adults. Behaviour & Information Technology 12(6), 330–335 (1993)
16. Stevens, R.D., Brewster, S.A.: Providing an audio glance at algebra for blind readers. In: Proceedings of ICAD (1994)
17. Turnbull, D., Barrington, L., Torres, D., Lanckriet, G.: Modeling the Semantics of Sound. Department of Computer Science and Engineering, UCSD (2006)
18. Moreno, R., Mayer, R.E.: Designing for Understanding: A Learner-Centered Approach to Multimedia Learning. Journal of Educational Psychology 92(1), 117–125 (2000)
19. Hughes, R.W., Jones, D.M.: Indispensible benefits and unavoidable costs of unattended sound for cognitive functioning. Noise and Health 6(21), 63–76 (2003)
20. Yates, F.A.: The Art of Memory. University of Chicago Press, Chicago (1966)
21. Jaynes, J.: The Origin of Consciousness in the Breakdown of the Bicameral Mind. Houghton Mifflin Company (1976)
22. Bellugi, U.: How Signs Express Complex Meanings. In: Baker, C., Battison, R. (eds.) Sign Language and the Deaf Community: Essays in Honor of William C. Stokoe, p. 72. National Association of the Deaf (1980)
23. Mannheimer, S., Ferati, M., Huckleberry, D., Palakal, M.: Using Audemes as a Learning Medium for the Visually Impaired. In: HealthINF 2009, Porto, Portugal (accepted, 2009)

Accessing User Information for Use in Design

Chris McGinley and Hua Dong

School of Engineering and Design,
Brunel University, Uxbridge UB8 3PH, UK
{chris.mcginley,hua.dong}@brunel.ac.uk

Abstract. This paper investigates the issue of accessibility of data and end user information in a typical design development project, the barriers that exist, and how relevant user information might be presented through ergonomic data tools. The barriers typically include a combination of financial outlet, time expenditure and lengthy sourcing of suitable user groups, all of which could be reduced through effective use of tools. Ergonomics information and data useful for 'inclusive' design outputs can be underused in design development at a professional level. This study reports on tool concept development and a co-design workshop, which were carried out as part of ongoing research into effective communication of user data to designers in more human and engaging ways.

Keywords: Inclusive design, universal access, tools, ergonomics, user data.

1   Introduction

1.1   User Input Incorporated into the Design Process

Data is used in varying ways through the course of a design project. It can be claimed that user data typically follows a path where the information needs peak and trough, as priorities in the development change. A hypothetical example of this occurrence is illustrated below (Figure 1) in relation to user data, with user data needs plotted as a dashed line against a double diamond model, produced by the Design Council UK, to represent a typical design process.

Figure 1 illustrates the user data needs which begin high and continue through the exploratory 'discover' phase, data needs become more specific through the 'define' phase, and with better understanding refinement occurs and the volume of data needs reduce. During the 'develop' phase concepts are tested and development of prototypes require testing, hence user data again peaks for interrogation and evaluation of proposed solutions with user requirements, before the 'deliver' phase, at which point all user data should be in place.

1.2   Ways of Gathering User Data with Inclusive Considerations

Where inclusive design is concerned, the underlying philosophy considers the needs of those that are often overlooked in the design process; the most effective means of doing this is to include 'extreme users' [1] in the design process, an approach often

C. Stephanidis (Ed.): Universal Access in HCI, Part I, HCII 2009, LNCS 5614, pp. 116–125, 2009.
© Springer-Verlag Berlin Heidelberg 2009

undertaken in the Helen Hamlyn Centre (HHC), based in the Royal College of Art, London. They use this approach in undergraduate projects through to their annual Design Business Association (DBA) Challenge, which pairs design companies with 'extreme' users in order to inform and inspire. This process often produces notable results, and challenges designers to include the requirements of underrepresented end users. However, this process can be difficult to set up without established access to specific user groups such as the HHC has, and hence at times proves both time-consuming and expensive.

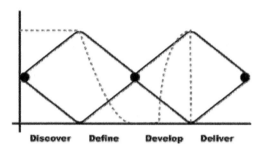

Fig. 1. 'Double Diamond' design process model, with plotted level of user data input

2 Designing Data for Designers

The intention of this study was to investigate the most effective means of gathering data and communicating it in a way that is easily accessible to designers helping to inform their definition and solutions of design problems. It is also intended to make the information inspiring and engaging, rather than lifeless, which tends to be a major hurdle with available tools and literature. Engaging with such tools would not only help designers interrogate issues during the design process, but would also assist them in forming new connections and insights, and encourage use of the tool(s) to supplement the creative phase of discovery at the front end of a design project.

There are many factors that are key to the uptake of information sources. It is essential that data tools are both intuitive and transparent, but also readily available. Ease of use is a huge factor, in the paper 'The many faces of accessibility: engineers' perception of information sources' [2] this ease of information search was described by engineers as "saving time, saving mental effort, convenience of use of format, and maximum physical proximity".

Existing information such as anthropometric data could be used as a resource for detailing users' capabilities and limitations, but rarely is. To explore this phenomenon research is underway within the Inclusive Design Research Group based at Brunel University. Eleven UK based design consultancies were interviewed early in the study to gain an insight into current use of anthropometric data [4], and explore suggestions for presentation of such data and preferences for data tools.

Throughout the design process designers gather a variety of information in numerous ways, often on an 'as needed' basis. When initial briefs are set there is often accompanying material relating to the subject area and/or design needs, this information typically forms part of a collection of prior internal research experience from within the design company, is supplied by the client group, or is a combination of both. The level of detail can vary greatly. However, a large proportion of information retrieval within design companies is not physically tangible, often deriving from 'designer intuition' or prior knowledge as demonstrated during an interview with Nina Warburton, Managing Director of The Alloy [4].

"I think one of the problems with design is that a lot of what we know is embedded in people we have in the company."

The interviews identified that the use of anthropometric data sources by designers is very limited, with experienced designers relying largely on experimental methods such as physical prototyping and engagement with people. They had preferences for more visually engaging and appealing means of data presentation, than the 'scientific' anthropometric data typically available to them. Based on these findings the researchers developed a series of data tool concepts using a highly visual format, and suggested means of data manipulation, which would be simple and intuitive. The intention being that the tools, could be readily included in the design process as a means of engaging designers with user information outside of their normal domain in terms of interaction and access, in a way that is time efficient and productive.

3   The Tool Concepts

A collection of 8 concept tools were developed and illustrated, based on the feedback received during the interviews mentioned in Section 2. The concepts were deliberately left under-defined, suggesting an overall principle, number of possible features and contents, but not detailing the data, means of manipulation, or means of presentation. This allowed the participants to place their own interpretations onto the concepts, which would help to flavour their feedback, allowing them to elaborate during the assessment and add unplanned features during the co-design task. This promoted development definition and change, whilst considered how the tools might or might not work for them. The tool concepts presented were as follows

2DPeople. 2DPeople is a searchable database of anthropometric data, with selectable variables such as sex, age and ethnicity. Upon selecting criteria a 2D subject is generated that can be manipulated for visualization, and accompanying data is generated for use in design.

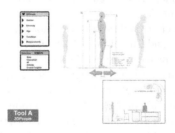

Fig. 2. 2DPeople

Posture Sourcebook. Posture sourcebook is a pictorial resource of common activities. It presents the full range of body movements typically used in everyday tasks. Taken from real life scenarios, instead of the rigid representations often found in books, a more natural 'lazy anthropometrics' with people represented in more natural way.

Fig. 3. Posture Sourcebook

ErgoLab. ErgoLab is a physical laboratory staffed by industry experts and extreme users, and brings together cutting edge expertise, resources and tools for user research and testing, a collaborative space for user centred design.

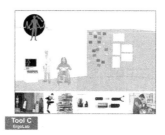

Fig. 4. ErgoLab

People Universe. People Universe is a user database of individual video profiles, images and measurements. It uses a highly visual browsing approach as well as conventional keyword search. It contains initial standard profiles but is also fully updatable, for new user profiles and data.

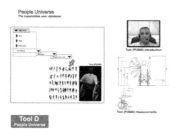

Fig. 5. People Universe

ErgoCES. ErgoCES incorporates large quantities of existing datasets based on people and products. These datasets can be browsed through, or parameters can be compared in a graphical manner. Axis categories are defined by the designer, which produces fast 2D data visualisation and comparisons.

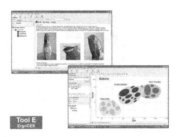

Fig. 6. ErgoCES

3DPeople. 3DPeople is a 3D human model generator. Variables such as sex, age and ethnicity can be input to generate 3D scale subjects for use within 3D CAD packages, and for visualisation and presentation purposes. It also offers sensory representations, through low vision render feature, which places representative filters over 3D CAD models.

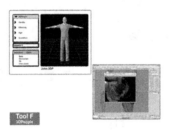

Fig. 7. 3DPeople

PeopleSpace. Peoplespace is a social networking tool, an online community and special interest group, with a key goal of bringing together real people and real designers. It allows discussion, assistance, and news in a general and product specific way. It allows the exploration of design issues without the need to leave the home or studio.

Fig. 8. PeopleSpace

Product Universe. Product universe is a searchable database of design examples, which can be used for comparison when designing. It lists the critical dimensions of products, to give an insight into the sizes adopted. Each sample has images, video and full dimensions, amongst other useful data.

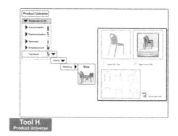

Fig. 9. Product Universe

4   The Evaluation Workshop with Designers

The tools were presented during 2 workshops, for discussion, assessment, and co-design. For the first workshop invitations were delivered largely to student partici-pants, then academic and finally industry professionals; for the second the opposite approach was adopted. This was to allow two perspectives to be obtained, and if they differentiated enough the reasons behind this could be further explored. For the pur-pose of this paper, the second workshop with industry focus will be considered.

Invitations were sent out to various design companies and to selected students, with an overview of the study and the goals. Approximately 25 participants attended each session, for a variety of reasons:

- new contacts/networking
- insights into the research
- participation/contribution to new tool development

4.1   Introduction to Tools

Workshop packs were given to each participant, which included an overview of the project, tool descriptions, attendee list, post-its, and feedback forms. Initially the overall project and previous research was presented to the audience, in order to set the scene. The tool concepts were then presented followed by a brief question session for any required clarification, before moving onto the more interactive sessions.

4.2   Individual Comments and Initial Feedback

The participants then began the individual feedback task by giving their first impres-sion ratings, which were given using a traffic light system of 'proceed' 'proceed with caution' and 'stop' represented by green, yellow and red post it notes consecutively. After the tool features were described during a presentation, participants were asked to write comments about the tools under the three categories, the intention being to assess which tools designers felt might be of benefit from first impressions and gut instinct, according to their own criteria of what might be useful for their work. The results of this session were used to create charts giving a quick indication of which tools created most positive interest, an example is presented below (Figure 10).

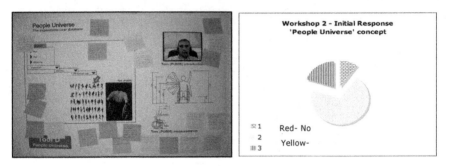

Fig. 10. Tool rating and derived feedback chart

4.3   Group Discussion, Rating and Co-design

After individual rating had been carried out, teams were formed for discussion of the tools. Each participant had been give a colour coded name tag dependent upon their company and role, people with different coloured tags were mixed in order that no table would have a particular bias. The teams were asked to discuss and write down the pros and cons of each concept and then to award a star rating (1 being the lowest, 5 being the highest) to the concepts. These discussions were recorded for later analysis, and the information obtained was analysed for consideration in later tool development.

The tools rating system varied immensely. Those that typically rated amongst the highest were 'ErgoLab', 'People Universe' and '3DPeople', and those typically rated amongst the lowest were '2DPeople' and 'Product Universe'. However, with these ratings there were suggestions for inclusions, exclusions and combinations. Some groups created their own rating systems, and example being a group that created their own rating criteria of 'usability', 'value to designer' and 'efficacy'.

The final workshop task was the co-design task. Having been presented with a number of concepts to discuss and rate the participants were then asked to remain in the teams which they had formed for discussion, to create a new tool concept, borrowing and combining features from the tools presented or developing their own ideas to create a completely new concept. The goal being to identify data tool features that could be useful in a typical design process. The co-designed tools were later presented by the teams, allowing them to explain the features they had included and the benefits they predicted they might have for the design process.

The tool concept example shown above (Figure 11) is an updatable visual and informational database, which combines the functionality of 4 of the tool concepts, however it is still stated that this is not a substitute for actual physical interaction with users, with statements such as, "do work yourself!" and "select volunteers for co-design."

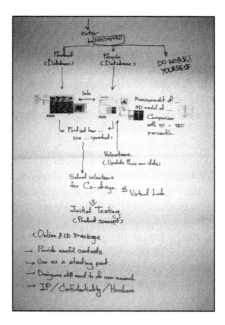

Fig. 11. Co-designed ergonomic tool concept

5 Discussion

Although there is an abundance of books and data on ergonomics and particularly anthropometrics, this opposes the fact that user based information gaps exist in the design process, and there is a clear reliance on intuition and experience. There is a prevalence of designers utilizing prior knowledge, unless the project is unique enough that they must engage with new scenarios, users and data.

This is not to say that this is an incorrect way to tackle design problems, it is a classic scenario found across most disciplines, with more experience, people become increasingly useful commodities. However, a tool that could collate this information and make it accessible to the less experienced designer, or a point of reference and tangible data source for the more experienced designer could have great value.

Typically designer skills and knowledge in the professional realm come from experience based learning, with designers gaining more knowledge as they complete more projects. Designers prefer to engage in experimental methods (e.g. prototypes and test rigs) and then interrogate these by working with actual users, even if this is very limited, even to the point where they might merely consult studio colleagues.

The tool concepts proved very effective in stimulating discussion, the two workshops had good attendance rates, and engaged participants in a lively way throughout, which demonstrates that topic itself provokes conversation. The eight concepts were deliberately varied, to touch upon many aspects of ergonomics from the more emotional to scientific, qualitative to quantitative. The hope was that this might polarise opinion and provoke definite answers, however the response demonstrated that there was value perceived in every tool, often relating to specific features, demonstrating that user data needs are wide and varied.

There was some deviation dependant on the nature of the design group. Clearly there is a wide range of design disciplines ranging from the more artistic design outputs which we could call 'designer' designs, to those more closely related to engineering, such as medical device design. The user needs vary correspondingly, from those looking for the pleasure of sitting on designer furniture, to the tight tolerances necessary for surgical tools.

There are two standpoints to consider, should a tool change the way designers work, or should it supplement their current methods? Is it even possible to impact a designer once they have reached the professional domain, or is this something that would be more suited to the educational sector, where the concepts and considerations can become part of the instinctive thinking that designers typically use in their day-to-day thinking process?

"We are wired to feel things for people, not for abstractions," [3]. This was demonstrated through several features of the tools such as visual impairment renderings, user videos, and figures based on real people, which repeatedly received positive feedback. It can be assumed that this is due in part to the fact that these features go some way towards creating a more 'human' representation. It is clear that a major obstacle to the uptake of tools is the preference for experimental and face-to-face interaction. According to David Fisher, Creative Director of Seymour Powell [4].

"Product design is now more tuned to marketing then engineering. We have moved, we are more part of a brand, and an absolute must within that is make a product as good as possible. But better could be better functionality, better ergonomics or more emotional connection! So emotional values are as important these days as good old fashioned engineering."

6 Conclusions

In summary this paper reported on ergonomic data requirements in professional design practice. It described tool concepts based on feedback from a study of the use of anthropometric data by professional designers in their design process. It then went on to discuss one of two workshops held to evaluate the tool concepts and co-design new tool concepts.

There is an abundance of ergonomic and anthropometric data currently available, however it is largely inflexible and difficult to access. Even when appropriate to a design project, most is not in a format that appeals to designers, hence there is scope to make use of this body of data by communicating it in a more engaging way. However, data on its own is not enough, it needs to be understood. The way data is presented should make understanding implicit, and naturally build on the knowledge a designer already possesses. A major step is talking the designers data language to allow them to add to the story of their design development in a natural way.

Ergonomics covers a huge range of information useful to design development projects, and designers typically use many elements of ergonomics dependant on the individual project. The concept of a holistic tool which meets all ergonomic needs in a design project is at best complex, and at worst both inappropriate and unusable. The criteria of an 'appropriate' and 'usable' tool need to be further explored. The features of a tool also require further development considering more specific criteria as indicated by designers, particular consideration being given to the stage of the design process in which such tools should be employed.

References

1. Dong, H., Cassim, J., Clarkson, J.: Best Practice of Critical User Forums. In: Paper presented at the Include Conference, Royal College of Art, London, UK (April 2007)
2. Green, M., Fidel, R.: The Many Faces of Accessibility: Engineers' Perception of Information Sources. Information Processing and Management: an International Journal 40(3), 563–581 (2004)
3. Heath, C., Heath, D.: Made to Stick: Why Some Ideas Survive and Others Die, p. 16. Random House, USA (2007)
4. Nickpour, F., Dong, H.: Designing Anthropometrics: Insights Into Designers Use of People Size Data. Technical Report, School of Engineering and Design, Brunel University (2008)
5. Nickpour, F., Dong, H.: Anthropometrics Without Numbers! An Investigation of Designers' Use of People Data. In: Paper to be presented at the Include 2009 Conference, Royal College of Art, London, UK (April 2009)

Engineering User Centered Interaction Systems for Semantic Visualizations

Kawa Nazemi, Thomas Daniel Ullmann, and Christoph Hornung

Fraunhofer Institute for Computer Graphics Research,
Fraunhoferstr. 5, 64283 Darmstadt, Germany
{Kawa.Nazemi,Thomas.Ullmann,Christoph.Hornung}@igd.fraunhofer.de

Abstract. For intuitive interaction with semantic visualizations, gesture-based interaction seems a promising way. However, the development of such ensembles is costly. To cut down the engineering effort, we propose a development model for interaction systems with semantic visualizations. In addition, we provide a set of evaluation tools to support the interaction developer engineer evaluating the engineering process.

Keywords: semantic visualization, gesture, interaction, universal access.

1 Semantic Visualizations and Gesture Based Interaction

The research questions we focus on are how people interact with semantic visualizations using other devices than traditional ones, and what types of gestures support users work with semantic information. We show a framework how semantic visualization interaction developer can engineer such ensembles efficiently.

Semantic visualization, or ontology-based visualizations [13], is a special field of information visualization [3][4][5] and focuses on visualizing classes, instances, properties, and their multiple relations. It is part of the top layer of the semantic web stack [15] - the user interface and application layer.

By now, the World Wide Web is designed for human reading and referencing of information through linking. The information and the context of information are not understandable for computers. The Semantic Web [2], as an extension of the WWW, computers will be capable to "understand" the information and thus will help to find and combine information more automatically. To avoid that only specialized people can participate in benefits of the Semantic Web, we have to provide tools, which abstract from the technical details. This is maybe similar to the development of the Web 1.0 to the Web 2.0. Within the early stages of the internet, people with some technical background were capable to use the technology for their needs. With the development of tools, like blogging systems or content management systems, who hide the details of the web technology, users can actively participate on the creation of content. For the Semantic Web, several approaches to visualize the relations of semantic information and to abstract from the technical details have been developed, for example, graph visualizations [6][7], hierarchies [8], facets [9][10], or timelines [11].

C. Stephanidis (Ed.): Universal Access in HCI, Part I, HCII 2009, LNCS 5614, pp. 126–134, 2009.

In addition to semantic visualization, we have to undertake efforts to providing users with intuitive ways to interact with the semantic web. The success of interaction devices apart from mouse and keyboard indicate a change of the user interaction needs with computer-based systems towards Post-WIMPs [20]. In contrast to WIMP GUIs, that is graphical user interfaces mainly based on menus, forms, icons, and pointing devices, like a mouse, Post-WIMPS rely on gesture and try to avoid using icons as representation for functionality. With the raise of mobile duo-touch displays, multi-user interactive walls and tabletops, with multi-touch sensing [1], or new controller for computer games, the master vendors of consumer hardware industry push the availability of such devices for a broader audience.

With these devices, new ways of interaction with the computer become possible. People will use a wide range of gestures, which are more natural to solve certain task, when possible with a mouse controller. We are following the notion of Kendon [22], that "… gesture is a name for visible actions, when it is used as an utterance or part of an utterance". We see gestures as natural form of humans to express themselves to achieve certain task. Humans developed a wide variety of gestures. According to a classification of gesture based computer interaction [21], we focus on gestures styles, enabling technology, and system response. For the solving of tasks within semantic visualizations, several gesture styles has to be considered, like deictic gestures (e.g. pointing to an object), manipulative gestures (e.g. moving a node by hand), semaphoric gestures (e.g. thump up for accepting an dialogue), or language gestures (e.g. sign language). In addition we take enabling technologies, like touch surfaces, electronic pens, or system response from e.g. visual displays or audio output enable multiple gestures into account.

2   Challenges of the Engineering of Interaction Systems for Semantic Visualizations

Considering the outlined trends, a broader audience will get access to semantic visualizations on modern devices. This also implies that the developer of semantic visualizations have to bear in mind the "average" typical user [2], who has few or no experiences with semantic visualizations or new interaction devices or computer interaction gestures, like hand-gestures, speech-interaction, multi-touch, and specialized intelligent objects.

In contrast to posteriori adaption of interactive software, we will present proactive strategies [2] for the design of semantic visualizations using formative and summative evaluation methods [14].

One of the problems of user interactions studies is that the sole working with a system a user is likely to adjust the user's behavior to the application logic and to the interactions styles necessary to use the interaction devices. A more human centered way would be to look first at the natural interactions styles of users and then adjust technology to serve users interaction styles. This bias between user adjustment and technology adjustment is not completely reducible, but we can strengthen user-centered approaches with an appropriate research design.

3 Research Design for the Development of Interactive Semantic Visualizations

To avoid that users adopt their interactions to technical parameters of the interaction devices or to the logic of the semantic visualization, we have developed a three-phase model to obtain the user interaction style. In the first phases, users have a high degree of freedom to interact with semantic visualizations and therefore can use gestures natural for them without dealing with technical constraints. Users do not have to adjust their behavior to the technology. Rather the opposite, technology is build step wise from stage to stage to serve the needs of users.

The Semantic Visualization Interaction Model comprises three phases in cyclic manner (see Fig. 1). Through formative evaluation of each stage, we use the results for continuous development of the product. During the formative evaluation stage, the interaction designer conducts short investigations with a small number of participants to gain insight of the usage of the users to solve tasks with gestures. If the development of the interaction design project reaches a satisfying level, the evaluation of the last phase serves as a summative evaluation of the whole development process. For this evaluation stage, an external team of evaluators tests a significant number of people. The goal of this evaluation is to rate the product efficacy. As an example for the product efficacy, this could be the usefulness of the supported interaction styles of the used gestures to solve certain tasks. In the following, we will discuss the cyclic development process of gesture-based interaction with semantic visualizations.

The interaction designer uses the first phase to get an early quick overview of the gestures people will naturally use for solving their tasks. At this stage, there is no need for a working software or hardware product. The requirements for building the products evolve from this early stage. This also helps, that we can tailor the product more to users needs. Thus we only provide the user on the one hand a static version of the visualization, for example a picture, and on the other hand an input device with no technical functionality, e.g. a switched of electronic pen, or a real pen. With these tools, we gave the user several tasks to solve. This task can include navigation, zooming, scrolling in an information space, or manipulating information. Since the visualization and the device have no functionality, we can minimize the feedback loops between the GUI and the user, which would shape the behavior of the user to the specific logic arising from the special usage of a working software or hardware. This frees the user from the product constraints and he can then use interaction styles natural for him solving given tasks.

Starting with this phase, the semantic visualization interaction developer gains an insight what interactions are intuitive for the user. With this information, the developer can generate assumptions about the logic of the semantic visualization and the technical possibilities the interaction device has to provide. Before the next stage, we formulate hypotheses derived from the first experiences. A hypothesis could be for example: "Most people will prefer using their hand, than an electronic pen to navigate from one concept to another", or "most people will move their body towards the visualization to zoom into it, than moving backwards". These hypotheses guide the next evaluation steps. The hypothesis will be proven, refined, dismissed, accepted, or even new hypotheses will be generated. The tools and methods supporting this process follow in the next section.

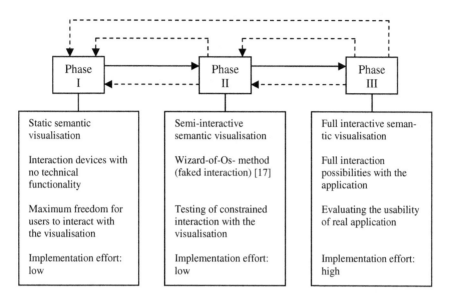

Fig. 1. The three phases of the cyclic development process of gesture-based interaction with semantic visualizations (dotted arrows indicate possible repetition steps for each phase, solid ones the optimal process without repetition steps)

The second phase is a proof of the assumptions of the first phase with the technical constraints of the future real application, but without developing the actual software or hardware. In this phase the developer can decide based on the information of the first phase what semantic visualization logic the user expects and what gestures the interaction device must be capable to track. To avoid high development effort and costs, this phase uses a wizard-of-oz method (see [17] for an example on natural-language dialogue systems), faking the real interaction with the semantic visualization. For this stage, we tell the user, with what gesture he can achieve a certain task. For example, we tell the user, that with a special move of both hands, he can zoom into the visualization. The special type of gesture bases on the experiences of the first stage. While the user tries to solve the given task with this gesture, we provide a visual feedback of the correctness of the gesture. We achieve this with another person watching the gesture and then according to the correctness provide the user the visualization for the right or for the wrong gesture. Since one person is faking the interaction for the user, we do not have to develop the software or hardware in depth. We use mainly prototypes. In this stage, we can evaluate the satisfaction of the users and the usability of the system as if they would work with a fully developed system, that reacts in the right way with a correct input or does not react with wrong input. Based on these new insights, we test the hypotheses of the first stage (see also the method section of this article), refine them, or add new one for the third stage. The developer repeats this process until reaching a satisfying solution. If this is not possible, he has to return to the first phase in order to change the initial hypotheses otherwise we can step to the next stage.

With the results of the first two phases, the developer can now build the logic of the semantic visualization and the interaction devices to a working system. This last phase is finished with the third observation of test users to refine and evaluate the final usability of the application. The test persons now interact with a full functioning application. The results of this phase serve as feedback for the next development loops for the further improvement of the product. The last step can serve as summative evaluation to assess qualities of the product.

During each phase, we support the interaction designer by a set of methods helping to gather relevant data for hypothesis guided designing decisions.

4 Methods

For each phase of the Semantic Visualization Interaction Model, a set of research methods is used. The method toolkit comprises video analysis [16], a newly developed questionnaire (Semantic Visualization Gesture Interaction Questionnaire, short SVGIQ), and a new developed Acceleration Gesture Tracking Device, for the unobtrusive recognition of accelerator values, generated by the interaction performed by users.

SVGIQ bases on general usability criteria [19] and gesture interaction research [18]. Based on this we extended the questionnaire to the needs of semantic visualizations. It consists of a set of three independent questionnaires. The first one is used before, one during, and the third after the treatment.

The first part collects data about sex, age, occupation, general experience with computers and computer games, semantic visualizations, and computer devices. We use this data for clustering users according to their background and experience. After the users have fulfilled one task within the semantic visualization with an interaction device, the investigator presents them the second questionnaire. It contains question about satisfaction, efficiency, and effectiveness with a semantic visualization and gesture. The third part gathers data about the general liking of the semantic visualizations and devices/gestures. In addition, subjective valuations of the interaction, like intuitive usability, learn ability, naturalness, controllability, practicability, and fun.

We record the interactions of the persons on video for a later video analysis. During the treatment, the investigator let the people describe why they use a certain gesture for solving a task, and what gesture "feels right" for this. The most significant gesture was later used for the analysis of the data. With standardized interview instructions, we assure a consistent way to provide the instructions to the subjects.

In addition to the video capturing, we developed a gesture-tracking device based on acceleration for the unobtrusive recognition of accelerator values, generated by the interaction of users. We use the video analysis, the SVGIQ data, and the data from gesture-tracking device for the analysis of statistical correlations of user characteristics with the semantic visualizations and input devices/gestures.

Each phases of the Semantic Visualization Interaction Model use these methods (see fig. 2).

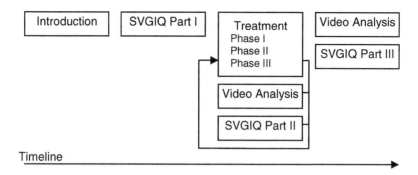

Fig. 2. Schedule of activities in each phase of the Semantic Visualization Interaction Model

After a short introduction into the general idea of semantic visualizations, the test users fill out the first part of the SVGIQ. After that every users becomes an interaction device and the order to fulfill a task within the semantic visualization. Depending of the phase of the process model, the shown visualization, and interaction device were more or less developed, as described above. During the treatment, the examiner asked several questions according to the standardized video instructions. In addition, we capture the whole treatment with a video camera for further examination. For acceleration-based devices we additionally use the gesture-tracking device. After the treatment, the users filled out the second part of the questionnaire, containing questions to the semantic visualization, the interaction device, and the task. For each task, we repeat the steps of the treatment phase. The examination ends with a short interview captured with video and the third part of the questionnaire containing questions to the general experience with semantic visualizations and interaction devices.

With this quantitative and qualitative measurement toolkit, we provided a framework for the empirical analysis of Semantic Visualization Interaction Model and an efficient software engineering process for developing semantic visualization interaction techniques.

5   Case Study

To exemplify the method we present the essential parts of an interaction study of semantic visualization conducted 2008. The goal of the study was to investigate gestures of users interacting with SeMap [23] and SemaSpace [24], semantic visualization for fast navigation in semantic knowledge worlds with several interaction devices and gestures. According to the first phase of our proposed process model, we showed a static semantic visualization (screenshots) and an option dialogue to our test persons (see fig. 3).

During the working on the tasks we record the persons on video, interviewed them, and they filled out the questionnaire. We gave the person the instruction to stand in front of a large screen, where we displayed the visualizations. We introduced the visualization with a short note about concepts, and that concepts have relations to other concepts. After that, the persons had some time to familiarize with the system (see fig. 4).

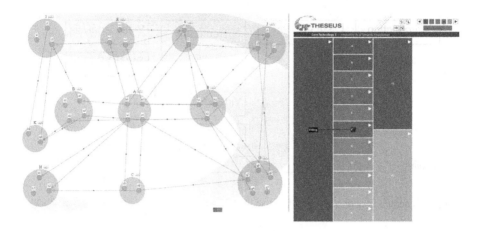

Fig. 3. Semantic Visualization SeMap and SemaSpace

Fig. 4. Interaction devices and gestures: Electronic pencil, hand gesture, accelerator based controller

They are supposed to use the electronic pencil like an ordinary pen and the controller like a bar. For hand gestures, we made no restriction. With these instructions, the persons fulfilled tasks like navigation from one concept to another, zoom in and zoom out, and accepting and declining options. The persons had some time to try several gestures to solve a task. After a while, we asked what the significant gesture was for them. We also asked them to verbalize why they chosen this gesture.

6 Discussion

In consequence of the complex nature of the relations between user interaction and semantic visualizations, we have to adjust the proposed methods to the special needs of each research setting. The proposed method of the Semantic Visualization Interaction Model can serve as a foundation for research, but for the individual requirements of each software product, we have to tailor the methods accordingly. A common set of methods could also serve as a way to compare different semantic visualization interaction studies. Further examinations with different visualizations and interaction devices are now necessary to examination universality of the proposed.

7 Conclusion

With this approach, we are able to build systems based on the preferences of users. We can reduce the problem that the users have to adjust their interaction to the needs of the technology. The users can use their natural gestures to interact with the semantic visualizations, and do not have to learn the logic of the system. Thus, we can lower the barriers to use such systems. This enables more people to participate and decreases the exclusion of people not capable or willing to learn the technical details of interactive semantic visualizations. The advantages in explicitly defining hypothesis at the beginning of each phase and then testing the hypotheses assures an empirical guided development process and help to make reasonable decisions.

References

1. Han, J.Y.: Low-Cost Multi-Touch Sensing through Frustrated Total Internal Reflection. In: Proceedings of the 18th Annual ACM Symposium on User Interface Software and Technology (2005)
2. Berners-Lee, T., Hendler, J., Lassila, O.: The Semantic Web. Scientific American (May 2001)
3. Card, S.K., Mackinlay, J.D., Shneiderman, B.: Readings in information visualization: using vision to think. Morgan Kaufmann Publishers, San Francisco (1999)
4. Ware, C.: Information Visualization: Perception for Design. Morgan Kaufmann Publishers Inc., San Francisco (2000)
5. Spence, R.: Information Visualization: Design for Interaction. Prentice Hall, Englewood Cliffs (2007)
6. Herman, I., Melançon, G., Marshall, M.S.: Graph Visualization and Navigation in Information Visualisation: a Survey. IEEE Transactions on Visualization and Computer Graphics 6(1), 24–43 (2000)
7. Battista, G., Eades, P., Tamassia, R., Tollis, I.G.: Graph Drawing: Algorithms for the Visualization of Graphs. Prentice Hall, Englewood Cliffs (1998)
8. Heer, J., Card, S.K.: DOITrees Revisited: Scalable, Space-Constrained Visualization of Hierarchical Data. Advanced Visual Interfaces, 421–424 (2004)
9. Hildebrand, M., Ossenbruggen, J., van, H.L., van: /facet: A Browser for Heterogeneous Semantic Web Repositories. In: Cruz, I., Decker, S., Allemang, D., Preist, C., Schwabe, D., Mika, P., Uschold, M., Aroyo, L.M. (eds.) ISWC 2006. LNCS, vol. 4273, pp. 272–285. Springer, Heidelberg (2006)
10. Hearst, M.: Clustering versus faceted categorization for information exploration. Communications of the ACM 49(4), 59–61 (2006)
11. http://simile.mit.edu/timeline/
12. Stephanidis, C.: User Interfaces for All: New perspectives into Human-Computer Interaction. In: Stephanidis, C. (ed.) User Interfaces for All - Concepts, Methods, and Tools, pp. 3–17. Lawrence Erlbaum Associates, Mahwah (2001)
13. Fluit, C., Sabou, M., van Harmelen, F.: Ontology-based Information Visualization. In: Geroimenko, V., Chen, C. (eds.) Visualizing the Semantic Web, pp. 36–48. Springer, London (2003)
14. Rossi, P.H., Freeman, H.E., Lipsey, M.W.: Evaluation. A Systematic Approach, 6th edn. Sage, Thousand Oaks (1999)

15. Berners-Lee, T: Semantic Web – XML2000. W3 Talks (2000),
    `http://www.w3.org/2000/Talks/1206-xml2k-tbl/`
16. Seidel, T., Prenzel, M., Kobarg, M.: How to run a video study: Technical report of the IPN Video Study. Waxmann, Münster (2005)
17. Dahlbäck, N., Jönsson, A., Ahrenberg, L.: Wizard of Oz studies—why and how. In: Maybury, M.T., Wahlster, W. (eds.) Readings in intelligent User interfaces. Morgan Kaufmann Publishers, San Francisco (1998)
18. Karam, M.: A framework for research and design of gesture-based human computer interaction (2006), `http://ecs.soton.ac.uk/~amrk03r/Thesis.pdf`
19. Shneiderman, B., Plaisant, C.: Designing the User Interface: Strategies for Effective Human-Computer Interaction, 4th edn. Addison Wesley, Reading (2004)
20. van Dam, A.: Post-WIMP user interfaces. Communications of the ACM 40(2), 63–67 (1997)
21. Karam, M., Schraefel, M.C.: A taxonomy of Gestures in Human Computer Interaction. Technical report, Electronics and Computer Science, University of Southampton (2005)
22. Kendon, A.: Gesture: Visible Action as Utterance. Cambridge University Press, Cambridge (2004)
23. Nazemi, K., Breyer, M., Hornung, C.: SEMAP: A Concept for the Visualization of Semantics as Maps. In: Proceedings of the 13th International Conference on Human-Computer Interaction (HCI International), San Diego, CA, USA (2009)
24. Bhatti, N.: Web Based Semantic Visualization to Explore Knowledge Spaces – An Approach for Learning by Exploring. In: Proceedings of World Conference on Educational Multimedia, Hypermedia and Telecommunications 2008, pp. 312–322. AACE, Chesapeake (2008)

An Open Source Tool for Simulating a Variety of Vision Impairments in Developing Swing Applications

Theofanis Oikonomou[1], Konstantinos Votis[1], Dimitrios Tzovaras[1], and Peter Korn[2]

[1] Informatics and Telematics Institute, 6th Km Charilaou-Thermi Road,
Thermi-Thessaloniki, PO BOX 60361, GR-57001, Greece
{thoikon,kvotis,tzovaras}@iti.gr
[2] Sun Microsystems, Inc., 17 Network Circle, MPK17-101,
Menlo Park, CA 94025, USA
Peter.Korn@Sun.COM

Abstract. A lot of tools have been created lately in order to simulate how a vision impaired or color-blind person would perceive web rich-client applications and content. In this work we propose a simulation tool for non-web Java ™ Swing applications. The aim is to assist the developers in preventing accessibility barriers and improving the overall quality throughout the design and implementation phases of the whole development process.

1 Introduction

It is important to realize that people with disabilities are not just a tiny minority of the population of the European Union. The lowest estimate, based on the extremes of currently defined disablement categories, puts their total number at around 40 Million persons (nearly 11% of the population of the EU[1]). Designing for people with disabilities is becoming an increasingly important topic for a variety of reasons, especially due to the recent legislation in many countries promoting their rights. Consequently, even if people with disabilities want to be independent and do things for themselves by themselves, unfortunately, most Information and Communication Technologies (ICT) applications and systems are not fully accessible today.

Assistive technologies such as screen readers, screen magnifiers, speech recognition systems and Braille terminals help make applications and content accessible to people with disabilities. To accomplish this goal, accessibility standardization activities have been actively performed in various areas, and many institutions and organizations [1,2,3,4,5,6] are introducing new criteria for assessing accessibility [7,8,9].

One of the problems in adopting these standards is the lack of tool support. In order to create documents and applications that are compliant with standards or guidelines, tools for accessibility checking, evaluation and simulation are needed to reduce the burdens on document authors and application/content developers. For the traditional HTML-based web content, various accessibility checking tools have been developed. Currently, sufficient tools do not exist for non-web rich-client applications and content.

---

[1] http://europa.eu.int/comm/eurostat/Public/datashop/printproduct/EN?catalogue=Eurostat product=3-11012002-EN-AP-EN mode=download

C. Stephanidis (Ed.): Universal Access in HCI, Part I, HCII 2009, LNCS 5614, pp. 135–144, 2009.
© Springer-Verlag Berlin Heidelberg 2009

To this end we propose a new vision impairment simulation tool for Java ^{TM} Swing applications.

The remaining of this paper is organized as follows: We briefly discuss the vision impairments that were included in our work in Sect. 2. We describe the most representative web rich-client content evaluation and simulation tools and Graphical User Interface (GUI) validation tools in Sect. 3. In Sect. 4 we present the proposed simulation tool followed by some screenshots. Final remarks are discussed in Sect. 5 which concludes this paper.

2 Vision Impairments

We simulate color blindness and various low vision impairments such as loss of central and peripheral vision, blurred vision, extreme light sensitivity and night blindness. These impairments, especially central and peripheral vision loss, have a negative impact on computer use, since modern operating systems employ GUIs which require the use of eye-to-hand coordination to operate the mouse.

The loss of central vision creates a blur or blind spot, but side (peripheral) vision remains intact. This makes it difficult to read, recognize faces, and distinguish most details in the distance. Mobility, however, is usually unaffected because side vision remains intact. Typical examples of central vision loss are cataract and macular degeneration.

Loss of peripheral vision is characterized by an inability to distinguish anything to one side or both sides, or anything directly above and/or below eye level. Central vision remains, however, making it possible to see directly ahead. Typically, loss of peripheral vision may affect mobility and if severe, can slow reading speed as a result of seeing only a few words at a time. This is sometimes referred to as "tunnel vision". Typical examples of peripheral vision loss are glaucoma and retinitis pigmentosa.

Blurred vision causes both near and far to appear to be out of focus, even with the best conventional spectacle correction possible. It may cause difficulties in reading texts with normal formal font size, mobility, everyday activities such as cooking, sewing, cleaning, using computers etc.

Extreme light sensitivity exists when standard levels of illumination overwhelm the visual system, producing a washed out image and/or glare disability. People with extreme light sensitivity may actually suffer pain or discomfort from relatively normal levels of illumination. Difficulties in activities either at dark or at a too bright light or in working in premises that are not properly lit.

Night blindness results in inability to see outside at night under starlight or moonlight, or in dimly lighted interior areas such as movie theaters or restaurants. There may be difficulties in a number of activities performed at dark after daylight such as crossing the street, reading signs etc.

Color blindness is a lack of sensitivity to certain colors. Common forms of color blindness include difficulty distinguishing between red and green, or between yellow and blue. Sometimes color blindness results in the inability to perceive any color. Color blindness is problematic in driving vehicles, reading signs or maps, watching TV, working on a computer, understanding colorful graphics and charts etc.

3 Related Work

In this section we briefly describe the most well known web accessibility evaluation tools, also known as testing or assessment tools (Sect. 3.1). Additionally, we enumerate the most technologically advanced web accessibility simulation tools (Sect. 3.2) and finally we elaborate on some GUI validation tools (Sect. 3.3).

3.1 Web Accessibility Evaluation Tools

Web accessibility evaluation tools check web pages against the two most commonly cited standards for web accessibility [2,10], point out errors or potential problems, and advise you to correct or double check them. Automated accessibility checking tools cannot make firm judgments about the accessibility of everything on a web page. Some of the most well known evaluation tools are:

A-Prompt [12]. A-Prompt is a downloadable software tool which first evaluates the web page to identify barriers to accessibility and then provides assistance in making the necessary repairs. You can check one page or focus on a particular element in a page.

Color Contrast Check [13]. This tool allows specifying a foreground and a background color and determining if they provide enough of a contrast when viewed by someone having color deficits or when viewed on a black and white screen.

Contrast Analyser [14]. It is primarily a tool for checking foreground and background color combinations to determine if they provide good color visibility. It also contains functionality to create simulations of certain visual conditions such as color blindness.

WAVE Web Accessibility Tool [11]. WAVE displays a web page graphically with icons that indicate errors or possible problems. You can even continue to browse within the site while using WAVE.

3.2 Web Accessibility Simulation Tools

Simulation tools present web pages as it would appear under specific circumstances, such as to someone using a text-only browser or to someone with color blindness. Simulation tools can help in some of the areas that accessibility testing tools leave to your judgement. Some of the most representative simulation tools are:

Accessibility Color Wheel [15]. This tool analyzes the contrast of a color pair. It simulates how people with three forms of color blindness might see the colors.

aDesigner [20]. aDesigner is a disability simulator that helps web designers ensure that their pages are accessible and usable by the visually impaired. The tool looks at such elements as the degree of color contrast on the page, the ability of users to change the font size, the appropriateness of alternate text for images, and the availability of links in the page to promote navigability. The tool also checks the pages' compliance with accessibility guidelines. The result of this analysis is a report listing the problems that would prevent accessibility and usability by visually impaired users. In addition, each page is given an overall score. With this information, web developers get immediate feedback and can address these obstacles before the pages are published.

Vischeck Color Blindness Simulation Tool [16]. A color blindness simulator that can be used online or as a Photoshop plug-in. The online tool simulates color blindness on an image that you upload or on a web page that you specify, while the Photoshop plug-in changes the colors of the document you are working on.

VIS [17]. Visual Impairment Simulator is an educational tool that simulates what it is like to use Microsoft Windows® with a visual impairment. When the program runs, it manipulates the images on the user's screen so that it seems like the user has a visual impairment such as color blindness or macular degeneration among others. The user is able to pick which visual impairment to use and the severity of the impairment.

WebAIM Low Vision Simulation Tool [18]. This tool provides an opportunity for web developers to experience a web page using simulated visual disabilities. While it certainly does not simulate low vision itself, it can be used to help understand how visual disabilities can impact web content and how web content can be better designed.

3.3 Graphical User Interface Validation Tools

a11y [23]. The a11y module is an accessibility checker Netbeans [22] plug-in that helps developers to make their GUI forms compliant with accessibility rules effectively and without unnecessary effort. It "listens" for any event in the Form Editor and checks whether all its components meet required criteria. If they don't, adequate message is generated and listed in a table with description or recommendation for the user.

RAVEN [21]. Raven, which stands for Rule-based Accessibility Validation Environment, is an Eclipse tool [24] for inspecting Java™ based GUIs and web pages and validating them for accessibility. It uses an innovative Aspect-Oriented Programming (AOP) technique to inspect the application as it is executed. This tool supports Java AWT or Swing and Eclipse Standard Widget Toolkit (SWT) GUIs, including Eclipse plug-ins.

4 Vision Impairment Simulator

As stated in Sec. 3.3 there is a tool (a11y) that helps the developer during the GUI implementation face by making sure all the accessibility information about every GUI component is set. This guarantees that the information will be available to an impaired user through the aid of an assistive technology. Having that in mind we devised two new modules for the Netbeans Integrated Development Environment (IDE) and one stand-alone application that can give the developer an idea of what would his GUI actually look like to a vision impaired user. In our work we used the Sun Java™ Standard Edition Development Kit (JDK), the Java Accessibility Application Programming Interface (JAAPI) and the Netbeans IDE.

4.1 Preview Design in Vision Impairment Simulator Module

As you design the User Interface (UI), the GUI builder shows the form in the design area of the NetBeans IDE (Fig. 2). This is an accurate but static representation of the UI form. You cannot interact with it as if it were actually running. Static and non-interactive views are fine while you are arranging components, but this view does not help you see how form components will behave as you resize the form, nor can you test the order of tabs. The "Preview Design in Vision Impairment Simulator" module (PreDeVIS) provides a visual design preview feature that allows you to see how the form will display in your application. You can activate the design preview by clicking on the preview icon, a small image of an eye with an arm-chair, at the IDE's Toolbar (Fig. 1).

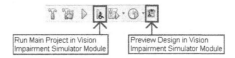

Run Main Project in Vision Impairment Simulator Module   Preview Design in Vision Impairment Simulator Module

Fig. 1. Netbeans toolbar with the two new modules installed

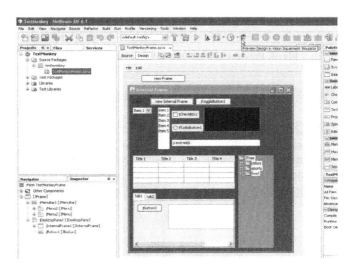

Fig. 2. Netbeans GUI builder

When you click on the preview icon, the GUI builder will activate the form in Preview mode. The preview gives an indication of whether the component alignments and anchors are set the way you want them. Preview mode lets you type information into text fields, tab from field to field, resize the form and simulate various visual deficiencies. We can identify four different regions. The first one, located in the upper left part of the PreDeVIS is the previewed form. The simulated form is located in the upper right part. Any action made in the previewed form is propagated in the simulated form. Furthermore, we can specify which impairment to simulate from the control panel found in the lower left part of the simulator and control various factors regarding the specific impairment from the controls located in the lower right part of

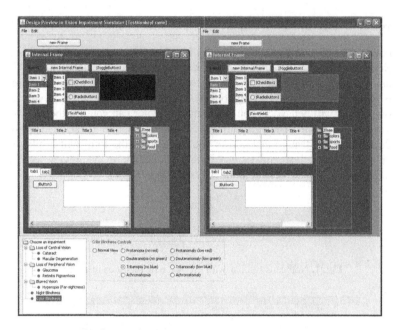

Fig. 3. Preview Design module simulating tritanopia

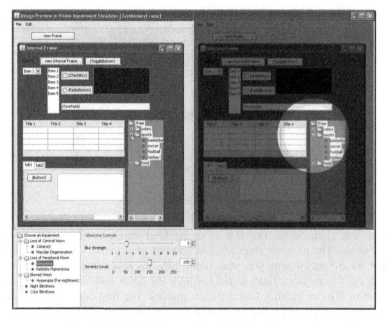

Fig. 4. Preview Design module simulating glaucoma

the preview simulator. For example we can choose to simulate how a color blind user with tritanopia [25] would perceive our form when he clicks on a combo-box (Fig. 3) or when a low vision user with glaucoma expands a tree (Fig. 4).

4.2 Run Main Project in Vision Impairment Simulator Module

The developer can use the PreDeVIS module in order to quickly preview the way the form he designs in the Netbeans IDE will look like. This way the functionality of the various GUI components present in the form cannot be tested. The "Run Main Project in Vision Impairment Simulator" module (RunVIS) comes to his aid. You can activate this module by clicking on the RunVIS icon, an image of a green triangle with an arm-chair, at the IDE's Toolbar (Fig. 1). With this module the developer has the ability to explore the application and test if the functionality he has programmatically set to each GUI component actually works. While the application is running new windows, such as dialogs, choosers or frames, may appear due to a user action. The module automatically simulates the window that has the user's focus. Another interesting feature is that the module inherits the Look and Feel (L&F) that was set to the application by the developer. For example the developer can see how a user with retinitis pigmentosa opens an internal frame while the application has the Metal L&F (Fig. 5) or how a user with cataract clicks on a check box while the application has the Windows L&F (Fig. 6). Notice that the Windows high contrast setting is turned on and the "High Contrast White" appearance scheme is activated.

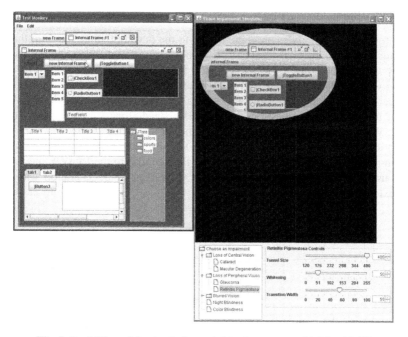

Fig. 5. RunVIS module simulating retinitis pigmentosa with Metal L&F

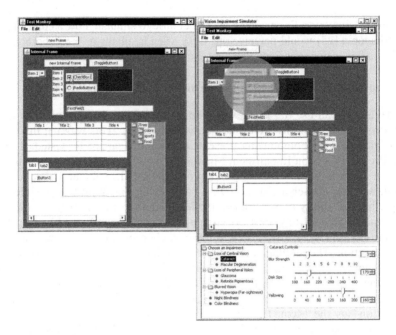

Fig. 6. RunVIS module simulating cataract with Windows L&F while having the "High Contrast White" appearance scheme activated

4.3   Vision Impairment Simulator Standalone Application

The aforementioned modules are a great help to the developer that give him the ability to quickly check any GUI form and eventually run the application and test its functionality while simulating a variety of vision impairments. These are all done while working with the Netbeans IDE. What happens when this IDE is not available to the developer or when someone else wants to evaluate the work done by the developer? In order to answer these questions we created a stand-alone version of the RunVIS module. With this application anyone, developer or not, can test any GUI application bundled in a jar file. As it is seen in Fig. 7 the user browses for a jar file of his choice and then starts the simulator. The interface is then similar to the RunVIS module and can be used for example to simulate a user with macular degeneration who types some text in a table's cell as can be seen in Fig. 8.

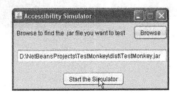

Fig. 7. Vision impairment simulator standalone application initial state

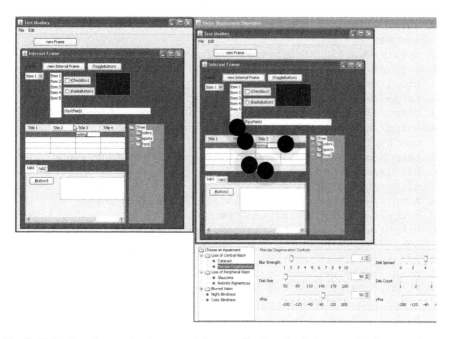

Fig. 8. Vision impairment simulator standalone application simulating macular degeneration

5   Conclusions – Future Work

In this paper a tool for simulating various vision impairments in developing Java ^{TM} swing applications is presented. This tool can be used as a part of the Netbeans IDE or as a standalone application, aiding the developers throughout the phases of the whole development process. This way they can overcome accessibility barriers and improve the overall quality of their applications. Feedback from user groups could be used to better simulate the implemented impairments or add more. Finally, the tool could be extended in order to apply the same simulation techniques to JavaFX [26] applications.

Acknowledgments. This work was partially funded by the EC FP7 project ACCESSIBLE - Accessibility Assessment Simulation Environment for New Applications Design and Development, Grant Agreement No. 224145.

References

1. http://www.w3.org
2. http://www.w3.org/WAI
3. http://www.sun.com
4. http://www.ibm.com
5. http://www.oasis-open.org
6. http://www.linux-foundation.org/en/Accessibility
7. http://www.w3.org/TR/aria-roadmap

8. http://java.sun.com/javase/technologies/accessibility/docs/jaccess-1.2/doc
9. http://www.linuxfoundation.org/en/Accessibility/IAccessible2
10. http://www.section508.gov
11. http://wave.webaim.org
12. http://aprompt.snow.utoronto.ca/overview.html
13. http://www.snook.ca/technical/colour_contrast/colour.html
14. http://www.paciellogroup.com/resources/contrast-analyser.html
15. http://gmazzocato.altervista.org/colorwheel/wheel.php
16. http://www.vischeck.com
17. http://vis.cita.uiuc.edu
18. http://www.webaim.org/simulations/lowvision.php
19. http://www.alphaworks.ibm.com
20. http://www.alphaworks.ibm.com/tech/adesigner
21. http://www.alphaworks.ibm.com/tech/raven
22. http://www.netbeans.org
23. http://a11y.netbeans.org
24. http://www.eclipse.org
25. http://en.wikipedia.org/wiki/Color_Blind
26. http://www.sun.com/software/javafx

Unexploited Resources in Interaction Design for Universal Access: People with Impairments as a Resource for Interaction Designers

Hans Persson, Kjell Ohlsson, Sigrid Petersén, and Anette Jonsäll

IHT (Institut for Humane Technology), Heden 128, 82134 Bollnäs, Sweden
{hans.persson,sigrid.pettersen,anette.jonsall}@iht.se
Linköping University, Department of Management and Engineering
kjell.ohlsson@liu.se

Abstract. A challenge to HCI-designers is to create simple, usable, and useful applications. The current paper addresses this problem and presents an innovative possibility to extract useful information from users rarely represented in contemporary participatory design approaches. The study was conducted from a Universal Access point of view.

The primary result of the study is that people with well defined intellectual (e.g. understanding and logical reasoning) difficulties provided the designers of web-pages with more valuable and elaborated answers to bottlenecks in the interaction than a more representative group of web-users.

With this result in mind Universal Access should not be an unreachable goal. This implies that people with intellectual difficulties can be regarded as an unexploited resource in HCI when using a participatory approach.

Keywords: Universal access, Design methods, Design for all, Universal Design.

1 Introduction

The aim of this study has been to develop a more effective design method enabling better understanding and an easy to use interface for net-based services, improving universal access.

Our emphasis is design support in early design phases. In traditional participatory design approaches users' diversity is not an issue in selection of participants.

An attempt to use a participatory design approach with the ambition to achieve universal access to net-based services has frequently been considered to be expensive as well as time consuming. However, is it possible to reach this goal with scarce resources? Participatory design has usually been applied for development of innovative services, whereas universal access has been more focused on finding problem areas and circumvention of these. In addition we strived to utilize opinions and experiences from a group of people with intellectual difficulties that usually is disregarded in design contexts.

The point of departure for the current study was the phase between the designer proposed paper prototype and before programming.

C. Stephanidis (Ed.): Universal Access in HCI, Part I, HCII 2009, LNCS 5614, pp. 145–153, 2009.
© Springer-Verlag Berlin Heidelberg 2009

2   Background

2.1   Strategies in Design

Is it possible to design "easy to use" interactive applications? Well, it should be, but where do we start? One strategy is to start with the most difficult part [1]. But, which one is the most difficult?

We have to define what we mean by "Easy to use". Is it just easy to navigate physically or is it easy to understand and easy to read? A simple and effective navigation system in interactive applications is one of the most important things when making it user-friendly.

We can approach the question in several ways. The one we have chosen is to involve the target users in the design process. This has been successful in User-Centered-Design (UCD) [2] and in co-operative [3]design processes. In genereal UCD projects, the end user is not usualy taking part as participant in the very design process, but the knowledg of the user is leading the design on the right track. On the other hand in Co-operative design processes the end user is participating in the process. One example is the project "KidStory" [4] were kids were equal partners in the workgroups. The objective of these workgroups was to build low-tech prototypes with an obvious focus on usability issues close to the participants.

2.2   Users in Design

The main issue in this paper is our critical attitude towards the use of "common user" or "representative user" and also the thinking that usability testing have to involve large groups of representative users to be valid.

One solution is to hold down the amount of individuals participating in the evaluation as Nielsen [5], suggests to use as few as 8 -10 experts in a "discount" usability test to get hold of up to 80% of the usability problems.

Most of the design approaches in order to make easy to use products for all people is to choose representative participants [6] [5] [7] (common users) to provide ample input to the design process.

The group "common users" consists of 'all users'. 'All users' include people with all possible variations of states and conditions [8]. There are very few efforts to explore alternative ways of choosing participants in design processes, despite the fact that individual's functioning is something that can change over time [9] or are tied to a certain situation.

Ohlsson, Persson & Östlin [1] advocate that individuals with limitations in their functioning could be a valuable asset in the design process to indicate difficult areas of the usage.

To use the concept 'functional difficulties' [10] instead of disabilities might give us another view on the design of products and services for all people that not always have to result in special solutions for certain kinds of groups. Special solution in itself can sometimes be considered as discrimination, while "broad" solutions, that are good for all, are experienced as natural solutions that fit the broader group as depicted in the TED – model [1].

The TED- model is compliant to ISO-standard 13407 [2], asserting four user centred design activities that need to start at the earliest stages of a project.

Most conventional models of usability testing in a user centred design approach, does not consider users with specific difficulties, is not sufficient for designing accessible, usable and use-worthy [11] services for a broad majority of users due to its focus on the main user.

The main difference compared to a conventional usability model to the TED-model is the introduction of a group comprising people with specific and defined difficulties. This group of people with defined difficulties are thought of as problem identifiers in the evaluation process, and a creative solution asset in the design process of new products and services.

3 Aim

The aim of this study is to determine how people with limitations in their functioning contribute to the design process in conjunction to other groups. The focus is to make the usability issue simpler to deploy in the design process of creating interactive-services.

The main research question in this study was:

How does the use of a group of persons with limitations in their functioning influence the design process of interactive services?

The secondary and more precise question is derived from the first question:

In which way do individuals with development disability enrich the development of easy to use interactive applications?

4 Method

This study was made in two phases; first phase used "Think aloud" protocols [12], where the user verbally describes the interactive sessions and their perception around them and the second phase was a group activity.[1]

A paper based prototype (sketches) of the interactive applications was used. The usability area of this study was primarily targeting the "Ease of understanding". Real navigation in the interactive applications was not possible due to the design phase (only paper based sketches was at hand), where not all information was available during testing. This was the first step in the development process, to give the designer some input on the layout and how understandable some of the conceivable/imagible functions were.

---

[1] In cases number one and five there was an additional iteration. The designer was present in the background in these two cases. A new paper based prototypes was presented to the participants based on the result of the previous iteration. The participants were then asked to "Think aloud" about both prototypes and asked for preferences and why, as the first step.

First phase; The method is based on "Think aloud" protocols [13] [14]. The method's main purpose is to let a user describe how to do a specific task. The user is also expected to verbally express his/her thoughts. The procedure allows the participants to express themselves as freely as possible and to let them talk as much as possible from their own point of view.

We asked the participants to "Think aloud", while he/she was looking at paper prototypes in solitude. Each participant was asked to describe how he/she navigates through the system and to describe his/her thoughts about what would happen when navigating through the system as the first part of the test.

Second phase; the group activity was made in two steps, A: one focus group discussion of their personal experience of the prototype, and B: the group made a simple prototype together.

Five different design cases where studied (Table 1). In all cases except one the intent was to use keyboard and mouse as input devices. In case number four a handheld control was used for potential navigation in the proposed main TV-media. Ethnographical data of presumptive users was collected by the designer prior to this study. The ethnographical data collection was not a part of this study.

Table 1. Descriptions of the five cases

Case 1	A web application aimed to promote a conference. The target for this site is politicians, organizations, companies and all other interested in the area. Target users for this site are all citizens in the county for the conference.
Case 2	A web application aimed to make pressure on manufacturers for certain consumer products. The target group is manufacturers and the entire group of consumers. The driving force behind this site is to increase the influence of consumers with a specific limitation of their hand function on the design of products.
Case 3	A web application targeting public information from a specific municipality. The target users are all citizens in the municipality. The municipality strives towards a site developed in a "Design for all" perspective.
Case 4	A interactive television (ITV) application intended to bring easy and understandable information to the guest of municipality driven elderly care centre and the guests' next of kin. This ITV-application should work both on a computer and on set top boxes for TV.
Case 5	A web application aimed for a small web shop with a limited number of products. Target group is all consumers that have access to Internet

The cases in the current study are aiming towards all as in "design for all". In case four the target users are elderly people and their next of kin, were the elderly are subjected to elderly care. This implicates that the first target group has severe difficulties due to the system of elderly care in Sweden, where elderly people live in their own homes as long as possible. The difficulties can be both of psychological and physiological nature.

4.1 Analyse Method of the Material

All activities was recorded and transcribed with Linell's second level of transcription [15]. The content from the transcribed material was analysed [16] [17]and categorized through the areas of remarks. The categorized material was compared between the tree groups of participants. Material from the first (individual) part was then compared to the second (group activity) part and the result was analysed both for each case and between the cases.

4.2 Participants

The study was conducted on one group persons with defined difficulties; In this case intellectually impaired, and one group with elderly and another group with school employees. All participants were recruited by referrals [18].

Table 2. Participants in the study

Participants	Case 1	Case 2	Case 3	Case 4	Case 5	Total all cases	
							Unique individuals
Defined difficulties(D)	9	6	6	6	7	34	31
Elderly (E)	6	6	0	6	8	26	20
School employees(S)	4	0	2	3	4	13	13
Total	19	12	8	15	19	73	64

In total 64 different persons participated in the study (Table 2). The group of people with defined difficulties (D) were 31[2] and they all have mild to moderate intellectual impairments. One group of elderly comprising 20[3] persons (over 63 years) and 13 school employees participated in the study.

People in the groups with defined difficulties (D) were in the ages between 17 and 20 years old. 60% of the participants in this group were female. All the participants were familiar with mobile phones, Internet and chat. None of the participants indicated that they were technique novices. At each site there were between 6 and 9 participants in the D group. Three persons participated in two different case studies. The total number of participants in the D groups was 31 individuals.

---

[2] Three of the persons participated in two different case studies. One person participated in case one and four and two persons in case one and five.

[3] The same group participated in case one and four.

In the groups comprising elderly persons the participants' ages were between 63 and 86. In this group there were 55% female and 25% of the participants indicated that they were technique novices. One of the groups of 6 elderly participated in two cases. The total number of participants, in the groups of elderly (E), was 14.

Another group with adults working in a school participated in the studies. Nine of the participants worked as teachers and the others worked as teaching assistants, without academic education. Of this group there were seven females. In this group two persons indicated that they were technique novices.

4.3 Ethics

All participants were informed that the participation of this study was strictly voluntary and that they could terminate the participation whenever they choose. They where also informed how the material should be used. The information allowed the participants to decide by themselves to participate or not. [19]

5 Results

The result of this study is described in two parts. The first part constitutes some examples of the design outcome of the two steps in the study. The second part consists of a comparison of the result between the groups in both steps of the study.

5.1 Examples of Design Result from the Different Cases

In the first case (Web application aimed to promote a conference), the D (defined difficulties) group stated that it should be easier to understand chosen menu items. This did not come up in the other groups. The D group came up with a design suggestion implemented in the second version that all groups considered as an improvement.

All individuals in the D group had trouble with the pictures in case two (Web application aimed to make pressure on manufacturers); they tried to give them some functionality. Half of the group in the E (elderly) group did the same thing. The designers' thought the pictures in the prototype were something that should emphasize the message of the site rather than being connected to any function.

In case number three (Web application targeting public information); the participants in the D group reacted to the menu text and the menu background colour. The S (school employed) group did not mention this at all.

Another thing that came up during step one in case three, for all participants in the D group, but not for all the participants in the S group, was a question about which of the menus that was the main menu.

In case four (ITV application); All participants in both the D group and the other groups could explain how to navigate by pointing at areas in the prototype. This differed, unfortunately from the designer's idea of how to navigate. Even the use of the handheld control: Two out of three in the S group and all in the D group explained how to use it in another way than the designer's way.

All participants reflected in case five (Web application aimed for a small web shop) step one (the individual part) that the menu system was easy to find. That the menu text was too small in relation to other text was also pointed out by all partici-pants in the D group, in the S group and four out of eight in E group.

All the individuals in the D group, seven in the E group and two of the S group in-dicated problems with some of the words used in the menu. The understanding of the words constituted difficulties for the members of the D group.

5.2 Study Result

The first question about how a group with people with limitation in their functioning influences the design process is illustrated by the following.

The method of using simple paper prototypes and to let the participant individually talk about what they are thinking and feeling seems to be very efficient. Especially the individuals with development disability were very focused during the "think aloud" activity. The E and S groups did not have the same focus in the individual parts and they seemed to have some form of psychological/social barrier to speak out loudly what they were thinking.

- It seems as the D group easily think aloud around the paper prototypes. For people in the S and E groups it took some time to get started.
- It was noticed that it takes significant longer time per individual in S and E groups than in the D group for both the individual part as well as the group activity.
- In the group activity the differences between the three groups were small. It seems to depend more on the group members' way of interacting with each other than which group they were in.

The second question outlined in the objective was in what way people with devel-opment disabilities could enrich the development of easy to use interfaces?

- The members of the D group came up with a wide range of suggestions, mainly through the group activity, to improvements that were of the kind that all individu-als, with or without disability, could take advantage of.
- Even smaller areas of difficulties were noticed by the D group, but not in the other groups.

6 Discussion

One result that might come as a surprise to designers was the ease of which the D group talked about how they perceived the tested prototype sites. The method of "think aloud" around paper prototypes seems to be very effective for the D group. The S and E groups did not seem to have the same immediate easiness to talk about what they perceived about the prototype pages.

The comments from people in the D groups were more homogenous than com-ments from people in the E and S groups. In almost every question, the D group was describing the same difficulties, but in a more instant way. The E groups had more life experience, which resulted in some unique points of view regarding the interpreta-tion of some menu items.

Using only the D group had resulted in the same result as the other control groups together in this study. This could be something that makes the UCD-process easier and shorter with fewer participants.

Also in the S control group the participants varied more in the individual part in their comments and reflections compared to the D group but still, all important comments also appeared in the D group. The S groups' diversity in reflection could depend on the fact that the participants in the former group varied in educational level and in life experiences. What is surprising is that the same reflection came up in the D group.

The D group's impact on the usability issues were actually mostly around the area pointed out in advance; the area of understanding the sites. The understanding of the text was one of the areas that the D group had a lot of comments about, probably because it is something that is important in their lives.

The method "Think aloud" was probably a very good way of receiving direct indication on the logic of the menu system. The members of the D group have a lack of logical thinking within their defined difficulties, which is probably the answer to why they so effectively point out the difficult parts of the menu system. They pointed this out without trying to describe what the menu item should mean. The members of the E and S groups tried to describe all the menu items even if they knew it was more or less a guess. This could be one of the things that make the use of D groups more effective.

With a "design for all" perspective in mind the result indicates that, having people with difficulties participating in the test/design groups, problems within the area of accessibility is automatically included in the process without having to include it separately. This was very obvious when a second prototype were presented to the participants built from the result from the design activity.

In the phase of designing the interactive services the approach using the method with people with defined difficulties in their functioning seems to be very effective.

In a Human Centred Design process the user is one of the main objectives. How do we describe a normal user in a normal environment? In design we often try to design with a representative user group in mind. Are these questions relevant? The result in this study points in the direction of rethinking how to select users that participates in design processes. We might end up with choosing participants according to the limitation in their functioning instead of a representative selection of participants. There can be contextual difficulties where specific knowledge is necessary. Maybe this result is more useful and efficient in applications meant to be used for the general public.

Universal Access should by this result not be an unreachable goal, but rather considering people with intellectual difficulties as an unexploited resource in HCI when using a participatory approach.

6.1   Future Areas of Research

Only a minor part of the design process has been covered in the present paper. Further research should focus on the whole design process from idea generation to product or service implementation and follow ups. The main group of the present study had cognitive impairments, whereas further studies will be augmented to embrace people with other impairments as well. Further studies should aim to provide designers and developers with practical knowledge about accessible design tools, and about the specific contribution from diverse user groups, and simultaneously enquire designers' further needs of how to utilize this knowledge.

References

1. Ohlsson, K., Persson, H., Östlin, O.: The Bollnäs' model for testing, evaluation and design of information and communication technology services. Online Deliberation 2005 / DIAC 2005. Stanford University Stanford, Stanford (2005)
2. ISO 13407, ISO 13407 Human-centred design processes for interactive systems. International Standard Organisation, Geneva (1999)
3. Bødker, S., Ehn, P., Sjögren, D., Sundblad, Y.: Co-operative Design — perspectives on 20 years with the Scandinavian IT Design Model. Stockholm: Invited paper, NordiCHI 2000 conference, pp.1–10 (2000)
4. Taxén, G., Druin, A., Fast, C., Kjellin, M.: KidStory: a technology design partnership with children. Behaviour and Information Technology, 119–125 (2001)
5. Nielsen, J.: Guerrilla HCI: using discount usability engineering to penetrate the intimidation barrier. Academic Press, Inc., Orlando (1994)
6. Bevan, N.: Measuring usability as quality of use. In W. Harrison. Software Quality Journal 4(2), 115–130 (1995)
7. Nielsen, J.: Usability Engineering. Academic Press Limited, London (1993)
8. Ohlsson, K., Persson, H., Östlin, O.: The concept of Normality and its impact on design of Information and Communication Technology. In: Proceedings of the biannual Human Factors Network conference in Linköping. Linköpings University of Technology, Linköping (2006)
9. Gregor, P., Newell, A.: Designing for dynamic diversity: making accessible interfaces for older people. In: Proceedings of the 2001 EC/NSF workshop on Universal accessibility of ubiquitous computing: providing for the elderly, pp. 90–92. ACM, New York (2001)
10. WHO. International Classification of Functioning, Disability and Health (ICF), World Health Organisation (2007), http://www.who.int/classifications/icf/en (retrieved November 20, 2007)
11. Eftring, H.: The Useworthiness of Robots for People with physical disabilities, Doctoral Dissertation. Certek, LTH, Lund (1999)
12. Ericsson, K., Simon, H.: How to study thinking in everyday life: Contrasting think-aloud protocols with descriptions and explanations of thinking. Mind, Culture, & Activity 5(3), 178–186 (1998)
13. Lewis, C.: Using the thinking-aloud method in cognitive interface design, Report RC 9265. IBM Research, Yorktown Heights (1982)
14. Lewis, C., Rieman, J.: Task-Centered User Interface Design - A Practical Introduction. Clayton Lewis and John Rieman as shareware, Boulder (1993)
15. Wibeck, V.: Fokusgrupper. Studentlitteratur, Lund (2000) (in Swedish)
16. Krippendorff, K.: Content Analysis, An Introduction to Its Methodology, 2nd edn. Sage Publications, Thousand Oaks (2004)
17. Ericsson, K.A., Simon, H.A.: Protocol analysis: Verbal reports as data. MIT Press, Cambridge (1984)
18. Morgan, D.: The Focus Group Guidebook. Book 1. The Focus Group Kit. Sage, Thousand Oaks (1998)
19. Eriksson, S.: Swedish Research Council. Codex, rules & guidlines for research (Januaruy 21, 2008) (2009),
http://www.codex.vr.se/codex_eng/codex/index.html
(retrieved February 24, 2009)

Older People and ICT: Towards Understanding Real-Life Usability and Experiences Created in Everyday Interactions with Interactive Technologies

Sergio Sayago and Josep Blat

Interactive Technologies Group, Department of Information and Communication
Technologies (DTIC), Universitat Pompeu Fabra
C/Tànger, 122-140, E-08018 Barcelona, Spain (4th floor, room 55.408)
{sergio.sayago,josep.blat}@upf.edu

Abstract. This paper reports key findings on an ethnographical study of every-day interactions of older people with ICT. The research questions addressed are what easy or difficult to use means for older people in their daily interactions with ICT and what the relationship between usability and experiences created between older people and ICT is. 388 older people were observed and conversed with while using a wide array of ICT during 3 years. The results reveal that usability is related to independency. When ICT are easy to use, older people are independent users. Independency (dependency) can be identified by the number and type of questions, environmental noise disturbing interactions and required practice to master ICT. Independency leads to experiences that are emotionally fulfilling, supportive of exploration and reassuring. Dependency results in very sad experiences. These results suggest another way of seeing the interactions of older people with ICT, far from traditional individual age-related changes in functional abilities.

Keywords: Ethnography, older people, real interaction, usability, experience.

1 Introduction

"The old computing was about what computers could do; the new computing is about what users can do" [16, pp: 2]. As Information and Communication Technologies (ICT) are penetrating our lives and no longer used by professionals for productivity purposes, there is a need to widen the traditional research focus from usability in labs and performance of tasks to real-life usability and experiences created in the everyday interactions with ICT. Traditional methods for ensuring usability, such as the traditional laboratory-based usability testing, are largely meaningless in ordinary interactions [17]. Much more deeply than ever before, we are aware that interacting with technology creates experiences. And those concerned with the design, use and evaluation of interactive systems need to be able to understand and analyze people's felt experiences with technology [11]. It is also unclear how well existing usability techniques and measures will perform if the focus is on designing experiences that people enjoy or value while doing a wide range of activities in which productivity is not the primary concern [9].

C. Stephanidis (Ed.): Universal Access in HCI, Part I, HCII 2009, LNCS 5614, pp. 154–163, 2009.

Yet, there has been surprisingly very little research on real-life usability and user experience in human-computer interaction (HCI) with older people. Much research on usability with older people has been focused on adapting methods to older people's special needs [1, 6]. The experiences created between older people and ICT seem not to have been addressed yet. A survey we did on leading HCI journals and conference proceedings show that no studies into user experience and older people have been published as yet[1]. Instead, the main concern is to compensate for individual age-related changes in functional abilities (sight, hearing, cognition and mobility). Nevertheless, older people are non-standard users in HCI research [4] and use ICT for non-productivity purposes [15]. Both facts provide a clear stimulus to explore usability "out of labs" and the felt experiences of older people with ICT.

This paper looks at everyday usability for older people and its relationship with their felt daily experiences with ICT. Older people are defined herein as adults ranging in age from 65 to 80 years old experiencing normal age-related changes in functional abilities. These changes do not have an impact on their ability to carry out ADL (Activities of Daily Living) and IADL (Instrumental Activities of Daily Living) on their own.

Regarding everyday usability, this paper aims to understand what easy or difficult to use mean for older people in their daily interactions with ICT. Within the traditional task performance model [9], easy and difficult to use are an indicator of productivity. The easier a system to use, the more tasks can be conducted in given period of time. Nevertheless, easy or difficult to use might have a completely different meaning for older people, since productivity is not their main concern when interacting with ICT.

With respect to user experience, this paper is intended to identify the relationship between usability and older people's experiences with ICT. As stated in [13], usability and user experiences are intertwined, being some combinations of usability and user experiences goals more compatible than others (e.g.; "it may not be possible or desirable to design a process control system that is both safe and fun" [pp: 20]). However, very little is known about the relationship (if any) between usability and user experience with older people.

Thus, the research questions addressed in this paper are:

1. What does easy or difficult to use mean for older people in their everyday interactions with ICT?
2. How does usability relate to the older people's felt daily experiences with ICT?

This paper has adopted an ethnographical approach in order to answer both questions. HCI has looked to ethnography in order to develop views of the interactions between people and technologies as they happen in naturally occurring settings. Gaining these insights is seen by academy, industry and corporate settings are an essential ingredient in design more useful and engaging technologies [2]. Ethnography allows designers

---

[1] Interacting with Computers; International Journal of Human-Computer Studies; Universal Access to the Information Society; ACM Transactions of Human-Computer Interaction; ACM Transactions of Accessible Computing; HCI – first issue – 2008; CHI ACM Proceedings, W4ALL, first conference – 2008. Keywords: experience, user experience, older people, older adults, elderly; ICT; interactive technologies; web; computers.

and researchers to explore technologies "in the wild" [5] in a way that is difficult to do by using other methods [2].

This paper reports the key findings of an ethnographical study of everyday interactions of older people with ICT (mainly, web and computer technologies). The ethnographical data consisted of in-situ observations of and conversations with 388 older people while using a wide array of ICT on a daily basis. This ethnographical data was collected over 3 years. We analyzed this data by using open, axial and selective coding and the constant comparison technique of the Grounded Theory approach for qualitative analysis [8].

The results indicated that easy (difficult) to use means independency (dependency) for older people in their day-to-day interactions with ICT. Independency is the ability of older people to interact with interactive technologies on their own. This ability can be characterized by the number and type of questions, environmental noise disturbing interactions and required practice. The experiences created between older people and technologies that are easy to use can be defined as emotionally fulfilling, supportive of exploration and reassuring. The experiences with technologies with poor usability are emotionally unfulfilling, unsupportive of exploration and pessimistic.

2   Description of the Ethnographical Study

2.1   Context

The study was carried out in Àgora from 2005 to 2008. Àgora is a 20-years-old association within La Verneda-St.Marti adult centre (Barcelona, Spain). Àgora has a strong commitment to the integration of sectors[2] that have been alienated from current society into the active fabric of it. Numerous courses in a wide array of subjects, ranging from languages to cooking, are offered on a daily basis. These courses are free of charge. Between 1000 and 1500 people (generally referred as 'participants') enroll on courses monthly.

Mastering ICT is regarded by Àgora and participants as an essential element for inclusion into contemporary society. Àgora offers a large number of courses in ICT, as well as daily Internet access and workshops. Most of these activities are aimed at older people, who are particularly disadvantaged. Older people decide what technologies they want to (learn to) use in courses and workshops. Their decision is grounded in the use they want to make of technologies in their daily lives (integration) rather than being imposed by pre-established syllabuses.

Participation is also a key pedagogical element. Àgora operates by using dialogic learning [7]. Agora is run by people who are deeply involved in activities. Agora blurs the traditional division between teachers and learners. A real scenario is that in which older people who started taking courses in ICT with little acquaintance with computers, now a command of them and become teachers for peers who are taking up ICT.

---

[2] About 50% of the current Catalan population has its origins from rural areas from elsewhere in Spain, the immigration taking place in the 1940-50s, immigrants having very low literacy levels, especially women. In the last 10 years a new (global) immigration wave has taken place with origins (mainly) in Morocco, South America and Romania, with an increase of about 10% of the existing population creating a new sector of potentially marginalized population, adding language problems to literacy issues.

2.2 Participants and Ethnographical Strategy

We wished to develop a first-hand view of the interactions of older people with ICT as a prerequisite for understanding real-life usability and the experiences that are created with between older people and ICT. To this end, we found a classical ethnographical approach very valuable[3]. The observations and conversations took place initially during the courses. They provided us with extensive material of real use of ICT, very far from more artificial "training" settings, due to the strong participative approach discussed above.

Even though participants were not a representative sample of the older population in some ways[4], they showed the real use that older people pioneers of ICT are making of these technologies. We think that this is likely to be the best approximation we can have to ethnography when introducing innovation. On the other hand, participants were very representative of ordinary people living in a developed country, as detailed next.

The participants were older Spanish people ranging in age from 65 to 80 years old. They hailed from Catalonia, the South and North of Spain. Participants lived in Barcelona and its outskirts. Participants experienced normal age-related changes in functional abilities (sight, hearing, cognition and mobility). However, these changes did not make them unable to carry out daily activities such as shopping, banking or cleaning on their own. They had different educational competencies and previous experience with ICT. 350 had low levels of education (i.e. degrees in primary school or basic literacy skills). These participants also had scant digital literacy skills, their experience being with calculators, cash registers and mobile phones. The rest of the participants (38) had higher educational levels (i.e. secondary school degrees or specific certificates related to their previous jobs). They were familiar with basic web and computer concepts, their experience being with specialized computer applications for their previous jobs (e.g. an internal e-mail system). Participants' main motives behind taking up ICT were not to lag behind in society, to be or remain closer to their children, grandchildren and friends, and to enjoy the opportunity of learning that they did not have in their childhood.

This profile was elaborated by conversing with the participants and other members of Àgora during the fieldwork. We also had access to the profile of the participants recorded and updated by Àgora.

2.3 Data and Methods

The data came from 388 participants. We observed and conversed with them 2 to 3 times per week. Each "contact time" lasted 2 hours. We used traditional paper and

---

[3] Ethnography consists of a long period (in anthropology, it has become relatively standard to think of a minimum of a year of fieldwork to gain sufficient insight) of immersion in people's everyday activities, combining observation with participation [3]. Other forms of ethnography (quick-and-dirty or lightweight, concurrent and evaluate ethnography) have been especially developed for HCI, to fit in with software engineering and user-centered design processes [12].

[4] Older people with a lack of experience with ICT constitute the majority of the older population living in Spain [10].

pencil to record observations and participant's in-situ comments. Other methods such as video cameras and tape recorders were found to be very intrusive, in addition to being difficult to use in Àgora[5]. Part of this fieldwork took place in courses and workshops coordinated by us (212 participants: all courses except those in first row on Table 1, plus workshops). Another relevant part of our fieldwork was realized in courses and meetings where we attended as observers (176 participants: public meetings plus three courses in first row on Table 1). Table 1 provides specific details of the fieldwork.

Table 1. Details of our ethnographical study

Course	Technologies	Participants	Duration
Gardens, Towns in the world and Internet	Yahoo! mail, Hotmail, Google, MS Word and PowerPoint, Websites (transport, health, TV)	72	1 course. 6 months. 2-hour session every week (Gardens and Towns in the World). The internet course lasted 1 month.
Online communication	Yahoo! mail, Hotmail, Chat, Blogs, Wikis, Forums, Google, Yahoo!	76	4 courses, which lasted 3 months. 2-hour session every week
Advanced aspects of the web and computers	MS Word, PowerPoint and Excel, Yahoo! mail, Hotmail, Google, Yahoo!, Yahoo! Flickr, Google Earth, Websites (flights booking; routes; medical assistance)	76	4 courses, which lasted 3 months. 2-hour session every week
Online resources	File management, Windows management, Google, Yahoo!, Blogs, Yahoo! Mail, Hotmail, websites (transport, TV, health, traveling)	18	1 course. It lasted 6 months. 2-hour session every week.
Workshops	Technologies	Participants	Duration
Workshop on web	Yahoo! mail, Hotmail, multimedia content edition, finding online information (directories, search engines), websites (transport, health, towns, news, TV)	18	3 workshops. 2-hour session every workshop
Workshop on recent technologies	Blogs, Yahoo! Flickr, Yahoo! mail, Hotmail, wikis, websites	24	2 workshops. 2-hour session
Public meetings	Technologies	Participants	Duration
7 meetings	Technologies used in courses and workshops	104	Between 2 and 3 hours

All this data was analyzed by using open, axial and selective coding and the constant comparison technique of the Grounded Theory approach for qualitative analysis [8]. This analysis initially involved one of the authors reading the entire field notes to gain an overall sense of the data. All the data was then read again and open-coded to produce an initial code list. This was done until, in the opinion of the two authors of

---

[5] Participants were used to seeing people taking notes with traditional technologies, viz. paper and pencil. They took their notes using these technologies, so this s was a natural practice in courses, meeting and workshops. However, participants were not used to seeing people taking notes by using laptops. They were also not used to being recorded while going online or using computers. Furthermore, Àgora did not allow video cameras in computer classes on the grounds that these technologies made people that are alienated from society feel very uncomfortable, as well as providing an unnatural environment for (learning to) using ICT.

this paper, analysis had reached theoretical saturation. Most of the codes were adapted from the language of the participants, rather than drawing solely on our review of literature. This reflected our attempt to tell the story of older people from their point of view, without theoretical preconceptions as to what will be found - which is the hallmark of ethnography. At the same time, axial coding was carried out to establish relationships between categories identified in open coding. From this basis, the data was then selectively coded in terms of core and subcategories categories identified with the initial and axial list of codes. The care and subcategories are listed below:

– Core category: Independency
  Easy to use: few questions; questions aimed at "knowing more"; environmental noise does not hinder interactions; older people are either engrossed in their activities or waiting for doing other tasks patiently; no extra practice is required

• Supportive of exploration: willingness to explore in the unknown
• Reassuring: showing a desire to comfort those who are having difficulties

– Core category: Dependency

• Difficult to use: many questions; need of support to carry out a task; environmental noise hinders interaction (mainly, concentration); extra practice is required before trying to do more activities
• Emotionally unfulfilling: unhappy and unsatisfied with their abilities; older people feel useless despite all their efforts put in mastering ICT
• Unsupportive of exploration: reluctance towards exploring the technology due to their reliance on others
• Pessimistic: give up using technology; end up being unwilling to use them (although they might considering giving it a go)

These categories (and related codes) were also used to analyze 20 in-depth interviews and 12 group-based discussions (8 focus groups and 7 workshops – different from those displayed in Table 1) about e-mail systems, relevance of accessibility barriers and social relationships. There aspects were found to be of great importance in the everyday interactions of older people with ICT.

The findings, which follow, are drawn from a large collection of observations and conversations. They summarize what usability means for older people and the relationship between usability and experiences created between older people and ICT. These findings were chosen as being of most relevance and likely interest to both researchers and designers. We use vignettes and real scenarios in an attempt to (i) situate the findings into their context and (ii) both capture and preserve the opinions and comments expressed by the participants as much as possible.

3 Key Findings

3.1 Dependency and Independency: A Matter of How Easy to Use ICT Are

Scenario: Maria is 68 years old. She is selecting an area of a picture with MS Paint. She has downloaded the picture from the web. She wants to send this part of the picture, which has a funny message, to her friend, Carmen. She was independent when she downloaded the picture. She did not ask us any question about how to do that. She was engrossed in this activity. When she finished, she came to us to know more about alternative strategies for downloading pictures from the web. She has seen people downloading pictures by using several methods and she is curious about that. Nevertheless, Maria is a dependent user when it comes to select the area of the picture she wants to share with Carmen. She asked us 10 questions in 20 minutes. This is the amount of time she required to select a portion of a picture. She thanked us for having been attentive to her and patient, at the same time. She acknowledged that she might have given the impression that she was stupid or useless. However, she thinks that the problem is that selecting an area of a picture is really difficult. She also apologised for having made noise or disturbed the interactions of the rest of the participants. She drawn our attention to the fact that she, as the rest of the participants, were working silently when downloading pictures from the Web. However, the environmental noise increased considerably in the second task, working with MS Paint. She pointed out that older people do not make noise when something is easy to use or do. However, when they have difficulties, older people start suddenly to ask a large number of questions about how to do things, using a loud voice to make their inquiries heard.

Scenario: At 12.15, a group of 8 older people are creating a web page. This web page contains a table with 3 rows and 2 columns. The participants were having difficulties inserting the table into the web page. They asked for help to the instructor. A member of the staff in Àgora popped in the computer room and asked both the instructor and the participants not to make so much noise. "Are we disturbing you? We did not realise, sorry", a participant exclaimed. "Yes, you are making so much noise that my students in the next room can not concentrate on their activities. I do no know what you are doing, but 30 minutes ago it seemed as if there were no people here", the member of Àgora said. "30 minutes ago we were doing something very easy. Now, we are working on web pages and tables, and this is very difficult. We talk a lot among ourselves and ask him lots of questions…we make a lot of noise when something is difficult to use!" the same participant replied.

3.2 Independency Leads to Emotionally Fulfilling, Supportive of Exploration and Reassuring Experiences

Vignette "Manolo". Manolo is 72 years-old. He finds e-mailing very valuable for him and his wife. Staying in touch with people they love, especially their children and grandchildren, is of immense value for them. He thinks that there are no words to express how useful the e-mail is for him and his wife. Receiving an e-mail from their grandchildren is the best things of the day; he tends to say to their friends. Despite his initial difficulties using e-mail, Manolo is nowadays able to communicate by e-mail independently. He opens the web browser, logs into his e-mail account and starts e-mailing on his own. Being able to master this technology and use it autonosmously makes him proud of himself. He thinks that when an older person realizes that he or she is able to do what many people think he or she will never be able to do, that person is very proud of him or herself. They can reply to these people with three words: yes, I can. Manolo is well aware of the fact that many older people are not so lucky. They have difficulties in e-mailing and he gives them a hand. He feels that it is very frustrating to see that you have managed to do many things in your life and now you get stuck with a simple machine. For this reason, Manolo thinks he must help peers to master e-mail. When he interacts with e-mail systems, he has every confidence in his ability to master the technology, even it something wrong or unexpected happens. This feeling has encouraged him to learn more aspects of e-mailing. He has learned many things about e-mailing on his own. Manolo was taught the basis of e-mailing in Àgora, and he is indebted to his instructor. However, as he found e-mailing both very useful and easy, he started to explore it at home. Nowadays, he is capable of doing numerous things. He thinks that he outdoes some instructors and friends of mine. Emailing creates a range of experiences and emotions, all of them positive.

3.3 Dependency Leads to Emotionally Unfulfilling, Unsupportive of Exploration and Pessimistic Experiences

Vignette "Jordi". Jordi is 73-years-old. He is able to use some interactive technologies on his own, such as mobile phones and e-mail systems. However, he is not able to use other technologies, which he would like to use in daily life, on his own. These technologies are tools for editing web pages and working with images. He finds it very frustrating not to be able to master the technologies they want to use. This lack of ability creates feelings of great unhappiness and sometimes loss of hope, especially when he sees that he is uncapable of using technologies that other people use daily. Being able to use his mobile phone and e-mail systems is not enough. He wants to use more technologies, and not being able to do it makes him feel stupid and very old. New technologies are not for older people, this is what he hears in the street. He is against this view, but interacting with certain technologies brings back this stereotype. Xavier tries to explore technologies that he finds it difficult to use. He thinks he is stubborn, many older people are stubborn, he also thinks. He explores these technologies with very little confidence, however. He knows that he is going to fail, and this idea puts him off keeping on trying. Xavier has even given up some technologies, especially creating web pages. This fact created a very sad experience with ICT. Despite his willingness to use them, because he thinks that they are the future and relatives and friends urge him to use them, he thought that it was better for him to stick to the technologies that he could use on his own. There is no point in making my live more complex than it is, he says.

4 Discussion

The above sections give some examples of the insights we obtained by a long and detailed ethnographic study of the everyday interactions of older people with ICT. What does easy or difficult to use mean for older people in their everyday interactions with ICT and why? Usability is related to independency. When ICT are easy to use, older people are independent users. However, when they are difficult to use, older people are dependent users. Both dependency and independency can be identified by a number of factors that emerge naturally from real interactions: the number and type of questions, the amount of environmental noise disturbing interactions and the perceived need of practice. How does usability (independency or lack of it) related to older people's felt daily experiences with ICT? Technologies are that easy to use create experiences that we have categorised as: emotionally fulfilling, supportive of exploration and reassuring. Technologies that are difficult to use create opposite experiences: emotionally unfulfilling, unsupportive of exploration and pessimistic.

Some of themes resonate with those identified by previous research. The core categories of our analyses stress the relevance of independency in order to understand usability in context and its relationship with the experiences created between people and ICT. Research on ageing has claimed that independency is a key condition in later life [14]. Nevertheless, other themes that have emerged are very different to those that are commonly used in human-computer interaction research with older people. The bulk of research is focused on compensating for age-related changes in functional abilities. And most of this research has taken place in either labs or real contexts but under controlled scenarios. We have adopted a different approach, the emphasis being on interactions "in the wild", which is in line with the growing awareness in academy, industry, corporate settings and human-computer interaction to the need to understand how people interact and make use of technologies in the daily lives [2, 16, 11]. This approach has enabled us to identify certain aspects of the interactions of older people with interactive technologies that seem to have been untapped so far. Nevertheless, it is no longer considered sufficient to produce a computer system that is effective, flexible, learnable or satisfying to use, it must also enrich the users' experiences [11].

The vignettes and scenarios presented on Section 4 draw attention to the importance of usability in everyday interactions and experiences in older person's daily interactions with ICT. This raises the question of how we can measure usability in real-life interactions using the parameters suggested in this study and how we can design ICT that enrich older people's experiences with these technologies. Answering both questions warrant much more research; this study was a first step towards this goal. We have uncovered aspects for measuring real usability that need to be validated in follow-up studies. We expect to record participants' interactions in terms of the factors presented herein and identify how well these factors allow us to measure usability (e.g. how many questions mean "difficult" or "easy"?). With respect to experience, 'designing for the full range of human experience may well be the theme for the next generation of discourse about software design' (cited in [11], pp: 183). We hope this paper makes a small contribution to this larger debate. At the very least we hope we will provoke researchers and designers to look at the interactions of older people with information and communication technologies in a different light.

Acknowledgments. We are indebted to Àgora and our participants for allowing a stranger into an important part of their lives. We also want to thank Ernesto Arroyo for his comments on early versions of the manuscript.

References

1. Barrett, J., Kirk, S.: Running focus groups with elderly and disabled elderly participants. Applied Ergonomics 31, 621–629 (2000)
2. Blomberg, J., Burrell, M., Guest, G.: An ethnographic Approach to Design. In: Jacko, J.A., Sears, A. (eds.) The Human-Computer Interaction Handbook: Fundamentals, Evolving Technologies and Emerging Applications, pp. 964–987. Lawrence Erlbaum Associates, London (2003)

3. Dewalt, K.M., Dewalt, B.R., Wayland, C.B.: Participant Observation. In: Bernard, H.R. (ed.) Handbook of Methods in Cultural Anthropology, pp. 259–301. AltaMira Press, California (2000)
4. Dickinson, A., Arnott, J.L., Prior, S.: Methods for human-computer interaction research with older people. Behaviour & Information Technology 26(4), 343–352 (2007)
5. Dourish, P.: Implications for Design. In: CHI 2006, Montréal, Québec, Canada, pp. 541–550 (2006)
6. Eisma, R., Dickinson, A., Goodman, J., Syme, A., Tiwari, L., Newell, A.F.: Early user involvement in the development of information technology-related products for older people. Universal Access in the Information Society 3, 131–140 (2004)
7. Flecha, R.: Sharing Words. Theory and practice of dialogic learning. Rosman & Littlefield Publications, Maryland (2000)
8. Glaser, B.G., Strauss, A.L.: The discovery of grounded theory: strategies for qualitative research. Aldine Transaction, New Jersey (2006)
9. Karat, J.: Beyond Task Completion: Evaluation of Affective Components of Use. In: Jacko, J.A., Sears, A. (eds.) The Human-Computer Interaction Handbook: Fundamentals, Evolving Technologies and Emerging Applications, pp. 1152–1163. Lawrence Erlbaum Associates, London (2003)
10. Larra, R.M.d.: Los Mayores en la Sociedad de la Información: situación actual y retos de futuro, Fundación AUNA, Madrid (2004)
11. McCarthy, J., Wright, P.: Technology as experience. MIT Press, Cambridge (2004)
12. Randall, D., Harper, R., Rouncefield, M.: Fieldwork for Design. Theory and Practice. Springer, London (2007)
13. Rogers, Y., Sharp, H., Preece, J.: Interaction design: beyond human-computer interaction. John Wiley & Sons, Chichester (2002)
14. Schaie, K.W., Boron, J.B., Willis, S.L.: Everyday Competence in Older Adults. In: Johnson, M.L. (ed.) The Cambridge Handbook of Age and Ageing, pp. 216–229. University Cambridge Press, Cambridge (2005)
15. Selwyn, N., Gorard, S., Furlong, J., Madden, L.: Older adults' use of information and communication technology in everyday life. Ageing & Society 23, 561–582 (2003)
16. Shneiderman, B.: Leonardo's Laptop. Human needs and the new computing technologies. MIT Press, Cambridge (2002)
17. Thomas, P., Macredie, R.D.: Introduction to the New Usability. ACM Transactions on Computer-Human Interaction 9(2), 69–73 (2002)

Interaction with Colored Graphical Representations on Braille Devices

Christiane Taras and Thomas Ertl

Institute of Visualization and Interactive Systems, Universität Stuttgart,
Universitätsstr. 38, 70569 Stuttgart, Germany
{taras,ertl}@vis.uni-stuttgart.de

Abstract. For several years there has been the wish to make colors accessible to blind people. Colors are all around us and sighted people often talk about colors as it is a simple means of distinguishing objects. They are used in educational materials to ease perception, support comprehension, and focus on different aspects. In this paper we present a new color code for viewing and editing colored graphics on Braille devices and report on our experiences with presenting graphics on Braille devices and our ongoing work on exploration strategies.

Keywords: tactile graphics display, Braille display, Braille color code, digital graphics, blind and visually impaired people, exploration strategies.

1 Introduction

The Institute for Visualization and Interactive Systems (VIS) is currently involved in a project called "HyperBraille" that aims to improve the access to graphical user interfaces for blind people [4]. One task in HyperBraille is to design representations of graphical user interfaces for the tactile display. This task is accomplished by a team of blind and sighted people. Hence, there was a desire to share ideas on which pins should be lifted and which not between sighted and blind people easily. No existing tool could fulfill our needs. Of course, for the sighted people the easiest way was to create ordinary bitmaps just showing the lifted pins as black pixels and the lowered as white pixels. The blind partners could utilize the textual format SVG (Scalable Vector Graphics) [14]. But the problem with this was that the blind partners had no means to check how the graphic would be presented on the Braille device. Existing tools did not provide pixel precise graphics embossing or presentation on a Braille display.

In the following chapters we report on a tool set called "HBGraphicsExchange" which we have developed to solve this problem. Together with this we have designed three file formats to facilitate the creation of graphics with the help of Braille devices. The first format, called "Elementary FigureBraille" (EFB), is a very simple one for creating and sharing monochrome images. This worked well until someone wanted to add text to the designs. Therefore, we created "Object FigureBraille" (OFB). In parallel we worked on presenting colors and defined "Detailed FirgureBraille" (DFB).

With this we continue our longtime research in providing graphics to the blind. VIS has several years of experiences with presenting graphics to blind people on the

C. Stephanidis (Ed.): Universal Access in HCI, Part I, HCII 2009, LNCS 5614, pp. 164–173, 2009.
© Springer-Verlag Berlin Heidelberg 2009

tactile graphics display called "Stuttgarter Stiftplatte". However, in former times, we mostly concentrated on presenting and exploring graphics and not on editing. Inspired through the work in HyperBraille we began targeting our work not only to Braille graphics displays like the new BrailleDis 9000 [11] but also on single-lined Braille displays. These are used in everyday life and so improvements for these devices bring direct benefit. We also further developed the presentation and exploration strategies presented by Rotard and Ertl in [6]. And we will report on our new ideas on this.

2   Related Work

Some work has been done on digital viewing and exploring of graphics for the blind (e.g. [6], [3]) and also on digital editing (e.g. [2]), but till now there is a lack of combining both parts interactively. Also SVG [14] and ASCII drawing [12] can be utilized for editing graphics on a Braille device. But the textual representation of SVG is rather long and for ASCII drawings no pixel-precise conversion to bitmaps is defined and the representation on the Braille device is not fully congruent to the created shapes.

Different approaches for coding colors for the blind have been presented. The most common ones are the conversion of colors into different textures (e.g. for swell paper) or gray scale (e.g. for embossers). Unfortunately, these methods are not standardized, often destruct the color information and are not suitable for Braille devices as with only two pin states only a few textures can be used and gray scale is not possible.

There are attempts to create a standardized color code like the Barker Color Code [1], the Tactile Colour Code [8], and the Tactile Vision Color Code System [9]. All these color codes have in common that they were only designed for presenting static graphics. The designers did not think of interaction with the graphics which means being able to explore and modify them. Of course, also things like paper-based tactile graphics reveal ways of exploring the graphics by preparing several views. But modifying a graphic and providing the new graphic to others is hard with these techniques. Braille displays reveal many possibilities for interacting with digital graphics. None of the color codes mentioned above is suitable for these devices.

3   Simple Braille Graphics – Elementary FigureBraille (EFB)

The EFB format is somehow the interactive form of drawing with a Braille writing machine. Each EFB sign represents six pixels. For monochrome images each black pixel is represented by a set dot (or lifted pin) and each white one by an unset dot (or lowered pin). For colored graphics the EFB representation depends on the applied color filter (see section 0). By default a colored graphic is converted to EFB by showing a dot for each pixel except white ones. The user creates a graphic by inputting Braille codes on the Braille keyboard or characters on the standard keyboard into an text file. EFB files can be converted to raster graphics by using the conversion table shown in Table 1 and drawing a pattern of black (for 1) and white (for 0) pixels that is aligned like a 6-dot Braille sign into a bitmap with no space between the dots, signs, or lines. Table 2 shows two example images and their EFB representations.

Table 1. EFB coding (matrix with first three dots in rows and last three dots in columns)

Dots	...456							
123...	...000	...100	...010	...110	...001	...101	...011	...111
000...	space	"	!	>	'	$	<	_
100...	a	c	e	d	1	3	5	4
010...	,	i	:	j	?	9	/	w
110...	b	f	h	g	2	6	8	7
001...	.	|	*	`	-	0	)	#
101...	k	m	o	n	u	x	z	y
011...	;	s	+	t	(	~	=	}
111...	l	p	r	q	v	&	{	%

Table 2. EFB coding of two sample images (The images in the left column are enlarged and their pixels are marked by a grid. The original sizes are 26×3 and 56×16 pixels).

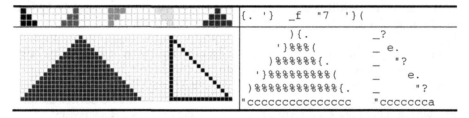

```
{. '}  _f    "7    '}(
               ){.              _?
            '}%%%(            _  e.
           )%%%%%%{.          _   "?
         '}%%%%%%%%%(         _     e.
        )%%%%%%%%%%%%{.       _      "?
       "ccccccccccccccc     "ccccccca
```

We have chosen a 6-dot Braille code for EFB as we wanted it to be as portable as possible. The files should look the same no matter which language, operating system, screen reader or Braille device is used. However, during our tests we have recognized that it would be nice if the full size of a single-lined device could be used. So we will evaluate in future if an 8-dot code can be used without too much configuration effort. For example by attaching Braille tables to our tool or the file extension ".efb".

When working with pixel-based graphics presentation on Braille devices, two aspects have to be taken in mind. The first arises from the low resolution and size of Braille displays compared to a computer screen. If one would simply take an ordinary graphic and convert it to EFB, much scrolling would be necessary to grasp the whole graphic. But if one uses to small graphics they may be misunderstood. For example a very small circle has the same shape as an octagon. The other aspect is that there is some space between the dots. They are not aligned as close to each other as pixels. So there is some more effort necessary to put the dots together than doing with pixels even if the pixels are enlarged like in Table 2. Additionally, on single-lined devices the dots are horizontally not equidistant but there is some additional space after each two dots. So there the graphic is also a bit stretched and lines are a bit bent. Of course, we gave special attention to these aspects during our user tests. And from this we can state that it is better to have a bit larger graphics where some scrolling is necessary than trying to make everything as small as possible. For example, for talking about triangles the larger graphic from Table 2 is preferable over the small on, although the small fits on the single-lined display at once. Furthermore, our user tests showed that the users overcome quite quickly the spacing problem. But of course, the problem of not being able to connect the dots does not occur that often on the graphics display as on the single-lined display. We also recognized that users performed better on the single-lined display if they had already worked with a graphics display.

4   Color Coding – Detailed FigureBraille (DFB)

After having successfully worked with EFB we thought about how we could enable the blind to also create colored graphics. The color of a bitmap's pixel had to be coded in a way that is suitable for viewing and editing and also for the different Braille devices. The color code should be compact. So we decided to use a 6-dot code where each 6-dot Braille sign represents a single pixel. As the code should also be easy to understand and to memorize, we based it on the color mixing known from primary school. This is much more common to most people than the RGB mixing. The primary colors, red, blue and yellow, are coded in one dot each. Mixed colors, violet, green, orange and brown, are coded as combinations of the primary color's dots. Furthermore, white is coded with no dots, black with all dots and gray as the middle with dots 1, 2 and 3. In our opinion these colors are sufficient for educational graphics. But to make the code also useful for more attractive images we have added light and dark shades by adding special dots to the code of the normal color.

To make the code usable on the graphics display, we added one dot for orientation. This is dot 1 which is set in every color code. Without this dot one could for example not distinguish between red, yellow and blue. On ordinary Braille displays the orientation is given by the modules. But, of course, we also use the orientation dot there to have the same touch impression as on the graphics display. Table 3 provides an overview of the color code that we have named "Detailed FigureBraille" (DFB). For the conversion of the dot patterns into signs we use the same table as for the EFB coding. Table 4 shows the DFB coding of the upper image in Table 2.

Table 3. Overview of the Braille Color Code – Detailed FigureBraille (DFB)

Name	Dots	Name	Dots	Name	Dots	Name	Dots
white	none	orange	145	light gray	12	light	+2
red	14	violet	146	dark gray	13	...	
yellow	15	green	156	gray	123	dark	+3
blue	16	brown	1456	black	all	...	

Table 4. DFB coding of the first sample image from Table 2

%	c	555	eee	1
%%	cc	55	ee	111
%%%	ccc	5	e	11111

For the visual representations of the colors we have defined color values that are clearly distinguishable and fit well to the DFB color names in a natural way so that talking about the colors is easy and does not reveal any misunderstandings.

Further-more, we tried to cover as much of the color space as possible and we have used colors that are likely to be used in graphics designed by sighted people. Of course, our tool can also load graphics with other colors. If so these colors are mapped to the nearest DFB color in the L*a*b* color space [5] according to Euclidean distance.

The colors were chosen through a multistep procedure. Firstly, we have chosen values for the normal DFB colors out of the HSV color space [7]. Then, we have lightened and darkened them by decreasing saturation or decreasing value, respectively. Finally, we tried to map the colors to known web colors [14]. This facilitates using them in different environments and talking about them. Table 5 shows the result of this process. Unfortunately, we could not find web colors for all DFB colors.

Table 5. Visual DFB colors (with web color name or Hex code and HSV values in °, % and %)

Light		Normal		Dark	
LightCoral	0,47,94	Red	0,100,100	Maroon	0,100,50
#ffff7f	60,50,100	Yellow	60,100,100	DarkKhaki	56,43,74
LightSkyB.	203,46,98	Blue	240,100,100	Navy	240,100,50
Gold	51,100,100	Orange	39,100,100	Ora.Red	16,100,100
#bf7fff	270,50,100	BlueViol.	271,81,89	#200040	270,100,25
PaleGreen	120,39,98	LimeGreen	120,76,80	DarkG.	120,100,39
Tan	34,33,82	SaddleBr.	25,86,55	#3f1a00	25,100,25
LightGrey	0,0,83	Gray	0,0,50	#3f3f3f	0,0,25

The selection of the HSV values was as follows. For the hues we have started with 0°, 30°, 60°, and 120° for red, orange, yellow, and green. For brown we have used 25° as it is less greenish than orange. For violet we used 270° as it should not look pink. For blue we started with 210° to clearly separate it from violet. Nevertheless, during the mapping step we observed that for normal and dark blue hue 240° is working well. For saturation and value we started with 100% both. Only green and brown were darkened right from the start as brown itself is a rather dark color and full RGB green looks neon like on screens. There we used value 50% and 75%, respectively. Darkening and lightning was done by adjusting saturation and value with respect to the perceived luminance. Special cases there were yellow and orange. A simply darkened yellow looks rather greenish, so it was mixed with brown (just as in real life). Orange was darkened with red and lightened with yellow. So it clearly differs from brown.

Unfortunately, using pink is not possible in our color code. If a graphic is converted to DFB pink will be mapped to red or violet which are both quite different from pink. We have not found that pink is that often used in graphics, but we will further evaluate if the absence of pink is a problem. Also cyan is not included in our color code. But this can be neglected. Cyan values will be mapped to light blue or light green which are mostly the names people use to describe cyan.

First user studies showed us that our color code is quite useful and really easy to memorize. We have also successfully used it to present colored games like "Same Game" (also known as "Bubble Breaker") on the tactile graphics display.

5 Text in Graphics – Object FigureBraille (OFB)

EFB and DFB were originally designed without special considerations for textual content in the graphic. If text should be included in a readable way, which means presenting Braille, two problems occur. The first originates from using the different Braille devices. Because of the equidistant pins on tactile graphics displays the Braille characters should be separated by one row of dots (pixels) right of each character and one line below to be readable on that device. However, on the single-lined display there should not be any additional space between the characters. The second problem is caused in using a 6-dot code for EFB. Through that, 8-dot texts have to be written by using two EFB signs for each character. When not using 8-dot Braille, the problem of split characters also occurs if the text is not aligned in an EFB line. Because of these problems, we decided that textual parts have to be stored in objects separated from the graphical parts. Therefore, we have defined "Object FigureBraille" (OFB) which is an XML format simply containing layers for text and graphic with their positions. Both, text and graphics are saved in plain text in the ".ofb" file. Graphics are saved as DFB. So the file is also readable and editable for a blind user without any special tool. Of course, without our tool a one cannot grasp the whole (combined) graphic directly. With OFB text can easily be integrated in DFB and the layers can be named and easily be reused in other graphics. Furthermore, using text objects reveals the possibility for searching for texts or showing it in normal font for sighted. As our ideas on OFB began sounding more and more like reinventing the SVG DOM [14], we decided to stop working on improving OFB as a stand-alone format but rather trying to extend SVG with an own namespace including OFB attributes in future.

Another aspect to text in graphics that we investigated was: "How to find the text?". As on Braille displays the dots for graphic and text are indistinguishable we thought that text would have to be marked to be recognized as text. However, our user tests showed that this is not necessary. Just like with the color codes all users recognized text elements without any hints.

6 Combining Views and Exploring Graphics

To fully grasp a colored graphic it is very helpful if one can utilize exploration techniques. Besides zooming and scrolling, one main technique is filtering the graphic by color. Therefore we also make use of our color code. The user can activate a color filter dialog in which the colors that are currently presented are shown with their codes as a text line. The user can now change the color filter by simply adding or removing color code signs. Furthermore, a contour filter can be applied which detects edges and presents only those. Fig. 1 shows some examples.

Fig. 1 also shows a problem with DFB: it stretches the graphic non-proportionally. Not only that each pixel is represented as 2×3 pins but further on the graphics display it is necessary to add space between the color code signs to separate them to get a clear presentation. So utilizing only DFB to understand a graphic is not possible. It has to be combined with a structural view of the graphic. One way to do this is providing views like shown in Fig. 1. But as we thought that permanently color filtering could be quite confusing we have also designed views like shown in Fig. 2. There the graphic is presented by its contours filled with a number of color codes and also combined with an even-odd filling algorithm. Our user test showed that these views are accepted by the user quite well as the user gets a lot of information about the graphic quickly without any extra activities like filtering or so. Even when we did not tell the user about what this view shows it was quickly recognized that there are color codes inside. The users preferred the views with lesser color codes. A similar technique could also be used for indicating the colors of lines in a line drawing. But we have not tested this yet. Of course, such views are not suitable for showing or creating single differently colored pixels. Therefore, one still needs DFB.

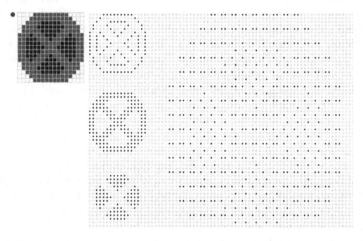

Fig. 1. Simple views of a traffic sign (top to bottom, left to right: original image of only 17×17 pixels, enlarged version of the original image, contour view on the tactile display, color filter view showing only red, color filter view showing only blue, DFB view)

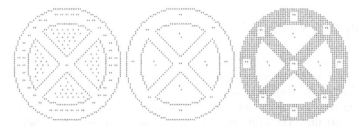

Fig. 2. Combined views of a traffic sign with 60×60 pixels on the tactile display, showing only the lifted pins (left to right: contour view with as much color code signs as possible, contour view with only a few color code signs, view with even-odd-filling and a few color code signs)

If the user works with an object-based graphical representation (like an OFB or a vector graphic) it is also possible to filter by objects or by object types like text elements. Of course, also meta-information about the objects like name, description and object type can be presented if they are included in the graphic. Furthermore, such graphics can be built up incrementally as described in [6]. In contrast to [6] we do not propose to always build up the graphic from left to right and top to bottom. For instance in this approach for a diagram like the one in Fig. 3 the blue box at the left border would be shown first which is not very useful. Such a diagram should rather be built from top to bottom and left to right, which means that in the example the blue box at the top is presented first. Of course, it is hard to decide automatically in which sequence a graphic's elements should be shown. Because of that we have decided to present the elements in the order of their appearance in the graphic's source code. If object-based graphics are created thoughtfully the elements' order is mostly quite useful. Further, ordering hints can be provided in such a graphic just like the tab order in GUI definitions. Our user test showed that telling where to start with the exploration is very helpful, especially on a single-lined display. If the user knows that a graphic is oriented to the bottom left or the center point, he or she can directly scroll there. Else the exploration will always start at the top right. Unfortunately, such information cannot be provided in raster graphics formats, EFB or DFB, respectively.

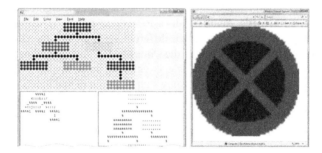

Fig. 3. Left: Screenshot of one of our tools showing the editing view for sighted at the top and the EFB and DFB views for the blind at the bottom, right: Example of a simple SVG (the traffic sign graphic of 60×60 pixels is included by an image tag with a size of 600×600 pixels)

All the exploration techniques have in common that there is a risk of getting lost in the exploration. For example when one has zoomed into a graphic and scrolled over it, it sometimes gets hard to go back to the point where one last saw something interesting. To solve this problem programs for sighted people often utilize a mini map. But this is not usable on Braille devices. So we have introduced a kind of bookmarking technique with which the user can save views or hotspots. If the whole view is saved all parameters of the different exploration techniques are recorded. So that the exact same view with its zooming level and the filter configurations can be recreated. Saving a hotspot means that only a special position is remembered e.g. an intersection point of two graphs. The user can navigate to a hotspot in every view while the configuration of the view is not changed (except of the current position). The saved views and hotspots can be named by the user and so selecting from a list.

A further technique that we will investigate in future is searching for interesting parts of the graphic like a special color, a pixel pattern or important objects. Therefore one needs an appropriate means of specifying the parameters and also to present the results in a useful way. Furthermore, we will investigate "folding" of graphics, which means that the user can specify several lines or columns of the graphic that should be hidden. By that, for example, one can show a diagram's axes next to a point of interest also in a zoom level that is suitable for figuring out the point's coordinates.

7 Sharing Graphics with Other People

A main interest of our research is the cooperation between blind and sighted people. This includes that blind people can provide their own graphics to sighted people e. g. via web pages like Wikipedia or e-learning portals easily.

With our tools EFB and DFB can be converted into bitmaps and vice versa. Two representations are provided. One is called "pixel view" and follows the original idea which means that it contains one pixel for each DFB sign (six pixels for each EFB sign). The other is called "swell paper view" and produces a circle for each pixel just as shown in Fig. 1 and 2. This is to provide sighted people with a larger version of the graphic. This was important in HyperBraille to give sighted people an impression of how large the graphic is for the blind people. We also use it in our tool supporting cooperation between blind and sighted as editable view for the sighted (see Fig. 3).

The best way to provide small graphics to sighted people is using a format that supports zooming. So we have evaluated different methods to save small graphics as SVG [14]. The simplest way is using the "image" tag and specifying the attributes "width" and "height" so that the graphic is enlarged to a size in which it is easily recognizable by sighted people. Fig. 3 shows an example of such an SVG opened in a web browser. The presentation is not beautiful but useful. Better looking SVGs can be generated with a raster to vector converter. First tests showed that the best results are achieved when filtering the graphic to just show one color, converting this to an SVG group and then combining the groups to one SVG. This has still to be implemented in our tool. Of course, both methods do not result in accessible SVGs. This is only possible when creating an object-based and annotated graphic right from the start.

8 Conclusion and Future Work

Our research showed us, that several blind people are curious about colored graphics and that the color information can also be useful for them. All subjects have learned the color code very quickly and had fun in playing colored games and creating their own colored graphics. Although most of them reported, that they have no impression what a color really is, as most of them had never seen colors, all were somehow proud to be able to work with and produce graphics that look nice to sighted people.

Currently, our tool consists of a set of prototypes covering different aspects. In future, we will work on integrating all our results into one single tool, which will then be available from our web site. We will also perform more user studies to evaluate our exploration strategies. Furthermore, we will evaluate the applicability of an 8-dot EFB code and we will examine how useful it is to fully integrate Object FigureBraille with SVG, so that our tool fully supports the creation of accessible graphics.

Acknowledgements. We thank the participants of our user study, especially Lydia Simon, Simone Müller, and Gerhard Jaworek for taking the time to tell us about their experiences with graphics and the hints on our research. We also thank our project partners, especially Wiebke Köhlmann, Oliver Nadig, Denise Prescher, Maria Schiewe, and Gerhard and Ursula Weber, for supporting our work with the extensive use of our tools. This research has been carried out in the context of the HyperBraille project which is financed by the German Federal Ministry of Economics and Technology (BMWi).

References

1. Barker, S.: The Barker Code of Color/Fabric Representation,
   `http://www.tactilecolor.com/`
2. Fujiyoshi, M., et al.: The Development of a Universal Design Tactile Graphics Production System BPLOT2. In: Miesenberger, K., Klaus, J., Zagler, W.L., Karshmer, A.I. (eds.) ICCHP 2008. LNCS, vol. 5105, pp. 938–945. Springer, Heidelberg (2008)
3. Gunzenhäuser, R., Weber, G.: Graphical User Interfaces for Blind People. In: Proceedings of the 13th World Computer Congress, pp. S.450–S.457 (1994)
4. HyperBraille, `http://www.hyperbraille.de/`
5. McLaren, K.: The development of the CIE 1976 (L*a*b*) uniform colour space and colour-difference formula. Journal of the Society of Dyers and Colourists 92, S.338–S.341 (1976)
6. Rotard, M., Ertl, T.: Tactile Access to Scalable Vector Graphics for People with Visual Impairment. In: SVG Open Conference (2004)
7. Smith, A.R.: Color gamut transform pairs. In: Proceedings of SIGGRAPH 1978, pp. 12–19. ACM, New York (1978)
8. Tactile Colour Communication Society, `http://www.tactile.org/`
9. Tactile Vision Inc.: Tactile Vision Color Code System,
   `http://www.tactilevisioninc.com/`
10. ViewPlus: Braille Embossers (Braille Printers) by ViewPlus,
    `http://www.viewplus.com/`
11. Völkel, T., Weber, G., Baumann, U.: Tactile Graphics Revised: The Novel BrailleDis 9000 Pin-Matrix Device with Multitouch Input. In: Miesenberger, K., Klaus, J., Zagler, W.L., Karshmer, A.I. (eds.) ICCHP 2008. LNCS, vol. 5105, pp. 835–842. Springer, Heidelberg (2008)
12. Wikipedia: ASCII Art, `http://en.wikipedia.org/wiki/ASCII_art`
13. Wikipedia: Web Colors, `http://en.wikipedia.org/wiki/Web_colors`
14. World Wide Web Consortium (W3C): Scalable Vector Graphics (SVG) – XML Graphics for the Web, `http://www.w3.org/Graphics/SVG/`

Living Labs as a Methodological Approach to Universal Access in Senior Design

Julie Christiane Thiesen Winthereik, Lone Malmborg, and Tanja Belinda Andersen

IT University of Copenhagen, Rued Langgaardsvej 7, 2300 Copenhagen S, Denmark
{jctw,malmborg,tanjabelinda}@itu.dk

Abstract. In this paper we discuss the potential of using the Living Lab methodology as an approach to ensuring universal access when designing for senior citizens. Our understanding of Living Labs is based on a recent study of 32 Living Labs cases, identifying central activities and issues in different applications of the methodology. We describe a Danish Living Lab project initiated to design for better quality of life for senior citizens in Sølund, a nursing home in Copenhagen. Two crucial concepts from the Living Lab methodology – co-creation and context – act as the core concepts for our analysis of user participation and universal access in Living Labs in general and in the Sølund Living Lab specifically. In our conclusion we suggest areas that should be given special attention when designing Living Lab projects and selecting user participants.

Keywords: Universal access, living labs, co-creation, participatory design.

1 Introduction

In order to design for universal access, it is crucial to reflect on the way we, as designers and researchers, represent the users that we wish to design for and consider what consequences this representation has for the given user group, which in this case is senior citizens.

The Living Lab phenomenon has its roots in very different traditions, which manifest themselves in various types of Living Labs. However these differences are rarely articulated and, despite the great interest for the Living Lab methodology, we find a profound lack of discussing the complexity of the processes and the different actors that the Living Labs involve. Central to the Living Lab thought is the user as the guarantor for successful innovation and development of the 'perfect' product that meets the actual user needs. Added to this is the idea of empowering the citizens and the communities through participation in the so-called innovation lifecycle [4].

We find there is a need for reflection on how the users are actually involved in the innovation process, how they are chosen and how this selective representation reflects back on the particular user group. Furthermore, it is our intention to deconstruct the essentialist image of user and product that is currently being reproduced in the Living Lab environment.

The article primarily finds its empirical basis in the work of Copenhagen Living Lab and their project at Sølund nursing home. We are looking at innovation of welfare technologies, which is characterized by a complex set of diverse strategies and

C. Stephanidis (Ed.): Universal Access in HCI, Part I, HCII 2009, LNCS 5614, pp. 174–183, 2009.
© Springer-Verlag Berlin Heidelberg 2009

values, e.g. the value of social responsibility, the strategies of political goals and agendas for re-election, the responsibility that follows with public funding etc. The complexity in this case very much has to do with the involvement of the Municipality of Copenhagen, but we still believe it is possible to draw parallels to other very different innovation syndicates, which may not be engaged in designing for senior citizens and public welfare, but still have to deal with the complexities of a user driven innovation process.

Our discussion is informed by literature on the Living Lab phenomenon, particularly the literature review made by Asbjørn Følstad [7]. We present a discussion of the concept of the users, setting out from two perspectives given by Følstad: *Co-creation* and *context* [7]. He identifies a lack of critical studies of the innovation and development processes [7, p. 120]. It is striking, though, that Følstad does not provide any new framework, but only underlines the fact that the span of Living Lab approaches is extremely wide, and that underneath the homogenizing discourse that is present in Europe exists a diverse and complex interpretation of central concepts, such as participants and context.

It is not our intention to reject the Living Lab idea as a fruitful and giving method within innovation and design, but to present a more nuanced gaze on the processes that are set in motion around the Living Lab concept and the different roles and agendas that takes place when working in a Living Lab setting. In the hype and excitement that is presently permeating the Living Lab environment, we see a risk of overlooking the complexity of the phenomenon, which could lead to failing processes and leaving the potential of the Living Lab methodology not fully tapped.

The theoretical foundation of this article and the authors themselves is grounded in anthropology and the Interaction Design tradition. This is not an anthropological study as such, but we are clearly inspired by the qualitative and hermeneutic approach that characterizes social science.

2 Conceptual Framework of Living Labs

Based on 32 publications on Living Labs, Følstad [7] categorizes European Living Labs in three categories: a. Living labs to experience and experiment with ubiquitous computing, b. Living Labs as open innovation platforms, and c. Living Labs exposing test bed applications to the users. He identifies main and divergent purposes, state-of-art processes and methods, and, finally, the theoretical foundations. When going through Følstad's findings, it is obvious that the different types of Living Labs have different purposes and methods, but it also becomes clear that it is not a prerequisite for Living Labs to either investigate the context of use or involve users as co-creators in any formal sense. Less than one third of the papers involve process descriptions of any forms of co-creation [7, p. 120] and the theoretical foundations described in the reviewed Living Lab articles are often rather weak or nonexistent. The theories are about co-creation and users as innovator, work from the field of Science and Technology Studies (STS) and ideas related to the field of Human-Computer Interaction [7].

Though it is not found to be the most common purposes of the living labs, the focus on context research and co-creation is, according to Følstad, the most substantial contribution to the state-of-art of Living Labs [7, p. 117]. According to Følstad's review there exists a general need for a thorough, but also critical, exploration of the potentials and pitfalls of user-involvement in Living Labs. This could appropriately include an exploration of the concepts of co-creation and context research. In the following we initiate such exploration by describing our case, the Sølund Living Lab.

3 The Case: Sølund Living Lab

The conceptual framework underlying Living Labs was discussed in the previous section. Here we present a Living Lab example from our local environment to illustrate the complexity of organization, processes and issues around a specific Living Lab case in the area of design for senior citizens.

The Sølund Living Lab is part of a project named "The Good Life of Elderly", focusing on user-centered development of the quality of life at nursing homes in Copenhagen municipality [3]. Supported by Danish research funding, the Care Department of the Municipality of Copenhagen initiated the project in autumn 2007. Project partners are from industry, rehabilitation, academic institutions and also a process facilitator (Copenhagen Living Lab – CLL). The goal is to develop solutions through innovation of new services that can make life better for elderly citizens. The Living Lab is based at the biggest nursing home in Denmark, Sølund. Staff members, residents and relatives are involved in the project. The Sølund Living Lab is situated in what Følstad would define as a "real-world context" (see section 4.2 for a more detailed discussion).

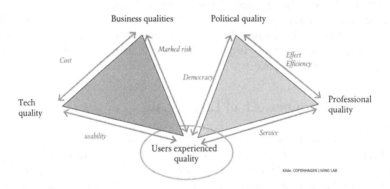

Fig. 1. Stakeholders and their relations in Sølund Living Lab [2]

In this Living Lab, the users' experiences and needs are explored and identified through ethnographic studies and qualitative analyses based on daily life practices.

3.1 Organization

One of the challenging issues of setting up a Living Lab is coping with multi-organizational collaboration [10] between a wide variety of stakeholders including public, industrial and academic stakeholders. Figure 1 illustrates the principles of how stakeholders in the project relate to each other. Sølund Living Lab is a construction of stakeholders from all "corners of the triangles". The right triangle represents public stakeholders associated with the Living Lab and the left triangle represents industrial stakeholders. This stakeholder model has been important for Copenhagen Living Lab in defining and understanding roles and power relations between stakeholders in the Sølund Living Lab initiative.

3.2 Sølund Living Lab Life Cycle

The life cycle maps the main activities around the Sølund Living Lab initiative. The driving force between these activities is the facilitator (CLL), but, of course, different stakeholders from the 'triangles' are involved in the activities. In the core of the life cycle is the daily life of the senior citizens.

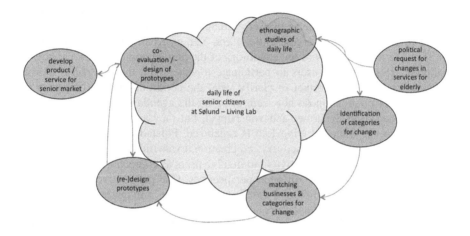

Fig 2. The Sølund Living Lab life cycle

As it becomes clear from this life cycle visualization of activities, the actual daily life of senior citizens is a central part of just two activities: the ethnographic studies of daily life and co-evaluation / -design of prototypes. If we look at the starting point and the planned ending point of the project life cycle, there is an obvious danger that the final products and services developed for the senior citizens and the senior market are not only far from the needs identified by ethnographic studies of daily life, but also far away from the original political request for change. The life cycle reveals several 'breaks', which primarily come from the fact that the seniors and their daily lives are left out of co-creation activities. The questions, that we will return to in our analysis, are by who, when and where will the interests of the residents be represented.

4   The Challenge of Co-creation and Context

Our analysis is divided into two parts. One part focuses on Følstad's analytical concept of co-creation and the other part on Følstad's notion of context.

4.1 Co-creation

When looking into details of specific examples of living labs like the Sølund Living Lab, we see that the concept of co-creation has many interpretations - interpretations that are probably grounded in the underlying political, ideological or philosophical paradigm of the methodological approach in the specific projects.

Theoretical foundations for co-creation in Følstad include von Hippel's [16] work on users as innovators and Scharmer's [14] work on innovation as a co-creation process involving multiple stakeholders. These conceptions and traditions of co-creation differ from the Scandinavian approach to user participation. Yngve Sundblad [15, p. 37] writes about the Scandinavian participatory design tradition that "...even at the early stages, where purpose of the design is not yet know, it is important to focus on multiple users and uses and on the experience of use. Post-design evaluation is not enough. (…) Often the problems of user participation are discussed from the point of view of researchers getting access to the users. Yet, user participation should also be seen from the point of view of the conditions of the participation process, i.e. how the conditions are set for the users to participate together with the designers." As this quote expresses it is important to clarify what the conditions for participation are. These issues of co-creation do not seem to be on the agenda in Følstad's theoretical framework, based on Scharmer and von Hippel, but they are relevant when we are analyzing how the Sølund Living Lab is organized. Følstad identifies five different activities, context research, discovery, co-creation, evaluation, and technical testing. He defines co-creation as the activity "to involve users as co-creators" [7, p. 106]. We discuss co-creation from two different perspectives. One perspective is dealing with the specific activities in which users are involved during a living lab life cycle. The second perspective regards how users are represented.

What is interesting when looking closer into the details of Følstad's activities compared with the Sølund activities is the role of technological services and products. The Sølund Living Lab process is deliberately designed in a way so that thinking in terms of new technological artifacts are not introduced to the users until very late in the process, whereas Følstad states that in many of the cases a "highly technology-driven research agenda may be the cause of the lack of activities aimed at providing general insight into end-users' context of use." [7, p. 107].

The (lack of) introduction of technological artifacts has important consequences for how co-creation takes place in the process. It seems that in most cases studied by Følstad possible technologies or services do already exist as either a concept idea or a prototype when entering the Living Lab project. This reduces the possibility of users having influence on the core idea behind the product or service.

If we look at the Discovery activity in Følstad's model, the purpose is described as gaining insight into unexpected ICT uses and new service opportunities. He mentions examples like gaining "insight through confronting (potential) users with (prototypes or demonstrators) of early technology early on in the innovation process." [7, p. 107]. He underlines that several authors do not include mechanisms for needs analysis and idea generation in their Living Lab. If we compare these two first steps with the ethnographic studies and identification of categories in the Sølund Living Lab process it is clear that the Sølund project identifies and categorizes needs among residents at the Sølund nursing home before thinking in terms of technology at all. In this way the conditions for user participation differ very much from the typical Living Labs in Følstad's material, where prototypes or demonstrators exist prior to the analysis of needs.

Følstad's report on co-creation activity reveals that premises or conditions for user participation in the innovation or development process are limited in most cases. He writes with reference to Mirijamdotter et al. [11] and Niitamo et al. [12], "In current Living Lab practices users are seen more as sources of (predefined) technology use, rather than sources of innovation." [7, p. 108]. Even if the Sølund Living Lab process leaves the initial forming of business concepts and design of prototypes with the industrial partners, these are still based on a shared understanding of the senior citizens' own experience and formulation of needs. This means that the following co-evaluation and co-design process still has this ethnographically informed material as the point of departure, whereas the typical co-creation activity reported in Følstad's study is strongly technology-driven. As an example of this Følstad mentions that Hoving [9] described the co-creative process as "being conducted through a series of action-research interventions, where end-users are provided with technology and the effects of the interventions are monitored by researchers." This is a vague and modest interpretation of co-creation compared with the Scandinavian participatory design tradition [7]. We are not able to make an analysis of the way this co-design is performed in the Sølund Living Lab as this activity is only now being planned and will take place early in autumn 2009. However, industrial partners are being invited for collaboration based on the categories for change, which in turn are based on ethnographic studies.

The issue of representation is closely related to the fundamental issue of democracy. In Pelle Ehn's early thoughts on designing for democracy at work it is stated that "the democratic ideal is a beautiful human invention, stating the right for every human to equally participate in decisions concerning his or her life. In practice, however, this freedom has always been limited." [5, p. 247]. In the participatory design tradition, with roots back to the Scandinavian tradition represented by Ehn, the selection of users to be part of the participatory design process is an issue that has received substantial attention. During the 70's and 80's when design of new information technology primarily focused on work place technologies this question was dealt with by unions. But how is this question dealt with in the Living Lab method, which always includes some selection of users, and which very often - at least in our case - deals with innovations for our homes and daily life?

In the Living Lab cases studied in Følstad the only issue brought up regarding representation is one case discussing what considerations are needed to decide the optimal number of participants in a specific Living Lab [7].

The question of representation in the Sølund case is complicated by the many stakeholders involved in the project (see figure 1). We cannot take for granted that the Municipality of Copenhagen will represent the interests of elderly, as one of the most important issues on the political agenda is how to solve the problem of the growing elderly population. This means that the perspective of the Municipality very often will be how to design and deliver more efficient services to senior citizens with fewer resources, whereas the perspective of elderly will be ensuring and enhancing their quality of life. In our interview with Thomas Hammer-Jacobsen [8] on how the Sølund Living Lab dealt with the question of representation of users' interests he said that the Copenhagen Living Lab became the ambassador for elderly by widening the scope of the Sølund Living Lab. The Municipality of Copenhagen had a narrow service goal focusing on how service is delivered to elderly, whereas Copenhagen Living Lab insisted that the perspective should be quality of life in a much wider sense. As a consequence of this, the selection of Living Lab participants included 7 elderly residents at Sølund, 4 care staff members at Sølund, 6 senior citizens who are preparing for their elderly life, and 6 relatives to residents at Sølund. Furthermore, CLL carefully selected participants in each of these groups on the basis of demographic variations. In this way, CLL has worked very consciously to ensure that all aspects relevant to the life of senior citizens have been explored, not just the relation between the public service provider and the residents at Sølund Living Lab.

Ensuring universal access, when using a Living Lab method, requires that the Living Lab facilitator is taking representation seriously. This means that it should be ensured that elderly and their organizations and informal ambassadors (like CLL) should have a say when participants for the Living Lab are selected. We should be aware that the public service providers have their 'efficiency'-agenda, just as the industry has their 'market'-agenda. Furthermore there is a tendency to see elderly as one single group, but the fact is that with a high number of elderly people reaching the age of 90 or 100 years, all having different experiences from long lives, they are a very varied group with many different needs that have to be considered in a design process.

4.2 Context

Følstad operates with three different notions of context. The first notion refers to the earlier mentioned context-research, the idea of studying the context of the users as such, for the purpose of contributions to the innovation and development process [7, p. 107]. The other two notions regard the setting of the Living Lab, namely "Familiar context" and "Real-world context". The distinction between "Familiar context" and "Real world context" is defining whether the Living Lab is set up to have the look and feel of a familiar context or if it is actually functioning in people's usual living spaces. To Følstad the familiar context setting can be seen as a threat to "ecological validity" [7, p. 110]. The idea of "ecological validity" is an interesting point to which we will return.

The process-oriented context definition "context-research" is only described and defined loosely by Følstad as research regarding context of use, including the users and their environment. Følstad argues that "context-research" is typically applied as an early research method, exactly as in the case of Sølund (as discussed in section 4.1). These context definitions that rely strongly on locality, point toward an understanding of the Living Lab as something that is both in the world and demarcated from it. This context interpretation makes it possible to believe that the well-structured Living Lab, located in a "real-world" setting, gives the developer first hand insight into a place where the developer imagines being able to find undisturbed "ecological validity" as Følstad argues for.

But the wish and hope that follow, by which some Living Lab managers believe to be able to find answers about the "real needs", are to ignore the complex realities influencing the practical set up of the Living Lab, its innovation methods and its outcome. The discipline of social anthropology has long ago disposed the idea of any authentic unspoiled cultural settings, in which it is possible to find the definite truth about certain people and their lives. The absolute ecological valid data is thus nowhere to be found.

The wish to overcome the problem of reductionism is exactly the common argument as to why to establish a Living Lab or other forms of "Real-World" innovation research. Researchers seek to understand and interpret lived life's complexities by looking at the users outside the usability lab – in their real life environment. However, they seem to forget that these users are not living on isolated islands and that the researchers themselves have certain perspectives with which to look. The problem of reductionism in the lab does not necessarily disappear by making a Living Lab – in practice you just install another type of lab with new forms of reductionism. We are aware that it is not possible to avoid reductionism, but it is crucial to stay reflective on the decisions made in the innovation process.

To take this argument further, we suggest an expansion, or even dissolution, of the concept of context within the Living Lab tradition. We suggest that the concept of context is re-designed to encompass what in figure 1 is called "Stakeholders and their relations". This is not so simple, both because "context" is a slippery concept and because the complexity of actors involved in doing Living Labs can be almost overwhelming, as it is revealed in figure 1. Many different stakeholders have interpreted what is good for the senior residents, but they also have their own different motives and agendas. Industry has to balance its business models towards profits, technological qualities and embedded use-qualities. Politicians have to balance the service of the citizens with resources and with upcoming elections, and care professionals have other interests, such as professional pride and values. Thus there are many diverging agendas and motives and they are negotiated in many different practices and certainly also in practices where no users are involved directly.

The discussion on context has deep roots in the social science tradition. Theoreticians have discussed at length how social scientists should encompass the "context" in research and analyses. We will not discuss such epistemological arguments at any length here, but only bring the possibly provoking standpoint – that there is no such thing as "context". By this we adopt a theoretical standpoint that seeks to overcome the split between structure, i.e. something that surrounds or frames certain practices, and situations. Instead every situation in all kind of practices must be seen as constitutive and made up by the constitutional elements present in the situation [1, p. 71]. There exists nothing else – the situation takes place simultaneously as both agency and structure happens, which leaves no meaning left to the distinction between practice and context. The way to go is, therefore, to give attention to the different actors constituting the situations in which Living Labs happen.

It is thereby necessary to rethink the way we understand where and how the innovation processes happens. The process is going on in many practices located at different places at different times and it surely also happens many other places than in the so-called "real-life-context" of the user. In complex innovation syndicates, such as the Sølund case, but also in all other Living Lab setups, much of the innovation process is happening far away from the user.

In Sølund, the goals of innovating for elderly residents are compromised in the process of innovation where, as we discussed in 4.1, the life cycle of the innovation process "forgets" to integrate the "users" all the way. There can be very good reasons for this and Thomas Hammer-Jacobsen agrees that in the innovation process there "is a lot in play that does not have anything to do with the quality of life for old people" [8]. The challenge is to be aware of how such diverging agendas are reflected in the decisions and thereby the outcome of the Living Lab activities; in practices directly involving co-construction activities as well as in other practices that do not directly involve users. The massive influence of various actors is thus embedded in many practices regarding the living lab life cycle in an ongoing changeable process. This does not leave room for findings of "real needs" or ecological valid data. A successful Living Lab is consequently not a simple question of the right set up; the complexity is universal, if nothing else is!

5 Conclusion

Through our analysis of the concepts of co-creation and context in the Living Lab literature and in the Sølund case, we have revealed crucial methodological issues when applying the method in the field of design for seniors. Ensuring universal access through user participation, when designing services and technologies for senior citizens, requires special attention on how this user group and its life situation is represented in the Living Lab setting.

Regarding representation in a co-creation process, it is important to take into account in which way, and by whom, the users are represented throughout the living lab life cycle. Seniors should not be considered as one homogeneous group. The various needs and life situations that exist among different groups of senior citizens should be taken into account along with decisions regarding delimitation of participants.

Regarding context, we consider the most important issue to be awareness of different conceptions of context and how to avoid unreflected reductionism. Many different stakeholders have interpretations of what is best for the senior citizens, but they also have different motives and agendas. Thus context should be understood in the complex landscape of stakeholders, their mutual relations and conflicting agendas.

We do not consider Living Labs a failed methodology, but we advocate for both academia and industry to bear in mind that no methodology or type of research is ever neutral, but is always a result of choice and ideological perspectives. It is such choices and ideologies that we, as researchers and product designers, should always be conscious about.

References

1. Clarke, A.E.: Situational Analysis - Grounded Theory After the Postmodern Turn. SAGE Publications, Inc., Thousand Oaks (2005)
2. Copenhagen Living Lab: Finding the positional match. Unpublished document (2009)
3. Copenhagen Living Lab: Det gode ældreliv - 8 innovationsspor, arbejdshæfte (2008)
4. Directorate-General for the Information Society and Media: Living Labs for User-driven Open Innovation – An Overview of the Living Labs Methodology, Activities and Achievements (2009),
   http://ec.europa.eu/information_society/activities/livinglabs/docs/brochure_jan09_en.pdf
5. Ehn, P.: Work-Oriented Design of Computer Artifacts. Swedish Center for Working Life (1988)

6. Erhvervs- og byggestyrelsen: Det gode ældreliv (2006),
   http://www.ebst.dk/brugerdreveninnovation.dk/aeldreliv
7. Følstad, A.: Living Labs for Innovation and Development of Information and Communication Technology: A Literature Review. eJOV 10 (2008)
8. Hammer-Jacobsen, T.: Interview with Thomas Hammer-Jacobsen about Copenhagen Living Lab and the Sølund case (2009)
9. Hoving, D.: Enhancing the quality of life in a living lab Moerwijk (The Hague), The New Media (2003)
10. Kviselius, N.Z., Ozan, H., Edenius, M., Andersson, P.: The Evolution of Living Labs - Propositions for Improved Design and Further Research. In: The 5th International Conference on Innovation and Management (ICIM 2008), aastricht, the Netherlands, December 10-11 (2008)
11. Mirijamdotter, A., Ståhlbröst, A., Sällström, A., Niitamo, V.-P., Kulkki, S.: The European Network of Living Labs for CWE - user-centric co-creation and innovation. In: E-Challenges 2006, Barcelona, Spain, October 25-27 (2006)
12. Niitamo, V.-P., Kulkki, S., Eriksson, M., Hribernik, K.A.: State-of-the-art and good practice in the field of living labs. In: The 12th International Conference on Concurrent Enterprising: Innovative Products and Services through Collaborative Networks, ICE 2006, Milan, Italy, June 26-28, pp. 349–357 (2006)
13. Pedersen, J.: Protocols of Participatory Design and Workplace Studies, ITU (2007)
14. Scharmer, O.: Theory U: Leading From the Future as it Emerges. Sol, Cambridge (2007)
15. Sundblad, Y.: From Utopia 1981 to Utopia 2008. In: Binder, L., Malmborg (eds.) (Re)Searching the Digital Bauhaus. Springer, Heidelberg (2009)
16. Von Hippel, E.: The Sources of Innovation. Oxford University Press, New York (1988)

A UCD Approach towards the Design, Development and Assessment of Accessible Applications in a Large Scale European Integrated Project

Karel Van Isacker[1], Karin Slegers[2], Maria Gemou[3], and Evangelos Bekiaris[4]

[1] European Platform for Rehabilitation, 15, rue de Spa, B-1000 Brussels, Belgium
[2] Centre for User Experience Research (CUO), IBBT / K.U. Leuven,
Parkstraat 45 Bus 3605 - 3000 Leuven - Belgium
[3,4] Centre for Research and Technology Hellas, Hellenic Institute of Transport,
17, Posidonos Av., 17455 Alimos, Greece
aegis@epr.eu, karin.slegers@soc.kuleuven.be,
{mgemou,abek}@certh.gr

Abstract. ÆGIS (Open Accessibility Everywhere: Groundwork, Infrastructure, Standards) is a user-centred project, involving several user groups (users with visual, hearing, motion, speech and cognitive impairments as well as application developers) throughout the design, development and assessment phases. In this paper the holistic UCD (User Centred Design) approach of the project is introduced. This approach ensures that the project's objectives to determine whether 3rd generation access techniques will provide a more accessible, more exploitable and deeply embeddable approach in mainstream ICT applications (desktop, rich Internet and mobile applications) are met, with the full support and involvement of a huge end-user group in every single step of the design, development and deployment of accessible mainstream ICT.

Keywords: accessible, mainstream ICT, Open Accessibility Framework, Holistic User Centred Design, design, development, assessment, end-user groups, desktop, rich web applications, Java-based mobile devices.

1 Introduction

Implementing a pan-European project, involving a wide plethora of stakeholders, and addressing one of the biggest needs for people with disabilities, namely affordable assistive technologies, would be an empty box, were it not for the in-depth involvement of these very end-users in every step of the project: its design, development and assessment. Following a holistic UCD (User Centred Design) approach, ÆGIS (Open Accessibility Everywhere: Groundwork, Infrastructure, Standards - http://www.aegis-project.eu/) aims to ensure that the user needs and interaction models for several user groups (users with visual, hearing, motion, speech and cognitive impairments as well as application developers) are identified and are considered throughout the entire project design, iterative development and assessment cycles. Based upon this approach, open source-based generalised accessibility support is developed into mainstream ICT

C. Stephanidis (Ed.): Universal Access in HCI, Part I, HCII 2009, LNCS, pp. 184–192, 2009.

devices/applications (desktop, rich web applications, and Java-based mobile devices), fully abiding to the needs of the end-user groups. All developments will be iteratively tested with hundreds of end users, developers and experts in four phases and four pilot sites across Europe (Belgium, Spain, Sweden and the UK).

2 Methodology

The User Centred Design approach for ÆGIS is planned in four phases. The first phase aims at gathering the needs for all user groups: end users with disabilities, and assistive technology experts. In the second phase the insights in the user needs will be translated into user requirements which will be the basis for the conceptual models that will be made in Phase three. In this phase, the model will be gradually and iteratively built into prototypes of increasing fidelity in a co-design approach. The result of the third phase, the working prototypes, will in the final and fourth phase be tested in the field.

2.1 Phase 1

To understand the users and to identify user needs, thorough analyses of the users, their tasks and their contexts will be done. A combination of quantitative and qualitative methods will be used to gather deep and rich insights on the one hand and to gather data of a substantial panel of users.

On a quantitative level, the user, task and context analysis will be performed by means of interviews that will be conducted by phone. For this purpose, separate questionnaires are made for end users with disabilities and for experts. In addition, different questionnaires are constructed for the ÆGIS application areas (desktop applications, mobile phone applications and rich internet applications).

On a qualitative level, a subset of the questionnaire participants will be interviewed face to face, allowing the discussion of relevant topics on a deeper level and doing contextual inquiries to observe the users while doing relevant tasks.

2.2 Phase 2

Aiming at translating the insights and user needs gathered in Phase 1 into user requirements, a number of User Centred Design techniques will be deployed. The main purpose of this phase is to set up the user requirements for AEGIS in a format usable for the remainder of the project. To achieve this, personas[1], use cases to be translated in UML diagrams, user scenarios and a list of user requirements will be created. To verify the relevance and accuracy of these formats, focus group meetings with end users and experts will be organised.

2.3 Phase 3

Starting from the personas, use cases, user scenarios and list of user requirements constructed in the previous phase, conceptual models of the assistive technologies,

---

[1] Personas are summaries of some typical real-user characteristics (i.e. age, family situations, motivations, behavior, personal experiences and end goals), collected during the user-and-task analysis of the end-users.

applications and developers' tools will be made. These models will present the high level functionalities and user interaction.

In the ÆGIS project, from the early beginning, a co-design (or participatory design) approach will be followed. In this respect, ÆGIS researchers, developers and designers will team up with target user representatives (both end users and experts). This team will follow an iterative process of designing, developing and iterating prototypes of increasing fidelity. Based on the created conceptual models, mock-ups of the intended applications will be co-designed. These mock-ups will be evaluated with end users on their usefulness, usability, and the user acceptance via qualitative techniques such as co-discovery, thinking aloud protocol, cognitive walkthrough, expert evaluations, etc. The feedback gathered on the mock-ups will be used for their optimisation on specifications and design level and the implementation of prototypes of progressively increasing fidelity, with regard to user requirements.

The process of co-design and evaluation is to be iteratively repeated until hifi, working prototypes are available. These working prototypes will then be extensively tested in the usability laboratories, allowing, in this case, the measurement of both objective measures – performance, eye tracking, psycho-physiological measures – and subjective measures – user experience, perceived usefulness, etc.

2.4 Phase 4

When working prototypes are available that are suitable for testing outside of the lab, extended field trials will be organised. In these field trials, end users will test the prototypes for a certain amount of time in their own contexts, for their own tasks. During the field trials, information about the user experience, usability issues, etc. will be collected by using diaries and by doing contextual inquiries. Both before and after the trial period, performance tests will be done to be able to assess whether the prototypes have improved end users' task performance. In addition to the automatic logging of the users' tasks performance, interviews through several types of questionnaires will be planned to collect extensive feedback on the final prototypes.

3 In Practice

This integrated and holistic UCD model will now be applied in three distinct evaluation iterations: (a) Initial concept testing (using simulation and storyboarding) with end users and other related stakeholders (UCD phase 2); (b) Creation of tentative content and user interfaces for initial baseline testing; and (c) Full testing and trialling of the demonstrators and applications by end users and experts (UCD phase 3 and 4). The UCD methodology was structured across all project phases to follow the modelled needs of people with disabilities, elderly and developers and the user interaction elements in using rich applications of mainstream ICT. The UCD methodology used for eliciting AT/AAC features and functionality within ÆGIS is heuristics-based, and will ensure that the different stakeholders are able to express their own priorities both with regard to which prototypes/products they would most like to see developed but also within that what these products should be capable of doing for them. More specifically, 3 specific phases can be identified: the design, development and assessment phase. Design (UCD phase 2): Defining some essential functionality and feel for each prototype on each platform. Development: Initial concept testing with users (using simulation or storyboarding to "set the scene") and creating some tentative content & user interfaces for initial user testing (UCD phase 3). Assessment: Testing & trialling the prototype demonstrators at recognised AT end user Centres (UCD phase 3 and 4).

3.1 Design

To apply UCD, a thorough understanding is needed of the targeted end-users. In the context of the project, end-users were identified as illustrated in Figure 1.

The analysis of the target groups was important since it guided the field studies with more than 160 end-users and experts which were undertaken via questionnaires and interviews in Sweden, UK, Belgium and Spain. The questionnaires were specifically adjusted to the targeted end-user, whether s/he was a person with a disability, or an expert user (expert, tutor, developer). During this phase, valid information about the context of use of ICT-based products and services was collected. The collected data provided the basis for prioritising user requirements for system and accessibility –oriented innovations.

The questionnaires and interviews covered various types of ICT applications, and identified misallocation of functions between users and existing mainstream technology (i.e. identify cases where a human skill is not used properly), and elucidated the different viewpoints and individuality among the current user base of ICT.

In order to bridge the outcomes of these field studies with the next stage of the ÆGIS user-centred approach, namely the creation of alternative accessibility solutions, user requirements were specified and modelled. A method to make information from user research more appropriate for use by designers is the design of personas [1]. This involves the creation of fictitious characters, built on user research data, which represent the most important user groups. The benefit of using specific characters is that they give the designers a more concrete item to work with. A concrete person is easier to focus on than user profiles or just all information about the users. The purpose of creating the persona is to get insight into the users and create empathy for them. It is also ideal for communicating this to all stakeholders in the organisations involved in creating a new application. It assures that everyone always has a reference to the same user.

To make these personas more concrete user scenarios [2] will be defined. Such scenarios are stories about a persona or more personas and their activities. It emphasises the goals users wants to reach with a specific product. Next to this, a scenario also describes the persons' expectations concerning a particular system, the most critical task(s) that s/he wants to execute, which task s/he executes frequently, etc. Each scenario will contain at least one actor and one goal. Within this task, it is also important to integrate the users' requirements model with the corresponding stakeholders' requirements model and combine them into one integrated model.

Based on the personas, user scenarios and user requirements, one or more conceptual model(s) are developed. A conceptual model is a translation of a number of integrated ideas and concepts about how a system should look like and what its functionalities should be for the end-user. In other words, it specifies the specific design of a

User Groups	Subgroups (1)	Limitations	Sub-groups (2)	Sub-groups (3)	Effects on activity	ICF code
People with disabilities & elderly	1. Blind and low-vision users	Vision limitations or other visual limitations	1.a Partly sighted	1.a1 Slight or moderate limitations (visual acuity, slow accommodation, etc)	Difficulties in reading (font size, contrast), identifying images.	b2100, b2101, b21020, b21021, b21022, b21023
				1.a2 Limited sight angle	Reduction of the peripheral vision (upper and lower)	
				1.a3 Limited color vision	Difficulties in the colour perception	
			1.b Fully blind		Communicating with - receiving – non-verbal messages (gestures, symbols and drawings). Use of screen readers and other assistive technologies.	
	2. Motor impairment users (Upper limbs)	Limitations in motion or strength or coordination or anthropometric limitations of upper limbs. Includes tetraplegic, hemiplegic, one-handed user, co-ordination and balance disorders, and varying degrees of neuromuscular impediment	2.a Dexterity difficulties or slight restriction on arms or hands		Difficulty in pressing keys, or requirements of accuracy in interacting with interfaces (screen, mouse, etc).	b750, b755, b760, b765, b780
			2.b Moderate restriction on hand use		Difficulty in pressing keys, or requirements of accuracy in interacting with interfaces (screen, mouse, etc).	
			2.c Severe or complete restriction on hand use		Difficulty or impossibility in pressing keys, or requirements of accuracy in interacting with interfaces (screen, mouse, etc). Needs of alternative ways of interaction: speech recognition, eyes, head mouse, etc	
	3. Cognitive impairment users / learning difficulties	Cognitive limitations in operating and performing tasks, learning, comprehension, adaptive behaviour and social skills. Includes Down Syndrome, Autism, Cerebral Palsy, Brain Injury and Alzheimer	3.a Slight cognitive limitation and low support need		Limitations in information processing, tasks organization, development, operating new technologies, moving on complex environments, limitations in short-term-memory, concentrating, learning, difficulties in use of language, recognition of signs and symbol	b117, b122, b140, b144, b160, b164, b172
			3.b Moderate and severe cognitive limitation and medium and high support need		Limitations in information processing, tasks organization, development, operating new technologies, moving on complex environments, limitations in short-term-memory, concentrating, learning, difficulties in use of language, recognition of signs and symbol	

Fig. 1. Identified end-users categories

User Groups	Subgroups (1)	Limitations	Sub-groups (2)	Sub-groups (3)	Effects on activity	ICF code
	4. Hearing impairment users	Hearing limitations or other audio limitations	4.a Slight or moderate limitation		Difficulties in hearing vocal information, audible signs, warning messages, etc	b230
			4.b Severe limitation or total deafness		No hearing vocal information, audible signs, warning messages, and sometimes in understanding verbal language	
	5. Speech / Communication impairment users	Limitations in speaking and conversation and sometimes in understanding verbal language	5.a Aphasia, loss of the ability to produce and/or comprehend language	5.a1 Slight and moderate comprehension and/or production difficulties	Difficulties in comprehension (simplified language, may need symbol/spoken support) and/or in production (simple cues to aid listeners and systems to assist communication)	b167
				5.a2 Severe and complete comprehension and/or production difficulties	Difficulties in comprehension (Symbolic communication and alternative methods) and/or in production (Alternative artificial speech alternatives)	
			5.b Stuttering & Dysarthria -motor speech disorder resulting from neurological injury, characterised by poor articulation.	5.b1 Slight and moderate	Slight and moderate difficulties in articulation. Use of augmentative systems and simple cues to aid listeners	b310, b320, b330
				5.b2 Severe and complete	Severe and complete difficulties in articulation. Use of artificial speech alternatives (only a few words discernible or cannot articulate)	
Developers	6. AT developers/experts					
	7. Mainstream software developers/experts					
	8. OS developers					
	9. Web application developers					
	10. Desktop developers					
	11. Mobile application developers					
	12. Accessibility assessors					

Fig. 1. (*continued*)

prototype based on the user and task analysis. In order to be able to develop a suitable (and useful) conceptual model, one needs to look at the icons and metaphors to use and at the mental models (which attempts to describe the structure of the mental representations that people use for everyday reasoning and problem solving) of the application that the users have built. This type of model is not supposed to be very detailed, but in the end the basic principles of the product must be present and clear.

The collected data are then transformed into distinct use cases [3] and application scenarios with reference to the different applications, environments and contexts (desktop accessibility, web application accessibility, cell phone and PDA accessibility). This involves the previously identified user groups. Based on the conceptual models, the corresponding use cases will be built, translating the model into a "description of sequences of events that, taken together, lead to a system doing something useful" [4]. Developing use cases is a joint task between users, usability engineers and software engineers. Therefore use cases should be understandable to end users and correspond with their idea of the application, while being concrete and task-oriented enough for software engineers to technically design and implement the application. Thus they will be iteratively evaluated by end-users via e.g. user workshops and dedicated user focus groups that will take place in each of the pilot testing sites (Sweden, UK, Belgium, Spain). These local national workshops aim at a better understanding of the user and organisational requirements, and at discussing and agreeing the details of the intended context of use. Participants range from end –users and their respective national representative organisations to product providers, managers, developers, marketing specialists, and evaluation specialists). These workshops will be used to validate the draft use cases and application scenarios.

After the needed fine-tuning the use cases will be finalised and captured into Unified Modelling Language (UML), for uptake by the developing workpackages. As proven successful already in previous projects (such as ASK-IT – IST-2003-511298, OASIS – IST-2007-215754), a methodology will be applied that provides a use cases model which is comprised of use cases descriptions and use cases diagrams. The description will contain actors/users, scope, preconditions, stakeholders elements, and the specific user scenarios in ÆGIS. For each use case a use case diagram will be designed, to graphically represent them, using UML. Subsequently, a pan-European workshop, gathering stakeholders and end-user groups is organised to review the use cases and scenarios, and gather feedback in order to adjust and finalise them.

3.2 Development

To achieve an on-going and practicable dialogue with the system developers during the embryonic development process, the project will work closely with a few experienced end users of AT/AAC products and their support teams. While they are small in number and pre-selected according to specific disability and level of AT experience (in order to be more effective contributors to the field work), they represent a good cross-section of the client group.

UCD in the context of AT/AAC prototype development places the end user, user organisations and support teams at the fulcrum of the design and testing process. This is essential for a genuinely iterative approach to AT/AAC design and will be strictly followed within ÆGIS.

Work starts by gathering the commitment of all concerned in the development process to the user-centred design philosophy, and to achieve consensus on the plan whereby there is ample time and opportunity for engaging in user requirements elicitation and testing as well as more technical aspects of development. Consensus needs to be gained also among the design and development teams (a) that active user involvement in the project is not simply at the end, (b) that user involvement in this project is a particularly challenging priority due to the extremely diverse nature of the target user audience and the inclusion goal, and (c) that everything users see, hear and touch shall be designed together, by a multidisciplinary team.

A UCD Implementation Plan will be the outcome, specifying how much iteration will be carried out and timelines for each, as well as when each method should be used, taking into account the budget, timescales, resources, skills and other constrains. A range of UCD principles and tried and tested interview tools will be included in the UCD Implementation Plan, drawing experience from previous UCD projects, such as PCAD (TIDE Project No. 3211 DE), WWAAC (IST-2000- 27518), and most recently COGAIN (IST-2003-5115). This Plan shall be a working document, which is first produced in outline terms and which is then reviewed, maintained, extended and updated during the design, development and assessment process.

First low-end prototypes (or mock-ups of the system) are considered as being good enough to evaluate the overall structure of the interface of the application and the products user-friendliness. Experts or end-users work (walk) through scenarios on the system while a facilitator shuffles the screens. The usability of such prototypes can be investigated with expert evaluations, user tests or a combination of both methods. During the expert test and user evaluation real usability problems will be investigated and listed up, ordered by priority and will be recommended to fix those problems.

3.3 Assessment

The project will ensure that representatives from all impaired end users as well as developers open source communities are actively and centrally engaged in ÆGIS' mission statement to provide "accessibility (that is) open, plug and play, personalised and configurable", including a focus on young, socially excluded impaired users and their hinterland of AT infrastructural support (facilitators, families, AT professionals and AT developers), as well as elderly and people who are not familiar with technology.

Relevant end-user partners will be vigilant through the various project phases, leading to the demonstration of applications and devices, so as "to be true to what they are" from an end user perspective. The accessible mainstream consumer products (desktop environment, web applications, new access tools, and mobile devices) will be thoroughly tested by strong cohorts of end users (over 160), experts (over 80) and developers (over 20) in the 4 sites across Europe. They will be engaged through focus groups, questionnaires, interviews and workshops, and actual testing to ensure that the promise of a "seamless integration of personalised assistive solutions for ICT access" is clearly met, fully matching the end-users' needs.

4 Conclusion

The UCD methodology and practical implementation as presented in the previous, heralds the full involvement of end-users in the ÆGIS project, thus ensures a fully user driven approach. The resulting project outcomes should as such accommodate at the highest extent the needs of end-users (persons with various disabilities and developers), and should set the path for further in-depth user involvement for any other projects that aim at having the end-user at the core of their development.

References

1. Pruitt, J., Adlin, T.: The persona lifecycle - Keeping people in mind throughout product design. Morgan Kaufmann Publishers, San Fransisco (2006)
2. Rosson, M.B., Carroll, J.M.: Usability engineering - scenario-based development of human-computer interaction. Morgan Kaufmann Publishers, San Fransisco (2002)
3. Overgaard, G., Palmkvist, K.: Use cases - patterns and blueprints. Addison Wesley Publishers, Reading (2005)
4. Bittner, K., Spence, I.: Use Case Modelling, pp. 2–3. Addison Wesley Professional, Reading (2002)
5. Annex, I.: Description of Work, Open Accessibility Everywhere: Groundwork, Infrastructure, Standards (ÆGIS). In: 7th FW, ICT-2007.7.1, ICT & Ageing, September 11 (2008)

Part II

Older Users and Technology

Lessons Learned from Developing Cognitive Support for Communication, Entertainment, and Creativity for Older People with Dementia

Norman Alm[1], Arlene Astell[2], Gary Gowans[3], Richard Dye[1], Maggie Ellis[2], Phillip Vaughan[3], and Philippa Riley[1]

[1] School of Computing, University of Dundee, Dundee, UK
[2] School of Psychology, University of St Andrews, St Andrews, Fife, UK
[3] School of Design, Duncan of Jordanstone College of Art and Design, University of Dundee, Dundee, UK
{nalm,g.m.gowans,r.dye,p.b.vaughan,p.j.riley}@dundee.ac.uk
{aja3,mpe2}@st-andrews.ac.uk

Abstract. We have developed cognitive support for people with dementia in three areas of activity : communication, entertainment and creativity. In each case the cognitive support was intended to in some way replace an effective working memory. With all three projects our findings have been a mix of expected results and surprises. We are still working out the implications of some of the surprising results. In this paper we set out some key findings from each of these projects, and the lessons learned.

Keywords: Dementia, cognitive prostheses, assistive technology, multimedia, multidisciplinary working.

1 Introduction

The increase in the numbers of people who have dementia is tied to the remarkable demographic shift which is taking place in most places in the world, with the proportion of older people in the population increasing at such a rate that the 'population pyramid' is in the process of inverting. The incidence of dementia increases from about 2% of those in their 60s to 33% or more of those in their 90s [1]. Dementia in older people involves the loss of cognitive abilities, in particular the use of working (short-term) memory. Without an operating working memory, many activities become problematic, including conversation, entertainment, and being creative. A cure for dementia still seems a considerable distance in the future. Until a way to reverse the effects of dementia can be found it is essential to maximise the quality of life of those who have the condition. The treatment of people with dementia has increasingly focused on keeping the personhood those who have dementia in the foreground, emphasising their positive capacities and looking for non-pharmacological approaches to helping them [2,3].

We have developed a number of computer-based systems to provide cognitive support for older people with dementia. Developing these systems has produced a number

C. Stephanidis (Ed.): Universal Access in HCI, Part I, HCII 2009, LNCS 5614, pp. 195–201, 2009.
© Springer-Verlag Berlin Heidelberg 2009

of findings, some of which were more or less expected, and a number of which were quite unexpected results.

2   A System to Support Communication

We have recently completed the development and evaluation of a computer-based communication support system which can assist older people with dementia to carry out conversations. Without an effective working memory, ordinary conversation becomes impossible. Long-term memory, however, can remain relatively well-preserved, so conversations based on reminiscence are possible, if long term memories can be prompted

Our system, called CIRCA, stimulates long term memories by providing the person with dementia and a carer with a touchscreen based hypermedia presentation of material from the past : photos, music, video clips, graphics and text, all accessible in a flexible and engaging manner. Using this system allows people with dementia to once again have a conversation on a more equal basis with relatives and carers. In evaluations the system was acceptable, and positively received by both staff and people with dementia, and people with dementia were able to take more control of the interaction than they could in reminiscence sessions run in the traditional way [4,5].

The system was developed a multidisciplinary team of software engineers, psychologists, and designers. Potential users and their families and professional carers were involved throughout the design process.

A number of design features have emerged from this work which are particularly important in systems which are to be used by people with dementia. Touchscreens are usable by this population, despite their unfamiliarity, whereas other forms of computer input would not be suitable. The interface was simple and uncluttered enough so as not to overwhelm the person with too much detail, while remaining interesting and engaging. Aesthetic considerations in the interface design were very important, in order to achieve engagement from a group with whom this can be problematic. If there is a rich enough selection of media items, we have found that long-term memories can be stimulated which are new to relatives and carers, and which might have remained unavailable without the prompting of a system such as this.

Some of the lessons learned from this project :

1. The importance of multidisciplinary working
It took equal contributions from all three disciplines : software engineering, psychology, and design to make this project a success. It was also important that such a disparate team worked cohesively. One practice that strengthened this was that contributions about all aspects of the project were welcomed from all members of the team, regardless of their home discipline. Given this approach, all team members learned a great deal throughout the project about the other aspects of the problem we were working on.

2. The key effect of aesthetics in interface design
We knew from the start that it would be important to engage and hold the attention of people with dementia, and the aesthetic aspect of he design was an important contributor to this. In addition the motivation to take part from the carers was

increased by the feeling that a great deal of thought and expertise had obviously gone into the interface they worked with.

3. The discovery that there was no need for personal material to trigger personal recollections

We had originally intended to create both a generic and personalised versions of CIRCA, but we found that the general version did an excellent job of eliciting personal recollections. In fact recounting personal recollections was all that the person with dementia could do. Also, we found that if the material was varied and rich enough, memories were triggered which none of the carers or relatives had heard before, which was a surprising and welcome bonus.

3 An Interactive Entertainment System

Finding ways to engage people with dementia in stimulating but safe activities on their own would be beneficial both to them and to their caregivers. The CIRCA project demonstrated that a simple but carefully designed computer-based touch screen interface can capture and hold the attention of people with dementia who are normally difficult to engage. With CIRCA, people with dementia used the system together with a caregiver to provide a shared activity. We are now developing a similar hypermedia system to be used alone by a person with dementia without caregiver assistance. The system is intended to focus on the 'living in the moment' state of people with dementia and make the most of their preserved skills. At the same time, the system will compensate for diminished abilities, such as working memory. We have piloted a number of virtual environments and activities and reported the results of this work [6,7].

Evaluation of three initial virtual reality environments by a group of dementia care professionals and a group of people with a diagnosis of dementia was positive and provided useful feedback for the initial development of the project. Of particular interest were the comments relating to the engaging properties of the stimuli. The dementia care professionals directly commented on the way the system captured attention and provided an engaging experience. These observations were further supported by the comments of the users with a diagnosis of dementia, who were able to imagine themselves in the environments, for example sitting on a bench in the botanic garden or having a pint of beer in the pub environment.

We then developed a wide range of virtual activities to try out with potential users. These included :

1. Short video clip presentations of activities, e.g. playing with a dog
2. Exploring environments, e.g. the Botanical Gardens
3. Creative activities, e.g. painting a virtual pot
4. Sport activities, e.g. bowling
5. Fair ground activities, e.g. coconut shy
6. Amusement arcade type games, e.g. pinball

We experimented with prompting methods, including spoken prompts with synthetic speech and real speech and text boxes.

Some of the lessons learned from this project :

1. Engagement is achieved through interactivity and not just passive appreciation
We had expected that some very beautiful and interesting virtual environments to explore would have been positively received. As a group activity and as a demo carried out by a researcher, these worked, but as a single unsupported activity, the users soon lost the thread of what they were supposed to be doing. Just 'having a look around' did not have enough structure to keep them engaged. On the other hand we were surprised at the impact that some very simple games had, as long as they required constant interaction. In this way the interaction itself acted as a kind of prompt.

2. Minimal prompting was needed
We planned to provide a range of prompts, from simple text boxes and voice prompts to having an avatar on the screen to guide the user. We discovered that spoken prompts and text boxes worked very well, and there was no need for the possible intrusive presence of an avatar. One unresolved issue was how best to deploy the text boxes, in particular how long to wait with the user not doing anything before prompting them. This will need further experimentation.

3. Having a 'mastery' aspect to activities was helpful even for people with working memory problems
This is one finding that was quite puzzling, and which definitely merits more investigation. We found that users would stick at a task that required mastery (e.g. the coconut shy game), trying very hard, and succeeding, in getting better at it, over a surprisingly long period of time (20 minutes or so). This seemed to require a degree of working memory usage that was surprising, given their condition. We speculate that the game may be helping them in some way to access procedural memory, which can be more persistent. But this requires a closer look.

4   System to Promote Creativity

Supporting communication and entertainment for people with dementia has involved considerable challenges. An even more ambitious aim would be to help people with dementia to be creative. We have begun to explore this possibility, beginning with a system to support the creation of original music.

It has been known for some time that music can be experienced and enjoyed by people with dementia, and recent research suggests this is evident even in the latter stages of the condition [8]. However, without a specialist music therapist present musical activities provided by caregivers tend to be passive , i.e. listening to music or to others singing. Where music therapists are available to provide active music making sessions for people with dementia, therapists often opt for simple percussion instruments for basic rhythm making [9]. This is because the use of traditional musical instruments for this group would be impractical : the symptoms of the condition make it difficult to learn to play such an instrument, and playing musical instruments successfully requires considerable prior training. Thus, although there are recognised benefits associated with the provision of musical activities, caregivers lack resources for them to support active music making sessions for people with dementia.

This project explored developing a system that could enable people with dementia to be creative with music-making, whether their skills were pre-existing or not. The system was intended to provide an engaging and enjoyable activity for those participating, with the added potential to increase social interactions if used in pairs or groups.

We have now developed a touchscreen based system called ExpressPlay that addresses the following requirements:

- Is easy and intuitive to use
- Plays music instantly, i.e. providing one-touch feedback
- Allows users to express themselves creatively
- Can be used on a one-to-one basis with a carer, or alone
- Does not require a prior knowledge of music

Music making is a pastime generally limited to people who have mastered playing an instrument. However, it is possible to use chords as a means of playing pleasant-sounding music regardless of prior musical knowledge. A chord is a set of three or more notes that are played simultaneously, and are usually the first, third and fifth notes taken from a musical scale. Any chord can follow another and usually sound reasonable. In Western culture we use chords that are split into two categories – major and minor - and this is an important way of giving an emotional effect to any music. Major chords are generally used to portray a happy, active mood, and minor chords, a melancholy or sad mood. This portrayal of emotion is recognisable within the culture regardless of musical training. Given the above, it would seem plausible that the system could be developed for people with dementia to not only do creative music making, but also as a way for them to express emotion.

We therefore decided to develop an initial system that could allow people with dementia to play music specific to three moods (happy, contemplative and angry). The design has an uncomplicated navigation system with a simple interface. Music is produced by the user dragging their finger around the touchscreen. Choices are kept to a minimum in order that users not become confused. Visual feedback is provided instantly during music play to help individuals with severe short-term memory loss to remain engaged while using the system [10].

Some of the lessons learned from this project :

1. Engagement was achieved to a high degree
   Users engaged for long periods of time with the system, whether the output they were creating was simple or complex. We were intrigued in particular to see users who were in fact producing very simple, minimal patterns locked in concentration for extended periods.

2. The system facilitated very individualized expression
   We logged the usage of the system and tracked all the finger movements on the touchscreen. The patterns of movement around the screen varied considerably from person to person, leaving a visual record that each person had an identifiable 'signature style' in expression.

3. Next we need to try other sound outputs to create more 'failure free' aesthetically pleasing results

The initial prototype had three different sound themes, which we intended to roughly suggest happy, contemplative, and angry moods. The 'angry tool' consisted of discords, and while a number of users enjoyed banging these out, most did not like it. Having established that we can achieve engagement and individual expression, we would like to experiment further to find ways that the system could always be relied on to produce aesthetically pleasing output as well.

5 Conclusions

Our work to provide cognitive support for people with dementia has thus far covered three areas of activity : communication, entertainment and creativity. In each case the cognitive support was intended to in some way replace an effective working memory. In the communication system, the system took over the executive function of guiding the user towards their relatively intact long-term memories. With the entertainment and creativity systems, the system supplied a visual and auditory scaffolding to prompt the user through the activity. We have focused on activities which relate to the social and expressive aspects of life, and hope this work can complement research into ways of supporting daily routines, in order to achieve a better quality of life for people with dementia, and their carers. The work is still in a relatively new area, and the findings so far have been a mixture of expected results and surprises, as is the nature of exploratory research. We plan to take all these projects further, and to follow up what seem to be the successful pathways towards supporting people with dementia and their carers in enjoying themselves, in addition to carrying out daily tasks.

Acknowledgments. This work was supported by three separate grants from the UK Engineering and Physical Sciences Research Council, and grants from The Royal Society of Edinburgh, Tenovus, and the Alzheimer's Research Trust.

References

1. Jorm, A.F., Korten, A.E., Henderson, A.S.: The prevalence of dementia: a quantitative integration of the literature. Acta Psychiatrica Scandinavica 76, 465–479 (1987)
2. Feil, N.: The Validation Breakthrough: Simple Techniques for Communicating with People with Alzheimer's-Type Dementia. Health Professions Press, New York (2002)
3. Kitwood, T.: Toward a theory of dementia care: Ethics and interaction. The Journal of Clinical Ethics 9(1), 23–34 (1998)
4. Alm, N., Dobinson, L., Massie, P., Hewines, I.: Computers as cognitive assistants for elderly people. In: Hirose, M. (ed.) Human-Computer Interaction - INTERACT 2001, pp. 692–693. IOS Press, Amsterdam (2001)
5. Alm, N., Dye, R., Gowans, G., Campbell, J., Astell, A., Ellis, M.: A communication support system for older people with dementia. IEEE Computer 40(5), 35–41 (2007)
6. Gowans, G., Dye, R., Alm, N., Vaughan, P., Astell, A., Ellis, M.: Designing the interface between dementia patients, caregivers and computer-based intervention. The Design Journal 10(1), 12–23 (2007)

7. Alm, N., Dye, R., Astell, A., Ellis, M., Gowans, G., Campbell, J.: Making software accessible for users with dementia. In: Lazar, J. (ed.) Universal Usability: Designing Computer Interfaces for Diverse Users, pp. 299–316. Wiley, New York (2007)
8. Clair, A.A., Mathews, R.M., Kosloski, K.: Assessment of active music participation as an indication of subsequent music making engagement for persons with midstage dementia. American Journal of Alzheimer's Disease and Other Dementias 20(1), 37–40 (2005)
9. Aldridge, D.: Dialogic-degenerative diseases and health as a performed aesthetic. In: Aldridge, D. (ed.) Music Therapy and Neurological Rehabilitation: Performing Health, pp. 39–60. Jessica Kingsley Publishers, London (2005)
10. Riley, P.J., Alm, N., Newell, A.F.: An interactive tool to support musical creativity in people with dementia. Journal of Computers in Human Behaviour (in Press)

The OASIS Concept

Evangelos Bekiaris[1] and Silvio Bonfiglio[2]

[1] Centre for Research and Technology Hellas, Hellenic Institute of Transport,
Thessaloniki, Greece
abek@certh.gr
[2] PHILIPS FIMI, Saronno, Italy
silvio.bonfiglio@philips.com

Abstract. OASIS is an Integrated Project with the aim to revolutionise the interoperability, quality, breadth and usability of services for all daily activities of the elderly, by developing and deploying innovative technological challenges, consisting of a new, open architecture and a hyper-ontological framework. A wide range of applications are integrated in the areas of independent living, socialization, autonomous mobility and smart workplaces. User friendliness and acceptability of OASIS services are a top priority of the project, ensured with a user-centered design approach and the development of interactive services.

Keywords: ontological framework, elderly users, independent living, autonomous mobility, smart workplaces.

1 Introduction to OASIS

OASIS is and Integrated Project that started in 2008. It is co-financed by the EC (7th FP) and encompasses 33 complementary partners (from 12 countries), addressing a very wide technological area (semantic web, knowledge representation, transport, tourism, health, domotics, UI design, e-Learning, e-Work, etc.), including leading industrial partners, multidisciplinary and strong research teams, including academic participation.

The project aims at an open and innovative reference architecture, based upon ontologies and semantic services, that will allow plug and play and cost-effective interconnection of existing and new services in all domains required for the independent and autonomous living of the elderly and their Quality of Life enhancement. Both the open reference architecture and the related tools will be made available as open source.

The OASIS System is open, modular, holistic, easy to use and standards abiding. It includes a set of novel tools for content/services connection and management, for user interfaces creation and adaptation and for service personalization and integration. Through this new Architecture, over 12 different types of services are connected with the OASIS System for the benefit of the elderly, covering user needs and wants in terms of Independent Living Applications, Autonomous Mobility and Smart Workplaces Applications. In detail, the following applications are foreseen within OASIS:

C. Stephanidis (Ed.): Universal Access in HCI, Part I, HCII 2009, LNCS 5614, pp. 202–209, 2009.

A. Independent Living Applications:

- nutritional advisor,
- activity coach,
- brain and skills trainers,
- social communities platform,
- health monitoring and environmental control.

B.   Autonomous Mobility and Smart Workplaces Applications

- elderly-friendly transport information services,
- elderly-friendly route guidance,
- personal mobility services,
- mobile devices,
- biometric authentication interface and multimodal dialogue mitigation and other smart workplace applications.

Applications are all integrated as a unified, dynamic service batch, managed by the OASIS Service Centre and supporting all types of mobile devices (tablet PC, PDA, smartphone, automotive device, ITV, infokiosk, etc.) and all types of environments (living labs, sheltered homes, private homes, two car demonstrators, public transport, etc.) in 4 Pilot sites Europewide. As user friendliness and acceptability is a top priority for the project, a user-centered-design approach is followed along the service and application development.

2 The Relevant Need

Age and disability are strongly correlated: 15% of the EU population has a disability; 70% of them will be over 60 by 2020.

There exist two main trends in the 21 century. One is the rapid development of ICT, which has affected all areas of life of people and radically changed the way-people live and tackle many activities. People have entered into digital times. The other is the trend of aging population, which has attracted attention from government as well as business firms. Potential business opportunities exist exactly at the crossing point of these two trends.

The older population is growing at a considerably faster rate than that of the world's total population. In absolute terms, the number of older persons has tripled over the last 50 years and will more than triple again over the next 50-year period. In relative terms, the percentage of older persons is projected to more than double worldwide over the next half century, to expand by more than three times, to reach nearly 2 billion, in 2050.

This rapid expansion in the older population affects practically all regions of the world and is increasing. Currently, the annual growth of the older population (1.9%) is significantly higher than that of the total population (1.02%). In the near future, the difference between those two rates is expected to become even larger, as the baby boom generation starts ageing in many parts of the world, including Europe. By

2025-2030, projections indicate that the population over 60 will be growing 3.5 times as rapidly as the total population (2.8% compared to 0.8%). Even though the growth rate of the over 60s age group is expected to decline to 1.6% in 2045-2050, it will still be more than 3 times the growth rate of the total population (0.5%) by mid century (see Figure 1). Below, the needs of the elderly population for specific areas is presented, together with OASIS plans and objectives in order to overcome them (United Nations).

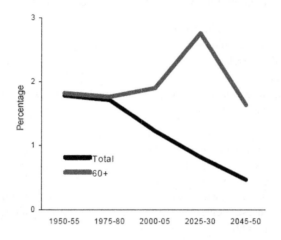

Fig. 1. Average annual growth rate of total population aged 60 or over, world, 1950-2050 (United Nations)

2.1 ICT and the Elderly

The profound, pervasive and enduring consequences of ageing population present enormous challenges as well as enormous opportunities for Information and Communication Technology. A typical example is the Internet that – according to many analysts – has become an enabler of social inclusion.

Social isolation is a common problem for senior people. Fortunately, the Internet offers new tools to address the problem. Internet users acknowledge that going on line is a good and convenient way to contact the outside world. Senior people can walk out of loneliness, through sending e-mails to family members and friends all over the world, chatting in forums to exchange feelings and ideas, etc. Indeed, many senior people are already benefiting from the Internet.

OASIS aims to utilise ICT and other key technologies in order to provide holistic services to the elderly to support their physical and psychological independence, stimulate their social or psychological engagement and foster their emotional well being. In doing so, OASIS thus addresses key areas of their activities encompassing: independent living and socialising, autonomous mobility, and flexible work-ability.

Table 1. Internet users in 2002 and 2005

Internet Users in 2002	18-29	30-49	50-64	65+	Internet Users in 2005	18-29	30-49	50-64	65+
	%	%	%	%		%	%	%	%
Canada	86	80	62	23	Canada	91	83	68	31
Germany	81	62	33	9	Germany	85	79	53	16
US	80	78	56	20	US	81	83	68	32
UK	72	63	30	10	UK	89	84	67	24
France	71	53	30	5	France	92	66	52	12
Poland	46	21	9	0	Poland	70	44	22	4
Russia	17	6	3	0	Russia	32	18	3	1

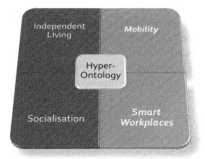

Fig. 2. OASIS targeted domains

3 OASIS Technological Developments

The following developments have already started in the project, aiming to assist the elderly users:

- A new Architectural Framework, called "COF-Common Ontological Framework" or "OASIS hyper-ontology", based upon the Common Algebraic Specification Language (CASL) of IFIP WG1.3 (Foundations of System Specification). The hyper-ontology is open, modular, holistic, easy-to-use and standards-abiding and allows the interoperability, seamless connectivity and sharing of content between not only single services but also competing ontologies of the same or different application domains.
- An Open Reference Architecture (also called 'OASIS Platform'), composed by the COF and its support tools (Content Connector Module-CCM and other ontology management modules), both available as open source, that allow the automatic or semi-automatic connection of existing and emerging ontologies and services to the OASIS Architectural Framework.

- The OASIS System, composed of the new Open Reference Architecture, enriched by an AmI Framework (a multi-Agents platform) and the Interaction Platform (allowing automatic UI self-creation for new connected services and self adaptation to the device used, the context of use and the user needs and preferences).
- A wide range of connected applications (over 12 different service types), all integrated within the OASIS System, and interoperating in integrated scenarios and Use Cases, covering the needs of the elderly and their caregivers in terms of Independent Living, Socialisation, Autonomous Mobility and Smart Workplaces.
- A Pilots test-bed, consisting of 4 sites Europewide and all potential test environments per site: Living Labs for technical verification and iterative development, Sheltered Homes for assisted living and user communities related real-world applications and Independent Living, namely private homes, for real world applications.

Thus, the OASIS system consists of the reference architecture, the Ambient Intelligence Framework and the Interaction Platform.

System efficiency and user acceptance are expected to increase through the development of a self-learning and adapting system to interactions, effective computing principles, models of human behaviour and human activity recognition, the flexibility of new mobile paradigms and devices, ontologies for sharing of contextual information between different services and objects and 3D based multi-media interaction systems and virtual community technologies, with appropriate privacy and ethical safeguards.

4 OASIS Interaction Principle

To facilitate the development of interactive services, the project will develop an interaction prototyping tool that will enable designers and developers to base interaction, accessibility and self-adaptation (user and context oriented) design on the semantic models in the Hyper-Ontology.

This tool will facilitate the connection of application task models (i.e., services) with accessibility solutions and adaptivity. Specifically, it will enable interaction designers to: create rough interaction models; connect user activity to monitoring; identify transformations and inferences leading from monitored data to (updates in) the dynamic models; encapsulate preliminary adaptation logic and effects; specify how adaptations are effected in the interactive front-end. In more detail, this tool allows the following very innovative functionalities:

a. Self-adaptation of interface to the specific device (device abstraction and device oriented customisation).
b. Self-adaptation of interface, to include new or modified applications (application and adaptation logic).
c. Self-adaptation of interface to the specific elderly needs, preferences and dynamically updated profile, according to his/her behaviour and services use pattern (user modelling and user oriented adaptability).
d. Self-adaptation of interface to the context of use, such as home, car, street, bus, etc. (context modelling and context oriented adaptability).

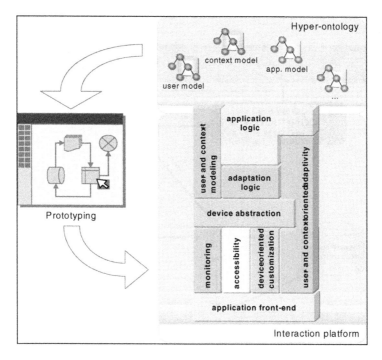

Fig. 3. Interaction platform of OASIS, to connect the hyper-ontology with the mobile devices

The output of the prototyping tool will be such as to facilitate further development of the interfaces, while preserving the possibility for full-cycle re-engineering of the modified output.

Also, an Ambient Intelligence (AMI) framework is developed, as key enabler of the project development platform, based upon a family of intelligent agents, to orchestrate, monitor, personalise and deliver the integrated services. The customization of devices according to own needs and preferences is facilitated by its AMI framework. Its architecture is shown below, where it can be clearly seen that the user personal AmI space relates directly to the user-computer interaction, through the various possible end-user devices supported by the OASIS platform.

Several sensors are being connected as part of the developed services, consisting of unobtrusive wireless acceleration sensor (for recognition of the type of movement if the elderly user, e.g. walking, sitting, climbing upstairs), physiological sensors (for accidents detection), wearable biometric and in-home positioning sensors (for health monitoring), ultrasound and radio-based localisation sensors (for in-door localisation), etc. The overall multisensorial platform architecture, showing their connection to OASIS hyperontology and its interface to the applications, is presented in the following figure.

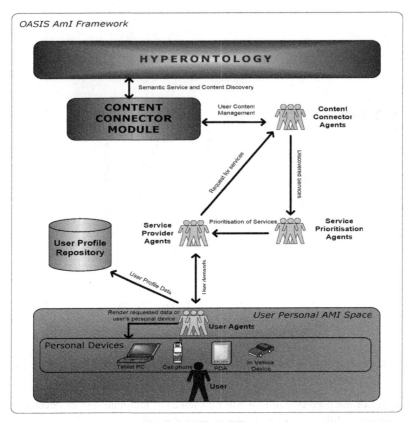

Fig. 4. OASIS AMI Framework

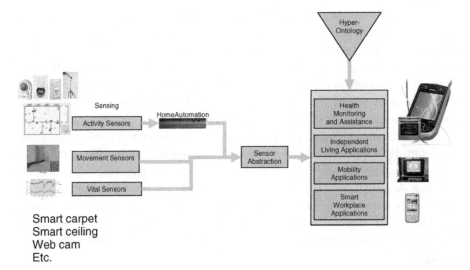

Fig. 5. OASIS multi-sensorial platform and its interface to applications

System efficiency and user acceptance are expected to increase through the development of a self-learning and adapting system to user interactions. Thus, among its goals, the following are directly relevant to the creation of an innovative and adaptive HCI concept for all types of users:

- To develop an intelligent interaction platform, to support the interaction between the user and the OASIS reference architecture, through self-adaptation of the interface layer to the type of device used (PC, tablet PC, PDA, smart phone, automotive device, infokiosk, …), the specific service layout, the context of use (i.e. at home, in the car, …) and the elderly user personal needs and preferences.
- To develop innovative multi-sensorial interface concepts, making use of visual, acoustic, haptic and even olfactoric elements and smart materials.
- To develop intelligent dialogues and interaction principles for user-system interaction seamless and concise adaptation according to the device, context of use and progressively changing user needs and preferences.

5 Conclusions

The objective of OASIS is the development of an innovative reference architecture ensuring a holistic approach to issues related to independent living and ageing. The System, which will be based on this innovative reference architecture, constitutes a complete system of sensors, content, services, devices and applications. Both the OASIS open architecture and the connected applications constitute a big step beyond the current state of the art, supporting seamless integration and plug-and-play operation of sensors, devices, sub-systems and integrated care services.

The user-centric approach of the OASIS applications, combined with their intuitive elderly-friendly design, minimises the intrusiveness of technology and offer users the opportunity to customise devices according to own needs and preferences. This customisation takes place through the user- and context- oriented adaptivity facilities of the OASIS framework and is facilitated by its AMI framework.

Eventually, the OASIS system is planned to be tested iteratively and thoroughly by hundreds of end users (in North, Central, South and East- Europe), their caregivers and other stakeholders, in order to optimize it and submit for standardization by the established OASIS world-wide Industrial Forum.

References

1. EUR 22532 Institute for prospective Technological studies European Commission User needs in ICT research for independent Living
2. OASIS Description of Work (2007)
3. Population Division, DESA, World Population Ageing 1950-2050, United Nations

Confronting the Transition: Improving Quality of Life for the Elderly with an Interactive Multisensory Environment–A Case Study

Phil Ellis and Lieselotte van Leeuwen

Faculty of Arts and Design, University of Sunderland, SR1 3PZ, UK
phil.ellis@sunderland.ac.uk

Abstract. Continuing developments in medical science are leading to a general increase in length of life. These have been accompanied by an increase in disabilities and diseases associated with ageing and the quality of life for the old and older old can be seen often to decline progressively. An interactive multisensory environment (*i*MUSE) has been developed, together with a particular methodology - vibroacoustic sound therapy – (VAST), to offer the possibility of amelioration for some of these conditions with the aim of providing the opportunity for an improvement of well-being for some elderly and older old people. This paper describes the development of this environment, its modus operandi, and concludes with a case study of an elderly frail man who provides a model for the application of *i*MUSE in care homes for the elderly frail and mentally infirm.

Keywords: elderly well being, successful ageing, multi sensory, vibroacoustic sound therapy.

1 Introduction

Across the developed world, people are living longer and life expectancy is set to continue increasing for the foreseeable future.

> '*According to the Office for National Statistics, life expectancy in the UK increased by 2.2 years during the last decade, but healthy-life expectancy increased by only 0.6 years. Death is currently preceded by about 10 years of chronic disease or disability, and this is increasing. Government health targets are contributing to this disaster by insistently targeting causes of death instead of chronic disease. This problem is one of the largest of the 21st century. If we do nothing about it, it will swallow up our health service, then our economy, and eventually ourselves. We must do something urgently to help the older old – before we join them*'. [1]

Care homes have to be run with fairly strict routines. Breakfast, lunch, tea, dinner structure the day of residents and often there are not many other meaningful or chosen activities in-between the meals. Residents feel a lack of meaning and control over their

C. Stephanidis (Ed.): Universal Access in HCI, Part I, HCII 2009, LNCS 5614, pp. 210–219, 2009.

lives, which leads to increasing dependency, lack of initiative, lethargy and depression. VAST and *i*MUSE have been specifically developed to provide a means of recovering, re-developing or retaining a sense of identity and agency through aesthetically based activities for interactive expression, communication, spontaneity and fun.

2 Conditions

Initially Vibroacoustic Sound Therapy (VAST) was developed for children with profound and multiple learning difficulties (PMLD) [2]. Following this a pilot project with the elderly was run for twelve months in 1997-8 to see whether there was potential for improving quality of life for the elderly frail and mentally infirm. Results were positive and further research and development has culminated in the development of an *i*nteractive MUltiSensory Environment (*i*MUSE), [3] within which a number of techniques have been developed and combined, resulting in a methodology – Vibroacoustic Sound Therapy [4]. The approach has been developed with elderly people with a range of conditions often associated with ageing, including stress, anxiety, depression, dementia, rheumatism and arthritis, cancer, stroke and (advanced) Alzheimer's.

3 Environment

Providing multisensory feedback for an action such as vocalization or hand movement can lead to powerful enhancement of experience. The *i*Muse environment evolved experimenting with combinations of real-time audio, tactile and visual feedback for action. When sound is created by a participant it can be heard, felt as vibration and 'seen' as changing graphical patterns.

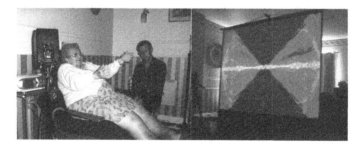

Fig. 1. A resident creating graphic displays from sound generated by hand/arm movements

The VAST room in a care home setting has a Soundchair set with two loudspeakers placed in front of the chair at around ear height. A 1.50 x1m projection screen is placed approximately two meters away from the chair. The room lighting level is kept generally quite low so that projected images are clear and distraction kept to a minimum. A Soundbeam sensor (see below) is placed beside the Soundchair. A Soundbeam controller unit, computer, sound mixer and projector are not normally visible to the participant, and these are controlled by the facilitator.

Fig. 2. The Soundchair, Soundbeam sensor, projector and computer

The Soundchair has acoustic chambers containing loudspeakers. There are three chambers corresponding to the areas of the upper body, seat and legs, a little like a three-part sun lounger. When sitting in this chair, any sound which is heard within the environment is heard and felt simultaneously in the back, seat and legs of the participant. This can reinforce the cause and effect experience and motivate further action and involvement from the participant.

The Soundbeam [5] is an unltrasonic distance sensor which is used for gestural capture. The sensor emits an ultrasonic beam. Any movement within this beam is registered by the device and converted into MIDI code, which subsequently can be used to generate any sound created in turn by a computer-based synthesizer or sampler. Large flowing movements, such as the sweep of an arm, or small movements, such as the flick of an eyelid, can be given expressive potential in this context, so enabling people with varying levels of physical disability the possibility for expression and control through movement. As any movement immediately generates a sound which corresponds to the speed and amount of the gesture, there is clear cause and effect – there is no apparent latency in the system and because the participant is sitting in a chair the field of movement is limited and therefore can easily be captured by the gesture sensor.

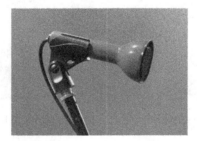

Fig. 3. The Soundbeam ultrasonic sensor

The visual output is generated in three ways: multi-coloured graphical patterns are generated from sounds made in the session using G-Force software [6]. Change of pattern shape and colour are mapped to change in pitch and amplitude of the sound, giving an immediate and intuitive sense of control. Arkaos VJ Midi software [7] is used to display pre-prepared sequences of images which can be customized for each individual. Signals (notes) from the Soundbeam change which picture is projected, and pictures can be merged and faded into each other in different ways. A third visual output is used, also utilizing Arkaos. In this, a camera is focused on the participant, and hand, arm and head movements form the basis of the projected image, which appears as a moving kaleidoscopic pattern. The colour of participant's clothing forms the colours of the projected kaleidoscope, and the feeling of control by the participant is enhanced, often resulting in intense immersion in the activity.

Fig. 4. Camera-based kaleidoscopic moving image from the participant's movements

The facilitator interacts with a participant in order to optimise the *i*MUSE environment according to individual preferences by adapting modes of inter-sensory mapping as well as types of sounds and colour schemes. On a technical level this involves operating the sound processor and Soundbeam settings and adjusting the various projection variables throughout the session.

The environment is a particular aesthetic, one in which the participant can explore and experience in a synaesthetic domain, and one in which there is no behaviour pattern more appropriate than another – everyone can find their own, most effective way of 'playing the environment'. The whole approach is dependent on technology, but is not technology led. The technology merely provides the tools, [8]. As pointed out by Strick [9]

> *'In digital media, .. music and visual art are truly united, not only by the experiencing subject, the listener/viewer, but by the artist. They are created out of the same stuff, bits of electronic information, infinitely interchangeable. ..the aspiration to novel experience created by the compounding of sensation and association has never been more possible'.*

The technology itself has to be used in a particular way, and the tools for *i*MUSE have been chosen carefully to be as open-ended as possible both in terms of operation and application. How the interaction is managed between the participant and facilitator is crucial, with the technology being as non-intrusive and as hidden from this as far as is possible.

4 Interactive Techniques

A Person-centred approach [10, 11] determines the nature of the interaction between participant and facilitator. Some interactive techniques which have been developed in VAST are reflected in the Intensive Interaction methods developed by Nind & Hewett [12].

The focus in VAST is always on the participant being active and as far as possible sharing control of any activity, and all the activities are designed to be intrinsically rewarding and motivating. The facilitator can encourage eye contact and turn taking and read and respond to facial expressions, always concentrating on and attending to the participant. It is important to accept people as they are and not to try to change them in a way which might seem better or more appropriate to an external observer. The focus is on what people WANT to do which allows us to concentrate on abilities rather than on the compensation for disability.

One fundamental feature of the approach is the phenomenon of *aesthetic resonation* [13], a fleeting state of well-being in which a feeling of 'rightness' or 'wholeness' can be experienced. These are special 'inner moments'. A combination of delight, discovery, wonder, intrigue, success, joy. External signs include spontaneous smiles, physical movements of no use – a wriggle of the shoulders – moments of arrival, actions not seen before and behaviour sometimes deemed not possible in normal life.

5 Session Structure

There are typically three parts to a VAST session :

1. Active or interactive activity centred upon use of a microphone;
2. Active or interactive activity centred upon the Soundbeam;
3. A receptive end section where the participant can 'let go' of aches and pains, anxieties and worries, and become immersed in a warm and enveloping 'bath of sound' in the Soundchair, which can often induce feelings of happiness, of soothing and care, calmness and well-being.

1. Sound is captured by a microphone and enhanced in different ways by using a sound processor. Even the quietest of sounds can be captured and subsequently given additional effect through the application of reverberation, delay patterns, and changes in pitch (pitch-shifting). Adding reverberation to sound encourages vocalization. Without this effect the tendency is to feel exposed or isolated, but adding reverberation somehow makes the sound warm and induces confidence and pleasure. Different delay patterns (echo) can induce self-confidence and sense of fun, with anticipation and turn-taking being encouraged. A pitch shifter can turn one pitch into an expanding chord, which leads to exploration, intrigue and playfulness. All vocalized sounds are visualized with the G-Force software.
2. The second experience is of generating sound merely through physical gesture or movement, voluntary or involuntary, and with the elderly this is most usually hand and arm movements. The abstract coloured graphics generated from sound via G-Force is the initial activity with the Soundbeam. Subsequently, using Arkaos

software, control over picture sequences personalized for the user and/or the kaleidoscopic projection follows. Customised picture sequences can trigger reminiscence as well as intense interest.

This part of the session can become energetic, so that the final phase of a session is designed to be less physically demanding.

3. In the final part the participant can adopt a more receptive mode. During this section, carefully selected pieces of music are played. These have been combined with a low frequency sine tone, typically between 30 – 80Hz. Skille [14], Wigram and Dileo [15] have extensively researched this aspect of using low frequency sound for therapeutic purposes, including many clinical trials. In this work a focus on the pitch has been associated with particular organs of the body which can alleviate numerous complaints, being independent of the music which may here be used as a 'cover'. In VAST however the exact pitch of the low frequency tone is determined by the music, its tonic key providing the pitch of the sine tone, and these tones regularly pulse for somewhere between 4 – 8 seconds in time with the music itself. The *aesthetic* of the music is thus the determining factor with regard to the pitch, speed and regularity of the pulsing. The choice of music is important and McClellan [16] and Williams [17] recommend music devoid of over-intellectualization, being calm and non-polemical, related to meditative states, possibly with a drone-like element and ostinato figures. Music without sudden changes of tempo, timbre or volume seems most effective and I have prepared music from a wide range of classical composers as well as 'music for relaxation' CDs.

Participants who experience this regularly report feeling happier, less stressful, more relaxed - generally an improved state of well-being.

Fig. 5. A resident 'playing' a picture sequence

6   Evaluation

All VAST sessions are recorded on video for analysis and archiving. Over a period of weeks and months, sometimes years, it is thus possible to chart the effects and responses from individuals and customise future sessions to target particular conditions or expressed wishes. From longitudinal observation of video recordings [13] it is possible to identify indicators of change and well-being. The chart below shows how it is possible to identify such changes. At the beginning of a sequence of therapy sessions the resident might well exhibit characteristics in the first column – 'Dependent'. Over time these can often change to those of the 'Responsive' column, and finally become those of the 'Independent' list. This is not a definitive or exhaustive catalogue of development, and it is of course qualitative rather than quantitative in nature, but in terms of aesthetic resonance and human happiness has its importance for well-being for this time of life.

Isaac Asimov [18] remarked that 'life is pleasant, death is peaceful. It's the transition that is troublesome'. It is this 'troublesome' phase which becomes more apparent in homes for the long-term care of the elderly, and the immediate feeling of well-being made possible is one focus of VAST sessions. In addition to this longer term benefits which might accrue from the activities can include anticipation together with residual feelings of well-being and the relief of aches, pains, stress, anxiety and depression.

Table 1. Markers for indicating progression

Dependent	Responsive	Independent
isolated	aware	contributing
indifferent	reactive	expressive
frowning	smiling	laughing
crying	laughing	expressing
silent	content	receptive
withdrawn	thoughtful	communicative
inward	poised	interactive

7 Case Study

During the past decade VAST has been experienced by more than 40 elderly people living in long-term care homes and also in sheltered accommodation. This case study illustrates the effectiveness of VAST with one man. The description of his responses is by no means atypical.

Robert was born in 1915, left school at 14 and had a long working life. He was married for more than 60 years and was devoted to his wife. I first met Robert in May 2006 when he was resident in a home for the long-term care of the elderly with dementia. He and his wife had moved into the home the previous year and their sitting room had been replicated for them in the home. Shortly before I met him his wife had died and he was devastated by this and was consequently very upset and low, in addition to being physically very frail.

Overall, Robert had 17 VAST sessions spread over 7 months with a six week break in the middle due to summer vacation. The study falls into three phases:

1. Accepting – Robert was understandably sad and generally lacked physical and mental energy or vitality. Walking to the session he needed two sticks and the assistance of a carer. At first there was little response to the microphone. He sat very still and appeared uninterested. With the Soundbeam at first he did not appear to like generating sound from his movements and was seemingly confused. However, he relaxed more when listening to the music and described this as 'restful and

soothing'. Gradually he became more vocal and began to smile and use more energy in vocalising, listening and responding to the sounds produced. Similarly with the Soundbeam his movements became more energetic and varied, with some focus being given to the visual projection, both of graphics and of picture sequences. The vibration became a significant feature for him, and after a few sessions he commented that

'I can feel the vibrations through my whole body – its soothing and relaxing'.
Having finished a session listening to the music he commented that 'the vibrations
were doing something – now sometimes I feel like going to sleep. I enjoy it'.

A few weeks later, at the end of his seventh session before we stopped for summer vacation he took a breath and said:

'I get something out of it
I don't know what it is, but there's something I'm getting out of it
Because I'm quieter now, and I'm taking things as they are – now – and –
I don't know what it is
I'm just carrying on
Taking things as they come and I'm not worrying about – I do worry –
But I'm not worrying so badly like it was before when it first happened (the death
of his wife)
But now I can look on it and face the wall and I can say
I'll be away soon'.

2. Becoming

I did not see Robert during the six week break over the summer vacation. During this time he apparently went into something of a decline, beginning to seriously worry again, although when we next met he seemed outward looking and quite bright, saying during the session 'that's very good – when I feel the vibrations'. However in another session he said:

'Feels good – feel the vibrations
When it stopped I had to go to the doctors – worse with worry
I've had depression – the doctor says badly
I'm going to give the doctor up
Today or tomorrow going for the last time
It is easing up
I think 1 or 2 doses of this and I'll be OK'.

In the sessions which followed he developed more energy and after two more sessions was walking to the Therapy room unaided and using just one stick.

3. Being expressive

No longer on medication, Robert was comparatively more active and energetic – his vocalisations could be heard for some distance from the therapy room, and he often smiled broadly showing real enjoyment. His physical gestures and control of sound were at times energetic and always purposeful. The enjoyment of listening to the music was self evident, and he focused on the benefit he felt he received from the vibrations. He commented 'very good, getting the vibrations going down my body'.

Fig. 6. Robert generating graphic displays from vocal activity

On his final session I asked him how he has found it, and he said;

'I enjoy the vibrations -
If it wasn't doing me good I wouldn't be having it'!

He then got an infection and was admitted to hospital.

In the final months of his life VAST gave him motivation, enjoyment, comfort and an improvement in physical and psychological well-being. Relating his time in VAST to the markers for progression table above in virtually every category we see a change from the first to the third column. From being sad, frail somewhat uninvolved and uncommunicative he had come to an acceptance of his situation, could look forward to the future without worry or fear. He gained pleasure from being expressive with sound both vocally and through movement, and experienced being moved aesthetically whilst feeling soothed and relaxed by the music with low frequency tones. These sessions provided for a stimulating, expressive, gentle and soothing transition.

8 Conclusion

Observed benefits from VAST can be short, medium and long term, and improvements in mood, perceived aches and pains, and communication often result from therapy sessions. Additionally, some residents talk about their sessions during the week, and actively look forward to the next visit. Many participants have shown that the vibrations received through the chair 'eases the pain' in joints, particularly the legs, hips and back regions.

Currently, two ladies in their 80s have been having regular weekly VAST sessions within *i*MUSE for more than three years. Both have various aches and pains from arthritis and other conditions, and both are adamant that the sessions improve their physical condition as well as contributing to an improvement in general psychological well-being. It is interesting to note periods of behaviour emanating from *aesthetic resonance* in these sessions; people with arthritis apparently forgetting how stiff or painful their hand or arm movements usually are, and 'playing' with sound for extended periods in the Soundbeam.

One lady who had a mild stroke and did not use her left arm spontaneously started to use this with the Soundbeam during one session, and continued to do so thereafter. The microphone seems to serve two purposes. It can help regenerate communication skills in a non-verbal way with people who have lost speech due to stroke; it can re-energise and motivate action and a sense of fun, and it can serve as a powerful way of generating the physical vibration which so many of the elderly in this project seem to value.

The elderly and the older old may not remember as younger people do, nor be as physically active. We allow and encourage the young to develop and enjoy life to the full. Asimov's 'troublesome transition' is an inescapable phenomenon. As increased ageing in society continues, so this awareness will generate more opportunities for giving positive support and emotional, expressive meaning through aesthetic engagement, with *i*MUSE perhaps being one way to enrich this time for some people during this stage of life.

References

1. Brown, G.: The Living End, The Future of Death, Aging and Immortality. Palgrave Macmillan, Basingstoke (2007)
2. Ellis, P.: Incidental Music: A Case Study in the Development of Sound Therapy. British Journal of Music Education 12(1), 59–70 (1997)
3. http://www.sunderland.ac.uk/imuse
4. Ellis, P., van Leeuwen, L., Brown, K.: Visual Music Vibrations, Digital Creativity. Routledge (2008)
5. http://www.soundbeam.co.uk
6. http://www.soundspectrum.com
7. http://www.arkaos.net
8. Ellis, P.: Moving Sound. In: MacLachlan, Gallagher (eds.) Enabling Technologies: Body, Image and Function. Churchill Livingstone (2004)
9. Strick, J.: Visual Music, in Visual Music: Synaesthesia in Art and Music Since 1900. Thames & Hudson (2003)
10. Kitwood, T.: Dementia Reconsidered: The Person Comes First. Open University Press, Philadelphia (1997)
11. Innes, A., Hatfield, K. (eds.): Healing Arts Therapies and Person-Centred Dementia Care. Jessica Kingsley (2002)
12. Nind, M., Hewitt, D.: A Practical Guide to Intensive Interaction. BILD (2001)
13. Ellis, P.: Layered Analysis: A Video-based Qualitative Reseacrh Tool to Support the Development of a new Approach for Children with Special Needs. In: Qualitative Methodologies in Music Education Research Conference II, Illinois (1996)
14. Skille, O., Wigram, T.: The effect of music, vocalisation and bibration on the brain and muscle tissue: studies in vivbroacoustic therapy: a handbook. Harwood Academic Publishers, Chur (1995)
15. Wigram, Dileo: Music Vibration and Health. Jeffrey (1997)
16. McClellan, R.: The Healing Forces of Music, Element (1991)
17. Williams, E.: An introduction to Vibroacoustic Therapy. The Soundbeam Project. Bristol (1997)
18. Asimov, I.: – cited in [1] above

Influences of Age and Experience on Web-Based Problem Solving Strategies

Peter G. Fairweather

IBM T.J. Watson Research Center
19 Skyline Drive, Hawthorne, NY 10532
pfairwea@us.ibm.com

Abstract. Older adults experience the World Wide Web differently than younger ones do. For example, they move more slowly from page to page, take more time to complete tasks, make more repeated visits to pages, and take more time to select link targets. Age-related cognitive and physical changes have been held responsible for these differences, engendering the view that older adults do the same sorts of things as younger ones but with less efficiency, speed and precision. This paper challenges that position. To accomplish their purposes, older adults may systematically undertake different activities and use different parts of websites than younger adults do. We examined the ways a group of adults aged 18 to 73 moved through an intricate website to solve a multipart problem. As they moved through the website, users followed different paths than younger ones. However, the number of years of their experience with computers and the web did not differentiate their paths. We discuss the results and reconsider our "tally sheet" definition of experience.

Keywords: World Wide Web, age, experience.

1 Introduction

The portion of adults over 65 who use the World Wide Web increased from 2% in 1995 to 33% in 2006 [1, 2, 3]. However, for this growth to reach the point where all capable older adults can access the web, we must solve more of the usage problems they experience [4, 5]. Although a few investigations have explored some of the socio–economic, cultural, and linguistic constraints on such access, most have limited their focus to the physical and cognitive dimensions of the problem. This paper will continue the thread of research into the differences between younger and older adult web users by contrasting the paths they followed through a complex website to solve a specific problem task. Moreover, it will assess whether and how users' prior experience mediates the effects of age.

Most explanations of the difficulties older adults experience with the web are based on age–related changes to their sensorimotor and cognitive capacities. Examples of disabilities associated with cognitive change include attention deficits, low-capacity working memory, reduced information processing speed, slow reaction time, reduced response inhibition strength, high-latency encoding rates, or low rate of inference production [6, 7, 8]. Furthermore, a weakness in one capacity may affect others and

C. Stephanidis (Ed.): Universal Access in HCI, Part I, HCII 2009, LNCS 5614, pp. 220–229, 2009.

diminish overall cognitive performance. For example, if the rate of information processing slows as an individual ages, the capacity of working memory may seem to deteriorate as it tries to keep some pieces of information active and usable while waiting for the sluggish retrieval of others [9].

As behaviors become automatic, they consume far less attention, long–term memory, working memory, executive control, or other cognitive resources than they do when performed mindfully or deliberately (see [11]) Such experience may help older adults [12, 13] to compensate for age–related cognitive deficits by "automatizing" some behaviors, lessening demands on cognitive resources. For example, they may develop heuristics that guide their activities on the web even without their awareness. They may learn, for example, that the left sides or the upper margins of web pages are the most likely regions to contain controls for navigation.

Web user behaviors can be analyzed at two levels of granularity. Web users can be thought of as performing extended transactions such as purchasing goods or retrieving weather information. In contrast, each of those transactions may be looked at as a collection of local behaviors, such as moving to the next page or following a hyperlink. Investigators have sought age-related performance differences by using measurements of unitary local behaviors even when they are integrated with others to form extended transactions [14]. Examples of typical findings show that older adults take more time to complete tasks, visit fewer pages overall, take more time to select link targets, make more unnecessary repeat visits to pages they have already seen, or return more frequently to the home page [14, 15, 16]. These findings have encouraged the widely shared belief that in terms of localized atomic behaviors, older users behave in the same way as younger ones although with less speed, efficiency, and precision.

To compare how older and younger users navigate a website in order to complete extended transactions such as locating a product or setting up the delivery of a purchase, the website must offer multiple routes to task completion. Breathtakingly obvious as it may seem, this procedure is surprisingly difficult to respect. Multiple paths by which to complete an extended transaction cost more to build and maintain than a single path. For that reason, only a small portion of websites implement multiple pathways with which to complete a task.

2 Method

2.1 Participants

The 16 female and 12 male participants ranged from 18 years to 73 years of age (M = 54.71, SD = 16.40). Participants' computer experience ranged from 1 to 25 years, (M = 4.78, SD = 4.48). They were required to have had at least one year of computer background and a computer that they used in their home regularly.

2.2 The Task

Overview of the assigned problem–solving task. Each of the participants was asked to solve a constructed but plausible problem by using resources that were located by navigating a website. Specifically, participants were to traverse the website of an online newspaper in order to find employment opportunities for a close friend or relative. The description of the sought–after job included reception, as well as logistical and clerical support for a hospital patient–care nursing station. Another problem constraint required the job to be within 75 miles of where the user was when participating in this experiment.

Equipment. To solve the assigned problem task, participants needed access to a particular website. They were to navigate through sequences of web pages seeking information about the job they sought. As they moved about, the URL for each page visited was logged to a file along with data needed to calculate the elapsed time for each page. We interposed a proxy server to intercept and log information sent from the website to the participants' browser so that the data could be collected automatically and unobtrusively.

In addition, to ensure that the participants navigated using page links, we made the "back" and "history" functions of the browser unavailable to them.

Materials. We asked participants to solve the problem task using the online version of a well–known newspaper. This particular newspaper was chosen for the following reasons:

1. All candidates for participation were familiar with the "paper version" of the newspaper.
2. Although the content of the online materials changed from day–to–day, the structure of the web pages remained constant. This included layout, controls and indicators and page URLs.
3. Every edition would provide two or more instances of advertisements for employment opportunities that fit the requirements as a solution to the task the participants were to complete.

3 Procedure

The session monitor described the purposes of the study for each of the participants with nonspecific phrasing such as "finding out how different people use a website". Then the monitor read a description of the problem–solving task. The participants were told that the session would end when they successfully completed the assigned problem or when they felt further search would be unproductive. Among the search options on the newspaper website were two links to external search engines — one for jobs, the other for general web searching. Using either of them would shunt the participant out of the website without any way to return that would not perturb the data collection process. We judged the participants to have completed their session if they followed one of the links that led outside the website.

Participants began the problem–solving session by responding to a computer program that collected their age, gender, and number of years of computer experience. As they had been told, no information about their identity was collected. Once they answered the last one of the biographical data questions, the program started a browser that loaded the "front page" of the newspaper.

4 Experimental Results

Of the 28 participants, 13 or 46.4% successfully completed the task. Fifteen or 53.6% did not successfully complete the task because either (a) they failed to locate information that accurately described the sought–for job, (b) they exited the newspaper website prematurely, or (c) they declared that further searching to be fruitless.

The mean values for age and experience for participants who completed the assigned problem did not differ significantly from those for the participants who did not. The average age of those completing the problem was 48.0 years while that of those who did not was 60.5 ($F(1, 26) = 3.63$, p =.068). Those who succeeded had an average of 6.46 years of experience with computers compared with 3.33 years for those who did not ($F(1,26) = 2.82$, p = .106). The comparison involving one user characteristic (e.g., age) used the other (e.g., experience) as a covariate.

However, the mean value for session elapsed time for participants who completed the assigned problem differed significantly from that of those who did not. Successful participants averaged 147.12 seconds compared with 243.87 seconds for the others ($F(1,26) = 5.317$, p < .05). The comparison involving session elapsed time used both age and experience as covariates.

Table 1. Associations between users' characteristics and their performance

	success	time
age	-.356	.503**
experience	.318	-.184

** $p < 0.01$

Table 1 echoes these results by showing the partial correlations of the two participant characteristics (age, years of experience) with the two measures of performance (task success, session elapsed time). Only the correlation between participants' age and the session elapsed time proved significant.

As participants tried to complete the problem task, they moved from page to page through the website. Pages and the connections among them were represented as the vertices and edges of a graph as illustrated in Figure 1. Figure 1 abstractly represents one of the participants' movements from the starting point at the "front page" (FP) to the point where he or she prematurely (and probably inadvertently) exited the newspaper site (EXIT). The other vertices, unlabeled here, correspond to web pages visited by this participant.

After collecting the paths followed by each of the 28 participants and constructing the corresponding graph in the manner depicted in Figure 1, we combined the graphs into a single meta–graph whose vertices represented the set of all pages visited by all of the participants. Its edges represented the set of all of the page–to–page transfers made by all of the participants.

We partitioned the combined graph into six sets constructed algorithmically to minimize the number of edges connecting different partitions and to maximize the number of edges contained within the same partitions, while keeping the partitions roughly the same size. In other words, the high density of the edges connecting

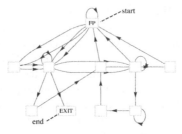

Fig. 1. Graph of a single participant's page sequence

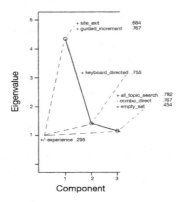

Fig. 2. Comparing the of each zone variable with that of experience

pairs of vertices, both of which were in the same set, contrasted with the sparseness of the edges connecting pairs of vertices where each member was in a different set. These partitions resembled neighborhoods in a large city that people might have visited for a distinct purpose such as finding a certain kind of restaurant or exploring a street fair. Each of the partitions represented a "neighborhood" or zone within the newspaper website where users might have gone for a particular reason. Table 2 identifies and describes each of the six website zones.

Each page transition placed the participants in one or another of the six zones listed in Table 2. Each page visited by a participant counted as a contact within the zone containing that page. The proportion of pages visited by a participant that were contained within a particular zone expressed the degree of alignment between that participant's purposes or actions and the overall purpose ascribed to that zone. To illustrate, if 85% of a participant's page visits came from the set labeled "guided incremental search", we would conclude that the participant chose to try to solve the assigned problem by using the search mechanism that prompted for information in small chunks. As Table 2 shows, all but two of the zones, "site exit" and "empty set" represent a purposeful activity. Each of the two exceptions represents a condition resulting from a purposeful activity rather than an activity itself.

Table 2. Zone names and descriptions

Name	Zone description
all-topic	This zone presents participants with a general search engine that operates over all articles and features in the current and past copies of the newspaper. It does not provide access to current employment opportunities.
combination-direct	This zone represents a direct search path using both selectable attributes and free responses to enter categorical information efficiently.
keyword-directed	This zone involves the exclusive use of a search dialog box that accepts words or phrases.
guided incremental search	This zone represents the use of the "conversational" search tool that prompts the participant to choose from alternative descriptions, advancing the search in small increments toward a target solution.
site exit	An entry into this zone means that the participant exited the site to an external search engine.
empty set	Any score within this zone means that the participant constructed a search query that produced no results.

5 Discussion

Neither age nor the number of years of experience with computers significantly affected whether or not a participant successfully completed the problem. We explain this result by considering how we decided who could participate in the study and by taking note of the different rates at which cognitive skills change with age.

Participants in this study were required to have had one year of experience with computers and to have a computer in their home that they used. Because early practice episodes exert such a disproportionately strong influence on performance compared to later ones [11] one year of experience may have provided the participants with the skills needed to attempt the assigned task. If so, then the requirement we imposed would have contributed to the dampening of the variation crucial to detect the influence of the amount experience on performance. Later in this paper, we will propose that to define experience simply as a quantity of time may mask the effects of knowledge acquired during that experience.

The assigned problem drew heavily upon participants' domain knowledge and, in particular, upon their knowledge of vocabulary concerning the task. To succeed, participants had to categorize and re–categorize what they were looking for by using terms drawn from the relevant domain (e.g., "clerk", "record", "chart", "logistics"). Because domain–related vocabulary knowledge is more robust in older adults than other areas of knowledge or skill [9], it may have had an effect on users success that may not be legitimately generalized to tasks involving maps or pictures.

5.1 Relationships between Users' Age, Experience and Path Selections

Table 3 shows three of the six zones attracted older participants significantly more strongly than younger or more experienced ones. In particular, Table 3 reveals the strong positive tendency for older participants to visit the "guided–incremental" zone, a set of pages that channeled participants in small steps toward the goal of their search. By firmly guiding them through the search, this set of pages relieved the older users of the resource demands brought on by navigation tasks.

The significant negative correlation between experience and "guided–incremental" suggests that more experienced participants actively avoided the "guided–incremental" zone. Moreover, the absence of correlation between experience and any other zone suggests that the strongest drive of the experienced participants was *away* from "guided–incremental" but not *toward* any other zone in particular.

Paradoxically, older users' frequent visits to this zone, while attesting to their preferences, bore a strong negative correlation with success with the assigned task $(r(28) = -0.506, p < .01)$. We observed that even though the pages in "guided–incremental" led participants with small, low–risk steps toward their goal, a mistake at an early step would prove too costly to salvage the possibility of a fruitful search.

For example, if participants selected "health care" instead of "administrative" as an initial rough categorization of the job, they might be asked to select from among categories such as "LPN" or "office nurse", choices far removed from the sought–after target. At least part of the apparent security of the "guided–incremental" search was illusory. The small steps seemed to guide them to successful task completion, but only if they chose accurately in the early parts of their search. We observed that in a few cases, participants abandoned the "guided–incremental" zone for another. This is not surprising because its slow pace may have given participants the impression that their searches were not converging on a successful conclusion. If participants failed after having abandoned the "guided–incremental" zone, their scores would properly link those pages to failure but conceal how that connection was mediated by a path through a different set of zones proximal to failure. Older users tended to exit the newspaper website inadvertently and prematurely more than younger ones did (see Table 3). They seemed to fail to recognize indicators of the nearby boundary, such as links that would take them to the external search engines. Another plausible explanation is that the older adults did recognize the indicators but did not consider the external search engines to lie outside the newspaper website. (This explanation illustrates how knowledge gained through experience may affect behavior rather than the length of that experience. We explore such possibilities in a later section).

Finally, the older users tended to visit the zone labeled "empty set", indicating that, one way or another, they had carried out a search that yielded no results. We found older adults solved the assigned problem with roughly the same success as the younger adults. However, Table 3 reveals a strong positive correlation between age and visits to the "empty set" zone. Although their overall success rate did not differ significantly from that of younger adult users, the older adult participants visited zones associated with fruitless searches more frequently. This implies that they often persevered, successfully reaching a solution in spite of one or more intervening failures.

5.2 Contrasting Experience with Knowledge

By migrating the definition of "experience" from a simple period of time to a measure of what users know at the end of that period, we may interpret our findings

Table 3. Correlations between users' zone visit scores and their age and experience

	all topic	combination direct	keyword– directed
age	.156	-.283	-.004
experience	-.264	.274	-.268

	guided incremental	site exit	empty set
age	.522**	.459**	.342*
experience	-.343*	-.117	-.087

$*\ p < 0.05$
$**\ p < 0.01$

differently. Defining experience as elapsed time seems simple, unambiguous and precise. However, experience defined that way is peripheral to user behavior and events. As Table 1 and Table 3 reveal, experience achieves a significant correlation with only one of the six zone visitation variables, "guided incremental," but with none of the other salient measures such as path length, age, total time, or success on the task. In other words, the quantity of experience had nothing to do with users' success on the task, the amount of time they took, how many pages they traversed, or, except in one case, zones they visited. Without much exaggeration, we could say that experience measured as the length of a period of time has little to do with any other values.

Principal components analysis (PCA) of all the variables confirms the tenuous contribution of experience to that portion of the overall variance they explain. In Figure 2, next to each variable name is the measure of its communality, the amount of variation in the extracted component structure it is responsible for. With the exception of experience, each variable name is strongly associated with one of the three substantive components (i.e., with an eigenvalues > 1.0). We depart from conventional applications of PCA, using it not to identify and label the three components but to illustrate how strongly each variable relates to one or another of those components. Experience, on the other hand, reveals through its low commonalities how little it has in common with them.

The six types of zone visits reflect differences in the users' behaviors. In turn, these behaviors imply differences in the users' states of knowledge. In other words, the six zone visitation variables are related to what the users know or do not know about how to solve the assigned problem using the web.

While the six visitation zone variables reflect what users know, they do so only indirectly. They are not direct measures of prior knowledge such as how to organize search terms or understanding what is meant by "logistical support". Nevertheless, in contrast to the simplistic definition of "experience" as "accumulated time", even such indirect measures are easily recognized   as being in the vicinity of familiar usage, such as "any forms of acquired knowledge that can influence behavior."

Throughout we have proposed explanations for the participants' behaviors. For example, we suggested that the failure to recognize a link to an external search engine might contribute to inadvertent exits of the newspaper site. To impute the cause for such inadvertent exits to having spent some number of months using computers would make little sense. However, we could legitimately link exiting/non-exiting to knowledge of the general features of search engine interfaces gleaned from some number of months using them. In contrast to the calendar-based measure of experience, those based on the type of experience (e.g., using search engines) as well its outcome would be expected to correlate strongly with user behaviors.

If experience-as-knowledge comes to explain much more of users' behavior, we speculate that the relationship between age and users' behavior observed in this experiment could weaken or even disappear.

6 Conclusion

We have presented evidence that when alternatives are available, older adults may follow routes and undertake activities on a website that differ from those of younger adults. The ways they can differ depend on the particular alternatives presented by a website. If the website environment tightly regulates what users do and coaxes them down a particular path, then it is not surprising that they seem to do that same thing. Under those circumstances, differences in the amount of time required for primitive localized actions will stand out to dominate comparisons of older and younger adult users.

In this study, older adults tended to use the least risky method of search to try to solve the assigned task, even as it frequently led them to failure. Older users may gravitate toward activities that do not support their problem–solving goals. They also tended to make choices that led to searches yielding no results. However, they recognized that an "empty" result did not necessarily mean that nothing fit the problem constraints so that another try might be productive. Older adults tended to fail to recognize the link to the external search engine for what it was, most likely because of its unfamiliarity.

However, we suspect that some of the effects of age, strong as they may appear, result from the level of knowledge these users had about how to solve the assigned problem using the web. More research using measures of what users know rather than measures of how long they have used computers will properly rank the contributions of age, experience and knowledge to the particular choices users make at the transaction level.

References

1. United States Census Bureau: Statistical Abstract of the United States, p. 719. U.S. Census Bureau, Washington, DC (2008)
2. United States Administration on Aging: Profile of older Americans,
   http://www.aoa.gov/prof/statistics/profile/profiles.aspx
3. Lee, S., Kim, J.: Has the internet changed the wage structure too? (2004)
4. Czaja, S.J., Lee, C.C.: The Internet and older adults: Design challenges and opportunities. In: Charness, N., Parks, D.C., Sabel, B.A. (eds.) Communication, technology, and aging: Opportunities and challenges, pp. 60–78. Springer, New York (2001)
5. Gregor, P., Newell, A.F.: Designing for dynamic diversity - making accessible interfaces for older people. In: Proceedings of the 2001 EC/NSF Workshop on Universal Accessibility of Ubiquitous Computing: Providing for the Elderly, Alcacer do Sal, Portuga, pp. 90–92 (2001)

6. Salthouse, T.A.: Constraints on theories of cognitive aging. Psychonomic Bulletin and Review 3(3), 287–299 (1996)
7. Craik, F., Salthouse, T.A.: Handbook of Aging and Cognition. Erlbaum, Mahwah (1996)
8. LaBerge, J.C., Scialfa, C.T.: Predictors of web navigation performance in a life span sample of adults: Aging and human performance. Human Factors 47(2), 289–302 (2005)
9. Park, D.C.: The basic mechanisms accounting for age-related decline in cognitive function. In: Park, D., Schwartz, N. (eds.) Cognitive Aging: A Primer. Taylor and Francis, New York (2000)
10. Sweller, J.: Cognitive load theory, learning difficulty, and instructional design. Learning and Instruction 4(4), 295–312 (1994)
11. Anderson, J.: Rules of the Mind. Lawrence Erlbaum, Mahwah (1993)
12. Chadwick-Dias, A., Tedesco, D., Tullis, T.: Older adults and web usability: Is web experience the same as web expertise? In: CHI 2004 extended abstracts on Human factors in computing systems, pp. 1391–1394. ACM, New York (2004)
13. Rogers, B.L.: Measuring online experience: It's about more than time! (2003)
14. Meyer, B., Sit, R.A., Spaulding, S.E.M., Walker, N.: Age group differences in world wide web navigation. In: Pemberton, S. (ed.) CHI 1997 extended abstracts on Human factors in computing systems: looking to the future, vol. 2, pp. 295–296. ACM, New York (1997)
15. Grahame, J., LaBerge, M., Scialfa, C.T.: Age differences in search of web pages: The effects of link size, link number, and clutter. Human Factors 46(3), 385–398 (2004)
16. Hart, T.A., Chaparro, B.S.: Evaluation of websites for older adults: How "senior-friendly" are they? Usability News 6(1),
    http://www.surl.org/usabilitynews/61/older_adults.asp

An Application for Active Elderly Follow-Up Based on DVB-T Platforms

Maria Jesus Falagan, Juan Luis Villalar, and Maria Teresa Arredondo

Life Supporting Technologies-Technical University of Madrid,
ETSI Telecomunicacion-Ciudad Universitaria,
28040-Madrid, Spain
{mfalagan,jlvillal,mta}@lst.tfo.upm.es

Abstract. This paper describes the T-CUIDA project, an ongoing collaborative initiative, partially funded by the Spanish Government, which aims at designing and developing an application for promoting active elderly in their habitual environments. The platform takes advantage of the DVB-T infrastructure, the European digital TV broadcasting system, recently deployed in Spain. Design for All principles are applied in a multimodal and personalized approach to provide a complementary set of services that help aged people to keep themselves physically and mentally dynamic. The final system is about to be conveniently evaluated during six months by more than a hundred of potential users in four different locations around the country.

Keywords: active elderly, usability, user acceptance, digital TV.

1 Introduction

Nowadays, long-living population is a rising fact in Spain, as well as in most developed countries where life expectancy has grown [1]. The elderly present specific needs due to their advanced age, and company gets profound importance. Because of western life rhythm, relatives are not always available for them, inducing loneliness feeling that makes them to let go. Moreover, considering their limited mobility, isolation may take old people to hard depression [2]. On the contrary, by helping them keeping physical and mentally active whereas enhancing their integration feeling, they would push themselves to maintain a healthy condition.

One of the most extended technological platforms is TV, and people of any age can easily manage through remote controls. The recent deployment of terrestrial digital TV (DVB-T) in Spain, which includes support for a wide range of interactive services [3], allows the design of applications especially devoted for elderly. The T-CUIDA consortium was shaped for this purpose, engaging complementary partners from technical business, university and assistance provision, supported by healthcare and psychology experts.

The aim of this paper is to present the functionality of the T-CUIDA research project, whose target is to design, develop and evaluate an easy-to-use TV-based application that stimulates cognitive and physical capabilities of the elderly from complementary approaches, trying to improve self-esteem and accompaniment. By

C. Stephanidis (Ed.): Universal Access in HCI, Part I, HCII 2009, LNCS 5614, pp. 230–235, 2009.
© Springer-Verlag Berlin Heidelberg 2009

assisting them in the daily organization of their time, promoting healthy lifestyle, a relevant first step is being taken towards the provision of interactive telecare support in the near future. The paper gives special emphasis to describe the user interaction strategy, as the key factor related to system acceptability.

2 Materials and Methods

In order to achieve project objectives, user interface requires an exhaustive analysis, mainly because of the special physical and mental condition of the target population. For this reason, an iterative User-Centered Design (UCD) methodology is being followed [4], involving final users along the whole design process. According to this scheme, a thorough literature revision was accomplished in search of ergonomics and usability design standards and guidelines, especially devoted to the elderly, complemented through an initial proof-of-concept validation phase arranged in Madrid with a dozen of potential users.

According to [5], ageing entails significant changes in individuals that affect their physical and cognitive abilities. In particular, elderly people usually suffer from vision deficiencies (yellowish and blurred image), auditory limitations (especially at high frequencies) and motor impairments (for selection, execution and feedback). Ergonomics design recommendations include clear and accessible environments, objects which are easy to handle and manipulate, large interfaces without superfluous decoration, error tolerant methods, high contrast between figures and background, combined usage of visual and auditory elements, selective acoustic amplification, etc.

The interviewed users put emphasis on simple and reliable applications as well as on non-threatening easy-to-learn technologies. They liked being informed about news, being encouraged to make exercise or being reminded about appointments. TV was considered a very convenient means for service provision due to its friendliness, as long as complicated hardware add-ons are avoided. Complementary sound messages were also highlighted to support accompaniment feeling. Besides, the combination of dark font colors on bright background is mostly preferred than the opposite (i.e. bright font colors on dark background).

According to user needs and preferences, the main functionalities of the T-CUIDA user interface are the following:

- Supply of an adapted interaction for common deficiencies of aged people, so as to motivate them and increase the use of the application.
- Design of a consistent "*Look and Feel*", to facilitate comprehension, legibility and navigation within the application.
- Supervision of exercise performance for each user, in order to follow up improvement/deterioration and personalize training plans.
- Provision of a simple method to communicate text messages through the TV, notifying them even if the device is turned off (e.g. led flickering).
- Protection of user privacy by avoiding messages that include sensitive information (i.e. TV is not a personal communication channel).
- Eventually, distribution of sporadic warnings for risk situations, especially for people who live alone or present mobility problems.

The rationale of the T-CUIDA application is to provide old people with preliminary telecare assistance and to introduce healthy habits into their daily life, as well as to warn people who can react quickly in case of trouble. Psychologists and experts will analyze user performance and determine the idle time to detonate automatic alarms to the telecare center and families. In order to provide this emergency service, the standardized intervention protocols have been established and followed by the assistance center involved.

3 Results

As shown in Fig. 1, the developed system takes advantage of the straightforward way of operation of interactive TV: access to the application is as easy as changing a TV channel with the usual remote control. The only atypical element for most Spanish aged people is the additional digital TV decoder, but once configured and after some minor training, it can be used without difficulty.

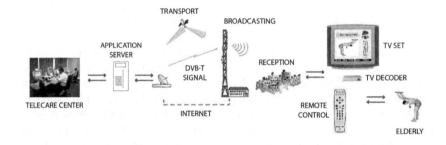

Fig. 1. T-CUIDA system architecture

The TV decoder is a terrestrial twin receiver called FTE Maximal PVR T150[1], which supplies two USB 2.0 high speed ports for connecting external hard drives, where the static part of the application is deployed. The dynamic elements of the application (e.g. videos, messages, exercises) are customized by the assistance center and updated from time to time through the TV broadcasting signal. Thanks to the high tuning sensitivity of the decoder, excellent results come out even with adverse signals. However, one of the drawbacks for this decoder is the low processing capability, so that images suffer from long loading times. It is expected that new models of the decoder will get through these limitations.

A singular remote control has been especially selected to interact with the application (Fig. 2). It is adapted to the common physical and cognitive handicaps of the elderly. It shows less and bigger buttons compared to typical devices. On top of that, the more eye-catching feature is that buttons present raised forms according to each figure (numbers, arrows, plus and minus signs, etc.), adding together the sense of touch to avoid confusions due to eyestrain and clumsiness.

---

[1] http://www.ftemaximal.com

Fig. 2. T-CUIDA remote control

The interaction strategy is as simple as the familiar videotext but presenting a more attractive appearance. Simple help messages are shown to support the user in case s/he gets lost while navigating along the application. Although most TV sets are still not available as touch screens, the graphical layout is conveniently prepared in case any user prefers direct tactile interaction modality in the near future.

The first integrated version of the T-CUIDA application comprises the following support services:

– Mental training: interactive intellectual exercises to keep mental activity.
– Physical training: videos of physical exercises to be replicated by the user.
– Agenda: list of relevant messages and appointments for the user.
– Information: updated collection of news, suggestions or general-purpose information.
– Events: compilation of events which may be of interest for the user.
– Health: specific recommendations about healthy lifestyle.

Apart from the dynamic content, the system supports personalization by several means. Two profiles may be selected: the advanced mode holds a small window for watching TV simultaneously and allows using numbers and arrows to navigate through the application screens; the basic mode completely hides the TV and goes sequentially over each option so as the user is just required to press the OK button. This option scanning interval is also customizable in the user profile. Furthermore, the set of services may be adapted according to user preferences, considering age, gender, physical skills, cognitive capabilities, etc. along with particular choices such as religion (e.g. an autonomous rosary praying assistant is included for Christians, as a proof of concept for including market-tailored applications). In addition, the system automatically extracts helpful information from user performance (e.g. number of activities carried out, success ratio, completion time), so as to permit professionals to analyze remotely the physical and mental condition of each user and adjust training plans in accordance.

The T-CUIDA client application is implemented as HTML pages while interaction events are handled through ECMAScript [6], a standardized version of JavaScript.

The web browser selected for handling this application is ANT Fresco[2], specifically designed for interactive TV, consumer electronics and embedded devices. However, due to the standard-based approach followed, a straightforward deployment of the application is possible in any common web browser. As shown in Fig. 3, a user-friendly style has been adopted for the user interface, incorporating some multimodal elements such as animations, videos and audios, which reinforce user motivation.

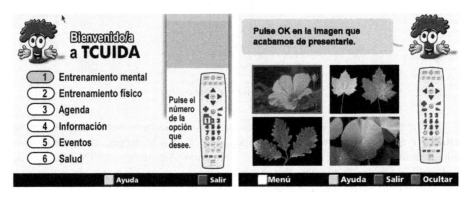

Fig. 3. Screenshots of the T-CUIDA user interface

4 Conclusions

This paper has described the application developed in the T-CUIDA project, which concentrates on improving elderly people life quality. Innovation has been sought by developing an inexpensive and easy-to-install solution, taking advantage of the recently deployed digital TV broadcasting infrastructure as a straight way to reach aged citizens. The application makes use of bidirectional communication through DVB-T by exchanging updated data in a seamless way between clients and assistance centers, giving support to non-invasive remote user monitoring as well as personalized services, exercises, information and messages. A careful user interaction design process has been followed, applying accessibility requirements and reinforcement methods coming from other high-interactive domains like Internet.

According to first impressions from elderly users, it appears that the usage of widespread technological devices such as TV facilitates user acceptance and mitigates the initial rejection to use modern technologies. This prototype is expected to be used at home, where people living alone could get proper assistance, while alleviating futility and loneliness feelings. Although the platform could also fit residences, in this kind of centers TV is a very impersonal means, and a priori it seems that people could not benefit from all the T-CUIDA follow-up and reinforcement functionalities.

After the first concept validations, a six-month pilot experiment is being prepared and is about to start with more than a hundred users at different regions in Spain (Valencia, Murcia, Galicia and Madrid), taking into account DVB-T coverage and existing home equipments. Different profiles of elderly users are considered, making

---

[2] http://www.antlimited.com

a thorough estimation of each person condition in order to personalize decoders and exercises, configuring the central database which will alert about risky situations. A sort of healthy style monitoring will be arranged to test, not only if users enjoy and make their best with the platform, but also if there are mid-term implications on their physical and mental conditions, self-esteem or isolation feeling. Professional assistants will be also part of the study so as to determine whether they find this kind of applications useful for client/patient supervision.

In the end, the T-CUIDA project intends to serve as a starting point for further implementation of interactive services over digital TV. If the ongoing initiative proves to be accepted by the elderly and assistants while commercially successful, a number of added-value services would shortly arise, including healthcare support videoconference, continuous user monitoring based on wearable sensors, customized social network applications, and so on.

Acknowledgments. T-CUIDA is a collaborative research project supported by the Spanish Ministry of Industry, Tourism and Commerce. Authors thank the T-CUIDA consortium partners (namely Secuenzia Pixels, Intercentros Ballesol and Instituto de Salud Carlos III) for their valuable contribution to this work.

References

1. United Nations, Department of Economic and Social Affairs, Population Division: World Population Prospects: The 2006 Revision, Highlights, Working Paper No. ESA/P/WP.202 (2007)
2. Lafortune, G., Balestat, G.: The Disability Study Expert Group Members: Trends in Severe Disability among Elderly People: Assessing the Evidence in 12 OECD Countries and the Future Implications. OECD Health Working Papers, DELSA/HEA/WD/HWP, 2 (2007)
3. Digital Video Broadcasting Project Consortium: Introduction to the DVB Project. Creating Global Standards for Digital Television, DVB Fact Sheet (June 2008)
4. ISO 13407:1999 Human-centred design processes for interactive systems
5. Moreira, H., Lillo, J.: Diseño ergonómico y envejecimiento. Boletín Digital de Factores Humanos, 26 (2004)
6. ECMA International: ECMAScript Language Specification, Standard ECMA-262, 3rd edn. (December 1999)

Preliminary Study on Remote Assistance for People with Dementia at Home by Using Multi-media Contents

Toshimi Hamada[1], Noriaki Kuwahara[1], Kazunari Morimoto[1], Kiyoshi Yasuda[2,3], Utsumi Akira[4], and Shinji Abe[4]

[1] Guraduate school of science and tehonology, Kyoto Institute of Techonology, Matsugasaki, Sakyouku, 606-8585, Japan
[2] Holistics Prosthetics Research Center, Kyoto Institute of Techonology, Matsugasaki, Sakyouku, 606-8585, Japan
[3] Rehabilitaiton department of Chiba Rosai Hospital, 2-16, Tatsumidai-Higashi, Ichiharashi, 290-0003, Japan
[4] ATR Intelligent Robotics and Communication Laboratories, 2-2, Hikari-dai, Keihanna Science City, Kyoto, 619-0288, Japan
{nkuwahar,morix}@kit.ac.jp, fwkk5911@mb.infoweb.ne.jp, {utsumi,sabe}@atr.jp

Abstract. We are developing the system that remotely support the daily living of people with dementia at home by using multi-media contents for bringing their peace of mind, for preventing their behavioural disturbances, and for guiding actions of their daily living, because a major problem in providing good care at home to people with dementia is that it must be constantly provided without interruption, which puts a great burden on family caregivers. At first, our developed system can provide dementia people with multi-media contents such as reminiscence photos and videos for instilling a sense of peacefulness in their minds. These contents are used in remote reminiscence therapy by using simultaneous photo and video sharing. Also, we developed video instruction system for guiding their actions in a toilet to help them. We evaluated the effectiveness of our system from viewpoints of relieving the stress of their family caregivers, and of the extent of their independence in daily living. According to the evaluation results, we discuss on essential problems to be overcome for supporting people with dementia remotely, and present our approach towards realizing the system that effectively guides and navigates people with dementia for living independently.

Keywords: Dementia, reminiscence, assistive technology, content.

1 Introduction

Providing a high standard of care for people with dementia and memory-impaired (patients) is becoming an increasingly important issue as societies continue to age. At the same time, supporting their daily living by handling various behavioral related disturbances, such as wandering, agitation, illusions, and incontinence, puts a great burden on caregivers, who are often family members [1]. Therefore, we are developing

C. Stephanidis (Ed.): Universal Access in HCI, Part I, HCII 2009, LNCS 5614, pp. 236–244, 2009.

the system that support patients' daily living by using multi-media contents because for bringing their peace of mind, for preventing their behavioural disturbances, and for guiding actions of their daily living.

Reminiscence therapy is reported to bring a sense of peacefulness to the minds of patients, which helps reduce behavioral disturbances [2]. Despite its effectiveness, reminiscence therapy is difficult to perform at home due to a shortage of experienced staff. Therefore, we developed the system for easily conducting reminiscence therapy with the patient at home [3, 4], and for enabling remote therapists to conduct audio-visual communication via the Internet and simultaneous reminiscence content sharing with the patient [5].

Also, the patients and family caregivers want to support the patients' independent life by automatically reminding them of routine chores such as medicine dosing and hospital visits, route guidance while going out, and so on. It is also important to not only remind patients who developed apractognosia of their household actions but also to present to them a sequence of actions in order to effectively support their daily living. We are currently developing and evaluating a system for instructing the patient to perform actions during a toilet visit [6]. This system provides systematic and de-tailed illustrations with voice instructions, such as where the patient should stand near the lavatory bowl, when he should pull down his pants, and so on. In this paper, we briefly introduce the systems that we developed.

Then, we present benefits and limitations of these systems based on our experiments. Based on these results, we discuss on essential problems to be overcome for supporting people with dementia by using contents, and present our approach towards realizing the system that effectively guides and navigates people with dementia for living independently.

2 Overview of Our Developed System

2.1 Reminiscence Video System

Reminiscence video has been experimentally proven to bring dementia patients peace of mind. It is a kind of slideshow video produced by using personal photos of patients. It comes with audio and visual effects. The latter include panning and zooming to the region containing the person the patient is interested in, and the former include background music (BGM) and suitable narration to make the video more engaging. We developed an authoring tool for easily producing various versions of reminiscence videos by simply choosing the set of photos with an aim to provide family caregivers with it. These effects are applied to each photo based on the meta-data annotated by the video author beforehand. The annotations are basically focused on the people in the photo. This is because the photos containing relatives and/or friends are often included in creating a reminiscence video. Fig. 1 is the GUI example of our authoring tool.

2.2 Networked Reminiscence Therapy System

Reminiscence therapy is reported to bring peace of mind to patients and to help re-duce behavioral disturbances. In a reminiscence therapy session, a therapist prepares

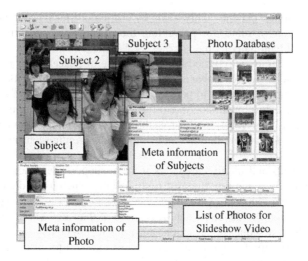

Fig. 1. GUI Example of Video Authoring Tool

old tools, toys, photos, and paintings to effectively stimulate memories. Despite its effectiveness, reminiscence therapy is difficult to perform at home due to a shortage of experienced staff. Therefore, we provided the patient with the system that conducts reminiscence therapy by delivering him reminiscence contents, while he talks with a remote volunteer via IP TV Phone (Fig.2). Our system provide remote talking partners with such ways for promoting the conversation with dementia patients as selecting photos, zooming-up subjects in the photo, feedback of pointing position from patient's terminal, and so on.

Fig. 2. Illustrative Example of Networked Reminiscence Therapy System

2.3 Video Instruction System for Toilet Actions

method and video contents, and are conducting preliminary evaluation. The posture-detection system using IR cameras and invisible IR dot pattern projector detects the user's state according to his/her 3-D appearance (Fig. 3). Video and voice instructions consist of scenes describing nine-step actions, such as asking the patient to stand in front of the lavatory bowl, and then pull down his pants, and so on.

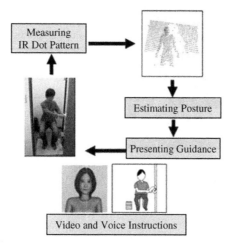

Fig. 3. Overview of Video Instruction System for Toilet Actions

3 Problems to Overcome for Realizing Effective Support for Daily Living of People with Dementia

We conducted some experiments for examining the effectiveness of our developed systems. Through our experiments, we found some essential problems to be overcome for realizing effective support for the daily living of people with dementia.

3.1 Reminiscence Video and Remote Reminiscence Therapy System

Our experiments proved that reminiscence video was effective to grab the attention of patients [3, 4]. Among audio-visual effects used in a reminiscence video, narrations were most important to gain a patient's attention. For example, usage of a person's name and names of places in narrations were highly desirable for holding patients' attention to reminiscence videos.

However, we should be very careful not to contain such error as wrong name of the subject in the photo because it might confuse patients' memory and thus cause an emotional disorder. Also, selecting photos that didn't recall sad memories for the reminiscence video was very important not to cause their emotional disorders. The same problems were pointed out for the remote reminiscence therapy [5].

3.2 Video Instruction System for Toilet Actions

We examined seven cases [6] and found that people with moderate dementia confused by instructions having such features that required patients to search for an object in their surrounding area, and then to interact with that object. For example, a patient has tried to open the paper box displayed in the screen as shown in Fig. 4. She had a difficulty to find the real box beside the display, even though we used beep sound and LED light for indicating the position of the real box. One of the reasons is that people with moderate and severe dementia usually lose their ability to switch their attention appropriately according to their situation.

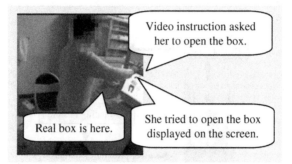

Fig. 4. Experimental Scene of Video Instruction System for Toilet Actions

3.3 Problems to Overcome

In order to add proper narrations to photos of the reminiscence video, it is necessary to interview with people with dementia and their family caregivers for gathering collect episode of all photos. Also, we need to remove photos that recall sad memories of people with dementia from the set of photos used for producing the reminiscence video. However, it costs much time and human resources to do so. On the other hand, in order to realize effective activity guidance, we need to prepare the proper video instructions according to patients' cognitive level. It also costs time and human resources.

Furthermore, it is necessary to switch the attention of people with dementia from the guidance video to the object that they interact with. We think that these are essential problems to realize effective support for their daily living by using contents.

4   Proposed Solutions

The first problem we pointed out is how to effectively produce contents for supporting patients' daily living. The second problem is how to realize the user interface for navigating the eye gaze of people with dementia to the object that they interact with, and for switching their attention to it in order to make them successfully perform tasks in their daily living. In order to overcome these problems, we propose the solutions as follows.

4.1 From Co-imagination to Co-creation

Through remote reminiscence therapy sessions by using our develop system, the remote talking partner stimulates patient's memory by asking him/her episodes on photos shared remotely with each other. Otake proposed "Co-imagination" program [7] for prevention of dementia where group of elderly people bring photos according to such themes as food, seasonal event, my favorites, and so on, and have face-to-face lively conversation on each photo. Selecting photos stimulates their planning ability, and conversation about photos develops their communication skill. From this viewpoint, our reminiscence therapy system is said to be the tool that provides remote "Co-imagination" field for people with dementia and remote talking partner. By talking with people with dementia in this remote "Co-imagination" field, remote talking partners will be able to gather episodes of their photos. Therefore, by providing remote talking partners with easy way to record such information of their photos as date, place, subjects, and so on, a reminiscence therapy session can be a part of the process of producing a reminiscence video. It is said to be "Co-creation" process of a reminiscence video where people with dementia and remote talking partners take part in. In order to realize remote "Co-creation" field, our remote reminiscence therapy system already has features as follows.

For engaging people with dementia in the conversation with the remote talking partner, the region in the photo that the talking partner specify is panned and zoomed in the display device of people with dementia. Also, for sharing the interest between people with dementia and the remote talking partner, the position in the photo where the remote talking partner points for asking the subject in the photo by using the pointing device is displayed as the marker on the photo shared in the display device of people with dementia (Fig. 5).

In order to make "Co-imagination" process a part of "Co-creation" process of a reminiscence video, we add such new feature to the remote reminiscence therapy system as pop-up dialog for inputting the information of the subject when the remote talking partner specifies the region in the photo (Fig. 6). This information is used in the video production process for searching the photo to be used in the video. Furthermore, the remote talking partner can select the narration related to the subject in specified region among typical narrations in the database. After specifying the region, input the information related to the region, and selecting the narration, only dragging and dropping photos in the timeline, we can produce the reminiscence video as shown in Fig. 7.

Fig. 5. Remote "Co-imagination" Field (Patient's Side)

4.2   Interface for Navigating Eye Gaze and Sifting Attention of People with Dementia

As mentioned before, patients with moderate and severe dementia can pay their attention to much narrower area than normal people, and tend to stick to one thing. Unless we successfully make their attention shift to the target object that they interact with, video guidance for helping patients perform tasks will not work well as we expect.

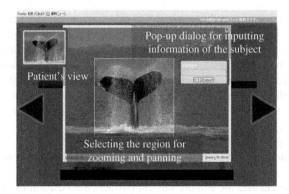

Fig. 6. Remote "Co-imagination" and "Co-creation" (Talking Partner's Side)

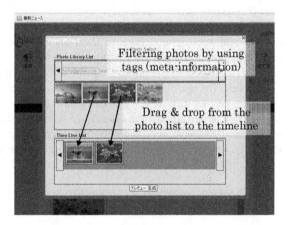

Fig. 7. GUI for reminiscence video production

In order to make patients' attention shift from the video guidance to the target object, it is necessary to make their eye gaze move to this object. For this purpose, the arrow showing the direction to it seems to be promising. The voice instruction showing the direction such as "right" or "left" are understood in the language area of the brain. On the other hand, graphic information like arrows to show the direction is perceived in the brain area for spatial cognition. The damaged part of the brain by a dementia or a brain injury is usually different from patient by patient. Therefore, combination use of voice date and graphic information showing the direction to the target object will be effective from the viewpoint of ensuring multi information paths for recognizing the direction to the target object.

However, it might be possible for the patient with very severe dementia that even such multi information paths possibly will not work for shifting their eye gaze. For such a case, we are studying the effectiveness to use a conjugated gaze. By using such reflexive response, we are now trying to navigate the eye gaze of people with very severe dementia because a reflexive response is likely to be kept well longer than higher brain functions like language comprehension and spatial cognition.

For evaluating the effectiveness of these methods, we are now conducting the preliminary experiment by using animations of arrows and eyes to indicate the direction target object as shown in Fig. 8.

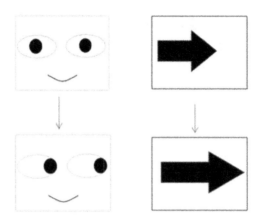

Fig. 8. Examples of Animations for Navigating Eye Gaze of People with Moderate and Severe Dementia

5 Conclusions

In this paper, we briefly introduce the systems that we developed for supporting the daily living of people with dementia at home. Based on experimental results, we discuss on essential problems to be overcome for making our system more effective. "From Co-imagination to Co-creation" and "Navigating Eye Gaze and Sifting Attention" are our key concept for overcoming these problems though we've only just begun.

Acknowledgments. This research was supported by research funds from Japan Science and Technology Agency.

References

1. Davis, R.N., Massman, P.J., Doody, R.S.: Cognitive intervention in Alzheimer disease: A randomized placebo-controlled study. Alzheimer Disease and Associated Disorders 15, 1–9 (2001)
2. Gräsel, E., Wiltfang, J., Kornhuber, J.: Non-Drug therapies for dementia: An overview of the current situation with regard to proof of effectiveness. Dementia and Geriatric Cognitive Disorders 15, 115–125 (2003)
3. Kuwahara, N., et al.: Reminiscence Video-Helping At-Home Caregivers of People with Dementia. In: Proceedings of Home-Oriented Informatics and Telematics, pp. 145–154. Springer, Heidelberg (2005)

4. Kuwahara, N., et al.: A Method for Producing Reminiscence Video by Using Photo Annotations –Application and Evaluation for Dementia Sufferers. Journal of The Japan Society for Artificial Intelligence 20(6), 396–405 (2005) (in Japanese)
5. Kuwahara, N., et al.: Networked Reminiscence Therapy for Individuals with Dementia by using Photo and Video Sharing. In: Proceedings of 8th International ACM SIGACCESS Conference on Computers & Accessibility, pp. 125–132 (2006)
6. Yasuda, K., et al.: Toilet task support system using 3-D human posture measurements: System evaluation in simulation environment. In: Proceedings of the 22nd Annual Conference of the Japanese Society for Artificial Intelligence (2008) (in Japanese)
7. Otake, M.: Establishment of Multisector Research Organization including Civil Society, Industry, Government and Academia named Fonobono Research Institute and Analysis of Memory Task with Coimagination Method - Development of Support Service for Prevention and Recovery from Dementia and Science of Lethe. In: Proceedings of the 22nd Annual Conference of the Japanese Society for Artificial Intelligence (2008) (in Japanese)

Cognition, Age, and Web Browsing

Vicki L Hanson

School of Computing, University of Dundee, Dundee, Scotland
vlh@computing.dundee.ac.uk

Abstract. The literature on Web browsing indicates that older adults exhibit a number of deficiencies when compared with younger users. But have we, perhaps, been looking at the question in the wrong way when considering technology skills of older users? What are the strengths of older users that can be leveraged to support technology use? This paper considers cognitive aging with respect to distinctions in abilities that decline, and those that do not, with age. A look at specific abilities and their interactions may serve to help designers create software that meets the needs of older users.

Keywords: older adults, Web, cognitive abilities.

1 Introduction

Currently there are neuroscientists who are investigating whether the high-paced constant bombardment of technologically-mediated input is changing the brains of today's youth [22]. While the focus of such work is on brain plasticity and changes in youth, the question can be turned around. That is, are the brains of older adults simply not able to cope with current technologies?

Subjectively, nearly every tech-savvy person has a story of an older relative or friend who has struggled with computers, mobile phones, or even the increasing technological sophistication of common household devices such as televisions and microwaves [17]. Is this inability to deal with technology an inevitable consequence of aging? Today's Gen-Xers believe that their ability to easily master current technology will not doom them to the same fate as the current generation of older adults. How realistic is this belief?

It is well known that aging brings about changes in a person's abilities. The fact of vision changes will cause most of us to begin to use glasses (often multi-focal) even if we have not previously done so. For others, vision changes will be more catastrophic, with major vision losses due to medical conditions such as macular degeneration that, in come cases, will lead to blindness. Similarly, losses in hearing as well as fine or gross motor skill will create a spectrum of difficulties for many as we age.

Of interest to the present discussion is the impact of cognitive aging on the ability to deal with technological complexity. Problems related to access and usability for people with vision, hearing, and physical disabilities are far from being solved, but are better understood than technologies needed for cognitive disability [2]. For example, guidelines exist for making the Web work with screen readers. When these guidelines are followed, people who use screen readers can access the Web [3]. This is not

C. Stephanidis (Ed.): Universal Access in HCI, Part I, HCII 2009, LNCS 5614, pp. 245–250, 2009.

to say that all problems for screen readers users are thus solved. Even for pages that conform to these standards, there are demonstrated usability problems [16, 18]. Older adults who have lost their vision late in life, in particular, need more help with Web browsing than is specified in guidelines for screen readers alone [26]. Cognitive issues, such as those to be discussed below, make it difficult for such older users to develop mental models of the browsing task and learn the commands needed to navigate with a screen reader. While the guidelines do not completely address all accessibility and usability issues for users of screen readers, there is at least a consensus that audio renderings of Web content are needed for this population.

In contrast, there is no general consensus of how to support the cognitive declines that accompany aging.

2 Fluid and Crystallized Intelligence

In healthy aging, there are number of declines in cognition that can affect ability to use technology. Looking at the population as a whole, these declines begin in middle age and continue throughout the rest of one's life [6, 8]. There is a great deal of variability from person to person, however, in the onset and rate and of these declines related to a number of factors [6, 8, 21].

To best understand the nature of these declines, we can look to information processing theories that deal with mental activities such as selection, storage, manipulation and organization of information [1, 20]. In work with older adults, a difference between *crystallized intelligence* and *fluid intelligence* is often made. Both are part of a general intelligence as differentiated by psychologists, but the two are broad categories that cover separate cognitive abilities. Crystallized intelligence commonly remains intact throughout one's lifetime and is not likely to be impaired as a result of brain trauma. It is measured through tests of verbal ability and reflects knowledge that we have gained through education and experience. A large-scale study spanning 66 years illustrates the stability of this form of intelligence. Deary and colleagues tested a cohort of 77 year olds in a region of Scotland [10]. This group had all been administered a battery of "verbal tests" in 1932 as part of a government testing program. Sixty-six years later, these researchers contacted survivors in the area and re-administered the tests. Results showed a high correlation in cognitive abilities in these verbal indicators over this large span of years.

Fluid intelligence refers to a set of cognitive abilities that includes short-term memory, speed of processing, and problem solving ability. Critically for older adults, these abilities are associated with aptitude for learning new technologies. In contrast to crystallized intelligence, fluid intelligence has been shown to decline with age and is can affected by brain trauma. Age-related declines due to fluid intelligence may help us understand the underlying reasons for patterns observed in Web use by older adults. Fluid intelligence, for example, is one of the strongest predictors of Web experience [8]. Specifically, older adults who measure high on tests of fluid intelligence engage in more types of Web activities (such as e-mail, games, news information, shopping) than those who measure low on these tests.

Difficulties with complex page navigation are interpretable in terms of short-term memory and processing changes, and some specific remedies to support users have been suggested. For example, consistent navigation of pages within a site and clearly structured information can reduce problems [3]. Providing feedback about the entire sequence of a multi-step event, such as when making online purchases could prove beneficial [11]. Searching can be improved for older adults by non-hierarchical interfaces [19]. Difficulties with browser basics such as the Back, History, Bookmarks and Search can all be understood as complex activities that tax limited cognitive systems. Better-supported information about visited sites and searched sites is crucial for older users. In terms of Web 2.0 content, difficulties of navigation are exacerbated by dynamic changes ("change blindness" being particularly strong for older adults), difficulty identifying clickable areas, lack of help for ever-changing content [4].

3 Technology for the Generations

A recent report found some surprising results in terms of Internet use by age: While there is still a digital divide between the youngest group studied (the Gen Y group, ages 18 – 32) and the older groups studied, the differences in use are shrinking [15]. For example, in 2005, only 26 % of the older adults ages 70 – 75 were online; today that number is 45%. Certainly this represents the gradual aging of the population, with the more technology oriented older users moving up the age scale. It does suggest, however, that ability to use the Web can continue even in the face of age-related changes.

What are these older users doing online? Not surprisingly, email is the number one use. This is followed by Internet searches, seeking of health information and making travel reservations [15]. Looking at the somewhat younger cohorts, we see that the boomers (ages 45 – 63) are more likely than their older counterparts to use the Web for online shopping and banking. Social networking appears relegated to the younger generations, however.

Changing demographics worldwide have created a workforce in which older workers are critical [9, 13]. The individual reasons for remaining in the workforce vary, including both financial needs and various needs for self-fulfillment [14]. Remaining in the workforce may be an important element of remaining technically savvy that is not typically considered [12]. Employment often requires workers to keep their skills up to date. Once retired, the pressures to keep up with the latest advances in technology are less. Use of technology by retired persons is for personal interests rather than an external demands by employers. For many older adults, the lack of use of the Internet and other technology is simply the fact that they see no need to use it [25]. Remaining in the workforce is one powerful motivator to stay current with technology.

The demographic make-up of today's workforce may well re-shape how technology, including the Web, is used [5]. In looking, for example, as the use of Instant Messaging (IM), the recent survey found IM used little (39% or less) by Boomers and older users [15]. In contrast, IM was reported used by 70 – 79% of the Gen Y users. For some workplaces, however, IM is a part of the work culture and employees, regardless of age will be using it. In one recent study at a large industrial company, administrative assistants were asked about their workday and the technology tools they used to perform their job [24]. All interviewed, regardless of age, used IM as a regular part of their day.

4 Uniquely Older

The literature on Web browsing suggests that older adults exhibit a number of deficiencies when compared with younger users. But have we, perhaps, not been looking at the right question? Of interest here is recent evidence that cognitively older adults bring specific skills and approaches to the task. A couple of recent studies about Web navigation by older adults will serve to illustrate this point.

In eye-tracking work, Tullis found that older and younger adults attend differentially to Web pages and parts of Web pages [23]. The task used by Tullis required participants to determine information about personal finances on a mock website. The older adults (ages 50 – 69) spent more time viewing nearly all Web pages than the younger participants (ages 20 – 39). They spent more time viewing both upper and left-side navigation areas on pages than the younger users. They read more text on pages than younger users.   Overall, they looked at parts of the Web pages that younger users seemed simply to ignore.

Tullis was not able to determine the underlying reason for this browsing difference between his two age groups, but he considered possibilities such a caution in selection and attentional issues associated with aging. While such factors may play a role, we can look at another study to get an additional interpretation. Fairweather examined the navigation paths of a group of users (ranging in age from 18 to 73 years old) [11]. The user task was to look for job openings in an online newspaper. This study showed that older and younger participants were not differentiated by their success on this task, but they were differentiated by how they arrived at the goals. Specifically, their paths through Web pages followed different courses.

Fairweather's hypothesis about his findings takes a new look at issues of cognition and aging. Specifically, he noted that the solution of the job task relied a great deal on participants' specialized knowledge, experience, and vocabulary about the domain, all of which are aspects of crystallized intelligence that generally do not decline with age.

Considering these two studies together, it is tantalizing to speculate as to the reasons for older participants' increased time attending to navigation, links, and text on a page. It may well be that this is related, at least in part, to their thinking about the problem task. In this, it might be considered that these users are savvy enough to use their strengths to support lesser abilities. Understanding such interactions, rather than simple statements of disability, may eventually prove crucial in being able to well support the technology needs of older adults.

5 Summary

Demographic trends show that people, worldwide, are living longer, with the greatest increase being in what could be considered the "oldest of the old". The impact of this is a clear need for technologies that are usable by older adults. The Web, as a technology that is becoming important in all aspects of life including social activities, commerce, and government services, provides an important application that needs to be understood from the perspective the abilities of older adults. Given specific cognitive changes that happen throughout life, cognitive factors in their relation to browsing represent an important and, to date, relatively little investigated issue for older users.

Recent suggestions that older adults are not simply deficient younger users may well re-define how technologists develop for older adults. Considerations of cognitive strengths and weakness are needed, with research investigating how older adults currently use their strengths to mitigate problems. This also suggests that technologists might consider how to design devices and interfaces, such as pages, that could use these strengths to help older users.

Acknowledgement. This paper was written was the author was also Research Staff Member Emeritus of IBM Research. Funding was provided, in part, from EPSRC grant EP/G002118/1.[1]

References

1. Adams, R.: Decision and stress: cognition and e-accessibility in the information workplace. Universal Access in the Information Society 5(4), 363–379 (2007)
2. Bodine, C., Sherer, M.: Technology for improving cognitive function. A workshop sponsored by the U.S. Interagency Committee on Disability Research (ICDR): Reports from working groups. Disability & Rehabilitation 28(24), 1567–1571 (2006)
3. Brewer, J.: Web Accessibility Initiative (2003), http://www.w3.org/WAI/ (retrieved February 20, 2009)
4. Chadwick-Dias, A., Bergel, M., Tullis, T.: Senior surfers 2.0: A re-examination of the older web user and the dynamic web. In: Stephanidis, C. (ed.) HCI 2007. LNCS, vol. 4554, pp. 868–876. Springer, Heidelberg (2007) (Appears as Volume 5 of the combined Proceedings of HCI International 2007)
5. Convertino, G., Farooq, U., Rosson, M.B., Carroll, J.M., Meyer, B.J.F.: Supporting intergenerational groups in computer-supported cooperative work (CSCW). Behaviour and Information Technology 26, 275–285 (2007)
6. Craik, F.I.M., Salthouse, T.A.: The handbook of aging and cognition (revised edn.). Erlbaum, Mahwah (2000)
7. Czaja, S.J., Charness, N., Fisk, A.D., Hertzog, C., Nair, S.N., Rogers, W.: Factors predicting the use of technology: Finding from the Center for Research and Education on Aging and Technology Enhancement (CREATE). Psychology of Aging 21(2), 333–352 (2006)
8. Czaja, S.J., Lee, C.C.: The impact of aging on access to technology. Universal Access in the Information Society 5, 341–349 (2007)
9. Czaja, S.J., Sharit, J.: Aging and work: Assessment and implications for the future. Johns Hopkins University Press, Baltimore (in press, 2009)
10. Deary, I.J., Whalley, L.J., Lemmon, H., Crawford, J.R., Starr, J.M.: The stability of individual differences in mental ability from childhood to old age: Follow-up of the 1932 Scottish Mental Survey. Intelligence 28, 49–55 (2000)
11. Fairweather, P.G.: How older and younger adults differ in their approach to problem solving on a complex website. In: Proceedings of the 10th international ACM SIGACCESS Conference on Computers and Accessibility, Assets 2008, Halifax, Nova Scotia, Canada, October 13-15, pp. 67–72. ACM, New York (2008), http://doi.acm.org/10.1145/1414471.1414485

---

[1] The *Digital Inclusion Network* was formed in the UK for the purpose of determining research priorities related to inclusion. For more information, see http:// www.iden.org.uk/

12. Hanson, V.L.: Age and web access: The next generation. In: Proceedings of the 2009 International Cross-Disciplinary Workshop on Web Accessibility, W4A, Madrid, Spain (2009)
13. Hanson, V.L., Lesser, E.: Implications of an Aging Workforce: An Industry Perspective. In: Czaja, S.J., Sharit, J. (eds.) Aging and work: Assessment and implications for the future. Johns Hopkins University Press, Baltimore (in press, 2009)
14. HSBC: The future of retirement (2008),
    http://www.ageing.ox.ac.uk/supporters/hsbc
    (retrieved September 20, 2009)
15. Jones, S., Fox, S.: Generations online in (2009),
    http://www.pewinternet.org/PPF/r/275/report_display.asp
    (retrieved February 20, 2009)
16. Leporini, B., Paternò, F.: Increasing usability when interacting through screen readers. Universal Access in the Information Society 3, 57–70 (2004)
17. Lewis, C., Menn, M.: Access tool? Accelerating treadmill? Technology and the aging popultion. In: Proceedings of HCI International (2009)
18. Miyashita, H., Sato, D., Takagi, H., Asakawa, C.: Aibrowser for multimedia: introducing multimedia content accessibility for visually impaired users. In: Proceedings of the 9th international ACM SIGACCESS Conference on Computers and Accessibility, Assets 2007, Tempe, Arizona, USA, October 15-17, pp. 91–98. ACM, New York (2007), http://doi.acm.org/10.1145/1296843.1296860
19. Pak, R., Price, M.M.: Designing an information search engine for younger and older adults. Journal of Human Factors and Ergonomics Society 50(4), 614–628 (2008)
20. Posner, M.I. (ed.): Foundations of Cognitive Science. MIT Press, Cambridge (1989)
21. Rabbitt, P.: Tales of the unexpected: 25 years of cognitive gerontology. The Psychologist 19(11), 674–676 (2006)
22. Small, G., Vorgan, G.: Surviving the technological alternation of the modern mind. Harper Collins, New York (2008)
23. Tullis, T.S.: Older adults and the web: Lessons learned from eye-tracking. In: Stephanidis, C. (ed.) HCI 2007. LNCS, vol. 4554, pp. 1030–1039. Springer, Heidelberg (2007) (Appears as Volume 5 of the combined Proceedings of HCI International 2007)
24. Vizer, L., Hanson, V.L.: Generations in the workplace: An exploratory study with administrative assistants. In: Proceedings of HCI International (2009)
25. Zajicek, M.: Web 2.0: Hype or happiness? In: Proceedings of the 2007 international Cross-Disciplinary Conference on Web Accessibility (W4A), W4A 2007, Banff, Canada, May 7-8, vol. 225, pp. 35–39. ACM, New York (2007)
26. Zajicek, M.: Patterns for encapsulating speech interface design solutions for older adults. In: Proceedings of the 2003 Conference on Universal Usability, CUU 2003, Vancouver, British Columbia, Canada, November 10-11, pp. 54–60. ACM, New York (2003), http://doi.acm.org/10.1145/957205.957215

Towards an Account of Sensorimotor Knowledge in Inclusive Product Design

Jörn Hurtienne[1], Patrick Langdon[2], and P. John Clarkson[2]

[1] Technische Universität Berlin, Institut für Psychologie und Arbeitswissenschaft,
FG Mensch-Maschine-Systeme, Sekr. FR 2-7/1, Franklinstraße 28/29, 10587 Berlin, Germany
`joern.hurtienne@tu-berlin.de`
[2] University of Cambridge, Department of Engineering, Engineering Design Centre,
Trumpington Street, Cambridge, UK
`{pml24,pjc10}@eng.cam.ac.uk`

Abstract. By 2020, one in every two European adults will be over 50 years in age. As old age brings along reductions in sensory, cognitive, and motor abilities, product development methodologies have to adjust. While sensory and motor abilities are relatively straightforward to measure, cognitive abilities are more elusive. The paper discusses how different sources of prior knowledge can inspire inclusive design. Special emphasis is put on knowledge derived from basic sensorimotor experiences. This is proposed to complement previous studies investigating the effects of tool knowledge on inclusiveness. Image schema theory as an account of sensorimotor knowledge is introduced and its universality, robustness, and multimodality are discussed. Current evidence for the usefulness of applying image schemas in user interface design is reviewed and implications for inclusive design research are derived. More specifically, a research program is developed that includes theoretical, empirical, as well as practical studies to promote the ideas developed in this paper.

Keywords: Inclusive Design, Image Schemas, Prior Knowledge, Cognitive Abilities, Embodied Cognition.

1 Introduction

Europe is getting older. Increased life expectancy and the demographic change in many countries of the European Union predict ageing populations and growing numbers of people with disabilities. By 2020, one in every two European adults will be over 50 years in age. As old age brings along reductions in sensory, cognitive, and motor abilities, product development methodologies have to adjust. It will not be sufficient to provide specialised products, also known as "assistive technology". The design of mainstream products needs to be inclusive.

Research into inclusive design has investigated the relationship between the capabilities of the population at large – derived from statistical data sets, and properties and features of the design of products [1, 2, 3]. Products meeting the ideals of inclusive design aim to minimise the number of people who have difficulty with, or are excluded from use, or to control such exclusion by manipulation of product features

C. Stephanidis (Ed.): Universal Access in HCI, Part I, HCII 2009, LNCS 5614, pp. 251–260, 2009.
© Springer-Verlag Berlin Heidelberg 2009

[4,5]. The cognitive capabilities of older users are one of the primary areas of concern. Particular attention is given to the effect of memory on learning a products' use and the ability of individual users to transfer learning from prior experience [6].

This paper introduces a model continuum of prior knowledge sources and argues that previous approaches to designing technology around prior knowledge about tools can be complemented by other, more subconsciously applied sources of knowledge. Image schemas as a special form of sensorimotor knowledge are introduced. The feasibility of the approach is illustrated by several examples. As the empirical evidence on the usefulness of the approach for inclusive design is rare, an agenda for further research is developed.

2 Different Sources of Knowledge

Prior knowledge is a critical factor of how easy the interaction with a new product is to learn [7]. If users can match their knowledge to what is presented at the user interface, the user interface will be easy to understand and be intuitive to use. To better understand the different sources prior knowledge can stem from, a continuum of knowledge sources has been proposed, shown in Figure 1 [8].

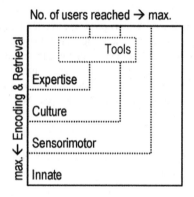

Fig. 1. Continuum of knowledge sources

The first and lowest level of the continuum consists of innate knowledge that is 'acquired' through the activation of genes or during the prenatal stage of development. Generally, this is what reflexes or instinctive behaviour draw upon. The sensorimotor level consists of general knowledge, which is acquired very early in childhood and is from then on used continuously through interaction with the world. Children learn for example to differentiate faces; they learn about gravitation; they build up concepts of speed and animation. Scientific notions like affordances [9], gestalt laws [10], and image schemas [11] (discussed below) reside at this level of knowledge.

The next level is about knowledge specific to the culture in which an individual lives. This knowledge can vary considerably between cultures and may influence how people approach technology. It touches, for instance, the realm of values (e.g. what constitutes a taboo), the styles of visual communication (cf. Japanese manga vs.

American comics), but also concerns knowledge about daily matters like the usual means of transportation (e.g. buses, trains, or bicycles) or the prevalent form of energy supply (e.g. by a public power line or by burning wood for heating).

The most specific level of knowledge is expertise, i.e. specialist knowledge acquired in one's profession, for example as a mechanical engineer, an air traffic controller, or a physician – and in hobbies (e.g. modelling, online-gaming, or serving as a fire-fighter).

Across the sensorimotor, culture, and expertise levels of knowledge, knowledge about tools can be distinguished. Tools at the sensorimotor level are primitive tools like sticks for extending one's reach and stones used as weights. Tools at the culture level are those shared by many people, like ballpoint pens for writing, pocket lamps for lighting, or cell phones for communication. Tools at the expertise level are professional tools like computer aided design (CAD) tools, enterprise resource planning (ERP) systems, or machine tools.

2.1 Inclusive Design at the Tool Level

Tool knowledge from the cultural or expertise level is an important reference when designing user interface metaphors. Tools at the sensorimotor level are rarely or never used explicitly [12]. Previous research on prior experience in inclusive design also focused at the cultural or expertise level of tool knowledge. These often are pragmatic decisions, because all products make some reference to either products extant during previous generations or products from different companies or product families.

Products that help the user make a reference to the same function on another device with which they are familiar should outperform those that make no such association – or worse still, make a different reference. Knowledge at the tool level has been researched in terms of 'computer literacy' [13], 'technology familiarity' [14], or simply 'prior experience' [6, 7]. These studies show that prior knowledge about similar tools decreases the time and errors in interacting with a new product (e.g. microwave ovens, digital cameras, motor cars). But performance measures (times and errors) were also influenced by age, usage frequency, and general cognitive capability.

2.2 Promises of the Sensorimotor Level

Relying on prior tool knowledge at the cultural or expertise levels is one strategy for inclusive design. However, designers then need to determine what prior tool experience the target user group has. Data on tool usage quickly becomes outdated as technology develops – statistics on the distribution of tool knowledge in the population would quickly be loosing their usefulness. Also, designing for prior knowledge about specific tools, like mobile phones or desktop PCs, may exclude many users that are not familiar with these tools. Finally, just repeating how existing products look and feel gives no guidance for designing new functionality and can even hamper innovation [15].

As the continuum of knowledge sources in Figure 1 suggests, there are types of knowledge that may not have these problems and therefore could complement the previous approaches. Specifically, we would like to focus on knowledge residing on the sensorimotor level of the continuum. This type of knowledge comes with two promises:

- Lower level sensorimotor knowledge is so basic and fundamental, that it should be available to a large range of people of different backgrounds – much more than tool knowledge or knowledge from the expertise or cultural level.
- Sensorimotor knowledge is acquired early in life and is frequently encoded and retrieved in a large number of different situations. Thus, its application has become automated and subconscious. It therefore should be less sensitive against individual differences in cognitive abilities like working memory capacity and attentional demands as well as injuries [16, 17].

It is the universality and robustness against differing levels of cognitive abilities that makes general knowledge on the sensorimotor level the ideal complement to previous research on prior knowledge at the tool-level (culture or expertise) in inclusive design.

2.3 Image Schemas as a Special Type of Sensorimotor Knowledge

Image schemas are a form of knowledge representation that encodes very basic and repeated sensorimotor experience [11]. The experience of vertically extended objects and of gravity, for instance, forms the image schema UP-DOWN. Other examples of image schemas include CONTAINER, BLOCKAGE, NEAR-FAR, and PATH (of a list of about 40 image schemas). They describe basic object properties (BRIGHT-DARK, BIG-SMALL), spatial relations (UP-DOWN, NEAR-FAR), or so-called force dynamics (BLOCKAGE, COMPULSION).

Many image schemas show experiential correlations with other sensorimotor experiences. For example, UP-DOWN correlates with quantity (the height of the water level correlates with the amount of water in a jar). NEAR-FAR correlates with similarity (similar objects or living things tend to occur together in space). These correlations are also encoded in memory and are re-used in the conceptualisation of abstract concepts, e.g. when talking about *rising inflation*, *sinking prices*, or *close colours*. In fact, most of these correlations have been first detected in language (about 250 of them are documented). The psychological reality of image schemas and their extensions to abstract concept has been validated by developmental research [18], by cognitive psychological experimentation [19, 20, 21, 22] and by neurocognitive findings [23].

3   Examples of Using Image Schemas in Product Design

Image schemas can be used in physical-to-physical mappings in user interfaces. This can be achieved by using simple principles of stimulus-response (or control-display) compatibility [24]. A highly successful application is Google Earth using the accelerometer and tilt sensors of the iPhone to navigate interactive 3D maps of the world. Maps are moved UP or LEFT by dragging a finger UP or LEFT on the screen. Zooming in is achieved by pinching the fingers as to stretch the surface of the map (BIG-SMALL). Tilting the phone leads to views of mountains or streets of houses in 3D (ROTATION).

Yet the most promising features of using image schemas in user interface design are physical-to-abstract mappings. Experimental results show that vertical sliders and button arrangements labelled in agreement with MORE IS UP – LESS IS DOWN and GOOD

IS UP – BAD IS DOWN mappings are operated faster and are more satisfying to use than the reverse mappings LESS IS UP – MORE IS DOWN and BAD IS UP – GOOD IS DOWN [8, 25]. Other research shows that under high cognitive workload the mapping SIMILAR IS NEAR – DIFFERENT IS FAR can explain results in user performance (times and errors) that can not be explained by previous design guidance like the proximity-compatibility principle of Wickens and Carswell [25, 26].

Lund [27] used physical-to-abstract mappings of image schemas to design a hierarchical collection of bookmarks in a virtual 3D space. Semitransparent cones in an information landscape represented different categories of bookmarks (using a CATE-GORIES-ARE-CONTAINERS mapping). The more bookmarks there were in one category, the taller the cone was (MORE IS UP). The relevance of single bookmarks in a category was conveyed by the mapping IMPORTANT IS CENTRAL, etc. This prototype was compared with an information-equivalent traditional hypertext prototype. The results show that the image-schematic mappings profoundly influenced what users thought about the interface. The image-schema prototype elicited significantly more comments containing the included image schemas than the hypertext prototype.

In two other studies [28, 29], image schemas were used during a context-of-use analysis of an invoice verification and posting software. The results were used to derive 29 image-schematic requirements for the re-design of the software. For instance, users often used FRONT-BACK relations to describe their use of additional information, e.g. lists of contact persons in the company or additional order information. Hence, in the re-designed solution the screen with additional information could be slid out from underneath the main screen (Figure 2.A). Credit and debit needed to be in BALANCE for an invoice to be booked, so a see-saw type widget was included to show the status of the invoice (Figure 2.B), etc. In the subsequent evaluation with users, the re-designed prototype was rated as significantly higher in hedonic and pragmatic quality compared to the users' current solution.

Although not explicitly intended to be an application of image schemas in product design, another study sheds light on the potential benefits of employing image schemas over tool knowledge at the cultural level. Figure 3.A shows the buttons of a common music player. The basic functionality is to start and stop the music, to navigate between tracks (previous/next), and to adjust the volume. The symbols on the buttons are the standard symbols found in other music and video players all over the world – whether they are realised as hardware (like in VHS players) or software. In this respect, these buttons draw on users' prior knowledge from the cultural/tool level of the knowledge continuum. The player also uses knowledge from the sensorimotor level that could be described by image schemas. Buttons are grouped according to their functionality (instances of a COLLECTION image schema). The *play*, *next* and *previous* symbols are pointing either RIGHTwards or LEFTwards in space indicating a virtual PATH. Tracks are assumed to be spread out in linear spatial order from the LEFT to the RIGHT. The volume control buttons are ordered in a way that the 'louder' control is on the RIGHT and the 'softer' is on the LEFT mirroring a mapping also found in the convention of the number line: MORE IS RIGHT and LESS IS LEFT.

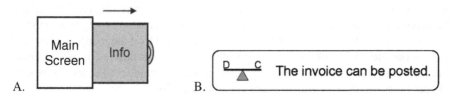

Fig. 2. Image schemas in a software application for invoice verification and posting. A. FRONT-BACK relations between main and supplementary information. B. A widget visualising BALANCE between debit and credit.

Fig. 3. Music player user interfaces A. common button arrangement, e.g. Microsoft Media Player Mobile, B. Touchplayer overview.

Pirhonen and colleagues [30] built a device called Touchplayer. It has a touch-sensitive display and can be operated without using vison. It is worn at the users' side, with a belt clip so that the screen is vertical and facing to the side (Figure 3.B). Forward or backward sweeps with the finger across the screen brought up the next or previous track, respectively. This embodies the PATH image schema as a FRONT-BACK gesture for track navigation (i.e. FRONT as in the direction of walking). Upward and downward sweeps turn the volume up or down (MORE IS UP – LESS IS DOWN). A single tap with the finger lets the music start or stop (COMPULSION). The difference between the Touchplayer and the common button arrangement in Fig 3.A. is that

- Touchplayer strongly relies on sensorimotor knowledge and embodies this in the interaction instead of presenting symbols with weak sensorimotor associations
- It uses stronger image schemas. UP-DOWN and FRONT-BACK are more powerful than the rather weak LEFT-RIGHT image schema (cf. [25]) for volume and navigation control.

Pirhonen et al. compared the Touchplayer to the standard version of the Microsoft Media Player. Users had to solve simple tasks with both players (e.g. "Move forward two tracks and increase the volume") while solving a secondary task (walking a pre-defined route). The results indicate an advantage of the Touchplayer over the standard player on several measures. The largest difference between the players was found for Mental Demand. Overall workload was reduced by 42% and the performance in the secondary task was 13% faster when using Touchplayer. Other significant differences in favour of the Touchplayer version were found for frustration, annoyance, physical demand, temporal demand, and effort.

Although not originally determined to investigate effects of knowledge level on interaction performance, the results of this study indicate a better and less cognitive demanding design is possible with a focussing on knowledge from the sensorimotor level of the continuum.

Taken together these examples show that there is value in regarding image schemas as a form of sensorimotor knowledge in user interface design. The Pirhonen et al. study shows that it can be advantageous to rely on image-schematic gestures over tool knowledge from the cultural level in terms of mental demand. Our own studies [8, 25] show that using image schematic designs lead to more effective, efficient and satisfying interaction with technology and using them can lead to an improved design lifecycle [28, 29]. Thus the approach seems promising for inclusive design as well. However, it still needs to be shown that image schemas are as advantageous as they promise to be for user populations with widely varying cognitive abilities. Plus it needs to be shown directly, how image-schema inspired designs fare in comparison to current approaches using knowledge from other levels of the continuum.

4 Implications for Inclusive Design: A Research Agenda

Image schemas are proposed to be universal, multimodal, and operating beneath consciousness. The universality predicts that user interface features designed with image schemas should be equally usable by members of different technology generations (cf. [31]). The multimodality predicts that also users with sensory impairments have image-schematic concepts. Blind users, for example, should have an understanding of what a CONTAINER is using haptic and acoustic cues. In fact, research has shown that the mental representations of blind people do not differ from those in sighted people, especially for spatial information (as opposed to purely visual information) [32, 33]. Most image schemas are abstractions of spatial relations [18], so image-schema based user interfaces should apply to blind users as well.

Finally, the subconscious application of image schemas predicts a certain robustness. Image-schematic designs should be less susceptible to variation in users' cognitive ability like working memory capacity, attentional resources, decision-making, etc. Similarly, cognitive losses should affect knowledge on the higher levels of the knowledge continuum earlier than image schemas that reside on a lower, earlier obtained and more strongly rehearsed level of knowledge.

Note that these predictions are different from those made for user interface features drawing on tool knowledge at the expertise or culture level. Research has shown that knowledge at the expertise/tool level is neither universal nor robust. Members of different technology generations perform differently and performance deteriorates with increasing age and decreasing ability [6, 7].

As these are interesting promises for the field of inclusive design and their empirical investigation is virtually non-existant, the following implications for inclusive design research arise:

1. Theoretical: The aim should be to integrate the theory of image schemas with a model of assessment of the prior-knowledge demand of a product user interface at the expertise/tool level of knowledge. Simple models of cognition were already

developed (cf. [34, 35]). As they are mostly inspired by information-processing approaches to cognition (e.g. [36]), they lack the subconscious, embodied, and sensorimotor accounts of knowledge that image schema theory can provide. An integrated theoretical framework would better account for the phenomena under study and would be a better guide to design than each of these theories alone.

2. Empirical: Then the objective is to test the predictions of the integrated theoretical framework for different products and to verify their fitness for practical purpose. Studies should verify the claims made about the universality, multimodality, and robustness of image schemas, compared to other levels of prior knowledge. This means including participants of different ages and degrees of cognitive capability who interact with different versions of everyday technology (e.g. microwave ovens, digital cameras, or music players). The outcomes of the empirical studies will show whether the strong predictions of image schema theory can be confirmed, must be rejected, or need refinement considering moderating effects by other factors.

3. Practical: Finally, the objective is to develop practical guidance for designers that results from the integrated theoretical framework and the empirical findings. This guidance could take the form of a design method. It will then be necessary to evaluate the usefulness of this guidance by applying it to a real-world design problem and assess its practicability.

These three objectives directly derive from the state of the art, because there is no common framework for inclusive design combining image schemas and general cognitive models of prior knowledge. Although data on the validity of image schemas in user interface design exist in general, it needs to be determined what their use for inclusive design is (see above). Ultimately, the growing demand for inclusive design makes it necessary to provide guidance to designers that is empirically validated.

5 Conclusions

A simple model of prior knowledge points out ways to analyse and design technology that have not been considered before. Current evidence shows that there is much potential in designing for more basic and subconscious forms of knowledge. Both, previous approaches to prior knowledge and the new approach can complement each other and can be integrated. More research needs to be undertaken on the theoretical, empirical, and practical level to make these ideas relevant for inclusive design. More generally, the results of such work will extend the knowledge, tools, and guidelines for engineering design and product development based on recent cognitive science findings.

References

1. Vanderheiden, G.C., Vanderheiden, K.: Guidelines for the design of consumer products to increase their accessibility to people with disabilities – working draft 1.7. Trace Research & Development Center, Madison, WI (1992)
2. Keates, S., Clarkson, P.J.: Countering Design Exclusion. An Introduction to Inclusive Design. Springer, London (2004)

3. Persad, U., Langdon, P.M., Clarkson, P.J.: Inclusive design evaluation and the capability-demand relationship. In: Clarkson, P.J., Langdon, P.M., Robinson, P. (eds.) Designing Accessible Technology, pp. 177–188. Springer, Berlin (2006)
4. Nicolle, C., Abascal, J. (eds.): Inclusive Design Guidelines for HCI. Taylor & Francis, London (2001)
5. Coleman, R.: Designing for our future selves. In: Preiser, W.F.E., Ostroff, E. (eds.) Universal Design Handbook, pp. 4.1–4.25. MacGraw-Hill, New York (2001)
6. Langdon, P.M., Lewis, T., Clarkson, P.J.: The effects of prior experience on the use of consumer products. UAIS 6, 179–191 (2007)
7. Lewis, T., Langdon, P.M., Clarkson, P.J.: Prior experience of domestic microwave cooker interfaces: A user study. In: Langdon, P.M., Clarkson, P.J., Robinson, P. (eds.) Designing Inclusive Futures, pp. 95–106. Springer, London (2008)
8. Hurtienne, J., Blessing, L.: Design for Intuitive Use - Testing image schema theory for user interface design. In: Proc. ICED, P_386, pp. 1–12. Ecole Centrale, Paris (2007)
9. Gibson, J.J.: The ecological approach to visual perception. Houghton Mifflin, Boston (1979)
10. Koffka, K.: Principles of gestalt psychology. Harcourt, Brace & Co., New York (1935)
11. Johnson, M.: The body in the mind: the bodily basis of meaning, imagination, and reason. University of Chicago Press, Chicago (1987)
12. Hurtienne, J., Blessing, L.: Metaphors as Tools for Intuitive Interaction with Technology. Metaphorik.de 12, 21–52 (2007)
13. Wandke, H., Struve, D., Sengpiel, M.: ALISA – Adaptive Lernumgebung zur Interaktiven Systemnutzung Älterer,
https://www.psychologie.hu-berlin.de/prof/ingpsy/forschung/ALISA/index_alt_html
14. Blackler, A.: Intuitive interaction with complex artefacts. Queensland University of Technology, Brisbane (2006)
15. Raskin, J.: Viewpoint: Intuitive equals familiar. CACM 37(9), 17–18 (1994)
16. Reber, A.S.: Implicit learning of artificial grammars. J. Verb. Learn. Verb. Behav. 6, 855–863 (1967)
17. Cleeremans, A.: Conscious and Unconscious Processes in Cognition. In: Smelser, N.J., Baltes, P.B. (eds.) International Encyclopedia of Social and Behavioral Sciences, pp. 2584–2589. Pergamon, Oxford (2001)
18. Mandler, J.M.: The foundations of mind: origins of conceptual thought. Oxford University Press, Oxford (2004)
19. Casasanto, D., Boroditsky, L.: Time in the mind: Using space to think about time. Cognition 106, 579–593 (2008)
20. Casasanto, D., Lozano, S.: Metaphor in the Mind and Hands. In: Sun, R., Miyake, N. (eds.) Proc. 28th Annual Conference of the Cognitive Science Society, pp. 142–147. Lawrence Erlbaum Associates, Hillsdale (2006)
21. Casasanto, D., Lozano, S.: Meaning and Motor Action. In: McNamara, D., Trafton, G. (eds.) Proc. 29th Annual Meeting of the Cognitive Science Society, pp. 149–154. Cognitive Science Society, Austin (2007)
22. Gibbs, R.W.: The psychological status of image schemas. In: Hampe, B., Grady, J.E. (eds.) From perception to meaning: image schemas in cognitive linguistics, pp. 113–135. Mouton de Gruyter, Berlin (2005)
23. Barsalou, L.W.: Perceptual symbol systems. BBS 22, 577–609 (1999)
24. Proctor, R.W., Vu, K.-P.L.: Stimulus-response compatibility principles: data, theory, and application. CRC/Taylor & Francis, Boca Raton, FL (2006)

25. Hurtienne, J.: Image Schemas and Design for Intuitive Use. Technische Universität, Berlin (in prep.)
26. Wickens, C.D., Carswell, C.M.: The Proximity Compatibility Principle: Its Psychological Foundation and Relevance to Display Design. Human Factors 37, 473–494 (1995)
27. Lund, A.: Massification of the intangible: an investigation into embodied meaning and information visualization. Umeå universitet, Umeå (2003)
28. Hurtienne, J., Israel, J.H., Weber, K.: Cooking up real world business applications combining physicality, digitality, and image schemas. In: Schmidt, A., Gellersen, H.v.d., Hoven, E., Mazalek, A., Holleis, P., Villar, N. (eds.) TEI 2008, pp. 239–246. ACM, New York (2008)
29. Hurtienne, J., Weber, K., Blessing, L.: Prior Experience and Intuitive Use: Image Schemas in User Centred Design. In: Langdon, P.M., Clarkson, P.J., Robinson, P. (eds.) Designing Inclusive Futures, pp. 107–116. Springer, London (2008)
30. Pirhonen, A., Brewster, S., Holguin, C.: Gestural and Audio Metaphors as a Means of Control for Mobile Devices. CHI Letters 4, 291–298 (2002)
31. Docampo, R.M.: Technology generations handling complex User Interfaces. Technische Universiteit, Eindhoven (2001)
32. Fleming, P., Ball, L.J., Collins, A.F., Ormerod, T.C.: Spatial representation and processing in the congenitally blind. In: Ballesteros, S., Heller, M.A. (eds.) Touch, blindness, and neuroscience, UNED Press, Madrid (2004)
33. Knauff, M., May, E.: Mental Imagery, Reasoning, and Blindness. Quarterly J. of Exp. Psychology 59, 161–177 (2006)
34. Persad, U., Langdon, P.M., Clarkson, P.J.: A framework for analytical inclusive design evaluation. In: Proc. ICED, P_536, pp. 1–12. Ecole Centrale, Paris (2007)
35. Langdon, P., Keates, S., Clarkson, P.: Developing cognitive capability scales for inclusive product design. In: Proc. ICED, P_1206, Stockholm, pp. 1–10 (2003)
36. Card, S., Moran, T., Newell, A.: The Psychology of Human-Computer Interaction. Lawrence Erlbaum, Hillsdale (1983)

A Touch Screen Button Size and Spacing Study
with Older Adults

Maria LaVictoire and Nick Everhart

Boston Scientific
Minneapolis, MN
{marie.lavictoire,nick.everhart}@bsci.com

In 2003 Boston Scientific was planning the release of a touch screen-based in-home monitor for patients with Boston Scientific Implanted Cardioverter Defibrillators (ICD). The demographic of these patients is heavily weighted towards older populations. The research, recommendations, and guidelines at that time were largely based on young healthy users. Hence, a need existed to determine acceptable button size and spacing for aged populations.

The purpose of this study was to determine a minimum touch screen button size for use by older participants with heart conditions. This study used a total of 16 participants: nine females and seven males. The age range was 51 to 79 years old, the mean age = 66.2 (SD=9.6). All of the participants were allowed to wear corrective eyewear if needed and self-reported their vision as 3 or better on a four point scale (with 4 being "excellent").

The results from this study were used to specify: (1) the optimal button height and vertical spacing for a set of buttons stacked vertically and (2) the optimal width and horizontal spacing for a set of buttons laid horizontally. A baseline button size (0.75" wide x 0.75" high) was approximated based on recommendations from the U.S. Army Weapons Systems Human-Computer Interface Style Guide (1999) and a "minimum" button size (0.5" x 0.5") was selected based on the size of the proposed touch screen and the needs of the interface. The optimal button height was determined by holding the button width constant (0.5") and varying the button height (0.5" and .75") while the optimal button width was determined by holding the button height constant (0.5") and varying the button width (0.5", 0.62" and 0.75"). The optimal between-button spacing was determined by randomly varying the between-button spacing (0.11", 0.18". 0.30", and 0.59") for each button size. Seated participants were presented with a touchscreen displaying a set of four identical buttons and a text sentence indicating which button they were to press. Each finger touch resulted in a new instruction being presented. Each participant had 560 button touches with each button/spacing combination having 20 button touches. It was possible for a participant to have more than 560 finger touches as a "miss" was not counted in the button touch total. The buttons were activated "on release". Participants were not allowed to practice with the touchscreen prior to the start of test. Participants were allowed to set the angle of the touchscreen to one that was comfortable and reduced the glare on the screen. The screen was placed on a "standard height" table in front of the participant and participants were allowed to position themselves to interact with the screen. Data from one of the participants was eliminated as they were unable to complete the tasks.

C. Stephanidis (Ed.): Universal Access in HCI, Part I, HCII 2009, LNCS 5614, pp. 261–262, 2009.
© Springer-Verlag Berlin Heidelberg 2009

Accuracy (errors, misses) was collected for every finger touch. An "error" was defined as when a participant pressed the incorrect button and a "miss" was defined as when the participant touched the touch screen but did not press a button. For this study, the following information was examined: (1) percentage of trials containing an error and (2) the overall number of misses. Analysis of the data indicated that there was a less than 1% difference in the number of incorrect button presses across all button sizes and between-button distances. Additional analysis was performed to determine if there was a notable number of button misses between the different button sizes and spacing. This analysis indicated that there was a less than 2% difference in the number of button misses across all button sizes and between-button distances. Therefore, we selected 0.5" x 0.5" for our minimum button size.

Reference

Department of the Army. U.S. Army Weapon Systems Human Computer Interface (WSHCI) Style Guide (Version 3), pp. 6.4–6.5 (1999),
http://www.pnl.gov/wshciweb/Wshciv3.exe (retrieved March 27, 2009)

Access Tool? Accelerating Treadmill?
Technology and the Aging Population

Clayton Lewis and Lise Menn

Institute of Cognitive Science, University of Colorado, Boulder, CO, USA
{Clayton.lewis,lise.menn}@colorado.edu

Abstract. Smart homes, smart cars, and electronic interactions with family, merchants, and service providers promise to make the lives of the elderly and people with disablities much easier. Paradoxically, the constantly accelerating pace of technological change will eventually make the machines we live with inaccessible to everyone who has a normal life span. Thought, planning, policy formulation, and action will be required to insure that everyday technology maintains interfaces that will be accessible to aging users, who are among the people who need it most. The User Access community is uniquely qualified to formulate and pioneer accessible design principles, and to bring these principles and policies to the attention of the public, relevant non-government organizations like the AARP, and public officials.

Keywords: older adults, Web, interface, design policy, disabilities.

1 Introduction

We and our family and friends – and even our children - will likely outlive our ability to cope with technology as we know it. As seniors, we may be unable to click or touch the right place on a panel; we will need more time to read, and to hear; we will need bigger print, clearer contrast, and more repetitions of instructions. We will forget that what we need might be something that we can't see because it's behind the active window, off the screen, or to be found in a different display mode. We will lose track of what mode we are in if something doesn't remind us. Incoming stimuli will make us lose track of what we were doing and overwhelm important top-down cognitive processing. At the same time, inappropriate top-down processing will distort incoming signals and make it difficult for us to react to them correctly.

Meanwhile, the pace of change will continue to accelerate. What we learned to do on version 6.1.2 of some program may not work a month later on version 6.1.3. People are already on an accelerating technological treadmill, and we will, sooner or later, fall off unless we die before we get old. Or unless enough people in the technology community are humane enough, foresighted enough, and savvy enough to create a technological safety net underneath that treadmill. That is, technology, appropriately directed, may be able to help us deal with its own challenges as we age. What is the potential for this, and how can it be realized?

Our focus is not on the wide range of services that technology can provide, important those these are. For example, many seniors, and their families, benefit from

C. Stephanidis (Ed.): Universal Access in HCI, Part I, HCII 2009, LNCS 5614, pp. 263–268, 2009.
© Springer-Verlag Berlin Heidelberg 2009

emergency alert bracelets or pendants that allow the wearer to summon help at the press of button, or even, in some cases, when the alert device senses that they have fallen. Services like this will become cheaper, and more widely available, as technology and communication infrastructure improve. But our special concern is how the problems *created by technology itself*, problems of access and control that emerge as we age, can be dealt with.

2 Technology-Driven Challenges

Household appliances. Digital technology has made it possible for appliances like microwaves, dishwashers, or washing machines, to support much more complex functions than their predecessors of a generation ago. This trend brings with it three challenges as we age.

First, there are more controls. Space constraints mean that their labels are small and hard to read unless you have excellent vision. The controls themselves are likely to be buttons, rather than knobs, and, especially in the case of popular membrane devices, often offer no tactile cues in operation. Did I push that or didn't I? Did I push the wrong one?

Second, operations are harder to understand. Few devices are simply "on" or "off". Rather, multiple modes of operation, combining different settings applied for different amounts of time in some sequence, are common.

Third, many controls have time constraints: home entry alarms must be armed and disarmed quickly, with no way to adjust the time allowed, and many devices with multiple modes of operation revert automatically to default mode, again without a way to slow that reversion time down or put it under manual control.

Communication devices. The simple term "phones" no longer does justice to this category. Our "phones" can send and receive text messages or emails, take and share photographs, play music, and more. The problems mentioned for appliances surface here, too, in more acute form. Because portability, and hence small size, is crucial, controls, and displays, are small, and impossible to use for many older people. The wealth of features is, likewise, hard to understand for many older people - and other people, too.

Computers. As we all know, computers are no longer just tools for work. Rather, because of the emergence of the Internet, including the World Wide Web as an important life resource, computers are crucial portals for many people in their private lives. But operating and maintaining a computer is a major challenge for many older people. The treadmill in our title barely seems metaphorical: One has to continually upgrade the operating system itself, and one's virus protection, to protect against cybersecurity threats that can be utterly disabling. One has to upgrade or replace one's computer itself at frequent intervals, to accommodate upgrades of common software that require more memory, and/or a current version of an operating system, to work.

The Internet and Web. The Internet exposes its users to threats that can be difficult for older people to understand and counter. Phishing attacks and other scams are sometimes aimed specifically at seniors, as in the case of a phishing attack that simulated email from the Social Security Administration [1]. Protecting personal information online is a challenge for users generally, not just older people for whom managing a stable of passwords may be especially difficult.

Websites can pose perceptual and cognitive difficulties. Small font sizes and cluttered screens can be difficult to read. Typical commercial sites feature multiple navigation paths, and multi-stage transactions, that can be difficult to follow.

Technology in public places. ATM's, elevators, vending machines, public transit ticket vendors, announcement boards, and even parking meters also present cognitive and sensory challenges.

3   Technology-Driven Remedies

We see we have quite a budget of challenges for older people posed by technology. How can technology itself help us to deal with these challenges?

Response of technology to market forces. As the population in many developed countries ages, we can expect that these challenges will be better met by new technology designed to appeal to older buyers. But progress may be slow. The economics of mass production, and the importance of insuring that there is very wide amortization of high design and development costs in meeting low price points for digital technology, work against products aimed at only a share of the market. Further, some vendors fear loss of trend-shaping "youth oriented" sales if they are associated with "granny" products.

Assistive add-ons. People with poor vision can buy screen magnifier software for their computer that increases font size, or software that allows them to have selected text read aloud. Blind users can buy screen readers that allow them some access to appropriately designed programs and Web sites. But many people who could use such aids do not have them, sometimes due to cost, and sometimes due to lack of awareness or help in understanding what tools are available and appropriate. Further, these tools are only beginning to be available for communication devices, and are not available at all for home appliances like microwaves.

The Universal Remote project [2], led by the TRACE Center at the University of Wisconsin, has developed a standard for home appliances and other devices that would change this situation, if adopted. The standard specifies an interface that would allow the device to be controlled by a remote controller, similar in concept to a TV remote. A user would have a single remote that could be used with all compliant devices, and that would be designed and configured with the user's needs in mind. For example, the buttons and display would be large and easy to see and operate, in the form of remote that would be chosen by many older people. The remote could help with the cognitive demands of operating complex appliances by offering simple controls only for basic operations.

Accessible infrastructure. Computer operating systems commonly offer some features that can ease use for older people, such as screen magnifiers and limited text-to-speech conversion. The Webanywhere project at the University of Washington builds on operating system support to demonstrate that screen reader support for blind users, can be provided in a wide range of settings, including many public computers. The Raising the Floor Initiative, led by Gregg Vanderheiden and Jim Fruchterman [3, 4], aims to build such support into all commonly-used information infrastructure, including communication devices.

Technology that monitors itself. The same advances that have given us increasingly complex appliances can also give us appliances that can tell when things are going wrong. A security system could detect that the user is barely getting out of the house in the time that is allowed before the alarm is armed, and increase the interval that is allowed. A stove with complicated timed operations could detect that food is burning and shut down before the smoke alarm goes off, or could perhaps detect that food has not reached a safe temperature.

Once a device detects a problem it may be able to respond itself, as in the examples above. But sometime the best response would be to communicate the problem to a caregiver or monitor. For example, if someone has misadjusted their heating system, so that the temperature falls into the freezing range, an alarm could be dispatched.

Design for extensibility. The escalating complexity of all kinds of devices, often called "featuritis", is driven by the reluctance of consumers to buy products that lack what they feel are potentially useful features. In market surveys consumers sometimes say they want simpler products, but they don't buy them when offered. A potential response to this problem is to configure a product to offer only basic functions initially, but with an easy way to add new features if they are wanted. This avoids the need to market a low-volume, "basic" product, while supporting both consumers who really need a basic product, and consumers who really want a lot of special features and functions.

The application stores that have rapidly become popular for the iPhone and the Android G1 phone [5] are attractive from this point of view. Literally hundreds of applications can be added to a phone by anyone who wants them, but these do not complicate the lives of users who do not want them.

User support. Many older people rely on family or friends to help them manage their computers, including carrying out upgrades and solving problems. Technology such as GoToMyPC [6] makes it possible for this support to be provided remotely, a great convenience factor in our mobile society. When a user is stuck or confused, someone else can view their computer screen and take the actions needed to sort out the difficulty.

Cognitive science and innovation in accessible technology design. Some barriers to using technology are sensory. These, as we indicated at the beginning of this paper, are not limited to difficulties with vision. Feedback for touch controls has already been mentioned; multimodal feedback (tactile, visual, and auditory) is desirable. Auditory feedback has to actually be hearable: loud enough and low enough in pitch. Visual feedback about something that needs attention ought to blink like a cursor.

Other barriers are based deeper in cognition. Against the desire for central controls for everything is the brain's need for controls with unique functions that are clearly linked to the context in which they will be used and that can't be confused with the controls for something else (what, you've never picked up the TV remote when the phone rang?) For people at risk of forgetting what they had intended to do by the time they get to the place to do it, stove controls should not look like the thermostat controls.

Security and updating. There are technical approaches emerging for many of these issues. Schemes for sharing authentication among different Web applications, like OpenID, can reduce the need for multiple passwords. Work at Intel Research is exploring ways to scan the information sent out from a computer, so that sending credit card numbers or bank information could be blocked, thwarting phishing attacks [7].

As mentioned earlier, keeping software up to date for security reasons is part of the treadmill we are all on. Cloud computing, in which nearly all of our software is stored on servers on the Internet, rather than our local machines, will simplify this problem, because updates will be done for us on the servers.

4 The Role of Regulation

Some of the supports just discussed cannot be provided without the cooperation of technology providers, and this cooperation isn't always forthcoming voluntarily. For example, improperly constructed Web sites fix the size of fonts, so that users cannot make them larger. Conscientious information providers avoid these problems by following Web accessibility guidelines [8], but not all providers are conscientious, or sufficiently knowledgeable, or prepared to deal with regulation [9].

Information technology in the US, including the Web, is subject to a patchwork of regulations at the federal and state levels. The Americans with Disabilities Act includes broad language about the rights of people with disabilities, including those with problems common among older people, like low vision, but whether these protections apply to the Web has been contentious. Recent legal action is encouraging, but not yet definitive [10]. Section 508 of the Rehabilitation Act [11] requires the federal government, and some other entities, to acquire and use only "accessible" technologies, and Section 255 of the Telecommunications Act [12] includes requirements for communication devices.

Section 255 provides a good illustration both of the need for regulation and the challenges of applying it effectively. The enormously popular iPhone cannot be used by many people with hearing aids, though hearing aid compatibility is a regulatory requirement. The iPhone has been held to be exempt from the regulation, because of a provision intended to ease the burden of regulation on small producers, those selling only one kind of phone. Apple sells only one kind of phone, but very many of them. (The iPhone also has other accessibility problems, including controls that are difficult to operate by touch – see [13].)

A good many technologists, including many in the Internet community, oppose regulation intended to increase access to technology for people with "impairments" on the grounds that innovations that are valuable for many people will be stifled. Other people argue that, without regulation, technologists will ignore the rights of participation by people with disabilities (including many older people). USACM, the policy arm of the ACM, the leading professional society for computer science, has adopted a resolution on Web access that attempts to balance these concerns [14].

The Universal Remote project, described earlier, may be an example of an initiative that will require regulation in order to succeed, because appliance manufacturers may see no benefit in entering a market in which consumers don't have remote controllers (which can't control appliances that aren't yet available.) But this chicken or egg dilemma may be broken by the possibility of applications for the iPhone or similar devices that would allow them to be used as remotes.

5 Agenda

What can we do to improve the situation for older people today, and for our future selves? Political action in support the UN Declaration on the Rights of Persons with Disabilities may improve the situation in many countries, including the US.

Consumer organization will also help. The action of market forces will be enhanced if consumers express their need and preference for appropriate technology. The AARP, the largest US advocacy group for older citizens, does not currently have an interest group on technology and aging, but one could be started, using the Web support for groups that the organization already provides. Such a group could identify constructive technology trends, and publicize products that embody or block them.

Many members of this audience will be able to contribute to the development of the technology we are describing, not just help to define the needs. An interest group could help organize that response, as well. And in recruiting allies, remember that what benefits the senior population is also likely to benefit children, and people of all ages with a wide range of physical and cognitive difficulties, and all of us when we are tired, overloaded, and multitasking, so starting by creating a broad coalition may be a good move.

References

1. http://www.ssa.gov/pressoffice/pr/colaPhishingScam-pr.htm (retrieved February 13, 2009)
2. http://trace.wisc.edu/urc/ (retrieved February 13, 2009)
3. http://www.raisingthefloor.net/ (retrieved February 13, 2009)
4. http://www.socialprofitnetwork.org/cs/jim.shtml (retrieved February 13, 2009)
5. http://www.androidg1.org/ (retrieved February 13, 2009)
6. http://www.GoToMyPC.com (retrieved February 13, 2009)
7. http://www.seattle.intel-research.net/projects.php#tw (retrieved February 13, 2009)
8. http://www.w3.org/TR/WCAG20/ (retrieved February 13, 2009)
9. http://www.alistapart.com/articles/tohellwithwcag2 (retrieved February 13, 2009)
10. http://www.law.com/jsp/article.jsp?id=1202424114568 (retrieved February 13, 2009)
11. http://www.section508.gov (retrieved February 13, 2009)
12. http://www.access-board.gov/telecomm/index.htm (retrieved February 13, 2009)
13. http://forums.macrumors.com/showthread.php?t=522071 (retrieved February 13, 2009)
14. http://www.acm.org/public-policy/accessibility (retrieved February 13, 2009)

Use Cases Functionality of the OASIS HCI

Maria Panou[1], Evangelos Bekiaris[1], Maria Fernanda Cabrera-Umpierrez[2],
Viveca Jiménez Mixco[2], and Maria Teresa Arredondo[2]

[1] Centre for Research and Technology Hellas, Hellenic Institute of Transport,
Thessaloniki, Greece
{mpanou,abek}@certh.gr
[2] Polythecnic University of Madrid, Madrid, Spain
{chiqui,vjimenez,mta}@lst.tfo.upm.es

Abstract. Within OASIS, a set of detailed Use Cases have been developed, after capturing the specific needs of elderly users on the use and acquisition of services for the support of their every day life. These use cases offer direct input to the design and development of the user interaction elements in terms of key characteristics, such as self-adaptivity and personalisation parameters that abide to the devices capabilities and environmental restrictions and satisfy the user personal needs and wants.

Keywords: use cases, personalisation, user needs, self-adaptation, independent living, autonomous mobility.

1 Introduction

OASIS Integrated Project (co-funded by the EC, under the 7th FP), introduces an innovative, Ontology-driven, Open Reference Architecture and System, which will enable and facilitate interoperability, seamless connectivity and sharing of content between different services and ontologies in all application domains relevant to applications for the elderly and beyond.

A Use Case, as a description of an actor's interaction with the system to be designed, is both a description of the system's user interface and an indirect description of some function that the system will provide (Ferg S., 2003). Thus, the use case is a powerful description to preview and analyze the functionality of a system and its human-computer interaction characteristics, to satisfy the user needs. There is a narrow area where the real world interacts directly with the system and this is exactly the use cases area.

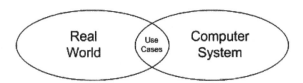

Fig. 1. Use cases as an interaction between the real world with the computer system (Ferg, 2003)

C. Stephanidis (Ed.): Universal Access in HCI, Part I, HCII 2009, LNCS 5614, pp. 269–277, 2009.
© Springer-Verlag Berlin Heidelberg 2009

A Use Case is made up of scenarios. Scenarios do not just refer to what the system can do, but also refer to those interactions that the system must be able to identify as invalid (e.g. error conditions and exceptions). Scenarios consist of a sequence of steps to achieve the goal, which define the interaction level between user-system; each step in a scenario is a sub goal of the use case. As such, each sub-goal represents an autonomous action that is at the lowest level desired by our use case decomposition. This hierarchical relationship is needed to properly model the requirements of a system being developed, including the technical characteristics of its operation and its interaction by the potential user. In addition, it helps avoid the explosion of scenarios that would occur if we were to try to simply list all possible ways of interacting with the system.

In the current paper, the OASIS Use Cases (UCs) are presented, discussing also their impact and contribution to the HMI design and development. Also, a sort explanation of the methodology followed for the definition of the UCs, is provided.

2 Methodology

The work started with a technological benchmarking on mobility issues and smart workplaces, which led to the identification of relevant gaps. Next, face-to-face interviews were realised in five countries (with 38 carers and 132 elderly users), in order to find the elderly users specific needs.

A thorough literature and market survey has been performed in the area of services for the every day support of elderly people. Not only past and existing systems have been collected and reviewed, but also relevant projects and services. Issues that have been considered are related to technological aids, systems and services to support the elderly in pre-trip and on-trip info, using public and private transportation means, as well as flexible on-demand services, utilizing specialized travel packages. Furthermore, the support of the elderly as tourists or workers, working from home or at the workplace without a fixed office, or even as mobile workers has been taken into account. Also, independent living applications and services are included, such as health monitoring, home automation, memory enhancement, physical activity management, etc.

All the retrieved results have been directly inserted in an on-line database that has been developed in the framework of OASIS, allowing clustering of and a structured presentation of the results. The database of relevant technologies provides useful information for each identified entity, such as relevant technical characteristics, costs and producer/promoter details, as well as - when available - information on compliance to an ontology, applications used in, type of users, method of use, usability issues, etc. Currently, the database consists of 601 Products, 33 Services and 46 Research Projects.

The main issue before extracting the Use Cases for OASIS was the development of an adequate format to describe them. Thus, an analytic template has been developed in order to identify and describe as thoroughly as possible the Use Cases, and the way they should be formally described. Most of the defined areas, constitute a significant source of input to the human-computer interaction design and development of the project, for the relevant system/module that each UC refers to. The following table presents these areas, including their relation to the HCI issues.

Table 1. OASIS UCs analysis areas and their relation to HCI issues

Issue	HCI relevance	Comments
Context of use (aim)	~	Partially relevant, i.e. only for those UCs the their aim depicts directly the HCI characteristics
Primary actor	√	Directly relevant, as the user specific needs and wants determine the self-adaptivity of content/info presentation and their accessibility parameters.
Secondary actor(s)	√	As above, but the needs of those actors in term of the UI will not be satisfied with the same details as above.
Connected UCs	~	Partially relevant, i.e. only in case that there are connected UCs that determine the design and behaviour of the human-computer interaction.
Priority Level	√	High priority UCs (see explanation on the prioritisation levels in section 2.3) fulfil all the OASIS goals in terms of the self-adaptive, personalisation interaction strategies.
Scenario(s)	√	The detailed scenarios (each UC consists of several scenarios) give more detailed info for the build-up elements and behaviour of the system-user interaction.
System output	√	Totally relevant to the system HCI design.
Relevant OASIS WP	-	
Services involved	√	The number and type of involved services give an insight on the system interface characteristics.
Devices & restrictions	√	This is one of the basic parameters that study on the level of user interaction needs to take into account. Also, alternative HCI concepts must exist for certain key services.
Critical success parameters	~	Partially relevant, i.e. if one or more of these parameters relate directly or indirectly with the HCI concepts.
Environmental restrictions	~	Such limitations need to be known by the system, in case of need to provide info to the user with alternative means/ components.
Interaction level	√	Self-evident that this issue is highly relevant to the HCI.
Personalisation/ adaptation level	√	Fully relevant, as the personalisation parameters relate also to the type and the way of info provision to the elderly user.
Quality of service indicators	~	Partially relevant, i.e. only if the indicator concerns HCI issues.
Potential input needed from other UCs (what input and which UCs?)	~	Only in case this input is related to the user interaction concept.
Important accessibility attributes (per UG)	√	These attributes affect directly the UI appearance and functionality.
Background info (reason on assigning the priority)	-	

Thus, the UCs analytical descriptions, based on the above fields, provide a significant contribution for the HCI development in terms of its functionality, adaptivity, interaction, personalization, etc.

2.1   Use Cases Clustering

An important feature of the Use Cases is that their "names" should reflect users' goals and should immediately convey meaning. Taking this into consideration through all processes, Use Cases provide a number of examples containing scenarios of use for OASIS, which should be of great utility for the work being developed by partners, but also for stakeholders and users.

Use Cases categorisation helps dealing with the large number of Use Cases for OASIS. This is considered as a clustering technique that separates UC's by subject area. The subject areas are according work distribution, being thus distinguished in two main fields:

- Independent living applications.
- Autonomous mobility and smart workplaces applications.

The use cases are presented (in section 3) based on the above fields. Furthermore, for each of these 2 fields, several sub-areas are defined, which consist of groups of UCs.

2.2 Use Cases Prioritisation

In order to distinguish Use Cases in terms of value or primacy for OASIS stake-holders (users, users' representatives or other interested entities) as well as in terms of importance for system operation, 3 categories of prioritization are set:

- Essential
- Secondary
- Supportive

Therefore, each Use Case description encloses a level of prioritization. The 'essential' and 'secondary' UCs are the ones that have to be tested in the project pilots, while the 'supportive' ones will be tested only if the specific UC is not covered/tested through another UC. The justification of assigning a specific priority level to the UCs has been provided from each UC provider. As said above, the 'essential' UCs are the ones that have to ensure the automatic adaptation and personalisation features of the system.

3 The OASIS Use Cases

The project UCs are presented in the next 2 sections, per area that they fall to.

3.1 Independent Living Applications Use Cases

There are 60 UCs determined for this area. Many of them relate to each other, by giving/getting input. All the UCs fall in 6 main groups. The list of the main and secondary groups is given below:

- **Category 1: Nutritional Advisor**

    - Nutritional profile definition & personalization
    - Nutritional Plan builder
    - Nutritional Empowerment & assessment
    - Shopping and cooking assistant

- **Category 2: Activity Coach**

  - Activity monitoring multisensorial system
  - Activity characterization
  - Activity Management
  - Rehabilitation support system
  - Fall and other accidents detection

- **Category 3: Brain and skills trainer**

  - Specific cognitive training exercises and activities
  - Stress management exercises
  - Daily activities simulation

- **Category 4: Social Communities platform**

  - Enhanced web experience
  - Collaborative web experience
  - E-learning and Infotainment environments
  - Recreation for the elderly

- **Category 5: Health monitoring**

  - Health profile definition& personalisation
  - Health remote monitoring
  - Health Coach
  - Alerting and assisting applications

- **Category 6: Environmental Control**

  - -n-door user localisation
  - Environmental control applications
  - Intelligent home management

Generic representation diagrams have be produced for each of the main categories above, but also per UC. An example of such a diagram follows below for Category 2: Activity Coach:

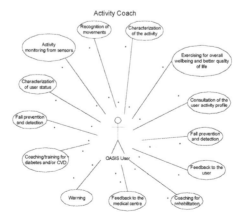

Fig. 2. Activity Coach generic Representation Diagram

The complete set of the UCs is shown below:

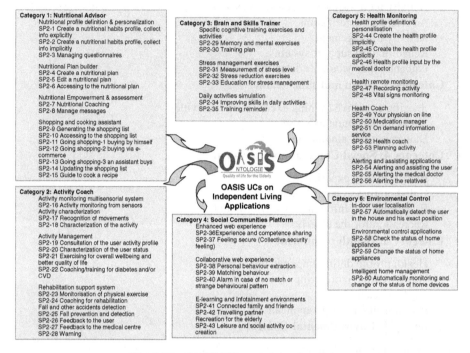

Fig. 3. The OASIS UCs on independent living

3.2 Autonomous Mobility and Smart Workplaces Applications Use Cases

There are 38 UCs determined for this area. Many of them relate to each other, by giving/getting input. All the UCs fall in 4 main groups. The list of the main and secondary groups is given below:

- **Category 1: Transport information services**
  - Pre-trip info
  - Short range trip info
  - Info in stations and hubs
  - TMIC interface
  - Long-range trip info
  - Multimodal trip planning
- **Category 2: Route guidance**
  - In-vehicle
  - Pedestrian
- **Category 3: Personal mobility**
  - On-demand services
  - Driver telematic support

- Driver comfort support
- Tourism and leisure

- **Category 4: Smart workplaces**

  - Smart workplaces
  - Telematic tools and technologies for flexi-work

As in section 3.1, generic representation diagrams have been built for the main categories, as well as each UC individually. The following figure shows the set of UCs:

Fig. 4. The OASIS UCs on autonomous mobility and smart workplaces

3.3 HCI and the OASIS Use Cases

The issue of HCI is involved in the majority of the defined use cases, both of sections 3.1 and 3.2. This was expected, as all UCs deal with the development of new systems, with innovative user interfaces, satisfying automatic self-adaptivity and personalisation concepts.

The need of appropriate HCI design is depicted in the presentation of a synthetic UC, combining the application areas of sections 3.1 and 3.2. The synthetic UC description is: Planning a trip (Fig. 5a), using route guidance, deciding to record a film on the DVD (Fig. 5b) while on trip (through the OASIS remote environmental control module), sharing the trip experience with a friend (OASIS social activities support;

Fig. 5c), and returning at home, using the nutritional advisor and health monitoring advice (Fig. 5d). This sequence of actions requires the use of a mobile device by the user, as shown below:

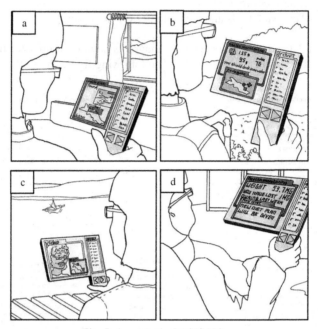

Fig. 5. A synthetic OASIS UC

The key device for the delivery of mobile services is the PDA, whereas other possible needed devices include smart PDA or smartphone, bus-stop information panel, etc. Their effective use will require several challenges to be considered beforehand. These are relisted below, along with some thoughts for consideration in OASIS:

• Challenge: Individual user needs and preferences

Personalisation of HCI should be performed automatically by the system, according to user type, profile (based on history if use, with the user being always the master of his/her profile), culture and context of use, but also progressively, following user actions (i.e. a user without car, now has also a car) and age-related deterioration characteristics (e.g. automatic adjustment of the size of the letters in the screen). Furthermore, cross-cultural factors are influencing human-computer interactions from different dimensions (perceptual, cognitive, and affective). Rather than cultural-specific appearance, a cultural-adaptive system should also adapt metaphors, navigation and interactions to the culture of target users, for better performance and higher satisfaction. Configurable and culture-adaptive interfaces are needed.

• Challenge: User navigation throughout the service chain.

Intelligent multimedia dialogues and high interaction level are absolutely needed, to allow the user to navigate easily from one service to another or within a service.

- Challenge: Device limitations.

Alternative HCI concepts must exist for some key services, to be able to be supported in "poorer" devices too (i.e. lacking vibration). Also external HCI modules (i.e. vibrating belt or seat belt) need to be available.

- Challenge: Services competing among them for users' attention or providing concurrently info or warnings by the same or different media.

Need for services hierarchy and HCI integration. Also, need for multi-sensual systems, to be able to handle multiple-warnings and support users with various problems in information retrieval channels.

4   Conclusions

The OASIS use cases (UC) and scenarios of use have been defined based upon literature review, on-site interviews, technological benchmarking and iterative consensus building among key stakeholders, already present in the OASIS Consortium and user group representatives.

As the use cases form an immediate reflection of user needs and relevant gaps in the area of services for the daily support of the elderly population definition of OASIS, they constitute the starting point of work for the definition of the user-computer interaction platform and properties, being the easy customisation and system reconfiguration (e.g. through assisted dialogues), personalisation to the individual need and preferences of the users, self-adaptivity of content presentation according to environmental constraints, devices restrictions, cultural characteristics, multi-services interconnection, etc.

References

1. Cabrera-Umpierrez, M.C., Jimenez-Mixco, V., Bonfiglio, S., Bekiaris, E., Panou, M., Pilar, M., Mocholí, J.B., Robledo, M., Van Isacker, K., Maza, C., Staehli, B.: OASIS Deliverable 2.1.1 Use Cases and application scenarios for independent living applications (March 2008)
2. Stephen, F.: What's wrong with use cases? (2003),
   http://www.jacksonworkbench.co.uk/stevefergspages/papers/
   ferg-whats_wrong_with_use_cases.html
3. Panou, M., Bekiaris, E., Van Isacker, K., Stamatov, M., Goranova, M., Lazarov, A., Otermin, A.M., Leonidis, A., Franken, V., Pachinis, T., Visintainer, F., Pantelopulos, S.: OASIS Deliverable 3.1.1, Use cases and application scenarios for mobility and smart workplaces (March 2008)

Keep It Simple! Assisting Older People with Mental and Physical Training

Herbert Plischke[1] and Niko Kohls[2]

[1] Peter-Schilffarth-Institut für Soziotechnologie, Prof.-Max-Lange-Platz 16,
83677 Bad Toelz, Germany
plischke@peter-schilffarth-institut.de
[2] Generation Research Program, Human Science Center, University of Munich,
83677 Bad Toelz, Germany
kohls@grp.hwz.uni-muenchen.de

Abstract. The demographic change is having a strong impact upon Europe's societies and upon our financial and social security systems. To avoid cost intensive retirement homes, one main goal for European governments is to build up and maintain a socio-technological infrastructure that allows elderly people to stay in their familiar surroundings and cultivate their social networks as long as possible, with support of assistive technologies. However, when deployed in real-life settings, i.e. "in the wild", it has been shown that these will only be accepted and therefore effective, when integrated into an environment that aims at enhancing people's health and well-being in general. Although it is well known that moderate physical training as well as mental exercising are crucial for maintaining health and well-being, lack of motivation frequently prevents individuals from exercising regularly. We introduce a simple way to motivate elderly people for mental jogging and physical training with assistive indoor and outdoor technology.

Keywords: demographic change, social interaction, social network, social technology, mental jogging, physical training, elderly care, AAL, ambient assisted living, Near Field Communication, NFC, senior playground.

1 Introduction

Most elderly people in Europe and elsewhere aspire to live in their own four walls and familiar surroundings in an independent and self determined way as long as possible. In comparison to the United States, resident areas exclusively for senior citizens are less common in Europe. The goal of senior areas is to provide living conditions in a secure and comfortable environment, frequently with several generations living together, so that tight social bonding can be combined with individual independency.

However, moving to a senior citizen home can become a necessity despite all individual and collective efforts, usually if an individual loses the ability to organize his or her independent living. Due to the demographic change and the continuously increasing live expectancy, Western societies are progressively forced to develop and maintain concepts, technologies and infrastructure that enable autonomy of senior

C. Stephanidis (Ed.): Universal Access in HCI, Part I, HCII 2009, LNCS 5614, pp. 278–287, 2009.

citizens in their homes, especially if high costs for elderly care in nursing homes are to be avoided.

The concept of salutogenesis developed by the American-Israelian sociologist Aaron Antonovsky (1923–1994) postulates that the experience of well-being is associated with a Sense of Coherence (SOC). Antonovsky considered SOC to consist of the three following core subcomponents [1]:

- Comprehensibility: The perception of the world as being structured, predictable, and explicable that allows an individual to understand his or her environment.
- Manageability: The conviction that resources that are necessary for an individual in order to meet the demands and requirements are available or can be made accessible.
- Meaningfulness: The profound experience of the individual life as being meaningful.

If Antonovsky`s theory is linked to the needs and demands of elderly populations, it is clear that in order to maintain the first two dimensions "comprehensibility" and "manageability" it seems to be essential to maintain physical and mental fitness, as well as mobility and communication as long as possible. Technology may thereby serve as a powerful tool for building and enriching infrastructure that aims at preserving, enhancing, protecting and maintaining mental and physical fitness. Mental and physical fitness is influenced by external and internal factors, such as possibilities to exercise the mind and the body alike (inside and outside) as well as developing, upholding and improving the motivation to do so. Meaningfulness however seems to be an existential dimension that bestows purpose to one's individual life that can only partially be substituted by means of technology.

2 A Biopsychophysiological Approach to Health and Well-Being

Let us first of all take a closer look at the consequences of regular mental training on the brain. In short, this relationship can be described as "use it or lose it", because the brain is actually very similar to a muscle that can be systematically trained by regular exercise and as we all know muscles gradually involute as a consequence of lack of exercise. Research has shown that lifelong learning is crucial for retaining mental fitness. However, systematic mental exercise has to start as early as possible, preferably even as early as the beginning of one's professional career. It is thereby important to highlight that the ability for livelong learning is not restricted to improving cognitive and metacognitive functions but that it may also have consequences on the social environment; one has only to recall that social isolation may occur due to the degrading possibility to develop new or adapt old forms of behavior as well as establish new contacts, for example when moving to a new setting (e.g. senior nursing home).

In addition to mental training for keeping the brain active, we see a strong synergistic effect for maintaining and improving important brain functions by means of physical training. As we know from brain research, the activation of the motor cortex while exercising bodily functions not only strengthens the peripheral muscles but also leads to an enhancement of cognitive functions. This effect is likely due to the increased blood flow in motor areas that results in a co-stimulating effect in related cognitive areas of the cortex. A recent study with eleven young test persons for example examined the effects of aerobic training on brain functions over 12 weeks. After the training program, participants scored significantly better in a memory task and a higher blood flow was detected in neuro-imaging of the Gyrus dentatus, an important region of the brain associated with memory and cognitive functions [2].

Another study found that walking showed a positive outcome for the prevention of dementia. A daily walk of more than 3000 meters leads to a better metabolism and heart and circulation parameters. Additionally, cognitive functions are less deteriorating as a consequence of aging. In a prospective trial with 2.257 healthy male individuals in the age of 71 to 93 a daily waking distance of less than 400 meters showed a 1.8 fold higher risk to develop dementia [3]. Unfortunately, lifestyle and dietary preferences were not considered in this study.

Women also benefit from extended walking. A survey in the Nurses Health Study evaluated 18,766 women between 70 and 81. A 20 percent risk reduction was found in the population with higher physical activity [4].

Examples like these show that the salutogenetic effects of physical and mental exercise go hand in hand. This means that retaining both a socially and existentially meaningful and stimulating atmosphere for the elderly is important, particularly for those with mobility constraints. One important stimulating factor is thereby the existential and spiritual anchoring, which may occur completely independent from denomination or religious affiliation. Empirical studies point to the fact that spirituality may act as a specific health resource, although it may sometimes also induce distress. Particularly some spiritual and meditative consciousness practices have not only been associated with an increased amount of resilience against stress but also proven to increase quality of life and well-being, even under difficult health and deteriorating life conditions.

However, although the pathways mediating the spirituality health connection remain largely unclear for the time being, some recent studies point to the fact that some aspects of spirituality such as the ability of self-transcendence may be associated with the configuration of important neurotransmitter subsystems in the brain such as the serotonin system. Since the serotonin system also plays a key role in mediating important psychophysiological, one might speculate that the ability to have spiritual experiences may also be associated with the ability to self-induce automatic healing responses of the body. In other words, since spiritually inclined or practicing individuals might be able to trigger so called "unspecific healing effects" by means of particular mind-body techniques, they might respond to medical treatment and intervention in a better way because they are able to exploit the psychologically induced unspecific effects in a more efficient way. Put simply, these individuals might be better responders to unspecific than specific effects. The holistic effect of a drug therapy therefore may not depend upon the active agent.

Kirsch et al. for example found in a recent metaanalysis that in mild depressive disorders placebo pills that simply consisted of sugar, have proven to be as effective as real drugs such as selective serotonin re-uptake inhibitors SSRI [5]. Thus the positive impact of the psychological mindset of an individual as it is mediated by psychological constructs such as expectancy or mindfulness can be considered to be a strongly underestimated field in health care and medicine. Ambient Assisted Living in the Wild might benefit a great deal from this approach.

3 Assisting Older People with Physical Training

Although details of the pathways from physical training to supporting and improving cognitive functions are not known for the time being, their existence cannot be questioned any longer in the light of the evidence. Thus, the question remains, how this insight may best be harnessed for improving and maintaining the well-being and health of elderly populations.

To begin with, let us take a look at state of the art in the indoor and outdoor home training systems. Apart from the traditional home exercisers with mostly mechanical parts, newer more sophisticated fitness devices that are also available for the elderly are computer programmable and monitor physiological parameters such as heart rate or blood pressure. The possibility of measurement of physiologic parameters allows individualizing the training in accordance with the actual fitness and strength level; an inbuilt-training history function systematically allows to analyse the effects of this training. However, technical functions like these are frequently not used by seniors due to a design that is not suitable for them e.g. haptic problems with plastic foil keypad and complicated menu navigation.

Newer concepts in Europe try to assist outdoor physical activity for seniors and kids by means of shared playgrounds that have been designed to fulfil both the needs and demands of kids and seniors. "Young at heart" or "moving seniors" is the new playground concept inspired by fitness parks in China. The first playground for seniors was opened in Berlin 2007. The idea was to encourage old people to keep themselves both fit and also allow them to socialize. This seems to work in the Berlin case, with the drawback that using the playground is only allowed for persons taller than 1.5 meters (5 feet). Unfortunately, this excludes the very young.

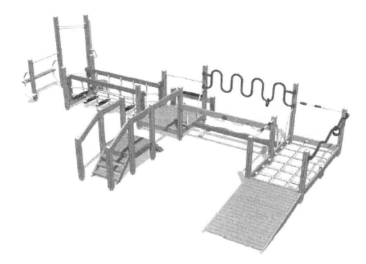

Fig. 1. The picture illustrates the concept "Moving Seniors" with easy to learn calisthenics and concentration training. Future concepts could integrate wireless sensors for documentation and visualization of training results (history function). The data transmission is realized over mobile phone with near field communication (NFC). User information direct or over a home based TV-application (Source: Sportkreativwerkstatt Munich).

A pilot project of the Peter-Schilffarth-Institute is to combine wireless sensors (near field communication) with outdoor and indoor training devices for visualization, documentation (history function) and a neuronal network feedback. It is simple to use, because the user just has to point with the mobile phone at the training gear and the stored parameters can be seen after the training in a TV-based health application at home with the possibility of receiving individualized feedback. Together with the parameters of mental training and change of nutritional behavior, a feedback for an individually optimized fitness program is possible.

4   Assisting Older People with Mental Training

It is common knowledge that brain jogging for patients suffering from dementia has positive effects [6]. Scientifically not yet proven is the effect of brain jogging programs for the maintenance and enhancement of the normal mental competence of healthy persons. One drawback in scientific studies is the selectivity of tasks in testing conditions, such as mental arithmetic or pattern recognition, where an improvement is obvious [7, 8].

In real life, however, we have to cope with multiple and complex tasks and activities of daily living (ADL) . Research has not found evidence for the amelioration of ADL through selective training. However, there is a growing body of evidence that so called mind-body techniques are associated with improved mental capacities and enhanced resilience against stress. These techniques have become increasingly popular among the public and researchers alike and can be considered to be a hall-mark of Integrative Medicine (IM), as the integration of psychological, medical, mental and physical approaches becomes most clearly visible. Mind-body practices embrace different methods that have one thing in common: they all use some sort of mental-behavioral training and involve modulating states of consciousness in order to influence bodily processes towards greater health and well-being and better functioning.

Possibly the best investigated Mind-Body technique is the „Mindfulness Based Stress Reduction Program" (MBSR) that was developed by Professor Jon Kabat-Zinn at the MIT more than twenty years ago in order to improve the compliance and stress resilience of chronic patients [16]. While the original mindfulness practice has its roots in Buddhist philosophy and correspondingly a religious connotation, the modern versions have to be considered as secular mind-body-techniques that frequently utilize only the meditation technique without the religious and philosophical background. Regular practice of mindfulness meditation should lead to a mindful awareness of one's mental activity and on the long run also to a non-judgmental attitude towards one's own mind and other people's actions. Systematic training of this state of mindfulness apparently allows an individual to develop a certain attitude of acceptance that seems to have salutogenetic effects [9]. MBSR programs have in common that they use principles of mindfulness and teach the patients formal mindfulness meditation, urging them to continue practicing at least within the 8 week program. In a meta-analysis of studies on MBSR we found that MBSR was effective in improving psychological and physical health outcomes across various diseases with an effect size of $d = 0.53$, which can be considered a medium effect that is remarkable when considering the chronicity of the diseases studied [10]. It is also noteworthy that a special adaption for preventing depression relapse has also proven to be effective in patients with recurrent depression in controlled studies [11].

Assistive technical systems for mental training are available, but the interactive form [12] is usually only for use with a personal computer, or the training has to be conducted with paper and pencil [13]. The computerized training however may be a barrier for some elderly individuals, as they may not be familiar with using a computer. Nevertheless, since 2006 a small device is available from Nintendo [14], which offers Brain Jogging for adults. Although this device has a user friendly intuitive graphical user interface and a wireless functionality, it can be connected with other devices of the same type. TV based brain jogging applications are still missing.

To sum up, for preserving the physical and mental functions even at an advanced age, three aspects can be considered to be crucial:, physical activity, brain jogging, relaxation and a reasonable diet (which is not addressed here). Optimal effects are supposed to occur when starting with this mix of prevention at an early age, possibly as integral part of a life philosophy. But still when starting at a later stage in life these three aspects –if observed not in an excessive but an adequate manner, with a sustainably high motivation - are quite effective for staying healthy both mentally and physically. Motivation can be enhanced and fostered by providing a suitable infrastructure.

5   NFC Technology to Keep It Simple

How can information technology assist in mental and physical training? Technology should offer functions that are similar to those that the human brain is accustomed to, for example control actions not only once but repeatedly. This is realized in brain by feedback loops and feedback-dependent reward systems. Using marketing as an analogy, in the same way that a product has to appear "sexy" in order to increase its chances to become a top seller, technology has to appear attractive to the brain. Adequate feedback helps generate "joy of use", and consequently feedback systems should aim at rewarding mental and physical training. How can technology provide feedback systems in physical training devices?

Indoor and outdoor training devices are usually „Stand alone units", i.e. they lack a standardized network connection with other training devices or with a central unit. NFC, or "near field communication" (NFC), is a new possibility to "virtually" connect remote devices (e.g. outdoor training devices) to a host for user feedback.. The principle has been derived from "radio frequency identification" (RFID) Technology. In short RFID is a technology that utilizes the use of electromagnetic or electrostatic coupling in the radio frequency (RF) portion of the electromagnetic spectrum in order to uniquely identify an object, place or organism. Using an additional chip in the mobile phone and a small software application, data from remote devices can be picked up from a physically extant electronic tag and sent to an internet based service. Implementing these tags in outdoor and indoor training gear could be a possibility to receive data from a device with self contained (low) energy supply. With usability optimized software for seniors the software application initiates a transfer of training parameters from the device to a host simply by touching the device with the mobile phone. This facilitates easy collection of outdoor training data for feedback.

Fig. 2. Near field communication (NFC) provides data transmission which is initiated simply by touching a surface with a integrated electronic tag. Applications with NFC for assisting seniors are now under development (Picture: www.smartnfc.com).

6 Assistive Technology with a Personal Touch

As with training devices, assistive systems for mental and physical training for seniors are nowadays only available as stand-alone components. The devices for physical training are electronically controllable and they have connections to transmit measured psychophysiological parameters. A central unit for collection and evaluation of the parameters (e.g. heart frequency, energy used) in connection with other parameters (e.g. calories intake) and with individualized user feedback has not been introduced to the market as yet.

Envisaging the ideal environment for mental and physical training, systems should visualize training data with a history function as well as evaluate data and provide feedback. The training should be possible outside and inside and the feedback device should work without barriers, maybe in the living room at home. Because all of the seniors can handle a TV Set, and a lot of time is spent watching TV, this medium seems to be almost ideal as a central unit for monitoring personal health activities. Moreover, brain jogging in a playful and exciting form could be realized comparatively easily by means of using the TV as a user interface. An individually configurable electronic "Wellness and Health Agent", with optional connection to a service center, in connection with a personal health manager (real person) would be an advance for ambient assistive technology and training support.

A project that aims at the personalization of assistive technology is ALADIN (Ambient lighting assistance for an ageing population), a project co-financed by the European Union . It has developed a platform for relaxation and activation in connection with dynamic lighting. The system provides a monitoring of mental training, which consists of brain jogging and relaxation tasks, biofeedback and history function with user feedback over TV with graphical user interface (TV-GUI). With a Bluetooth

Fig. 3. Communication and information portal implemented on interactive TV and videophone with call center connection. (Source: Sophia GmbH, Germany)

sensor glove biofeedback training over TV-Screen is possible and a usability optimized interface can be easily operated by seniors. Field tests with 12 seniors (age over 65 years) in Austria, Germany and Italy showed a high acceptance of the mental training device and a good effect of dynamic lighting on activation and relaxation.

In addition to already available possibilities for seniors to communicate and interact over their TV-Set [15], the ALADIN System additionally allows to incorporate a biofeedback and mental jogging device. A history function with a neuronal network designed to compute target values provides individualized real-time feedback to the user for mental and physical training support. The combination of technology and personal service, health management and technical attendance creates added value not only for the manufacturer but also for the local service provider economy.

Like in a call center, a bundle of functionalities can be integrated, e.g. personalized health services such as advice for health and well-being , a professional service and social interaction by counseling patrons both face-to-face and by TV-phone communication.. Computer based programs via a TV-based graphical user interface aim at supporting mental and physical fitness at a comparably low cost rate as they can be efficiently be realized by local providers with the assistance of peer-group and call-center.

7   Summary

Specifically designed technological devices for elderly populations, which allow easy to handle mental and physical training support are currently only available as stand-alone gadgets such as home trainers or brain jogging devices and the like. However, these devices are frequently connected to a personal computer, which are sometimes difficult to operate for older individuals. Thus an easy to operate system that is able to facilitate mental and physical exercise, monitor and record progress as well as provide feedback would be desirable. Possibly, one could also think of devices that are able to provide feedback concerning psychophysiological states associated with states of mindfulness or other relaxation states, so that the individual gets feedback at home, even if he or she is not instructed by a mindfulness trainer. Systems like these, although they are not able to substitute for a mind-body technique trainer, could prove to be helpful for upholding the motivation for regular mental and physical exercise.

For user acceptance it is essential to create graphical interfaces, which can be intuitively and effortlessly operated by older individuals. It is desirable that the system is linked with a communication device that allows individuals with mobility constraints to conduct videophone conferences with other people or call centres. This would turn the television not only into a platform for information, communication and interaction but actually into a personal assistant. Even data generated remotely, such as training data from outdoor training facilities could easily be fed into the home systems, for example an USB-stick or alternatively by near-field communication technology.

However, it has to be acknowledged that despite all the fascinating options that state-of-the-art technology can offer, technology cannot be used as a substitute for meaningfulness. Despite these reservations we believe that the prudent use of technology has much to offer for improving the health, well-being and quality of life of senior citizens. And from our field trials we know that the elderly do accept very complex technology, provided it is kept simple. This means that the technology has to provide easy access, effortless processing and efficient action.

References

1. Antonovsky, A.: The salutogenic model as a theory to guide health promotion 1. Health Promotion International 11(1), 11–18 (1996)
2. Pereira, A.C., Huddleston, D.E., Brickman, A.M., Sosunov, A.A., Hen, R., McKhann, G.M., Sloan, R., Gage, F.H., Brown, T.R., Small, S.A.: An in vivo correlate of exercise-induced neurogenesis in the adult dentate gyrus. Proc. Natl. Acad. Sci. 104(13), 5638–5643 (2007)
3. Abbott, R.D., et al.: Walking and dementia in physically capable elderly men. JAMA (292), 1447–1453 (2004)
4. Weuve, J., et al.: Physical activity, including walking, and cognitive function in older women. JAMA (292), 1454–1461 (2004)
5. Kirsch, I., Deacon, B.J., Huedo-Medina, T.B., Scoboria, A., Moore, T.J., et al.: Initial Severity and Antidepressant Benefits: A Meta-Analysis of Data Submitted to the Food and Drug Administration. PLoS Medicine 5(2), e45 (2008)
6. Kawashima, R., Okita, K., Yamazaki, R., Tajima, N., Yoshida, H., Taira, M., Iwata, K., Sasaki, T., Maeyama, K., Usui, N., Sugimoto, K.: Reading Aloud and Arithmetic Calculation Improve Frontal Function of People With Dementia. Journals of Gerontology Series A: Biological Sciences and Medical Sciences 60(3), 380–384 (2005)
7. Mahncke, H.W., Connor, B.B., Appelman, J., Ahsanuddin, O.N., Hardy, J.L., Wood, R.A., Joyce, N.M., Boniske, T., Atkins, S.M., Merzenich, M.M.: Memory enhancement in healthy older adults using a brain plasticity-based training program: A randomized, controlled study. Proc. Natl. Acad. Sci. 103(33), 12523–12528 (2006)

8. Willis, S.L., Tennstedt, S.L., Marsiske, M., Ball, K., Elias, J., Mann-Koepke, K., Morris, J.N., Rebok, G.W., Unverzagt, F.W., Stoddard, A.M., Wright, E.: Long-term Effects of Cognitive Training on Everyday Functional Outcomes in Older Adults. Journal of the American Medical Association 296(30), 2805–2814 (2006)
9. Kohls, N., Sauer, S., Walach, H.: Facets of mindfulness - Results of an online study investigating the Freiburg mindfulness inventory. Personality and Individual Differences (2008)
10. Grossman, P., Niemann, L., Schmidt, S., Walach, H.: Mindfulness-based stress reduction and health benefits A meta-analysis. Journal of Psychosomatic Research 57(1), 35–43 (2004)
11. Teasdale, J.D., Segal, Z.V., Ridgeway, V.A., Soulsby, J.M.: Prevention of Relapse/Recurrence in Major Depression by Mindfulness-Based Cognitive Therapy. Prevention 68(4), 615–623 (2000)
12. Brainwizard, http://www.brainwizard.de
13. Lehrl, Siegfried, Gesellschaft für Gehirntraining e.V, http://www.gfg-online.de/lehrl.html
14. Nintendo, D.S.: http://www.nintendo.de
15. SOPHIA FRANKEN GmbH & Co KG, http://www.sophia-tv.de
16. University of Massachusetts Medical School, Center for Mindfulness (CFM), http://www.umassmed.edu/cfm
17. ALADIN, Ambient Lighting Assistance for an Ageing Population, http://www.ambient-lighting.eu

RACE: Towards Exploring the Design Dimensions of a Route Assisting and Communicating System for Elderly

Suleman Shahid[1], Omar Mubin[2], and Abdullah Al Mahmud[2]

[1] Tilburg centre for Creative Computing,
Department of Information and Communication Sciences
University of Tilburg, Tilburg, The Netherlands
[2] Department of Industrial Design,
Eindhoven University of Technology
Den Dolech 2, 5600 MB, Eindhoven, The Netherlands
s.shahid@uvt.nl, {o.mubin,a.al-mahmud}@tue.nl

Abstract. This paper explores the usability requirements of a navigation system for older adults by identifying the key usability and ergonomic problems in existing navigation systems and proposing a set of new guidelines for designing such systems. We also discuss the design of a new Route Assisting and Communication system for Elderly (RACE) in which design guidelines are incorporated. Our results are primarily obtained from a series of usability evaluations undertaken with the elderly. This paper also identifies a number of advance features that a routing system should have for satisfying older adults on road. We suggest design implications for navigation systems based on our research and lay the path for future work.

Keywords: Elderly, Navigation Systems, Usability, Design Guidelines, Communication.

1 Introduction

The advancements in mobile technology are known to all. An after effect of this has been the swift deployment of navigation aids built on top of mobile technology. Of course this progress and growth has also been rendered possible by the initiation of the Global Positioning System (GPS). Now, users have access to route information that lets them manoeuvre themselves with ease whether in their car, bike, or even just walking. Nearly all state-of-the-art mobile devices provide some navigation feature. With the proliferation of automobiles in our society, there is a certain need of assisting these drivers with modern but easy to use navigation systems which not only help them in driving with ease but also at the same time ensure that their life is in safe hands [2], [10]. Therefore, a number of applications have been built to help in navigation for able and disabled people such as mentioned in [5].

Our research concentrates on filling an existing gap that exists in relation to providing senior citizens with user-friendly navigation systems. Senior citizens are known to be reluctant to accept hi tech systems and thus any navigation system built specifically for the elderly must cater their individual requirements. The elderly are

C. Stephanidis (Ed.): Universal Access in HCI, Part I, HCII 2009, LNCS 5614, pp. 288–296, 2009.

known to be susceptible to confuse interaction with complex interfaces, navigation system being one of them. If they are distracted or occupied with the interaction, it can be hazardous to their life. The issues with GUI based navigation aids for general users have been contemplated elsewhere [4].

Assistive Technology is the talk of the town in modern Human Computer Interaction and our research is a step in its direction. Concerning navigation systems, most of the effort has concentrated on assisting blind and visually impaired users to walk [3, 6]. Even so, there are several examples of map navigation and route finding concepts for pedestrians in general [1], [7] and more interestingly for the elderly walkers [8]. However, to the best of our knowledge not much has been written about navigation aids for the general elderly car driving user group.

We argue for offering the elderly with car navigation aids that are specially tailored for them. The design of such systems must take into account that the elderly are faced with cognitive, sensory disabilities and general impairments occurring with age. The desirable features in a navigation system may not be the same for the young and the old. For example, the best route for the elderly might not be the shortest path but rather the route that has the least traffic [9].

2 User Research

\In order to start off the user requirements gathering phase, we first conducted a series of informal interviews with the elderly. This was followed by a collective focus group discussion amongst the senior citizens. We summarize the findings from both sessions.

2.1 Participants

In total, we held interviews with seven users. Their average age was 72 years, ranging from 67 to 78 years old. Generally, the users were healthy and had no severe disability. All of them had more than 20 years of driving experience and all of them had renewed their driving license. The entire pool of participants had a basic knowledge of navigation systems. Concerning the focus group session, six of the earlier mentioned seven users participated. Two researchers acted as facilitators in the session.

2.2 Method

Firstly, an informal interview session was conducted with every user individually and different questions related to their driving skills were asked. Questions addressed various aspects such as driving habits, driving and finding way in unknown/new places and experience with navigation systems with respect to general likes and dislikes. Secondly, the discussion in the focus group session revolved around almost identical aspects, with the main aim being to arrive at a consensus amongst the participants. As a last supplementary task, we asked participants of the focus group to draw maps (including landmarks) of common travels.

2.3 Results

In this section, we summarize the results from both sessions of the user requirement-gathering phase. It was revealed that the main medium of navigation employed by the elderly was paper maps. Occasionally the spouse of the driver would act as a helper in the navigation process. When the elderly would be completely lost they would ask other commuters as a last resort. They were seemingly not entirely confident with manual navigation, as they would tend to avoid long trips on cars (especially between countries). This was precisely the reason why they highlighted the importance of improving the quality of city maps. For them maps of the city they lived in and of surrounding cities were the most important.

As a part of the focus group, we also asked participants to draw the map of their favourite or most visited route on the paper in as much detail as possible. Upon analyzing maps, it was observed that elderly extensively used landmarks for navigation aid and during discussion; they identified some important landmarks (e.g. station, hospital and church). Interestingly, many participants also drew the major speed limits on the edges of road, which shows the importance of such road signs to them. Few participants also drew the street names but interestingly they only drew the street names, which were either around the starting point or the destination.

With regards to navigation systems they have used in past, the elderly pointed out that they are very complex for them to use and to make it for the first time is quite hard. They also pointed out the continuous voice as feedback was quite irritating. What they missed in the feedback was an affirmative signal that they were going in the right direction or doing the right thing [5]. One person said, "Twice I was stopped by control because I was driving below speed limit". Similarly, another was quoted to say: "Over-speeding is no problem because I usually do not do such ventures anymore but driving slow is, so the system should tell me about this". Most of the users were intimidated by the amount of information presented at one time on the screen, which hampered their user experience.

3   User Evaluation

As a step forward, we organized practical user evaluations within the setup of the cars owned by the elderly users. All our users had their own cars and all them were regular drivers.

3.1   Participants

Six participants took part in this interesting evaluation session. These were the same six participants who participated in the focus group session.

3.2   Method

A facilitator accompanied each participant as they set out to complete two tasks. A camera was installed at the back seat for recording. The task of the participant was to reach particular specified locations both with and without the use of a navigation system. It was ensured that the locations were never visited prior by the elderly. In the case of finding route using paper maps, participants were provided with a task book explaining their task. They were allowed to bring assistive material with them, this included maps and printouts. In the latter case, the navigation system that was used in the test was handed over to them a day before the actual test. There were given time to explore the system. Almost all the elderly had used a navigation system in one way or the other but all of them had used different models of two companies. To achieve consistency, we selected one navigation system for all participants.

3.3 Location/Test Route Features

In order to maintain consistency the two routes chosen were carefully balanced. They had the following three features:

- Equal left and right turns and roundabouts
- Roughly equal checks on speed limits, priority junctions and specially common and high ranked landmarks
- Three side by side turns in both routes

It is arguable that both locations were not the same so results from paper maps condition can be different from the results of navigation system. But an important aspect to consider is that the focus of the study was not go at a detailed level of road structure (with all nodes and connections) but rather to ascertain what is missing in existing navigation systems. Moreover, our goal was to determine how the transition from paper to electronic maps could be ensured in safer and usable manner and at the same time reducing the learning curve to a minimum.

3.4 Evaluation Goal

Our evaluation aimed to answer several questions. Such as, how older adults use paper maps and navigation systems. Secondly, what do they perceive as missing from navigation systems and thirdly, what are the usability problems of such systems.

Fig. 1. Participant interacting with the system in his car

4 Results

In the situation when participants did not use the assistance of a navigation system, they were observed to carry out comprehensive pre-planning. Number of participants marked the paper map with different tags (left from here or taken a U-turn from church). Few participants also prepared a concise version of the map (using pen and small paper), where only the most important roads and name of interesting landmarks were shown. They were easily consulting these sticky notes while driving and placed them on the top of the car steering. It was also observed that although the participants used text for comprehending and augmenting the paper maps but pictorial representation (signs, landmarks, turns) was extremely important to them, which is also clear from their hand drawn maps. Three participants brought very interesting maps with them where important attractions and landmarks were represented using big pictorial icons. These participants informed researchers that had such road maps for all big cities. These participants had a detailed city map with them as well.

Interestingly, on average the participants spent more time on the road when they used the paper-based maps as compare to navigation system. On average participants spent 17 minutes (21 minutes maximum and 15 minutes minimum) on road while using paper maps and 14 minutes on road while using navigation systems. Average time is the time spent on the road. Initial tasks related to the start-up of the navigation system and adding the destination address is not the part of this time. There were more wrong turns in the case of the navigation system but most of these were early turns (participants took early turn on the first street instead of the second one). The elderly were not able to judge the exact distance in meters (based on the speech instructions) and occasionally took a wrong turn sometimes without even looking at the screen. There were less wrong turns in the case of paper maps as elderly took time in deciding where to go and occasionally even stop their car for making sure the exact turn.

Although overall people were satisfactory while using paper based maps and everyone was able to find the correct locations, we ascertained that there was an overall clear need for an automatic navigation system but with a tailored user interface design for the elderly. Elderly were quite optimistic about various features of the navigation system. They really liked the idea of saving their home address and just by pressing one button the system would start guiding them to home. They also appreciated in time instructions from the system such as to keep to their lane, advice about early turns, etc.

However, the participants complained that using any existing navigation system was not entirely easy due to various reasons. In the coming sub-sections we will explain these usability problems in detail.

4.1 Usability Problems with the Navigation System

Once again, the issue of continuous feedback emerged. The elderly wanted to have feedback once they are on the right direction [3]. Another problem faced by the elderly was the ambiguity in automatic calculation of the new route when they took a wrong turn. We realized that when elderly accidently took a wrong turn, the system calculated the new route started giving new instructions but did not explicitly inform the driver about what has occurred. This was extremely confusing and almost all drivers in way or the other reported this. One quote from the participant confirms their feeling: "I took a wrong turn and I would go back now but it is saying go ahead instead of asking me to go back"? On the contrary, too much or unnecessary feedback can be misleading. One driver said while driving on a trunk road: "The system is telling me to do something after 1.5 KM when I am only going at 60 km p/h".

4.2 Evaluation with Respect to Speech Interaction

The participants liked the voice instruction but were also annoyed by the over excitement of the narrator especially in the case of error. We observed that the elderly had a tendency to forget the list of instructions (go straight 200 meters, turn right and then immediate left etc.). The elderly demanded that there should be an option of repeating the previous instruction specially without focusing too much attention on the screen (probably using a speech instruction). They wanted to have a more mild and polite tone once they have done a mistake. One user said "The voice should reflect the situation in a friendly and sensible manner". They also wanted to have an opportunity to change the voice (dialect and most importantly gender). Few of them showed interest in recording their own voice and thought that it would be much more trust worthy.

4.3 GUI Interaction

The evaluation of the general GUI interaction was quite stimulating. We can conclude that not all the displayed information is required or important for the elderly at a certain time. What would be beneficial is to support modes of information display (all, reduced, no), preferably by providing a zooming feature. Entering the point of interest (POI) was also a bit tricky for many drivers. They tried to enter the address in a typical manner (by writing it down all in one row with comma separation) without knowing the fact that system is asking for this information step by step.

Almost all drivers and particularly all women repeatedly showed an interest in displaying the landmarks on the calculated routes. They also said that these landmarks should be as specific as possible (e.g. churches, hospitals, stations etc.). These landmarks ensure that they are on the right track. They also reported that landmark icons (such as hotels, café, etc) as displayed on the interface were indistinguishable. On paper maps, when they gaze at the final destination, they have a possibility to look at the surroundings and have complete glance of the route but they miss this overall view in typical navigation systems. Their main wish is to have a clean and simple screen design supported by on demand supplementary information such as surrounding areas or current path details.

Sensitivity of the touch screen was sometimes a problem. It was over sensitive and a single touch or click was registered two or three times. If the system response was a bit slow then users would start tapping many times which disturbed the interaction. A major drawback of the interaction was unclear initiation feedback. After entering the POI, elderly were not sure what to do. There was no clear feedback that everything was ready. The font size of the text was rather too small for most of our participants. Occasionally they would grab the system out of the stand at the front dashboard. If they system was brought forward, there was a threat of the device obscuring their view. When the system was placed further back, video recordings revealed that the elderly would gradually just rely on audio instructions and avoid glancing at the device.

The glancing time was also dangerously increased for some participants when the system was installed a bit further. Almost all elderly complained about the position of the system on the windscreen. Majority of the participants said that installing the system on the windscreen was a bad idea as it disturbs their field of view (fov) but two of them said that they have no problem in installing system on the windscreen as they can see both the system and the traffic outside. Almost all were agreed that system should be installed between 60 to 80 degrees of the FOV.

5 Design Implications

Based on the results from the user research and user evaluation, early design guidelines of a navigation system are proposed, which explicitly focus on design problems faced by older adults. We also include the feature wish list proposed by elderly in these guidelines. We also briefly describe our implemented system.

5.1 Design Guidelines

The *physical placement of the navigation device* is a vital requirement. There should be an option of *switching between a map or instruction based layout* via a single click (text based instruction are every important for them when they have almost reached destination). There should be an option of *switching between regular map and landmark-based map*. In order to reduce the clutter on a map upon the navigation system, it would be advisable to *use only famous, well-known and easily identifiable landmarks*. All *additional information* (battery life, GPS strength, time etc.) *should be visible on demand. Street names should be announced* when a driver is in the vicinity of his/her destination. *The system should announce the exact location after reaching the destination* (you have reach your destination "ABC" which is on your left side). *Improved auto-fill functionality* should be provided based on the previous history, in order to save effort and time on behalf of the elderly. *Audio and visual information should be synchronized* (keeping in mind the delay between hearing the audio instruction and looking at the screen). Enough information *should be given about wrong turns and recalculating the route* (Ask for "calculate new route or continue on the previous one"). *The system's speech (dialect and gender) should be customizable.* The system should step by step guide elderly from beginning to end and *should give sufficient feedback once everything is ready.*

In the post evaluation focus group, elderly also identified some key features, which a modern navigation should have. It should be an option of *locating the closet emergency response* by either activating hard (physical) or soft buttons. The system should *show (flash) and announce the major road signs.* The system should *keep track of their speed* and *inform them when they are over or specially under speeding.* The system should *inform about the give priority junction* explicitly. The system *should inform about the blind spots* while taking right turn. It would be beneficial to *provide a connection with a family member* while the elderly are on the road. This would simply serve the purpose of informing a family member of where the elderly driver is at a point in time.

5.2 System Design and Implementation

On the base of these user tests and guidelines, an early prototype of our own navigation system RACE (Route Assistant and communication system) was developed. The core system was developed in VC++ and interface was developed using Flash (action script for communicating to VC application). A snapshot of the architecture of the system is given below.

We implemented the features based on our earlier research with the elderly. The system operates on the principle of wizard of oz, as it is not fully implemented yet. It is functional for an area of 3 km only, which was extracted from a standard map application. It supports pre-recorded narrator messages. Substantial feedback is provided in the case of wrong turns and the system waits for the response from the user before recalculating the new route. The system can track users and place this information on an authenticated website. There is also an option of switching between standard maps, textual instruction and landmark-based navigation. System also shows and announces all major road signs automatically. User can also hide and show related information on demand (as shown in the below screens).

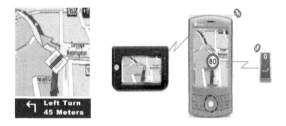

Fig. 2. Screen with sign (left), System Architecture (Right)

We carried out an initial testing of our prototype with three users during a design workshop and we report the results of that elsewhere. We were controlling the system with a tablet PC and the navigation system was placed in a PDA. Our focus was not on altering the basic framework on which navigation systems are built but rather support efficient presentation of information and improve audio video synchronization. The application is still under enhancement and further user tests are planned.

6 Conclusion

In summary, we feel that there is an imperative need of providing a usable navigation system that is primarily tailored for the use of the elderly population. We not only emphasize basic usability, but more so issues such as multimodal information presentation, which are directly influenced by the physical and cognitive state of the elderly.

Acknowledgments. We thank all our participants for their time and cooperation.

References

1. Beeharee, A.K., Steed, A.: A natural way finding exploiting photos in pedestrian navigation systems. In: Proceedings of the 8th Conference on Human-Computer interaction with Mobile Devices and Services. MobileHCI 2006, vol. 159, pp. 81–88. ACM, New York (2006)

2. Burnett, G., Summerskill, S., Porter, J.: On-the-move destination entry for vehicle navigation systems: Unsafe by any means? Behaviour & Information Technology 23, 265–272 (2004)
3. Heuten, W., Wichmann, D., Boll, S.: Interactive 3D sonification for the exploration of city maps. In: Proceedings of the 4th Nordic Conference on Human-Computer interaction: Changing Roles, NordiCHI 2006, vol. 189, pp. 155–164. ACM, New York (2006)
4. Holland, S., Morse, D.R., et al.: Audio GPS: Spatial Audio Navigation with a Minimal Attention Interface. J. Personal and Ubiquitous Computing 6(4), 253–259 (2002)
5. Holone, H., Misund, G., Tolsby, H., Kristoffersen, S.: Aspects of personal navigation with collaborative user feedback. In: Proceedings of the 5th Nordic Conference on Human-Computer interaction: Building Bridges, NordiCHI 2008, vol. 358, pp. 182–191. ACM, New York (2008)
6. Marston, J.R., Loomis, J.M.: Evaluation of Spatial Displays for Navigation without Sight. ACM Transactions on Applied Perception 3(2), 110–124 (2006)
7. May, A.J., Roass, T., et al.: Pedestrian Navigation Aids: Information requirements and design implications. J. Personal and Ubiquitous Computing 7, 331–338 (2003)
8. Pittarello, F., De Faveri, A.: Improving access of elderly people to real environments: a semantic based approach. In: Proceedings of the Working Conference on Advanced Visual interfaces, AVI 2006, pp. 364–368. ACM, New York (2006)
9. Völkel, T.: Personalized and adaptive navigation based on multimodal annotation. J. SIGACCESS Access. Comput. 86, 4–7 (2006)
10. Young, M.S., Stanton, N.A., Walker, G.H., Jenkins, D.P., Smart, W.: Where do we go from here? An assessment of navigation performance using a compass versus a GPS unit. J. Cogn. Technol. Work 10(3), 231–236 (2008)

The Effects of Camera System on Caregivers' Behaviors to Persons with Dementia

Taro Sugihara[1], Kenichi Nakagawa[2], Xi Liu[1], and Tsutomu Fujinami[1]

[1] Japan Advanced Institute of Science and Technology, Ishikawa, Japan
{sugihara,fuji,s0750215}@jaist.ac.jp
[2] Freelance programmer
macsi@m2.spacelan.ne.jp

Abstract. We installed a camera system into a group home to investigate how such a device may help caregivers in responding to the behaviors of the persons with dementia. We studied how their behaviors have changed by introducing the system into the home through video recording and a series of interviews. We found that the system enables caregivers to optimize their responses to the persons with dementia depending on their degree of mobility.

Keywords: group home, persons with dementia, caregiving, and camera system.

1 Introduction

Japan is a super-aged society. Despite the urgent need for care support systems and for eligible care workers at group homes, neither qualified persons nor any type of systems has caught up with the rapid social change.

There are methodologies such as human-centered design [1] and user-centered design [2] that reflect users' needs, and improve usability in terms of custom-made design. However, dementia care is a difficult field because it depends heavily on contexts such as residents' behaviors and their surroundings including the equipments employed to help them. Davenport argues that knowledge management systems should be embedded into the flow of job processes of expert workers [3]. It is necessary to adopt his argument for supporting caregiving, too.

Most researches of caring persons with dementia (PWD) focus on supporting the communication problems [4][5][6], but it is also important to help caregivers to improve the quality of life for the elderly with dementia, some of whom reside in group homes. We have conducted several field researches by introducing camera systems into group homes and employed a qualitative method for analyzing the effects of the system, with a hope to develop useful systems for caregivers [7][8]. By supporting caregivers, we can not only develop their abilities but also lead them to improving the quality of life for residents, which in turn result in easing caregivers' physical and mental work stress.

In this article, we describe a field research to investigate the effects due to the introduction of a camera system for helping caregivers at a group home. We conducted interviews to five caregivers and a couple of managers as well as a video observation for our research.

C. Stephanidis (Ed.): Universal Access in HCI, Part I, HCII 2009, LNCS 5614, pp. 297–303, 2009.
© Springer-Verlag Berlin Heidelberg 2009

As for the ethical issue, our research has been approved to carry out the experiment by the ethics committee at Japan Advanced Institute of Science and Technology.

2 Methods

2.1 Interview

A series of semi-structured interviews were carried out before and after installing the camera system. We interviewed caregivers to ask what they think of the system and which aspects they regard most effective in terms of dementia care. In the interviews we asked the following questions:

- What is the burden for dementia care? (before)
- What is/are the most important factor(s) for dementia care? (before)
- How do you use the camera system? (after)
- How do you think about using the system? (after)
- How does the system change your work stress? (after)

Table 1 shows the overview of our field study. The group home accommodated nine residents to its full capacity and the number of caregivers was as required by the law. The profile of the interviewees is illustrated in Table 2. We graded the caregivers to three groups depending on their work experience, that is, one group with less than three year experience, another with 3-7 year experience, and the other with more than 7 year experience. Every caregiver has worked for at least three years as caregiver at a group home and was qualified to care the elderly. Three of them were qualified as a nurse, too.

Table 1. Overview of the group home and this research

Feature		Data
Residents		9
Total of caregivers		8
Intervewees		5
Caregivers in the daytime		2 or 3
Caregivers in the nighttime		1
Residential area		first floor
Start of operation		2008 March
Timing of interview	before	2007 Noveber to December
	after	2008 May
Timing of video observation	before	2008 March
	after	2008 Decmber

2.2 Video Observation and Analysis

We observed behaviors of the caregivers and the residents by recording them. The caregivers and the managers allowed us to record their images with two extra video cameras, not as part of the camera system. We carried out the data collection for one day before installation and another day after installation. We analyzed behaviors of a

Table 2. Profiles of interviewees

Intervewees	Sex	Experience level	Qualification of nurse	Prior job
c1	female	high	eligible	Nurse of hospital for dementia care
c2	female	moderate		Caregiver of carehouse for dementia care
c3	female	high	eligible	Nurse of hospital for dementia care
c4	female	moderate		Housewife
c5	female	moderate		Another group home

caregiver and residents observed in the corridor (V1 in Fig. 1) and in the living room (V2) to concentrate our investigation to the events closely related to daily activities such as the assistance in the restroom.

We counted how often each resident took an action and how the caregiver responded to it for every ninety minutes from four o'clock in the evening to half past five in the early morning (16:00 to 5:30). We studied the behaviors observed in the evening and at night because we expected the effects of the system to be best evaluated for the time period. The number of caregivers is limited to one at night and the camera system is thus expected to be most effective then. Preceding studies also suggest that caregivers are most benefited from the kind of system during the night [8][9].

We eliminated some behaviors of the residents of our data analysis when they were just wondering in the corridor or living room because such behaviors do not particularly require reactions by caregivers.

3 System Installation to a Group Home

3.1 Overview of Camera System

Since the caregivers were inexperienced with computers, we designed the system with four wireless cameras, a portable monitor and a note PC as a server. The server gathered visual data from the cameras and a Web browser was used to display the information collected from four video signals. The information was converted into signal of TV footage by a down-scan converter to be emitted to the portable monitor. Malfunctions due to mishandling by the caregivers or residents were reduced because they did not operate the system through the monitor.

3.2 Installation Process

We respected the privacy issue because the manager and caregivers were both concerned with the matter. They were particularly worried about video recording. The recording function was therefore not included in the camera system and its cameras were only placed in common spaces such as entrance hall, corridor and living room. The cameras and the monitor were placed as shown in Fig. 1.

Through the interview before installation, the caregivers mentioned their demands for the system. Their comments were mostly about toileting assistance. That is, when some resident enters the restroom, caregivers have to check who it is and how many times she used it. Caregivers were also anxious of possible accidents at night due to the lack of sights. The cameras were thus placed to cover caregivers' blind spots such as the corridor (Z1). The camera at the living room (Z2) was for monitoring the falling accidents. The other cameras, Z3 and Z4, were for monitoring unnoticed walkout of residents and checking visitors. The portable monitor was usually placed by the sink in the kitchen because one of the caregivers always worked there.

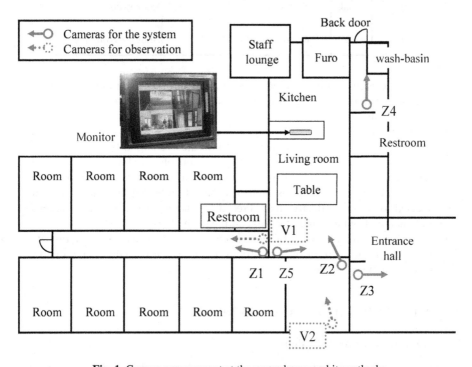

Fig. 1. Camera arrangement at the group home and its outlooks

After three months we began to operate the system, a new camera was set up to watch the entrance hall (Z5). This issue was raised by a manager and caregivers alike; they noted that the place was a serious blind spot because a resident may walk out unnoticed. They wanted to be warned when a resident walks into the entrance hall so that they can prepare for her walkout.

4 Results

The series of interviews revealed that the system reduced caregivers' physical and mental stresses because they could judge the appropriate timing for taking actions by watching the monitor. They appreciated the system, especially owing to the elimination of blind spots. When some resident shows up from her room, approaching to the restroom (depicted in the center of Fig. 1), caregivers in the kitchen may not be aware of the incident. If they notice it, they suspend their work in progress to come to the place and see who has entered there.

A veteran caregiver told us that she realized the system to be valuable although she use to believe that caregivers should only rely on manpower. She roughly estimated that mental stress was decreased by 20 to 40 percent and the physical one by 20 percent. Other caregivers appreciated its positive effects, too. They felt the system improved their work styles significantly because it enabled them to focus on the task at hand such as writing residents' daily records, washing dishes and cooking.

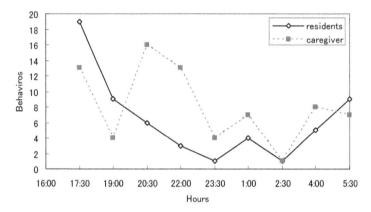

Fig. 2. Behavior patterns before system installation

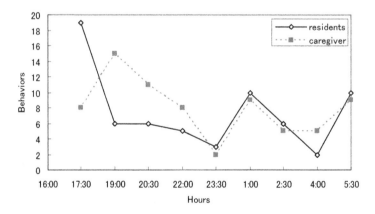

Fig. 3. Behavior patterns of after system installation

The video analysis validated their testimony. Fig. 2 shows the behaviors of the residents and the caregiver, respectively, in March, before we installed the camera system in the group home and Fig. 3 shows those in December after the caregiver had used the system for nine months. Those figures indicate that the caregiver's responses to the residents' behaviors have been optimized to some extent as the difference between the behaviors of the residents and those of the caregiver was decreased, especially between 23:30 and 5:30. Note that the total number of their actions did not differ so much. That is, the camera system has not reduced the workload, but helped the caregiver to adjust her efforts to the residents' demands.

5 Discussion

It is rather surprising that the caregiver's workload did not differ before and after the installation of the camera system. The system helped her to optimize her efforts to taking care of the residents. The question is whether the change found in the caregiver's responses is desirable for her. We believe that the caregiver is benefitted from the installation of the camera system because she can take things under control by adjusting her behaviors depending on the demands from the residents. She can continue her work at hand, i.e., writing a daily record of each resident, if she thinks that she does not need to take an immediate action to a resident's particular acts such as using the restroom as long as she can manage it by herself.

We were told that the caregivers had to run up to the place when they noticed that someone entered the restroom. They had no means to see who entered the restroom before the camera system was installed. They felt a stress in doing so because they believed that such reactions might make the residents feel awkward. That is why the system contributed to easing the stress which the caregiver felt when such a system was not available although the overall workload did not particularly change.

6 Conclusion

We analyzed how the camera system affects on the caregiver. Our observation using two video cameras showed no distinctive difference to the caregiver's behavior before and after the installation of the camera system. A series of interviews, however, revealed that the stress they felt was removed whose reason we believe lies in that they can take things under control by monitoring the residents' behaviors with the camera system.

Data collection is further required to verify our findings as we only carried out our experiments several times. We also need to improve the camera system by investigating the caregivers' needs with additional field studies.

Acknowledgements. Our research is partly supported by the fund from Ministry of Education, Culture, Sports, Science and Technology, Japan, under the name of Cluster for Promotion of Science and Technology in Regional Areas. We would like to thank caregivers and managers, residents, and their families for their kind cooperation.

References

1. Norman, D.A.: The Design of Everyday Things. Doubleday, New York (1990)
2. Schuler, N.A.: Participatory Design Principles and Practices, Hillsdale, NJ (1993)

3. Davenport, T.H.: Thinking for a Living: How to Get Better Performances and Results from Knowledge Workers. Harvard Business School Press (2005)
4. Kuwahara, N., Kuwabara, K., Abe, S.: Networked Reminiscence Content Authoring and Delivery for Elderly People with Dementia. In: Proceedings of International Workshop on Cognitive Prostheses and Assisted Communication, pp. 20–25 (2006)
5. Kuwahara, N., Abe, S., Yasuda, K., Kuwabara, K.: Networked Reminiscence Therapy for Individuals with Dementia by using Photo and Video Sharing. In: ASSETS 2006: The 8th International ACM SIGACCESS Conference on Computers and Accessibility 2006, pp. 125–132 (2006)
6. Alm, N., Dye, R., Gowans, G., Campbell, J., Astell, A., Ellis, M.: A Communication Support System for Older People with Dementia. Computer 40(5), 35–41 (2007)
7. Takatsuka, R., Fujinami, T.: Aware Group Home: Person-Centered Care as Creative Problem Solving. In: Khosla, R., Howlett, R.J., Jain, L.C. (eds.) KES 2005. LNCS, vol. 3684, pp. 451–457. Springer, Heidelberg (2005)
8. Sugihara, T., Nakagawa, K., Fujinami, T., Takatsuka, R.: Evaluation of a Prototype of the Mimamori-care System for Persons with Dementia. In: Lovrek, I., Howlett, R.J., Jain, L.C. (eds.) KES 2008, Part II. LNCS (LNAI), vol. 5178, pp. 839–846. Springer, Heidelberg (2008)
9. Nakagawa, K., Sugihara, T., Koshiba, H., Takatsuka, R., Kato, N., Kunifuji, S.: Development of a Mimamori-Care System for Persons with Dementia Based on the Real World-Oriented Approach. In: Apolloni, B., Howlett, R.J., Jain, L. (eds.) KES 2007, Part II. LNCS (LNAI), vol. 4693, pp. 1261–1268. Springer, Heidelberg (2007)

A Function Based Approach towards Adaptive Interfaces for Elderly Users

Edmund Wascher, Gerhard Rinkenauer, and Michael Falkenstein

Leibniz Research Centre for Working Environment and Human Factors
{wascher,rinkenauer,falkenstein}@ifado.de

Abstract. Recent information technologies may support elderly people in living independently even when they become immobile. Most computer systems, however, are hard to use when age-related impairments increase. While sensory and motor deficits can be alleviated by built in accessibility tools, cognitive alterations with increasing age are often not addressed. Here, we present an approach that intends to evaluate the adaptation of interfaces based on individual capabilities.

Keywords: Accessibility, information technologies, higher age, cognitive functions.

1 Introduction

Because of current social and demographic trends, an increasing amount of seniors may be at risk of being socially isolated or lonely [31]. The trend towards smaller families and higher mobility in young generations cause that it is rare to have many members of a family living in close proximity [15]. When elderly people additionally become limited in personal mobility due to driving cessation, out-of-home activities decrease [20], which may have negative consequences also for cognitive functioning [19].

Using current information technologies such as computers or mobile phones may help elderly people to maintain a social network and to live on their own even when mobility is alleviated. These systems, however, are hardly adjusted to the needs of elderly people, inevitably resulting in a poor usability of the system for this user group. Besides impairments in sensory and motor systems, elderly people often experience a decline in cognitive abilities and, possibly as a consequence of all factors mentioned so far, a fearful relationship to modern technologies. Therefore they might dismiss even obviously helpful tools due to overall poor design.

Technical systems, in particular commercial ones, which are adjusted to elderly users have not been established so far. This is not surprising since the needs of elderly users are not easy to define. The decline in cognitive functions is quite selective. Two people of the same age might both be impaired in some sense but the kind of impairment might be quite different. Also the time course of decline varies individually. Thus, the "group" of elderly people is quite heterogeneous.

The present study intends to evaluate issues in usability for elderly users based on an exhaustive analysis of physiological and psychological alterations with increasing age.

C. Stephanidis (Ed.): Universal Access in HCI, Part I, HCII 2009, LNCS 5614, pp. 304–311, 2009.

2 Functional Ageing

Aging goes along with a potential decline in numerous functions. Most important for the area of computer usability are changes in sensory functions, motor behavior and cognitive abilities.

2.1 Elementary Deficits

Visual abilities decline during normal (non-pathological) aging. Most prominent are deficits in visual acuity and spatial contrast sensitivity (especially for low luminance levels), suprathreshold contrast vision and contrast gain, temporal-frequency contrast sensitivity and resolution, spatial-temporal interactions, hyperacuity, binocular processing, and sensitivity to motion [26]. The decline might be of peripheral as well as of cortical origin [10]. Besides visual deficits, 30 to 35 % of adults aged 65 to 75 years have age-related hearing loss, as do 40% of those older than 75 [8]. It seems to be noteworthy that decline in these sensory functions appears to be correlated to impairments in intelligence [17].

Also basic motor abilities suffer from an age-related decline [27]. Loss of muscular strength, endurance and tone [12] impair the execution of physically demanding tasks at older age.   Furthermore, coordination, that is the ability to control multiple movement components at any one particular time, becomes increasingly difficult with advanced age. The loss of coordination affects a variety of movements including aiming, reaching and grasping, drawing, handwriting, and bimanual coordination tasks [4], [6], [29].

One of the most conspicuous age-related changes, however, is generalized slowing that affects also physical performance. Slowing has been found already for the time needed to initiate and execute very simple movements [23]. Motor slowing already begins to develop in early adulthood [28], [33] and thus slowing is not merely a problem at higher age, but also prominent in adults below retirement age.

2.2 Cognitive Deficits

Results of a large number of studies on cognitive ageing suggest that cognitive performance does deteriorate with age, but that there are also domains that remain intact for a long time. As mentioned above, the speed at which the mind operates in general decreases [24]. Such global slowing that affects behavior at all levels is accompanied by more specific deficits in working memory capacity [21], [22], [25] and long-term memory functions [22]. But also the selective processing of relevant against irrelevant information is disturbed with increasing age [2]. On the other hand, knowledge about the world, vocabulary and semantic knowledge, remains largely intact, or may even grow with age [22].

Since the selection is essential in environments that are rich of information, such as a computer interface, this issue will be discussed here in more detail. Many studies have shown that elderly subjects have problems to ignore irrelevant information [13]. Thus, elderly people are always prone to get overwhelmed by incoming signals. Such a deficit might not only impair the identification of target items, as evident from research on visual search [18]. Additionally, impaired suppression of irrelevant information may influence higher cognitive processing such as working memory [9]. Age-related decline in selective attention has been even proposed to be the basis for generalized slowing.

These and many more cognitive functions, such as the ability to flexibly switch between tasks, to detect errors, or to perform two or more tasks at the same time, are related to frontal structures of the human brain. These regions are especially vulnerable to physiological and metabolic age-related changes [32]. Therefore, functional processes being linked to the frontal lobe and especially to dorsolateral prefrontal areas are particularly subject to age-related deterioration. These structures play an important regulatory role for cognition by distributing information across other cortical regions [5], [30].

3   System Adaptation

3.1   Accessibility Tools

Common operating systems (Windows, Linux, Mac OS-X) include a number of accessibility tools that intend to help the elderly user to overcome deficits, in particular with respect to elementary cognitive functions.

The size of display items as well as the contrast of elements presented can be adjusted to individual needs. For more severe deficits in visual acuity, display utilities are available that make the computer screen more readable by creating a separate window that displays a magnified portion of the screen. Text to speech utilities may enable even blind users to extract reliable information.

On the motor side, deficits can be covered by adjusting the behavior of the mouse or even substitute mouse actions by keyboard commands. Adjusting keyboard repeat rates may compensate for severe motor slowing and speech recognition may completely substitute manual interaction with the computer.

However, adapting the system cannot be done by the impaired user autonomously for several reasons:

1. People are often not aware or do not want to be aware of their deficits [11]. They may attribute problems that arise when interacting with a computer to the machine and not to an individual deficit of themselves. Therefore, accessibility tools are often not used.
2. Accessibility tools are often not approachable for those who need compensation for a particular deficit. For a demonstration see two examples regarding the configuration tool for the visual display below (figure 1). Within the dialog fonts are huge and buttons large. However, up to this point the user has to navigate through dialogs that are of regular fonts and not accessible if vision is impaired.
3. Those features need to be found. For example, the double click interval that has to be adjusted for many elderly users who suffer from motoric slowing cannot be found in the accessibility tools in OS-X. There is a separate mouse configuration tool that might easily be neglected when the intention is to increase accessibility.

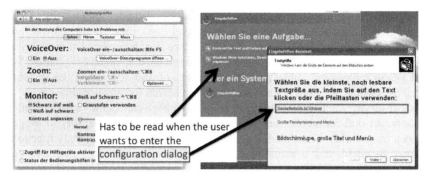

Fig. 1. Configuration tools for increasing accessibility for visually impaired persons (left: Mac OS-X; right: WindowsXP). In both cases, regular (small) font sizes have to be processed until the user enters the final configuration menu. Only at that level, font sizes are increased in order to support the handicapped user.

3.2 Advanced System Adaptation

Already basic installations of common operating systems include an incredible number of programs installed. They all have strange names (Outlook, Thunderbird, Entourage) which are not self explaining and in the worst case the user has to list all in order to find the correct tool to accomplish a particular goal.

As outlined above, one of the core cognitive deficits with increasing age is the inability to separate relevant from irrelevant information (see also [1], [3]). Thus, visual search for a particular feature (e.g. a launch button) may become really hard and time consuming and therefore potentially frustrating. In addition, if the user is not familiar with the English language, he/she experiences the program names as nonsense syllables.

As for elementary functions, there are numerous tools to alleviate the access also at this higher level. Menu lists may be edited easily in most operating systems, however, again an expert is needed to do this. Also, program names may be replaced by functional descriptions for example in KDE. But also this feature requires profound knowledge of the operating system, which lacks before most in novices and elderly users. Thus, adaptation requires the help of an expert, shaping the system based on knowledge of the actual user.

3.3 Substantiating the User Model

The user model that underlies the configuration of a computer system may be based on usability surveys or solely on assumptions about the potential users (or user groups).

The latter may fail when a system should be adjusted to elderly people. Alterations of both physiological as well as cognitive functions vary enormously across this group. Global setting might therefore be experienced as if the system would be created for heavily impaired subjects. Surveys might be helpful when the complexity of the system is to be reduced to individual needs but will, for already mentioned reasons, never be able to capture physiological decline.

Thus, deficits in elementary functions should be evaluated empirically. Simple psychological in situ tests may measure individual capabilities in all relevant areas and adjust the system accordingly. Such a procedure may be embedded in a way that most users are able to access it autonomously even when e.g. vision is impaired. Such a tool would circumvent subjective misjudgments of abilities, shape the system as optimal as possible and does not require a difficult search for functionality.

A short survey would be in particular helpful to cover the cognitive deficits of elderly users. As outlined above, one of the main problems is the inability to suppress irrelevant information. Thus, menus need to be as simple as possible. Only functionality should be visible that is actually needed. If the number of entries exceeds a comfortable size, they should be organized in suitable groups to reduce the effort needed to accomplish a goal as much as possible.

3.4 Considering Emotions

Computers came into the private use in the mid 80s. Today's 35 to 45 years old are the first generation that was confronted with information technologies already at school. Additionally, people retiring now have less experience with computers from their working life if compared to the younger generation. Therefore, it is not surprising that computer anxiety, which is strongly related to experience, is more common in the elderly [7], [16].

Function based adjustment may help to overcome this problem, may help elderly users to be more confident with computers. However, systems that had already addressed this point did not succeed on the market. In 2006, Fujitsu-Siemens introduced a Linux desktop computer, which was called "Simplico". Visible functionality was reduced to surfing the net, use e-mail, write letters, play along and look pictures and videos. These features were additionally organized into contend defined groups which were color-coded.

Although initial critics were enthusiastic, the system did not become a top seller. Besides possible technical problems with a linux based system (some complaints have been raised regarding the possibility to connect any desired hardware), the system appeared to be too obviously fitted to senior use which is generally known to be a major obstacle for purchasing a system. As with other technologies, shaped for the elderly should not mean that it has to look like it. There should be no obvious connotation to disabilities.

3.5 Evolving Systems

Since elderly users are often inexperienced when starting to use a computer, their capabilities to improve performance are sometimes larger than those of younger users. Thus, when they had started off with an individually adjusted system that covers all possible impairments, they may soon wish to use more of the potential of the machine.

Adaptive (or evolving) systems [16] might detect changes in the user's level of expertise and optimize the system accordingly. More features might be activated or parameters of accessibility setting might be changed. Such mechanisms might nicely add on the initial configuration. However, some problems may raise with such modification that are not well understood yet:

1. Elderly people may be irritated by sudden changes of the system that are not due to their own interaction with the machine. Especially in early stages of experience, when confidence in the technology has not established yet, unexpected modifications may decrease the efficiency of interaction.
2. Usage of the system by any other person (e.g. a visiting, a younger family member that enters the system on the same user profile) may recalibrate the system in an unpredictable way.

Thus, it has to be evaluated whether automatic adaptation or rather proposal-based variation should adapt the system to increasing experience [14]. In any case, as can be learned from the Simplico disaster, potential availability of full functionality is necessary to avoid the image of disabilities and give the opportunity to adjust for any increase in experience.

4 Summary

Elderly people represent the fastest growing group in our society. Using recent information technologies might essentially increase live quality and, before most, help them to remain independent even when mobility is limited. These technologies, however, are hardly adopted to special needs and to age-related functional decline. Accessibility tools as implemented in all operation systems address this problem only superficially, by widely ignoring individual levels of sensory and motor functioning, cognitive changes with age and computer experience. Thinking on adjusted systems is confronted with the enormous heterogeneity of this group with respect to all determinants.

The fact that more and more elderly people use computers for many purposes does not mean that their interaction with this technology is efficient. Elderly people tend to adapt to the system in order to accomplish a particular goal. Often, they need to learn processes by rote since they have no mental model of the machine. Adjusting the system to individual capabilities and reducing the amount of information that needs to be processed might not only increase accessibility for those who already use computers, but also help not-users to overcome the fear of the unknown.

References

1. Akatsu, H., Miki, H., Hosono, N.: Design Principles Based on Cognitive Aging. HCI 1, 3–10 (2007)
2. Andrés, P., Parmentier, F.B.R., Escera, C.: The effect of age on involuntary capture of attention by irrelevant sounds: A test of the frontal hypothesis of aging. Neuropsychologia 44, 2564–2568 (2006)
3. Ball, T., Schreiber, A., Feige, B., et al.: The role of higher-order motor areas in voluntary movement as revealed by high resolution EEG and fMRI. Neuroimage 10, 682–694 (1999)
4. Bennett, K.M., Castiello, U.: Reach to grasp: Changes with age. Journal of Gerontology 49, 1–7 (1994)
5. Botvinick, M.M., Cohen, D.C., Carter, C.S.: Conflict monitoring and anterior cingulate cortex: an update. Trends in Cognitive Science 8, 539–546 (2004)

6. Carnahan, H., Vandervoort, A.A., Swanson, L.R.: The influence of aging and target motion on the control of prehension. Experimental Aging Research 24, 289–306 (1998)
7. Chua, S.L., Chen, D.T., Wong, A.F.L.: Computer anxiety and its correlates: a meta- analysis. Computers in Human Behavior 15, 609–623 (1999)
8. Davison, M., Dean, W.A.: Hearing loss in adults. Clinician Review 12, 62–67 (2002)
9. Gazzaley, A., Cooney, J.W., Rissmann, J., et al.: Top-down suppression deficits underlies working memory impairment in normal aging. Nature Neuroscience 8, 1200–1298 (2005)
10. Gazzaley, A., Clapp, W., Kelley, J., et al.: Age-related top-down suppression deficit in the early stages of cortical visual memory processing. PNAS 105, 13122–13126 (2008)
11. Holland, C.A., Rabbitt, P.M.A.: People's Awareness of their Age-related Sensory and Cognitive Deficits and the Implications for Road Safety. Applied Cognitive Psychology 6, 17–23 (1992)
12. Khalil, T.M., Abdel-Moty, E., Diaz, E.L., et al.: Efficacy of physical restoration in the elderly. Experimental Aging Research 20, 189–199 (1994)
13. Kok, A.: Varieties of Inhibition: manifestations in cognition, event-related potentials and aging. Acta Psychologica 101, 129–158 (1999)
14. Kules, B.: User Modeling for Adaptive and Adaptable Software Systems (2005), http://www.otal.umd.edu/uuguide/wmk/
15. Lafreniere, S., Carriere, Y., Martel, L., et al.: Dependent seniors at home- formal and informal help. Health Reports 14, 31–40 (2003)
16. Laguna, K., Babcock, R.L.: Computer Anxiety in Young and Older Adults: Implications for Human-Computer Interactions in Older Populations. Computers in Human Behavior 13, 317–326 (1997)
17. Lindenberger, U., Baltes, P.B.: Sensory functioning and intelligence in old age: A strong connection. Psychology and Aging 9, 339–355 (1994)
18. Madden, D.J., Gottlob, L.R., Allen, P.A.: Adult age differences in visual search accuracy: Attentional guidance and target detectability. Psychology & Aging 14, 683–694 (1999)
19. Marattoli, R., Mendes de Leon, C., Glass, T., et al.: Consequences of Driving Cessation: Decreased Out-of-Home Activity Levels. Journal of Gerontology: Social Sciences 55B, 334–340 (2000)
20. Mooney, J.: Driving Status and out-of-home social activity levels: The case of older male veterans. GRC News 22, 3 (2003)
21. Morris, R.G., Craik, F.I.M., Gick, M.L.: Age differences in working memory tasks: The role of secondary memory and the central executive. Quarterly Journal of Experimental Psychology 42, 67–86 (1990)
22. Park, D.C., Smith, A.D., Lautenschlager, G., et al.: Mediators of long-term memory performance across the life span. Psychology & Aging 11, 621–637 (1996)
23. Proctor, R.W., Vu, K.L., Pick, D.F.: Aging and response selection in spatial choice tasks. Human Factors 47, 250–270 (2005)
24. Salthouse, T.A.: The processing-speed theory of adult age differences in cognition. Psychological Review 103, 403–428 (1996)
25. Salthouse, T.A., Babcock, R.L.: Decomposing adult age differences in working memory. Developmental Psychology 27, 763–776 (1991)
26. Spear, P.D.: Neural bases of visual deficits during aging. Vision Research 33, 2589–2609 (1993)
27. Spirduso, W.W., MacRae, P.G.: Motor performance and aging. In: Birren, J.E., Schaie, K.W. (eds.) Handbook of the psychology of aging, pp. 183–200. Academic Press, San Diego (1990)

28. Teeken, J.C., Adam, J.J., Paas, F.G.W.C., et al.: Effects of age and gender on discrete and reciprocal aiming movements. Psychology & Aging 11, 195–198 (1996)
29. Teulings, H.L., Stelmach, G.E.: Signal-to-noise ratio of handwriting size, force, and time: Cues to early markers of Parkinson's disease. In: Stelmach, G.E., Homberg, V. (eds.) Sensorimotor impairment in the elderly, pp. 311–327. Kluver Academic, Dordrecht (1993)
30. Thompson-Schill, S.L., Bedny, M., Goldberg, R.F.: The frontal lobes and the regulation of mental activity. Current Opinion in Neurobiology 15, 219–224 (2005)
31. Tijhuis, M.A., De Jong-Gierveld, J., Feskens, E.J., et al.: Changes in and factors related to loneliness in older men. The Zutphen Elderly Study. Age and ageing 28, 491–495 (1999)
32. Tisserand, D.J., Pruessner, J.C., Sanz Arigita, E.J., et al.: Regional Frontal Cortical Volumes Decrease Differentially in Aging: An MRI Study to Compare Volumetric Approaches and Voxel-Based Morphometry. Neuroimage 17 (2002)
33. Yan, J.H., Thomas, J.R., Stelmach, G.E.: Aging and rapid aiming arm movement control. Experimental Aging Research 24, 155–168 (1998)

Part III

Interaction and Support for People with Cognitive Impairments

Cognitive Chance Discovery

Akinori Abe

ATR Knowledge Science Laboratories
2-2-2, Hikaridai, Seika-cho, Soraku-gun, Kyoto 619-0288 Japan
ave@ultimaVI.arc.net.my

Abstract. Dementia is the progressive decline in cognitive function due to damage or disease in the body beyond what might be expected from normal aging. Dementia persons cannot reasonably live their lives. In order to support dementia persons' lives, various approaches are proposed. Bozeat and Hodges showed affordance might give a certain support to (semantic) dementia persons of understanding (meanings of) objects. In this paper, based on the concept of affordance, abduction, and chance discovery, a dementia care under the concept of affordance is proposed.

1 Introduction

Due to the advanced and innovative medical treatment, we are able to live longer. It will be happy to live long, but the other problems are caused by such long lives. One of the most famous problems is increasing patients who are suffered from cancer. It will be able to be overcome by the advancement of medical treatment and is a problem for individuals. Furthermore serious problem for a person and even for his/her family and surroundings will be dementia. It is the progressive decline in cognitive function due to damage or disease in the body beyond what might be expected from normal aging. Dementia persons cannot reasonably live their lives. It is said that the current medical treatment cannot cure dementia completely. Even in the near future, it will be negative to cure dementia. Dementia is caused by problems in a brain. Accordingly, it is more difficult to cure dementia than cancer. Currently, some methods to delay the progress of dementia are proposed. For instance, a therapy room or house will be one of the solution to take care of dementia person [21]. Actually, it is rather a support system for dementia person's everyday life.

In addition, several researches and experiments are conducted to analyze the feature of dementia. Bozeat and Hodges showed affordance might give a certain support to (semantic) dementia persons of understanding (meanings of) objects [4,13]. Actually, it covers a limited situation, but it would be better to introduce a concept of affordance to a dementia care. Affordance has been discussed in Artificial Intelligence or philosophy as well as in cognitive science. For instance, Magnani discussed manipulation of affordances in the abduction framework [17]. Thus strategies for dementia care can be discussed and built in the framework of affordance theory. Affordance theory is a natural processing in actual environments. In addition, affordance can be dealt with abduction framework and

C. Stephanidis (Ed.): Universal Access in HCI, Part I, HCII 2009, LNCS 5614, pp. 315–323, 2009.

since affrodance is not explicitly displayed but hidden in the environments. Accordingly, chance discovery [19] can be one of the strategies to a dementia care problems.

In this paper, based on the above discussion, a dementia care under the concept of affordance, abduction, and chance discovery is discussed.

Section 2 reviews the feature of dementia. Section 3 illustrates the concept of affordance, abduction, and chance discovery which are discovery reasoning or knowledge processing. Section 4 proposes a system based on the concept of affordance. It will be discussed in the context of chance discovery.

2 Dementia

Dementia is the progressive decline in cognitive function, such as memory, attention, language, and problem solving, due to damage or disease in the body beyond what might be expected from normal aging. In the later stages, dementia persons will not be able to recognize time (day of the week, day of the month, and year etc.), place, and person. Phenomena due to aging and dementia are different. For instance, for memory, aged person does not forget all of his/her experiences, on the other hand, dementia person forgets whole of his/her experiences. Dementia is roughly categorized to cortical and subcortical. For instance, several types of cortical dementia are reported such as Alzheimer's disease. Except for the treatable types, there is no cure to dementia, although scientists are progressing in making a type of medication that will slow down the process. For instance, For the medication of Alzheimer, actions such as cheerful communication and proper stimulation are recommend [15]. For instance, some studies have found that music therapy which stimulates emotion as well as brain may be useful in helping patients with dementia [3]. Alternative therapies are also discussed for the care of Alzheimer's disease and dementia [5,6].

Bozeat and Hodges analyzed the feature of mapping between objects and their meaning for semantic dementia person from four factors — affordance, presence of recipient, familiarity, and problem solving [4,13]. They showed very interesting results For instance, they pointed out "as a group, the patients did not achieve better performance on a subset of affordanced objects when use of these was compared with a familiarity-matched subset of objects lacking such affordances. This absence of a general group benefit applied both to overall use and to the specific component of use afforded by the object's structure.[...]it became clear that there was a reliable benefit of affordance on the specific components of use, but only for the most impaired patients." They also pointed out "The impact of recipient, like affordance, was found to be modulated by the degree of semantic impairment. The patients with a moderate level of conceptual impairment demonstrated significantly better use with the recipient present, whereas the patients with mild and severe impairment showed no effect. [...] It was not surprising, therefore, to find that familiarity also influenced performance on object use assessments."

These observations and analyses show that proper affordance might give a certain support to dementia persons understanding (meanings of) objects.

3 Affordance

3.1 Affordance

Gibson ecologically introduced concept of affordance for perceptional phenomena [10,11]. It emphasizes the environmental information available in extended spatial and temporal pattern in optic arrays, for guiding the behaviors of animals, and for specifying ecological events. Thus he defined the affordance of something as "a specific combination of the properties of its substance and its surfaces taken with reference to an animal." For instance, the affordance of climbing a stair step in a bipedal fashion has been described in terms of the height of a stair riser taken with reference to a person's leg length [22]. That is, if a stair riser is less than 88% of a person's leg length, then that means that the person can climb that stair. On the other hand, if a stair riser is greater than 88% of the person's leg length, then that means that the person cannot climb that stair, at least not in a bipedal fashion. For that Jones pointed out that "it should be noted also that this is true regardless of whether the person is aware of the relation between his or her leg length and the stair riser's height, which suggests further that the meaning is not internally constructed and stored but rather is inherent in the person's environment system" [14].

In the context of human-machine interaction Norman extended the concept of affordance from Gibson's definition. He pointed our that "...the term affordance refers to the perceived and actual properties of the thing, primarily those fundamental properties that determine just how the thing could possibly be used. [...] Affordances provide strong clues to the operations of things. Plates are for pushing. Knobs are for turning. Slots are for inserting things into. Balls are for throwing or bouncing. When affordances are taken advantage of, the user knows what to do just by looking: no picture, label, or instruction needed" [18]. Thus Norman defined affordance as something of both actual and perceivable properties. Accordingly his interpretation has effectively been introduced to interaction designs.

Zhang categorized several types of affordance into the following categories [23]:

- Biological Affordance
  For instance, a healthy mushroom affords nutrition, while a toxic mushroom affords dying.
- Physical Affordance
  For instance, the flat horizontal panel on a door can only be pushed. Many of this type of affordances can be found in Norman [18].
- Perceptual Affordance
  In this category, affordances are mainly provided by spatial mappings. For instance, if the switches of the stovetop burners have the same spatial layout as the burners themselves, the switches provide affordances for controlling the burners. Examples of this type include the pictorial signs for ladies' and men's restrooms.

- Cognitive Affordance
  Affordances of this type are provided by cultural conventions. For instance, for traffic lights, red means "stop," yellow means "prepare to stop," and green means "go."
- Mixed Affordance
  For instance, a mailbox, which is one of the examples used by Gibson, does not provide the affordance of mailing letters at all for a person who has no knowledge about postal systems. In this case, internal knowledge is involved in constructing the affordance in a great degree.

Thus since Gibson's introduction, affordance has been widely discussed, and the other perspective and extensions have been added. Especially, it has been effectively introduced to interface designs after several extensions.

3.2   Affordance, Abduction and Chance Discovery

It is important to deal with rare or novel phenomena which might lead us to risk or opportunity. We call this type of activity as chance discovery and discuss theories and methods to discover such chances. A chance is dedined as "*a novel or rare event/situation that can be conceived either as an opportunity or a risk in the future*" [19]. Thus it is rather difficult to discover a chance by usual statistical strategies. We adpot abduction and analogy (Abducitve Analogical Reasoning) to perform chance discovery [1,2]. Where chance discovery is regarded as an explanatory reasoning for the unknown or unfamiliar observations, and a chance is therefore defined as followings:

1. **Chance** is a set of unknown hypotheses. Therefore, explanation of an observation is not influenced by it. Accordingly, a possible observation that should be explained cannot be explained. In this case, a hypotheses base or a knowledge base lacks necessary hypotheses. Therefore, it is necessary to generate missing hypotheses. Missing hypotheses are characterized as chance.
2. **Chance** itself is a set of known facts, but it is unknown how to use them to explain an observation. That is, a certain set of rules is missing. Accordingly, an observation cannot be explained by the facts. Since rules are usually generated by inductive ways, rules that are different from the trend cannot be generated. In this case, rules are generated by abductive methods, so trends are not considered. Abductively generated rules are characterized as chance.

Magnani also discussed application of abduction to chance discovery. Especially, he pointed out "manipulative abduction happens when we are thinking through doing and not only, in a pragmatic sense, about doing. So the idea of manipulative abduction goes beyond the well-known role of experiments as capable of forming new scientific laws by means of the results (the nature's answers to the investigator's question) they present, or of merely playing a predictive role (in confirmation and in falsification). Manipulative abduction refers to an extra-theoretical behavior that aims at creating communicable accounts of new experiences to integrate them into previously existing systems of experimental and linguistic (theoretical) practices. The existence of this kind of extra-theoretical cognitive behavior is also testified by the many everyday situations in which humans are perfectly able to perform very efficacious (and habitual) tasks without the immediate possibility of realizing their conceptual explanation" [16]. Then he pointed out that "in dealing with the exploitation of cognitive resources and chances embedded in the environment, the notion of affordance, originally proposed by Gibson to illustrate the hybrid character of visual perception, can be extremely relevant. [...] In order to solve various controversies on the concept of affordance, we will take advantage of some useful insights that come from the study on abduction. Abduction may fruitfully describe all those human and animal hypothetical inferences that are operated through actions which consist in smart manipulations to both detect new affordances and to create manufactured external objects that offer new affordances" [17]. Thus he suggests the application of abduction to detect affordances which can be regarded as chances embedded in the environment.

4   Dementia Care Inspired by Affordance

It is not possible to prepare all necessary things in every places. Sometimes an alternative or an extended usage of things will be necessary. For a proper and an extended usage of a thing, it is necessary to present proper information of it. At least, it is necessary to suggest such information. Sometimes it can be presented as a memorandum or a sign. In the other case, it can be received as hidden information inside of the thing. Actually it is not always necessary to provide such hidden information. For a progressive and promising system, it is not realistic to prepare all the necessary information to things. Sometimes such information is not correct and will change in the future. For instance, it is ridiculous to attach a sign such as "You can sit here." to tree stumps. It is rather realistic to suggest information about its hidden functions.

In this section we discuss how to present such hidden information in dementia care situation. Such hidden information can be presented as certain stimuli in such situations. Because, as shown in the previous section, even for dementia person, if he/she receives certain stimuli, he/she sometimes achieve better performance. The problem is that what type of stimulus will be better to present and how to make it recognize. Actually such stimulus should be "afforded" by the user. That is, it can be regarded as "affordance" in an environment. Accordingly we introduce concept of affordance to a dementia care system. Proper affordance might give a certain support to dementia persons understanding (meanings of) objects. Thus affordance is a fruitful concept for recognizing objects and using them as tools. According to Gibson's definition, affordance is hidden in the nature and it should be accepted by us naturally. For instance, if an object's upper side is flat and it has a certain height, the observer will be able to afford it as something to sit, rest or sleep. Of course, the level of affordance will be change according to observer's acceptance ability. For a certain person a tree stump will function as a chair, but for the other person it will not. If they are able to regard a tree stump as a chair, it will be necessary to provide a proper guidance to discover an affordance as a something to sit.

For normal persons, it is not so difficult to provide such guidances. They can also understand analogy, so that they can extend the meaning to the other materials. For instance, after finding that a tree stump functions as a chair, they can also understand a wooden board or box can also function as a chair. That is, they can extend or map the meaning to the other situations. However, for dementia persons, it is not easy to provide a proper guidance with which they can afford the function of an object. Actually, for person who does not have common knowledge or context, it is also not easy to provide a proper guidance for affordance discovery. For them affordance is something rare or novel. Accordingly, it is rather difficult to be aware of "affordance" as an afforded matter. In therapy houses, there should be many things which are not able to properly used by dementia persons. In the case, it is necessary to provide certain guidances to lead the user to the correct direction to use things properly. The simplest method will be to attach the name and usage of things. It will functions well for normal persons. However, for impaired persons, sometimes even such attachment will not function well. For them, it will be necessary to apply the other strategy to suggest or instruct the meaning or usage of things. For semantic dementia persons, it is observed that they did not achieve better performance on a subset of affordanced objects when use of these was compared with a familiarity-matched subset of objects lacking such affordances. Therefore, when we design an environment for dementia persons, it is necessary to consider such unhappy situations. It is necessary to prepare specialized affordances to dementia person. Even if they can detect affordance, they might not understand what it will emerge.

For affordance, according to the Gibson's definition, an *Object* is observed and affordance is detected in the environment to understand its meaning. Accordingly, the affordance situation can be logically described as follows:

$$F \cup affordance \models Object \tag{1}$$

$$F \cup affordance \not\models \Box \tag{2}$$

The above is described based on the formalization of Theorist [20].F is so called facts which involves fundamental knowledge in the world. The obtained affordance is consistent with F (equation (2)) and gives life (meaning) to the *Object*. Thus *Object* involves invisible *meaning* and by adopting discovered affordance, potential meaning appears. Therefore, in the above formalization, *meaning* does not appear explicitly.

However, in the above application, we would like to give a certain meaning to the *Object* explicitly. Though meaning exists inside of the *Object*, in this framework meaning is explicitly described. That is, meaning should be observed and affordance functions as a type of link to *Objects*. When meaning is fixed, the affordance determination situation will be logically described as follows:

$$Object \cup affordance \models meaning \tag{3}$$

$$Object \cup affordance \not\models \Box \tag{4}$$

That is, affordance can be regarded as a hypothesis. We can select consistent affordance ((equation (4))) in the environment (hypothesis base) to explain meaning. In addition, for understanding subset of or similar affordanced objects (*Object'*), the affordance determination situation will be logically described as follows:

$$Object \cup Object' \cup M \cup affordance \models meaning \tag{5}$$

In fact, the above description is based on Goebel's formalization of analogy [12]. M is a mapping function from *Object* to *Object'*. That is, to understand the same meaning of the subset of or similar affordanced objects, an additional mapping function M is required. Thus if M can be determined and the usage of *Object* is known, *Object'* can also be understood. In fact, for normal persons, M is easy to understand. However, for dementia persons, it is pointed out that it is rather difficult to understand and determine M. Then the issue becomes how to suggest a mapping function M as an additional hypothesis. For typical analogical mapping, objects in the source domain and the target domain are quite different. In fact, the typical analogical mapping is determined based on conceptual structure as pointed out by Gentner [7,8,9]. For instance, if we know about the water flow system where water flows from a place with greater pressure to a place with less pressure, we can guess or find the heat flow system where heat flows from a place with greater temperature to a place with less temperature. However, for the applications shown in this paper, a mapping function will not so complex as typical analogical mapping. For the proposed application, expected situations are very simple. For instance, to give a hint (mapping function) of sitting on a wooden box to dementia person who could use a tree stump as a chair. In fact, the situation is structured, but for an application, we can only focus on an aspect such that the upper side is flat. . This type of mapping will be one dimensional mapping and not so confusing. Thus theoretically a mapping function becomes simple.

The final issue is how to suggest hidden information as affordance. This type of information is usually hidden in the environment. Thus the proposed type of application can be discussed under the context of chance discovery. As Abe mentioned, chance discovery can be performed by a combination of abduction and analogy. Also as Magnani pointed out, affordnace can be performed by a certain type of abduction. In the above, the concept of affordance is also described in the framework of Theorist that is hypothetical reasoning (limited version of abduction). Accordingly, all procedures can be described in abduction's framework. In addition, it is happy for us that we can simplify our problems to one dimensional mapping. Of course, in this section, for the first step, a very simple case is discussed. For the actual usage, much more complex situation should be considered. My assumption is that such complex situation can be transformed to a combination of simple situations. To deal with complex situations, it is necessary to develop a mechanism to transform complex situation to a combination of simple situations such as polynomial.

5   Conclusions

In this paper, I introduced the concept of affordance to support dementia persons. Limited merits of affordance for supporting dementia persons are pointed out by Bozeat and Hodges. In addition, after the extension of Gibson's concept of affordance, it is mainly applied to the interface design. Based on the concept of affordance, I proposed a dementia person support mechanism in which functions of things can be suggested. It is based on abduction framework and performed under the context of chance discovery to determine affordance. In this paper, I only described logical framework and dealt with very simple situation. In fact, actual sisuations should be more complex. To deal with such complex situation, additional treatments are necessary. I showed my assumption that complex situation can be transformed to a combination of simple situations and necessasity of develop a mechanism to transform complex situation to a combination of simple situations.

References

1. Abe, A.: The Role of Abduction in Chance Discovery. New Generation Computing 21(1), 61–71 (2003)
2. Abe, A.: Abduction and Analogy in Chance Discovery. In: [19], ch. 16, pp. 231–248 (2003)
3. Aldridge, D.: Music Therapy in Dementia Care. Jessica Kingsley Publishers (2000)
4. Bozeat, S., Ralph, M.A.L., Patterson, K., Hodges, J.R.: When objects lose their meaning: Waht happens to their use? Cognitive, Affecgtive, & Behavioral Neurosciences 2(3), 236–251 (2002)
5. Cafalu, C.A.: The Role of Alternative Therapies in the Management of Alzheimer's Disease and Dementia, Part I. Annals of Long-Term Care 13(7), 34–41 (2005)
6. Cafalu, C.A.: The Role of Alternative Therapies in the Management of Alzheimer's Disease and Dementia, Part II. Annals of Long-Term Care 13(8), 33–39 (2005)
7. Gentner, D.: Structure-Mapping: A Theoretical Framework for Analogy. Cognitive Science 7, 155–170 (1983)
8. Gentner, D.: Analogical Inference and Analogical Access. Analogica, 63–88 (1988)
9. Gentner, D.: The mechanisms of analogical learning. Similarity and Analogical Reasoning, 199–241 (1989)
10. Gibson, J.J.: The Theory of Affordances. In: Shaw, R., Bransford, J. (eds.) Perceiving, Acting, and Knowing (1977)
11. Gibson, J.J.: The Ecological Approach to Visual Perception. Houghton Mifflin (1979)
12. Goebel, R.: A sketch of analogy as reasoning with equality hypotheses. In: Jantke, K.P. (ed.) AII 1989. LNCS (LNAI), vol. 397, pp. 243–253. Springer, Heidelberg (1989)
13. Hodges, J.R., et al.: The role of conceptual knowledge in object use evidence from semantic dementia. Brain 123, 1913–1925 (2000)
14. Jones, K.S.: What Is an Affordance? Ecological Psychology 15(2), 107–114 (2003)
15. Kasama A.: Dementia, http://www.inetmie.or.jp/~Ekasamie/dementia.html

16. Magnani, L.: Epistemic Mediators and Chance Morphodynamics. In: Abe, A., Oh-sawa, Y. (eds.) Readings in Chance Discovery. International Series on Natural and Artificial Intelligence, vol. 3, Advanced Knowledge Intelligence, ch. 13, pp. 140–155 (2005)
17. Magnani, L.: Chances, Affordances, and Cognitive Niche Construction: The Plasticity of Environmental Situatedness. International Journal on Advanced Intelligence Paradigms (to appear, 2009)
18. Norman, D.: The Design of Everyday Things. Addison-Wesley, Reading (1988)
19. Ohsawa, Y., McBurney, P. (eds.): Chance Discovery. Springer, Heidelberg (2003)
20. Poole, D., Goebel, R., Aleliunas, R.: Theorist: A Logical Reasoning System for Defaults and Diagnosis. In: Cercone, N.J., McCalla, G. (eds.) The Knowledge Frontier: Essays in the Representation of Knowledge, pp. 331–352. Springer, Heidelberg (1987)
21. Sloane, P.D., et al.: The Therapeutic Environment Screening Survey for Nursing Homes (TESS-NH): An Observational Instrument for Assessing the Physical Environment of Institutional Settings for Persons With Dementia. Journal of Gerontology: Social Sciences 57B(2), S69–S78 (2002)
22. Warren, W.H.: Perceiving affordances: Visual guidance of stair-climbing. Journal of Experimental Psychology: Human Perception and Performance 10, 683–703 (1984)
23. Zhang, J., Patel, V.L.: Distributed cognition, representation, and affordance. Cognition & Pragmatics (2006)

Efficacy of Cognitive Training Experiences
in the Elderly: Can Technology Help?

Cristina Buiza, Mari Feli Gonzalez, David Facal, Valeria Martinez, Unai Diaz,
Aitziber Etxaniz, Elena Urdaneta, and Javier Yanguas

Fundación Instituto Gerontológico Matia – INGEMA, Camino de los Pinos,
27-bajo, 20018. Donostia – San Sebastián, Spain
{cbuiza,fgonzalez,dfacal,vmartinez,udiaz,aetxaniz,
eurdaneta,jyanguas}@fmatia.net

Abstract. Cognitive training has been a growing field in recent years. It is established that training improves cognitive abilities in healthy elderly people.
Specialized software and commercial devices including the possibility of cognitive gaming has been placed into the market; most of them are based on neuropsychological models of cognitive aging, but few have been scientifically
tested. Computerized cognitive games are being developed in "HERMES –
Cognitive Care and Guidance for Active Aging", a research project co-funded
by the European Union under the Seventh Framework Program (FP7). Cognitive training designed for HERMES includes daily live events introduced by the
user into the system, allowing the stimulation of prospective memory with their
own information. Gaming model, concepts and assessment aims (including usability, subjective value and efficacy) are described.

Keywords: Cognitive training, cognitive stimulation, cognitive games, elderly,
aging.

1 Introduction

Cognitive training for older adults has been a growing field in recent years, with increasing scientific knowledge about efficacy of cognitive stimulation programs [1].
This is not surprising attending to cognitive changes in an increasing older population,
specially observing implications of cognitive aging for basic and instrumental
daily-life activities. For example, cognitive abilities are critical in technological tasks
common in daily live, such as operating a mobile phone or buying a train-ticket in a
vending machine [2].

Research in the efficacy of cognitive training is pointing to some extent to the
achievement of the goals comprised by the concept of successful aging, as described
by Rowe & Kahn [3]: a) the preservation of physical and cognitive functions, b) an
active engagement with life; and, to some extent, c) the absence of pathology, disability and risk factors. The contribution of cognitive functioning to this ideal of successful aging comes from the consideration that elderly people with a preserved cognitive
functioning have healthier lifestyles. In a 20 years follow up study, Gale et al. [4]

C. Stephanidis (Ed.): Universal Access in HCI, Part I, HCII 2009, LNCS 5614, pp. 324–333, 2009.

found that cognitive impairment was associated with an increase of mortality, specially, in association to isquemic cerebral vascular disease. On the other hand, McGuire et al. [5] examined the relative contribution of cognitive function to mortality for a 2 year period in a sample of 559 adults elder than 70 years old with diabetes without cognitive impairment by the time of the initial assessment. They found that elders with diabetes and low cognitive function (even within the normality range) had an increased probability of 20% for dying than those diabetics with a better cognitive function.

The first two sections of this paper describe empirical studies on the efficacy of cognitive training and its computerized applications respectively. Hereinafter, "HERMES: Cognitive Care and Guidance for Active Aging" is described, including sections about HERMES Cognitive games concept, its evaluation plan and the differential values HERMES add in the growing field of computerized cognitive training.

1.1 Efficacy of Cognitive Training

It has been established that cognitive training improves cognitive abilities in healthy elderly people. It includes specific stimulation regarding to concrete processes such as memory or language, as well as more general tasks based on broad constructs such as attention or speed of processing [6]. As a principle, cognitive stimulation must be adapted to the cognitive abilities of each person, which means that the level of difficulty must be in accordance with capabilities [7]: difficult enough to mean a challenge for the elder, but not so difficult that becomes frustrating.

Regarding the question about how cognitive stimulation can work in the maintenance of cognitive function in older adults, Tranter et al. [8] have determined that fluid intelligence, the portion of intelligence which implies an active resolution of problems in tasks for which cannot be derived simple solutions based on formal training or in previous knowledge, shows frequently an almost linear deterioration associated to the ageing process. -Nevertheless, it is not clear that fluid intelligence decline is, indeed, inevitable. Many evidences suggest that elderly people, under appropriate conditions, show a much more flexible thinking and adaptation than what it could have been expected.

Little attention has been placed in this field on older adults' prospective memory stimulation, despite its importance on their daily living. Prospective memory refers to the ability to become aware of previous plans, executing them at the right time and place [9]. Recent research and reviews point out the variability of age-related declines on prospective memory regarding to test setting and sub-domains. On natural settings, age declines are weaker than in laboratory, probably because of contextual information available on daily routines. Using meta-analysis [9], age-significant declines were observed in 1) proper prospective memory, which implies the awareness of previous plans mentioned above, and also in 2) vigilance, in which plans remain on consciousness; significant differences were not found in 3) habitual prospective memory, in which the plan has to be brought back to consciousness repeatedly as long as the cue is presented.

In elderly persons suffering from a neurodegenerative dementia such as Alzheimer's disease, cognitive stimulation maximizes their performance in specific domains such as verbal and visual learning, and also has a significant impact on related behavioral disturbances and caregiver's quality of life. In these patients, restorative cognitive training strategies, which attempt to directly improve functioning in specific domains – i.e. errorless learning, vanishing cues or spaced retrieval- have achieved larger effects than compensatory approaches [10]. Ideal memory training should target information useful for the everyday functioning of the patients and their caregivers, such as activities of daily living, and use similar training procedures or techniques for every subject involved in a given program. A posterior meta-analysis [11] reviewed the literature and summarized the effect of cognitive training for Alzheimer's disease patients on multiple functional domains. They concluded that cognitive training evidenced promise in the treatment of Alzheimer's disease, having the restorative strategies larger effect sizes than compensatory strategies, with primarily medium effect sizes for learning, memory, executive functioning, activities of daily living, general cognitive problems, depression, and self-rated general functioning.

About the use of cognitive training in the field of dementia, two major limitations have been pointed [12]: the transfer of improvement to other cognitive areas and the durability of the effects. Emerging clinical results indicate that cognitive training do not only slow the cognitive decline for a specific area, but also slows the deterioration of more general indexes of global dementia function. By means of animal models, it has been observed that mental stimulation is a strong signal for the induction of Brain Derived Neurotrophic Factor (BDNF) [13].

1.2 Efficacy of Computerized-Cognitive Training

In parallel to the increasing knowledge about cognitive training, a great amount of specialized software and commercial devices including the possibility of cognitive training have been placed into the market. Most of these programs are based on neuropsychological models of cognitive functioning and cognitive aging, but few of them have been scientifically tested through empirical studies with healthy older people, highlighting the need of more research efforts and publications in order to empirically establish the efficacy of computerized stimulation.

Scientific research in computerized cognitive training with healthy adults has focused on executive functions [14]. Executive functioning implies, for example, the knowingly processing of internal and external problems. It includes processes such as problem solving – to determine concrete aims, to plan actions concerned with these aims and to use feedback from this actions-, mental flexibility –to evaluate behaviors in terms of successful or failure and to change actions planned in the light of these evaluations- and verbal fluency. VitalMind project [15] designs tasks to train these three cognitive functions supported by frontal regions and particularly compromised with age. It also includes four training components: a brain fitness component, a life-skill component, an integrated component and a personal memory and enrichment component. Each component contains activities which train each specific mental function separately and uniquely.

Cogmed Working Memory Training is a home-based program to improve executive function by training working memory capacity, first developed by a team of researchers at the Karolinska Institute in Sweden [16]. In brain injured patients after stroke, Cogmed Working Memory Training was found to have an effect on short-term memory tests, on a paced auditory serial-addition task and also on a selective attention task –to select numbers 2 and 7 with letters or numbers as distracters- chosen as non-trained test because it is very close but not exactly identical to tasks in the program. In young healthy adults, after this working memory training, authors found an increase in brain activity in the middle frontal gyrus and superior and inferior parietal cortices [17].

In mild and moderate stages of dementia, computerized cognitive training in combination with other cognitive stimulation programs has shown improved outcome scores in cognitive performance. Smartbrain is a system developed for the treatment of cognitive impairment –Alzheimer's disease and other dementias, brain damage and so on. Its efficacy with the cognitive stimulation in Alzheimer's disease has been demonstrated in a single-blind randomized study [18] comparing 12 patients receiving only pharmacological treatment –cholinesterase inhibitors-, 16 patients receiving both pharmacological and non-pharmacological treatment – integrated psycho stimulation program and, finally, 15 patients in an experimental group receiving both treatment and also training in Smartbrain as a interactive multimedia internet-based system. Patients receiving Smartbrain training began at the lowest level of difficulty from 15 levels, increasing the level of difficulty automatically after three consecutive performances and decreasing it when his or her performance fell below 15% correct for three consecutive sessions. No differences were found at baseline; after 12 weeks and also after 24 weeks, significant differences were found in standardized measures of cognitive function, but not in functional assessment nor in specific neuropsychological tests.

In addition to its efficacy on cognitive functioning, computerized games may offer elderly users new ways of social interaction. ElderGames project [19] develops games using digital object interaction with the aim of stimulating the social interaction and participation of elderly people. The social interaction underlying computerized games could be a central motivator to engage elderly people in daily cognitive stimulation routines, as well as an important key to get older adults without experience closer to digital technologies [14].

2 HERMES – Cognitive Care and Guidance for Active Aging

"HERMES: Cognitive Care and Guidance for Active Aging" is a project co-funded by the European Commission within the 7th Framework Program [20]. HERMES has been developed with the aim of reducing age-related cognitive decline. It provides assistance but also promotes the autonomy and independence of users in their daily lives, employing pervasive non obtrusive technology.

The main aims of the HERMES project are facilitation of episodic memory, advanced activities reminding and cognitive training. Regarding age related cognitive decline, the episodic memory may present gaps or some details of the past can be lost. In fact, the autobiographical information memory is weaker than published information memory [21]. HERMES captures user's daily life information through audio and video means as well as information on the context. HERMES also provides reminders through visual and audio patterns in order to strengthen prospective memory, facilitating the information previously captured when it is essential. In this sense, HERMES cognitive games are designed to stimulate not only processing resources and episodic memory, but also prospective memory related to users' daily life. Additionally, conversation support through everyday conversation recording and mobility support are included into the project.

The first step in the HERMES project was to clearly identify the user's needs as well as their preferences about the new technologies, including computerized cognitive games, with the goal of checking the feasibility of the application [22]. Technical complexity of the product has to be adapted to a very specific population from a user-centred design point of view, providing maximum functionality while being easy to use. In order to achieve this aim, information about users was collected through questionnaires, interviews, cultural probes, diaries of memory failures and memory assessments.

Questionnaires employed in the user's requirements collection were completed by 99 people over 60 years old. The results showed that most of the healthy older adults studied stated they would appreciate a device to play some cognitive games. Older adults want a device to remind them the following issues: shopping list (48.3%), conversations with a doctor (31.0%) or their families (24.1%), things they have to do (48.1%). The situations in which they feel most uncomfortable due to forgetfulness are buying something or doing any task (42.85%); how to get somewhere (22.22%), forget names (61.9%); an important appointment (39.68%) and conversations (28.5%).

On the characteristics of these technological devices, utility is perceived as the most important feature, followed by simplicity. Aesthetics were the least rated feature. Qualitative techniques showed that elderly people of this generation are reluctant to use any technology that may reduce their autonomy or minimize their cognitive or functional efforts. Technology plays a minor role in their life and they did not explicitly see how technology could help them with this but were open to give it a try should they be in need of it. In this sense, technological external aids should be easier and simpler than the aids currently used.

Other important conclusion from user-requirements study was that older adults perceived to maintain the cognitive function as the most needful requirement for an independent living [22]. On cognitive functioning, diary studies on daily memory failures showed that most of the participants forgot from 5 to 7 events per week, while objective cognitive assessment showed low scores in working memory and attention measures [23]. Memory and attentional changes may cause problems in developing conceptual representation and strategies to cope with computerized tasks [24].

2.1 HERMES Cognitive Games Concept

Cognitive games included in HERMES have been designed taking into account age-related changes in memory, executive processing, visual attention and visual-manual coordination, avoiding burden on these functions but stimulating them. HERMES cognitive training games are offered through novel ergonomic interfaces, which provide to aged users comfort, flexibility and natural interaction. In particular the HERMES end-user interface for cognitive training is implemented on multi-touch surface interface based on leading edge finger tracking technology [26], which enhances interaction, motivation and allows complex game features.

Two phases of games implementation have been designed. The first phase takes into account cognitive changes related to aging as well as the multi-touch system potentials. The second phase, following user-requirement study [24] in a narrower sense, will include both attentional and language games.

The two first games to be developed are the "HERMES Maze" and the "HERMES Puzzle". Both take information introduced into the system by the HERMES user and employ it as stimulus for cognitive stimulation, and both stimulate visual-hand and bimanual coordination.

In the "HERMES Maze", the HERMES system asks the user to match an appointment clue (e.g. Doctor visit) and a time clue (e.g. 10:00 h.) from two different start points to an Appointment Sheet, which is inside a maze and serve as a reaching point (see Figure 1).

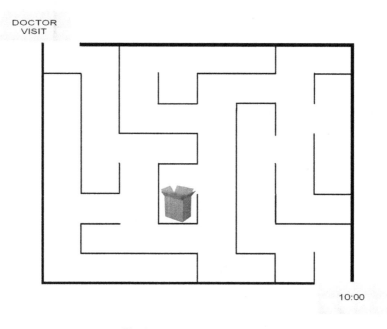

Fig. 1. "HERMES Maze" layout

The user has to move the "clues" (letters in a box or cube) along the maze, each clue with a hand (Figure 2). If the user withdraws a hand, the clue returns to the start point. Once he or she has matched the clues putting them both inside the Appointment Sheet, both clues change in a single Appointment message and a Congratulations message is displayed and another pair of clues is displayed. In this game, difficulty level is varied manipulating the number of appointments (e.g. three appointment clues and three time clues are displayed and the user has to select one appointment clue and its corresponding time clue and then match them across the Maze) and/or the complexity of the mazes.

For its part, the HERMES Puzzle (Figure 3) uses pictures already store at the HERMES database and related to the appointments of the next day (e.g. his son picture if she will meet him tomorrow). The distinctiveness of this task is the movement of the pieces of the puzzle, which can be simple (up-down or left-down) or complex

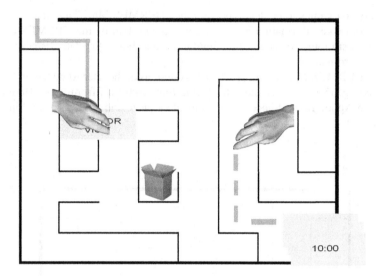

Fig. 2. "HERMES Maze" gaming schedule

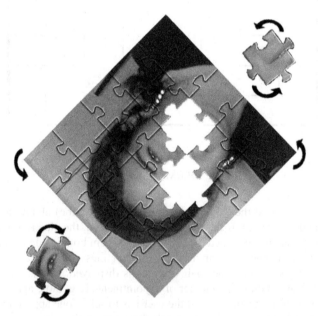

Fig. 3. "HERMES Puzzle" layout

(rotation) according to the difficulty of the task. Besides the number of pieces, other dimensions of the difficulty of the task would be the speed of the movements, and the combination of both direction and speed. HERMES direct the assembly of pieces presenting two or more pieces assembled at the start of the game. Pieces do not stop movement unless you touch them so, in order to assemble a piece into the puzzle, users have to simultaneous touch them both. If the user does not progress towards the resolution, HERMES can facilitate the performance drawing the related pieces near each other. When the puzzle is finished, HERMES reinforces the user and stimulates prospective memory showing the appointment related to the completed picture in a marked way.

2.2 HERMES Cognitive Games Evaluation Plan

The users will be taken into account in the phases of development and implementation, defining game requirements together with them. The games will be tested in three different phases.

In the first phase, an expert group -composed mainly by neuropsychologists and gerontologists- will be invited in a focus group session in order to give their opinion about cognitive games.

In the second phase, the user-target group will be assessed in terms of games' usability and subjective value by means of a focus group and individual interviews. Exploration of both gaming experience [14] and assessment tools [25] are observed.

Focus groups are six to ten person meetings to discuss experiences or opinions around topics introduced by a moderator. This qualitative research method has been used extensively in marketing studies, social research and, more recently, in user-requirements studies [26]. In the assessment of games usability and subjective value, this qualitative technique can show priorities, interests, motivations or anxieties, as well as identify potential steps on efficacy assessment and new scenarios for potential developments.

Finally, the efficacy of these games will be tested in a third phase using prototypes of the games and the devices developed into the HERMES Project. Performance on computerized cognitive training could be a valuable tool for trend detection, complementing neuropsychological evaluation though frequent data acquisition, also avoiding biases due to education, culture and experience [27].

2.3 HERMES Cognitive Games Uniqueness

Taking the user's requirement study results into account [22, 23], flexibility and adaptability of the HERMES System have been reinforced. HERMES will employ cognitive training to strength their autonomy rather than their dependence on technology, allowing users to work with their personal information, instead of offering reminders without any cognitive effort. As older adults have pointed out, HERMES games have been designed to be easy to use, intuitive, and available highly interactive.

While other devices have a fixed database as a source of information for presented games, with the subsequent lack of any game personalization other than an arbitrary level of difficulty, games developed in HERMES have the goal of encouraging autonomy and sense of independence by means of making use of information introduced into the system by HERMES users about their own daily life. This distinctive aspect will allow us stimulate prospective memory directly addressed to daily events.

Users' motivation has been taken into account, especially in order to promote user long-term motivation and adherence to daily gaming experience. In this sense, computerized cognitive training has the potential of parallel using a big amount of visual and acoustic stimulus and also the possibility of personalized levels of difficulty, adapting them automatically from users' previous performance (successes and failures, reaction times, gaming routines).

Acknowledgements. This work is part of the EU HERMES project (FP7-216709), partially funded by the European Commission in the scope of the 7th ICT Framework. Special thanks to CURE – Center for Usability Research and Engineering and AIT – Athens Information Technology for the great work done in the user requirements and games developments described in this document.

References

1. Yanguas, J.J., Buiza, C., Etxeberria, I., Urdaneta, E., Galdona, N., González, M.F.: Effectiveness of a non pharmacological cognitive intervention on elderly factorial analysis of Donostia Longitudinal Study. Adv. Gerontol. 3, 30–41 (2008)
2. Slegers, K., Van Boxtel, M.P., Jolles, J.: The efficiency of using everyday technological devices by older adults: the role of cognitive functions. Aging Soc. 29, 309–325 (2009)
3. Rowe, J.W., Kahn, R.L.: Successful aging. Dell, New York (1998)
4. Gale, C.R., Martyn, C.N., Cooper, C.: Cognitive impairment and mortality in a cohort of elderly people. BMJ 312, 608–611 (1996)
5. McGuire, L.C., Ford, E.S., Ajani, U.A.: The impact of cognitive functioning on mortality and the development of functional disability in older adults with diabetes: the second longitudinal study on aging, http://www.biomedcentral.com/1471-2318/6/8 (March 26, 2008)
6. Ball, K., Edwards, J.D., Ross, L.A.: The impact of speed of processing training on cognitive and everyday functions. J. Gerontol. B Psychol. Sci. Soc. Sci. 62, 19–31 (2007)
7. Yanguas, J.J., Buiza, C., González, M.F.: Programas de psicoestimulación en demencias. In: Fdez Ballesteros, R. (ed.) Psicología de la vejez: una psicogerontología aplicada, pp. 187–214. Pirámide, Madrid (2009)
8. Tranter, L.J., Koutstaal, W.: Age and flexible thinking: an experimental demonstration of the beneficial effects of increased cognitively stimulating activity on fluid intelligence in healthy older adults. Aging Neuropsychol. Cogn. 15, 184–207 (2008)
9. Uttl, B.: Transparent meta-analysis of prospective memory and aging. Plos ONE 3(2), e1568 (2008)
10. Sitzer, D.I., Twamley, E.W., Jeste, D.V.: Cognitive training in Alzheimer's disease: a meta-analysis of the literature. Acta Psychiatr Scand 114, 75–90 (2006)
11. Olesen, P.J., Westerberg, H., Klingberg, T.: Increased prefrontal and parietal activity after training of working memory. Nat. Neurosci. 7, 75–79 (2004)
12. Valenzuela, M.J.: Brain reserve and the prevention of dementia. Curr. Opin. Psychiatry. 21(3), 296–302 (2008)
13. Valenzuela, M.J., Sachdev, P.: Brain reserve and dementia: a systematic review. Psychol. Med. 36, 441–454 (2006)
14. IJsselsteijn, W., Nap, H.H., de Kort, Y.: Digital game design for elderly users. In: Proceedings of the 2007 conference on Future Play, pp. 17–22. ACM, New York (2007)
15. http://www.vitalmind-project.eu/
16. Westerberg, H., Jacobaeus, H., Hirvikoski, T., Clevberger, P., Östensson, M.-L., Bartfai, A., Kingberg, T.: Computerized working memory training after stroke – A pilot study. Brain Inj. 21(1), 21–29 (2007)

17. Olesen, P.J., Westerberg, H., Klingberg, T.: Increased prefrontal and parietal activity after training of working memory. Nat. Neurosci. 7, 75–79 (2004)
18. Tárraga, L., Boada, M., Modinos, G., Espinosa, A., Diego, S., Morera, A., Guitart, M., Balcells, J., López, O.L., Becker, J.T.: A randomised pilot study to assess the efficacy of an interactive, multimedia tool of cognitive stimulation in Alzheimer's disease. J. Neurol. Neurosurg. Psychiatry. 77, 1116–1121 (2006)
19. Gamberini, L., Alcaniz, M., Barresi, G., Fabregat, M., Ibanez, F., Prontu, L.: Cognition, technology and games for the elderly: An introduction to ELDERGAMES Project. PsychNology. J. 4(3), 285–308 (2006)
20. http://www.fp7-hermes.eu/
21. Craik, F.I.M.: Changes in memory with normal aging: a functional view. Adv. Neurol. 51, 201–205 (1990)
22. Buiza, C., Gonzalez, M., Etxaniz, A., Urdaneta, E., Yanguas, J., Geven, A., Höller, N., Tscheligi, M.: Technology Support for Cognitive Decline and Independent Living – Presenting the HERMES Project. In: Gerontological Society of America Conference (2008)
23. Buiza, C., Diaz, U., Gonzalez, M.F., Etxaniz, A., Prieto, L., Urdaneta, E., Yanguas, J.: Age relates accurately to reported estimation of memory abilities. In: 37th Meeting of the International Neuropsychological Society Lifespan Neuropsychology: Transdisciplinary Issues and New Horizons, Atlanta, Georgia (2009)
24. Zajicek, M.: Interface support for elderly people with impaired sight and memory. In: 6th ERCIM Workshop User Interfaces for All. CNR-IROE, Florence, Italy (2000)
25. IJsselsteijn, W.A., de Kort, Y.A.W., Poels, K.: The Game Experience Questionnaire: Development of a self-report measure to assess the psychological impact of digital games (manuscript in preparation)
26. Courage, C., Baxter, K.: Understanding your users. A practical guide to user requirements. Methods, tools, and techniques. Elsevier, San Francisco (2005)
27. Jimison, H.: Unobtrusive monitoring of computer interactions to detect cognitive status in elders. IEEE Trans. Inf. Technol. Biomed. 8, 248–252 (2006)

Distributed Intelligence and Scaffolding in Support of Cognitive Health

Stefan P. Carmien and Randal A. Koene

Department of Neuroengineering, Fatronik Foundation
Mikeletegi Pasealekua 7, 20009 Donostia (Gipuzkoa) Spain
{scarmien,rkoene}@fatronik.com

Abstract. Computers have dramatically changed the social landscape and living practices in the 21st century. Most of those changes have empowered typically abled adults, while it is only in the last few years that platforms and frameworks have been developed to extend support to those with diminished cognitive capacity. In this paper we discuses the use of scaffolding and distributed intelligence in assistive technology design. Four examples are presented, in domains from education to cognitive orthotics. We discuss the technology of such applications and the problems that technology designers must be aware of. Finally, we specify how these support frameworks fit into overall efforts toward a culture that supports cognitive health.

Keywords: assistive technology, distributed intelligence, scaffolding, design frameworks.

1 Introduction

The human use of computers use have significantly affected the social landscape and living practices in the 21st century. Most of the changes have empowered typically-able adults and it is only in the last few years that platforms and frameworks have been developed to extend support to those with diminished cognitive capacity. This paper reviews the issues and opportunities for Activities of Daily Living (ADL) support for an aging population, where many deal with decreasing cognitive ability. Our target populations are those elders who experience a characteristic decline of cognitive and mnemonic ability with age as well as those elders with minimal cognitive impairment and in the mild stage of onset of Alzheimer's dementia [1].

1.1 Target population

One of the research areas of the department of neuroengineering at Fatronik-Tecnalia is technologies that support seniors' quality of life and extend autonomous aging in place. We are particularly interested in those elders transitioning into reduced cognitive abilities. Our technology research ranges from supporting spatial orientation to supporting finical independence in making day-to-day economic decisions. These elders may be experiencing what is considered normal cognitive decline. This includes a range of decrease in mnemonic ability from the decrease typically associated

C. Stephanidis (Ed.): Universal Access in HCI, Part I, HCII 2009, LNCS 5614, pp. 334–343, 2009.

with Age Associated Memory Impairment (AAMI) up to the more severe forms of memory loss associated with Mild Cognitive Impairment (MCI) and the onset of Alzheimer's dementia.

1.2 ADL Support

As neuroengineers, we target the broad domain of supported tasks, in addition to end users. We are most interested in the day-to-day tasks that make up the structure of independent living. Occupational therapists often refer to these tasks as Activities of Daily Living and, supporting them, Instrumental Activities of Daily Living (IADL). ADLs are ambulating (walking), transferring (getting up from a chair), dressing, eating, drinking, personal hygiene, taking medication. IADLs are driving, preparing meals, doing housework, shopping, managing finances, managing medication, and using the telephone. By focusing on the core tasks of autonomous living, we aspire to enable aging-in-place, living in ones own home and acting autonomously, as long as possible. The technology we are currently working on deals with orientation, financial decisions support and mitigating forgetfulness.

2 A Context of Cognitive Heath

In this time, we have an active culture of awareness of physical health, but no "Culture of Cognitive Health", as evidenced for example by a glance on this date at the main page of the U.S. Government multi-agency site http://www.health.gov, at http://www.healthierus.gov or at http://www.nutrition.gov. Mandatory school attendance insures close monitoring of cognitive health in childhood, yet there is no equivalent structure in place for aging adults. To improve this situation will require action by governments, by physicians, and by researchers in fields of study that include cognition, aging and the field of neuroengineering. In neuroengineering, an important part of our effort is directed towards early detection of problems with cognitive health, since early detection enables early intervention, and early intervention is often the strongest predictor of successful treatment. We develop and advocate the use of intelligent technologies that support the persisting cognitive capabilities of the user. We aim at a minimally invasive integration of technological support in terms of the least possible disruption of normal processes in the recipient's daily life. Therefore, assistive technology must be designed to be co-adaptive, not to take control of activities that pose cognitive challenges.

3 A Framework of Support

Computational support of ADLs can be implemented in two ways: replacing functionality and augmenting exiting functionality. We believe that the second alternative is preferable. We can call these two modalities artificial cognition and cognitive augmentation. By leveraging existing abilities, such systems more naturally conform to the needs, abilities, and habits of the user, which may also result in reduced abandonment of the assistive technology.

The design space for such assistive technology is by necessity a socio-technical environment (STE) [15], which treats the user, the user's social environment, the user's artifacts and her interactions all as deserving of specific attention. The STE is often understood through ethnographic studies done before and during the design and adoption phases. Grounding the design in its STE helps the designer to understand the system in place. By contrast, many computer applications are developed with environmental assumptions that implicitly include end users with characteristics similar to those of the designer, which leads to poor adoption and utilization of the application by the end user with disabilities [12]. Technology in support of ADLs that is intended to be used by elders or persons with cognitive disabilities will be intimately and critically involved with the lives of end-users and their caregivers. The system may not be adopted if its development does not include an understanding of the dynamic environment or of the ways in which the technology could affect activities and individual roles in the STE.

There are two primary theoretical perspectives from which to approach this problem: 1) distributed cognition and 2) scaffolding. These together inform the manner of support and the dynamic of changing use patterns in the end-user (e.g. as caused by elders' declining cognitive ability) and the environment over time.

3.1 Distributed Intelligence

Gregory Bateson remarked that memory is half in the head and half in the world[2]. We exist in a world full of examples of this distributed cognition: the shopping list that "remembers" for us, the speedometer on our car, the position of the toggle on our light switch (down for on in UK, up for on in USA), the very words that we are reading right now. Distributed cognition is the view that both the internal assets of the person and the cultural structures and artifacts support the intelligence or cognition in a given human action. The knowledge and skill put into building a house are drawn not only from the builder's internal knowledge and abilities, but also from his tools, tape measure, saws, and hammer, and also his cultural support, language, and customs [17]. Acts and knowledge are not constructed unilaterally [19]. Distributed cognition is an approach that views the cognitive act as a result of a system comprising an actor, the artifacts in the actor's environment, and possibly other people. These artifacts can be as concrete as a notebook and as ethereal as language. Viewing cognition in this fashion can enable analysis and prediction of cognitive behavior that has a basis beyond the solitary human mind.

Distributed intelligence (DI) [10] considers the support that enables persons to accomplish activities that would be error prone, challenging, or impossible to achieve alone. DI often implies learning a different set of skills to accomplish with support that which was previously done unaided. By designing aids for daily living for cognitively and mnemonically impaired persons, those persons may gain some of the capabilities of unimpaired persons that would otherwise be unattainable (e.g.. using internet banking to pay bills).

3.2 Scaffolding

Scaffolding [3] describes a technique of providing the appropriate level of cognitive orthotic (assistive technology to correct cognitive function) for a given user to accomplish a task. Grounding technology design in a "scaffolding with extending" perspective leads to abilities comparable to autonomous performance by persons without impairment [16]. Scaffolding is also a technique for implementing DI design. A critical problem in long-term design for elders is that there is an inevitable decline in ability that leads to a choice: abandon the technology and use a more 'invasive' one or design technology that can adapt to the user's needs as long as possible.

Scaffolding is an approach that attempts to support a changing end-user. This change can either require retractive scaffolding or extendible scaffolding that takes over more function as abilities decline. Retractive scaffolding may be used in a learning environment where scaffolding retracts as the student learns the task at [6],. In fact, continued use of the technology after successful learning may impair further progress (e.g. continued use of training wheels while attempting to ride a mountain bike in the hills). In this case, the scaffolding tool is used then dismantled [9, 16] as its function is internalized by the user.

An example of a design domain that benefits from extendable scaffolding is technology to support elders who experience cognitive decline with the making and execution of financial. Extending scaffolding also lends itself to providing assessment functions by opportunistically collecting performance information, and using the analysis of this information to inform or alert caregivers about an elder's cognitive state.

4   Technological Foundations of Distributed Intelligence and Scaffolding

Supporting successful scaffolding involves both an *adaptable* aspect [21], one that can be flexibly reconfigured by the user or proxy, and an *adaptive* facility, i.e. one that tailors itself automatically to an individual user profile based on usage characteristics or other factors [23].

The technology of adaptable systems primarily enables fitting the system to the slowly changing attributes of a user, and is often implemented with configuration files that are read at start-up. Initial configuration to the user's needs and skills is made possible by designing systems that can be configured in depth. The configuration may be carried out by a proxy rather than the user. In assistive technology systems a caregiver usually updates the configuration with some provision for end-users participation Configuration interfaces must be very flexible yet useable by those who are not computer professionals.

The technology used in adaptive systems allows the interface and functionality to change rapidly, depending on changing user needs and the use environment. Such a system needs input from the user's interactions and from the changing environment of the application. Adaptation must proceed cautiously, as the literature is replete with examples of unusable adaptive systems, e.g. Microsoft's paperclip utility and programs with vanishing menus. Some of these design mistakes involve adaptation based on too little data. False positives and false negatives in adaptation can have significant implications, which need to be taken into consideration. Another approach to adaptive systems includes the users agent, an example being a web browser on a PDA, as part of the data to base content adaptation on.

4.1   Examples of Scaffolding and Distributed Intelligence

WISE Collaborative Scripts. The Web-based Inquiry Science Environment "WISE" system (see Figure 1) supports the learning of scientific argumentation by providing scripts to follow that lead dyads of students to produce valid arguments and thus learn *how* to produce valid arguments [6]. The system guides the construction of complete arguments and longer argumentation sequences in a web-based collaborative inquiry learning environment. As students internalize the technique of properly constructing scientific arguments the scaffolding retracts by removing elements of instruction in making the argument. The key to its pedagogical impact is the system's recognition of the acquisition of the portion of the argumentation's generation process that must fade out for the next use by of the same users. Critical to the applicability of this technique was the generalizability of the skill learned.

MAPS Task support environment. The Memory Aiding Prompting System (MAPS) provides external cueing to guide a young adult with cognitive disabilities through a task in step-wise fashion, which she would not be able to accomplish unaided. The system is based on the "Universe of One" principle, which states that the set of disabilities and contexts that persons with cognitive disabilities bring to a problem are unique. Applications consequently require customization to extraordinary depth, in effect presenting an end-user programming problem [5] that requires intimate knowledge of the user that only a caregiver can provide.

MAPS [4] consists of two major subsystems that share the same fundamental data structure but present different affordances to caregivers and system users: (1) The MAPS designer/editor (MAPS-DE) for caregivers employs web-based script and

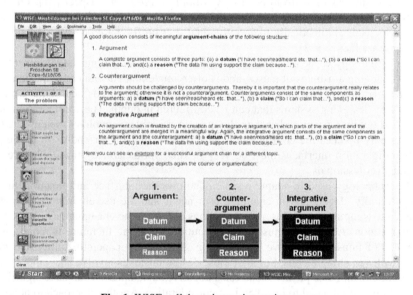

Fig. 1. WISE collaborative script environment

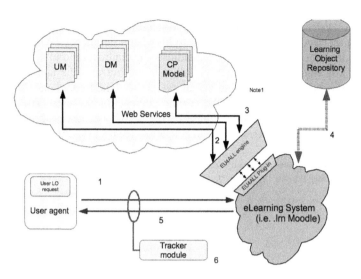

Fig. 2. EU4LL adapting of content for all

template repositories that allow content to be created and shared by caregivers of the end-users different abilities and experiences. (2) The MAPS prompter (MAPS-PR) for end-users, provides the display of the external scripts with a cognitive demand that is reduced as needed for a particular user, changing the task from memorization to the use of MAPS-PR. The MAPS-PR gives step-by-step instructions to the user with cognitive disabilities. Thus, the cognitive act is composed of a combination of the cognitive ability of the end-user, the MAPS-PR prompter, and the task environment an example of distributed intelligence. Further, as an end-user's ability changes, the caregiver can modify the set of prompts to fit, changing the scaffolding to fit the current need. This means there are more steps for a given task when the user needs more help, fewer if the end-user has learned the details of the task.

EU4ALL, access to learning. The European Unified Approach to Accessible Lifetime Learning (EU4ALL http://www.eu4all-project.eu/index) is an EC funded project with the goal of providing universal access to distance education [7], and a critical part of the project is the provision of an automatic adapting interface for a user's needs and abilities, as well as for the capabilities of the device used [22]. By taking into account the user preferences and the device capabilities, the user is no longer chained to a single (type of) device through which to receive and interact with learning materials.

Any system that can do automatic user adaptation requires a deep and complete set of standards for the content providers to work with. Given sufficient properly annotated content for the adaptation engine, a user can seamlessly switch from machine to machine and receive education content that is adapted specifically to his unique set of disabilities. Thus EU4ALL provides dynamic and automatic appropriate scaffolding.

In Figure 2 above, the set of models labeled UM and DM stand for the stored user models and device models that form the basis for delivery of appropriate content by the EU4LL system. As an example, take a young man using a laptop that has been presenting material especially formatted to his vision deficiency. When he goes outside and continues his study, the system adjusts the contrast ratio to accommodate the high levels of ambient light. When his blind friend borrows the laptop the machine switches to verbal presentation and verbal navigation. The figure below illustrates the gross level process of producing the correct content for the user. The core of this technology is the extensive work done in the W3C web accessibility group [24, 25]and in the several universal access to education groups [18, 26].

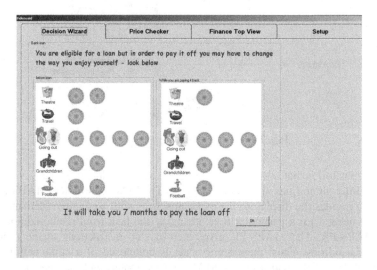

Fig. 3. Fidemaid loan feedback example

Fidemaid financial support tool. The Fidemaid system is designed to help elders age in their own homes as long as possible, to delay the need for a transition to a nursing home. Two of the main criteria that are used to consider a move to supported living [13, 14] are health issues and financial ability. Therefore, Fidemaid intends to achieve its goal by focusing on support with critical aspects of the finances of the elder.

Fidemaid provides help with the making of decisions about major expenditures by using information that is collected from the user, that is provided by various databases and other information sources, and by presenting a likely scenario given one decision or another (see Figure 3). At the same time, caregivers are kept informed of this and other interactions that the elder has with the Fidemaid system, especially any anomalous behaviors that might indicate a fraudulent event. The activities, icons and counters in the above display are specifically tailored to a user's current lifestyle and cognitive ability. As financial abilities decline the system takes note of the change, so that a caregiver can change the configuration to match a new set of end-user needs and skills. In this way, the scaffolding changes according to collected data. Beyond financial support, this form of data driven scaffolding retraction and extension may be useful in many ADL areas [18].

5 Possible Problems with This Approach

The technology described above operates in a realm that involves fluctuating personal abilities and the needs of day-to-day activities. A set of tools with such an intimate significance needs to be designed with possible failures in mind, since the consequences of a mis-match, mis-application or inappropriate use could affect the user in ways that range from discomfort to danger.

5.1 Learned Helplessness

An inappropriate over-reliance on tools for accomplishing ADLs can lead to learned helplessness and deskilling [6], which displaces a user's existing abilities by making the user dependent on the tool. This has been observed in the case of screen reader use by dyslexics, who were thereby impeded in the learning of reading skills [18]. Similarly, the use of calculators in the classroom may be inhibiting the learning of basic calculation skills. In 1989, the US National Council of Teachers of Mathematics (NCTM) issued a position paper stating that their recommendation in response to calculator technologies is to dramatically transform the objectives and timing of the entire course of mathematics education [17] to include appropriate use.

5.2 Device Failure

Reliance on a device can lead the leveraged user to find herself in a situation that would have been inaccessible without support. In that circumstance, device failure or malfunction may cause discomfort or danger. Consider the case where a spatial navigation system fails when an elder is in a frightening location. During the development of MAPS, groups of caregivers repeatedly expressed concern that using a tool such as MAPS as an orienting device could place their charge in more harm that she could have been in before MAPS. They based their arguments on the well-known fragility of computers, especially that of the software, the unreliability of battery power and the known lack of robustness in the entire technological infrastructure (i.e. wireless networks, GPS cell phones). That which is an inconvenience for the typical population may constitute serious danger for less capable populations.

5.3 Selection and Adoption

This sort of assistive technology is not just a snap-in-place prosthetic [11], but requires an entire socio-technical adoption process of selection. The system must suit the characteristics of the person who will use it. An example of this issue is illustrated by the MAPS project. MAPS was intentionally put on a platform with which one could play games and listen to music. This was important to the single adults who had so often been forced to use 'dorky' AT. Improper selection of AT is ranked high among the causes for technology abandonment [20].

6 Broader Implications

Distributed intelligence and scaffolding as described above, meet the criteria for use of neuroengineering in a Culture of Cognitive Health as proposed: Scaffolding provides support without displacing persisting cognitive capabilities that apply to a task (co-adaptation, not control). The retracting and expanding of scaffolding may be regarded as a substrate of ambient intelligence (AmI) [8], where the scaffolding must be based on an accurate assessment of the distributed cognition that a situation allows. Furthermore, the concept of distributed intelligence can minimize the degree to which the integration of technological support is perceived as invasive of a user's environment and daily activities, and ongoing data collection (e.g. in Fidemaid) enables early detection of new cognitive problems.

Acknowledgments. The authors wish to thank the Fatronik Foundation for providing the ground to pull these various strands together. We also wish to thank our co-workers at the Center for Lifelong Learning and Design, especially Gerhard Fischer and Anja Kintsch; Fraunhofer's Web Compliance Group especially Carlos Velasco and Yehya Mohamad; and Frank Fischer and Ingo Kollar of the Knowledge Media Research Center in Tübingen, Germany, for their collaborative script study.

References

1. Alzheimer's: Alzheimer's Association,
   http://www.alz.org/alzheimers_disease_research_ad.asp
   (accessed 2007)
2. Bateson, G.: Steps to an Ecology of Mind. Publishing Company (1972)
3. Carmien, S.: MAPS: Dynamic scaffolding for independence for persons with cognitive impairments. In: Brusilovsky, P., Corbett, A.T., de Rosis, F. (eds.) UM 2003. LNCS, vol. 2702, pp. 408–410. Springer, Heidelberg (2003)
4. Carmien, S.: End User Programming and Context Responsiveness in Handheld Prompting Systems for Persons with Cognitive Disabilities and Caregivers. In: Human Factors in Computing Systems, CHI 2004, Portland Oregon USA. ACM, New York (2005)
5. Carmien, S.: Leveraging Skills into Independent Living- Distributed Cognition and Cognitive Disability. VDM Verlag Dr. Mueller e.K., Saarbrücken (2007)
6. Carmien, S., Kollar, I., Fischer, G., Fischer, F.: The interplay of internal and external scripts — a distributed cognition perspective. In: Fischer, F., Kollar, I., Mandl, H., Haake, J.M. (eds.) Scripting Computer-Supported Learning – Cognitive, Computational, and Educational Perspectives, pp. 303–326. Springer, New York (2007)
7. EU4ALL: EU4ALL Project Public Web Site, http://www.eu4all-project.eu/ (accessed 2006)
8. Riva, G., Davide, F.V.F., Alcañiz, M. (eds.): Ambient Intelligence. IOS Press, Amsterdam (2005)
9. Guzdial, M.: Software-Realized Scaffolding to Facilitate Programming for Science Learning. Interactive Learning Environments (1994)
10. Hollan, J., Hutchins, E., Kirsch, D.: Distributed Cognition: Toward a New Foundation for Human-Computer Interaction Research. In: Carroll, J.M. (ed.) Human-Computer Interaction in the New Millennium, pp. 75–94. ACM Press, New York (2001)

11. Kintsch, A., de Paula, R.: A Framework for the Adoption of Assistive Technology. In: Bodine, C. (ed.) Proc. SWAAAC 2002: Supporting Learning Through Assistive Technology, pp. E3, 1–10. Assistive Technology Partners, Winter Park (2002)

12. LoPresti, E.F.B., Lewis, C.: Assistive technology for cognition [Understanding the Needs of Persons with Disabilities]. IEEE Engineering in Medicine and Biology Magazine 27(2), 29–39 (2008)

13. Mather, M.: A review of decision making processes: Weighing the risks and benefits of aging. In: Carstensen, L.L., Hartel, C.R. (eds.) When I'm 64, pp. 145–173. The National Academies Press, Washington (2006)

14. Moye, J., Marson, D.: Assessment of Decision-Making Capacity in Older Adults: An Emerging Area of Practice and Research. Journal of Gerontology: Psychoiogical Sciences 62B(1), 3–11 (2007)

15. Mumford, E.: Sociotechnical Systems Design: Evolving Theory and Practice. In: Bjerknes, G., Ehn, P., Kyng, M. (eds.) Computers and Democracy, pp. 59–76. Avebury, Aldershot (1987)

16. Pea, R.D.: The Social and Technological Dimensions of Scaffolding and Related Theoretical Concepts for Learning, Education, and Human Activity. The Journal of the Learning Sciences 13(3), 423–451 (2004)

17. Perkins, D.N.: Person-plus: A distributed view of thinking and learning. In: Solomon, G. (ed.) Distributed Cognitions Psychological and educational conciderations, pp. 88–110. Cambridge University Press, Cambridge (1993)

18. Sakai: The Sakai project, http://sakaiproject.org/portal(accessed 2009)

19. Salomon, G. (ed.): Distributed Cognitions: Psychological and Educational Considerations. Cambridge University Press, Cambridge (1993)

20. Scherer, M.J., Galvin, J.C.: An outcomes perspective of quality pathways to the most appropriate technology. In: Scherer, M.J., Galvin, J.C. (eds.) Evaluating, selecting and using appropriate assistive, pp. 1–26. Aspen Publishers, Inc., Gaithersburg (1996)

21. Stephanidis, C.: Adaptive Techniques for Universal Access. User Modeling and User-Adapted Interaction 11(1-2), 159–179 (2000)

22. Velasco, C.A., Mohamad, Y., Gappa, H., Nordbrock, G., Pieper, M., Darzentas, J., Darzentas, J.S., Koutsabasis, P., Spyrou, T.: IRIS: Toward An Environment That Supports Internet Design For All. In: Proc. Proceedings of International Conference on Assistive Technology (ICAT 2002), pp. 1–7. Pride Park Stadium, Derby (2002)

23. Velasco, C.A., Mohamad, Y., Gilman, A.S., Viorres, N., Vlachogiannis, E., Arnellos, A., Darzentas, J.: Universal access to information services – the need for user information and its relationship to device profiles. Universal Access in the Information Society 3(1), 88–95 (2004)

24. W3C: Composite Capability/Preference Profiles (CC/PP): Structure and Vocabularies 2.0, http://www.w3.org/TR/2007/WD-CCPP-struct-vocab2-20070430/: (accessed 2007)

25. W3C: Web Accessibility Initiative (WAI), http://www.w3.org/WAI/ (accessed 2009)

26. Wiley, D.A.: Connecting learning objects to instructional design theory: A definition, a metaphor, and a taxonomy, http://reusability.org/read/chapters/wiley.doc (accessed 2000)

Asperger Syndrome and Mobile Phone Behavior

Laura Daley[1], Shaun Lawson[1], and Emile van der Zee[2]

[1] Lincoln Social Computing (LiSC) Research Centre,
Department of Computing & Informatics
{Ladaley,Slawson}@lincoln.ac.uk
[2] Department of Psychology,
University of Lincoln, Brayford Pool, Lincoln, LN6 7TS
Evanderzee@lincoln.ac.uk

Abstract. This paper introduces the idea of using modern technology to work as an assistive tool for adults with Asperger's Syndrome (AS) and Higher-Functioning Autism (HFA) The study investigated the use of mobile phones by a neurotypical control group. Participants reported their pattern of phone use given specific social scenarios. Results showed that participants were more likely to use the text messaging facility on their phone to contact someone rather than call them. It also showed that their choice of communication mode did not differ given different social scenarios and neither did it when the information was given from the recipients' perspective. Further investigation is described where this information will be compared to a group of AS individuals.

Keywords: Asperger's Syndrome, Autism, Computer mediated communication, mobile phones.

1 Introduction

This paper describes research which is investigating how advances in computer mediated communication (CMC), such as mobile phone calls and texting, may be used to benefit individuals with Asperger Syndrome (AS) or Higher-functioning Autism (HFA)[1]. Hans Asperger, 1944 paper, first described the neurodevelopment disorder of Asperger Syndrome (AS), a classic literature of child psychiatry [1]. However up until 1981 AS was considered to be covered within the term Autism, Frith (1991) explains that this was partly due to Asperger's pioneering paper only being available German. Wing (1981) recognized and emphasized the differences between Classic Autism and AS. From her work, AS began to be considered as being on the spectrum of Autism i.e. an Autism Spectrum Condition (ASC) on which AS lay towards the high functioning end [2].

Asperger Syndrome has been described as having a 'triad of impairments' [3], this model consists of Social and Emotional impairments, Language and Communication impairments and Flexibility of Thought impairments. Figure 1 shows the triad and its subcategories.

---

[1] From this point references to AS will include HFA.

C. Stephanidis (Ed.): Universal Access in HCI, Part I, HCII 2009, LNCS 5614, pp. 344–352, 2009.
© Springer-Verlag Berlin Heidelberg 2009

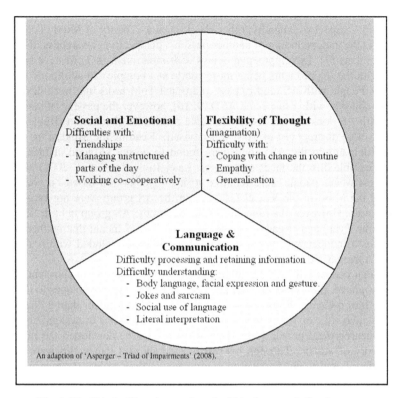

Fig. 1. The Triad of Impairment found within Asperger's Syndrome

This triad has shown to be a well standing general framework for the understanding of AS. These impairments are not always present in each and every individual with AS; with this in mind the model can increases our understanding of AS in general as well as on an individual level.

The research described in this paper is concerned with a one aspect of each of the triad, namely friendships, social use of language, and empathy. This paper investigates empathy is a core element of successful communication.

Empathy is notoriously difficult to define [4], but simplified is the understanding of another persons view point, from an emotional and cognitive perspective. Classic autism is associated with significant impairments in empathetic skills. This deficit manifests within the individuals behaviors in such ways as: lack of interest in others, lack of consideration of other peoples opinions, lack of awareness and understanding of body language and unspoken cues, lacking the ability to envisage another persons metal state; 'metalizing' etc[5]. Although this is not an exhaustive list of the possible effects a deficit of empathy can have, these are really at the root of the problem that autistic individuals have when interacting with others. When it comes to AS these impairments are generally to a lesser degree and more discreet, hence why it is helpful here to understand the problems given the most extreme case scenario.

Empathy is said to have several levels [6], the specific level this paper looks at is the cognitive aspect of empathy; otherwise known as Theory of Mind (ToM). Theory of Mind is the understanding of another person's perspective; awareness of the mental states of others [7]. Developmental delays and impairment in ToM have been shown in AS, with the impairments being more subtle and complex in adulthood than childhood [8]. People with AS tend to pass traditional ToM tasks that were developed for use with children with a suspected ASD [9, 10], however the passing of these tasks by adults with AS does not necessarily indicate normal ToM function (Rutherford et al, 2002). A more discreet test of ToM was devised; 'Reading the Mind in the Eyes' task [11]. Participants in the AS group were found to be not so good at identifying the emotion exhibited in the faces of pictures. Later Rutherford et al (2002) developed a similar test where people were required to identify emotion based on vocalizations; 'Reading the Mind in the Voice' task. Again the AS group were not as good as the control group. However, the range of results within the AS group in both 'Reading the Mind in the Eyes' and 'Reading the Mind in the Voice' meant that neither test could be used as a independent diagnostic tool, but could be included within a battery of tests for Asperger's diagnosis (Rutherford et al, 2002).

Although people with AS are often spoken about as having impairments or weaknesses, as above, these traits are not always perceived as disadvantages to the individual [12]. Baron-Cohen discusses AS as being a condition rather than a disorder [13]. One particular trait of AS is that on average they are better at systemizing than the average neurotypical person [14]. Baron-Cohen (2002b) developed the male-female brain theory of autism. Through his research he showed that males were more systematic than females and females more empathetic than males. He then went on the show that autistic individuals where even more systematic than the average male and even less empathetic than them too; hence the terminology 'the extreme male brain' explanation of autism. The poor ability of empathizing has already been discussed, be in a negative light. However, on the positive side people with an ASC have a greater ability to systemize.

There are many forms of systemizing; musical systemizing, spatial systemizing, natural systemizing just to name a few. A high ability to systemize helps people in many ways; from being organized on a day to day basis, to the understanding of physical processes and mathematical practices. Within the AS population this skill is reflected in their commonly seen fixated interests, e.g. train locomotives, computers, and routines, this is because natural systemizers investigate only varying one thing whilst everything else stays constant (Baron-Cohen, 2002). On an anecdotal level the magazine Wired in 2001 reported that ASC was rather prevalent in Silicon Valley California in work that heightened systemizing skills could be taken into the workplace, from this they coined the term 'the geek syndrome' as reference to AS[2].

1.1 Asperger's Syndrome and Technology

The heightened systemizing ability of people with AS could be drawn upon to benefit the social interaction skills of people with AS, in which they tend to be inhibited. This

---

[2] Wired magazine article available at
http://www.wired.com/wired/archive/9.12/aspergers_pr.html

idea of drawing on systematic tools, as aids for people with AS, has been used in previous research. Quite a considerable amount of research has gone into technology as learning tools in the field of humanoid robotics [15-18]. Along side this, research has taken place that has led to the development of computer applications that aim to assist individuals with social deficits such as the understanding of emotions expressed through facial expressions (e.g. Mind Reading [19] and The Transporters [20]). However the majority of these tools are aimed at children with ASC's rather than adults.

Previous computer applications that have been developed to date have also been based around desktop computers and therefore not available to the individual at all times. A technology that would be in the ideal position as a platform for an assistive tool would be the mobile phone; a prevalent social tool that is widely accepted within society [21]. With mobile phone use having risen dramatically in the past 10 years; reaching the impressive mile stone, in 2002, of having more subscribers than the traditional landline telephone [22]. Indeed Srivastava goes on to describe the mobile phones as having become a key social object, being both a social and technological phenomena.

The 'digital divide' is a phrase that is commonly used to describe the notion of the divide between those who have access to technology and those who don't. Jones and Marsden [21], talk about the 'digital divide' as being something that is important to bridge otherwise it adds to the barriers that come between the developed and developing world. Although in this sense it is spoken about having physical access this concept could also be applied to accessibility. Considering that people with AS often experience social difficulty this may lead to difficulties or hesitations using social technologies such as the mobile phone. As mobile phones are targeted at the mass market, the majority of phone applications are too. Mobile phone use by the AS population, has previously lacked research therefore how people with AS use and would like to use the mobile phone, which would need to be investigated before any AS targeted applications be developed.

Whilst the mobile phone is still new technology it would be an appropriate time to develop a more AS user friendly mobile phone application as anecdotal data (e.g. Srivastava, 2005) indicates that social etiquette for phones, in general, is still developing. For the individual with AS this would mean that they would be free to use the phone when and where they thought suitable and learn the social etiquette at the same time as other, Neurotypical (NT), phone users.

1.2 Aims of This Research

The intention of this study was to establish how NT people use their phones. In doing so it was investigate whether a stable social etiquette has been established for use of mobile phones within the NT population. It will look into whether people consider the other recipients perspective when using their mobile phones. Another aspect of the study will check that NT people are using mobile phones in the way they would like to and that nothing in constricting their use. Combined this information will form the baseline information needed in order to continue to identify any differences in needs from or use of mobile phones people with AS have compared to the NT population.

2 Method

Participants were recruited from the University of Lincoln and surrounding area. Some of the University participants received a reward in the form of a credit for the Psychology Department credit pool system, the remaining were entered into a draw to win a Nintendo Wii games console. 65 participants were tested; one participant's results were removed from the analysis as the participant did not fall within the control criteria (see measures section). Data sets from 64 participant's were analyzed; 15 males and 49 females (mean age of 22.89 (2dp)). Each participant carried out the same questionnaire.

This study took the form of a questionnaire carried out in a one to one interview setting. The Questionnaire consisted of three sections; demographic information, scenario questions and opinion questions.

2.1 Demographic Information

A modest amount of information about the participant were acquired; age, gender, education and employment. This information was collected in an interview format where the experimenter asked the same set of question to each participant. This demographic information was taken for future use in the aim to acquire matched participants from an Asperger population

2.2 Scenario Questions

The scenario section of the study was in questionnaire format. The experimenter first gave a verbal brief about the task, participant then worked through the questions with no experimenter intervention.

The questionnaire consisted of seventeen, two part questions. Each question set out a scenario to which the participants had to respond. The scenario gave information either from the participant or the prospected recipient perspective. A small amount of social information was given; whether they or the recipient were either with a single person or within a crowd of five people. This social information about their company was given in form of a list of people around at the time; this information was balanced for sex across the questions. Figure 2 shows one question from each perspective.

Participants were required to respond on two 6-point Likert scales; one reporting their likelihood of using a voice call, the other their likelihood of using a text message to contact the person mentioned in the scenario.

2.3 Opinion Questions

Three questions were asked by the experimenter. Participants' responses were recorded for accurate transcription. All participants were asked the same questions, with the experimenter asking standard prompts if the question was not fully answered.

The questions were designed to investigate whether the participants use their mobile phones in the way wished to; if not, what is constraining their use.

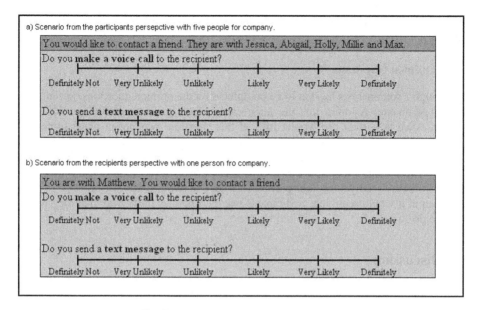

a) Scenario from the participants persepctive with five people for company.

You would like to contact a friend. They are with Jessica, Abigail, Holly, Millie and Max.

Do you **make a voice call** to the recipient?

Definitely Not	Very Unlikely	Unlikely	Likely	Very Likely	Definitely

Do you send a **text message** to the recipient?

Definitely Not	Very Unlikely	Unlikely	Likely	Very Likely	Definitely

b) Scenario from the recipients perspective with one person fro company.

You are with Matthew. You would like to contact a friend

Do you **make a voice call** to the recipient?

Definitely Not	Very Unlikely	Unlikely	Likely	Very Likely	Definitely

Do you send a **text message** to the recipient?

Definitely Not	Very Unlikely	Unlikely	Likely	Very Likely	Definitely

Fig. 2. Examples of the scenario questions

2.4 Measures

All participants were required to fill out the Autism Spectrum Quotient [23]. The AQ was used to ensure participants fell within the control population for further investigations. Participants that had a high number of traits in common with AS were not considered a control population. This was given to participants after the main batch of questionnaires to ensure it had no effect on the main experiment.

Results

3.1 Scenario Questions

The Likert scale responses were analyzed using a 2 (Perspective; Participant, Recipient) x 2 (Company; One, Five) x 2 (Mode, Call, Text) repeated measures analysis of variance. The results indicated a significant main effect of Mode, $[F (1,63) = 70.72, p < 0.001]$, showing that participants likelihood of using the different Modes of communication differed. A mean score from the 'Text' questions $[\mu = 4.620 (3dp)]$ compared with those from the 'Call' questions $[\mu = 3.368 (3dp)]$ indicates that text messages were more likely to be used than voice calls.

No main effect of Company was found $[F (1,63) = 0.039, p = 0.843]$, indicating no difference in phone use in the different social settings used. No main effect was found of Perspective $[F (1,63) = 0.234, p = 0.631]$, showing no difference in use when information was given from their own or the recipients perspective.

There were no significant interaction effect between Perspective and Company $[F (1,63) = 0.480, p = 0.491]$, Perspective and Mode $[F (1,63) = 0.020, p = 0.888]$,

Company and Mode [F (1,63) = 0.432, p = 0.513], or between all three [F (1,63) = 2.564, p = 0.114].

3.2 Opinion Questions

Although a full analysis has yet to be completed on the opinion questions, anecdotally the experimenter reported that the main cause of constrain to phone use was cost. When asked how their use would differ if this constrain was not in place some participants reported that their general use would increase, others said it would not differ however the overall impression was that this constraint didn't effect their use drastically. A few people reported social situations such as lectures as constraining their use, but these socially conscious participants were in the minority.

Overall it would seem that participants use their phones in the way that they would like to do so.

4 Discussion

There are three main findings from this study. Firstly, very simply, our participants reported that they are more likely to use text messages to contact people. Secondly that whether they are in company of a crowd or an individual does not make a difference on the communication mode (be it voice call or text message) they are likely to choose to use. And finally that when given information from their own perspective, or from the recipients, does not influence their choice of communication mode to use. The findings from this study make a simple base line for comparison to an AS population at a later date as no interaction effects were found with only one main effect found.

The results support the anecdotal literature [22] and show that a social etiquette does not seem to have been developed as regards to being in company. For people with AS this may have positive implications; to use their mobile phone in a social setting at any time they like would therefore not be inappropriate as there are no set social rules that they will be breaking or for that matter confused by. To use a device that has already been accepted within society, and that is not yet surrounded by unsaid social rules, would mean the use of an application on the mobile phone would be discreet.

It was also interesting that text messaging was the preferred choice of the NT participants. This means that if people with AS find synchronous communication difficult, because of the complex social cues [14, 24], asynchronous chat via text messaging again can be used discreetly.

To find no difference in choice of mode when scenarios are from the senders or the recipient's perspective indicates that the NT population empathize with the recipient in these circumstances. It will therefore be interesting to see whether this real world use of ToM is challenging for people with AS. As the literature suggests ToM deficits in AS are not strikingly obvious and it would be interesting to see whether the difficulties that Rutherford et al found through his 'Reading the Mind in the Voice' task [8] translate to mobile phone use

4.1 Further Work

From these findings further research will be done on establishing a fuller view of how NT people use their mobile phones and progress to compare this to the mobile phone use of people with AS. Current work is underway looking at actual phone use of NT people, this will be compared with there projected use reported in this study.

Another area that will be investigated is phone use given the recipients familiarity to the participants. Individuals with AS may find it difficult to adopt a socially appropriate language given the context and relationship of recipient [24]. Difficulties in adopting appropriate language and understanding friendships are two subcategories that lie within the 'triad of impairment', mentioned earlier; both being useful for successful social communication [3].

Acknowledgements

Laura Daley is funded by an EPSRC CASE award. We thank the participants from the University of Lincoln and surrounding area for taking part in this study.

References

1. Frith, U. (ed.): Autism and Asperger Syndrome. Cambridge University Press, Cambridge (1991)
2. Attwood, T.: Aspergers Syndrome; A Guide for Parents and Professionals. Jessica Kingsley, London (2006)
3. Wing, L., Gould, J.: Severe impairments of social interaction and associated abnormalities in children: Epidemiology and classification. Journal of Autism and Developmental Disorders 9(1), 11–29 (1979)
4. Baron-Cohen, S., Wheelwright, S.: The Empathy Quotient: An Investigation of Adults with Asperger Syndrome or High Functioning Autism, and Normal Sex Differences. Journal of Autism and Developmental Disorders 34(2), 163–175 (2004)
5. Wing, L.: Asperger's syndrome. A clinical account. Psychological Medicine 11, 115–129 (1981)
6. Lawrence, E.J., et al.: Measuring empathy: reliability and validity of the Empathy Quotient. Psychological Medicine 34(5), 911–924 (2004)
7. Premack, D., Woodruff, G.: Does the chimpanzee have a theory of mind? Behavioral and Brain Sciences 4, 515–526 (1978)
8. Rutherford, M.D., Baron-Cohen, S., Wheelwright, S.: Reading the Mind in the Voice: A Study with Normal Adults and Adults with Asperger Syndrome and High Functioning Autism. Journal of Autism and Developmental Disorders 32, 189–194 (2002)
9. Bowler, D.M.: Theory of Mind in Asperger's Syndrome. Journal of Child Psychology & Psychiatry & Allied Disciplines 33(5), 877–893 (1992)
10. Ozonoff, S., Pennington, B.F., Rogers, S.J.: Executive function deficits in high-functioning autistic individuals: relationship to theory of mind. Journal of Child Psychology And Psychiatry, And Allied Disciplines 32(7), 1081–1105 (1991)
11. Baron-Cohen, S., et al.: Reading the Mind in the Face: A Cross-cultural and Developmental Study. Visual Cognition 3, 39–60 (1996)

12. Baron-Cohen, S.: Is Asperger Syndrome Necessarily Viewed as a Disability? Focus on Autism and Other Developmental Disabilities 17(3), 186–191 (2002a)
13. Baron-Cohen, S.: Autism and Asperger Syndrome. The Facts. Oxford University Press, Oxford (2008)
14. Baron-Cohen, S.: The extreme male brain theory of autism. Trends in Cognitive Sciences 6(6), 248–254 (2002b)
15. Egan, L.M.-A.: Students with Asperger's syndrome in the CS classroom. In: Proceedings of the 36th SIGCSE technical symposium on Computer science education. ACM Press, St. Louis (2005)
16. Robins, B., et al.: Robotic assistants in therapy and education of children with autism: can a small humanoid robot help encourage social interaction skills? pp. 105–120. Springer, Heidelberg (2005)
17. Robins, B., Dautenhahn, K., Dubowski, J.: Does appearance matter in the interaction of children with autism with a humanoid robot? Interaction Studies. Social Behaviour and Communication in Biological and Artificial Systems 7(3), 479–512 (2006)
18. Robins, B., et al.: Robot-mediated joint attention in children with autism: A case study in robot-human interaction. Interaction Studies: Social Behaviour and Communication in Biological and Artificial Systems 5(2), 161–198 (2004)
19. Baron-Cohen, S., et al.: Mind Reading: The interactive guide to emotions. Jessica Kingsley Limited, London (2004)
20. Caroline, M.: The Transporters. Child and Adolescent Mental Health 12(4), 197 (2007), http://www.transporters.tv
21. Jones, M., Marsden, G.: Mobile Interaction Design. John Wiley & Sons Ltd., Chichester (2006)
22. Srivastava, L.: Mobile phones and the evolution of social behaviour. Behaviour and Information Technology, 2005 24(2), 189–201 (2005)
23. Baron-Cohen, S., et al.: The Autism-Spectrum Quotient (AQ): Evidence from Asperger Syndrome/High-Functioning Autism, Malesand Females, Scientists and Mathematicians. Journal of Autism and Developmental Disorders 31, 5–17 (2001)
24. Attwood, T.: The complete guide to Asperger's Syndrome. Jessica Kingsley Publishers, London (2008)

Age Related Cognitive Impairments and Diffusion of Assistive Web-Base Technologies

Senaka Fernando, Tony Elliman, Arthur Money, and Lorna Lines

The School of Information Systems, Computing and Mathematics, Brunel University,
Middlesex, UB8 3PH, UK
{senaka.fernando,tony.elliman,Arthur.money,
lorna.lines}@brunel.ac.uk

Abstract. Several researchers argue that age related cognitive impairments have detrimental affect on use of web services by older adults. However little and systematic applied research has been conducted on how age related cognitive impairments might affect the usage of web services by older adults. Undoubtedly, understanding the relationship between the cognitive changes that accompany aging and their impact on older adults' usage of web services will be beneficial for designing web services for this group. The paper demonstrates how such understanding has been employed to develop an assistive technology in order to improve older adults' interaction with online forms (e.g. state benefit application form). However the paper acknowledges that this new assistive technology does not guarantee that people with age related cognitive impairments accept it, as diffusion of innovation research shows that getting a new technology adopted even when it has noticeable advantage is often very difficult. Consequently the paper identifies critical factors that need to be considered when adopting this new assistive technology, drawing on Rogers (2003) theory of Diffusion of Innovations.

Keywords: age related cognitive impairments, older adults, assistive technology, online forms and web services, innovation, diffusion.

1 Introduction

Recent surveys show that the number of people over the age of 65 is increasing worldwide. For example by 2030, the percentage of people over the age 65 in Europe will be about 24% of the total population [1]. However research indicates that the growing numbers of these older adults are living in their homes with limitations in mobility, dexterity, and cognitive ability[2]. Currently there is considerable discussion about the scope of improving the older adults' autonomy and independence that is restricted by age related impairments, using recent developments in information technology[3]. One of such development is web services and it is rapidly becoming a major means of accessing health, care in the community and many government services for the older adults[4]. The web services are also becoming a vehicle for older adults in engaging activities such as employment and educational opportunities[5]. However the older adults use web services less often and have less experience with them than

C. Stephanidis (Ed.): Universal Access in HCI, Part I, HCII 2009, LNCS 5614, pp. 353–360, 2009.
© Springer-Verlag Berlin Heidelberg 2009

younger adults. For example the recent surveys show that web service users among those 16-24 years of age are three times higher than among adults 55-74 of age[see 5].

Although there are many reasons for the lack of use of web services by older adults, one major reason noted in the literate is the age related impairments which hinder the visual, auditory, motor and cognitive abilities of older adults[6]. The research indicates that such impairments have detrimental affect on use of web services by older adults. Many researchers and practitioners made attempt to address the implications of age related visual, auditory and motor impairments that have impact on information technology based systems and developed technology to minimise the negative impact of such impairments on usage of such systems by older adults[see 7, 8]. However little research has been conducted on how age related cognitive impairment might affect the usage of information technology based systems such as web services[see 9]. Consequently this paper focus on age related cognitive impairments.

With reference to the age related cognitive impairments the paper discusses the implications of impairments in working memory, spatial cognition, attention and perceptual speed on usage of web services by older adults. These impairments are briefly discussed below:

Working memory. Working memory is usually conceptualized as "the temporary storage of information that is necessary for such activities as learning, reasoning, and comprehension"[10]. The usual tasks carried out by working memory are those in which the individual must hold a small amount of material in mind for a short period of time while at the same time performing further cognitive operations (e.g. comprehension), either on the material held or on other incoming materials [11]. The decline of working memory holds a number of implications for the use of web services/applications by older adults. For example older adults can have difficulties in (1) understanding instructions in an online form (2) performing a large number of steps in an online transaction.

Perceptual speed. The age related cognitive impairment make older adults to have a general slowing of perceptual and motor processes involved in perceiving and responding to items. In other words the perceptual speed (the speed at which mental operations are performed) is decreased with increased age. Such slowness is raised, when task complexity increases. As a result older adults have difficulties performing complex tasks on websites which must be done externally imposed time constraints [see 12]. For example older adults may take considerable time to submit an online form after completing it.

Spatial abilities. Spatial ability refers to skill in perceiving the visual world, transforming and modifying initial perceptions, and mentally recreating spatial aspects of one's visual experience. [13]. Spatial abilities boost during adolescence, reach their height during the second or third decade of life, and shrink steadily thereafter. Thus older adults have lower levels of abilities in performing tasks which require spatial visualisations, integration of spatial information, and ongoing information processing [14]. As many websites have complex computer screens which contains complex menu structures, banners, animations, three dimensional presentations etc which demands high degree of spatial abilities, older adults will have difficulties in using existing websites [see 15]. For example older adults may have difficulties in understanding how to move to next page when next page button is available on an online form.

Attention. Attention refers to the process which enable individual to allocate cognitive resources when two or more distinct cognitive tasks[16]. As existing web pages present scenarios where users require doing more than one thing at time older adults who have impaired attention will have difficulties in using them.

Although there is very little research was conducted on implications of age related cognitive impairments on usage of web services/applications by older adults, some research demonstrate that the difficulties that older adults having when using web services, can be mediated by the manner in which web services are designed. Such research demonstrates that designing web services that take into consider age related cognitive impairments would consequently enhance the usage of web services and other computer applications by older adults [17, 18]. For example Holt and Morrell[17] demonstrate that efficiency of text comprehension by older adults is improved when the text is well organised and clearly presented in short segments on web pages.

2 The Project

The project, Delivering Inclusive Access to Disabled and Elderly Members of the community (DIADEM), used systematic effort to understand older adults' needs related to web services that are shaped by their declined cognitive impairments and incorporate them into design solutions. DIADEM project is developing an assistive technology to help the older adults with age related cognitive impairments, to use the web services more effectively. The project focuses on the problem of accessing services online where older adult users need to fill in online forms (e.g. housing benefits applications). The DIADEM is currently being undertaken in the UK, Norway and Italy and funded by the European Union (EU). The following EU project partners are involved in the project:
1. Brunel University (Brunel) in the UK
2. Norsk Regnesentral (NR) in Norway
3. Bluegarden (BG) in Norway
4. More Optimised Registration Elements(More) in Norway
5. CSI Piemonte (CSI) in Italy
6. Sheffield City Council (Sheffield) in the UK
7. Comune di Torino (Torino) in Italy

3 Methodology

The methodology consists the key stakeholder focus group interviews, the older adult user interviews and the older adult user trials. Key-stakeholders comprised not only the developers and the service providers but also representatives from government agencies, private care/medical agencies and charities that support the older adults in each partner country (the UK, Norway and Italy). From the analysis of the key stakeholder focus group and the older adult user interviews, core functional and us-ability requirements was identified for all applications as they are presented and ac-cessed through DIADEM. The software specification is the main output from the gathering and analysis of the functional and usability requirements. The main focus of this software specification was a description of what all the functions of the software of the DIADEM are. These were defined in grate length to ensure that the developers understand what the older adult users require from the DIADEM and prioritise the requirements to pay considerable attention to the items that were perceived by the older adult users as very important. The DIADEM technology was developed using these specifications. The older user trials were employed to evaluate the efficiency, effectiveness, usability of the technology developed and the older users' satisfaction with it. Using the various results from these older user trials the DIADEM technology is being further improved

4 The DIADEM Technology

To respond to the challenges faced by older adults with age related cognitive impair-ments DIADEM employs Expert System techniques to analyse user behaviour and adapt the presentation of the transaction dialogue to mitigate the cognitive problems exhibited by the user. To ensure that a single user sees every online form in a consis-tent and personalised style this client component is data driven. It takes XML control files, which contain an abstract transaction description from the server, and generates an appropriate user interface using a rich set of multimedia devices (e.g. sound, video, document scanning and smart cards) to reduce the cognitive load on the user.

All user interaction with DIADEM takes place through a web browser. DIADEM is responsible for providing immediate help functionality in a consistent way across all services. In addition, if the DIADEM system fails to provide adequate "on screen" assistance it has access to external means of help desk support.

To respond to the security and trust issues around user identification and profiles DIADEM allows the end-user's computer to have a facility for user authentication that is not password-based (e.g., fingerprint, retina, smartcard, signature recognition). The DIADEM system keeps all user profiles confidential from other parties other than their respective users. It also protects the integrity of all user profiles so that the pro-file can only be modified by the system or by an authorised individual.

5 Diffusion of Assistive Technology

All the characteristics mentioned in section 4 will reduce the impact of age related cognitive impairments on usage of web services by older adults. However, as this assistive technology has never been seen before, there will be inherent uncertainty to this untested innovation. Rogers[19] argues that getting a new innovation adopted even when it has noticeably advantages, is often not easy as the decision to adopt an innovation take time. As a result, during the project the partners of the projects (the research teams) will have the responsibility of determining how best to progress the DIADEM technology to form the basis of future commercial products. For example

MORE intends to adopt DIADEM technology in their forms based information-capture services for public authorities (both local and central) and financial institutions. Similarly, Bluegarden intends to adopt the same technology in their HR-services for the employees of large companies in Norway and Denmark. Also, CSI, Sheffield, and Torino all anticipate being able to adopt DIADEM technology for their current public service provisions. These commitments are to exploit this technology, subject to business environment and market conditions, as a matter of urgency as soon as practically possible either within the project timeframe or after it. All these activities will be major components of the diffusion of DIADEM technology.

According to Rogers (2003), the diffusion of innovations is "the process by which an innovation is communicated through certain channels over time among the members of a social system." Innovation is used more generally here to mean an item, thought, or process that is new and diffusion is the process by which innovations spread one social group to another. Diffusion of innovation theory suggests that consumers of new technology make their adoption decisions base on several factors [20].

Relative advantage: The benefits of adopting the new technology compared to the cost.

Compatibility: The extent to which adopting and using the innovation is based on existing ways of doing things and standards cultural norms.

Complexity: How difficult the new product is.

Trialability: The extent to which a new product can be tried on a limited basis.

Ability to communicate product benefits: The ease and clarity with which the benefits of owning and using the new product can be communicated to prospective customers.

Observability: How observable the benefits are to the customer using the new product, and how easily other customers can observe the benefits being received by a customer who has already adopted the product.

Each factor affects the rate of adoption of a innovation differently. However, empirical evidence suggests that relative advantage is consistently the best forecaster of adoption of new technology [21-23]. Consequently, the key issue related to diffusion of DIADEM technology is to assess the relative advantage that DIADEM technology brings to application and service providers. The perceived advantages of adopting DIADEM, when weighed against the associated costs and risks, need to justify a provider in adopting DIADEM technology as one of their service delivery channels. The questions need to be addressed in this context are discussed in more detail below.

Does DIADEM demonstrate advantages for an application provider? This question goes to the issue of assessing the benefits of DIADEM from a provider's perspective. It is accepted that direct cash flow benefits are hard to quantify and the innovators are expected to address this question from a broader qualitative standpoint rather than a strictly financial one.

One such approach to evaluating technology adoption is to consider the observability or awareness of advantages to various stakeholders. The premise here is that the more clearly observable the benefits then the greater the likelihood of technology adoption. In the first instance there is the need to consider how observable the benefits are to an elderly person using DIADEM to access online services. Second is the question of how easily an application or service provider can observe such benefits being transferred or translated into benefits for them.

Is the effort required to adopt DIADEM technology reasonable? The effort required to adopt DIADEM technology goes to the other side of the relative advantage equation. Since technological complexity is a barrier to adoption it is necessary to consider the perceived simplicity of adopting and using DIADEM. From the provider's perspective this amounts to the simplicity of creating and maintaining the interface between their information systems and the DIADEM software. However, for success the technology also needs to be adopted by the elderly user group and it is also necessary to consider whether they will find difficulties in using DIADEM. In so far as the technology does present complex characteristics they need to be demonstrable as absolutely necessary, in terms of the elderly users' requirements.

However, the adoption effort required will also vary from one application or service provider to another depending on DIADEMs compatibility with their existing provision. This raises the question of the extent to which providers may have to learn new skills, gain new knowledge and make change in their existing way of working to enable their legacy systems to use DIADEM software.

Is the business model and licensing appropriate? The other main element on the down side of the relative advantage equation is the market or business model and the availability of appropriate software licences. In addition to the direct cost of licensing providers need to minimise the risks they take when adopting a new technology. Critical risk factors are first the existence of an adequate "market demand" and second the ability to control the initial take up costs.

The DIADEM supplier's ability to communicate product benefits positively influences market demand and reduces the risk of an inadequate return on investment for the application or service provider. Consequently there is the need to evaluate whether the project partners effectively convey the benefits of DIADEM to the market place in such a way as to generate a reasonable demand for the technology.

Minimising the risk of incurring significant take-up costs depends upon the extent to which DIADEM can be tried on a limited basis. This is a major issue with new technological products or innovations that might at first be perceived as complex and incompatible with existing technologies. Thus, there is the need to evaluate whether the business model and licensing makes it feasible for application and service providers to try DIADEM on a limited basis prior to making a long term commitment.

6 Conclusion

The paper present that how age related cognitive impairments would affect the use of web services by older adults. It emphasis that developers and providers of web services need to have significant understanding of the impact of age related cognitive impairment on usage of web services. The paper demonstrates how such understanding has been employed to develop an assistive technology in order to provide an adaptable web browser for the older adults with age related cognitive impairments to improve their interaction with web base forms. This improvement is achieved by developing an Expert System, which monitors the user's behaviour to adapt and personalise the computer interface as the user interacts with web based forms whilst providing privacy and security. Drawing on Diffusion of innovation theory the paper suggests that several factors need to be considered when adopting this new technology. It argues that major factor that influences the process of adoption is relative advantage. The papers shows that detail understanding of these factors would help innovators of the DIADEM to assess (1) how quickly the DIADEM might take off in the unconventional marketplace (2) critical barriers to commercialisation and diffusion of the DIADEM. Such assessment would help the innovators of the DIADEM and similar technologies to develop effective marketing strategies to improve the commercialisation and diffusion of such technologies.

However diffusion arenas of assistive technologies such as DIADEM are highly complicated. The institutional (e.g. governments) policies and practices would shape in defining the scope and authorization for the diffusion process of these technologies. For example governments' social policies related to elderly and their political commitments to improve the quality of life of elderly can radically affect the diffusion process. Nevertheless diffusion of innovation theory does not seem to offer adequate knowledge to deal with highly complex political and institutional issues in diffusion arenas. Consequently future research on assertive technologies such as DIADEM would be much more effective if they extend their studies combining the diffusion of innovation theory with other theoretical perspectives that can be employed to address such issues in diffusion arenas.

Acknowledgements. The authors wish to acknowledge the European Union funding of DIADEM as a Framework 6 project (034106). They also wish to acknowledge the contributions of the other DIADEM consortium members - Norsk Regnesentral (Norway), Bluegarden AS (Norway), More Optimised Registration Elements AS (Norway), CSI-Piemonte (Italy) Sheffield City Council (UK), and Citta di Torino (Italy) - in supporting this research.

References

1. Kinsella, K.: An Aging World. US Government Printing Office, Washington (2001)
2. Grundy, E.: The epidemiology of aging. In: Tallis, R.C., Fillit, H.M. (eds.) Brocklehurst's Textbook of Geriatric Medicine and Gerontology, pp. 3–20. Churchill Livingstone, Edinburgh (2003)
3. McMellon, C.A., Schiffman, L.G.: Cybersenior Empowerment: How some older inviduals are taking control of their lives. The Journal of Applied Gerontology 21(2), 157–175 (2002)
4. Morrel, R.W., Mayhorn, C.B., Bennett, J.: A survey of World Wide Web in Middle Age and Older Adults. Human Factors 42(2), 175–185 (2000)
5. Czaja, S.J., Lee, C.C.: The impact of aging on access to technology. Universal Access in the Information Society (5), 341–349 (2007)
6. Czaja, S.J., Lee, C.C.: Information systems and older adults. In: Sears, A., Jacko, J.A. (eds.) The Human Computer Interaction Handbook, pp. 777–792. Lawrence Erlbaum Associate, London (2008)
7. Fisk, A.D., et al.: Designing for older adults; Principles and creative human factors approaches. Taylor and Francis, London (2004)

8. Smith, N.W., Sharit, J., Czaja, S.J.: Aging, motor control and performance of computer mouse tasks. Human Factors 41(3), 389–396 (1999)
9. Czaja, S.J., et al.: Factors predicting the use of technology: Finding from the centre for research and education on aging and technology enhancement. Psychology and Aging 21(2), 333–352 (2006)
10. Bradeley, A.D.: Working Memory. Oxford Scientific Publications, Oxford (1986)
11. Morris, R.G., Craik, F.I.M., Gick, M.L.: Age difference in working memory tasks. The role of secondray memory and the central executive system. Quarterly Journal of Experimental Psychology 42A, 67–86 (1990)
12. Newell, A.F., et al.: Information technology for cognitive support. In: Sears, A., Jacko, J.A. (eds.) The Human Computer Interaction Handbook, pp. 811–828. Lawrence Erlbaum Associate, London (2008)
13. Howard, G.: Frames of mind: The theory of multiple intelligences. Basic Books, New York (1985)
14. Morrell, R.W., Echt, K.V.: Instructional design for older computer users: The influence of cognitive factors. In: Rogers, W.A., Fisk, A.D., Walker, N. (eds.) Aging and skilled performance, pp. 241–265. Lawrence Erlbaum Associate, New Jersey (1996)
15. Kurniawan, S.H., et al.: Personalising web page presentation for older people. Interacting with Computers 18, 457–477 (2006)
16. Gross, R.: Psychology: The science of mind and behaviour. Hodder and Stoughton Educational, London (2001)
17. Holt, B.J., Morrell, R.W.: Guidelines for web site design for older adults: The ultimate influence of cognitive factors. In: Older Adults, Health Information, World Wide Web, pp. 109–129. Lawrence Erlbaum Associate, London (2002)
18. Sharit, J., et al.: The effect of age and environmental support in using telephone voice menu systems. Human Factors 41(3), 389–396 (2003)
19. Rogers, E.: Diffusion of Innovation, p. 512. Simon and Schuster International, New York (2003)
20. Mohr, J., Sengupta, S., Slater, S.: Marketing of High-Technology Products and Innovation. Pearson Education, New Jersey (2005)
21. Choudhury, V., Karahanna, E.: The Relative Advantage of Electronic Channnels: A Multidimensional View. MIS Quarterly 32(1), 179–200 (2008)
22. Moore, G., Benbasat, I.: Development of an Instrument to measure the perceptions of adopting information technology innovation. Information Systems Research 2, 192–222 (1991)
23. Plouffe, C., Hulland, J., Vandenbosch, M.: Research Report: Richness verses parsimony in modelling technology adoption decisions-Understanding merchant adoption of a smart card-based payment systems. Information Systems Research 12, 208–222 (2002)

Does Health Related Quality of Life Differ between People with Chronic Mental Illness Who Use Computers and Those Who Do Not?

Yan-hua Huang[1] and I-Ju Su[2,3]

[1] Department of Occupational Therapy
College of Professional Studies, California State University, Dominguez Hills
1000 East Victoria Street, Carson, CA 90747
[2] Department of Occupational Therapy & Graduate Institute of Clinical Behavioral Science,
College of Medicine, Chang Gung University
259 Wen-Hwa 1st Road, Kwei-Shan Tao-Yuan 333, Taiwan
[3] Department of Psychiatry, Taipei Medical University- Wanfang Hospital
No.111 Section 3 Hsing-Long Road, Taipei, 116, Taiwan
{Yan-huaHuang,yhuang}@csudh.edu

Abstract. Occupational therapists are increasingly interested in promoting quality of life and digital divides in people with chronic mental illness. This study aims to compare quality of life between people with chronic mental illness who use and do not use computer. Twenty-four participants were recruited from a medical center in northern Taiwan. Two assessments were used including 1) a Quality of life questionnaire (WHOQOL-BREF Taiwan) and 2) a questionnaire relating to computer and internet use developed specifically for this study. The results show that there was a statistically significant difference in environment domain of quality of life between people who use computers and people who do not use computers in their daily life (p=.029). There was no statistically significant difference in the physical, psychological and social relationship domains of quality of life. Occupational therapists may help people with chronic mental illness to engage in meaningful activities through using the computer as ordinary part of their daily lives and in order to improve their perception of quality of life.

Keywords: Computer Use, Digital Divide, Mental Illness, Occupational Therapy, Quality of life.

1 Introduction

1.1 Background

Health professionals, especially occupational therapists, are increasingly interested in promoting quality of life and digital divides in people with chronic mental illness. People with chronic mental illness often suffer setbacks in information access and communication due to their symptoms. Although internet and computer use may improve patients' accessibility to information, the disability makes them the least privileged group in utilizing information technology. However the relationship between computer use and quality of life is not well understood.

C. Stephanidis (Ed.): Universal Access in HCI, Part I, HCII 2009, LNCS 5614, pp. 361–365, 2009.
© Springer-Verlag Berlin Heidelberg 2009

1.2 Purpose and Significance

This study aims to understand the difference in health related quality of life between people with chronic mental illness who use computers and those who do not use computers. We hope to help health professionals or other professionals have more understanding of digital use and digital divide of this population in order to help people with mental illness improve their life quality. It will assist health professionals in their work with these people with chronic mental illness by enabling an understanding of the effect of computer use in their quality of life.

2 Literature Review

People with chronic mental illness have low computer use rate. According to The Research, Development and Evaluation Commission of the Executive Yuan in Taiwan [1], the percentage of families in Taiwan that own computers, have internet access and use computers in the general population are 82.6%, 74.7% and 71% respectively. However, the percentages of families with people with mental illness that own computers and have internet access are 63.6% and 53.8% respectively. And 22.6% of individuals with mental illness use computers. The computer use rate (22.6 %) in people with mental illness is even lower than people with visual impairment (23.1%). People with mental illness are the second lowest group in computer using rate in the people with either physical or psychological disabilities.

Huang et al. [2] stated that there are five factors affecting computer use of people with schizophrenia. These are information access, information literacy, information application, family information agency, and personal clinical characteristic. As the world fills up with more and more digital information, people who do not use computers in their daily lives will experience greater digital divide and disengagement in society.

Currently, there is little research related to computer use or computer training in people with mental illness. Salzer, Simiriglia and Solomon [3] examined computer use among 262 people with mental disability and their interest in receiving computer training. 71% of the participants indicated that they had previously used a computer for at least one activity, though only 39% for at least three or more activities in their lives. 67% said that they have very little computer experience and 56% were very interested in receiving computer training. Chang [4] studied the effect of the computer training and the employment rate after computer skills training in 24 persons with various psychiatric disabilities. The results of this study indicated that the computer skills training not only increased their computer skills but also expanded job opportunities in people with psychiatric disabilities. The results also showed that 67% of the participants improved their attention and 79% increased their performance in keyboard typing.

Computer and internet use may provide social interaction, work opportunities and leisure opportunities, which may further improve people's quality of life especially for people who have chronic mental illness. Mayers [5] indicated that lack of personal achievement, lack of employment, difficulty in forming and maintaining relationships, loneliness and lack of leisure activities are key areas that were negatively affecting quality of life in people with mental illness. However, there is no study that addresses computer use and quality of life in people with mental illness, so the relationship between the two is unclear.

To understand the difference in health related quality of life between people with chronic mental illness who use and who do not use computers is the focus in this study. This study hypothesized that there will be a difference in quality of life between these two groups.

3 Methods

Twenty-four people with chronic mental illness were recruited from a medical center in northern Taiwan. Participants lived at home and attended a day-care ward in the medical center on the weekdays. All participants were unemployed during the study. The inclusion criteria include people who live in the community and who is able to fill in or understand the quality of life measurement. The exclusion criteria include people with schizophrenia who are in the acute mental illness stage. People who cannot understand the question items in quality of life measurement due to cognitive deficits were also excluded. The 24 participants were in a stable phase of their illness and received regular medical treatment. Participants were assessed by occupational therapists using questionnaires to understand their digital use and quality of life. Two assessments were used, including (1) a Health Related Quality of life (HRQoL) questionnaire (WHOQOL-BREF Taiwan) [6] and (2) a questionnaire relating to computer and internet use developed specifically for this study. Participants were divided into two groups of people. The first group is participants who use computers in their daily lives and the second is participants that do not. Independent T tests were used for statistical analysis to compare the quality of life between the two groups.

4 Results

There were thirteen males and eleven females that participated in this research. Fifty percent have a college degree or higher degree. Fifty-eight percent of the participants use computers and forty-two percent of the participants do not use computers in their daily life. The two groups were homogeneous and no statistically significant difference was found with regards to age and gender and education background. The results show that there was a statistically significant difference in environment domain of quality of life between people who use computers and people who do not use computers in their daily lives (p=.029). There was no statistically significant difference in the physical, psychological and social relationship domains of quality of life. Table 1 shows the statistical analysis of the results.

Table 1. Health related quality of life between people with chronic mental illness who use and do not use computer

WHOQOL-BREF DOMAINS	Use Computer		Do Not Use Computer		F	p
	Mean	SD	Mean	SD		
Physical	60.00	16.09	57.00	12.88	0.44	.631
Psychological	58.29	12.10	51.30	14.51	0.15	.213
Social Relationship	48.86	19.86	45.10	18.31	0.38	.642
Environment	62.14	17.69	45.00	17.69	0.16	.029*

*p < .05

5 Discussions

The perception of HRQoL in environment domain showed lower scores in those people with mental illness and who do not use computer in their daily life. In the WHO-QOL-BREF questionnaire, 5 of the 8 facets of the environment domain are directly or indirectly related to computer use. They are: 1) financial resource, 2) health and social care accessibility, 3) opportunities for acquiring new information and skills, 4) participation and opportunities for leisure activities and 5) transport. Financial resource may relate to the ability to afford a computer or other meaningful things that related to quality of life. A computer is not only a tool that most jobs require, it is also a tool for searching and accessing health and social care, acquiring new information and skills, participating in leisure activities and providing diverse transportation information. Study shows that engagement in meaningful activities is significantly correlated with quality of life in persons disabled by mental illness [7]. Health professionals may help people with chronic mental illness engage in meaningful activities through using the computer as an ordinary part of their daily lives and thus improve their perception of quality of life.

The reason that there was no significant difference found in the domains of physical, psychological and social relationship HRQoL is probably due to the small sample size. One limitation of this study is the small sample size. Another limitation is that the participants were recruited from the day care ward of one medical hospital in Northern Taiwan, which means that the present result do not necessarily apply to all individuals living with mental illness. A longitudinal quantitative study with larger sample sizes that observe people with mental illness over longer period of time undergoing a computer intervention program is needed in order to further explore the relationship between quality of life and computer use. Future qualitative studies to understand the experience of computer use that contribute to improve QOL for people with mental illness are also needed.

6 Conclusion

People with chronic mental illness who use computers in their daily lives have a better environment domain of quality of life comparing to people with chronic mental illness who do not use computers. Many health professionals, such as occupational therapists, not only want to decrease the dysfunction resulting from the illness, but want the people with chronic mental illness to have better quality of life. As society fills up with digital information, the manner through which we can reduce the digital divide and improve quality of life in people with mental disorder is a necessary focus. A vital finding showed that computer use is related to better environment domains of quality of life. The findings of this pilot study can serve as the basis for future computer intervention studies that target the needs of the people with mental illness.

7 Application

Few studies focus on computer use in people with mental illness. This study is one of the first to describe the computer use and quality of life for people with mental illness.

The finding can help health professional especially occupational therapist in their clinical practice. People with mental illness have different education and support needs. When occupational therapists promote digital life in the people with mental illness, they should make sure they have computer access in the hospital or in the community and help to set up stable and reliable computer hardware and software.

Computer training can be used as a medium to improve cognitive abilities, performance of activities of daily living, and social/vocational performance. The digital world provides equalized status, temporal flexibility and recordability for each user [8]. The internet democracy [8] allows equalized status for internet users and provides an environment without stigma resulting from chronic mental illness. Computer and internet use do not require face to face interaction and immediate response. Also, people with mental illness can keep a record of communications in computer applications such as email. Those characteristics of the digital world can compensate for their limitations such as cognition, memory, communication and expression. In designing occupational therapy group treatment such as computer and internet training, we need to know the digital needs and digital divides for the population and also tailor the treatment specialized for this group and to their needs. A suitable computer training program could be implemented to promote these clients' quality of life.

Acknowledgement. This study was supported by National Science Council grant 96-2520-S-182-002. We are grateful to the participants in this study for their participation.

References

1. Digital Divide in Taiwan,
   http://www.rdec.gov.tw/public/Attachment/81714551671.pdf
2. Huang, Y.-H., Wu, C.-Y., Chang, T.-C., Lai, Y.-J., Lee, W.-S.: Factors Relating to Computer Use for People with Mental Illness. In: Dainoff, M.J. (ed.) HCII 2007 and EHAWC 2007. LNCS, vol. 4566, pp. 225–230. Springer, Heidelberg (2007)
3. Salzer, M.S., Simiriglia, C., Solomon, A.: Computer Experience and Training Interests of Psychosocial Rehabilitation Program Participants. Psychiatric Rehabilitation Journal 26(4), 417–421 (2003)
4. Chang, T.C., Cheng, N.P., Lin, Y.W., Lee, D.M.: The Application of Computer Skills Training on Clients with Psychiatric Disabilities. Formosa Journal of Mental Health 14(2), 87–98 (2001)
5. Mayers, C.A.: Quality of life: priorities for people with enduring mental health problems. British Journal of Occupational Therapy 63(2), 50–58 (2000)
6. WHOQOL-Taiwan Group: The development and user manual of WHOQOL-BREF Taiwan version. Taipei (2001)
7. Goldberg, B., Brintnell, E., Goldberg, J.: The relationship between engagement in meaningful activities and quality of life in persons disabled by mental illness. Occupational Therapy in Mental Health 18(2), 17–44 (2002)
8. Essential Issues in Cyberphychology: Comprehensive Overview,
   http://www.truecenterpoint.com/ce/essentials.html

Cognitive Impairments, HCI and Daily Living

Simeon Keates[1], James Kozloski[2], and Philip Varker[3]

[1] IT University of Copenhagen, Rued Langgaards Vej 7, DK-2300 Copenhagen S, Denmark
[2] IBM T.J. Watson Research Center, 1101 Kitchawan Road, Route 134,
Yorktown Heights, NY 10598 USA
[3] IBM Human Ability and Accessibility Center, IBM Research, 19 Skyline Drive,
Hawthorne, NY 10532 USA
skea@itu.dk, {kozloski,varker}@us.ibm.com

Abstract. As computer systems become increasingly more pervasive in every-day life, it is simultaneously becoming ever more important that the concept of universal access is accepted as a design mantra. While many physical impairments and their implications for human-computer interaction are well understood, cognitive impairments have received comparatively little attention. One of the reasons for this is the general lack of sufficiently detailed cognitive models. This paper examines how cognitive impairments can affect human-computer interaction in everyday life and the issues involved in trying to make information technology more accessible to users with cognitive impairments.

1 Introduction

In a paper presented to the 4th International Conference on Universal Access in Human-Computer Interaction it was observed that cognitive impairments and the related issue of learning difficulties are often overlooked in much of the research performed into enabling Universal Access (UA) to information technology (IT) [1].

The IBM Human Ability and Accessibility Center, along with IBM T.J. Watson Research Center, has a longstanding interest in addressing the needs of users with cognitive impairments and learning difficulties. After sponsoring an international symposium of leading experts in the field in October 2005, a series of follow-up meetings has been held over a number of years to identify potential areas of research. This paper discusses much of the background thinking that is informing the ongoing development of a strategy to improve access to HCI for users with cognitive impairments.

1.1 Terminology

In this paper, the term "cognitive impairments" will be used as an umbrella term for the more usual interpretations of cognitive impairments (e.g. memory loss) as well as learning difficulties (e.g. dyslexia) and also behavioural disorders (e.g. attention-deficit/hyperactivity disorder – ADHD). The following is an example list of conditions considered:

- Attention-Deficit/Hyperactivity Disorder
- Auditory Processing Disorder

C. Stephanidis (Ed.): Universal Access in HCI, Part I, HCII 2009, LNCS 5614, pp. 366–374, 2009.
© Springer-Verlag Berlin Heidelberg 2009

- Asperger's Syndrome
- Autism Spectrum
- Childhood Disintegrative Disorder
- Dementia
- Depression
- Dyscalculia
- Dysgraphia
- Dyslexia
- Dyspraxia
- Rett Syndrome
- Visual Processing Disorder

This paper examines the role of cognition in accessing IT systems, especially in the context of daily living activities and how those activities are affected for those with cognitive impairments.

2   Cognitive Impairments and UA Research

There are several reasons why cognitive impairments are often overlooked:

- They are "invisible" – whereas many sensory or motor impairments are often easily discernible by other people, cognitive impairments are not necessarily
- They are difficult to diagnose – while some symptoms of cognitive impairments can be identified (e.g. memory tests), not all can be
- They are not universally defined – some researchers believe that learning difficulties and (especially) behavioural disorders should be treated separately from cognitive impairments.
- They are not easy to design for – the lack of a clear understanding of the design problem to be addressed (what is the impairment and what are the implications of it?) makes it difficult to solve.

This last point is arguably the most significant. Common attempts to address the issue of how to design for users with cognitive impairments focus on providing best practice guidelines.

2.1   Example Best Practice Guidelines

Keates and Varker [1] proposed the following best practice guidelines gathered from an international symposium held at the IBM T.J. Watson Research Center in October 2005:

- Find the required set of demands to complete the range of tasks compared with what the IT system demands and ensure that the IT system does not introduce new demands.
- Involve users with cognitive and learning difficulties in the design process.
- Use clear, unambiguous language and reinforce with images where appropriate.

- Use "scaffolding" techniques that build a support structure beneath each new concept, which consists of strong links to other, already learned, bits of knowledge.
- Use positive reinforcement and provide feedback.
- Recognise the use of coping strategies by users and try to complement, support and augment these wherever possible.
- Design for people's learning strengths, not for their weaknesses.
- Design for flexibility, e.g. provide information in multiple formats or with sliding levels of complexity.
- "Chunk" information into more manageable pieces.
- Keep menu hierarchy depths to a minimum.
- "Help" systems and documentation needs to be concrete, repeatable and consistent.
- Present assistance options carefully to avoid potential stigma.
- Avoid "feature creep" and only add new functionality that is required.
- Try to be consistent with design features.

While design best practice guidelines such as these are very important for designers, they are only part of the solution. To successfully design an IT system that is accessible to a user with a cognitive impairment requires a full understanding of the IT system and the user's wants, needs and aspirations.

Much research in usability in human-computer interaction (HCI) focuses on "the extent to which a product can be used by specified users to achieve specified goals with effectiveness, efficiency and satisfaction in a specified context of use" [2]. For many users with moderate or severe cognitive impairments, their aim is usable access to the activities of daily living.

2.2 Activities of Daily Living

Most discussion of the activities of daily living (ADLs) focuses on a medical perspective, specifically helping someone get through the day. ADLs are often considered at 2 levels:

1. **Basic/self-care ADLs** – these are related to day-to-day basic requirements for living, for example: bathing, eating, using the toilet and so on.
2. **Instrumental ADLs** – these are more advanced ADLs that are required for successful independent living, for example: housework, preparing food, shopping, managing money

From an IT perspective, especially for a company such as IBM, these definitions of ADLs are too basic. A new classification is required.

2.3 Areas of Life Endeavour

A better approach to the issue of cognitive impairments and HCI is to consider areas of life endeavour and five such areas have been identified as being of interest, specifically:

1. Lifelong learning and education
2. Workplace
3. Real world (i.e. extended ADLs)

4. Entertainment
5. Socialising

It is worth looking at each of these areas in more detail.

Lifelong learning and education. While traditional classroom (K12) learning environments are the most obvious examples of a learning context, they are not the only ones of interest here. The concept of "lifelong learning" mandates that learning continue long after a person leaves school. Access to learning is especially important for users with cognitive impairments, where the very nature of the impairment may make acquiring and retaining learned knowledge especially challenging.

It is important to consider the rate of acquisition of knowledge here, along with the level of retention.

Workplace. There are two perspectives to consider for the workplace:

1. Gaining initial access to the workplace – how to secure a job
2. Maintaining employability – how to keep a job

In the first case, it is often necessary to acquire brand new skills and knowledge to enter the job market, especially for someone with a congenital condition present from early life. In the second case, the basic skills will have been acquired some time ago. However, due to a change in circumstances (such as a traumatic brain injury or even the ageing process), the user may need to reacquire some of the skills, adapt existing skills or learn alternative skills to compensate for the acquired impairment.

Common tasks to be considered include:

- Learning / acquiring new skills – (discussed above)
- Workflow management – ensuring that tasks are identified and addressed in a timely and consistent manner
- Collaboration – identifying the appropriate team members to work with and communicating concepts and ideas correctly and efficiently
- Creative problem solving – identifying all of the key points and interrelationships of a problem and developing innovative and appropriate solutions
- Task efficiency – identifying the key goals of a task and maintaining focus on those goals
- Personnel management – supporting typical everyday management activities

Real world / extended ADLs. This category is an extended concept of the more typical interpretation of ADLs as described earlier in this paper. Access to real world activities, as defined here, includes:

- Transportation/travel
- Daily living/personal care
- Self-organisation
- Commerce/shopping
- Crisis management

Socialising. The ability to socialise is a required capability in many common daily activities for independent living. Socialising, as defined here, includes:

- Verbal communication – person-to-person
- Non-verbal communication – person-to-person and including gestures, body language and emotions
- Remote communication – communication conducted via an attenuating medium (e.g. a phone line)
- Social Networking Software (for example, Facebook with accessibility enhancements, such as icons to indicate emotional content for an autistic person)

Entertainment. Not all aspects of IT are focused on accomplishing tasks. Entertainment is a key activity for many domestic IT users. Indeed the games market is now larger than the market for many of forms of entertainment [3]. As different forms of media continue to converge and become more powerful, in terms of their computing capability, media consumption is increasingly becoming more reliant on IT access solutions.

3 Decomposing the Areas of Life Endeavour

Having identified a number of prospective areas for future research, it is necessary to consider methods of decomposing them into more manageable concepts for designers and researchers to consider. Fundamentally, issuing the design challenge "Design a new game for someone with a cognitive impairment" is too vague to be meaningful. A more pragmatic approach is to consider functional capabilities to be considered. For example, Adams proposed a model of cognitive operation that consists of 8 components moderated by a ninth element that ties them all together [4]:

- Working memory
- Emotions and drives
- Perception
- Output
- Feedback
- Complex output sequences
- Cognitive models
- Long-term memory
- Executive functions (moderating component)

For the purposes of this discussion, though, a different set of cognitive capabilities has been identified as being of most relevance and usefulness. The principal areas of focus are:

- Attention
- Memory
- Organisational skills
- Language skills
- Social skills

This is by no means a full description of all areas of potential interest, though, simply the ones that are thought to be most appropriate for this discussion. Other additional areas of potential interest that we do not cover in this discussion include, but are not limited to:

- Mood and emotion
- Impulse control
- Visual-motor and spatial processing
- Abstract thought

Having identified the areas of life endeavour and the five principal areas of cognitive capabilities that are of most interest, the next step is to relate these to one another in a matrix describing the scale of the solution design problem to be addressed.

3.1 The Shape of the Matrix

The next stage was to produce a matrix that identifies how the different cognitive capabilities affect a user's ability to interact with an IT system to accomplish a particular task (or set of tasks) within an area of life endeavour. Table 1 shows the basic shape of the matrix.

Table 1. The basic layout of a matrix relating areas of life endeavour to the principal cognitive capabilities identified

	Attention	Memory	Organisational skills	Language skills	Social skills
Learning					
Workplace					
Real world					
Socialising					
Entertainment					

Having established the basic layout of the matrix, the next step is to begin populating it.

3.2 Populating the Matrix

Taking Table 1 as a guide, the next step is to identify specifically which actions and abilities each cognitive capability may affect and facilitate within each area of life endeavour. Table 2 shows an example of this for the Workplace.

3.3 Completing the Matrix

Knowing how different cognitive capabilities are relevant for particular actions and abilities is a good starting point, but needs to be developed further to be useful for designers and researchers. Having identified a particular capability as being of interest, several steps are required to target specific technological capabilities to enhancing

Table 2. The decomposition of the workplace area of life endeavour into component actions and abilitiesaffected and facilitated by each cognitive capability

Workplace	Attention	Memory	Organisational skills	Language skills	Social skills
- Workflow management - Collabora-tion - Creative problem solving - Task efficiency - Personnel management	- Identify and maintain focus on what is to be done - Avoid anxiety and distraction - Manage interruptions	- Maximise access to information that has been applied successfully in the past (professional knowledge base) - Remember what didn't work - Remember roles, procedures, individuals, etc.	- Decompose, sequence, prioritize problems/tasks - Maintain self-awareness of capabilities and limitations - Structure environment in way that is conducive to attention and memory - Identify criticality of specific things (and what can be safely forgotten, "to-do"/reminder mgmt)	- Allow language (written, spoken, affective) to affect the cognitive process — "listening" - Communicate lack of understanding or intent - Present, persuade, influence, negotiate, etc. — "outbound" language skills	- Observe, acquire and then behave appropriately in workplace environment - Interpret and respond appropriately to others, incl. mgmt - Understand personal work objectives and priorities in context of the larger whole - Ask for and obtain support - Empathize with colleagues

Table 3. A completed matrix for Lifelong learning and education

Learning	Attention	Memory	Organisational Skills	Language Skills	Social Skills
-K12 -Higher Ed -Professional education -Continuing/just in time education -Immersive learning -Rehabilitation	•Maintain focus on what is to be learned •Avoid anxiety and distraction	•Maximise access to information that is already learned; relate new material to that •Retain information / relevance of learning to problem context •Remember roles, procedures, individuals, etc.	•Decompose, sequence, prioritise learning problems/tasks •Maintain self-awareness of capabilities and limitations •Structure environment in way that is conducive to attention and memory (meaning "learning")	•Allow language (written, spoken, affective) to affect the cognitive process — "listening" •Communicate levels of understanding or lack thereof (e.g., through interrogation) •Acquire and apply extended language skills	•Behave appropriately in learning settings •Interpret and respond appropriately to others, incl. the teacher •Understand personal learning objectives in context of the group
Need to Identify…	•User's level of capability •Underlying motivations •Objects in the environment	•User's level of capability •Elements of what the query might be •Existing user knowledge base	•User's level of capability •User's native strategy	•User's level of capability •Desired outcome of communication	•User's level of capability •Representation of social network
Possible solution capabilities	•Signposting (tactical support) •Suppress unnecessary distractors	•Chunking of information •Signposting and Scaffolding •Use positive reinforcement and feedback •Offer multiple, alternative representations •Deploy alternative memory cues	•Assist with problem identification (strategic support) •Complement user's strategy •Timetabling and organizational support •Keep hierarchy depths to a minimum •"Help"/Wizards/Task automation	•Use of clear language, simple language •Use of multimedia •Be consistent	•Use positive reinforcement and feedback •Be consistent

or supporting individuals' capabilities and the specific actions supported. It is therefore necessary to identify the level of the potential user's capability and other information about the user in order to model their abilities. Finally, potential solution options can also be identified building on the best practice guidance discussed earlier in this paper, to match the modeled level of capability and needs for each action supported.

Table 3 shows a completed matrix for the "Lifelong learning and education" area of life endeavour.

4 Summary

This paper has shown that cognitive impairments, along with learning difficulties and behavioural disorders, can affect a person's quality of life. IT offers a potential means of assisting in a number of key areas of daily living and also areas of life endeavour. This latter concept is more useful when considering IT because it moves away from the more mundane issues of basic existence, which would most often benefit from "lo-tech" solutions, to considering more ambitious goals to which "hi-tech" solutions offer more appropriate solutions.

A basic framework for relating a person's cognitive capabilities to those areas of life endeavour has been presented and extended to identify possible design guidance for developing solutions.

5 Further Work

The most obvious conclusion of this research is to begin working on projects that take this framework as their inspiration, identify a clear need and develop a viable solution. It is expected that this will be the next phase of this work.

References

1. Keates, S., Varker, P.: Establishing design best practices for users with cognitive and learning difficulties. In: Stephanidis, C. (ed.) Proceedings of 4th International Conference on Universal Access and Human computer Interaction, Beijing China, July 22-27 (2007)
2. ISO. Ergonomic requirements for office work with visual display terminals (VDTs) Part 11: Guidance on usability. International Organization for Standardization. ISO Press, Geneva (1998)
3. Yi, M.: They got game. San Francisco Chronicle (2004), http://www.sfgate.com/cgi-bin/article.cgi?f=/chronicle/archive/2004/12/18/MNGUOAE36I1.DTL (accessed February 20, 2009)
4. Adams, R.: Decision and stress: Cognition and e-Accessibility in the information workplace. Universal Access in the Information Society (UAIS) 5(4), 363–379 (2006)

Remote Conversation Support for People with Aphasia: Some Experiments and Lessons Learned

Kazuhiro Kuwabara[1], Shohei Hayashi[1], Takafumi Uesato[1], Kohei Umadome[1], and Keisuke Takenaka[2]

[1] College of Information Science and Engineering, Ritsumeikan University
1-1-1 Nojihigashi, Kusatsu, Shiga 525-8577 Japan
kuwabara@is.ritsumei.ac.jp
[2] Abiko City Welfare Center for the Handicapped
1637 Araki, Abiko, Chiba 270-1112 Japan

Abstract. This paper describes a system for supporting remote conversation for people with aphasia. We have constructed an initial prototype using Skype for video chat and the RemoteX plug-in for screen sharing over a network. Preliminary experiments conducted using the prototype have revealed that simply providing video chat and screen-sharing functions is not sufficient for supporting remote conversation with people with aphasia. We propose various simple communication tools to facilitate questioning and answering in the remote conversation, where a person with aphasia can reply by marking an appropriate portion of a window provided by the tool. Their effectiveness is demonstrated through experiments.

Keywords: remote conversation support, people with aphasia, screen sharing, video phone.

1 Introduction

Advancements in communication technologies allow people to communicate virtually anywhere at any time. People with communication handicaps, such as aphasia, however, cannot fully benefit from those technologies. For people with aphasia, an audio phone and text chat are difficult to use because their communication media depend on the use of language. A video phone allows us to see a person in a remote place. However, due to the limited image size and resolution, video chat is basically designed to show the face of a person. Thus, it is difficult, for example, to point at a thing such as a word on a piece of paper, which is easily accomplished in face-to-face communication.

To remedy this problem, we are investigating a way to enhance remote communication support over a network, targeted at people with aphasia. The remote conversation support system is based on a video chat system for audio and visual communication. In addition, we use a personal computer to share a variety of information over the network. The supporting information items for conversation are shown on the PC display and shared over the network. A touch panel display is also used on the side of the person with aphasia. We assume that a person with aphasia can point at an item displayed on

C. Stephanidis (Ed.): Universal Access in HCI, Part I, HCII 2009, LNCS 5614, pp. 375–384, 2009.
© Springer-Verlag Berlin Heidelberg 2009

the PC display by touching the screen. The position of the touch is sent over the network to the conversation partner's PC.

In order to acquire specific requirements for this type of remote conversation support, we have implemented an initial prototype using Skype for the video chat function, and the RemoteX Skype plug-in for the screen-sharing function. This paper first describes this prototype, and discusses preliminary experiments using the prototype. Through the experiments, we realized that simple screen sharing is not sufficient for remote conversation support for people with aphasia. Therefore, several simple communication tools to assist remote communication are proposed. Finally, experiments conducted to evaluate the effectiveness of the proposed tools are described.

2 Remote Conversation Support

2.1 System Overview

In order to demonstrate the possibility of remote conversation support, we set up an initial prototype as shown in Fig. 1. Skype is used as a video phone and the RemoteX plug-in is used for screen sharing. Using the screen-sharing tool, the conversation partner can share information to facilitate conversation. A hands-free microphone is used to make it easier to use the video chat. A touch panel display is also introduced on the side of a person with aphasia, so that the patient can point at the PC screen by touch.

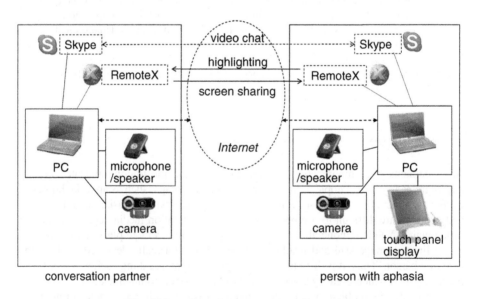

Fig. 1. Overview of remote conversation system

The PC screen (desktop image) on the conversation partner side is sent to the PC of the person with aphasia ("patient"). With RemoteX, the entire desktop is transferred to the remote PC, including a window for Skype. Since this might confuse the patient, we adjusted the position of the RemoteX window on the remote PC (on the patient side) so that only the portion of the desktop that is intended to be shared appears in the remote PC display, and the rest of the desktop of the conversation partner's PC (including the window for Skype) is off the screen on the patient's side.

Though the RemoteX plug-in also allows a remote user to control the remote PC, we decided not to let the patient control the PC at the conversation partner's side in order to simplify operation. The patient only observes the desktop of the conversation partner's PC. In order to communicate which item on the shared desktop the patient is interested in, the patient is asked to use a pen tool (included with RemoteX) to mark the corresponding area in the window. Marking is done by touching the touch panel display.

2.2 Preliminary Experiments

With this initial prototype, we conducted a remote conversation experiment with people with aphasia. The participants can basically understand spoken words, but have difficulty expressing their thoughts verbally. The conversation is conducted in the following way. First, a conversation partner considers a question to ask, and prepares the contents to be displayed on the PC, which contains possible answers to the question. The conversation partner, then, asks a question verbally and shows the contents containing possible answers in the PC screen. The contents will also be shown on the patient's PC screen (by RemoteX screen sharing), and the patient can answer the question by marking the word (or item) displayed on the screen with the pen tool. The conversation partner can then recognize the answer to the original question by seeing which word or item is marked.

As for the contents to support conversation, we used a vocabulary data file called 'Rakuraku-JiyuuKaiwa'[1]. This vocabulary list categorizes words useful in supporting conversation with people with aphasia. Since the vocabulary list is available on the Internet, we used a web browser to show a list of words. We also utilized 'communication notes' that consist of many paper cards on which various (personal) topics and frequently used words are written. We digitized the communication notes of the experiment participants and made them accessible from the web browser locally. In addition, we used search engines to search the Internet for appropriate web pages for the conversation. In this case, the conversation partner uses the search engine to obtain more detailed information on the current conversation topic. When the appropriate web page is found, the page is then shared with the patient's PC.

The preliminary remote conversation using the prototype described above revealed that simply sharing the PC screen is not sufficient for supporting remote conversation with people with aphasia. One of the reasons is that it is somewhat cumbersome to prepare a list of possible answers. The vocabulary list is designed to be used for this purpose, and is useful for starting a conversation by selecting a topic from the list. As the conversation progresses, the vocabulary list itself often fails to cover all the topics. The Internet offers a wealth of information, but it takes time to search for the appropriate web page during the conversation. While the conversation partner searches the Internet, the conversation with the patient stops, and this disrupts smooth communication.

Table 1. Categories of typical questions

Type of Question	Tool	Functions to be Provided
Yes-No question	Yes-No tool	The window containing Yes / No or not-understood buttons.
Asking the degree of something	Scale tool	The scale bar is shown.
Asking from among several items	Choice tool	Several text areas for a conversation partner to type in during the conversation.
Asking about a place	Map tool	The web-based map system (such as Google, Yahoo) to be presented is shown.
Asking about a date	Calendar tool	A blank calendar is shown.
Asking about a time	Clock tool	A clock without hands is shown.
Asking about the number of times	Number tool	A group of numbers is shown.

2.3 Conversation Support Tools

In order to facilitate the conversation, we categorized the typical conversation into several types [2], and devised a simple tool for each conversation type as shown in Table 1. These simple tools are written in HTML and are intended to be used with a web browser. The person with aphasia can answer the question by simply marking the relevant portion of the tool shown in the web browser using the RemoteX pen tool.

Each tool is stored as an HTML file in the conversation partner's PC. The Google Chrome browser is used to display the HTML file, because the Chrome browser allows us to create a short-cut icon to show the HTML file without any address bar or menu bar. We placed short-cut icons on the conversation partner's desktop to make it easy to use the tools.

1. Yes-No tool

The Yes-No tool is intended to be used for a simple Yes-No type question (Fig. 2). This tool presents three buttons for answering 'Yes,' 'No,' and 'not understood.' The last button was necessary to clearly indicate that the question posed by a conversation partner is not understood by the patient.

Fig. 2. "Yes-No" tool

When the conversation partner asks a question that can be answered by yes or no, the partner brings this window to the front. The same window will appear on the patient's PC display, and the patient can reply by marking the corresponding part of the window with the pen tool.

2. Scale tool

The scale tool (Fig. 3) is intended to be used for answering questions such as "How much do you like it?" The scale bar is shown on the screen, and the patient is expected to respond with the degree by marking the corresponding position in the scale bar.

3. Choice tool

The choice tool is used for preparing a list of possible questions on the fly. This is simply an HTML document with several text area boxes. The conversation partner types a possible

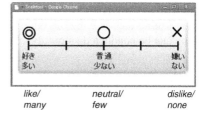

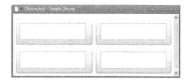

Fig. 3. Scale tool

answer in each text box. Fig. 4 shows the choice tool, which contains four choices. The patient will mark the item using the pen tool to answer the question.

4. Map tool

A map is very useful when talking about places. There are several map services available on the Internet. We made a simple tool to make it easier to utilize the map service (specifically Yahoo! Japan Maps). One of the

Fig. 4. Choice tool

problems in using a map is to communicate in which direction the map is to be scrolled. Since a patient cannot directly control the partner's PC, s/he cannot scroll the map by him/herself. Instead, eight arrows are placed around the map as shown in Fig. 5. When the patient wants to scroll the map, s/he marks the corresponding arrow. Then, the conversation partner scrolls the map on his/her PC. This may sound

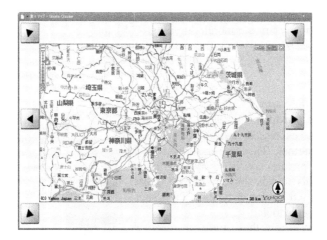

Fig. 5. Map tool

somewhat cumbersome, but if the conversation partner leads the conversation well by confirming the scrolling direction each time the patient marks an arrow, the conversation can be conducted smoothly.

5. Calendar/Clock/Number tool

In order to talk about the date, the calendar tool is designed as shown Fig. 6. It has areas for selecting year and month along with the monthly view of the particular month.

Fig. 6. Calendar tool

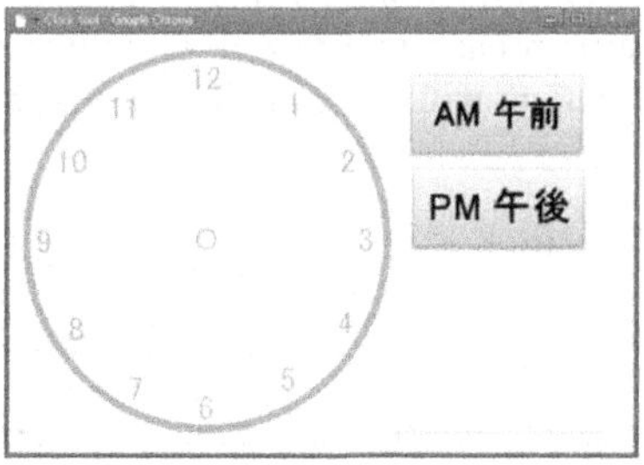

Fig. 7. Clock tool

Similarly the clock tool is provided as shown in Fig. 7. The patient is expected to draw the clock hand on the figure to respond with the time. In addition, the number tool is provided for questions involving numbers (Fig. 8). In this example, the partner can ask a question such as "How many times a month do you go?" by putting a word in each box.

Fig. 8. Number tool

6. Drawing tool

In addition to the various tools described above, a free drawing tool is provided (Fig. 9) to convey information that cannot be expressed well verbally by a conversation partner. The conversation partner can draw a picture as in a typical paint application. This tool is universal in the sense that it can be used like other types of tools such as Yes-No, or scale tools.

Fig. 10 shows how these tools are used in the conversation. The patient is supposed to mark the corresponding portion on the screen by the pen tool provided by RemoteX.

Fig. 9. Drawing tool

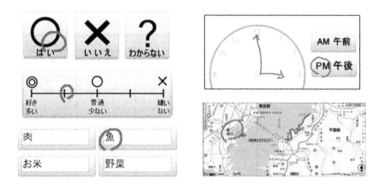

Fig. 10. Sample usage of tools

3 Experiments

3.1 Method

In order to investigate the proposed tool, we conducted the following experiment. Three persons with aphasia participated in the experiments as shown in Table 2. The-experiments were conducted in connection with the Abiko City Welfare Center for the Handicapped and Ritsumeikan University, which are about 500 km apart. As explained in the previous sections, we used the Skype video chat system for audio-visual communication and the RemoteX plug-in for screen sharing. The two places were connected by the Internet.

In order to investigate the effectiveness of the proposed tools, we used the A-B design. Basically method A involves only a Skype video chat system. However, since it is very difficult to conduct remote conversation using just video chat, we also utilized a drawing tool if necessary. Method B introduces the tools proposed in the previous section. Each conversation lasted about half an hour to one hour. First, method A was tried, and then one week (or more) later, method B was tried. The conversations were recorded and analyzed later.

3.2 Results

We counted the number of questions asked in each trial. The number of uncertain answers by a participant and the number of repeated questions were also counted. The results are shown in Table 3.

Table 2. Participants

participant	gender	age	symptom	drive for communication
P1	male	51	non-fluent aphasia (severe)	high
P2	male	59	non-fluent aphasia (severe)	low
P3	male	71	transcortical motor aphasia (moderate to severe)	low

Table 3. Experiment Results

participant	P1		P2		P3	
method	A	B	A	B	A	B
duration	42 min.	52 min.	58 min.	47 min.	24 min.	50 min.
number of questions asked	58	96	73	104	33	105
number of uncertain answers	11	4	8	3	0	0
number of repeated questions	8	4	5	1	2	0

The number of questions per minute for each trial was calculated and shown in Fig. 11. In the method A trial, we ended up using the map tool temporarily for the conversation involving questions regarding places for participants P2 and P3 in order to carry on the conversation. For participant P3, a calendar tool was also used temporarily for method A. Even when we take these factors into consideration, we can infer that the proposed tool allows us to ask more questions. This is because less time was needed for composing the questions with the proposed tools available.

As for uncertain answers, the proposed tools could reduce their number. The tools, in a sense, present an answer form to be filled out by the patient. Thus, the ambiguity in the answers can be reduced. As a result, the number of repeated questions can also be reduced. Uncertain answers were not observed for participant P3. This may be because P3 tended to be passive in conversation, thus, most of the questions were yes-no or multiple choice types. This is reflected in Fig. 12, which shows the ratios of the individual tools used in the experiment. For P3, most of the questions were yes-no types. Also note that all the tools were utilized in the experiment as shown in the graph.

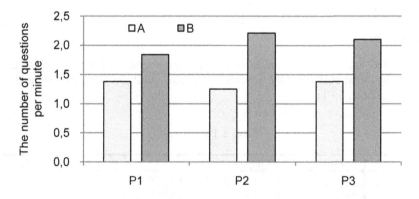

Fig. 11. Number of questions per minute for each participant

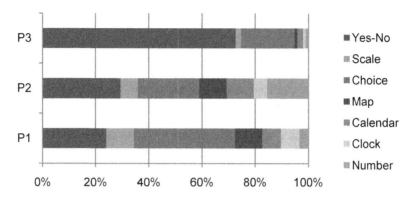

Fig. 12. The ratio of the number of usage of each tool

4 Discussion

The experiment results indicate that the time needed for preparing the questions can be shortened with the proposed tools. Thus, the proposed tools can increase the number of questions we can ask and more information can be obtained from the conversation within the same amount of time.

In addition, we observed that miscommunication can be reduced with the proposed tools. This is partly because the participant can easily understand the intent of the question when the proposed tools show a window (answer box) that the patient uses to make a reply. It can also reduce the number of repeated questions.

With the proposed tools, we can also ask more elaborate questions, for example, we can ask the degree of things. For instance, it becomes easier to ask "How much do you like the movie?" with the answer box containing the scale bar in which the participant can express his or her answer. These factors contribute to smoother remote conversation with people with aphasia.

One of the additional benefits of the proposed tools is that for a novice conversation partner, the proposed tools can act as a kind of template for conversation to be conducted. A novice conversation partner can compose questions with the tools to use in mind.

5 Conclusion

In this paper, we have proposed several tools to facilitate remote conversation over a network. The tools are simple HTML files to be used with a web browser. The experiments using a Skype video phone and its RemoteX screen-sharing plug-in suggest that the proposed tools are effective.

We are also developing a remote conversation support system that utilizes a word database [3]. We plan to integrate the proposed tools with the word database, which can be accessed over the network. In addition, in order to make it easier to use, we are designing a web browser-based system to replace the RemoteX screen-sharing tool.

Screen sharing is very convenient, but it has some drawbacks. For example, it is difficult to play the same video clip or audio file in the remote location. In addition, we cannot easily control which part of the screen is to be shared and when to share it. In the case of remote conversation with people with aphasia, the conversation partner often searches the Internet for information related to the current conversation topics. It is not advisable to share this kind of search process with the patient because it may provide too much information and confuse him or her. It is necessary to be able to easily determine which information should be shared and when. Taking these points into consideration, we plan to extend the proposed tools to support remote conversation for people with aphasia.

Acknowledgements

The authors wish to thank participants of the remote conversation experiments. They also thank Dr. Kiyoshi Yasuda of the Chiba Rosai Hospital for his advice and discussion on the support of conversation with people with aphasia.

References

1. Yasuda, K., Nemoto, T., Takenaka, K., Mitachi, M., Kuwabara, K.: Effectiveness of a vocabulary data file, encyclopaedia, and Internet homepages in a conversation-support system for people with moderate-to-severe aphasia. Aphasiology 21(9), 867–882 (2007)
2. Non-Profit Cooperation WAON: Let's talk with people with Aphasia, 2nd edn., Chuo Houki (2008) (in Japanese)
3. Aye, N., Ito, T., Hattori, F., Kuwabara, K., Yasuda, K.: Conversation Support for People with Aphasia in Distant Communication. In: The 7th IEEE International Conference on Cognitive Informatics, pp. 294–299 (2008)

Mobile Technology for People with Cognitive Disabilities and Their Caregivers – HCI Issues

Clayton Lewis, James Sullivan, and Jeffery Hoehl

Coleman Institute for Cognitive Disabilities and
Department of Computer Science
University of Colorado
Boulder, Colorado USA 80309
{Clayton.Lewis,James.Sullivan,Jeffery.Hoehl}@colorado.edu

Abstract. Smart phone technology is evolving to become more open to application developers. This trend is opening the way to development of personalized assistive technologies, location-aware services, and enhanced person-to-person communications. This paper presents findings from an international workshop, with participants from industry, policy, education, and private organizations. Participants mapped future directions for exploiting technical opportunities, with a focus on people with cognitive disabilities. HCI issues that emerged as critical include profile-based configuration of user interfaces and functionality, support for spoken presentation of text content, support for viewing web content on devices with small screens, and support for remote assistance, so that users can get help when they get stuck. In addition to technical issues, key process and methodology issues were identified, including more inclusion of self-advocates in design development and user testing, and increased recognition of and support for the overall "value chain" throughout system deployment and use.

Keywords: mobile technology, persons with cognitive disabilities, caregivers, assistive technology.

1 Introduction

The 2008 Coleman Workshop on Mobile Technologies was held on October 15, 2008 in Boulder, Colorado to discuss near and long-term strategies for utilizing information technologies to improve choice, independence, and quality of life for those living with cognitive disabilities and their caregivers. The workshop was conducted under charterhouse rules, allowing all members to freely speak their minds without individual attribution. Participants from industry, policy, education, clinical care delivery and private organizations addressed both technical opportunities and process issues in improving assistive mobile technologies. In this paper, we summarize the discussions at the workshop to encourage interest in this topic and participation in the work of development that is needed.

C. Stephanidis (Ed.): Universal Access in HCI, Part I, HCII 2009, LNCS 5614, pp. 385–394, 2009.
© Springer-Verlag Berlin Heidelberg 2009

2   Recent Developments and Opportunities in Smart Phone Technologies

Mobile smart phones are evolving to become more open for development with applications of value to people with disabilities. In the past, mobile phones were sold with a fixed repertoire of functions. While these devices contained powerful microprocessors, users could not easily install new software. More recently, Apple's iPhone and many new smart phones running Windows Mobile, Symbian, PalmWebOS, or Java ME allow users to install any of a very wide range of applications. For example, many smart phones support text to speech applications that can be useful for people who have difficulty reading.

Conditions are still evolving with respect to control of the particular applications available to users. Apple limits installation of "native" iPhone applications, those that can access the full range of phone features, to those approved by Apple and made available through the iTunes system. Other manufacturers and service providers do not impose this kind of control, but they may require applications to be tested and registered in order to access some functions.

As of October 2008, the operating system software for Google's Android smart phone platform is "open source". This means that a community can freely make an extension or modification to the platform software code, and it can also make enhancements available to others. Nokia has announced plans to make the Symbian software open source as well.

These developments are potentially very important for people with disabilities. Due to the limited market size, the commercial industry rarely supplies assistive applications except as required by regulations such as Section 508 of the Rehabilitation Act, or Section 255 of the Telecommunications Act in the USA. Allowing end users to dynamically install applications makes it possible for and encourages user communities, students, and other volunteers to develop and distribute useful applications. Making the underlying software platforms open source enables further important developments, since interested communities can design and implement significant extensions to the platforms that provide useful support for people with disabilities.

3   Technical Opportunities

Workshop participants explored a variety of developments that have the potential to support a broad range of mobile products and services. These technical developments include: profile-based configuration of user interfaces and services, support for spoken presentations of information, cross-platform software support, and support for viewing web content on small screens.

3.1   Profile-Based Configuration of User Interfaces and Services

Current personalization approaches emphasize independently configuring a large number of potentially confusing interface settings, including preferences for sound, display, messaging, and single key commands (speed dial, mute, etc.). In contrast, a profile-based approach offers the potential for users to easily select a range of information displays and services tailored to their needs and capabilities. Once one or more profiles have been configured, the user can set multiple parameters to appropriate values by simply selecting a profile.

If combined with available contextual information, such as day of week, time, and GPS location, a profile-based approach could offer the possibility to appropriately adjust or even change information modalities. For example, sound volume can be automatically turned up while traveling or switched to vibrate when at a doctor's office. If a user interface architecture is designed to support this tailoring, it could also promote the modular sharing of UI services across applications and smart phone platforms.

Profiles for smart phones could be specified using the same schema being developed for computers and based on the AccessForAll framework (http://dublincore.org/accessibilitywiki/AccessForAllFramework/). Such profiles can be stored online and delivered by an identity provider to any device a user is operating.

3.2 Support for Spoken Presentation of Information

An overwhelming volume of information, both on the Web and in the world, is provided in text format. People with cognitive disabilities often cannot read and require a different presentation of text content, including textual controls. Unless some option for modality shift and augmentation are provided, this can create a significant barrier to information access and comprehension.

Smart phones can be used as translation devices by allowing such information to be converted from text to speech. Translation is not limited to web-based information sources; Kurzweil text to speech reading technologies are now available in Nokia smart phones so that users can read signage as they navigate the world. As smart phones become more powerful, they offer the possibility to translate complex information into simpler, more comprehensible forms that are appropriate to an individual's abilities.

3.3 Cross-Platform Software Support

Today, an application developed for a particular phone will usually not work on another model. This means that the cost of supporting a diverse range of users, who have different phones, is generally high. Applications that do not use phone-specific features, such as a camera or GPS sensor, and do not require information storage on the phone, can be developed as web applications and run via web browsers in a phone-agnostic way. The technical limitations of web applications, however, rule out many applications that could be useful to people with cognitive disabilities.

The emerging HTML5 standard (http://dev.w3.org/html5/spec/Overview.html/) will change this situation, and implementations of some HTML5 features are now available in Google Gears (http://gears.google.com/) for select smart phones. HTML5 provides means for applications running in a browser to use phone features and store information on the phone, so that applications can run without being online. This development will be important for reducing the cost, and increasing the availability of many applications, including some of interest to people with cognitive disabilities.

3.4   Support for Viewing Web Content on Devices with Small Screens

The Web offers tremendous opportunities for "on-the-go, anywhere, anytime" information access and sharing, and especially for people with cognitive disabilities with limited attention or memory. While market pressure for small screens may creates difficulties for people with vision difficulties, adaptive techniques are also emerging [1] that can automatically tailor presentations to fit limited screen real estate. We need to develop these techniques, with additional attention to supporting navigation and controls.

A promising technology, already demonstrated for screen reader users, is predicting what part of a webpage is most likely of interest to a user, based on their interaction history [2]. For screen reader users this can save considerable time and effort, since it is difficult for these users to scan from the top of a page looking for the desired content. The same technique should be valuable for people who can see but who cannot read well, saving them the effort of reading irrelevant material while searching for what they need. It should be especially helpful on devices with small screens, on which only a small amount of content can be viewed at a time.

3.5   Support for Remote Assistance

One of the most significant opportunities for people with cognitive disabilities is the potential to leverage smart phones as a lifeline for increased independence, by linking them and their caregiver community network. If technologies can be developed to support unobtrusive and secure monitoring services between at-risk users and trusted caregivers, new opportunities for independence can be explored, while providing a robust safety net when mobile users need assistance. In order to make this a reality, smart phone technologies and services must be reliable, robust, secure, and have the ability to alert caregivers either when a mobile user requests help or the system detects an unusual anomaly, such as the user wandering off course, a person who is no longer near their smart phone, or a system failure.

Smart phones should also allow enable users to remotely get assistance in using the device itself when needed. On desktop machines, technologies like GoToMyPC (http://www.gotomypc.com/) allow a remote user to view and control one's machine, and this approach would be useful for many users with cognitive disabilities. Comparable tools should be provided for smart phone devices.

4   Process and Methodology Issues

Exploiting the opportunities just discussed, and others that will emerge, requires a *process* that will shape the underlying technology of smart phones in appropriate ways, and promote the development of applications that support people with cognitive disabilities. How can this process be promoted?

4.1   More Inclusion of Self-advocates in Design, Development, and User Testing

It has long been understood that development of effective computational tools and services requires deep understanding of the interests and needs of users. This understanding cannot be developed without the participation of those users themselves. Unfortunately, software developers have been reluctant to include people with disabilities in activities like user focus groups and user test sessions [3]. Partly for this reason, it is too common that new devices and programs are developed with serious accessibility problems, as happened with the release of a popular smart phone [4] and a new web browser [5].

On the other hand, progress is being made. Shawn Henry [6] has published helpful information for those uncertain about how to be inclusive in user testing. The WebAnywhere project (http://webanywhere.cs.washington.edu/), developing a Web-based screen reader, has included blind people in each stage of development. Organizations like TEITAC (http://www.webaim.org/teitac/) and the Web Content Accessibility Guidelines working group (http://www.w3.org/TR/WCAG20/) have pushed for more representation of people with disabilities, including cognitive disabilities, in their work. The National Institute on Disability and Rehabilitation Research (http://www.rerc-act.org/) has funded device usage research programs explicitly designed to incorporate user focus groups, in vivo usage trials, and post-usage feedback from both users and caregivers.

This progress has to come for application development for smart phones too. In grasping the opportunities provided by increased openness, we have to develop organizations and work processes that include self-advocates as participants throughout the design, development, and testing process. Partnerships with national and local self-advocate organizations must be forged. Technology like York University's VULab (http://www.vulab.ca/), that allows user testing to be performed remotely, may have a valuable role to play in enabling participation by a geographically scattered user community.

4.2 Increased Recognition and Support for the Overall "Value Chain"

Successful use of assistive technology (AT), when it occurs, is the culmination of a long chain of events, with many participants. For a person with a cognitive disability to become aware of appropriate technology, caregivers, advisers, and support staff usually have to be aware of it too. Choice of an appropriate device or application also requires knowledgeable assistance in nearly all cases, as does configuring a device or application once it is acquired. Often, training and follow-up adjustments are necessary since people with cognitive disabilities often cannot tailor a smart phone to suit their own needs. Further follow-up is often needed during long-term use, if that is achieved, since user needs and capabilities change over time.

For new technology to be successfully applied, all of the participants in this long value chain need to know about the technology and understand their roles in the chain. Clearly, these requirements go far beyond simply developing a "valuable" technology in the research lab, or even creating a product from it that can be made and delivered economically. Rather, the effort has to include substantial outreach and education to prepare a large supporting cast. This is a challenge to traditional models of R&D and funding, requiring new development models and processes.

4.3 Open Source Opportunities

The open source model of design and development provides considerable potential in creating better AT in both hardware and software. In this model, a community of developers works collaboratively to develop or enhance software tools.

Since these communities can be formed by anyone, and can be open to new participants, potentially anyone can contribute knowledge or resources to improving a product. In particular, a community of people with needs that are important to them can organize to produce software, without requiring the involvement of a commercial organization or research lab.

The open source model also allows persons living with cognitive disabilities, caregivers, and advocates to more directly provide input and feedback into the design and development process. This allows for software and hardware that is more attuned to the actual needs of the end users.

Once developed, open source software can be adapted by anyone with the desire and means to do it as needs arise. If someone wants a program to run on a different device, for example, they are free to adapt it. Because the same program is being adapted for the new device, rather than a new program being developed, a useful application may be made available on new devices as they appear, taking advantage of lower cost or improved performance.

This happy picture may not always be realized. It may be too difficult to create a program for a given purpose, or too hard to adapt it to a new device. Many successful open source projects receive substantial investment of paid work from corporate sponsors. Communities of people with cognitive disabilities, and those who support them, may not command these resources.

4.4 Education

Developing software for people with cognitive disabilities, or other disabilities, is largely neglected in current computing curricula. Thus, when students become professional developers they seldom have relevant skills or even awareness. But this problem can and should be addressed.

Student Projects. Many computer science curricula include substantial student projects, often with clients outside the university, as a way of introducing students to development "in the real world". Since faculty often have to work hard to identify interesting project opportunities, connecting these project courses with software needs in AT offers a substantial benefit on both sides.

One project approach is to consider how senior projects and capstone courses can be structured to focus on long-term projects that incorporate accessibility needs. Using this approach, the focus is not how to manage a single student group working on a project over a long period of time, but instead how to create course focus on a long-term project that rotates through several groups of students. This would also allow students to develop and extend an existing code base rather than developing new code from scratch.

Open source software, as described earlier, also has advantages in this connection, because students have free access to the software they need to work with, and the open source project will have ways to evaluate and adopt student contributions. A thorny problem with student projects is long-term maintenance. Software always needs work over time to fix defects as they are found, to adapt to new devices, and to address new user needs. Student projects cannot meet these needs. Framing student projects within established open source communities would make it possible to take advantage of what the students can contribute, while relying on the larger community to meet the long-term needs.

Similarly, students working on a project cannot provide ongoing user support, training, and the like, including the needs identified in our discussion of the value chain. Here, too, framing student projects within a larger community can solve the problem.

Courses. Material on accessibility, including relevant standards, should be included in courses in human-computer interaction (HCI) in computer science curricula. Other technology and engineering courses covering diverse topics such as software engineering, universal design, pervasive and ubiquitous computing, and hardware design should likewise include topics concerning design standards and accessibility needs of people with disabilities. Information School programs, which have emerged at many universities in the last several years, should also include these topics in their curricula. Likewise, courses in the social systems, communications, and cognitive sciences also have strong reasons to include discussions of cognitive and physical disabilities and opportunities for interdisciplinary project collaborations should be broadly explored and encouraged.

4.5 Integration with the Raising the Floor Initiative

Grasping the opportunities described here will require large-scale cooperation. An organization is taking shape that promises to provide an effective framework for this, the Raising the Floor initiative (http://www.raisingthefloor.net/), led by Gregg Vanderheiden of the University of Wisconsin and Jim Fruchterman of Benetech. The central aim of Raising the Floor (RTF) is building essential AT into the basic information infrastructure we all use. RTF will not only make AT available to all who need it, but will also provide a higher level platform for AT than now exists, supporting enhanced applications developed by commercial AT providers, as well as by other developers.

Because of the critical role of the Web in our information infrastructure, web accessibility is the initial focus of RTF. But trends show that Web access from mobile devices is rapidly increasing, and mobile devices represent a larger share of our infrastructure. In response, RTF will seek to promote the availability of quality AT on mobile platforms as well as in traditional browsers.

As discussed earlier, web technology is rapidly changing and implementations of HTML5, like Google Gears, are starting to appear. This technology will further blur the boundaries separating mobile applications from traditional desktop applications. For example, it will be possible to automatically download and store data and applications on the smart phone when the device is not being used, just as is routine for desktop applications.

For AT applications, this attractive scenario requires that basic AT functionality, such as text to speech conversion, be available in any browser, in a uniform way. Once this is accomplished, applications like reading aids for people who can see but cannot read well, can be developed and provided at low cost, by commercial or non-commercial entities. This is a good example of the promise of the RTF initiative.

4.6 Standards and Regulation

With today's interconnected technologies, standardization is essential to progress. Operation of the World Wide Web depends entirely on the use of standard protocols; without these the whole fabric of communication that it supports would be impossible. As already mentioned, HTML5, which holds great promise for helping meet the goals outlined here, is an emerging standard of this kind.

Experience has shown that there is sometimes a need for regulation, as well as standardization, where access to technology for users with disabilities is concerned. One example is hearing aid compatibility, where most vendors have welcomed regulations to ensure smart phones are available that can be used by hearing aid users. Regulations mean that all vendors share the cost of serving this public purpose, and that vendors who make the needed investment are not thereby put at a competitive disadvantage. Regrettably, a popular smart phone that is not hearing aid compatible represents a regulatory failure in this respect, exploiting a loophole intended to exempt small industry participants [7].

The workshop participants agreed that regulation should be minimized. But what will a workable minimum represent? In the USA, current regulations do not require that most websites comply with accessibility guidelines, or, more accurately, court decisions have not made clear how existing law, in particular the Americans with Disabilities Act [8], will or will not apply to the Web. These matters may affect our ability to provide good access to web content on smart phones, as well as via more familiar browsers.

The Raising the Floor initiative will provide a useful setting for deliberation, and cooperative action, with respect to regulation. It may emerge that meeting the goals of RTF will require that smart phones meet some technical standards, in more or less the same way that hearing aid compatibility imposes technical requirements. Or this may not happen. Participants in RTF will be in a good position to identify and define such needs, should they emerge, and help frame appropriate regulations in response.

5 Expanded Opportunities, Collaborations, and Participatory Design

The workshop suggests the value of increased collaboration across discipline, organizational, and national boundaries in addressing these opportunities. The participants represented a wide variety of organizations, including academic, clinical, commercial, for profit and non-profit. A roadmap for progress emerged from the exchange among technologists, who have a sense of that can be done; clinicians and others knowledgeable about people with cognitive disabilities, and people with long experience in the promotion of accessibility, including the realm of regulation and standards. Notably, there is great potential for sharing technology across efforts to support people with different kinds of disabilities.

The workshop would have been even more fruitful had we had participation by self-advocates (one self-advocate planned to attend but had to cancel at the last moment). As mentioned earlier, such participation should be a priority in these efforts.

Broader international participation will also be helpful. Attendance at the workshop shows cooperation in North America, as well as involvement of companies that operate on a global level. Even in its early days, the Raising the Floor initiative has participation from eight countries on three continents. Mobile technology is a global system, and work to make it more useful to people with cognitive disabilities will be a global effort.

Acknowledgements. The authors would like to thank all of the participants who contributed to the success of the workshop:

- Budris, Michele (Sun Microsystems, Inc)
- Caves, Kevin (Wireless RERC)
- Coleman, Bill (Cassatt Corporation)
- Davies, Dan (AbleLink)
- Dowds, Murdo (Spaulding Hospital)
- Dougall, David (Research in Motion)
- Dzumba, David (Nokia)
- Hoehl, Jeffery (University of Colorado)
- Lewis, Clayton (University of Colorado)
- LoPresti, Ed (AT Sciences)
- Paciello, Mike (Paciello Group)
- Prideaux Jason (University of Oregon)
- Ramakrishnan, IV (SUNY)
- Rowland, Cyndi (Utah State University)
- Sullivan, Jim (University of Colorado)
- Treviranus, Jutta (University of Toronto)
- Vanderheiden, Gregg (TRACE)
- Waddell, Cynthia (International Center for Disability Resources on Internet)
- Wilson, Cameron (Association for Computing Machinery)

The authors also wish to acknowledge the generous support from the Coleman Institute for Cognitive Disabilities (http://www.colemaninstitute.org/) for hosting this workshop. Clayton Lewis also acknowledges research support from the Rehabilitation Engineering Research Center for the Advancement of Cognitive Technologies (RERC-ACT).

References

1. Gajos, K.Z., Wobbrock, J.O., Weld, D.S.: Automatically generating user interfaces adapted to users' motor and vision capabilities. In: Proceedings of the 20th Annual ACM Symposium on User interface Software and Technology, pp. 231–240. ACM, New York (2007)
2. Mahmud, J., Borodin, Y., Ramakrishnan, I.V.: Assistive browser for conducting web transactions. In: Proceedings of the 13th International Conference on Intelligent User Interfaces, pp. 265–368. ACM, New York (2008)
3. Lewis, C., Bodine, C., LoPresti, E.: Including people with cognitive disabilities in user testing of technology. Workshop, RESNA Annual Conference, Atlanta (2006)
4. The Apple iPhone voluntary accessibility information document states the following: "Effective use of the iPhone requires a minimal level of visual acuity, motor skills, and an ability to operate a few mechanical buttons. Use of iPhone by someone who relies solely on audible and tactile input is not recommended",
   http://images.apple.com/accessibility/pdf/iPhone_vpat.pdf
5. Faulkner, S.: Google Chrome Accessibility,
   http://www.paciellogroup.com/blog/?p=92
6. Henry, S.L.: Just Ask: Integrating Accessibility Throughout Design. ET\Lawton, Madison (2006)
7. Battat, B.: National Update: Apple iPhone Not Hearing Aid Compatible. Hearing Loss Magazine, 22 (November / December 2007),
   http://www.hearingloss.org/magazine/2007NovDec/
   HL%20NovDec%202007.pdf
8. Americans with Disabilities Act (ADA), http://www.ada.gov/

ESSE: Learning Disability Classification System for Autism and Dyslexia

Nor'ain Mohd Yusoff[1,2], Muhammad Hafiz Abdul Wahab[2],
Mohamad Azrulnisyam Aziz[2], and Fauzul Jalil Asha'ari[2]

[1] Faculty of Computer Science and Information Technology, University of Malaya,
Kuala Lumpur, Malaysia
norain.yusoff@mmu.edu.my
[2] Faculty of Information Science and Technology, Multimedia University,
Melaka, Malaysia
seefueq@yahoo.com, motorbreth_03@yahoo.co.uk

Abstract. This paper presents an Expert System for Special Education (ESSE) based on scenario in Malaysia. This system is developed through the process of knowledge-gaining which is gathered from various expertise in chosen domain. Realizing the limitation of traditional classification system that teachers adopted, we developed ESSE to automate a centralized decision making system. ESSE is also able to provide consistent answers for repetitive decisions, processes and tasks. Besides, teachers using this system hold and maintain significant level of information pertaining both learning disabilities, thus reduce amount of human errors. ESSE knowledge-based resulted from the knowledge engineering called Qualifiers and Choice. Both are gathered from the analysis of symptoms that are experienced by Autism and Dyslexia patients. Every type of disability is divided to several categories and sub-category to facilitate question's arrangement. This paper presents a review of Expert System for Special Education (ESSE), problems arises and the knowledge-based classification systems.

Keywords: Qualifiers, Choice, Autism, Dyslexia, Knowledge Engineering.

1 Introduction

Nowadays, expert system application is the field that has a high demand in Human-Computer Interaction. There are a lot of demands in developing the expert system as an alternative of the human expertise especially in the domain of special education system.

In special education field, the new teachers need to know what type of disability that each of their students have, and they need to categorize the students into a suitable curriculum activity based on the students disability. Therefore, the result from this classification system can be a guideline and knowledge interpretation to their disabilities. Expert System for Special Education (ESSE) that we proposed is developed by using Incremental Expert System Prototyping Model, and adopting the Qualifiers and Choices for Autism and Dyslexia. The strength of this model is that users are

C. Stephanidis (Ed.): Universal Access in HCI, Part I, HCII 2009, LNCS 5614, pp. 395–402, 2009.
© Springer-Verlag Berlin Heidelberg 2009

allowed to recognize changes that are needed in future enhancement based on information and knowledge added by expertise. This paper presents a review of Expert System for Special Education (ESSE), problems arises and the knowledge-based classification systems.

1.1 Background

Malaysian Education Ministry provides education services to students that need special education in visual problem, hearing problem, learning problem, and student rehabilitation. Learning problem services under the Malaysian Education Ministry responsible can be categorized into Syndrome Down, Mild Autism, Attention Deficit Hyperactive Disorder (ADHD), Cerebral Palsy, and Specific Learning Problem (example : Dyslexia and Autism) [1].

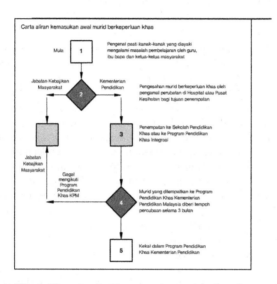

Fig. 1. The entry level process in special education

Remark

Process 1: The flow starts when the student is suspected to have learning problem by teachers, parents, or society leaders. Process 2: The student needs a disability approve letter from the doctors. Process 3: The student then is placed at Special Education School or enters the Special Education Integration Program. Process 4: Students who follow the Special Education Program will be tested in three months whether he will continued the program or not. Process 5: Students need to stay in special education program.

Our ESSE covered two out of five learning problem disabilities i.e. Autism and Dyslexia. Dyslexia and Autism is chosen among other type of learning problem because both of have higher number of children registered under the Malaysian Education Ministry. Syndrome Down was not chosen for this system because they can be categorized by recognition of faces and features.

1.2 Related Work

Research in the screening and diagnosis of learning disabilities in Autism and Dyslexia is growing. Research by [4] concluded that DSM-III-R (American Psychiatric Association, 1994) and DSM-IV (American Psychiatric Association, 1994), together with ICD-10 (World Health Organization, 1993), had achieved agreed standardized measures in Autism. The first of these was the autism diagnostic interview, developed with [3]. The Autism Diagnostic Observation Schedule (ADOS) [5] was developed to determine social and communicative interaction what sorts of spontaneous interactions were initiated by the child and what kind of responses were made to the overtures of the investigator. [6] described two United Kingdom (UK) screening tests for dyslexia: the Dyslexia Early Screening Test (DEST) and the Cognitive Profiling System (COPS 1). Both normed and designed to be administered by teachers to children four years and older. There is a study to compare visual perception between both people in dyslexia and autistic spectrum disorders. [8] conduct a comparison of form and motion coherence processing in Autistic and Dyslexia. All of the above systems employ clinical interview and observation by experienced psychologists to screen and diagnose Autism and Dyslexia. None was done to classify both groups if they were mixed in the classroom. The screening process is relatively difficult when involve new teachers who do not have enough experiences and skills.

2 Problem Statement

Special Education Department does not have a system to help new teachers who lack of experience and information to identify the learning problems among students. Teachers were given short briefings or a motivations before they started to teach special education students. Therefore, problems will appear when the teachers' especially new teachers who did not have any experience or expertise to categorize type of disability and failed to understand the learning problem symptoms and to decide which curriculums activities are suitable for their students. Hence, curriculums activities that have been outlined by Malaysian Educational Ministry cannot be affectively applied to the students.

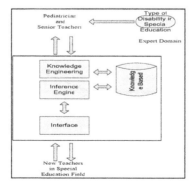

Fig. 2. The Scenario of Special Education System

The objectives of ESSE as follows:
Build an expert system for special education i.e. Autism and Dyslexia

1 To categorize type of disability for special education students which is under Malaysian Educational Ministry
2 To find out related symptoms based on Qualifiers triggered in the Expert System
3 To associate Autism and Dyslexia students with appropriate special education according to their needs.

The result from the expert system will help new teachers in special education field categorized their students according to their disability. Thus, the teachers can decide which type of learning method is suitable for the students.

3 Methodology

ESSE that we proposed is developed by using Incremental Expert System Prototyping Model. The strength of his model is that users are allowed to recognize changes that are needed in future enhancement based on information and knowledge added by expertise.

Knowledge based is a combination of facts and knowledge. The function of knowledge based is to connect the facts and knowledge. Facts consist of qualifier and choice. While knowledge is consist of rules. Rules is generated from combination of qualifier and choice through the IF and THEN statement. Please refer to Table 1.

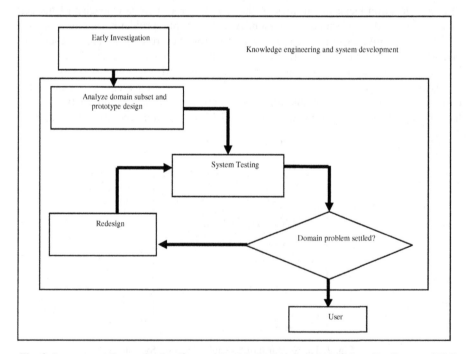

Fig. 3. Incremental Expert System Prototyping Methodology (Adapted from Darlington, 2000)

Table 1. A Part of Qualifiers and Choice for Autism and Dyslexia

<u>**List of Qualifier**</u>

AUTISME
1. Do the students always keep repeating words that heard literally?
2. Do the students prefer to pronounce a word repeatedly?
3. Do the students cannot give any meaning for some words with simple explanation?

DYSLEXIA
1. Do the students difficult to spell a simple word like in KBSR syllabus?
   Standard 1: shirt, mom, house, face
   Standard 2: event, like, baby, thirsty
   Standard 3: cage, bunch, brother, cold
2. Do the students spell words that have no correlation with the original word?
   Example:

Correct Alphabet	Student's Spelling
Flag	fleg
Same	sane
Bat	baj
Plate	pleat

<u>**Lists of Choices**</u>

AUTISME
1. Students always repeat the same words.
2. Students were slow in conversation and mastering the language skills.
3. Students have difficulties to orally express their feeling to others

DYSLEXIA
1. Students difficult to spell simple word and always spell word that have other meaning with the original word.
2. Students always do spelling mistakes and confused to differentiate an alphabet that has similar pronunciations in one syllable.

Rules List (Autism)
1. IF Do the students always keep repeating words that heard literally YES
   OR Do the students prefer to pronounce a word repeatedly YES
   THEN Students always repeat the same words.
2. IF Do the students cannot give the meaning for some words with a simple explanation YES
   OR Do the students cannot be able to sing a children's song itself after been taught YES
   OR Do the students not be able to tell exactly the daily experience of their selves to teachers and friends YES
   THEN Students were slow in conversation and mastering the language skills.

Rules List (Dyslexia)
1. IF Do the students difficult to spell a simple word like in KBSR syllabus
   OR Do the students spell words that have no correlation with the original word
   THEN Students difficult to spell simple word and always spell word that have other meaning with the original word.
2. IF Do the students always confused with arrangement of alphabet in a word YES
   OR Do the students always make mistake like insert or combine a syllable of a word reversely YES
   OR Do the student not able or confused on differentiating alphabets that sound exactly same in a syllable YES
   THEN Students always do spelling mistakes and confused to differentiate an alphabet that have similar pronunciations in one syllable.

4 ESSE System

ESSE System supports the clinical diagnostic features in learning disabilities. Screening activities are crucial to early diagnosis. The purpose of screening is to identify children appropriately for autism and dyslexia as soon as possible so that they can be rapidly referred for suitable learning modules and interventions [7]. As such, ESSE further to assist to automate the decision-making system, and classify both learning disabilities to different learning modules. Fig. 4 shows the display of ESSE interfaces.

A Cognitive Map [see Fig. 5] is developed to summarize the overall movement and progress of the system nodes. We implement the system using Macromedia MX, ASP, and MYSQL.

Table 2. Schedule of Functionality and Unit Testing

Criteria Tested	Expected Output	Result Output
Autism Information Module		
- Able to display Autism Information's interface	Interface of Autism's disabilities will be displayed when user clicks "Autism?" menu in the "Main Menu".	Successful
- Navigate to next page	Interface of Autism information can be linked to main menu when user clicks "Main Menu".	Successful
Dyslexia Information Module		
- Able to display Dyslexia Information's interface	Interface of Dyslexia's information disability will be displayed when user clicks "Dyslexia?" menu in the "Main Menu".	Successful
- Navigate to next page	Interface of Autism information can be linked to main menu when user clicks "Main Menu".	Successful
Question Module		
-Able to display question	Interface of Question appear when user clicks "Expert System" menu in the Main Menu.	Successful
- Able to go to next page	Interface of the 1st question's page can be linked to next question by clicking on "Next" button.	Successful
- Able to go to the next page	Interface of result can be linked to "Main Menu" when user clicks to the "Main Menu" button.	Successful
Result Module		
- Able to display result	Interface of displaying student which belongs to either group of Autism or Dyslexia.	Successful
- Able to go to the next page	Interface of result can be linked to the "Main Menu" if user clicks "Main Menu" button.	Successful

Fig. 4. Main Interface and Result Display Interface

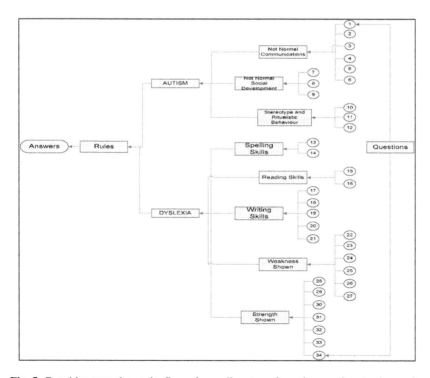

Fig. 5. Cognitive map shows the flow of overall system, from the questions to the result

Test of Unit and the Functionality. Modules of information are tested on its ability to display the interface to user while using the system. Page that display information are static.

5 Conclusion

This system helps new teachers to recognize and categorize two groups of learning problems. This system also gives extra information to user through information module of Autism and Dyslexia. With this, the objective to develop this system finally achieved by helping new teachers in Special Education in categorizing type of disability among Special Education that state under the responsibility of Ministry of Education, Malaysia.

Further development of the system include, enhance more categories for type of disabilities for Special Education such as Down Syndrome, Minimal Mental Disorder and Attention Deficit Hyperactive Disorder (ADHD). Besides, additional information module like methodology of treatment and suitable education are to be added in this expert system as for the user's reference. Meanwhile, the design of this system interface can also be improved to make it more attractive, for example; the integration of animation and audio to add commercial value to this system.

References

1. Jabatan Pendidikan Khas,
   http://apps2.emoe.gov.my/jpkhas/htm/web/profil_program.php
2. Darlington, K.: The Essence of Expert System. Prentice Hall, England (2000)
3. Le Couteur, A., Rutter, M., Lord, C., Rios, P., Robertson, S., Holdgrafer, M., McLennan, J.: Autism Diagnostic Interview: A standardized investigator-based instrument. Journal of Autism and Developmental Disorders 19, 363–387 (1989)
4. Rutter, M.: Autism Research: Lessons from the Past and Prospects for the Future. Journal of Autism and Developmental Disorders 35(2) (April 2005)
5. Lord, C., Rutter, M., Goode, S., Heemsbergen, J., Jordan, H., Mawhood, L., Schopler, E.: Autism Diagnostic Observation Schedule: A standardardized observation of communicative and social behaviour. Journal of Autism and Developmental Disorders 19, 185–212 (1989)
6. Fawcett, J., Singleton, C.H., Peer, L.: Advances in early years screening for dyslexia in the United Kingdom. Annals of Dyslexia 48(1) (December 1998)
7. Filipek, P.A., Accardo, P.J., Baranek, G.T., Cook, E.H., Dawson, G., Gordon, B., Gravel, J.S., Johnson, C.P., Kallen, R.J., Levy, S.E., Minshew, N.J., Prizant, B.M., Rapin, I., Rogers, S.J., Stone, W.L., Teplin, S., Tuchman, R.F., Volkmar, F.R.: The Screening and Diagnosis of Autistic Spectrum Disorders. Journal of Autism and Developmental Disorders 29(2) (December 1999)
8. Tsermentseli, S., O'Brien, J.M., Spencer, J.V.: Comparison of Form and Motion Coherence Processing in Autistic Spectrum Disorders and Dyslexia. Journal of Autism and Developmental Disorders 38(7) (August 2008)

Coimagination Method: Communication Support System with Collected Images and Its Evaluation via Memory Task

Mihoko Otake[1], Motoichiro Kato[2], Toshihisa Takagi[3,4], and Hajime Asama[1]

[1] Research into Artifacts, Center for Engineering The University of Tokyo,
5-1-5 Kashiwa-no-ha, Kashiwa-shi, Chiba 277-8568, Japan
[2] Department of Neuropsychiatry, School of Medicine, Keio University,
35 Shinanomachi, Shinjuku-ku, Tokyo 160-0016, Japan
[3] Database Center for Life Science, Research Organization
of Information and Systems, 2-11-16 Yayoi, Bunkyo-ku, Tokyo 113-0032, Japan
[4] Department of Frontier Science, The University of Tokyo,
5-1-5 Kashiwa-no-ha, Kashiwa-shi, Chiba 277-8568, Japan

Abstract. Prevention of dementia is a crucial issue in this aged society. We propose coimagination method for prevention of dementia through supporting interactive communication with images. Coimagination method aims to activate three cognitive functions: episode memory, division of attention, and planning function, which decline at mild cognitive impairment (MCI). Participants of the coimagination program bring images according to the theme and communicate with them. They share feeling rather than memory, which is a major difference between coimagination and reminiscence. They take memory task whether they remember the owner or theme of images after the series of sessions. We held coimagination program successfully at the welfare institution for elderly people in Kashiwa city, Japan. Each session was held one hour per week for five times. The result of the task indicates that the subjects showed empathy with each other. The effectiveness of the proposed method was validated through the experiment.

1 Introduction

The number of people suffering from dementia is expected to quadruple by the year 2050. Prevention and suppression of the progress of dementia are crucial issues in this century. More than eighty percent of patients with dementia are with Alzheimer's disease or cerebral vascular disease. Therefore, the major strategy for prevention of dementia is to reduce risk factors for these two diseases. There are two approaches for prevention of dementia. One is physiological approach and another is cognitive approach. Former approach includes dietary habits and physical activities. It is based on the fact that use of nonsteroidal anti-inflammatory drugs, wine consumption, coffee consumption, and regular physical activity were associated with a reduced risk of Alzheimer's disease[1].

C. Stephanidis (Ed.): Universal Access in HCI, Part I, HCII 2009, LNCS 5614, pp. 403–411, 2009.

Fig. 1. Subjects Surrounding the Image on the Screen during Coimagination Program

Latter approach includes intellectual activities and development of social network. There is an evidence that a long-term cognitive-motor intervention in cholinesterase inhibiter-treated early Alzheimer disease patients produced additional mood and cognitive benefits[2], and an extensive social network seems to protect against dementia[3]. The effectiveness and durability of the cognitive training interventions were validated in improving targeted cognitive abilities[4]. There is a hypothesis that activation of three cognitive functions which decline at mild cognitive impairment (MCI) is effective for prevention of dementia[5,6]. The cognitive functions include episode memory, division of attention, and planning function. Interactive communication activates above three functions. Reminiscence therapy is known as effective methods for the enhancement of psychological well-being in older adults[7]. However, its focus is not on activation of cognitive functions although it is based on communication. A replication of effectiveness studies of the well-defined protocols is warranted. This study proposes novel method with a measure, supporting interactive communication for activating three cognitive functions.

2   Coimagination Method

In this study, we propose coimagination method towards prevention of dementia through supporting interactive communication with images. The method is named after that we can share (co-) imagination through interactive communication with images. The basic concept of the method is listed below.

1. Communication is one of the typical intelectual activities. The method should support interactive communication so that three cognitive functions of subjects including episodic memory, division of attention, and planning function are activated as a whole.

2. Communication is a foundation for social network. The method should contribute to generate social network among the subjects through communication. Social network provides opportunity for sustainable communication among the subjects.
3. The method should have measures for effectiveness. It requires both long term and short term measures. Short term measure should evaluate whether the activities required three cognitive functions.

The first strategy comes from the fact that interactive communication requires division of attention to listening, understanding, estimating intentions, asking questions, making comments. If the allocated time is fixed, division of attention to keep time is also required. Planning function is required if the theme of the communication is determined beforehand. The subjects have to prepare topics of conversation according to the theme. We made rule to bring images according to the theme for communication so that both episodic memory and planning functions are activated. The subjects have to remember which images they have and to plan which images they bring.

In order to achieve second strategy, we extended theme of communication. Theme of communication of reminiscence has been past while theme of communication of coimagination is past, present, and future. The subjects bring feelings rather than memories, which is a major difference between the coimagination method and the reminiscence method, so that subjects who don't want to remember anything from the past can participate. For sustainable communication, forward-looking thinking towards future is better than backward-looking one towards past.

The third strategy is based on the fact that activation of cognitive functions leads to enhance the cognitive functions, although it takes time to alter cognitive functions. Activation of cognitive functions is measured by memory task. We make rule for subjects to take memory task in order to make clear whether communications themselves form episodic memory. Subjects guess the owner and the theme of the collected images after a series of communications. Division of attentions and episodic memories are assumed to be activated when the topics of surrounding subjects are remembered by each subject. In the same way, planning is successful when the topics of each subject are remembered by surrounding subjects.

To summarize, we define coimagination method and typical coimagination program as follows:

Definition 1. *Coimagination method supports interactive communication through bringing feelings with images according to the theme. Allocated time for each subject is predetermined. Subjects take turns so as to play both roles of speakers and listeners. The themes of communication are examined considering the effects for social networking. Cognitive activities which require episodic memory, division of attention, and planning are measured by memory task.*

Definition 2. *Typical coimagination program includes five series of sessions. Each session is held for an hour per week. Theme of each session is different.*

Average number of subjects is six. There are two rounds for each session. The first round is for brief speech, and the second round is for questions and answers. Average allocated time is five minutes for each subject and round during first four weeks. On the fifth week, the session for memory task is held. Images of the series of four sessions are displayed one after the other. Subjects guess the owner and the theme of the collected images.

3   Coimagination Support System

There are three requirements for coimagination support system.

1. The system dynamically displays the images corresponding to the stories of subjects.

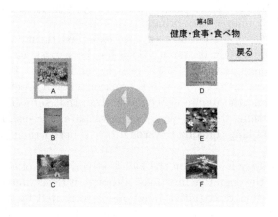

Fig. 2. Displayed Images for the Group of Subjects

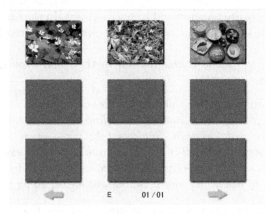

Fig. 3. Displayed Images for One Subject

Fig. 4. Enlarged Displayed Image of One Subject

Fig. 5. Displayed Image for Memory Task

2. Users of the system easily register the images. The registered images are accumulated for each subject.
3. Operations of the system are logged so as to be analyzed afterwards. Questions for the memory task are generated from the registered data for display.

We developed coimagination support system which meets the above requirements. The system consists of a laptop computer for the chair of the session, a projector for displaying the images, and a screen.

Before starting the session, the chair of the session scans pictures into the computer and registers them for each subject. Once the session starts, the chair selects the images of the speaker. The initial window is shown in Fig. 2. Images for the group of subjects are arranged according to the seating order. The number of subjects is six. Allotted time for each speaker is five minutes. When one subject is a speaker, other five subjects are listner. The chair of the session selects images considering the elapsed time. When subject E is a speaker, the chair clicks on the image of subject E of Fig. 2. The images brought by the subject E are displayed, which is shown in Fig. 3. The speaker selects the image to talk about, and ask the chair to click on the image to enlarge. The image is enlarged after the image in the center of Fig. 3 is clicked, which is shown in Fig. 4. The next speaker is subject F after five minutes has passed for subject E. Then, the chair operates the system so as to go back to the initial window, and clicks on the image of subject F of Fig. 2.

A number of images are collected after the series of four sessions in four weeks. On the fifth week, the fifth session for memory task is held. The window for memory task is shown in Fig. 5. It is operated by each subject rather than the chair of the session. The collected images are displayed one after the other. Subjects select the owner and the theme of the displayed image. The subject clicks on the "next" button after click on the buttons of the owner and the theme. Different images randomly appear until the all images are displayed. The scores of the memory task are recorded so as to be analyzed after the session.

4   Coimagination Programs at Welfare Institution

Coimagination programs for elderly people have been provided at welfare institution in Kashiwa city. In this section, we analyze two programs which were held for the first and the second time. Both programs include series of five sessions. Each session was held one hour per week. The last session provided memory task while other four were conversation sessions. The themes of each session are shown in Table 1. The theme of the first session was "favorite things", that of the second session was "work, purpose of life, and hobbies", that of the third session was "memorable or recommended places", and that of the fourth session was "health, dishes and foods". The last session was for memory task. Six normal subjects (3 men and 3 women; mean age= 74 years) for the first program and six normal subjects (3 men and 3 women; mean age= 70 years) participated in the second program. In total, twelve subjects participated in the two programs.

Table 1. Themes for Each Session

First Session	Favorite Things
Second Session	Work, Purpose of Life, and Hobbies
Third Session	Memorable or Recommended Places
Fourth Session	Health, Meals, and Foods
Fifth Session	Memory Task

5   Quantitative Evaluation of Coimagination Programs via Memory Task

Percentages of memorized images by self and others for each subject of the first and second coimagination programs are shown in Fig. 6 and 7. Numbers of

Table 2. Number of Images for the First Coimagination Program

Subjects	A	B	C	D	E	F	Total
First Session	1	2	4	5	1	6	18
Second Session	4	9	2	5	5	4	29
Third Session	3	4	6	3	2	5	23
Fourth Session	1	3	3	3	3	3	16
Total	9	18	15	16	11	17	86

Table 3. Number of Images for the Second Coimagination Program

Subjects	A	B	C	D	E	F	Total
First Session	4	3	3	3	6	4	23
Second Session	2	6	3	6	2	3	22
Third Session	5	5	7	4	7	1	29
Fourth Session	3	4	3	4	2	4	20
Total	14	18	16	17	17	12	94

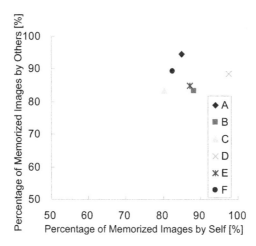

Fig. 6. Percentage of Memorized Images by Self and Others for Each Subjects of the First Coimagination Program

images in total were 86 for the first program and 94 for the second program. Numbers of images for each participants are shown in Table 2 and 3.

Horizontal axis shows the percentage of memorized images of other subjects by each subject. This indicates whether the subject listened carefully and remembered other subjects' stories with images. Episodic memory and division of attention functions are assumed to be activated if the percentage of memorized images of other subjects is high. Percentage of memorized images of other subjects was high for subject D of the first program in Fig. 6, and subject C of the second program in Fig. 7. They have good memories.

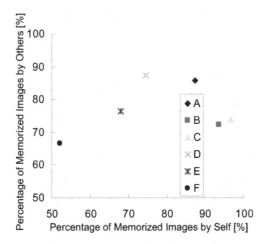

Fig. 7. Percentage of Memorized Images by Self and Others for Each Subjects of the Second Coimagination Program

Vertical axis shows the percentage of memorized images of each subject by other subjects. This indicates whether other subjects listened carefully and remembered the subject's stories. Planning of stories with images by each subject was successful when the percentage of memorized images by other subjects is high, although this depends on the efforts of other subjects. Percentage of memorized images by other subjects was high for subject A of the first program in Fig. 6, and subject D of the second program in Fig. 7. Their stories were memorable and attracted attentions of other subjects.

Overall, percentage of memorized images by both self and others were high. Interactive communications were achieved for both programs, so that cognitive functions including episodic memory, division of attentions and planning were supposed to be activated. The result indicates that the subjects showed empathy with each other. The effectiveness of the proposed method was validated through the experiment.

6   Conclusion

We have proposed coimagination method towards prevention of dementia through supporting interactive communication with images. Characteristics of the method are described as follows.

- Coimagination method supports interactive communication through bringing feelings with images according to the theme.
- Allocated time for each subject is predetermined. Subjects take turns so as to play both roles of speakers and listeners. The themes of communication are examined considering the effects for social networking.

– Cognitive activities which require episodic memory, division of attention, and planning are measured by memory task.

The method was validated through providing programs for elderly people at welfare institution in Kashiwa city. Percentage of memorized images by both self and others were high. The result indicates that the subjects showed empathy with each other. We succeeded in achieving interactive communication during the programs, so that cognitive functions were supposed to be activated. Future work includes evaluation of the method through direct measurement of the cognitive functions, change in size of social network, and longer follow-up to observe effects on everyday function.

Acknowledgements

This work was supported by a Grant-in-Aid for Scientific Research on priority area Systems Genomics (#014), Mobilligence (#454) and Information Explosion (#456) from the Ministry of Education, Culture, Sports, Science and Technology of Japan (MEXT).

References

1. Lindsay, J., Laurin, D., Verreault, R., et al.: Risk factors for alzheimer's disease: A prospective analysis from the canadian study of health and aging. American Journal of Epidemiology 156(5), 445–453 (2002)
2. Laurin, D., Verreault, R., Lindsay, J., et al.: Physical activity and risk of cognitive impairment and dementia in elderly persons. Archives of Neurology 58 (2001)
3. Fratiglioni, L., Wang, H.X., Ericsson, K., et al.: Influence of social network on occurrence of dementia: a community-based longitudinal study. Lancet 355 (2000)
4. Ball, K., Berch, D.B., Helmers, K.F., et al.: Effects of cognitive training interventions with older adults. Journal of American Medical Association 288(18), 2271–2281 (2002)
5. Rentz, D.M., Weintraub, S.: Neuropsychological detection of early probable alzheimer's disease. In: Scinto, L.F.M., Daffner, K.R. (eds.) Early Diagnosis and treatment of Alzheimer's disease, pp. 69–189. Humana Press, Totowa (2000)
6. Barberger-Gateau, P., Fabrigoule, C., Rouch, I., et al.: Neuropsychological correlates of self-reported performance in instrumental activities of daily living and prediction of dementia. Journal of Gerontology Series B: Psychological Sciences and Social Sciences 54(5), 293–303 (1999)
7. Bohlmeijer, E., Roemer, M., Cuijpers, P., et al.: The effects of reminiscence on psychological well-being in older adults: A meta-analysis. Aging and Mental Health 11(3), 291–300 (2007)

Intelligent Mobile Interaction: A Learning System for Mentally Disabled People (IMLIS)

Heidi Schelhowe and Saeed Zare

dimeb (Digital Media in Education)
Department of Mathematics and Informatics
University of Bremen, Germany
{schelhow,zare}@informatik.uni-bremen.de

Abstract. This paper describes the main ideas and the architecture of a system called Intelligent Mobile Learning Interaction system (IMLIS) that provides a mobile learning environment for mentally disabled people. The design of IMLIS is based on the idea to adjust its content, the kind of tasks and the mode of display to specific needs of individuals and to engage them for learning activities with new learning motivations due to IMLIS' dynamic structure and flexible patterns. We apply knowledge from the field of research and practice with mentally disabled people as well as pedagogical and didactical aspects in the design.

Keywords: Mobile Learning, Mobile Technology, Mentally Disabled People, Pedagogy, Learning Process, Interactive Learning Environments, Inclusive Design, Tacit Knowledge, Accessibility.

1 Introduction

Usage of mobile technology is growing and affects other technologies with new motivations and methods. At the same time, the difference between mobile phones and handheld computers is becoming less and less evident. Convergence offers the opportunity of learning anytime, anywhere. Kevin Walker (Institute of Education) [11] says: "Mobile learning is not something that people do; learning is what people do. With technology getting smaller, more personal, ubiquitous, and powerful, it better supports a mobile society. Mobile learning is not just about learning using portable devices, but learning across contexts."

There exist already some systems and projects which use mobile devices for e-learning. In other projects the adoption to the context of a real working situation is targeted. But there does not seem to be projects aiming at the exploitation of mobile learning environment for the needs of a person with mental disabilities.

The aim of our project is to develop a dynamic learning system, which provides customized learning material for people with mental disabilities based on their specific abilities. We want especially to recognize the factors that make limitations and influence the learning processes of mentally disabled people, in order to improve their learning opportunities. The objective of this paper is to show first results designing a mobile application for people with special needs (focusing on mentally disabled) highlighting active learning to arouse their motivation and to improve their learning results.

C. Stephanidis (Ed.): Universal Access in HCI, Part I, HCII 2009, LNCS 5614, pp. 412–421, 2009.

Chapters 2 and 3 provide the state-of-the-art knowledge about mentally disabled people and mobile learning. Chapter 4 provides the approach taken within our IMLIS system and in chapter 5 the architecture and customization method in IMLIS are discussed.

2 Mentally Disabled People

According to the World Health Organization (WHO) definitions, a disability is "any restriction or lack (resulting from any impairment) of ability to perform an activity in the manner or within the range considered normal for a human being"[15].

It is scientifically proven that a mental disability is an intellectual impairment [2]. It is called commonly cognitive disability [4] that points to the mental process of knowing. Most of these people have difficulties in thought processes (perception, awareness, reasoning, memory and judgment) and to gain new knowledge to be applied in daily work. Especially, transferring knowledge learned from the classroom to real life or workplace, a loss of parts of it has to be expected.

The target group of mentally disabled people can be classified based on the classification of the American Association on Mental Deficiency (AAMD). This classification is based on IQ testing, which shows the Intelligence Quotient, function performance of a person and the score, which someone gets on an IQ test. People with the average score between 70 and 85 are considered as slow learners, but not learning disabled, and people under 70 are called learning disabled [9]. The following table shows the classification.

Table 1. AAMD Classification for IQ categories [1&12] (table redesigned)

Levels of Mental Ability	Theoretical IQ	Stanford-Binet IQ	Our Target Group
Normal	85 - 115		
Borderline	70 - 85		
Mild	55 - 70	67 - 52	*
Moderate	40 - 55	51 - 36	*
Severe	25 - 40	35 - 20	*
Profound	< 25	< 20	

In our case, the preparation of learning material has to be different from group to group. Our target group ranges from mild to severe level.

3 Possible Benefits of Mobile Learning

3.1 General Aspects of Mobile Learning

Mobile learning can be seen as a bridge between practical exercises and theoretical knowledge. It can support several functions that enable orientation in context and space of a certain field or task. "A new m-learning architecture will support creation, brokerage, delivery and tracking of learning and information contents, using ambient intelligence, location-dependence, personalization, multi-media, instant messaging (text, video) and distributed databases" [8]. Six reasons why mobile learning might be motivating and fruitful for learners were suggested by Jones [11, 5] as following:

- Control (over goals)
- Ownership
- Fun
- Communication
- Learning-in-context
- Continuity between contexts

As mobile learning can be considered as self-paced learning, learners are able to control their learning process in relation to speed and content on their own. This can provide an easier way to reach our goals, although learning by current mobile technology is affected by many constraints that enforce us to limit our user interface design in specific cases. Mobile learning systems represent a variety of learning interactions in mobile environment and can be used for a dynamic learning context. It also enables to combine cooperation and exchange of advices with self-determined action in real live situation during solving a task. With mobile learning, waiting time can become more easily a learning time.

3.2 Considering Mobile Learning for Mentally Disabled People

According to the six points mentioned in 3.1, mobile learning can be considered as an appropriate solution for mentally disabled people. "The mentally disabled learn less through listening, writing down, reading and understanding than through watching and imitating, or having their movements physically guided by the teacher or trainer or steered through demonstration." [9] So mobile learning could help mentally disabled people to keep their physical movements, environment observations when at the same time learning trough mobile contexts instead of sitting at a desktop computer and learning isolated from the real situation where learning should be applied.

As a consequence of the special difficulties to transfer knowledge from the classroom to context, our approach fosters learning processes directly within the context of use (in real life with mobile devices). To ensure that the learner gets engaged with the learning material, he/she becomes part of the learning application. This should provide better memorization and recalling of work procedures.

Current technology provides mostly an opportunity for learners to control their learning process [6]. This option gives learners the chance to adopt themselves with the learning environment and learn at their own learning speed and favorable way. But in the learning process for mentally disabled people this option should be changed and limited: they should be guided by the program towards the learning steps and exercises, but not in respect to learning speed. In other words, they need a flexible learning speed but a fixed structure.

"Psychic (mental) processes like sensation, perception, representation, thinking and imagination are fundamentals for the learning ability. The efficiency of learning activities depends on the specific features of these mental processes and functions, which are part of the complex structure of the personality of each pupil." [13]

Chen [3] points to the following principles of pedagogy, which should be considered in a learning process:

- Urgency of learning need
- Initiative of knowledge acquisition
- Mobility of learning setting
- Interactivity of learning process
- Situatedness of instructional activities
- Integration of instructional content

From the principles mentioned, the last three are immensely important for learning processes of mentally disabled people. As we discussed with experts in our workshops, the learning process for mentally disabled does not mean too slow learning, but mainly presenting the learning material in a way which is understandable for learners; although it might be presented slow in special points.

4 The IMLIS Approach

In our project, we considered the idea of mobile computing as a learning context, which is embedded in everyday working environments for mentally disabled people. The integration of working and learning in one and the same process is supposed to support the acquisition and revelation of tacit knowledge [10] that seems to play a crucial role in this context. We are in the process of developing a system called IMLIS. The main ideas and how we developed these in a cooperative process with the target group itself are described in the following.

IMLIS firstly analyzes and identifies specific requirements, constraints and conditions of the person through interaction. Commonly, they have delay in their physical, cognitive and social activities and have less stamina than normal people. They should be able to associate perception with concepts and contents. Hence, dividing the learning activities and interactions into smaller, controllable and manageable workload, repetition of learning material in a period of time, using an easy language and preparing more visualized material facilitate the learning process for these people.

Martinshof (Est. 1953) [7] is one of the largest sheltered workshops for people with mental disabilities and is located in Bremen, Germany. Martinshof trains the mentally disabled individually in various activities and adapts the workplace according to the disability of the workers instead of assigning people to the workplace. Due to our cooperation with Martinshof over the past two years, they supported us in different activities.

Between April 2008 and January 2009 we accomplished different workshops (every workshop with 4 to 8 participants, 15–40 years old) in cooperation with Martinshof and a school for people with special needs. The first workshops focused on the role of digital media in their everyday life. We wanted to understand their first impression and how they use and what they know about mobile devices. Later with the workshops, we tried to ask them about their learning activities and how they get adapted to new technologies. We presented them different quizzes on mobile devices and asked them to try out the quizzes. In the last workshops we confronted them with different mobile phones to get feedbacks on their interaction with mobile devices.

We recognized that nearly all knew something about mobile devices. Most of them have seen advertisements and knew pretty much about device brands. For them a mobile device symbolizes the world to get connected to. A lot of them had a private cell phone and they knew how to use them. In most cases they need a mobile to organize help if needed or to get useful information. Some could work with other functions of cell phones like SMS or using the camera.

The small quizzes were not complicated for most of them, in contrary, they liked to take the quiz, although some of them had to do the quiz several times in order to understand how it works. In some cases, we could give enough attention to the groups, which had difficulties to get success in the quiz. Easily they learned to use the simple functions of new mobiles, and they helped each other to use the mobiles in the proper way. They told that they learned to use many functions of their private cell phones by using and observing how others to it or by trying in groups.

Based on the principles mentioned above and our experiences in different workshops with samples of our target group, we studied their special learning behaviours and distinguished the following four parameters:

Attention: This parameter is the absorption of information in a learning process. The lack of attention is regarded as a huge problem with mentally disabled; they can often hardly aim their attention to the important parts of a task and can be easily disturbed and distracted from what they are doing. In our approach, we tried to recognize the times, which the learner is distracted, and try to invite the learner again towards the learning process.

Recall: It refers to a call for stored information to bring it back to mind. The percentage of this factor is too much different with mentally disabled. The improvement of this factor can be defined somehow as a success in a learning process.

Memory: Mentally disabled have always problems in reproducing information. It is not the problem to save the information, but to reach the information. The process should contain an imperative and structured workload.

Speech: Experts proved that it gets easier to keep something in mind when you can name it [14]. In our system, we tried to design the learning process in a way that requests from the learner to name or repeat the objects and events in different periods of time.

Due to our observations, mentally disabled people who attended in our tests in different workshops, play once a week a memory game at school that trains their ability of recall, memory and communication. Their teachers and advisers emphasized the importance of encouragement, which seems to be immensely important for those who have problems in learning. According to our experiences during the tests, mentally disabled people often get disappointed and exhausted because of their limitations in reaching their goals. The learning program should be so designed that motivates them to go forward and not to give up in middle way. Every small mistake should be corrected with an appropriate feedback (usually positive and in a motivating way) and every favorable outcome and success should be appreciated by the system. In many cases a small effort or advance should be considered as a success.

5 IMLIS – The System

5.1 Organizing Learning Content

Generally in mobile learning scenarios, as other learning solutions, one of the most important parts is the learning content. It is presented in a context and might influence different feedbacks and interactions of the learner based on system behaviour. Learning content is extremely sensible and important for mentally disabled people.

Our system provides different outputs according to the user, which is due to his disability, the history of usage, and the suitable learning method. For example, if the learner has slow reaction time, the time for the presentation of the learning material in the output is affected by this factor. On the other hand, the feedback at the end of the learning process and applying the results for the next decisions will also influence the process. This is like in traditional learning when teachers get familiar with students' backgrounds after several sessions and will interact with them according to their abilities. IMLIS tries to cover such kind of issues dynamically according to the level of weakness and cognitive disabilities.

When inserting learning material in our system, the learning assets are assigned with special pedagogical metadata by the author according to specific questions. This metadata shows how, where and when a specific learning asset can be used.

In order to cover the pedagogical aspects, we have tried to apply the following aspects for the learning material, based on World Health Organization (WHO) classification, expert's advises and our experiences in different workshops.

- Urgency of learning need
- Using supportive learning behaviors
- Using stress and attention on special words and phrases
- Using clear, easy comprehensible and self adaptive interactions
- Categorizing of interactions based on disability
- Using simple animation guides based on the environment
- Audio integration (clear and distinct) for all material
- Using direct, accurate and unique names for terms, avoiding abstract naming if possible
- Using gestures (e.g. sympathy's avatar)
- Avoid subjunctive sentences and using more indicative, concise and simple language
- Applying invisible checkpoints to control user concentration and attention

5.2 Architecture

The IMILS concept is based on an idea that emphasises a dynamic structure for learning contents instead of a fixed structure. By adapting to mentally disabled learners and their special abilities, the system should be able to prepare an appropriate profile or model for the learners, which can actuate the way for an adapted-learning process in presenting and memorizing the learning material. The system architecture consists of two parts, a mobile client and a server. The client is a mobile device, which is connected via a wireless protocol to the server, and the server is a standalone device that feeds the client with appropriate learning materials.

To support the mentioned description and cover all the requirements of the user, the following architecture is designed.

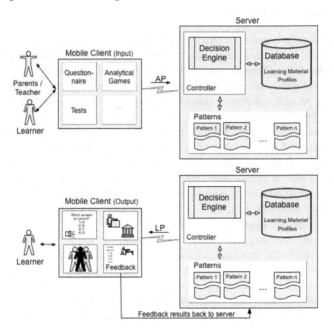

Fig. 1. IMLIS client-server based architecture

As it is shown in figure 1, a user's request is captured by the system and the analytical material will be sent from the server to the client for analysis and profile creation. This profile registration is just for one time at the beginning of the usage. The learner is asked to answer the questions, or play analytical games (if necessary assisted by a teacher or parents) that are provided by the program. The information gathered during this interaction is recorded and classified automatically according to a categorizing system based on the World Health Organization (WHO) standards (International Classification of Functioning or International Classification of Diseases-10). Additionally a profile key is generated and sent to the server as an "Analytical Package" (called AP).

The server receives the AP from the client and starts to analyze the package according to the predefined algorithms and definitions. A decision engine decides - according to the AP information and criteria - about the learning material and didactically appropriate format for this particular category of learner that is specified, and available in the database in order to present a coherent package related to the analysis. A "Learning Package" (called LP) will be composed and sent to the mobile client. The mobile client receives the LP and presents the learning material to the learner.

At the end of the learning process, a feedback test will be offered to the learner to verify the performance of the process. The result of this feedback will be synchronized at the same time with the server to update the profile key and to be applied for the next decision on the same (type of) user.

A web-based administration portal provides access via a normal web browser for data entry and editing of learning materials.

5.3 Customization and Decision Engine

As mentioned in section 5.1, every learning asset is assigned to a key with identifiable tags, priority flags and pedagogical metadata. These metadata should be defined by data entry of learning assets based on parameters, which are available in analytical information and shows the criteria of usage for the specific learning asset. In this system, "Decision Engine" decides about the output-learning package based on the analytical information, which is collected in profile registration. The analytical information appears as an identifiable profile key for decision engine.

Table 2. Sample profile and learning assets keys, used in IMLIS for decision engine

Key for profile ID: 374	45	0.75	36	74	95	0	1	1

Learning Assets (LA)	C1: IQ	C2: RT	C3: MA	C4: PS	C5: PA	C6: AA	C7: VA	C8: RA
LA1: intro.jpeg	40-55	0.25-1	20-50	35-85	10-99	Void	1	Void
LA2: main.txt	25-40	0.15-1	20-40	30-80	50-99	Void	1	1
LA3: movie.avi	40-55	Void	20-90	30-80	Void	1	1	Void
.	.	.	.	.	.	.	.	.
.	.	.	.	.	.	.	.	.
LAn	...	...	...	...	...	...	...	...

Sample criteria (C) used in IMLIS. IQ. Intelligence Quotient, **RT**: Reaction Time, **MA**: Memory Ability, **PS**: Problem Solving, **PA.** Physical Abilities, **AA**: Audio Ability, **VA**: Visual Ability and **RA**: Reading Ability

For preparing a learning package, decision engine compares the profile key with the learning assets keys according to available search algorithms and selects some of learning assets. The selected assets at this stage should be reviewed based on user history table. The remaining assets should be sorted by priority and appropriate category, lesson and page. The final selected assets in this phase will be integrated to the adaptive patterns to be packaged as a learning package (LP) and sending to the client.

The received learning package will be presented in mobile client for learning process. The profile key also can be updated (in some cases) based on the result of feedbacks.

6   Conclusion and Future Work

Our system can take the role of a flexible companion that is embedded in daily live of a person with special needs. As a kind of tutor it guides the learning experiences of the person. By an embedded situated help system, the users should get encouraged to face new tasks with higher degree of complexity. Prospectively, this virtual supported reliability could foster their autonomy and independence from advisers. The development consists on several iterative steps evaluated with tests. In the relevant step of basic system, database with decision engine connected to templates, patterns and the learning data are designed and mobile client is built. By a first range of learning materials the process of evaluation started. The evaluation is designed in order to foster autonomous and self-confidently work accesses in the sheltered workshop. One main focus of the evaluation is in which way the system adapts to the needs of users, the functionalities and the usability.

Often one learner can handle a certain problem unexpectedly fast and can become an expert that helps the other colleagues to accomplish the goals as well. This person might create a visual or audio-visual help-description of his accomplished task. The communicative functionalities and social self-determined mobile activities will be a challenge for future. Thus the target group might form communities that can explore their world together.

Acknowledgments. We would like to thank Michael Lund, Dennis Krannich and Yuriy Yepifanov for their valuable comments and advises. Also special thanks to Digital Media in Education group at University of Bremen and sheltered workshops Martinshof for their support.

References

1. American Association on Intellectual and Developmental Disabilities (AAIDD) & American Association on Mental Retardation (AAMR), http://www.aamr.org
2. Barbotte, E., Guillemin, F., Chau, N.: The Lorhandicap Group: Bulletin of the World Health Organization (WHO): Prevalence of impairments, disabilities, handicaps and quality of life in the general population: a review of recent literature. Genebra 79(11) (2001) ISSN 0042-9686
3. Chen, Y.S., Kao, T.C., Sheu, J.P., Chang, C.Y.: A Mobile Scaffolding-Aid-Based Bird-Watching Learning system. In: Milrad, M., Hoppe, H.U., Kinshuk (eds.) IEEE International Workshop on Wireless and Mobile Technologies in Education, pp. 152–156. IEEE Computer Society, Los Alimatos (2002)
4. Clark, J.: How Do Disabled People Use Computers. In: Building Accessible Websites (2002) ISBN 0-7357-1150-X
5. Jones, A., Issroff, K., Scanlon, E., Clough, G., McAndrew, P.: Using mobile devices for learning in Informal Settings: Is it Motivating? In: Paper to be presented at IADIS International conference Mobile Learning, Dublin, July 14-16 (2006)
6. Laurillard, D.: Rethinking University Teaching: a conversational framework for the effective use of learning technologies, 2nd edn. Routledge Falmer, London (2002)
7. Martinshof, Werkstaetten fuer Menschen mit Behinderungen, http://www.martinshof-bremen.de
8. Mobilearn, Worldwide European-led research and development project, http://www.mobilearn.org
9. Pitsch, H.J.: How does a trainer working with the mentally disabled differ from any other teacher or trainer?: Agora XII. Training for mentally disabled people and their trainers. In: Permitting the mentally disabled a genuine and appropriate exercise of their rights. Cedefop Hrsg.: Thessaloniki, July 5-6, pp. 127–140. Office for Official Publications of the European Communities, Luxembourg (2003)

10. Polanyi, M.: The Tacit Dimension. First published Doubleday & Co. (1966); Reprinted Mass.: Peter S. (1983)
11. Sharples, M., Walker, K., et al.: Big Issues in Mobile Learning: Report of a workshop by the Kaleidoscope Network of Excellence Mobile Learning Initiative. The Learning Sciences Research Institute. University of Nottingham (2007)
12. Speck, O.: Menschen mit geistiger Behinderung und ihre Erziehung: ein heilpaedagogisches Lehrbuch, 7th edn. Ernst Reinhardt, Munich (1993)
13. Suta, V., Suta, L., Vasile, M.: Study on the ICT Application in the Didactical Activity of Children with Mental Deficiency - ICT. In: Education: Reflections and Perspectives - FISTE - A Future Way for In-Service Teacher Training Across Europe (2007)
14. Wendeler, J.: Geistige Behinderung: Paedagogische und psychologische Aufgaben Weinheim. BELZ Gruene Reihe, Basel (1993)
15. World Health Organization (WHO), Publications and Documents,
    http://www.who.int

Studying Point-Select-Drag Interaction Techniques for Older People with Cognitive Impairment

Nadine Vigouroux[2], Pierre Rumeau[1], Frédéric Vella[1,2], and Bruno Vellas[1]

[1] Laboratoire de Gérontechnologie La Grave CHU Toulouse / Inserm U 558 / Gérontopôle,
37 Allées Jules Guesde, 31073 Toulouse Cedex
[2] Institut de Recherche en informatique de Toulouse, Université Paul Sabatier, 118 Route de
Narbonne, 31062 Toulouse cedex 9, France
{vigourou,vella}@irit.fr,
{rumeau.p,vella.f,vellas.b}@chu-toulouse.fr

Abstract. Graphical user interfaces and interactions that involve pointing to items and dragging them are becoming more common in rehabilitation and assistive technologies. We are currently investigating interaction techniques to understand point-select-drag interactions for older people with cognitive impairment. In particular, this study reports how older perform such tasks. Significant differences in behavior between all of the interaction techniques are observed and the reasons for these differences are discussed according the cognitive impairment.

Keywords: Cognitive impairment, older people, interaction technique, task duration, Alzheimer disease.

1 Introduction

Introducing Information Communication Technology (ICT) for aging population raises promises and challenges. The challenges are the accessibility of ICT even if there are physical, emotional and cognitive barriers that may inhibit use of the technologies. For example, computer's using may raise physical and cognitive demands depending on the interaction devices and/or the input/output interaction [11].

Improved pointing techniques selection has been the subject of many studies in the mainstream human-computer interaction (HCI) community, where the techniques may also be applied in the interfaces to assistive systems. One of the key challenges in developing assistive and rehabilitation systems for older people is finding some easy and effective means of interaction. However, there is some research into the design of novel interaction and in the behavior understanding.

[3] and [4] reported studies on age-related differences in movement control. [5] and [6] discussed the use and the investigating of novel point-select techniques for older people. [1] examined the influence of age related changes in the component skills required to use a mouse, specifically processing speed, visuo-spatial abilities and motor coordination. They defined slip errors as events when the cursor left the target without completing the task (either clicking or double clicking on the target). These errors proved to be a major source of age-related differences in movement time and distance travelled. The hypothesis was motor co-ordination.

C. Stephanidis (Ed.): Universal Access in HCI, Part I, HCII 2009, LNCS 5614, pp. 422–428, 2009.
© Springer-Verlag Berlin Heidelberg 2009

[2] also shown movement time as an result age-related linked to cognition; in fact older people tend to take longer time to process incoming information and typically require more time to respond. Then [77] reported twenty-one difficulties with mouse use like losing the cursor, running out of the application window, or the mouse click getting stuck.

A major point from this literature is that older subjects take longer to realize selections, and require a greater proportion of time and a higher number of corrective movements to reach the targets with the same level of accuracy as younger subjects. So, compared with younger users, older subjects can have greater difficulty to perform the aiming, clicking, and movements required to point-select-drag interactions.

Based on the researches reported above, this paper investigates how older people with cognitive impairment respond to Point-Select-Drag interaction techniques. This ongoing study presents our experiment and aims to provide an understanding of how the performance of older people with cognitive impairment is affected by three interaction techniques to move an item to another item. Actually this knowledge could be useful toward the design of adequate computer interaction that could be used in the development of cognitive rehabilitation systems.

This paper describes the methods that will be used in upcoming experiments on three interaction techniques to point and drag virtual items on a screen. Then, we report the significant differences in task duration observed according the cognitive impairment.

2   Experimental Design

This experiment studies three interaction techniques to select and to move an item to another one with a mouse. The aims of this experiment are to:

- Analyse performance differences between older subjects without cognitive impairment and with cognitive impairment;
- Identify and analyse factors that can explain any preference or better efficiency observed between these interaction classes.

Fig. 1. Exercise view

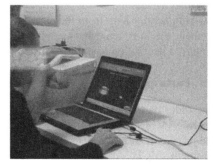

Fig. 2. A subject doing the exercise

The experiments were conducted on a Satellite Pro A200Toshiba laptop with a 15 inch widescreen, 1024*768 TFT display. An optical computer mouse was used as an input device. The right button was deactivated. The mouse was selected to be representative of an input device that would be typical for personal use. A hand cursor was preferred as a good metaphor.

2.1 Task

Study participants (Figure 2) have been asked to perform some serial pointing and moving tasks (Figure 1). They have been asked to select the item (the piece of sugar) and to put it in the coffee. Three interaction techniques have been defined:

- The *clicking* interaction (CL): The subject selects the sugar by clicking it, moves the cursor to the coffee cup top, and clicks the area of coffee ; then the piece of sugar is falling down;
- The *dragging* interaction (DR): This technique corresponds to the usual *drag and drop*. The subject selects the sugar by clicking it, maintains the pressure on the mouse button until the cursor is over the cup of the coffee, then the sugar is falling down;
- The *clicking and magnetization* interaction (CAM): The subject selects the sugar by clicking it, then the sugar is automatically attached to the cursor; secondly the subject is asked to move the cursor without pressure over the cup of the coffee, then the sugar is falling down.

A sound feedback is playing to inform that the sugar is taken by hands during the clicking action. A splash sound is playing when the piece of the sugar is over the coffee.

2.2 Method

Participant sessions involved a set of training and test computer sessions using a program recording cursor movement, and a semi-structured questionnaire. The training phase consisted in: firstly, describing the run of the mouse (moving and clicking principles), secondly doing the exercise with each interaction technique. We have considered that the technique was mastered when the subject was capable of using it without any comment or help from the experimenter. The questionnaire was designed to complement the movement behaviour and to address issues such as computer expertise, preferred interaction technique, difficulties of computer use, etc.

2.3 Participants

The older participants were recruited at Toulouse geriatric hospital. A Mini Mental Scoring (MMS) examination was made by an expert doctor in Alzheimer disease. Subjects were regrouped in three cognitive impairment groups: Mild cognitive impairment (MCI), Alzheimer's disease (AD), control (C) without cognitive problem. The subjects never used a computer before the experiment.

Table 1. Participants characteristic

N°	MMS	Gender	Age	Pathology simplified	Preferred model	Best efficient mode
1	26	F	65	MCI	1	3
2	25	F	76	MCI	1	1
3	14	M	82	Alzheimer's disease	3	3
4	15	F	71	Alzheimer's disease	3	3
5	27	F	74	MCI	1	2
6	12	M	73	Alzheimer's disease	3	3
7	26	F	67	MCI	1	3
8	20	M	89	Alzheimer's disease	4	3
9	-	M	81	Control	4	3
10	-	M	74	Control	2	1
11	-	M	83	Control	3	2
12	10	W	81	Frontal temporal dementia	0	-
13	15	W	75	Alzheimer's disease	0	-
14	7	M	69	Alzheimer's disease	0	-
15	8	W	88	Alzheimer's disease	0	-

3   Results and Discussions

From the empirical observations, we identify several difficulties with mouse, such as:

- Keeping the mouse steady when moving;
- Losing the cursor out of the exercise map;
- Bad control in moving in the adequate direction;
- Running out of the room on the mouse cursor
- And the mouse cursor getting stuck.

This study proves that, for low MMS (<10), the subject does not remember the instructions (Table 1). The results for CAM technique and the CL one are equivalent concerning points (four occurrences).

The CAM interaction is well appreciated because the technique represents well the natural actions (taking and moving). It is a good metaphor. The DR was rejected by subjects because it requests too much workload: this fact can be explained because two simultaneous processes (moving and pressure) are involved in the task.

When the subject was falling in one of the part of exercise (clicking or moving with or without pressure), he/she developed two main behaviours: one is asking help (for instance, can you show me, can you explain me, what do must do now?), another is doing with hand as he/she would have done in a real world.

Although the number of participants was too small to allow statistical analysis it is worth noting the difficulty in doing the task.

One major significant (Figure 3) result is that the duration factor is significantly different for the three interaction techniques: the DR duration is much longer than this CAM one (for MCI, -40s towards 17,8s- and for DA -43 s towards 12,9s- user groups. CAM duration (Figure 6), around 20 seconds per action, is stable for all patients. This result is independent of the age.

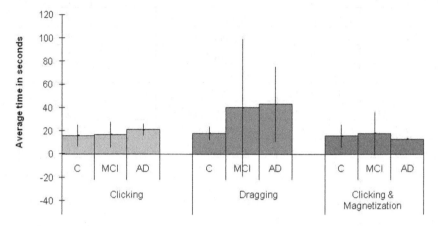

Fig. 3. Average Time for the 3 interactions techniques according to the cognitive impairment

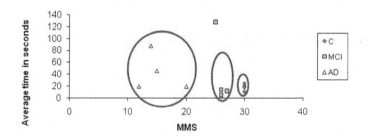

Fig. 4. Average time in seconds for the *clicking* interaction

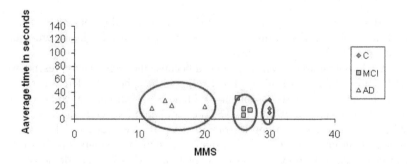

Fig. 5. Average time in seconds for the *dragging* interaction

Another important result is that the duration increase is correlated to the decrease of the Mini Mental Score (MMS) for DR ((Figure 5).We observe also large behaviour variability for a MMS comprised between 15 and 20.

CL ((Figure 4) duration is also dependant of the MMS (the more MMS is low, the more duration is long).

From the empirical observations, we identify several difficulties with mouse, such as losing the cursor and bad control in moving with DR.

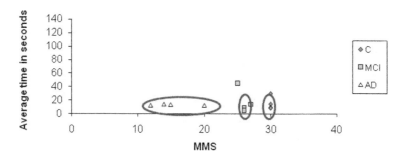

Fig. 6. Average time in seconds for the clicking and *magnetization* interaction

4   Conclusion and Future Works

The population of older people is a rapidly-growing group of users of assistive and rehabilitation technologies. As such, the development of interfaces that are usable by older people is of high importance. While a number of novel pointing techniques have been assessed in the HCI literature, the activity of older users remains to be investigated. We have described an ongoing research which aims to provide a fundamental understanding of how older subjects with and without cognitive disabilities react to interaction techniques by pointing. This point is vital in particular to design interactive rehabilitation system based on suitable interaction techniques for older adults with cognitive impairment.

This paper has focused on presenting the experiment experiments on point-select-drag interactions. One of the most important point is that the pointing interaction technique has an important impact on the cognitive activity of the subject. We plan to analyse the number of clicks missed and those of target re-entry to select the object. The aim is to differentiate between the point-and-click behaviour of able-bodied users and users with quite severe motion impairments, as already done by Mackenzie et al. [99].

Acknowledgement

We thank the patients and caregivers of the Department of Geriatric Medicine of the Toulouse University Hospital, Gerontopole, who accepted to take part in trying the interfaces and the staff who introduced us to them. This research is partially funded by ANR TECSAN as part of TANDEM project.

References

1. Smith, M., Sharit, J., Czaja, S.: Aging motor control, and the performance of computer mouse tasks. Human Factors 41(3), 389–396 (1999)
2. Czaja, S.J., Lee, C.C.: Designing computer system for older adults. In: Jacko, J., Sears, A. (eds.) Handbook of Human-Computer Interaction, pp. 413–428. Lawrence Erlbaum and Associates, New York (2003)
3. Walker, N., Philbin, A., Fisk, A.D.: Age-related differences in movement control: Adjusting submovement structure to optimize performance. Journal of Gerontology: Psychological Sciences 52B(1), 40–52 (1997)
4. Ktecham, C.J., Seidler, R.D., Van Gemmert, A.W., Stelmach: Age-related kinematic differences as influenced by task difficulty, target size and movement amplitude. Journal of Gerontology: Psychological Sciences 57B(1), 54–64 (2002)
5. Wood, E., Willoughby, T., Rushing, A., Bechtel, L., Gilbert, J.: Use of Computers Input Devices by Older Adults. The Journal of Applied gerontology 24(5), 419–438 (2005)
6. Williams, N., Hwang, F.: Investigating Novel Point-Select techniques for Older People. In: Proceedings of the 2007 IEEE 10th International Conference on Rehabilitation Robotics, Noordwjk, The Netherlands, pp. 614–618 (2007)
7. Paradise, J., Trewin, S., Keates, S.: Using pointing devices: difficulties encountered and strategies employed. In: Proceedings of 3rd International Conference on Universal Access and Human-Computer Interaction (UAHCI) (2005)
8. Worden, A., Walker, N., Bharat, K., Hudson, S.: Making computers easier for older adults to use: Area cursors and sticky icons. In: Proceedings of CHI 1997, Atlanta, GA, USA, pp. 266–271. ACM Press, New York (1997)
9. MacKenzie, I.S., Kauppinen, T., Silfverberg, M.: Accuracy measures for evaluating computer pointing devices. In: Proceedings of CHI 2001, pp. 9–15 (2001)

Remote Reminiscence Talking and Scheduling Prompter for Individuals with Dementia Using Video Phone

Kiyoshi Yasuda[1,2], Noriaki Kuwahara[2], and Kazunari Morimoto[2]

[1] Rehabilitaiton department of Chiba Rosai Hospital, 2-16, Tatsumidai-Higashi,
Ichiharashi, 290-0003, Japan
fwkk5911@mb.infoweb.ne.jp
[2] Kyoto Institute of Techonology, Matsugasaki, Sakyouku, 606-8585, Japan
{nkuwahar,morix}@kit.ac.jp

Abstract. Caring for individuals with dementia is very difficult and frustrating task, especially for home caregivers. We have created two remote assisting systems, the remote reminiscence talking and scheduling prompter using video phone, and used them with four individuals with dementia living in their homes. For two out of four individuals, reminiscence talking and scheduling prompter are effective respectably, compared to TV watching and care giver's instructions. The psychological stability of one individual has continued for three hours even after the remote reminiscence talking finished. We suggest that remote reminiscence talking and scheduling prompter are very promising for caring individuals with dementia, although further revisions are required.

Keywords: Remote, reminiscence, scheduling, dementia, video phone.

1 Introduction

The onset of dementia usually starts with mild anterograde amnesia and proceeds to develop a variety of behavioral disturbances such as wandering, agitation, illusions, and incontinence [1]. These behavioral disturbances arise from inactivity, discomfort, and a need for social contact [2]. Since individuals with dementia and their caregivers bear a heavy burden, they urgently need rest time [3]. To reduce their stress, various interventions have been introduced, such as memory training, music therapy, validation therapy, and behavioral therapy, as well as pharmacotherapy [4].

1.1 Reminiscence Video

Reminiscence therapy is reported to stabilize individuals with dementia and to help reduce behavioral disturbances [4]. Despite its effectiveness, reminiscence therapy is difficult to perform at home. This is because a reminiscence therapy session is usually conducted in a group led by experienced staff at institutions, using various items such as old tools, toys, photos, and paintings. Therefore, we have explored the personal reminiscence photo videos [5].

This photo video is a kind of slideshow produced from their personal photos. The video includes background music, comfortable narration to make the video more

C. Stephanidis (Ed.): Universal Access in HCI, Part I, HCII 2009, LNCS 5614, pp. 429–438, 2009.
© Springer-Verlag Berlin Heidelberg 2009

engaging, and panning/zooming effects to the regions which the individual with dementia is interested in. Through our experiments, family caregivers were very pleased that individuals' utterances increased when they watched this reminiscence video [5]. Since creating such personal reminiscence photo videos requires much labour, we have introduced a simple way to make the videos by connecting a digital video camera to a TV set with an integrated VCR function. With this system, the photo video can be made on the spot without any editing time and labor [6]. We also explored an half automatic authoring tool for easily producing by simply choosing the set of photos [7].

1.2 Networked Interaction Therapy for Memory-Impaired and Dementia Individuals

Recently, the use of computer-based intervention is also being explored for individuals with dementia [8]. We are currently proposing *a networked interaction therapy,* intended to provide various types of communicative intervention such as talking on video phones, providing appropriate contents, and managing daily-life scheduling through a TV monitor [9]. This system uses a set-top box with a camera and microphone for monitoring the user's status and controls various types of intervention. If these forms of intervention can increase individuals' quality of life and reduce behavioral disturbances, caregivers will be able to gains some respite while individuals with dementia are engaged in the networked interaction therapy.

1.3 Experiment for Face to Face Talking and Video Phone Talking

Communication, especially verbal conversation, is an easy, common, and enjoyable activity for most of us. Individuals with dementia, however, tend to be alone and poorly informed, with few chances to talk. One of the most important interventions in the networked interaction therapy is to provide them with talking partners on the Internet, such as friends, partners, and family members living in remote locations. A simple interface would thus enable individuals with dementia to talk with partners on the video phone whenever they want [9].

However, there were no studies on how long and how eagerly individuals with dementia could talk with a partner on the video phone, in comparison with the face to face settings. Yasuda et al. have conducted an experiment in which nine individuals with dementia talked with a partner on a video phone and in a face-to-face session [10]. The individuals were requested to reply to 20 questions asked by a partner. The results revealed that there was no difference in the total response time and in the eagerness observed between the two sessions. This suggested that the video phone talking could potentially have the same effects as face-to-face talking.

2   Two Remote Assisting Systems

2.1   Remote Reminiscence Talking System

The researches discussed so far suggest that the combination of video phone and reminiscence interventions would be effective for psychological stability. Kuwahara et al.

[11] created a system to incorporate video phone and reminiscence photo sharing. In this system, the start of intervention is triggered by operation of a remote partner. The size of the photos on the monitor is manipulated by the partner. The part of photos pointed by an individual or partner is also shown as a red small circle in the same picture on both monitors. Kuwahara et al [11] conducted an experiment on effectiveness of this system in an institution for elderly residents. A satisfactory result was gained from individuals with severe dementia.

2.2 Scheduling Prompter System

Recently, we have also developed the scheduling prompter system. This system is to deliver individuals video contents for prompting the individual's willingness to keep the schedule, such as medicine dosing, hospital visits, and so on.

Figure 1 illustrates an overview of the scheduling prompter system. Our system is implemented via a server on the Internet. An individual or caregiver can ask a volunteer to input their schedule time if she/he is having difficulty in operating their PC. After the volunteer inputs the schedule time (① in Fig. 1), the server delivers the video content in which a memory clinic therapist explains and encourages to perform a scheduled task on the individual's PC (②). We have prepared more than ten kinds of video contents, including dosing, meals, bathing, and so on. The length of video content was about one minute.

The five-minute automatic recording system was also installed. Since some scheduled tasks such as, medicine dosing, are important for maintaining the individual's health, the "dosing" video content includes a portion of asking an individual to take her/his medicine in front of the PC. After the video presentation, the system shoots video for five minutes with the Web camera as the evidence of the individual's taking the medicine. Then, this video is sent to the server (③), allowing the caregiver (who is out of home) to check it (④). If the individual does not take her/his medicine, the caregiver, or the volunteer can make a call to the individual by using the IP video phone or a cellular phone (⑤, ⑥).

Usually, the present time, date, the day of the week, year are always shown on the monitor. These presentations automatically disappear when the video contents begin.

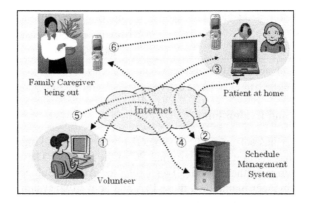

Fig. 1. The overview of schedule management system

3 Field Experiment for Individuals with Dementia

There have been no reports using video phone to assist individuals with dementia living in their home. We conducted the experiment to evaluate the above two systems, the remote reminiscence talking and the scheduling prompter systems for individuals with dementia living in their home, although this field experiment may be more challenging in the way that various factors will affect the results.

3.1 Subjects

The inclusion criteria for subjects were as follows: (1) the subject who was considered to be able to sit and watch the TV monitor for 45 minutes, (2) the subject who had an appropriate number of old photos, and agreed to use them for remote reminiscence talking. The subjects with hearing and vision impairment to watch the TV monitors were excluded from this experiment. Four subjects with moderate and mild dementia had satisfied these criteria. They were outpatients in a hospital's memory clinic. The Mini Mental State Examination (MMSE)[12] was performed to determine their dementia severity. Table 1 shows the demographic and assessment data for the four subjects. Figure 2 (left) shows the scheduled tasks for the subject 1, Figure 2 (right) shows that the subject 1 is talking with a partner, while watching her own old photos.

Table 1. Subjects

Subject	Age	Gender	MMSE	Etiology	Behaviors
1	86	F	27	AD	frequently forgets to take medicines, to eat meals, and what she was just told, living alone
2	74	M	16	AD	forgetful, easily excited or gets angry at his wife, living with his wife
3	72	F	23	unknown	visual illusions, asks the same questions, sometimes uneasiness, doubtful, living alone
4	84	F	22	AD	dislikes taking a bath, asks the same questions, forgets neighbors' faces, living with her son's family

Note: F=female;   M=male;   AD=Alzheimer's   disease;   unknown=unknown   dementia   type
Behaviors=behaviors reported by caregivers at their home

3.2 Procedures and Evaluation

A system engineer has set up a PC at subject' home, and a talking partner's home, respectively. He has also set up the terminal PC at the hospital. These three PCs were connected by Internet with the optic fiver cables or ADSL (Subject 4). During the experiment, the engineer maintained these PCs and above two systems. A special key board cover was attached to the subject's PC, in order to prevent the subject from

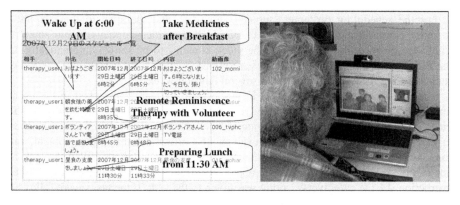

Fig. 2. Example of scheduled tasks and remote reminiscence talking scene

As the preparation of the remote reminiscence talking, the subjects and caregiver submitted their old photos. Then, the engineer digitized them on the terminal PC. The subject, caregiver and talking partner decided on the time for remote talking. In order to check the effect of psychological stability of the remote talking, we used the D section of the GBS check sheet [13]. In this sheet, psychological status was evaluated with 0-7 grading points by the care giver, while the subject was talking with the partner. The score 7 was the worst psychological status, and score 0 was the most concentrated and stabilized status.

The first week was the A period. In this period, the subject was requested to see the TV programs which they like. The next week was the B period. In this period, the partner made a call to the subject PC (video phone), asked the subject to sit in front of the PC, and had some conversation. The partner was asked to use the photos when she could not find any topics to talk.

The subject 1 talked for 60 minutes with the partner, and other three subjects talked for 45minutes. The conversation started at 9:00 for Subject 1, at 12:30 for Subject 2, at 18:00 for Subject 3, and at 16:00 for Subject 4. For both periods, the care giver was asked to fill out a GBS check sheet. We compared the grades of GBS between watching TV and talking with a partner.

Table 2. Scheduled tasks for subjects

Subject	Tasks
1	Take medicine, write on accounting note, prepare for meals
2	Take medicine, throw garbage away, take a walk, do gardening
3	Take medicine, throw garbage away, hang out washing, boiling water, shutting the window
4	Take medicine, write diary, washing her hair, informing her why family member are absent

For the scheduling prompter, subject, caregiver, and therapist in the hospital's memory clinic decided on the daily tasks which the video contents would support. They also decided on the timing of the video contents to be shown automatically on the PC monitor (table 2). They were several tasks which were carried out every day such as taking medicine, or output on several days on week.

The first week was the A period. In this period, the caregiver asked in the usual manner the subject to carry out the above tasks. The next week was the B period. The video content for scheduled task was output automatically. The subject was also asked to carry out the tasks. In order to evaluate the effects of this video content, the caregiver was required to check whether the subject successfully fulfilled the task or not in the A and B periods. If the subject performed the task without any further instructions by the caregivers, 1 point was given to the task. If the tasks were followed by any additional instruction by the caregivers, 0.5 point was given to the task. If the task was not completed, 0 was given.

4   Results

4.1   Results of Remote Reminiscence Talking

The psychological stability was compared between the watching the TV program and remote talking with the video phone on the GBS check sheets observed by the caregivers. In this check sheets, lower points mean more psychological stability. The psychological stability while talking with partner was apparently effective in subject 2 and 4 (Fig.3). The psychological stability continued for even three hours after the remote talking in the subject 4 (* in Fig. 3). The subject 1 got the score 0 in the both periods. The subject 2 refused to talk on the second day. The experiment was cancelled. .

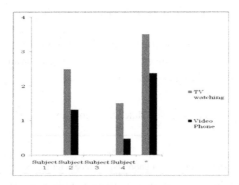

Fig. 3. The points of psychological stability between TV watching and remote talking
note: * = the psychological stability of subject after three hours.

4.2   Summary of Observation by Care Givers

Subject 1: She was at the beginning strained to talk on the video phone. She would also be worried about who the partner was, although the partner introduced herself every time. She was also wondered why her photos were shown on the monitor. If this talking will continue, the psychological effects will be increased.

Subject 2: He was worried about the cost when he would continue the remote talking, although he enjoyed the talking very much.

Subject 3: She became uneasy in talking with the partner□She doubted as if she was questioned on her personal matter by "an stranger", although she had met the partner in the hospital a month ago. On the next day, she refused to talk on the video phone.

Subject 4: She enjoyed talking on the video phone, looked energetic for 45 minutes. The care giver could get a respite time. This chatting kept her from become uneasy in the evening.

4.3 Results of the Scheduling System

The figure 4 is the average percentage of accomplished scheduled tasks observed by the care giver. Compared to the care giver's usual instruction, the automatic output of the video content was more effective in subject 1 and 3. On the other hand, it was completely ineffective for the subject 4.

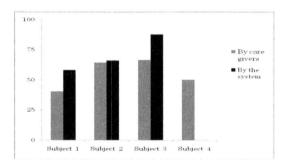

Fig. 4. The percentage of scheduling accompleshment

4.4 Summary of Observation by Care Givers

Subject 1: The audio part of the video content were not heard in the kitchen, or during watching the TV. Sometime she looked the video contents as if the content was given to the other person. If this presentation will continue for longer periods, the effects will increase. After the video content was provided, she was easy to accept the caregiver's additional instructions.

Subject 2: His daily activities were irregular, and did not follow the given time table. So, the automatic output of prompter did not often match his actual activities. At first, he replied to the video content, but he stopped replying to the video afterwards.

Subject 3.(We asked her daughter to appear in the video) She was glad to see her daughter on the monitor, and replied to her in the monitor by saying "thank you for your advice". The video content such as shutting the door did not match the weather of the day.

Subject 4. Continual presentation of the present time and day was helpful to give her time orientation. She was deeply involved into watching the video content, saying "it is helpful for me", but she did not carry out the scheduled tasks as instructed by the video contents. When we used an IC recorder for automatic verbal reminder, the effect was higher than that of the video content.

5 Discussion

The remote reminiscence talking was effective for the subject 2 and 4 in the terms of psychological stability. As the subject 4 sometime becomes uneasy in the evening, the remote talking in the evening could stabilize her and give the caregiver the respite. This system will have possibility to prevent the syndromes such as wandering in evening, agitation etc. Furthermore, she was stable even for three hours after the talking. This may be the most valuable finding in this experiment, and for future research.

For the subject 1, there was no difference in psychological stability between the watching TV and the remote talking. Her dementia was still mild so she could also enjoy the usual TV programs. This might be a reason why there was no difference in the psychological stability. According to the daughter of the subject 3, her skeptical attitude was maintained, though. She felt as if her personal matter was asked by "stranger".

The scheduling prompter was effective for subject 1 and 3. Both of them were living alone. This might be the reason why the automatic and regular output of video content worked well. The subject 3 enjoyed to see her daughter on the monitor. This video content may have lessened her loneliness. On the other hand, the subject 2 and 4 were living with their wife or, family. Since the instructions usually were given to them by their caregivers, the additional effect from the video content was less than those of subject 1 and 3.

The scheduling prompter was completely ineffective for the subject 4, although she was deeply interested in watching the video content. She may have regarded the video content as something like TV commercial.

As indicated in the results of the subject 2, automatic prompting of the scheduled tasks often did not match his actual time table and the day's weather. For example, the individual would not go out for walking when it was raining. It is better to take the individual's behavior and weather into consideration when the prompt is given.

Though the number of subjects was limited in this experiment, our remote reminiscence talking and scheduling prompter system seems to be promising. The experiment also revealed several points for further improvements.

In this experiment, we used only subjects' old photos. However, individuals with severe dementia have difficulty in comprehending verbal stimulus. These impairments often prevent continued talking. To cope with this problem, presentation of emotional contents is required. Yasuda et al [10] have created the "Talk Video," in which a woman talks on various topics such as hometowns, old customs etc, and sings old songs. Several DVD movies on the markets can also be used as additional contents, such as the short movies depicting old foods, traditional events etc., or broadcasted social news movies [10].

Yasuda et al. also developed a conversation-support system consists of three electronic resources: a vocabulary data file, an encyclopedia, and homepages on the Internet [14]. This system is now converted into a remote conversation system by Aye et al. [15]. These contents will strengthen the function of remote assisting systems.

Acknowledgments. This research was supported by research funds from the hospital functions of Japan Labour Health and Welfare Organization. We appreciate four patients and their caregivers, and Hirotaka Kagami, Tetsuo Nakamura, Akiko Iwamoto.

References

1. Davis, R.N., et al.: Cognitive intervention in Alzheimer disease: A randomized placebo-controlled study. Alzheimer Disease and Associated Disorders 15, 1–9 (2001)
2. Cohen-Mansfiled, J.: The impact of environmental interventions on behavioral symptoms in person with dementia. Les Cahiers De La Fondation Me'de'ric Alzheimer 3, 154–163 (2007)
3. Lund, D.A., Hill, R.D., Caserta, M.S., Wright, S.D.: Video RespiteTM; An innovative resource for family, professional caregivers, and persons with dementia. The Gerontologist 35, 683–687 (1995)
4. Gräsel, E., et al.: Non-drug therapies for dementia: An overview of the current situation with regard to proof of effectiveness. Dementia and Geriatric Cognitive Disorders 15, 115–125 (2003)
5. Yasuda, K., Kuwahara, K., Kuwahara, N., Abe, S., Tetutani, N.: Personalized Reminiscence photo video for individuals with dementia. Neuropsychological Rehabilitation (in press)
6. Yasuda, K., Abe, S., Kuwahara, N.: Effect of personal reminiscence video for dementia and its simple production method. Nihon Ninchisyo Kea Gakkaishi (Journal of Japanese Society for Dementia Care) 5, 206 (2006b) (in Japanese)
7. Kuwahara, N., et al.: Semantic Synchronization: Producing Effective Reminiscence Videos. In: 4th International Semantic Web Conference 2005, Demo Papers, PID-14 (2005b)
8. Alm, N., Astell, A., Ellis, M., Dye, R., Gowans, G., Campbell, J.A.: Cognitive prosthesis and communication support for individuals with dementia. Neuropsychological Rehabilitation 14, 117–134 (2004)
9. Kuwahara, N., et al.: Networked Interaction Therapy: Relieving Stress in Memory-Impaired Individuals and Their Family Members. In: Proceedings of 26th Annual International Conference IEEE EMBS, pp. 3140–3143 (2004)
10. Yasuda, K., Kuwahara, K., Kuwahara, N., Abe, S., Tetsutani, N.: Talking with individuals with dementia on a video phone; A preliminary study for networked interaction therapy. In: International Workshop on Cognitive Prostheses and Assisted Communication, in International conference on Intelligent User Interfaces, pp. 43–46 (2006)
11. Kuwahara, N.: Effects on Presenting Reminiscence Video to Individuals with Dementia. In: Proceedings of 4th International Symposium for Material and Kansei in Textile - Fashion, pp. 3140–3143 (2007)

12. Folstein, M.F., Folstein, S.E., McHugh, P.R.: Mini–Mental state; A practical method for grading the cognitive state of patients for the clinician. Journal of Psychiatric Research 12, 189–198 (1975)
13. Gottfries, C.G., Brane, G., Gullberg, B., Steen, G.: A new rating scale for dementia syndromes. Archives of Gerontology and Geriatrics 1, 311–330 (1982)
14. Yasuda, K., Nemoto, T., Takenaka, K., Mitachi, M., Kuwabara, K.: Effectiveness of vocabulary data file, encyclopedia, and internet homepages in a conversation support system for people with moderate-severe aphasia. Aphasiology 21(9), 867–882 (2007)
15. Aye, N., Ito, T., Hattori, F., Kuwabara, K., Yasuda, K.: Conversation Support for People with Aphasia in Distant Communication. In: The 7th IEEE International Conference on Cognitive Informatics, pp. 294–299 (2008)

Part IV

Design Knowledge and Approaches for Accessibility and Universal Access

A Modern Integration of Cognitive and Computer Sciences

G. Susanne Bahr, Matthew G. Bell, Jason Metz, Sarah Sowle, and Elizabeth Beasley

Florida Institute of Technology, Melbourne, Florida 32901, U.S.A.
gbahr@fit.edu

Abstract. Cognitive and Computer sciences have a long history of shared concepts and shared terminology. This paper explores a radical way of interdisciplinary thinking that ventures beyond loosely modeled metaphorical applications of computer systems and the use of terminology with mere face validity. Our focus is on interdisciplinary conceptual, structure and process commonalities. We provide an example of the discovery of shared concepts, knowledge structures and a common mental model using semantic memory organization in humans and object oriented programming, in particular the principle of inheritance. We discuss whether JAVA applications forget and suggest further research topics.

Keywords: Cognitive Science, Computer Sciences, Interdisciplinary, Cross-cutting, Common Concepts, Hierarchical Network Model, Inheritance, Memory, Forgetting.A Modern Integration of Cognitive and Computer Sciences.

1 Brief Historical Context

The concept of the "brain as a computational system" has been part of popular culture for decades. See for instance the 1960s U.S. television series Star Treck and its alien but human like, Vulcan life form Mr. Spock. His persona became exemplary for equating cognitive processing with computational system's activity: In [22] Captain Kirk comments, 'You'd make a splendid computer, Mr. Spock.', to which a flattered Spock replies, 'Thank you, Captain!' Ten years later, in the classic British television series "The Sweeney" [15] and "Open all hours" [5], the characters refer to *human* cognitive activity as "running things through the biological computer".The human mind as an information processing system whose performance is measureable dates back to the Dutch physiologist, and perhaps the first psychometrician, Franciscus Cornelius Donders (1818–89) [12]. Donders measured reaction times and decision making latencies, and interpreted them as processing times of human cognition [12]; Based his model of additive processing times he developed the subtraction method which allowed him to compute the time it takes to make a decision about visual stimuli; (For contemporary evidence see [14].) Similarly Wilhelm Wundt, founder of the first psychology laboratory (1879), measured awareness (attention) as a serial process using his thought meter paradigm [12], [17]. The core research concepts of information processing and their emphases on understanding mechanisms and measuring performance were displaced temporarily in the first half of the 20th century by behaviorist

C. Stephanidis (Ed.): Universal Access in HCI, Part I, HCII 2009, LNCS 5614, pp. 441–449, 2009.
© Springer-Verlag Berlin Heidelberg 2009

dogma, which delegated perception and cognition to the black box. The renaissance of cognitive sciences began in the 1950s with a re-evaluation of human information processing in parallel with the growing discipline of computer sciences [3]. Regardless of one's acceptance of the computer metaphor [9], [16], the synergy between cognitive psychology and computer sciences acted as a catalyst to advance our understanding of human cognitive performance: For instance, Miller's seminal paper on short term memory provides us with generalized finding about its capacity [20], [34]; Broadbent's work established the serial nature of attention [4] which later informed Simon's seminal work on attention economics [1]; and Baddeley's model of working memory discovered the modular nature and parallel processing of distinct modality inputs in working memory [1], [2].

2 Surface Commonalities: A Not so Common Vocabulary

Based on the shared concept of information processing, the analogy between neurological webs and logic circuits has guided the development of constructs, measurements and vocabulary in cognitive science. For instance, cognitive psychologists have been generously employing the terms of input, output, storage, capacity, modules, buffers, primary memory, secondary memory, prototype, etc. While one might surmise that word sharing provides a basis for interdisciplinary integration, the operational definitions of the same terms in computer and cognitive science vary and potentially lead to mutual confusion. For example in 2007, Unsworth and Engle [34] introduced the terms primary and secondary memory to investigate individual differences in working memory capacity. They refer to primary memory as an active workspace that holds approximately four items that can be replaced by incoming information (new input). Items in primary memory can also be replaced by retrieving items from secondary memory which is considered permanent, long term and searchable. Their terminology is derived from primary and secondary memory or storage in computers: Here, primary memory refers to a temporary and quickly accessible data that is directly linked to the central processing unit [21]; secondary memory is often referred to as *storage* and it is not directly accessible by the central processing unit. Data access and retrieval are comparatively slower than accessing data in primary memory. Unlike primary memory, secondary storage is not volatile: one does not lose one's data when the device is powered down [18]. The similarity between cognitive and computer science uses of these memory related terms is at the surface level and lacks conceptual integration which is necessary for interdisciplinary exchange.

Another example of cosmetic use of computer science derived terminology is Baddeley's [2] use of the term *buffer* for the concept of episodic buffer. The episodic buffer links information across long term memory and working memory module to form integrated units of visual, spatial, and verbal information with chronological ordering; This use of buffer coveys more sophisticated functions than that the computer science buffer concept, which is limited to data being held temporarily after they have been retrieved from an input device (such as a mouse) or before they are sent to an output device (such as a printer) [18]. Data integration at the buffer level is not accomplished but the passing of data between different units that require synchronization.

This section has been intended to pique interdisciplinary awareness and to evaluate the utility of cosmetic word usage. So far the state of the sciences seems to indicate that modern commonality is limited to the same words pointing to different models and definitions. However, further examination in the next section provides an example of an existing, common conceptual architecture that has given rise to a divergent terminology.

3 Below the Surface: Common Concept

This section provides an example of a modern integration based on the commonality of two mature areas in cognitive and computer sciences, respectively: Semantic memory organization and object oriented programming.

3.1 Semantic Memory Organization

Tulving [33] defines semantic memory as the storage of generalized world knowledge that is not attached to autobiographical or temporal codes. The Hierarchical Network Model [33] conceptualizes that within memory, categorical information is stored though its associations. In this model, categories are arranged according to their relations. This is done so that general categories (like food) are stored at higher levels, more specific categories (like fruit) are stored at intermediate levels, and highly specific items (like tangerine) are stored at lower levels.

A group of these related items makes up a network. The associations are represented by arrows which show the relation between the category represented by nodes. For example, the item tangerine may point towards the category fruit, because tangerines are an example of fruit. However, this relationship is unidirectional, and an arrow would not point from fruit towards tangerine, because fruit are not an example of tangerines. Characteristics that apply to all the categories would be stored at the highest level of the hierarchy, while lower level characteristics would only apply to that particular item and not to all in the hierarchy. For example, "plant life" may be a high level characteristic applying to all fruit, but "segmented", "round", "orange in color", "easy to peel" may be more lower level characteristics applying specific fruits.

Collins & Quillian [6] developed the hierarchical network model to conceptualize human semantic memory. They proposed two main features: The first is that moving from one level to another in the hierarchy takes time. The second is that retrieving features stored at another level also takes time. The data collected in their studies supported both feature assumptions about human memory. Conrad [7] noted that this model is economical because all characteristics do not need to be stored at each category, but can be stored at the most general category that applies. Further, these characteristics are "inherited" by the lower level categories that apply.

Related to hierarchical network modeling, Rosch et al. [23] hypothesized that there are at least three hierarchical semantic categories: the largest and most general are the superordinate categories, the intermediate categories are the basic-level categories, and the highly specific are the subordinate categories. Differentiation of categories is difficult at the superordinate and subordinate levels because they represent items that have either very few attributes, or that have very specific attributes, respectively. The basic level categories provide an intermediate level of categorization. The reason for their frequent is likely the result of their high degree of differentiation, their prominence in language and early acquisition during cognitive development [23]. However, with increasing domain expertise, differentiation and classification abilities are enhanced and refined and it appears that subordinate categories may rise to the level of basic categories; this hypothesis was confirmed by subsequent research [28]: Experts classified birds and dogs and then vice versa; the subordinate level classifications were made just as quickly as the basic-level classifications by experts compared to novices who exhibited increased latency for subordinate classification.

In summary, hierarchical network models employ at least three levels of semantic categories, they rely on at least two semantic relationships (category level membership and attribute relation) and they store attributes parsimoniously at the highest level applicable without redundancy at lower levels in the hierarchy.

3.2 What Is Object-Oriented Programming?

The object-oriented programming (OOP) paradigm involves the categorization of data and code and can be conceptualized as programming with taxonomically organized data [13]. Object-oriented programming first appeared in the programming language Simula and was focused towards the simulation of real-world phenomena [29].

OOP divides the data being processed into objects with both "static aspects", the object's characteristics, and "dynamic aspects", the object's behaviors [10], [13]. A "class" is a blueprint for a set of objects that share some characteristics [10], [13]. Each of an object's static characteristics has a value and a type; According to [13] a type is a set of values, and a value is a mathematical abstraction. A class is required to create an instance of an object. The object instances created from the same class are distinct from one another. An object instance is considered a labeled set of labeled constants [13] and can accept parameters unique to the instance [10]. Thus, an instance of a class may contain the same or different values as another instance while having a different label.

Since a proposed class may include static and dynamic aspects that closely resemble another concept that requires a class definition, the object-oriented idea of inheritance was developed. Inheritance is the mechanism that combines the specific properties of a newly-defined class with the properties of one of more existing classes from which it inherits; in this way, a programmer only needs to develop the differences between the more specific class and the more general class [2]. For example, the class convertible may inherit the properties from the class car and hence is equipped with four wheels, an engine, a steering wheel, etc. Although different definitions of relationships between classes resulting from inheritance have been defined, in general inheritance seems to be tied to the concept of specialization, meaning that new concepts can be derived from less specific classes [10], [29]. Taivalsaari [29] clarifies that the distinction between the inheritance and specialization: specialization appears to be abstract, while inheritance appears to be a tool of convenience. Formica & Missikoff [13] note that specialization may also be called *subtyping*. An additional distinction can be made that nonstrict inheritance is based on programming language convenience, whereas "strict inheritance" requires that the derived class and the more general class are "behaviorally compatible" [35],, [36]. The latter rely on the implementations of inheritance with restrictions [13].

A restrictive relation supporting strict inheritance is the "is a" relation. The "is a" relation expresses belonging of a class to superclass. For instance, superclass car and subclass convertible are related such that the convertible "is a" car. The "is a" relation appears to create ambiguity in cases of a union between two classes which have different behavior for two properties of the same name. Such ambiguity appears to be solved, however, by "overriding" (redefining the domain of) the conflicting properties [13], [29]. Unlike single inheritance, multiple inheritance allows a subclass to derive from multiple superclasses. Singh [26] describes a few uses for multiple inheritance that vary across their purposes and the relatedness of the classes involved. The main advantage however is that single inheritance might not accurately represent the data for real world simulations because realistic classes tend to share attributes and behaviors.

In summary, class definition in OOP are hierarchically organized blueprints of objects who store a set of attributes at the class level; these sets can be inherited by subclasses without the necessity of duplication and may be further refined or specialized as needed. Strict inheritance requires the "is a" relationship which is a onedirectional relationship pointing from subclass to a superclass: a convertible is (always) a car but not all cars are convertibles.

4 Common Structure and Process

Four points of commonality, the last being initially in the guise of a difference between object oriented programming (OOP) and the hierarchal networks of semantic memory, are the subject of this section. We present the equivalency of classes and categories, semantic relations and attribute storage, and the reverse engineering of their processes.

1. OOP's classes are equivalent to categories or levels of classification, where superclasses serve as superordinate or basic levels and subclasses as subordinate levels or highly specific categories.
2. Hierarchical network models and OOP make use of relations. Specifically, the "is a" relation is structurally and semantically equivalent to the subordinate to basic to superordinate classification in semantic memory. (See the tangerine example as a subordinate example in semantic memory section.)
3. Both approaches rely on graph structures and traversal time across the network with focus on optimization. In particular, both concepts appear to make use of distributing information across several layers of their network structures. This economical allocation of class or category attributes and behaviors (characteristics) allows both inheritance and the hierarchical network model of semantic memory to reduce processing time for information retrieval.
4. OOP is focused on generating new objects or exemplars; Hierarchical network models were developed to explain classification and organization of existing knowledge. The main difference between OOP class structures and semantic memory networks lies in the directionality of their application and function. Classes are defined in order to create new instances of objects with certain attributes and behaviors that exist, e.g., in a virtual world. Semantic hierarchical networks provide

categories for the classification of the real world. They have been experimentally investigated in sentence verification paradigms collecting response latencies to test whether memory is indeed organized as hypothesized. For example, a participant judges the following statements, one at a time, to be true or false: A robin is a bird; a robin is an animal. The process of using a structure for generating objects is the reversal of testing the structure for its properties. Hence, while the applications in cognitive and computer sciences appear different they have reverse engineered each others processes.

5   Synthesis Example: Forgetting

What appears to be a distinction may well be the impetus for venturing to a new perspective on the utility of OOP class structures and semantic networks. We suggest that concept such as creativity (creating new instances) and forgetting (loss of objects) will be relevant for the growing understanding and development in network structure research with benefits for both fields. For instance, we were reminded that OOP has the express purpose of creating objects. Objects as instances (or class exemplars) consume memory resources. JAVA is a popular OOP language that makes use of automatic garbage collection. Garbage collection is a mechanism that allows for memory that is being consumed by an object and its values, to be given back to the system by destroying the object. While a *destructor* can be invoked deliberately in the code, automated *destruction* is handled by the garbage collector and relies on the absence of pointers. This means that an object is considered unused and marked for garbage collection if it is no longer referenced, referred to, pointed to, or associated (all synonymous). One might infer that JAVA applications *forget*.

Human memory as a connectionist semantic organization relies on its associations. In order to retrieve information we step through a series of associated items. Likewise, recall of memories or knowledge in general is triggered by associations. By this explanation, one might concur that in the absence of any association (even those supplied by sensory data) the memory has been destroyed. The implication of the analogy between JAVA destructors and loss of memories is that poorly associated contents in long term memory are more likely to decay. This is not a new proposition: The acquisition of new knowledge requires semantic relation building also referred to as semantic elaboration. The more connected a concept is the easier it is to retrieve. Conversely, we suggest that items without semantic relations can be considered non-existent.

6   Common Research Topics and Conclusions

This paper explored a radical way of interdisciplinary thinking with the emphasis on discovering commonalities. We suggest that a modern integration between computer and cognitive sciences must venture beyond loosely modeled metaphorical applications of computer systems and the use of terminology with mere face validity. In this paper we provided an example of the discovery our shared concepts, knowledge structure and a common mental model of semantic structure and process. A problem space of particular interest for joint research appears to be parallel processing and programming.

The human brain is a sophisticated, albeit poorly understood system built on parallel processes with perceptual and cognitive components [24], [30]. One of the hard problems in perception and cognitive sciences is the binding problem: How are features or data processed by separate neurological pathways and/or in separate areas of the brain *integrated* and perceived as a gestalt? Stryker [27] proposed the synchronization hypotheses where features of the same object, processed separately, are integrated with a synchronized neurological firing rate. Furthermore it appears that attention increases synchronous firing [11]. Related problems dealing with how to synchronize data, how to design data storage (unitary vs. multiple memory stores) and delays resulting from synchronization and communication between multiple processing streams are currently under investigation in computer sciences [24]. An interdisciplinary investigation to address these issues may focus on the phenomenon of illusory conjunctions. Illusory conjunctions illustrate the break down of the binding process where features (color, shape, hairstyle, glasses) are associated incorrect objects (or people) [11], [32]. Illusory conjunctions appear as memory errors resulting form *parallel process integration errors.* It appears reasonable that by investigating how the human brain manages the parallel process we may discover meaningful solutions to the questions currently under investigation in parallel computing.

While processor speed enhancements are asymptotic, the next enhancement is the optimization and development of efficient robust parallel programs. Given the "biological computer concept" and our current set of questions as cognitive and computer scientist, some of our options are to reverse engineer existing phenomena and potential solutions and to advance the state of modern artificial intelligence by continued efforts to model human processing *authentically.* Hence, the inevitable conclusion to this paper is that interdisciplinary exchange on the findings and hypotheses in our respective fields may inspire all parties involved to follow new lines of investigation and to experiment with new ways of problem solving.

References

1. Baddeley, A.D., Hitch, G.: Working memory. In: Bower, G.H. (ed.) The psychology of learning and motivation: Advances in research and theory, vol. 8, pp. 47–89. Academic Press, New York (1974)
2. Baddeley, A.D.: The episodic buffer: A new component of working memory? Trends in Cognitive Science 4, 417–423 (2000)
3. Boden, M.: Mind as Machine: A history of cognitive science, vols. 1 and 2. Oxford University Press, New York (2006)
4. Broadbent, D.E.: A mechanical model for human attention and immediate memory. Psychological Review 64, 205–215 (1957)
5. Clarke, R.(Writer), Lotterby, S.(Director).: A Mattress on Wheels [Television series episde]. In: Lotterby, S. (Producer)(ed.) Open all hours. BBC Two, London (1976)
6. Collins, A.M., Quillian, M.R.: Retrieval time from semantic memory. Journal of Verbal Learning and Verbal Behavior 8, 240–247 (1969)
7. Conrad, C.: Cognitive economy in semantic memory. Journal of Experimental Psychology 92, 149–154 (1972)

8. Cowan, N.: The magical number 4 in short-term memory: A reconsideration of mental storage capacity. Behavioral and Brain Sciences 24, 87–185 (2001)
9. Crowther-Heyck, H.: George A. Miller, language, and the computer metaphor of mind Dispelling the "mystery" of computational cognitive science. History of Psychology 2, 37–64 (1999)
10. Deitel, P.J., Deitel, H.M.: JAVA: How to program, 7th edn. Pearson, Upper Saddle River (2007)
11. Engel, S., Fries, P., Konig, P., Brecht, M., Singer, W.: Consciousness & Cognition 8, 128–151 (1999)
12. Fancher, R.E.: Pioneers of Psychology, 3rd edn. Norton, New York (1996)
13. Formica, A., Missikoff, M.: Inheritance processing and conflicts in structural generalization hierarchies. ACM Computing Surveys 36, 263–290 (2004)
14. Gottsdanker, R., Shragg, G.P.: Verification of Donders' subtraction method. Journal of Experimental Psychology Human Perception and Performance 11, 765–776 (1985)
15. Graham, R.(Writer), Ritelis, V.(Director).: Queen's Pawn [Television series episode]. In: Childs, T. (Producer) (ed.) The Sweeney. Thames Television, London (1976)
16. Green, C.D.: Dispelling the "mystery" of computational cognitive science. History of Psychology 3, 62–70 (2000)
17. Hunt, M.: The Story of Psychology. Anchor, New York (2008)
18. Laplante, P.: Dictionary of Computer Science, Engineering and Technology. CRC Press-Taylor & Francis Group, Boca Raton (2000)
19. Lester, B.P.: The art of parallel programming. First World Publishing, Fairfield, Iowa (2006)
20. Miller, G.A.: The Magical Number Seven, Plus or Minus Two: Some Limits on Our Capacity for Processing Information. Psychological Review 63, 81–97 (1956)
21. Mogle, J.A., Lovett, B.J., Stawski, R.S., Sliwinski, M.J.: What's So Special About Working Memory? An Examination of the Relationships Among Working Memory, Secondary Memory, and Fluid Intelligence. Psychological Science 19, 71–77 (2008)
22. Roddenberry, G.(Writer), Pevney, J.(Director): Return of the Archons [Television series episode]. In: Roddenberry, G.(Producer) (ed.) Star Treck. Desilu, Los Angeles (1967)
23. Rosch, E., Mervis, C.B., Gray, W.D., Johnson, D.M., Boyes-Braem, P.: Basic objects in natural categories. Cognitive Psychology 8, 382–439 (1976)
24. Salvucci, D.D., Taatgen, N.: Threaded Cognition: An Integrated Theory of Concurrent Multitasking. Psychological Review 115, 101–130 (2008)
25. Simon, A.: Designing organizations for an information rich world. In: Greenberger, M. (ed.) Computers, communications and the public interest, pp. 38–52. Johns Hopkins Press (1971)
26. Singh, G.B.: Single versus multiple inheritance in object oriented programming. ACM SIGPLAN OOPS Messenger 6, 30–39 (1995)
27. Stryker, M.P.: Is grandmother an oscillation? Nature 338, 297–298 (1989)
28. Tanaka, J.W., Taylor, M.: Object Categories and expertise: Is the basic level in the eye of the beholder? Cognitive Psychology 23, 457–482 (1991)
29. Taivalsaari, A.: On the notion of inheritance. ACM Computing Surveys 28, 438–479 (1996)
30. Thornton, T.L., Gilden, D.L.: Parallel and Serial Processes in Visual Search. Psychological Review 114, 71–103 (2007)
31. Treisman, A.M.: Features and objects. Quarterly Journal of Experimental Psychology 40A, 207–237 (1988)

32. Treisman, A.M.: Attention and binding. Presentation to the cognitive science group. University of Arizona (February 5, 2005)
33. Tulving, E.: Episodic and semantic memory. In: Tulving, E., Donaldson, W. (eds.) Organization of memory, pp. 381–403. Academic Press, New York (1972)
34. Unsworth, N., Engle, R.W.: The Nature of Individual Differences in Working Memory Capacity: Active Maintenance in Primary Memory and Controlled Search From Secondary Memory. Psychological Review 114, 104–132 (2007)
35. Wegner, P.: The object-oriented classification paradigm. In: Shriver, B., Wegner, P. (eds.) Research directions in Object-Oriented Programming, pp. 479–560. MIT Press, Cambridge (1987)
36. Wegner, P., Zdonik, S.B.: Inheritance as an incremental modification mechanism or what Like is and isn't like. In: ECOOP 1988: European Conference on Object-Oriented Programming, Oslo, Norway, August 15-17. Lecture Notes in Computer Sci., vol. 276, pp. 55–77. Springer, Heidelberg (1988)

Evolutionary Changes in the Traditional Ergonomics

Jerzy Charytonowicz

Wroclaw Univeristy of Technology
53 Prus St., 50-317 Wroclaw, Poland
jerzy.charytonowicz@pwr.wroc.pl

Abstract. To an average user the term *ergonomics* means first of all comfort and convenience, and only then safety, orientation to health, functionality and efficiency of a system. On the one hand such a sequence of associations and 'knowledge of ergonomics' undoubtedly results from marketing strategies and intensity of influence of advertisements of various commodities, but on the other hand it shows a still low level of ergonomic consciousness of society. From prehistory, man has always taken care of their comfort and convenience by making the first tools and successively transforming the material environment, in order to adjust them to their own needs and thus subconsciously initializing paraergonomic activities. The time from prehistory to the second half of the nineteenth century can be described as a period of intuitive ergonomics or subconscious ergonomics. Formulating principles of a new field of a new science, which W. Jastrzębowski called ergonomics, has begun a stage which I call a period of rational ergonomics, or fully conscious ergonomics. It was at this time, lasting from the beginning of World War II, when areas of application, tools, research methods were defined and attempts to apply them in practice were made. Preparations for the war intensified the scientific research in the field of applied ergonomics, starting a new stage in its development lasting untill the present moment, which I call a period of scientific ergonomics.

Keywords: intuitive ergonomics, rational ergonomics, scientific ergonomics, static ergonomics, dynamic ergonomics, ecology.

1 Introduction

The great and sudden dynamic economic and social changes in the nineteenth century have been often called the *Industrial Revolution* or the *electricity, steam and steam engine era*. They were characterized by inventiveness and a common application of machines in different industrial branches. That resulted in a switch from individual craft production to cheap serial industrial production. Industrialisation changed human life patterns. Craftsmen and merchants were eliminated from the market by cheap manufacturing industries and trade companies and they had to seek employment in factories, increasing cheap workforce at the same time. The change of production methods and common application of machines caused a fall in employment and a rise in unemployment. That, in turn, finally led to revolutionary movements at the beginning of the 20th century and the subsequent wave of economic and social changes.

C. Stephanidis (Ed.): Universal Access in HCI, Part I, HCII 2009, LNCS 5614, pp. 450–459, 2009.
© Springer-Verlag Berlin Heidelberg 2009

A common practice in that period was employing women and children for heavy and dangerous work (e.g. in mines). Although employing children as chimney sweeps in England was banned in 1840 and women and children in mines in 1842, employing the under-aged children still continued for a long time. [5]

Work was more and more often subject to mechanisation. Workers employed at production lines manufactured still the same articles, and employers did not bear responsibility for accidents caused by monotonous long lasting work performed without any protecting clothing at machines lacking shields of their moving parts. The lack of shields was a consequence of fascination with inventions, development of technology and specific understanding of machines aesthetics, which apart from efficiency of their mechanisms and solid construction were also supposed to meet their owner's aesthetic needs.

For the lack of ideas for the entire appliances aesthetics, they sought satisfaction of aesthetic needs mainly in observing some working parts of machines. Decorative elements, usually applied on furniture and products made of wood, then repeated on elements made of cast iron and being suppport for machines provide evidence for that. Similar aesthetics represented other products manufactured with machines, whose ugliness could have been seen on the London Exhibition organized in 1851. That fact provoked a general discussion on the matter leading to a birth of industrial aesthetics and industrial design.

An average man associates the word *ergonomics* first with comfort and convenience, and later with safety, health, efficiency and effectiveness of a system, etc. On the one hand such a sequence of associations and "knowledge of ergonomics" results undoubtedly from marketing strategies and influence of advertisments of various goods. However, on the other hand it shows a still low level of social ergonomic consciousness.

Ergonomics has been formulated into various definitions, which reflect its multi thread and flexible nature and purposes the definitions were supposed to serve, being a derivative of subsequent development stages of the science. What all the definitions have in common is emphasising its main purpose, which is adjusting the material environment of man to their needs and possibilities. The purpose, however, was pursued regardless of needs and possibilities of the natural environment, whose man is just a mere element.

Beginning with prehistory, people have always taken care of their own comfort and convenience by creating the first tools and transforming successively the material surroundings to adjust them to their own needs and at the same time initiating paraergonomic activities. Thus the time from prehistory untill the 19th century can be called a period of intuitive or subconscious ergonomics. Formulating rules of a new science that W. Jastrzębowski called ergonomics started a new stage, called a period of rational ergonomics, the fully aware ergonomics. At that time, lasting from the beginning of World War II, new areas of application of the new science, its tools, research methods were defined and attempts to implement ergonomics into practice were made. War preparations intensified academic research on ergonomics, beginning the next stage of its development lasting up to now – scientific ergonomics.

2   Rational Ergonomics as a Social Product of the Industrial Revolution

Interest in the work issue aroused significantly during the Industrial Revolution, when the epoch of craft production came to an end and the era of industrial production came. Significance of human work as an important production factor was noticed. However, fascination with manufacturing capabilities of machines steered the thinking towards a number of goods manufactured frequently at the cost of their quality, as observed on the London Exhibition in 1851. Division of work process into specialised tasks realised by carefully selected and trained workers contributed to a new style of manufacturing whose purpose was a high productivity, and further increased efficiency at the minimum manufacturing costs.

A growing number of accidents at work resulting from lack of organizational experiences in the machine production technology, work processes organization and lack of rules governing the man and machine interaction in the 19th century became a social problem. Striving for efficiency, increasing work pace and a frequent organizational chaos led to a growing number of accidents. That fact can be regarded as a factor contributing to emergence of ergonomics as a science of work. Its main purpose generally speaking was protecting man against the "machine" whose pace was difficult for people to adjust to and follow.

A Polish academic, a professor of natural science and a philosopher, Wojciech Jastrzębowski was concerned with the work issues in his research. In 1857, in the weekly *Nature and Industry* he published an article *Outline of ergonomics that is science about work based upon principles derived from nature*, where he defined the science on work as ergonomics and delineated its rules. [2] He defined the role work plays in man's life, analysing in detail its social aspects from a philospoher's point of view.

Social interest in the issues of work and working man was intended to improve work conditions in factories and work safety in their interaction with machines. We can assume then that Jastrzębowski pursued "protection of man against machines."

Development of industrial manufacturing generated a growing number of post-production waste of all kinds most frequently stored in accidental places. Further, that practice caused a successive contamination of the natural environment, affecting at the same time man's health condition. As health risk to people working with machines incurred immediately in the form of numerous work accidents, the consequences of the natural environment contamination and degradation and their negative influence on health emerged with delay. Twelve years after defining ergonomics, a German biologist and philosopher Ernst Haeckel noticed those relations and in 1869 he formulated principles of a new science which he called *ecology*. Simplifying, in his research he pursued protection of the natural environment against destructive influence of industrial production.

The end of the 19th century was not favourable to developing new sciences such as ergonomics and ecology because of the growing social, economic and political problems in most European countries.

At that time increasing efficient manufacturing was the main interest, not safety of the employed. That was the aim of analyses of human work processes conducted in

1898 – 1901 by a French engineer Francis W. Taylor, whose activities were defined as attempts to adjust man to a machine.

The issue of rational work in a household was much earlier dealt with in a work by an American housekeeper who published *A Treatise on Domestic Economy for the Use of Young Ladies at Home and at a School* in 1849, where she discussed some health issues, comfort and convenience in planning and arranging home interiors. In 1869, she and her sister published the book *The American woman's Home*, and then in 1873 she published another book *Miss Beecher's Housekeeper and Healthkeeper* concerning the economical work issues, health and safety in a household. [6]

Roots of the contemporary ergonomics can be also traced back to the 19-century philosophy (George W. F. Hegel), arising from psychology, which as an academic discipline took shape in the middle of the 19th century, and also to development of anthropology and arising anthropometry.

3   Beginnings of the Contemporary Scientific Ergonomics

The beginning of the 20th century is marked, among other things, by Frank and Lilian Gilbreth's work researching ways of performing work from the aspects of movements and time of performance. As a result of the research in 1911, they formulated principles of economics movements, delineating conditions of reducing physiological cost of work, which in turn led to activities increasing work safety.

Francis W. Taylor's method concerning rationalisation and scientific organization of work processes has also found its application in a household, partly thanks to studies by Christine Frederic, the author of *Household Engineering: Scientific Management in the Home* published in 1923 and exploring household and household work organisation, and thanks to Mary Pattison's *The Principles of Domestic Engineering* published in the same time. American housekeepers' initiatives applying Taylor's methods further led to emergence of a new scientific discipline called household engineering. [6]

Beginning with 1903, aviation started to develop and the first tanks came into use in 1916. The beginning of War World I encouraged development of complicated military machinery. Primitive Bleriot's *flying machines* (one of French aviation pioneers) were converted into Spad, Neuport and Fokker *fighter planes*. Complexity of the military equipment required training and selection of the equipment operators on the basis of psychological tests, which contributed to establishment of the first aeromedical research laboratories using *experimental psychology*.

In Germany, the first centre of psychological tests was established in 1915 for a selection of lorry drivers, pilots and artillerists. In Russia, Rudniev conducted research on standard plane cockpits (1915). In England, *Department of Scientific and Industrial Research* and *Medical Research Council* began research into work conditions in weapons factories in 1917 and in 1921 *National Institute of Industrial Psychology* was established. The American military psychology started in 1917. When the USA joined World War I, *Council of the American Psychological Association* brought *Committee on Psychological Problems of Aviation* into being in 1918. It was at the same time the beginning of *engineering psychology*. In the USA the first two aeronautical laboratories were established (Brooks/Texas and Dayton/Ohio) at the end of

World War I. Anthropometric works were initialised and their influence on plane design and crew actions were researched there.

In the USSR, Dmitrij Mendelejew was considered an ergonomics pioneer who already researched a possibility of adjusting machines to man in 1888. Another pioneer was Arendt studying adaptation problems in aeronautics. In 1928, Rosenberg, using an anthropometric atlas, specified parametres of a cockpit design. In 1929, Bernstein designed a workplace for a tram driver, and in 1934, Platonov and Michajlovsky designed an adjustable seat for a driver. In the 20. and 30., in the USSR many psychologists exploring work physiology and psychology conducted research on the basis of the Marxism philosophy.

In the USA the first flight simulator was designed (Edwin Link) in 1930, which was later, in 1934, used in *Army Air Corps*. In 1924-1933, *Western Electric Company* conducted research on the influence of the illumination effect on workers' efficiency. In 1939, in the American army *Personnel Testing Section* and *Emergency Committee on Psychology* were formed for selecting and testing personnel. In 1941, *Air Army Force Aviation Psychology Program* was developed and directed by John Flanagan. In that time, Fius and Jones carried out research on optimal configuration of knobs, steering dials and control desks used in cockpits. As a result of cooperation of engineers and psychologists, a new discipline emerged called the *applied experimental psychology* (1949), later renamed as *human factors*. That was the beginning of the contemporary stage of scientific ergonomics.

The postwar years is a period of the Cold War, tensions in the East and West relations and a time of dynamic development of studies and laboratories funded by the army. In the USA, for example, in that time *US Navy Electronics Laboratory*, *Naval Ocean System Center* or *RAND Cooperation* were established. Also, in the same time, the military ergonomics started to penetrate the civil industry. Big aviation companies, such as *North American*, *McDonell-Douglas*, *Boeing and Grumman* created the first interdisciplinary ergonomic teams in their design departments created. [3]

Anthropometric data were introduced in the design of various kinds of artefacts only in 20. of the last century, when the Scandinavian designers (Kaare Klint) began to include measurements of the human body in designing objects of daily use. Application of the anthropometirc data in design became more popular only after World War II. The American industrial designer Henry Dreyfuss was one of leading designers accepting anthropometry as a basic ergonomic tool for designing. He developed flat models of a man and a woman (called Joe and Josephine) used for verification of anthropometric parameters in designed objects. In 1955, he published the study *Designing for People*, and in 1960 the book *The Measure of Man: Human Factors in Design*, containing a collection of anthropometric data for design.

The 60s are the beginning of space exploration, space industry and spatial medicine laboratories. They brought into life new materials, new technologies, and new issues in relations man-technology emerged. That period also marked the beginning of common application of computers in American research centres and schools. In the second half of the 60s Paul Baran from *RAND Corporation* developed a conception of a *new system of computer communication* and its practical application in the form of *ARPANET*, the forerunner of the contemporary *INTERNET*. The development of computers and their application in technology contributed to emergence of a new area of study for ergonomics, whose researchers started empirical research on software after 1970, when the first personal computers appeared. The 90s is the time of introducing another technical inventions such as a fax machine, a modem, cordless digital telephony GSM, World Wide Web, the Internet, and virtual reality.

4   Complex and Dynamic Ergonomics of the Future

The above mentioned facts and examples imply that since the beginning of the 20th century the military and space industry has been the generator of the technical and technological progress. The needs of the industry determined research directions, scientific goals, tools and research methods. The main role in the resaerch was played by psychology, physiology, anthropometry and engineering sciences. One of the effects of the studies was emergence of new scientific disciplines, such as engineering psychology and experimental applied psychology.

The computer, such as a steam machine in the era of the Industrial Revolution, brought about significant changes. At the end of the 80s, the development of the digital technology and microprocessors initiated a new stage in the engineering development called the *information technology revolution* or the *computer era*, which, in turn, initiated another race but this time not with a steam machine, but with a digital machine. The latter unlike the former one affects the human psyche creating **stress** that results from fears both of substituting computer robot's work for human work and of failure to follow a pace of machine work.

Protection of man against stress resulting from interaction with technology achievements seems to be a direction of utmost priority in the contemporary ergonomics, especially as various bodily ailments connected with long lasting operation of computers have already been quite well recognised and identified (wrist, spine, circulatory problems, etc.) in contrast to psychological and social influences that have been omitted in the ergonomic studies so far. Since the contemporary information science offers such superb means of creating synthetic and mobile images reacting simultanously to viewers' presence (*virtual reality*), it has become a serious concern to psychiatrists and psychologists. As they claim, spending a lot of time in the apparent reality may discourage from living a real life and tackling real daily problems.

The technical progress is usually evolutionary in nature, its changes are rapid and dynamic unlike social changes, which usually have evolutionary nature and are gradual, gentle and placid. Reconciling a rapid tempo of the technical development with the process of social acceptance of new technological achievements that change common habits and life style of society have become a serious challenge. Technical development has always stayed ahead of development of social consciousness and this important fact has to be remembered when implementing new inventions since it is their *social acceptance* that determines efficiency and tempo of technological progress in particular social circles. The technical progress, despite its undoubtful convenience, carries hazards of various kinds, both to a man's proper personal development and equilibrium maintained in the natural ecosystem, whose man is an active participant.

Frequently, people sensing potential threats defend themselves instinctively against some of the technological achievements (e.g. nuclear weapons, nuclear power stations, genetic experiments, etc.) However, they easily succumb fascination with opportunities the developing technology provides not thinking about possible negative effects of their activity. Social acceptance of technical innovations of all kinds to a large degree depend on their main intended use and extent to which they affect man's imagination as far as potential risk is concerned. Sociologists, psychiatrists and psychologists more and more often indicate that an impetuous technical development destroys sources and grounds related to shaping man's personality and appropriate shaping of social relationships. Therefore, making and accepting technical progress, people have to at the same time introduce mechanisms that would enable controlling new technologies, taking into consideration a wide spectrum of their social influences, which, in turn, should be another challenge to the future ergonomics.

Technology reveals also man's attitude towards nature and creates new conditions for social relationships, since each product of technology carries some ideological implications connected to shaping the surrounding reality. Technological changes the technical progress conveys have an "ecological" character, which means that one significant technological change, like in the natural ecosystems, generates in consequence overall changes throughout a structure of the "technical ecosystem". New technologies change the structure of social interests, ways of behaving and thinking, cultural patterns and even nature of an entire society. Therefore, departure from the historical ergonomic model of man-technology for the sake of the modern model man-technology-environment will help reduce negative effects of technology on the two latter elements of the system and will enable faster implementation of principles of the sustainable development. Further, what may serve that purpose is including ecological issues in a scope of the future ergonomics thanks to closer integration of ergonomics with sozology, a complex science dealing with basic principles of the environment protection.

The changing environment which moulded the biological profile of the modern man is optimal to maintain efficiency of their physiological mechanisms. Man cannot be isolated from influence of the environment, although the technical development allows it, since not each and every new technological achievement facilitating life comprises progress in terms of both man's health and the environment protection.

Difficulties ergonomics has been facing so far in its efficient application in every day life may result from delimiting its scope exclusively to the *work environment*, which can be justified by the fact that ergonomics grew out of "a science of work." If we realise that man spends merely a third of day and night time in the work environment, and the rest of time in the *rest environment,* a need for expanding the area to be encompassed in the ergonomic activity appears obvious. Ergonomics expanded its influence into the rest environment, including the living environment. If problems of the professional work environment apply exclusively to a group of working people, the problems of the living environment apply to a full (in terms of age and efficiency) spectrum of society (children, the aged, people with a various degree of psychophysical efficiency, etc.).

As a result of progressing computerisation, common work forms and methods are also subject to change causing a gradual overlap of the both mentioned living environments. Forecasts suggest change in forms of the office work through moving workers to their homes (a virtual office).

Therefore, in order to provide society with full adjustment of their material environment to needs and possibilities of an average man and to increase the efficiency of ergonomic activity and winning a wide social acceptance for it, a shift must take place from the traditional *work ergonomics* to *complex ergonomics*, encompassing all social groups in all kinds of life situations. It will broaden out a group of professional ergonomics specialists into other professionals. It will let include representatives of various professions in the family of ergonomists, who deal not only with moulding the *work environment*, but also the *rest environment* (e.g. architects and town planners). Also, people professionally dealing with the issues of man's safety and health will belong to the ergonomists society.

As results from the analysis of the origins, the programme assumptions, main features of the contemporary ergonomics, as well as extent to which society accepts it, it is a *static ergonomics*. The ergonomics is still oriented towards issues which inspired its existence in the past. The present time, however, shows that the scope of ergonomics is in fact much wider than it was originally assumed and it results mainly from its underlying features of humanocentrism and interdisciplinary nature. In new social and economic conditions all over the world the basic problems ergonomics has tackled, e.g. environment optimalisation and work conditions (mainly industrial), lose their priority for the sake of loads and threats specific to professions predominant in the era of postindustrial civilization, characterized by a fall in employment in industrial sectors for the sake of employment in the information technology sector.

The technological progress is accompanied by new problems which appeared in connection with it and are related to psychological loads (stress), general threats derived from facilities of the technical civilization and a decrease in man's general physical activity (e.g. reducing physical effort) closely connected with the former factor.

A complex nature of ideas and aims that ergonomics pursues is a focus for specialists of various disciplines who create specific specializations within the ergonomics itself related to domains of their professional activity. This, in turn, provides evidence for the fact that ergonomics has all features of a science and that there is a social demand for it. Natural emergence of subsequent specializations within ergonomics proves that there is a need for its transformation into so called *dynamic ergonomics*, being an antonym of the traditional static ergonomics. Dynamics in this case needs to be understood both according to the dictionary definition /as power, impetus, vigour, ability to act, movement, vitality, energy/ and according to the definition of *dynamism* /in philosophy/. The latter one assumes an internal activity of matter itself /nature/, its continual movement and development, and interaction of objects. Close relationships between ergonomics, ecology and architecture provide examples of such interrelations.

I think making ergonomics more "dynamic" is necessary on the assumption that the area of its activity will encompass the entire living environment and all areas of human activity both in the work and rest environments.

Some ergonomists oppose the division of ergonomics into specializations, considering creating overall academic compilations common to all professional specializations. It does not seem to be sensible considering a wide diversity of issues addressed in numerous professions. Modern lifestyles confirm that ergonomics needs to encompass a wider area than so far. It does not only refer to designing selected elements of man's material environment or optimalisation of workplaces and work processes, but also to broader interrelations man-the environment, technology – nature, or to issues of shaping the "ergonomic consciousness" (ergonomic thinking) in the entire society and among designers of all kinds of specializations.

Ergonomics is an interdisciplinary science, which is emphasised by its ample scope and complexity of issues it addresses and knowledge it conveys that one person cannot tackle and explore. Specialization amounted to a group of scientific domains directly connected with a practised profession seems to be more sensible, since professional motivation may, in turn, efficiently encourage a deepened ergonomic understanding. A general division of scientific works amounted to basic, applied, development and implementation works also supports specialization within ergonomics which naturally derives from specificity of professions and problems connected with them. The division would reflect areas of potential activity for ergonomics supporters according to specific nature of various professions and workplaces.

5 Conclusion

The history of technology proves that only breakdowns and disasters make societies aware of unreliability seemingly even the most perfect technology. Although their originators do not deny that fact, but still do not discuss it frequently enough, focusing mainly on prospects offered by new constructions and global systems.

New technologies change structure of social interests, behaviour and thinking patterns, cultural patterns and nature of societies.

Technology cannot be considered the only universal panacea for all problems societies face nowadays. The human instinct for self-preservation suggests that we should expect more and more sophisticated manners of defence against threats from sophisticated technology. In this place importance of ergonomics should be emphasized which must remember that the new information technology civilization with its technological achievements undoubtedly facilitating man's life also carries some threats to their privacy, a sense of integrity and autonomy, cultural traditions and customs, etc. The main purpose of *the future ergonomics* should be protection of the human psyche against dangers of rapid cybernetisation and cyborgisation of social life.

Ergonomics of the information technology epoch should be thus a *dynamic ergonomics* rapidly responding to technical and technological transformations occurring in societies, and also ought to be a *complex ergonomics* encompassing all areas of man and technology interaction and the environment, with particular emphasis on protection of the psychological sphere of life both of an individual man and whole societies.

The simplest way to forecast the future directions in ergonomics can be exploration of present needs and pursuits on the assumption that ergonomics represent man in their interactions with systems of the world they are immersed in. However, it is impossible to plan the future, being ignorant of achievements and heritage of the past and presence.

The fundamental purpose of ergonomics should be therefore shaping the natural environment in a way that provides man with proper standards and comfort of life respecting at the same time needs and possiblities of the natural environment, thus respecting the principles of ergonomics and ecology.

In the future, undoubtedly an answer to the old question what is ergonomics and what issues it should address will still be sought. It can be expected that the internal division of the discipline in question into specializations will further proceed and the specializations will derive from professions practised by ergonomists. It can be expected that the computer techology, researched by ergonomics at present, will become an integral part of the ergonomic methodology. The future also lies in the need for quantitive and qualitative development of methods of forecasting technological changes, in development of theory of ergonomics and application of ergonomic models of human activity, and what is more, developing efficient methods of teaching ergonomics. The future will show which of the purposes will be accomplished.

References

1. Fiell, C.P.: Design handbook: concepts, materials, styles, Taschen, pp. 16–17. GmbH, Köln (2006)
2. Koradecka, D., Karwowski, W.: Wojciech Jastrzębowski – an outline of ergonomics or the science of work based upon the thruths drawn from the science of nature. In: Commemorative edition of the 14th Triennale Congress of the IEA, CIOP, San Diego/Warsaw, Poland (2000)
3. Meister, D.: The History of Human Factors and Ergonomics, LEA, London, pp. 148–152, 161–162, 176–177 (1999)
4. Meister, D.: History of Human Factors in United States, International Encyclopedia of Ergonomics and Human Factors, pp. 73–75. Taylor & Francis, London (2001)
5. Roberts, J.M.: An illustrated World history: One World: Europe the Maker ..., Polish edition by Wydawnictwo Łódzkie, Łódź, pp. 18–37 (1991)
6. Rybczyński, W.: Home. A short history of an idea, Polish edition by Oficyna Wydawnicza Wolumen, Warszawa, pp. 161–165 (1996)

Affordance Conditions of Product Parts in User-Product Interaction

Li-Hao Chen[1], Chang-Franw Lee[1], and Sy-Gia Kiong[2]

[1] Graduate School of Design, National Yunlin University of Science and Technology,
123 University Road Sec 3, Douliu, Yunlin 64002, Taiwan
[2] Department of Industrial Design, National Yunlin University of Science and Technology,
123 University Road Sec 3, Douliu, Yunlin 64002, Taiwan
hao55@mail2000.com.tw, leecf@yuntech.edu.tw,
sheqakiong@hotmail.com

Abstract. The purpose of this study is to identify the influences of affordance conditions, both perceptible and hidden affordances, in product interfaces on user-product interactions. An analysis scheme was used to analysis the affordance conditions of a digital camera's parts used as example. Moreover, a usability evaluation was carried out to examine what affordance conditions would influence users' operations while they practiced the operational tasks. The results show that affordances for functionality should not only be perceptible, but more importantly, also should be lucid for users in user-product interactions; the evidence presented by other comprehensive perceptual information and conventional layouts can deal with affordances being hidden in interfaces of a product.

Keywords: Affordance, Perceptual information, User-product interaction.

1 Introduction

In interface design, the affordance concept proposed by Gibson [7] as a design idiom would often be mentioned to state how it works in user-product interaction. The affordance concept was introduced into product design by Norman [13], in his book, *The Design of Everyday Things,* and illustrates how the affordance concept can be applied to everyday objects. For example, just by looking at them, plates can be pushed by hands and knobs can be turned by hands. However, affordance is not totally mature and is still without a formal-agreed definition in design [11] and it is difficult to define in precise analytic terms [1]. In recent years, in terms of the application to product design, the affordance concept has been extended as being related to observers' cultures and experiences. It has diverged from Gibson's original idea [15] [18]. The affordance concept we discuss in this study is in part far from Gibson's affordance.

Affordance refers to function or usefulness of an object [4], [14], [17]. An object can have various affordances [14], and behavioral possibilities for users [18]. Actions of people do depend on the goal context [16]. What affordances are perceived by users that influence their behaviours depends on perceivers' current psychological

C. Stephanidis (Ed.): Universal Access in HCI, Part I, HCII 2009, LNCS 5614, pp. 460–469, 2009.

states at the moment [3], [4]. In design, there are two viewpoints in terms of affordance referring to function or usefulness of an object, operability and functionality. Operability refers to physical-behavioural possibilities in user-product interaction. As Hartson [9] has noted, the term "physical affordance" is what helps the users in doing physical tasks. In addition, outside of the physical relationship between objects and human parts, the physical-corresponding relationship for two certain parts can be regarded as a kind of affordance for operability to suggest the function for assembly-ability of the parts [10]. Functionality refers to intended functions of a product and perceiving it might be related to users' cultures and experiences. Users have to learn which affordances will satisfy particular goals, and they need to learn to attend to the appropriate aspects of the visual environment [4].

Affordance is independent of perception [5], [6] and information [12], [18]. That is, affordance is separate from perceptual information [6], [12], [18]. Moreover, affordance of an object can be specified by perceptual information [6], [12], [14]. Thus, perceptual information is not necessary for existence of affordance but essential for perception of affordance. The central question for affordances is not whether they exist and are real but whether information is available in ambient light for perceiving them [7]. Perception of affordance depends on the process of picking up information directly. As Greeno [8] notes, Gibson developed an interactionist view of perception and action that focused on information that is available in the environment.

Perceptual information is the definitely important factor for perception of affordance. Affordance conditions in the affordance-information framework suggested by Gaver [6] illustrate affordance could be perceptible, hidden or false in terms of the existent-absent relationships between perceptual information and affordance. Based on the affordance conditions, the aim of this study is to explore and evaluate the influences in terms of product parts' affordances are perceptible and hidden in user-product interaction.

2 Method

A digital camera was used as the test sample to explore the influences of product parts' affordance conditions on user-product interaction. Affordance-information analysis and usability evaluation were carried out in this study to manifest the influences of the product parts' affordance conditions in user-product interaction.

2.1 Affordance-Information Analysis

This was to find out what affordances the product parts required for the operational tasks, and to see if the product parts' affordances are perceptible, hidden or false based on the affordance-information framework proposed by Gaver [6] (see Fig. 1). Lee et al [10] further considered the corresponding relationships between affordance viewpoints in design, operability and functionality, and the three categories of perceptual information in operating products proposed by [3], Behavioural information, Assemblage information and Conventional information, to explain product parts' affordance conditions in user-product interaction.

For example, Table 1a shows that the operability and functionality are perceptible when behavioural information and conventional information are available for them; the operability is false if the behavioural information indicates a nonexistent affordance for operability (Table 1b); Table 2c shows that the functionality is hidden if there is no conventional information for it; if the part is not only operated by users' body parts but also needs to be assembled with other certain parts for a certain task, the behavioural and assemblage information can present the affordances for operability (Table 1d). Table 1 can serve to clearly present product parts' affordance conditions caused by the affordance-information relationships.

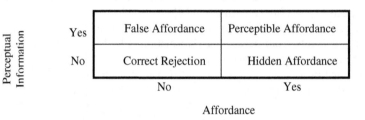

Fig. 1. Affordance-information framework ([6])

Table 1. Example of affordance-information analysis ([10])

	Affordance conditions	Affordances		Perceptual information		
		Operability	Functionality	BI	AI	CI
a	Perceptible	■		■		
	Perceptible		■			■
b	False			■		
	Perceptible		■			■
c	Perceptible	■		■		
	Hidden		■			
d	Perceptible	■		■		
	Perceptible	■			■	
e	Correct Rejection					

■: existent; BI: behavioural information; AI: assemblage information; CI: conventional information

2.2 Usability Evaluation

Procedure and material. In order to limit the users' behavioural possibilities and intentions for operations to the product parts, seven immovable tasks were set in this study. The participants were asked to operate the digital camera according to the tasks set in this study and then determined subjectively the difficult-easy level for practicing the subtasks within the tasks. The subtasks were carried out in a within-subject design. A seven-level Likert scale was used as the measurement technique in this study, with 1 for quite difficult; 7 for quite easy for the subtasks. The processes of the participants' operations were videoed and their operational faults were noted as well. After finishing the tasks, the subjects were asked the reasons for the operational faults during interviews. A digital camera was placed on a desk and the participants sat on a chair to operate it without time limitation.

Subjects and tasks. Thus study had thirty subjects including seventeen females and thirteen males (mean age 22.1, SD=3.1) who had experience using digital cameras. Five tasks were set up in this study as follows: 1) Insert memory card and load battery; 2) turn on; 3) adjust zoom and take pictures with non-flash mode; 4) view pictures and delete one taken picture; 5) insert USB cable. For the tasks set up in this study, the related parts of the digital camera that needed to be operated by the subjects are as shown in Fig. 2.

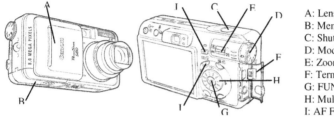

A: Lens cover
B: Memory card/battery slots
C: Shutter button
D: Mode dial
E: Zoom lever
F: Terminal connectors
G: FUNC/SET button
H: Multi control dial
I: AF Frame selector

Fig. 2. Parts of digital camera (user manual)

3 Results

3.1 Affordance-Information Analysis

In this study, the five tasks included separate subtasks for completing the tasks. Moreover, each subtask was concerned with related parts of the digital camera as shown in Table 2. For instance, task 1 consisted of one subtask and involved one part. In the subtask, users needed to practice operational behaviour upon the related part, Part A. For task 3, four subtasks needed to be practiced completely by users and the subtasks separately corresponded to the related parts, Parts D, E, H and C.

From the analysis in Table 3, required affordances of each part within the subtasks could be identified through their corresponding tasks and the behaviours in the subtasks. For example, for Part A, users needed to push it with their fingers to turn on the digital camera. Thus, push-ability is required for the part affording the operational behaviour. Affordance for functionality refers to a part's intended function such as Part A affords the function of turning on the digital camera. Turning on the digital camera is the part's functionality for task 2. Therefore, the affordances for push-ability and functionality are required for subtask 2.1. In addition, as mentioned before, affordance for operability refers to physical-behavioural possibilities in user-product interaction. Assembling two certain parts can be regarded as a kind of physical-behavioural operation. For instance, in subtask 1.1, users needed to insert a memory card and battery into the slots.

Table 2. Task analysis

Task	Subtasks	Related parts
1.Insert memory card and load battery	1.1 Open memory card/battery slot cover, insert memory card and load battery	B: Memory card/battery slot
2.Turn on	2.1 Push the lens cover	A: Lens cover
3. Adjust zoom and take pictures with non-flash mode	3.1 Select scene mode	D: Mode dial
	3.2 Adjust zoom;	E: Zoom lever
	3.3 Select flash mode	H: Multi control dial
	3.4 Take pictures	C: Shutter button
4. View pictures and delete one taken picture	4.1 Press playback button	J: Playback button
	4.2 View pictures	H: Multi control dial
	4.3 Press AF Frame selector	I: AF Frame selector
	4.4 Press Func/Set button	G: Func/Set button
5.Insert USB cable	5.1 Open terminal cover and insert USB cable	F: Terminal connector

Table 3. Analysis of the parts' required affordances for the subtasks

Part		Subtasks	Behaviours for the subtasks	Required affordances
A		2.1	Push with finger	Push-ability; functionality
B		1.1	Push memory card/battery slot cover with finger and insert memory card and battery into the slots	Push-ability;assembly-ability
C		3.4	Press with finger	Press-ability; functionality
D		3.1	Grasp and turn with fingers	Grasp-ability; turn-ability; functionality
E		3.2	Push with finger	Push-ability; functionality
F		5.1	Pull terminal cover with finger and insert USB cable into USB connector	Push-ability; assembly-ability
G		4.4	Press with finger	Press-ability; functionality
H		3.3	Press with finger	Press-ability; functionality
		4.2	Press or turn multi control dial with finger	Press-ability; turn-ability; functionality
I		4.3	Press with finger	Press-ability; functionality
J		4.1	Press with finger	Press-ability; functionality

The parts' affordance conditions can be identified through analyzing the absent-existent relationship between the affordances and the perceptual information. Based on the affordance-information analysis scheme, affordances might be perceptible, hidden or false in terms of existence or absence of perceptual information for the affordances, as shown in Table 4. For subtask 2.1, affordances for push-ability and functionality are required for Part A. Furthermore, Part A's physical properties as the behavioural information are available for the push-ability, but there is no conventional information for the functionality. Hence, its affordance conditions can clearly be shown as push-ability is perceptible; the functionality is hidden.

Table 4. Affordance-information analysis

Part	Subtask	Affordances		Perceptual information			Affordance conditions
		Operability	Functionality	BI	AI	CI	
A	2.1	■	■	■			Push-ability is perceptible
							Functionality is hidden
B	1.1	■		■			Push-ability is perceptible
		■					Assembly-ability is hidden
			■			■	Functionality is perceptible
C	3.4	■	■	■			Press-ability is perceptible
							Functionality is hidden
D	3.1	■		■			Grasp-ability is perceptible
		■		■			Turn-ability is perceptible
			■			■	Functionality is perceptible
E	3.2	■	■	■		■	Push-ability is perceptible
							Functionality is perceptible
F	5.1	■		■			Push-ability is perceptible
		■					Assembly-ability is hidden
			■			■	Functionality is perceptible
G	4.4	■	■	■		■	Press-ability is perceptible
							Functionality is perceptible
H	3.3	■	■			■	Press-ability is hidden
							Functionality is perceptible
	4.2	■					Press-ability is hidden;
		■		■			Turn-ability is perceptible
			■			■	Functionality is perceptible
I	4.3	■	■	■		■	Press-ability is perceptible
							Functionality is perceptible
J	4.1	■	■	■		■	Press-ability is perceptible
							Functionality is perceptible

■: existent; BI: behavioural information; AI: assemblage information; CI: conventional information

In subtasks 1.1 and 5.1, the affordances for push-ability and assembly-ability are required for the following parts, Parts B and F. The two parts' affordance conditions both show that push-abilities are perceptible; assembly-abilities are hidden. Moreover, there is conventional information on the parts to present their functionality, the functions of memory card/battery loading and USB cable connection. However, in fact, the affordances for functionality are not necessary for subtasks 1.1 and 5.1. The affordance for press-ability of Part H is hidden in subtasks 3.3 and 4.2. In subtask 3.3, Part H's affordance for press-ability is hidden since the protruding strips on the round dial suggest users to turn it with their fingers naturally. However, turning Part H is not workable for subtask 3.3. Both the affordances for turn-ability and press-ability are usable in subtask 4.2. That is, users can press or turn Part H to practice viewing pictures. The form of Part H tends to suggest turn-ability so that its press-ability is hidden in subtask 4.2.

3.2 Usability Evaluation

Table 5 shows the mean of the evaluation from the subjects' subjective judgments on the subtasks with the seven-level Likert scale used in this study and the numbers of operational faults for each subtask from the thirty subjects. Otherwise, corresponding to the parts' affordance conditions in each subtask, the influences of the affordance conditions on user-product interaction can be analyzed. From the interviews, the major operational faults that were the major reasons for why the subjects made the operational mistakes in the subtasks are shown in Table 5.

The data of difficult-easy level for the subtasks from the thirty subjects was analyzed with Repeated Measures ANOVA in SPSS software to examine the significance level among the subtasks. As shown in Table 6, for the thirty subjects, the results show the difficult-easy level for the subtasks reached a significant difference ($p <$ 0.001). Table 6 shows the significance level between each subtask. From the analysis shown in Tables 5 and 6, comparing subtask 2.1 with 3.4, the easy-difficult levels reached a significant difference ($p < 0.001$). Part A's functionality could not be suggested to users because there is no information for it. Therefore, the subjects had difficulty to find out how to turn on the digital camera. Part C's functionality was hidden as well in subtask3.4. However, most subjects had no problem in doing subtask 3.4. The reason might be that the convention of using a digital camera in society suggests that Part C should be the "shutter button" for users.

Affordances are perceptible for subtasks 3.1, 3.2, 4.1, 4.3 and 4.4. Comparing subtask 3.1 with 3.2, 4.1, 4.3 and 4.4, the results show that the easy-difficult level reached significant differences. In subtask 3.1, Part D's affordances for grasp-ability, turn-ability and functionality are perceptible, but the icons and texts on Part D are not lucid for users to understand the part's functionalities. That is, the perceptual information should not only be perceptible but also clear and straightforward for the functionalities.

Comparing subtasks 1.1 with 5.1, both the assembly-abilities of Parts B and F were hidden by the covers. However, the easy-difficult level of subtasks 1.1 and 5.1 reached a significant difference ($p \square 0.001$). For Part F, there is conventional information, an index and texts, on the cover to suggest to users its function and how to open it. However, the meaning the texts on Part F's cover presented are not lucid for users so that they still had difficult to find the USB connector. For Part B, the texts "battery" is presented clearly on its cover so that users can perceive clearly what function the part actually affords. In doing so, the problem of affordance for assembly-ability being hidden could be solved.

Table 5. Usability evaluations

Subtask	Mean of evaluation (SD)	Numbers of operational faults		Related parts' affordance conditions
1.1	5.3 (1.0)	0	B	Push-ability is perceptible Assembly-ability is hidden
2.1	3.8 (1.4)	12	A	Push-ability is perceptible; Functionality is hidden
3.1	4.1 (1.2)	16	D	Grasp-ability is perceptible; Turn-ability is perceptible; Functionality is perceptible
3.2	4.7 (1.0)	4	E	Push-ability is perceptible; Functionality is perceptible
3.3	4.8 (1.3)	5	H	Press-ability is hidden; Functionality is perceptible
3.4	5.2 (1.1)	1	C	Press-ability is perceptible; Functionality is hidden
4.1	4.7 (1.1)	12	J	Press-ability is perceptible; Functionality is perceptible
4.2	4.7 (1.2)	5	H	Press-ability is hidden; Turn-ability is perceptible; Functionality is perceptible
4.3	4.6 (1.1)	7	I	Press-ability is perceptible; Functionality is perceptible
4.4	4.9 (1.1)	1	G	Press-ability is perceptible; Functionality is perceptible
5.1	4.2 (1.1)	16	F	Push-ability is perceptible Assembly-ability is hidden

For Part H, the easy-difficult level of subtask 3.3 and 4.2 does not reach a significant difference ($p > 0.05$). In subtask 3.3, the form of Part H suggests a turn affordance so that some subjects tended to turn it with fingers. Actually, for setting the flash mode, users needed to press Part H rather than to turn it. Although the form of Part H tends to present its turn-ability, the icons or texts around the part could suggest users to press it after they turn it. In subtask 4.2, there are two ways for viewing pictures, turning Part H or pressing it with left-right direction. Some subjects did not know that Part H could be pressed as well or that it should be pressed with a left-right direction. However, for subtask 4.2, it does not matter if it is not pressed.

4   Discussions

Part A in subtask 2.1 and Part C in subtask 3.4, there is no conventional information for the parts' affordances for functionalities. Most users know about the locations of shutter button on digital cameras in the artificial world. Therefore, users could easily figure out Part C's functionality and they had no problem in operating the part. For the digital camera used in this study, the way of turning on the digital camera is quite different from other cameras. In general, there is usually an icon or texts on the on-off button of a digital camera to present the functionality. Therefore, users had difficulty to find out that pushing Part A was for turning on the digital camera. As the cases above illustrate, affordance for functionality can be hidden when the design of interface conforms to the conventions and experiences of the users. As Eysenck and Keane [4] stated that Gibson would have been forced to admit that the meaning of objects is stored in long-term memory. That is, the conventional factors as strong cues can effectively guide users to perceive a product's affordances in user-product interaction.

Gaver [6] stated that users must make inferences from other evidence if affordance is hidden. As Part H in subtask 3.3, the icons or texts around the part could imply the affordance for press-ability that is hidden. Moreover, the assembly-abilities of Parts B and F are hidden by the covers, and the texts on the covers could suggest users to find out the affordances. However, the conventional information of Part F is not comprehensible for users to perceive the affordance immediately. Users would not directly know that the USB connector is hidden by the cover. The hidden affordance could be coped with by evidence presented by other perceptual information that is comprehensible for users. As the results above show, in brief, affordances for operability and functionality being hidden in product interfaces would influence user-product interaction if there is no other comprehensible perceptual information for users to infer the affordances; or the designs of interface layouts do not fit in with the conventions in the artificial world.

The affordances are perceptible in subtasks 3.1, 3.2, 4.1, 4.3 and 4.4. However, for subtask 3.1, the results show that it seems not to be an easy operation for the subjects. Uncertainly, affordances are perceptible in product interfaces that would facilitate user-product interaction. For subtasks 4.1 and 4.3, the colors of icons of Parts I and J are not obvious so that users had to take more time to perceive them. The results show that subtasks 4.1 and 4.3 are easier than subtask 3.1 in terms of the easy-difficult level of the operations. The icons or texts on Part D in subtask 3.1 are not lucid for the comprehension of affordance for functionality. For affordances for functionality in product interfaces, the perceptual information for affordances should not only be obvious, more importantly, but also they should also be lucid for users in user-product interaction.

Table 6. ANOVA analysis. (∗: p<0.05, ∗∗:p<0.01, ∗∗∗:p<0.001, -: non significant

Subtask	1.1	2.1	3.1	3.2	3.3	3.4	4.1	4.2	4.3	4.4	5.1
1.1		** *	** *	**	*	- *	**	*	**	** *	**
2.1			-	**	** *	**	**	**	**	**	-
3.1				** *	*	** *	*	*	*	**	-
3.2					-	**	-	-	-	-	-
3.3						*	-	-	-	-	-
3.4							*	*	**	-	**
4.1								-	-	-	*
4.2									-	-	-
4.3										-	-
4.4											*
5.1											

5 Conclusion

This study only considers visual-perceptual information. Other types of perceptual information might be worthy to consider in the analysis scheme, such as using sounds. There are not any cases of false affordance in this study. As Gaver [6] states, hidden and false affordances lead to mistakes. It is worthy to further study the influence of false affordances on user-product interaction.

References

1. Amant, R.S.: User interface affordances in a planning representation. Human-Computer Interaction 14, 317–355 (1999)
2. Chen, L.H., Lee, C.F.: Perceptual information for user-product interaction: using vacuum cleaner as example. International Journal of Design 2(1), 45–53 (2008)
3. Chen, L.H., Lee, C.F., Ho, M.C.: Application of affordance concept on product design. Journal of Science and Technology 16(2), 143–151 (2007)
4. Eysenck, M.W., Keane, M.T.: Cognitive psychology, 4th edn. Psychology Press, New York (2000)
5. Galvao, A.B., Sato, K.: Affordance in product architecture: linking technical functions and users' tasks. In: Proceedings of 17th International Conference on Design Theory and Methodology, pp. 1–11. ASME Press, Long Beach (2005)
6. Gaver, W.: Technology affordances. In: Proceedings of the SIGCHI Conference on Human Factors in Computing System: Reaching Through, pp. 79–84. ACM Press, New York (1991)
7. Gibson, J.J.: The ecological approach to visual perception. Houghton Mifflin Company, Boston (1979)
8. Greeno, J.G.: Gibson's affordances. Psychological Review 101(2), 336–342 (1994)
9. Hartson, H.R.: Cognitive, physical, and perceptual affordances in Interaction Design. Behaviour and Information Technology 22(5), 315–338 (2003)
10. Lee, C.F., Chen, L.H., You, M.L.: Framework of product affordances and perceptual information. Bulletin of Japanese Society for the Science of Design 56(2) (accepted, 2009)
11. Maier, J.R.A., Fadel, G.M.: Comparing function and affordance as bases for design. In: Proceedings of 2002 ASME Design Engineering Technical Conferences, Paper no. DETC2002/DTM-34029, Montreal, Canada (2002)
12. McGrenere, J., Ho, W.: Affordance: clarifying and evolving a concept. In: Proceedings of Graphics Interface 2000 Conference, pp. 179–186. Lawrence Erlbaum Associates Press, Montreal (2000)
13. Norman, D.A.: The design of everyday things. MIT, London (1990)
14. Reed, E.: James J. Gibson and the psychology of perception. Yale University Press, New Haven (1988)
15. Stone, D., Jarrett, C., Woodroff, M., Minocha, S.: User interface design and evaluation. Morgan Kaufmann Publishers, San Francisco (2005)
16. Van Vugt, H.C., Hoorn, J.F., Konijn, E.A., Dimitriadou, A.B.: Affective affordances: improving interface character engagement through interaction. Int. J. Human-Computer Studies 64, 874–888 (2006)
17. Vihma, S.: Products as representations: a semiotic and aesthetic study of design products. University of Art and Design, Helsinki (1995)
18. You, H., Chen, K.: Application of affordance and semantics in product design. Design Studies 28(1), 22–38 (2007)

Conformity Assessment in the Public Procurement of Accessible ICT

Stephan Corvers[1], Loïc Martínez-Normand [2], Clas Thorén[3], Enrique Varela[4],
Eric Velleman[5], and Klaus-Peter Wegge[6]

[1] Corvers Procurement Services BV, 's Hertogenbosch, Netherlands
[2] DLSIIS, Facultad de Informática, Universidad Politécnica de Madrid, Spain
[3] Clas Thorén Consulting, Ekerö, Sweden
[4] Fundación ONCE and freelance consultant, Madrid, Spain
[5] Bartiméus Accessibility Foundation, Utrecht, Netherlands
[6] Siemens Accessibility Competence Center, Paderborn, Germany
s.corvers@corvers.com, loic@fi.upm.es, clas.thoren@gmail.com,
evarelac@gmail.com, e.velleman@bartimeus.nl, wegge@c-lab.de

Abstract. Public procurement is an important instrument for improving the accessibility of the information society. In Europe, in December 2005, the European Commission issued mandate M/376 to CEN, CENELEC and ETSI, to harmonize and facilitate the public procurement of accessible ICT products and services by identifying a set of functional European accessibility requirements for public procurement of products and services in the ICT domain. The mandate is to be carried out in two phases: Phase I – inventory of accessibility requirements and assessment of suitable testing and conformity schemes, and Phase II – standardization activities. This paper presents an overview of the technical report produced by the authors as members of a CEN and CENELEC project team assigned to carry out "an analysis of testing and conformity schemes of products and services meeting accessibility requirements". The work was developed from October 2007 until October 2008.

1 Introduction

In Europe, USA, Canada, Australia, Japan and many other countries public procurement is regarded as an important instrument for improving the accessibility of the information society.

In December 2005 the European Commission issued a mandate M/376 [1] to CEN, CENELEC and ETSI. One key objective of this mandate was to harmonize and facilitate the public procurement of accessible products and services in the field of information and communication technologies (ICT) by identifying a set of functional European accessibility requirements.

A crucial element of public procurement processes is to verify that the products offered in the tenders fulfill the requirements set out in the call-for-tender. In particular, the procurer has to be confident that the statements on conformity claimed by the awarded supplier are true. Preferably, such statements should be the result of a conformity assessment process compliant to international standards.

C. Stephanidis (Ed.): Universal Access in HCI, Part I, HCII 2009, LNCS 5614, pp. 470–479, 2009.
© Springer-Verlag Berlin Heidelberg 2009

By conformity assessment is meant a demonstration that a product (in a general sense) fulfils specified requirements [5]. In most cases this demonstration is carried out either by the manufacturer of the product (called "first party" in the conformity assessment field) or an independent third party organization.

A conformity assessment system is a set of rules, procedures and management for carrying out conformity assessment. A conformity assessment scheme is a conformity assessment system related to specified objects to which the same specified requirements, rules and procedures apply. This means that a conformity assessment scheme is the application of a conformity assessment system to a specific situation in which the type of objects (products) and the requirements are always the same.

Mandate M/376 is to be carried out in two phases: Phase I – Inventory of European and international accessibility requirements and assessment of suitable testing and conformity schemes, and Phase II – Standardization activities.

This paper presents an overview of the technical report produced by the authors as members of a CEN and CENELEC project team assigned to carry out "an analysis of testing and conformity schemes of products and services meeting accessibility requirements". The work was developed from October 2007 until October 2008 and can be found in the complete report [2]. Another report focused on functional accessibility requirements, standards, and the current state of public procurement of accessible ICT was produced by ETSI specialist task force 333 [3].

2 Approach

The approach taken by our team consisted of the following six steps:

1. Search for existing schemes in the field of ICT product accessibility.
2. Search for systems or schemes in other domains that could be applicable to the accessibility of ICT products.
3. Define a model to analyze the different properties of a conformity assessment system or scheme, the "dimensions".
4. Apply this model to describe the conformity assessment systems and schemes that have been found in steps 1 and 2.
5. Define a model to analyze the properties of a public procurement context, the "criteria". They are means for determination of the type of conformity assessment scheme that best fits each procurement situation.
6. Apply this model of public procurement analysis to describe a small set of scenarios. The details of the influence of the public procurement context criteria on the dimensions of conformity assessment schemes are confined to these scenarios.

The dimensions and criteria together make up a multi-criteria decision support system, aimed at assisting the procurer to find the conformity assessment system or scheme that best fits the procurement in question.

The rest of this paper will present the main results of our research. Section 3 will describe the dimensions to analyze conformity assessment systems and schemes. Section 4 will summarize information of existing conformity assessment systems and schemes, using the dimensions of section 3. Then, section 5 will describe the criteria used to analyze the properties of a public procurement context, and section 6 will present an overview of the scenarios that were defined in the complete report. Finally, section 7 will present some conclusions and indications of future work.

3 The Dimensions

The initial goal of the analysis of conformity assessment systems and schemes for public procurement of accessible ICT products was to generate a matrix similar to the one presented in the IDC report [4]. That report presents a table of criteria for consideration in evaluating and making an informed decision about a conformity assessment approach appropriate for the circumstances.

The IDC report applied several criteria to only two types of conformity assessment: mandatory third-party certification vs. voluntary self- declaration of conformity. This was considered to be a limited approach given the diversity of conformity assessment systems that can be applied. For instance, a distinction has to be made between the involved parties (first, third) and whether the assessment is mandatory or voluntary.

After an in-depth study of the components of conformity assessment systems and schemes, the project team decided to further decompose conformity assessment systems into several dimensions. This decomposition was made based on the functional approach to conformity assessments defined by EN ISO/IEC 17000 [5], which is comprised of four functions (Figure 1).

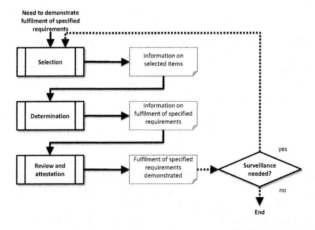

Fig. 1. The functional model of conformity assessment (EN ISO/IEC 17000:2004)

The first function is *selection*: it involves planning and preparing activities in order to collect or produce all the information and input needed for the subsequent determination function. Such activities may concern the object of assessment (e.g. whether sampling is needed), the specified requirements (are all requirements applicable?) and the methods of determination (e.g. inspection or testing). The second function is *determination:* it includes the evaluation activities that are undertaken to develop complete information regarding fulfillment of the specified requirements by the object of conformity assessment or its sample. The third function is *review and attestation.*

Review is the final stage of checking before taking the important decision as to whether or not the object of conformity assessment has been reliably demonstrated to fulfill the specified requirements. Attestation is the conformity statement, usually presented in a form that most readily reaches all of the potential users. The fourth function is *surveillance*. Conformity assessment can end when attestation is performed. In some cases, however, the assessment functions may need to be systematically iterated to maintain the validity of the statements.

Table 1 provides an overview of the dimensions identified in our work, with a short description of each of them. Full detail can be found in the complete report [2].

Table 1. The dimensions defined to describe conformity assessment systems and schemes

Selection	
Type of requirements (TR)	The type of requirements that will be used in the assessment. The requirements can be based on international standards, on European standards, on national standards, on de facto standards or on other sources. For the definition of standard, see annex VI of the Directive 2004/18/EC [6].
Scalability (SC)	Whether the conformity assessment scheme is scalable. Scalability is a capability of a scheme to enable its application to products of varying degrees of complexity. Scalability depends on the selection of the object of assessment (or parts or functions of it) and on the selection of the determination methods to be used. A scalable scheme can be applied equally well to simple and complex products.
Determination	
Method of determination (MD)	The method that is used to determine the resulting value for each requirement. Some types of determination activities defined in EN ISO/IEC 17000:2004 are testing, inspection, audit and peer assessment. The value of this dimension can be "mixed" if several determination methods can be used in one system or scheme.
External (EX)	Whether the determination activities are done by the same organization that will provide the attestation (external=no) or by an external entity (like a laboratory) that is contracted by the organization providing the attestation (external=yes).
Type of party (TP)	Type of party doing the determination. It can be: a first party: (the person or organization that provides the object), a second party: (person or organization that has a user interest in the object, like purchasers, users of products, potential customers...) and a third party: (person or body that is independent of the person or organization that provides the object and of user interests in that object). For third parties, their independence will be measured using the types identified in EN ISO/IEC 17020, from type A (fully independent) to type C (not independent).
Review and Attestation	
Type of party (TP)	Type of party responsible for the attestation. Same values as above.
Detail of attestation (DA)	This dimension represents the level of detail of the attestation that is generated as a result of the conformity assessment process.
Publicity (PU)	This dimension indicates whether the resulting attestation is made publicly available to external bodies (such as, for example, the public procurers or users).
Surveillance	
Existence (ES)	This dimension indicates whether or not the conformity assessment scheme includes surveillance.
Complaint system (CS)	This dimension indicates whether the conformity assessment scheme includes a complaint system that is maintained by the customer (the contracting authority), by the provider of the attestation or by a mediation party (like a disability rights office).
Other	
Mandatory (MA)	This dimension indicates whether or not the conformity assessment scheme is mandatory. Mandatory systems are the ones regulated by national laws.

4 Existing Conformity Assessment Systems and Schemes

During the preparation of the full report, several conformity assessment systems and schemes were found. These were divided into three groups: general systems as described by standards, existing schemes for ICT accessibility and, finally, systems or schemes outside the ICT domain that could be of interest.

4.1 General Conformity Assessment Systems

The first group contains conformity assessment systems as defined by international and European standards and, in addition, a generic methodology for conformity assessment of the accessibility of web sites. The systems described in this group are: generic first party assessment (as defined in ISO/IEC 17000:2004), Supplier's declaration of conformity (EN ISO/IEC 17050-1:2004), generic second party assessment (as defined in ISO/IEC 17000:2004), generic third party assessment (as defined in ISO/IEC 17000:2004), inspection (EN ISO/IEC 17020:1998), product certification (EN 45011:1998) and, finally, UWEM [7].

As the listed systems are generic, most of the dimensions don't have defined values and the main differences are on the type of parties doing the assessment and the details of the attestations. Detailed information can be found in the full report [2].

4.2 Existing Schemes Specific to ICT Accessibility

The second group is based on the research carried out to find and describe existing conformity assessment schemes in the field of ICT accessibility. Several examples were found, and they were grouped into categories, depending of the type of product, the type of party, mandatory and public funding. Each category has a key example, although most of the categories contain several examples. Table 2 summarizes the values assigned for each dimension in the scheme categories:

1. *Web sites. Certification by accredited type A third party* (WCERT). In Spain there is one official accessibility certification of websites, offered by AENOR and conforming to EN 45011:1998 and ISO/IEC Guide 65.
2. *Web sites. Inspection by accredited type A third party* (WINSP). In the Netherlands there are two examples of inspection performed by accredited type A third parties (conforming to ISO/IEC 17020): Foundation Quality Mark "drempelvrij.nl" and the Accessibility Foundation. Both use UWEM as a conformity assessment system.
3. *Web sites. Publicly-funded assessment* (WPUBL). In Germany there is one project, BIK (*Barrierefrei Informieren und Kommunizieren*), funded by the German Federal Ministry of Labour and social affairs, that defines a complete test to evaluate conformity with the Amendment BITV of the German equal opportunities act (based on WCAG 1.0).
4. *Web sites. Assessment by type C third party* (WCTHRD). This is the most common example: a conformity assessment scheme offered by an organization that is not fully independent. The one described in the report is offered by Segala.
5. *Web sites. Mutual recognition between European parties* (WMUT). Euracert is a unique example of mutual recognition between conformity assessment bodies. It is

Table 2. Values assigned for each dimension in existing schemes specific to ICT accessibility

	WCERT	WINSP	WPUBL	WCTHRD	WMUT	WSCND	IMAND	IPTHRD	IFIRST
Selection									
TR	National Std.	De facto	National legislat.	Variable (de facto, legislation)	De facto	Other	National legislat.	Internat. Std.	National legislat.
SC	Yes	Yes	Yes	Yes	Yes	Yes	No	No	-
Determination									
MD	Inspection & audit	Inspection	Mixed	Mixed	Mixed	Mixed	Mixed	Testing	Mixed
EX	Yes	No	No	No	No	No	No	Yes	-
TP	3rd (C)	-	-	-	-	-	-	3rd (A)	-
Review and Attestation									
TP	Accred. 3rd (A)	Accred. 3rd (A)	Accred. 3rd (A)	3rd (B)	3rd (C)	Second	3rd (A)	3rd (A)	First
DA	No	No	Detailed	Detailed (machine)	Detailed	Detailed	Detailed	Detailed	Detailed
PU	Yes	Yes	Yes	Yes	Yes	Yes	Yes	Yes	Yes
Surveillance									
ES	Yes	Yes	No	Yes	Yes	No	-	Yes	No
SC	Yes	Yes	No	Yes	Yes	No	-	-	Supplier
Other									
MA	No	No	No	No	No	No	Yes	No	No

an agreement between three private organizations: AnySurfer in Belgium, Accessiweb in France and Technosite in Spain. They share the same requirements (WCAG 1.0) and the same method for accessibility evaluation (UWEM)).

6. *Web sites. Assessment by second party* (WSCND). There is only one example in this category: the See it Right audit. It is a service provided by the RNIB in the UK. As RNIB is an organization representing blind and visually impaired users, it can be considered to be a second party: it is an organization that has a user interest in the object of assessment.

7. *ICT. Mandatory conformity assessment scheme* (IMAND). In Italy there are several legislation pieces that establish a mandatory conformity assessment scheme for accessibility of ICT, including the definition of requirements, a registry system of accredited third parties registry system and an assessment methodology.

8. *ICT hardware. Assessment by privately-recognized third party* (IPTHRD). There are few conformity assessment schemes that apply outside the web domain. The most recognized is the TCO label, from Sweden, that includes some accessibility aspects in their quality mark.

9. *ICT. First party attestation* (IFIRST). In the USA there exists the Voluntary Product Accessibility Template (VPAT), which was developed by US industry and government to show conformance to Section 508. It is a document generated by the supplier (or manufacturer) to disclose to what extent the product addresses requirements. Therefore, a VPAT does not provide a clear yes/no answer for each requirement and for product accessibility.

As a conclusion to the analysis of this group of conformity assessment schemes, it has to be noted that most of them deal with web content and thus use a de facto standard (the Web Content Accessibility Guidelines - WCAG) as requirements for the conformity assessment, or national legislation that adapts the content of the WCAG.

4.3 Conformity Assessment Systems and Schemes in Other Domains

The third group includes conformity assessment systems or schemes existing in other domains that could be applied to the context of public procurement of accessible ICT products. The examples are of very different types and characteristics, and they are grouped here only because they do not apply to the ICT domain. The full report describes the following: CE marking, Cencer, Common criteria and Keymark.

Table 3. Product-dependent criteria

Criteria	Description
Type of product	The type of product, as defined in EN ISO 9000, combined with the applicable CPV codes (Common Procurement Vocabulary [8], amended by [9]).
State of technology	Describes the state of the product's technology on the market. It may be an existing technology, an existing technology applied to a new domain or a completely new technology.
Time to market	The time that a new product is under development before it reaches the market.
Life span	The time that a product remains on the market before being replaced. Several things may affect life span: legislation, security, user requirements, etc.
Rate of changes	How often the product can change (e.g. new features be added) during its use.
Adaptability	Whether the product can be adapted to better suit the needs of its users. Adaptations can be easy (like user preferences) or hard (like major changes to user interface behavior) to make
Interoperability with assistive technologies	Whether the product can be connected to assistive technologies
Total cost of ownership	The addition of product-related direct and indirect costs. Not only does it reflect the cost of purchase but also aspects in the further use and maintenance of the equipment, device, or system considered

Table 4. Market-dependent criteria

Criteria	Description
Competition	The degree of product market competitiveness
Market awareness	Level of awareness of accessibility issues among companies, customers and users
Market surveillance	Existence of product conformity assessment after the product goes to the market. This criterion also covers who is responsible for the market surveillance.
Competitor's surveillance	Existence of conformity surveillance performed by the competitors.
Barriers to trade	Whether the assessment of accessibility could generate barriers to trade by promoting local suppliers
Independent expertise on accessibility	Whether there is expertise on product accessibility and accessibility conformity assessment. This expertise has to be independent of suppliers and manufacturers for accessibility requirements to be defined for public procurement.
Size of product suppliers	The type of enterprises dominating the marketplace by size. SMEs and big worldwide companies do not all have the same resources for conducting conformity assessments. Remember that at least 95 per cent of the enterprises in the EU are SMEs.

As in the first group, the elements of this third group are generic and most of the dimensions don't have an assigned value. Details are provided in the full report [2].

5 The Criteria

The context of a public procurement process can be divided into several elements: (a) the product to be procured; (b) the market the product belongs to; (c) the public administration procuring the product (i.e. the contracting authority); (d) the users that will be using the product; and (e) the public procurement characteristics. We have identified criteria for each of these elements, summarized below in tables 3 to 7.

Table 5. Public administration-dependent criteria

Criteria	Description
Public task	The tasks of the public administration. They can be driven by policy, execution or control.
Geographical focus	The geographical level of competence of the contracting authority: local, regional, Member State or European.
In-house expertise on accessibility	Whether the contracting authority has expertise for evaluating suppliers' accessibility claims in-house.
Legal requirements	Whether the public administration has to comply with accessibility-related legal requirements

Table 6. User-dependent criteria

Criteria	Description
Risk of harm	Level of potential risk of producing adverse effects on users. In this report the 'risk-of-harm' criteria is related only to accessibility-based adverse effects, and not to safety regulations
Risk of social exclusion	The risk of a non-accessible ICT product producing social exclusion of users with disabilities, because there are no alternatives
Confidence	The users' level of confidence in accessibility attestations

Table 7. Public procurement characteristics-dependent criteria

Criteria	Description
Type of procurement	According to Hommen's matrix [10]: direct procurement (based on needs intrinsic to the procuring organization, e.g. e-government services), cooperative procurement (based on shared needs, congeneric to multiple users, e.g. energy efficient lighting or buildings), catalytic procurement (based on needs extrinsic to the procuring organization, i.e. needs of other users, e.g. new sustainable technologies).
Type of procedure	The type of public procurement process, from direct purchase to fully fledged procurement.
Electronic procurement	Whether or not the procurement is electronic. Electronic procurements have specific characteristics and should be analyzed separately. There are electronic procurements both below and above the threshold amount.
Prior existence of the product	Whether the product to be procured exists on the market or has to be developed.
Number of units	The number of product units (or licenses) to be procured. This information is part of the needs analysis performed in preparation for public procurement.
Budget	The amount of money that the procurer is expecting to invest.
Liability and accountability	Whether the supplier is liable for not providing an accessible product (risk mitigation procedure...).

6 The Scenarios

The intention of the scenarios is to apply the analysis model of the procurement contexts (the criteria). These scenarios detail the influence of the criteria of the public procurement contexts on the dimensions of conformity assessment systems. The scenarios are hypothetical and merely illustrative. The intention is to show how the criteria are used within the decision-making process and the type of possibilities they output concerning the best conformity scheme to adopt. This reasoning is only illustrative and was not subjected to formal evaluation.

Notice also that tenderers have the option of using another method of proof as long as they can demonstrate that it produces equivalent results. So, even though the scenarios recommend conformity assessment systems or schemes, the public procurer should accept alternative means of proof.

The scenarios were selected to cover four different procurement cases, which are fully described in the report [2]. Here only the potential conformity assessment system or scheme is listed:

- A set of units of desktop laser printers, which is a procurement of off-the-shelf products. Potential system: supplier's declaration of conformity, plus third party determination made by external laboratories.
- A frame contract for mobile communication, including a set of units of mobile phones, which is a procurement of a service including off-the-shelf products. Potential system: supplier's declaration of conformity.
- Development of a web site, which is a common procurement case. Potential system: product inspection according to ISO/IEC 17020.
- A road traffic management system, which is a complex object of procurement. Potential system: certification (for individual components) and self declaration of conformity (for the full system).

7 Conclusions and Further Work

The CEN/CENELEC report [2] has presented an analysis of conformity assessment systems and schemes that could be applied in the domain of the public procurement of accessible ICT products and services. Some conclusions can be drawn.

First the procurement of ICT is a highly complex process with many variables. Due to this complexity and diversity one conformity assessment system (and less so a scheme) is unlikely to be applicable across all the situations covered by the public procurement of accessible ICT.

A second key concept is that the European Public Procurement Directives give the contracting authority limited freedom of choice as to require what means the suppliers can use to demonstrate the accessibility of the offered products: the contracting authority has to accept equivalent means of proof of conformity.

A third extremely important concept is that assessment of conformity to specified requirements is a fundamental element of the evaluation of tenders. The contracting authority has to be able to analyze the different tenders and rank them with respect to conformity to the accessibility requirements.

References

1. European Commission. M/376, Standardisation Mandate to CEN, CENELEC and ETSI in support of European accessibility requirements for public procurement of products and services in the ICT domain (December 2005)
2. CEN/BT WG 185 Project Team Final Report for Approval. European accessibility requirements for public procurement of products and services in the ICT domain (European Commission Mandate M 376, Phase 1) (September 2008),
   http://econformance.eu/
3. ETSI DTR 102 612 V 50. Human Factors (HF); European accessibility requirements for public procurement of products and services in the ICT domain (European Commission Mandate M 376, Phase 1). Final draft for ESO TB cross-approval (September 2008),
   http://portal.etsi.org/stfs/STF_HomePages/STF333/STF333.asp
4. IDC White Paper Using Appropriate Conformity Assessment Tools to Ensure Effective Consumer Protections (2007),
   http://www.itic.org/archives/articles/2007b/
   IDC_White_Paper_on_Conformance_Assessment_Nov2007.pdf
5. EN ISO/IEC 17000:2004 Conformity assessment – Vocabulary and general principles (2004)
6. Directive 2004/18/EC of the European Parliament and of the Council of 31 March 2004 on the coordination of procedures for the award of public works contracts, public supply contracts and public service contracts (2004),
   http://eur-lex.europa.eu/LexUriServ/LexUriServ.do?uri=
   CELEX:32004L0018:EN:NOT
7. WAB Cluster. Unified Web Evaluation Methodology version 1.2 (2007),
   http://www.wabcluster.org/uwem1_2/
8. Regulation (EC) No 2195/2002 of the European Parliament and of the Council of 5 November 2002 on the Common Procurement Vocabulary (CPV) [Official Journal L 340 of 16.12.2002]
9. Commission Regulation (EC) No 2151/2003 of 16 December 2003 [Official Journal L 329 of 17.12.2003]
10. Hommen, L., Rolfstam, M.: Public Procurement and Innovation: Towards a Taxonomy. Journal of Public Procurement 9(1), 17–56 (2009)

Evaluation Framework towards All Inclusive Mainstream ICT

Maria Gemou and Evangelos Bekiaris

Centre for Research and Technology Hellas Hellenic Institute of Transport,
17, Poseidonos Av., 17455 Alimos, Greece
{mgemou,abek}@certh.gr

Abstract. The current paper presents the evaluation framework and plans developed for the evaluation of the applications to be developed in the context of the ÆGIS Integrating Project (Grant Agreement: 224348) of the 7th Framework Programme, which aims to embed support for accessibility through the development of an Open Accessibility Framework, upon which open source accessibility interfaces and applications for the users as well as accessibility toolkits for the developers will be built. Within ÆGIS, three mainstream markets are targeted, namely the desktop, rich Internet applications and mobile devices/applications market segments. Upon the basis of an overall user-centred approach, the developed evaluation framework will involve all types of targeted end-users, namely persons with disabilities as well as experts in Assistive Technology, trainers/tutors and developers as well as a series of other related stakeholders. Evaluation will be held in three iterative phases and across 4 Pilot sites (Belgium, Spain, Sweden and in the UK), providing in-between each phase, feedback to the development teams for debugging and optimization.

Keywords: Evaluation, accessibility, iterative testing, user-centred approach, mainstream ICT, Open Accessibility Framework.

1 Introduction

The ÆGIS project (Open Accessibility Everywhere: Groundwork, Infrastructure, Standards; http://www.aegis-project.eu) of the 7th European Framework Programme seeks to determine whether 3rd generation access techniques will provide a more accessible, more exploitable and deeply embeddable approach in mainstream Information and Communication Technologies (ICT). This approach is developed and explored with the Open Accessibility Framework (OAF) through which aspects of the design, development and deployment of accessible mainstream ICT are addressed. The OAF provides embedded and built-in accessibility solutions, as well as toolkits for developers, for "engraving" accessibility in existing and emerging mass-market ICT-based products, thus making accessibility open, plug & play, personalised & configurable, realistic & applicable in various contexts; ÆGIS is placing users and their needs at the centre of all ICT developments. Based on a holistic User Centred Approach (UCD), ÆGIS identifies user needs and interaction models for several user groups (users with visual, hearing, motion, speech and cognitive impairments as well

C. Stephanidis (Ed.): Universal Access in HCI, Part I, HCII 2009, LNCS 5614, pp. 480–488, 2009.

as application developers) and develops open source based generalised accessibility support into mainstream ICT devices/applications:

- desktop,
- rich web applications, and,
- Java-based mobile devices.

All developments will be iteratively tested with a significant number of end users, developers and experts in 3 phases and 4 Pilot sites Europe wide (in Belgium, Spain, Sweden and the UK).

The project includes strong industrial and end user participation (the participating industries are among the market leaders in the corresponding mainstream ICT markets). The project results' uptake is promoted by strong standardisation activities, as well as the fact that much of the technology results will be either new open source applications or will be built into existing and already widely adopted open source ICT.

2 Overall Approach

The whole ÆGIS project is driven by a User Centred Design approach, and the extraction, based on it, of representative Use Cases. According to ISO 9241-11, User Centred Design stands for "*The extent to which a product can be used by <u>specified users</u> to achieve <u>specified goals</u> with effectiveness, efficiency and satisfaction in a <u>specified context of use</u>"*, where (1) effectiveness is the accuracy and completeness with which users can achieve their goals; (2) efficiency of an application stands for the resources expended in relation to the accuracy and completeness of goals achieved and (3) concept satisfaction stands for the comfort and acceptability of the work system to its users and other people affected by its use [10, 11].

When using the user centred design approach we start from the users, determine their present needs and expectations and convert them into an appropriate user interface design [6] (see the following figure). The interface of an application will offer different levels of access (e.g. simple and expert search) always trying to morph into a self explanatory interface characterized by minimal usage of technical language.

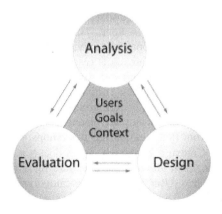

Fig. 1. The user centred design approach

One of the key challenges addressed by ÆGIS is to provide appropriate design solutions that will contribute to reducing the 30% of the European population currently not using ICT. In order to address this issue effectively, ÆGIS is committed to develop solutions that will receive wide acceptance from intended users. For this purpose, the project will define and follow an appropriate user-centered development process, in which needs, wants, and limitations of the end user are given extensive attention at each stage of the development process. The ÆGIS approach requires designers to analyse and foresee how users are likely to use a design solution, as well as to test the validity of their assumptions with regards to user behaviour in real world tests with actual users.

A number of models of a user-centered design process have been made available to allow user requirements to be considered right from the beginning and included into the whole product cycle. For defining the ÆGIS integrated approach, various relevant models will be taken into account, including, but not limited to, Cooperative design [5], Participatory design, Contextual design [2], INCLUDE, Universal Design [4], COST219 [3], and other ISO (see footnote[1]) compliant approaches. Finally, additional user-oriented issues shall be explored as research suggests that, for instance, different forms of behaviour and pleasure should be included in a user-centered approach in addition to traditional definitions of usability and accessibility (e.g., see Emotional Design [12], User-orientation framework [9]).

Experience has demonstrated the important role that distributed project settings play in Participatory Design. This is particularly true of many of the applications proposed in relation both to selecting relevant users for the design process, and where distributed groups of developers and users are engaged in a design process. The problems of geographical distribution will be explored though the development of best practice in relation to Distributed Participatory Design. This is likely to include the proposal of a number of approaches to bridge geographic division, including: use of groupware; technical or personal media to gather feedback; surveys to involve unknown users; video-based interaction analysis; e-prototypes or electronic paper prototypes to get feedback from distant users; and combining distributed and non-distributed phases.

Based on the ÆGIS user centered approach, a conduct of interviews, focused questionnaires and observations made in the user's context of use will follow. It is important to take under consideration that the social behaviour of a user group is different in situations where the key end user is alone. The prime focus of the User workshops and field studies will be on collaborative activities, user to user communication and situations where multiple users share some resources (e.g. shared computer in a lab, communication devices). Such activities are typical in situations like schools, nursing homes-houses, day centres and during communication with care-givers. The workshops will consist of meetings with user groups, seminars and focus groups. Both national and a pan-European workshop are planned.

The data collected from field studies and workshops will also be used for the assessment of the User Centered Approach, as well as for the modeling of the user needs. For each user segment identified,a procedure for assigning a user to a particular segment will be created. User needs will be categorized by user segments (based on the kind of impairment). The user needs will be summarized according to [6]:

---

[1] http://www.usabilitynet.org/tools/r_international.htm#9241x (ISO 9221-11).

- What the user is trying to achieve and how?
- How users are influenced by their context of use, their previous knowledge and experience?
- What the users appreciate most when using ICT (e.g. speed, accuracy, error recovery, fun)?

Usability goals and objectives will be defined, in order to be able to assess the success of the Open Accessibility Framework (OAF) during testing.

The Open Accessibility Framework is a comprehensive, holistic approach to programmatic support for assistive technologies. This is in stark contrast to the 2nd generation approach to accessibility via assistive technologies on the proprietary Windows platform. Building on the pioneering 3rd generation of the state of the art Open Desktop in UNIX and GNU/Linux systems, the Open Accessibility Framework extends the concepts of programmatic accessibility in two directions: "upstream" into the developer tools for creating accessible applications, and "downstream" into further use and deployment – into Internet technologies and mobile devices.

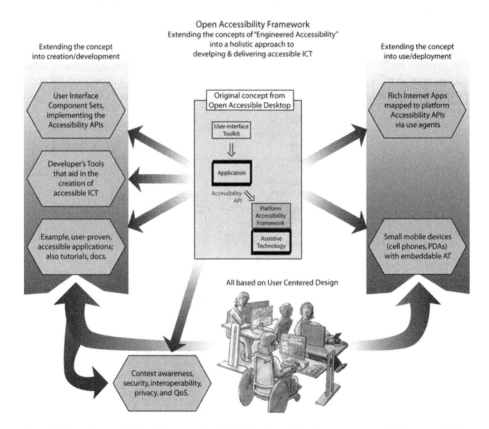

Fig. 2. Open Accessibility Framework of ÆGIS: Extending the concepts of "Engineered Accessibility" into a holistic approach to developing & delivering accessible ICT

All developments of the project, namely the Open Accessibility Framework as well as the research prototypes of all application areas domains will be finally evaluated, across three phases. More specifically, ÆGIS is committed to build evaluation with sample users and user-based validation into all stages of the development lifecycle, from the very first prototypes till the pre-release stage. It should be noted that evaluation in ÆGIS focuses on both user- and expert-based evaluation, including also technical validation of the prototypes and the Open Accessibility Framework.

Regarding evaluation, ÆGIS will review traditional evaluation approaches, methods and tools and develop improved means for assessing the prototypes and applications in question, including a generic framework for the evaluation of inclusive ICT-based solutions. Evaluation criteria will include, but not be limited to: the quality of the user experience of the ÆGIS applications under validation, the desirability and utility of the project results.

Clearly this approach will provide valuable feedback to various design and development teams of the project; nonetheless, the experience to be gained by a number of spread evaluation groups will be consolidated and documented appropriately in order to serve as reliable, yet raw, input to standards and exploitation plans.

In summary, ÆGIS has developed a horizontal evaluation plan, involving several sequential evaluations that shall involve both experts and users, as appropriate, at various stages of the development lifecycle of all the proposed prototypes and applications. As implied by its name, sequential evaluations involve a series of evaluation techniques that run in sequence (see following figure), such as cognitive walkthrough [14], heuristic evaluation [11], formative and summative evaluation [13].

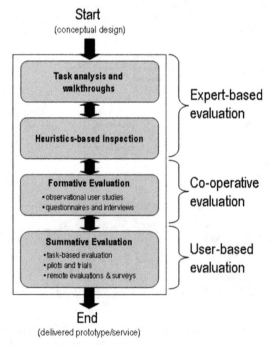

Fig. 3. Example of sequential evaluation to be followed within ÆGIS

The plan will be realised from several independent and multidisciplinary evaluation specialists at various partner sites, and monitored centrally in order to minimise contingencies. An example of the sequential evaluation to be followed within ÆGIS is reflected in the following figure.

3   Evaluation in ÆGIS

Four distinct pilots are planned in Belgium, Spain, Sweden, and the UK within the project. As described in the previous chapter, the User Centred Design model adopted will have three distinct evaluation iterations following the initial defining of essential functionality:

- Initial concept testing (using simulation and storyboarding) with end users and other related stakeholders.
- Creating some tentative content & user interfaces for initial baseline testing.
- Full testing and trialling of the demonstrators and applications by end users and experts.

Each pilot will undertake evaluation across the aforementioned 3 phases and aims to involve people with vision, mobility, cognitive, hearing and speaking impairments. Experts, tutors and developers will also be involved. All feedback received from each of the 3 evaluation phases will be brought back into the development process that will take place in the project period following the respective evaluation phase.

The first phase will focus on Wizard of Oz trials and trials with mock-ups. The Swedish Pilot site will involve the following users:

- 10 persons with cognitive impairments
- 10 persons with motor impairments
- 10 persons with speech impairments
- 5 experts
- 5 tutors

The Pilot site in the UK will involve the following users:

- 10 blind/low vision users
- 10 with motor impairments
- 10 with speech impairments
- 5 experts
- 5 tutors

The Pilot site in Belgium will involve the following users:

- 10 blind/low vision users
- 10 with motor impairments
- 10 with cognitive impairments
- 10 with hearing impairments
- 10 with speech impairments

- 5 experts
- 5 tutors

  The Spanish Pilot site will involve the following users:

- 10 blind/low vision users
- 10 with motor impairments
- 10 with cognitive impairments
- 10 with hearing impairments
- 10 with speech impairments
- 5 experts
- 5 tutors

The second phase of the evaluation will focus on the assessment of the early proto-types produced until then. The same numbers and types of users will be engaged in each case with the addition of 5 developers in each Pilot site. The third phase, which constitutes the evaluation of the final prototypes will engage 5 more experts and tutors in each case in comparison to the 2nd phase.

A series of novel tools and methods will be developed, not excluding traditional methods like log files, questionnaires, event diaries, etc., to ensure the recording of the measurements, objective (users' performance) and subjective (usability and user acceptance aspects), collected during each evaluation phase and during the evaluation of any type of application (mobile, desktop, rich Internet).

4   User Selection, Involvement and Recruitment in ÆGIS

ÆGIS efforts occur in the following important domains:

- Desktop and mobile user agents and web browsers
- "Web 2.0" applications - rich Internet applications built with technologies like AJAX, DHTML, JavaScript, and JavaFX
- Mobile applications and devices (e.g. smart phones, PDAs, etc.)
- Developer's tools
- Document authoring applications
- Communications products
  In this context, ÆGIS addresses 2 main categories of end users:
- Developers of ICT infrastructure, applications and services –referred to hereinafter as "developers"
- People with disabilities –referred to hereinafter as "end users"– who experience one or more of the following mild to severe impairments:

  o   Blind and low-vision users
  o   Motor impairment users
  o   Cognitive impairment users
  o   Hearing impairment users
  o   Speech impairment users

It is worth noting that the target end user groups include also the elderly, given that the vast majority of elderly people experiences one or more of the above impairments.

Individual end users (people with disabilities) as well as various other stakeholders such as accessibility assessors and developers, service providers, and where applicable relevant accessibility units within public bodies, will actively participate in the project's User Centered Approach and iterative evaluations and will be recruited through Partner networks and contacts of the end user representatives in the Consortium (RNIB, FONCE, EPR, ACE, SUDART) and key individual specialists working with people with disabilities.

It should be noted that a participants pool has been created from the early beginning of the project, which will enable the Pilot sites to engage the same participants (all categories of them), as far as possible, throughout the whole evaluation cycle, even since the initial field trials conducted before the first evaluation phase.

From the pool of end users and experts of the project, a "hard core" of ten end users and experts will be identified. At least two of them experts will also be classified as "expert end users" – that is they have a lot of knowledge both as end users of Assistive Technology (AT) and as experts in the field of AT. This "hard core" will engage in the process of rapid, iterative testing based on home/school/work visits and via workshops. Some equipment and demonstrators will also be loaned out for short periods of time, once they are robust and useful enough for this to happen. As each significant change is made in the development cycle of an demonstrator or application prototype, individual visits will be made to the "hard core" test team, some of whom will be switch users with very complex needs and who may require novel tools and evaluation methods to elicit their opinions. This group will also need a great deal of time and support in order to be genuinely and actively engaged in the iterative test cycle. The remaining end users and experts within the pool will be engaged and consulted during the iterative pilot testing through annual workshops where small group testing, discussion groups and plenary meetings will ensure a breadth and range of feedback from this bigger pool of end users, experts and developers.

5 Conclusions

This paper presented the approach and plans of the evaluation activities to be followed within ÆGIS FP7 Integrating Project. ÆGIS is anticipated to constitute a breakthrough in the eInclusion area, embedding accessibility support by default in mainstream ICT applications (desktop, mobile, rich Internet). In the context of the overall User Centred Approach to be adopted in the project, evaluation of the Open Accessibility Framework to be developed and all research prototypes will take place in three iterative phases and in 4 Pilot sites across Europe (Belgium, Spain, Sweden and the UK). In addition to the testing that will take place in a laboratory environment (pilot sites), close observation of user interaction with technology is a critical component of "real usability testing", and forms the cornerstone of the pilot programs in the project. That said, many of the ÆGIS-developed prototypes and technologies are designed explicitly for use outside of a "lab environment". These include a part of the open desktop work (including the realtime-text application), part of the rich Internet applications being developed, and the accessible mobile devices. Towards the end of the project (when the technologies are in their second iteration cycle), prolonged end-user evaluation of usage scenarios and sample applications (over a period of weeks, used as part of the related daily life activities) will be scheduled, gathering feedback during and after the trial period. The open desktop and a number of rich Internet applications will be evaluated in this extended trial, and will do so at least with vision and hearing impaired end-users. The possibility of including longer term evaluation of mobile device accessibility will be further explored (to the extent that secure cell phone connectivity where the end-user trials are taking place is secured; otherwise existing end-user cell phone connectivity will be re-used). In addition, the possibility of longer term evaluations by people with cognitive impairments will be explored, to the extent that ethical safeguards are taken on-board.

References

1. Annex, I.: Description of Work, Open Accessibility Everywhere: Groundwork, Infrastructure, Standards (ÆGIS). In: 7th FW, ICT-2007.7.1, ICT & Ageing (September 11, 2008)
2. Beyer, H., Holtzblatt, K.: Contextual Design: Defining Customer-centered Systems. Morgan Kaufmann, San Francisco (1998)
3. COST 219ter Accessibility for All to Services and Terminals for Next Generation Networks Patrick Roe, Chairman COST 219ter, LEMA-Ecole Polytechnique Fédérale de Lausanne
4. Emiliani, P.L., Stephanidis, C.: Universal access to ambient intelligence environments: opportunities and challenges for people with disabilities. IBM Systems Journal 44(3), 605–619 (2005)
5. Greenbaum, J.M., Kyng, M.: Design at Work: Cooperative Design of Computer Systems. Lawrence Erlbaum Associates, Mahwah (1991)
6. Hackos, J.T., Redish, J.C.: User and Task Analysis for Interface Design. John Wiley &Sons, Inc., Chichester (1997)
7. Hix, D., Hartson, H.R.: Developing User Interfaces: Ensuring Usability through Product & Process. John Wiley and Sons, Inc., Chichester (1993)
8. Jacko, J.A., Sears, A.: The Human-computer Interaction Handbook: Fundamentals, Evolving Technologies, and Emerging Applications. Lawrence Erlbaum Associates, Mahwah (2003)
9. Mourouzis, A., Antona, M., Boutsakis, E., Stephanidis, C.: A User-Orientation Evaluation Framework: Assessing Accessibility Throughout the User Experience Lifecycle (2006)
10. Nielsen, J.: Usability Engineering, 13th edn. Morgan Kaufmann, San Francisco (1994)
11. Nielsen, J.: Heuristic evaluation. John Wiley & Sons, Inc., Chichester (1994)
12. Norman, D.A.: Emotional Design: Why We Love (or Hate) Everyday Things. Basic Books (2003) ISBN: 978-0465051359
13. Scriven, M.: The methodology of evaluation. In: Stake, R.E. (ed.) Perspectives of curriculum evaluation, American Educational Research Association Monograph. Rand McNally, Chicago (1967)
14. Wharton, C., Rieman, J., Lewis, C., Polson, P.: The cognitive walkthrough method: A practitioner's guide (1994)
15. http://www.usabilitynet.org/tools/r_international.htm#9241x (ISO 9221-11)

Digital Design Mobile Virtual Laboratory Implementation: A Pragmatic Approach

Vlado Glavinic[1], Mihael Kukec[2], and Sandi Ljubic[3]

[1] Faculty of Electrical Engineering and Computing, University of Zagreb,
Unska 3, HR-10000 Zagreb, Croatia
[2] College of Applied Sciences,
Jurja Krizanica 33, HR-42000 Varazdin, Croatia
[3] Faculty of Engineering, University of Rijeka,
Vukovarska 58, HR-51000 Rijeka, Croatia
vlado.glavinic@fer.hr, mihael.kukec@velv.hr,
sandi.ljubic@riteh.hr

Abstract. The omnipresence of m-devices, and especially those of the cellular phones type, certainly makes the basis for the introduction and use of m-learning systems, but their implementation heavily depends on the area to be covered hence showing a different degree of complexity. This especially holds for the area of digital design, where there is the need for handling logic schemes which includes both displaying and modifying them in addition to the usual imaging of text and graphics. In this paper we discuss essential HCI issues, which are related to the implementation of a Mobile Virtual Laboratory for digital logic design. We make use of a pragmatic approach by blending a number of interaction methods known from other application fields hopefully providing a holistic effect in the process of learning and teaching in the mobile.

Keywords: digital logic design, m-devices, m-learning, touch sensitive screen, virtual laboratories.

1 Introduction

Present technological developments prompted by an ever increasing demand of mobile services on the telecom market have brought to an equally intensive development of mobile devices (m-devices) [24], such that the generational gap between m-devices and desktop computers is been constantly reduced. As the technological progress of both computers and the Internet has favored the expansion of e-learning systems, the development and proliferation of m-devices enables, although with a slower pace, the advancement of m-learning systems. The fundamental hindrance for a faster and smoother introduction of m-learning systems lies in limitations imposed by m-devices themselves [23], which mostly arise from their reduced dimensions.

The advantage of the m-learning concept has led us to the inception of the Mobile Virtual Laboratory (MVL) that would support the process of teaching and learning on the move for the area of digital design [10]. According to the domain specificity, the major requirements to be put in front of the respective MDA (Mobile Device

C. Stephanidis (Ed.): Universal Access in HCI, Part I, HCII 2009, LNCS 5614, pp. 489–498, 2009.

Application) implementation should include the following: (i) display of digital schemes on reduced area screens typical of m-devices, (ii) successful navigation within digital schemes which are not necessarily displayed on an m-device screen as a whole, (iii) easy creation/modification of digital schemes possibly using new techno- logical enhancements (as e.g. touch sensitive screens), and (iv) simultaneously run- ning simulations coupled to the digital circuit being developed on-screen. As the latter subject is beyond the scope of this paper, we focus on usability [11] and HCI prob- lems concerning display, managing, and navigation within digital circuitry on the mobile device screen (Fig. 1). In solving the abovementioned issues we make a prag- matic use of already known techniques, which we consider to have a holistic impact to the solution of the digital design MVL problem.

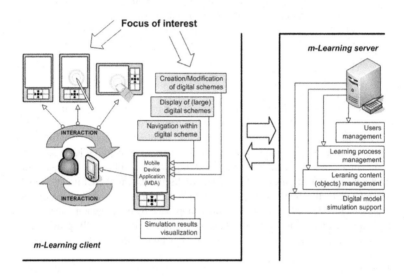

Fig. 1. Focus of interest within a digital design MVL system

2   Related Work on M-Learning and Our Motivation

The potentiality of m-learning overall success lies in the omnipresence of mobile devices in classrooms and university halls. In fact, it has been noticed that "there is no doubt that one of the ways of motivating people such as the typical 20 or 30 year old is by using Information and Communication Technology" [2]. A research conducted at University of Birmingham on a sample of seventeen MSc students [7] with the goal of "investigating whether students would find a handheld computer useful for sup- porting their learning" has shown that although technology has been useful to stu- dents, "mobile learning organizers used in this study did not 'revolutionize' student's styles or patterns of learning". However, the authors acknowledged this study as just the first attempt at designing integrated learning organizers.

Mobile Learning Engine (MLE) [12] represents a multimedia mobile device appli- cation which supports many features, some of them being display of formatted text with integrated images and hyperlinks, audio and video playback, single/multiple choice quizzes and graphical marking questions. Strong multimedia capabilities have been developed to partially overcome limitations of screen size, as authors believe that replacing continuous text with different kinds of multimedia brings better results in the learning process. MLE has been tested for the medical knowledge domain but it can easily be utilized for other domain environments, too. Deficiencies of mobile devices have been reduced with the usage of Mobile Interaction Learning Objects (MILOs) and strong emphasis on multimedia, resulting with new benefits in transforming mobile devices into mobile *learning* devices.

Cellular phones and/or PDA based MDAs developed for performing virtual experiments by remote controlling real hardware is an interesting concept presented in [1]. Concerning HCI issues, while commenting virtual laboratories in general, the authors found that "action of wiring and rewiring offers the true challenge" while working with digital components.

Apparently, both usability challenges and HCI issues represent a common problem in the abovementioned work. Some of them can be reduced through technological advancement of mobile devices (more computing power and storage capability, better screen resolution, communication channels of larger bandwidth), but others require much more effort to be even partially solved. Firstly, it is obvious that the learning content should be presented in the most appropriate way for mobile users. One of the possible solutions is to create small units of domain knowledge containing as much as possible multimedia content adapted to target mobile device. If an m-Learning system is to be used in a special knowledge domain requiring practice and training (such as a laboratory environment), it should then include special MDAs tailored to support interactive examples and simulations from this particular area. Such interactive techniques can be very helpful in the learning process, because "a number of studies indicated that interactive, dynamic computer simulations have been successfully applied in promoting exploratory learning of new concepts as well as in changing existing mental representations" [13].

3 Design and Implementation of an MVL

This section discusses in more detail our implementation of a mobile virtual laboratory, the component of our m-Learning system which is to be used as a "support MDA" for teaching digital design, and emphasizing both user interface design and HCI issues.

Mobile applications are becoming more versatile, with many options and functions being lately offered to the user. To be able to efficiently use all of the offered options, the MDA user should be able to find the required option quickly and without much effort. Some of the mobile applications and related functions are self explanatory and intuitive (e.g. the picture browser), and as such they do not have much options. On the other hand, a digital design MVL application represents a complex software unit with many options and modes of behavior. Such an application must provide the user with a method of swiftly browsing through its options and eventually of finding the desired one. The described functionality is provided by our transformable menu component (TMC) for mobile device applications [8]. TMC development is motivated by our goal to improve mobile user interaction with menu navigation and provide our MDA with a rich GUI component capable of managing a large number of functions and options which the user can apply during her/his work without having to invest much effort in the interaction. The TMC has the same form as PC desktop application menus, as well as suitable size and shape with respect to limitations of mobile device displays. The abovementioned motivation goals (i.e. HCI issues) are encompassed by using both adaptable and adaptive procedures, thus making the menu component both personalized and easy to use. Recent improvements to the TMC, which are currently under development, include support to touchscreen events and actions.

3.1 Creation and Modification of Digital Schemes

Creation and modification of digital schemes in any type of simulator or even CAD system are a painstaking task. Applications for simulating digital logic running on desktop computers, having at their disposal all of the respective luxuries, can be very complex to use, and encompass numerous menus and toolbars, such that creating a logic scheme of an even moderate size can be a time consuming task. The user has to place a number of components, move them to different locations, align them manually or by means of some tools, connect (or virtually wire) them, and then iterate the cycle. The procedure for creating digital logic schemes in our MDA is the same as in any other simulation or CAD tool but with a reduced number of actions the user has to take. Interconnection routes between components are automatically routed using the A* search algorithm, eliminating the need of user intervention here [15], [25].

Having at disposal minimal input capabilities, we had to reduce the number of actions the user has to take to activate certain functions. Different input methods have been implemented and combined so far, some of them specially tuned for specific task [17]. From the standpoint of graphical imaging, TMC and other interface components are designed to be partially, and in some cases even fully transparent, in order to limit occlusion of background objects as less as possible. A feature that additionally limits the occlusion of background object is the ability to relocate TMC to four different locations [8]. As TMC uses icons, we expect it to be more usable through implementation of icons usage guidelines [14]: textual information is replaced wherever possible, with icons, using icons familiar in the domain of digital schematics (mostly logic symbols), see Fig. 2.

On the other hand, we note that many contemporary mobile devices are already equipped with touchscreens, a technology which undoubtedly is going to improve the input capabilities of mobile device but yet remains to be thoroughly investigated [20]. Motivated by the existing research done in the area of touchscreen usage we have implemented the MDA interface so as to be able to concurrently use interaction events from both keypads and touchscreens of mobile devices. In any moment, without need to explicitly change mode of operation from keypad to touchscreen and vice versa, both input methods can be used. Using a touchscreen fewer actions are needed to obtain the same result than using the keypad, which requires navigating to an option before activating it. Within the touchscreen environment all of the on-screen options are displayed just one tap distant from their activation, in order to avoid navigation to the item. Conversely, when using the keypad, both adaptive and adaptable algorithms can be used to decrease the number of actions to be carried out [10].

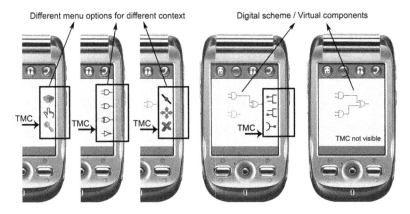

Fig. 2. TMC is a semitransparent GUI component imaged only when required, thus minimizing occlusion of background objects

When using a touchscreen we assume that the user is tapping the screen using her/his fingers and not the stylus (if present), hence for TMC we are using the Direct Touch technique. Because of the relatively large size of fingers in comparison to the screen size, screen targets must have adequate sizes for the user to be able to tap on them with the required degree of precision. According to [19], mobile device touchscreen targets should have a size of at least 9.2 mm, which in pixels varies considerably from one device to another. Pixel size is important in the design phase, when user interface components are modeled. Because of big variations between different devices, accommodation must be provided by implementing adaptability and adaptivity in order to create interface components with adequate sizes for a particular touchscreen [9]. TMC uses raster icons which also need to be adapted to different screen sizes to conform to the 9.2 mm rule. Rather than resizing raster icons, we have taken a much simpler approach: the margin belonging to the icon is resized, thus improving tapping accuracy on small screens with higher resolution. The change in size of the icon margin can be calculated by the MDA (adaptive behavior), while subsequently the margin size can be changed by a suitable user action (adaptable behavior).

Iconic interaction [5] is not used only by the TMC but also by the MDA's virtual breadboard. *Breadboards* are tools used to assemble electronic circuitry during the experimental phase, resulting in prototypes being built without soldering the components. This enables their subsequent disassembly and reassembly as required in the design process. A *virtual breadboard* uses icons (in fact logic symbols) to represent real digital components, as shown in Fig. 2 and Fig. 3. The respective icon (logic symbol) here stands for a representation of the underneath data structures carrying semantics and related component data. Icons/logic symbols pertinent to a touchscreen environment should also adhere to the 9.2 mm guideline for target size [19], what is achieved by the virtual breadboard zooming feature. The zooming factor can be automatically calculated by the MDA (adaptive behavior) and subsequently possibly changed by the user (adaptable behavior).

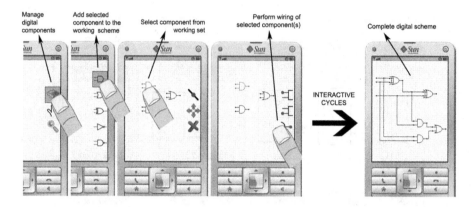

Fig. 3. From left to right: creation of a simple digital logic scheme. Using the touchscreen the user points to the first icon of a vertical TMC hence opening a submenu, then points again to the logic gate to be placed, and eventually places it by again tapping the screen. The A* algorithm is subsequently used to calculate the routes and connect the symbols.

The latter two paragraphs illustrate how to accommodate the user interface to touchscreen actions by resizing the interface widgets, however some of them due to their nature cannot be magnified enough like e.g. interconnection lines in the MVL setting. Users planning to create interconnections between two virtual wires must select a point in a pixel-wide wire where the connection is to be made. Using a finger a user would probably tap correctly on the line, but the accurate tap position will be somewhere in the range of the abovementioned 9.2 mm. Zooming the line (in both dimensions) as any other graphical element will make it wider on the screen, resulting with a smaller length imaged on-screen with the surrounding interconnected symbols possibly out of screen, thus loosing the schematic context. The precise selection of a target having dimensions of just a few pixels is very difficult when using Direct Touch on touchscreens, hence warranting a completely new approach. For instance, techniques like TapTap and MagStick are experimentally proven to successfully tackle with the "selection of targets with the thumb on small tactile screens: screen accessibility, visual occlusion and accuracy" [22]. TapTap uses one tap to generally determine the region of interest and a second one to precisely select the target in the previously selected region of interest which is zoomed in the middle of the screen. However, selection of points on a line by zooming it is not applicable in our case, and consequently we cannot use the TapTap. Conversely, because of its "magneticity" feature, MagStick can be very successfully applied for selection of connection points on lines, since it supports sticking to a line but allow also movements of the selection point, as opposite to sticking and holding to the closest selected point on the line.

3.2 Display and Navigation Issues Associated with Small Screens

The display of digital schemes on reduced area screens presents problems related to the impossibility of having imaged the whole circuit, since digital schemes can very easily be large and complex, exceeding the imaging capabilities of m-devices (and especially of cellular phones). In this context we rely on some known techniques, which are used quite successfully for displaying both (regular) Web pages [3] and geographic maps [16]. Both from a conceptual and an implementation view, regarding digital schemes as vector graphics enables an easier display scaling (i.e. zooming in/out), see Fig. 4, a characteristic that is considered important for such contents. Additionally, simple vector graphics manipulations also support an easier adaptation to various m-devices with differing screen resolutions; this also involves the possibility of a subsequent implementation of fish-eye techniques for highlighting the focus of manipulation.

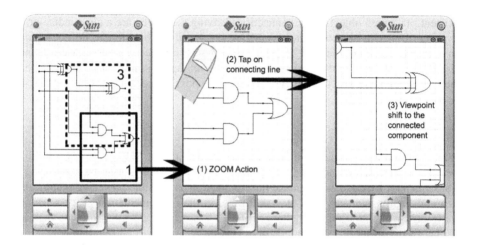

Fig. 4. Navigation to off-screen elements using interconnection lines

Implementing an effective navigation is a general issue in m-device screens [18], [21]; in digital design (and in our MVL implementation) it should get a more considerate attention because of the specific content to be displayed. Here the analogy with navigating (digital) geographic maps cannot be assumed to hold fully. Namely, spatial relationships are the core of the information to be relayed to the user of maps, while this is not the case in digital schemes where the information lies in interconnecting of digital components. Therefore, navigation to digital components (represented by logic symbols) relies either on classic window panning or on using information about components' internal relationships; this latter is especially helpful when trying to reach digital components not imaged on-screen.

Performing manipulations on digital schemes (creation and/or modification) is certainly not an easy task, and is quite demanding for an MDA because of limited input capabilities provided by an m-device, which are presently constrained on arrow keys navigation. Hence the rationale for using a pointing device based interaction style, using a suitable touch sensitive screen, what comes especially useful when handling unconnected components. Such an approach could also be interpreted as syntactic sugar for a digital circuitry visual language.

The virtual breadboard implements only basic methods for navigating to off-screen objects, which includes scrolling, panning and zooming (the latter is supported by the usage of vector graphics). Some more advanced methods, on the other hand, include techniques like Halo and HOP. Halo is a technique interesting "for pointing users to the presence of off-screen objects" [4] by drawing circles around them while HOP is an "interaction technique that enables quick access to off-screen objects" [16]. A comparative evaluation of Halo and simple direction arrows pointing hasn't found significant differences in performing simple spatial tasks [6]. This fact together with the prospect of occluding much of the screen by Halo arcs (visible parts of circles drawn around off-screen object) in the case of larger number of components prompted us to implement a simpler technique much closer to the direction arrows, which uses information on component internal relationships to make the user aware of possibly existent off-screen objects. Interconnections leaving the screen are a clear indicator of existing off-screen objects; hence the MDA and its virtual breadboard do not require any special graphical element for showing off-screen objects. Interconnections are also used to navigate to the next connected element: tapping on the outgoing line near the screen boundary will shift the viewpoint to the next connected element, see Fig. 4.

4   Conclusion

While developing a particular mobile device application for MVL, a strong ambition to take advantage of improved capabilities of present day mobile devices occurs. Consequently, we endeavor to make this application as possible powerful, graphically rich and highly interactive. In the same time, in the implementation process we are confronted with the usability challenges and HCI issues, hence our efforts are focused on the quality of mobile user interaction. Having in mind special requirements in the digital design domain, we have considered and evaluated a number of well-known interaction methods, trying to pragmatically adapt them in our MDA, while at the same time keeping in mind both features and type of contents our application handles.

Our work targets the implementation of a suitable MDA with (i) iconic interaction which enables easy creation and modification of digital logic schemes on mobile device screens, and (ii) the possibility to use both device keypad and touch sensitive screen (if available), without special need to explicitly change interaction mode. We deem that such an approach, which consists of using a visual language (digital schemes) and bimodal interaction (arrow keys and fingers), accomplishes a didactically innovative and effective m-learning concept for teaching digital design.

Acknowledgments. This paper describes the results of research being carried out within the project 036-0361994-1995 *Universal Middleware Platform for e-Learning Systems*, as well as within the program 036-1994 *Intelligent Support to Omnipresence of e-Learning Systems*, both funded by the Ministry of Science, Education and Sports of the Republic of Croatia.

References

1. Alkouz, A., Al-Zoubi, A.Y., Otair, M.: J2ME-Based Mobile Virtual Laboratory for Engineering Education. International Journal of Interactive Mobile Technologies (iJIM) 2(2), 5–10 (2008)

2. Attewell, J., Gustafsson, M.: Mobile Communications Technology for Young Adult Learning and Skills Development (m-Learning). In: Milrad, M., Hoppe, H.U., Kinshuk (eds.) Proc. IEEE Int'l Workshop on Wireless and Mobile Technologies in Education (WMTE 2002), pp. 158–160. IEEE Computer Society, Washington (2002)

3. Baluja, S.: Browsing on small screens: recasting web-page segmentation into an efficient machine learning framework. In: Proc. 15th Int'l Conf. World Wide Web (WWW 2006), pp. 33–42. ACM, New York (2006)

4. Baudisch, P., Rosenholtz, R.: Halo: a technique for visualizing off-screen objects. In: Proc. SIGCHI Conf. on Human Factors in Computing Systems (CHI 2003), pp. 481–488. ACM, New York (2003)

5. Beaudouin-Lafon, M.: User interface support for the integration of software tools: an iconic model of interaction. ACM SIGSOFT Software Engineering Notes 13(5), 143–152 (1988)

6. Burigat, S., Chittaro, L., Gabrielli, S.: Visualizing locations of off-screen objects on mobile devices: a comparative evaluation of three approaches. In: Proc. 8th Conf. Human-Computer Interaction with Mobile Devices and Services (MobileHCI 2006), pp. 239–246. ACM, New York (2006)

7. Corlett, D., Sharples, M., Chan, T., Bull, S.: A Mobile Learning Organiser for University Students. In: Proc. 2nd IEEE Int'l Workshop on Wireless and Mobile Technologies in Education (WMTE 2004), p. 35. IEEE Computer Society, Washington (2004)

8. Glavinic, V., Ljubic, S., Kukec, M.: Transformable Menu Component for Mobile Device Applications: Working with both Adaptive and Adaptable User Interfaces. International Journal of Interactive Mobile Technologies (iJIM) 2(3), 22–27 (2008)

9. Glavinic, V., Granic, A.: HCI Research for e-Learning: Adaptability and Adaptivity to Support Better User Interaction. In: USAB 2008. LNCS, vol. 5298, pp. 359–376. Springer, Heidelberg (2008)

10. Glavinic, V., Ljubic, S., Kukec, M.: Mobile Virtual Laboratory: Learning Digital Design. In: Luzar, S.V., Hljuz, D.V. (eds.) Proc. 29th Int'l Conf. Information Technology Interfaces (ITI 2007), pp. 325–410. SRCE University of Zagreb, Zagreb (2007)

11. Glavinic, V., Ljubic, S., Kukec, M.: A Holistic Approach to Enhance Universal Usability in m-Learning. In: Mauri, J.L., Narcis, C., Chen, K.C., Popescu, M. (eds.) Proc. 2nd Int'l Conf. Mobile Ubiquitous Computing, Systems, Services and Technologies (UBICOMM 2008), pp. 305–310. IEEE Computer Society, Los Alamitos (2008)

12. Holzinger, A., Nischelwitzer, A., Meisenberger, M.: Mobile Phones as a Challenge for m-Learning: Examples for Mobile Interaction Learning Objects (MILOs). In: Proc. 3rd IEEE Int'l Conf. Pervasive Computing and Communications Workshops (PerCom 2005), pp. 307–311. IEEE Computer Society, Washington (2005)

13. Holzinger, A., Kickmeier-Rust, M.D., Wassertheurer, S., Hessinger, M.: Learning Performance with Interactive Simulations in Medical Education: Lessons Learned from Results of Learning Complex Physiological Models with the HAEMOdynamics SIMulator. Computers & Education 52(2), 292–301 (2008)

14. Holzinger, A., Errath, M.: Mobile Computer Web-Application Design in Medicine: Research Based Guidelines. Int'l Journal Universal Access in Information Society 6(1), 31–41 (2007)

15. Johann, M., Reis, R.: Net by Net Routing with a New Path Search Algorithm. In: Proc. 13th Symposium on Integrated Circuits and Systems Design (SBCCI 2000), p. 144. IEEE Computer Society, Washington (2000)

16. Irani, P., Gutwin, C., Yang, X.D.: Improving selection of off-screen targets with hopping. In: Proc. SIGCHI Conf. Human Factors in Computing Systems (CHI 2006), pp. 299–308. ACM, New York (2006)
17. Karlson, A.K., Bederson, B.B.: One–handed Touchscreen Input for Legacy Applications. In: Proc. 26th SIGCHI Conf. Human Factors in Computing Systems (CHI 2008), pp. 1399–1408. ACM, New York (2008)
18. Mehra, S., Werkhoven, P., Worring, M.: Navigating on handheld displays: Dynamic versus static peephole navigation. ACM Transactions on Computer-Human Interaction (TOCHI) 13(4), 448–457 (2006)
19. Parhi, P., Karlson, A.K., Bederson, B.B.: Target Size Study for One-Handed Thumb Use on Small Touchscreen Devices. In: Proc. 8th Conf. Human-Computer Interaction with Mobile Devices and Services (MobileHCI 2006), pp. 203–210. ACM, New York (2006)
20. Perry, K.B., Hourcade, J.P.: Evaluating one handed thumb tapping on mobile touchscreen devices. In: Proc. Graphics Interface (GI 2008). ACM Int'l Conf. Proc. Series, vol. 322, pp. 57–64. Canadian Information Processing Society, Toronto (2008)
21. Roto, V., Popescu, A., Koivisto, A., Vartiainen, E.: Minimap: a web page visualization method for mobile phones. In: Proc. SIGCHI Conf. Human Factors in Computing Systems (CHI 2006), pp. 35–44. ACM, New York (2006)
22. Roudaut, A., Hout, S., Lecolinet, E.: TapTap and MagStick: improving one-handed target acquisition on small touch-screens. In: Proc. Working Conf. Advanced Visual Interfaces (AVI 2008), pp. 146–153. ACM, New York (2008)
23. Shudong, W., Higgins, M.: Limitations of Mobile Phone Learning. In: Proc. IEEE Int'l Workshop on Wireless and Mobile Technologies in Education (WMTE 2005), pp. 179–181. IEEE Computer Society, Washington (2005)
24. The GSM Association (GSMA),
    http://www.gsmworld.com/europe_observatory/
25. Xing, Z., Kao, R.: A Minimum Cost Path Search Algorithm through Tile Obstacles. In: Proc. 2001 Int'l Symposium on Physical Design (ISPD 2001), pp. 192–197. ACM, New York (2001)

Eliciting Mental Models of User Methods for Product and Communications Design

Joy Goodman-Deane[1], Patrick Langdon[1], P. John Clarkson[1], and Susannah Clarke[2]

[1] Engineering Design Centre, Department of Engineering, University of Cambridge,
Cambridge CB2 1PZ, UK
{jag76,pml24,pjc10}@Springer.com
[2] Department of Civil and Environmental Engineering, Imperial College, London
susannah.clarke05@imperial.ac.uk

Abstract. In order for products and services to be designed inclusively, designers need to understand users' capabilities and needs Thus methods for involving and understanding users are of key importance for inclusive design. However, many of these methods have limited uptake, possibly because of a poor fit with design practice. We conducted a card-sorting study with twenty-one product and communications designers, examining how they view user-centred methods, and how they relate them to other design methods. Results were analysed using hierarchical agglommerative cluster analysis to try to identify groups of methods that are considered similar to each other. This paper particularly examines the differences between product and communications designers. We found that product designers perceive a larger distinction between user involvement and other design methods, and communications designers are less structured in their approach to methods. We conclude that inclusive design methods and their presentation need to be adapted for different groups of designers.

Keywords: Inclusive design, user methods, design practice.

1 Introduction

In order to design useful and usable products and services inclusively, designers must keep in mind the end-users' needs, capabilities and desires [1]. This is especially important in inclusive design because the users have a wide range of capabilities and situations, which are often very different from the designer's own [2, 3]. However, doing this can often be difficult. Therefore, many methods have been developed to support this, including both methods for involving users directly and ones for helping designers to consider and understand users more remotely.

However, many of these methods have had a mixed and limited uptake in design practice [4, 5, 6]. Our previous research [3] identified various possible reasons for this, particularly a poor fit between many of the methods and the ways in which designers think and work (c.f. [4, 5, 13]).

In order to improve the uptake of user methods, it is therefore important to understand more about design practice, particularly about how designers think about design methods. We therefore conducted a card-sorting study to investigate designers' views

C. Stephanidis (Ed.): Universal Access in HCI, Part I, HCII 2009, LNCS 5614, pp. 499–505, 2009.

of design methods, particularly examining how user methods of various types fit into this picture. This was part of a larger study which examined design practice more generally, with the aim of understanding how best to equip designers to carry out inclusive design. The larger study indicated differences between product and communications designers in how they approach and carry out design [7, 14], and the card-sorting study indicated that these differences also affect the ways in which they view design methods. In this paper, we focus on these differences and their implications for developing and disseminating inclusive design methods to these communities. Some initial results from this study, examining the sample as a whole, were previously published in [8].

1.1 Related Work

Other researchers have also investigated the use of user methods in design, describing what methods are or are not used and for what purposes (e.g. [9, 10]). Informal approaches appear to dominate [11], with more formal user research often being constrained by limited resources and difficulties in applying the research results [9].

These findings describe the kinds of user methods that are commonly used, and some of the reasons for this, but they do not examine how the designers themselves perceive the methods. Some researchers have addressed this by asking designers to explain the reasons for their use (or non-use) of methods (e.g. [9]) or to rate a selection of methods (e.g. [10]). This provides some useful insight into designers' perceptions of the methods, but does not tend to examine their underlying assumptions about them. In addition, some of the studies focused on relatively small selections of methods.

We therefore sought to augment the previous work by examining designers' underlying views of a wider range of user methods. The study aimed to uncover more about designers' underlying perceptions of the relationships between different design methods, and of the roles played by user methods in particular.

2 Method

Over 330 design methods and techniques were identified through a literature review of fields such as product design, HCI and ergonomics. A subset of 57 methods was then chosen. Care was taken to ensure a representative range of method types, and a wide selection of methods for understanding and involving users. Each method was then described on a card, as shown in Fig. 1.

The card set was given to fourteen product designers and seven communications designers. The product designers had between 1 and 27 years of design practice experience (mean 8), and the communications designers had between 2 and 20 years of experience (mean 11.5). They were asked to organise the cards into groups using any criteria they liked and with any number of groups and sub-groups. Care was taken to avoid influencing the judgments. They then labelled these groups, as shown in Fig. 1. By allowing the designers flexibility in grouping and labelling the methods, we aimed to uncover their perceptions of design methods and the considerations that they felt were important in categorising them.

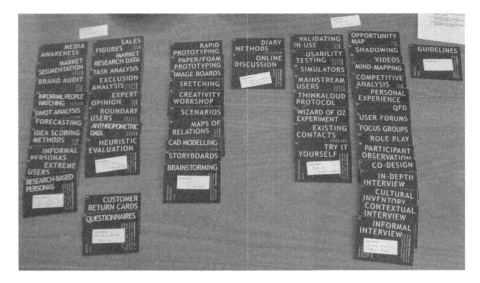

Fig. 1. An example card and a completed card sort

The results were analysed using cluster analysis; an exploratory multivariate statistical technique that is traditionally used to group and classify subjects or variables. By using iterative numerical methods of classification, it is possible to extract the underlying structure in data without any prior assumptions. Clustering methods are primarily descriptive and exploratory in nature [12]. They were used in this study to identify groups of methods that participants considered similar to each other, thus uncovering common perceptions of the relationships between the methods.

In order to identify differences between product and communications designers, these two sub-samples were analysed separately. Hierarchical agglomerative cluster analysis was used on the probabilities of methods co-occurring in the same sorting groups. The resulting probability data were clustered in SPSS using the squared Euclidian distance measure, and a number of agglomerative clustering algorithms or linkage rules run: (1) complete linkage (furthest neighbour) and (2) Ward's method. The results of these analyses were compared for agreement and examined to identify stable clusters and sub-clusters of methods. The output was then collated in the form of clustering dendrograms, which are graphical representations of the clustering process. These were then named by the researchers, based on the methods within each cluster. In some cases, there was no clear connection between the constituent methods, so they were given labels such as "Other" (see Figs. 2 and 3). Wards's method was chosen as the best method for characterising the data, and the resulting clustering dendrograms using this method are shown in Figure 3. It should be noted that figure 2 and 3 represent the main hierarchical cluster relationships in a simpler visualisation and do not reflect an arbitrary choice of clusters. In fact, no cluster choice has been made; the results presented represent the strong evident grouping of the data. Unstable peripheral group members across the two methods were simply omitted.

3 Results

3.1 Product Designers

The clusters of methods used by the product designers are shown in Fig. 2. Both the clusters and the relationships between them were extremely stable, indicating that the product designers held a strong common view of design methods. Because the relationships were stable, the diagram has a detailed hierarchical structure, showing how the clusters are related to each other.

3.2 Communications Designers

The clusters of methods used by the communications designers are shown in Fig. 3. As before, the clusters were stable; however, the relationships between them were not. As a result, only a limited amount can be concluded about the relationships between the clusters, and the resulting cluster structure shown is relatively undeveloped.

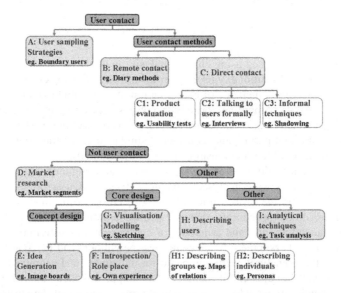

Fig. 2. Common clustering pattern of methods for the product designers in the study. The main clusters are indicated by light grey boxes, and sub-clusters by white boxes. Dark grey boxes indicate how the clusters are related to each other; labels on them are tentative.

In addition, the communications designers identified a large cluster (H, with 14 out of the 57 methods), containing a wide range of methods. Almost all of the communications designers scattered the methods in H across several groups. This indicates that H does not represent a coherent cluster, but rather a set of methods inconsistently categorised across the sample.

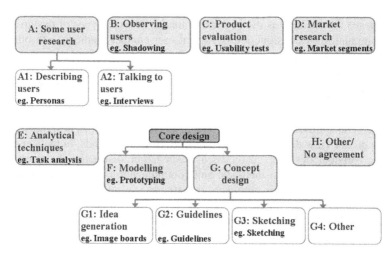

Fig. 3. Common clustering pattern of methods for the communications designers in the study. The main clusters are indicated by light grey boxes, and sub-clusters by white boxes. Dark grey boxes indicate how the clusters are related to each other; labels on them are tentative.

4   Discussion

Both product and communications designers identified clear clusters of design methods. Furthermore, some of these clusters were similar: Product evaluation (clusters C1 and C), Market research (D, D), Idea generation (E, G1) and Modelling (G, F) contained similar methods for both product and communications designers. Both kinds of designers also identified clusters for Describing users (H, A1) and Analysis (I, E), although these only shared a third to a half of their members. Both also identified a higher-level group of "Core design" methods, containing Modelling and several Concept design methods, particularly methods for Idea generation.

However, communications designers had fewer consensuses about design methods, with several of the methods being inconsistently categorised across the sample. Moreover, product and communications designers differed in their views of the relationships between the clusters. Product designers had a common, detailed view of how the clusters were related. Communications designers, on the other hand, did not tend to agree about this, as shown in the flat structure in Fig. 3. Thus, although communications designers have some shared understanding of design methods, this is much weaker than for product designers. The shared understanding does not cover all methods, nor does it extend to the relationships between groups of methods.

The two kinds of designers also differed in their perceptions of user involvement. The product designers had a clear, top-level split between methods with and without user contact. In contrast, although the communications designers had some clusters of user contact methods (A2, B and most of C), these clusters did not group together, and several user contact methods were located in H (Other/No agreement).

We conclude that within the constraints of the small sample, designers tend to think of user contact methods separately from other methods, but this tendency is much stronger for product designers than communications designers. In fact, product designers see user contact as the key discriminator between types of design methods, while communications designers mix several user contact methods with other methods in cluster H and (to some extent) cluster B.

5   Implications

Despite several similarities between product and communications designers, it is clear that they do not view design methods, particularly user methods, in the same way. In particular, product designers perceive a much larger distinction between user involvement and other design methods, and communications designers have less consensus and structure in their approach to methods. As unequal numbers of product (14) and communication (7) designers were involved in this study it is necessary to consider whether the different numbers of each type of designer may have had an impact on the results. For example, it is possible that the outcome may have been different if the number of designers of each type were equal.

This has implications for developing and disseminating inclusive design methods, particularly ones for involving users. It indicates that different design disciplines will respond in different ways. Methods that are suited to one group may need to be adapted or presented differently before they are accepted and used by another group. Although communications designers may benefit from a more flexible approach that allows them to examine method sets in a variety of ways it is also possible that they may really need more guidance on whether and how users are involved. Our results indicate that product designers would benefit from a structured presentation of inclusive design methods and clear guidance on whether and how users are involved. It would also be helpful to place new user methods within the designers' existing conceptual framework. In contrast, communications designers may benefit from a more flexible approach that allows them to examine method sets in a variety of ways and makes less distinction between user methods and other design methods. The framework being developed in the next stage of this research will help to address these issues.

6   Further Work

The results of this study are being used to assist in constructing a framework to help designers to think about methods for inclusive design and to choose ones that are appropriate for their needs.

Acknowledgement. This work was carried out under the UK EPSRC funded Inclusive Design project at the University of Cambridge Engineering Department.

References

1. Langdon, P.M., Clarkson, P.J., And Robinson, P. (eds.): Designing Inclusive Futures. Springer, London (2008)
2. Keates, S., Clarkson, P.J.: Countering design exclusion: An introduction to inclusive design. Springer, London (2003)

3. Langdon, P., Clarkson, P.J., Robinson, P.: Designing accessible technology. Universal Access in the Information Society 6(2), 117–217 (2007) (1615–5289)
4. Dong, H.: Barriers to Inclusive Design in the UK. PhD thesis, Cambridge University (2005)
5. Dong, H., Clarkson, P.J., Cassim, J., Keates, S.: Critical User Forums - An Effective User Research Method for Inclusive Design. The Design Journal 8(2), 49–59 (2005)
6. Gyi, D.E., Sims, R.E., Porter, J.M., Marshall, R., Case, K.: Representing older and disabled people in virtual user trials: data collection methods. Applied Ergonomics 35(5), 443–451 (2004)
7. Goodman, J., Langdon, P.M., Clarkson, P.J.: Equipping Designers for Inclusive Design. Gerontechnology 4(4), 229–233 (2006)
8. Goodman-Deane, J., Langdon, P., Clarke, S., Clarkson, P.J.: Categorising design methods: how designers view the roles of user methods in design. Ergonomics, 273–278 (2008)
9. Crilly, N., Clarkson, P.J.: The influence of consumer research on product aesthetics. In: DESIGN 2006, pp. 689–696. The Design Society (2006)
10. Gulliksen, J., Boivie, I., Persson, J., Hektor, A., Herulf, L.: Making a Difference - a Survey of the Usability Profession in Sweden. In: NordiCHI 2004. ACM Press, New York (2004)
11. Hasdoğan, G.: The Role of User Models in Product Design for Assessment of User Needs. Design Studies 17(1), 19–33 (1996)
12. Everitt, B., Landau, S., Leese, M.: Cluster Analysis, 4th edn. Arnold, London (2001)
13. Cardello, A.V.: Terminology, reliability, validity, and subjectivity in the search for the "voice of the consumer". Food Quality and Preference 16(3), 203–205 (2005)
14. Goodman-Deane, J., Langdon, P., Clarkson, P.J.: Key Influences on the User-Centred Design Process. Journal of Engineering Design (accepted) (in press)
15. Porter, C.S., Chibber, S., Porter, J.M., Healey, L.: RealPeople; Encouraging Inclusive Design through Empathy. In: Include 2005. Royal College of Art, London (2005)

Functional Accessibility Testing Using Best Practices

Jon Gunderson

Division of Disability Resources and Educational Services, University of Illinois,
1207 South Oak Street, Champaign, Illinois, USA, 61820
jongund@illinois.edu

Abstract. The problem with many automated web accessibility testing tools is that they assume a repair oriented approach to web accessibility. The functional web accessibility approach is based on best practices design approach to creating web resources. The best practices build upon the use of web standards to increase developer acceptance, since developers benefit from the design efficiencies of web standards while they build highly accessible websites based on best practices coding techniques. Automated testing tools can be used to look for the best practices coding patterns to verify accessibility. The best practices are essentially effective techniques to implement web accessibility standards like Section 508 or guidelines like the W3C Web Content Accessibility Guidelines.

Keywords: web accessibility, section 508, web content accessibility guidelines, automated testing, html, xhtml, best practices, disability, wcag.

1 Introduction

The best practices approach at the University of Illinois has been developed over a period of ten years and has become the primary means to increase the accessibility of web resources at the university. The work started as a part of accessibility awareness events at the university to encourage web developers to consider accessibility as part of developing web resources. Presentations on the W3C Web Content Accessibility Guidelines 1.0 [1] and Section 508 [2] led developers to start asking questions about coding practices for accessibility. The web was a new technology and most web developers had little, if any, formal training in web technologies. Many were coming from a graphics design background so the visual look and feel of a website was a dominate design requirement. The techniques at that time being used to create web resources were based on the use of graphical images to control styling and tables to control layout and positioning. Developers had little knowledge of the semantic markup available in HTML [3] and the use of Cascading Style Sheets [4] to control styling and layout that is so important for creating web sites the support the principles of interoperability and accessibility [5]. Web developers mostly were considering accessibility at the end of the development process, often the last "check" before they published the website. The results was that the website was so intrinsically inaccessible that the small changes that could be made to improve accessibility, like ALT text for images, would make little difference to people with disabilities. Automated tools used for the "check" highlighted certain accessibility requirements like ALT text for

C. Stephanidis (Ed.): Universal Access in HCI, Part I, HCII 2009, LNCS 5614, pp. 506–514, 2009.
© Springer-Verlag Berlin Heidelberg 2009

images over just as important use of structural markup like headings (H1-H6). Automated tools did this because it is easier to detect and report a missing ALT attribute than to report missing or incorrect use of heading structure of a web resource. Automated web accessibility testing tools generated long lists of manual tests (including use of headers) that overwhelmed web developers so they focused their limited resources on fixing the known problems like ALT text for images. Often fixing ALT for images would remove the "known" accessibility problems from an automated report, even though many of the manual checks would have failed. It was clear that the repair approach was giving accessibility a "bad" name on campus and reinforced stereotypes of accessibility being hard and resource intensive process that limited developer creativity and artistic expression. The repair model was not leading to significant improvements in website accessibility or widespread adoption by developers on campus.

1.1 Designing for Accessibility

A new design oriented model was needed that could be embraced and even endorsed by web developers to not only make their resources more accessible, but also benefit them in terms of making it easier for them to create and maintain websites. This required a different view of the accessibility problem. The repair approach was looking at whatever markup the developer decided to use to create their web resources and look for known or potential sources of accessibility problems. The design approach asks what is needed in the design of web resources to make them not only accessible, but functionally usable by people with disabilities. This turns out to be a much different question than the repair approach and requires us to look at web page design in general to understand the key features of the web pages. The following sections are the issues that arose as we started working with web developers during the design phase of their web development and building accessibility into templates being used to create the web site.

1.2 Titling

One of the first issues in a design oriented approach is the concept of titling a page. Titling is a critical usability feature whether you have a disability or not. The requirement is not a part of Section 508 and only recently became a direct part of the W3C Web Content Accessibility Guidelines 2.0 [6]. Web developers put a lot of time into using graphical styling to let users know what website they are on and most web developers use some type of text styling and placement to make it easy for people to know the purpose of a particular page in their web site. These two pieces of information therefore need to be represented in HTML markup in a way for people with disabilities to also perceive titling information. Looking at the available mark in HTML there were two elements that seem well suited for titling a page, the TITLE element in the HEAD section of the HTML resource and the H1 heading element. In the best practices the TITLE element should provide information on both the web site and the sub page information. The H1 element should contain the sub page information. With this as a best practice now rules can be developed to test whether a page is using the best practices for titling. For example pages that are missing either the TITLE or the H1 element can now be marked as Failing. The H1 sub page content can be compared to the TITLE content to see if the H1 content is a subset of the TITLE content, if the not the page can generate a failure or warning to the developer. The rule is based on the TITLE element containing both web site and sub page information and the H1 element containing sub page information. People with disabilities can use header navigation features of their browser [8] or the header navigation features of screen readers to easily find the title of a web page. The title should be placed right before the main content, making it easy for people with disabilities to find and explore the main content of the page.

An unexpected result of these types of rules is the embracing of this type of feedback by developers. In automated web accessibility evaluation systems that report manual testing of headers it was difficult for developers to know exactly what they should do, but now with the best practices rules they have much more detailed information about the markup patterns they should use for TITLE and H1 elements. Developers also benefit from the efficiencies of using CSS to style H1 element across web resources making it easy to change the styling of sub page titles and to create new pages with consistent styling for titles.

1.3 Navigation Bars

Navigation bars and menus are another important feature of a website that web developers spend a considerable amount of time and effort. The Section 508 [2] requirements indicate the importance of navigation bars through the "1194.22 (o) A method shall be provided that permits users to skip repetitive navigation links" requirement. Yet there is no consensus in the web accessibility community on how developers should code navigation bars [9]. Users with disabilities also may want to do more than just skip over navigation bars, they may also want to move directly to the links of a navigation bar and also be able to differentiate links in navigation bars from other links on the page. The best practices adopted the web standards practice of marking up navigation bars, which uses the UL and LI elements to create navigation bars. The use of unordered list markup seems reasonable, but the tricky part is how to label the navigation bar for identification by people with disabilities. Most web resources have more than one navigation bar and there may be other lists of links that are a part of the main content of the web resource. The first thought was to use the TITLE attribute of the unordered list (UL) to provide a label for the list of links, but this was rejected primarily because assistive technologies like screen readers need to be configured for a special mode to read the title of elements. So the best solution available is using heading elements placed immediately before the unordered list. This allows users to easily navigate to navigation bars using header navigation commands of browsers and assistive technologies and the header content can provide a label for the collection of links.

The rules for navigation bars are not as straight forward as the rules for titling, but the central requirement of the rule is that a heading be placed before the navigation bar to provide a landmark to users. The first step is simple by creating a rule for navigation bars based on requiring a list element that contains mostly link content to have a heading (h2-h6) element immediately preceding the list markup [10]. It cannot be assumed every web page has a navigation bar, so creating another rule requiring a page to have at least one navigation bar seemed like it would lead to false errors, reducing the credibility with developers. Many times a web page may be a simple document that is linked to from another page in the website and does not contain a navigation bar. Developers also may be using tables or other types of markup to create navigation bars which would not even be detected with this rule, essentially eliminating any feedback to them on using headers before the start of the navigation bar. So at best the rule only applies to web resources developed using the web standards technique of using lists to create navigation bars. Another issue found when the rule was initially implemented is the problem of navigation bars not being the only lists on the web page that were mostly links. Developers were confused when other lists of links on the page that were not thought of as navigation bars were identified as navigation bars and warned them of missing header markup. This actually led some developers to put in empty headers before the lists, just to satisfy the requirements of the evaluation tool. This was clearly counter-productive, since the best practices wanted to make sure that accessibility requirements make sense to web developers and this did not make sense to them. So the rule was modified to only identify unordered lists that were mostly links that were before the last H1 element in the web resource. This change was based on the assumption that most navigation bars are before (i.e. document order) the main content in a web resource and the H1 is just before of the main content. This change to the rule was much more palatable to web developers and helped them think more clearly about marking up navigation bars with headings. But the issue remains that this rule is only effective if the developer is using a web standards based approach to web design and places their navigation bars before the last H1 on a page. Authors who don't use unordered lists or have arranged their pages so navigation bars are after the last H1 will not get any feedback on placing headings before navigation bars.

1.4 Form Control Labels

Form control labels brought up other issues in developing rules for the best practices. The form control labeling rules brought into interaction of markup, browser accessibility API mapping and assistive technologies. There are two ways to the LABEL element to label form controls:

LABEL using encapsulation:

```
<label>Name: <input type='text' id='textbox1'
size='30'/></label>
```

LABEL using FOR attribute reference:

```
<label for='textbox1'>Name: </label><input type='text'
id='textbox1' size='30'/>
```

The first code example demonstrates form labeling by encapsulating the INPUT element with the LABEL element and the second example uses the FOR attribute of the LABEL element to reference the ID attribute of the INPUT element. Both these techniques are valid HTML markup, but the encapsulation technique has an unfortunate side effect for assistive technology when using Internet Explorer. The browser includes the value of the form control as part of the communicating the label information to assistive technologies like screen readers. So if there is any initial value in the input text content the content will be included as part of the label. This is clearly a problem since the value content may confuse screen reader users, especially as they start to fill in text boxes on the page and the entered information modifies the label. Using the reference technique does not have this artifact of modifying the label information communicated to assistive technologies, making it a much better practice than the encapsulation technique, especially when you realize this problem also occurs for the SELECT/OPTION and TEXTAREA elements. It is clearly better for developers to use the reference technique to label form controls and the rules developed for form controls must warn the user of the avoiding the use of the encapsulation technique.

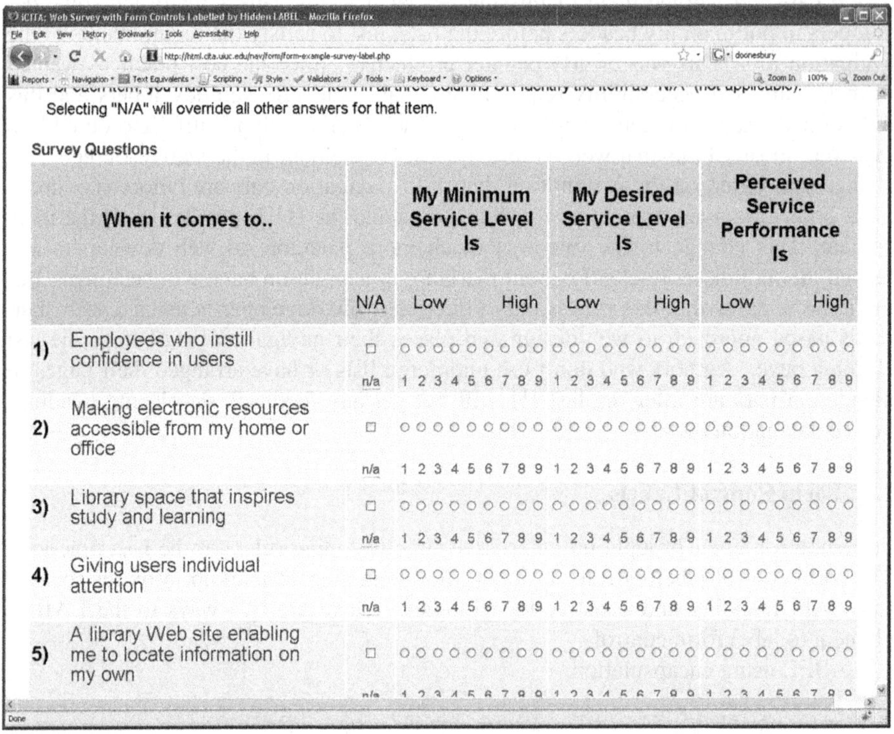

Fig. 1. Screen shot of a survey with high density form controls

In addition to enforcing the labeling rules it is also important to include a uniqueness rule for form controls, especially for high density form controls used in surveys, as seen in Figure 1. The figure shows a web based survey with a question and a set of 31 form controls in *each* row of a table. The 31 controls are organized in four groups of responses. The first column is a checkbox related to the question not being applicable. The next 30 controls are divided into 3 groups with each group of ten radio buttons used to rate the quality and importance to the user on a 10 point scale, with 1 being the lowest rating and 10 being the highest rating. A developer approaching the accessibility of this form (and they did in this example) just used the numbers 1-10 to label the radio buttons in each group. There were no references to the question or to the response categories. Technically each form control had a label, but the labels were not usable to a screen reader user, since they would only hear the numbers 1 through 10. In this case hidden labels need to be created to uniquely identify each potential response and to make it clear to users what question and type of rating they are selecting.

1.5 HTML Best Practices

The rest of the iCITA HTML Best Practices [11] are grouped in a markup centric view that is more familiar to web developers than the grouping used for the W3C Web Content Accessibility Guidelines and the Section 508 requirements. The current grouping of the best practices includes:

Navigation and Orientation. The navigation and orientation features center on the use of HTML markup in a consistent and uniform way to represent major topics and relationships between the content on the page. The examples in the beginning of this paper are part of the navigation and orientation section.

Text Equivalents. Text equivalents current includes images and other non-text content and include requirements to remove decorative images and instead use CSS styling techniques.

Scripting: Scripting is a complex web accessibility topic, but the initial rules in the best practices focus on providing keyboard support for dynamic web. One of the challenges of testing dynamic web content is that even handlers are added dynamically and it is difficult to analyze this information unless you have access to the event handlers in the DOM. There is no standard way in the DOM to enumerate event handlers.

Styling. A fundamental aspect of the accessibility best practices is to support web standards through the separation of content from styling. The styling section includes the use of the CSS to create graphical effects and to minimize and even eliminate the use of tables for the graphical layout of content. It emphasizes creating interoperable content that can adjust to a wide range of renderings by use relative and proportional sizes for fonts and the widths of columns. This allows content to fit small and large screens without needing to use horizontal scroll bars.

Standards. The inclusion of DOCTYPE, language and character encoding information is checked to see if the author is considering validation of their web resources. These pieces of information are needed by validators to check validity to DOC-TYPEs.

2 Web Best Practices Working Group

The iCITA HTML Accessibility Best Practices working group was formed to bring together both disability access specialists and web developers who are trying to implement the web accessibility requirements of the Illinois Information Technology Accessibility Act (IITAA). The IITTA requirements are base on Section 508 and WCAG 1.0 requirements, but provide more specific markup requirements that web developers in Illinois wanted. The working group develops best practice resources to help web developers with specific information on the HTML, scripting and CSS markup needed to create accessible web resources that comply with the IITAA requirements. The web site is design oriented to provide developers with both the accessibility principles and specific techniques that integrate accessible graphical styling and automation into web designs. The best practices resources implement forward looking web design concepts to make sure web resources are not only compatible with current and legacy web browsing technologies, but will also seamlessly support emerging and future web technologies through the use of interoperable web standards. The use of web standard based implementation techniques allows resources to adapt to the rendering capabilities of a wide range of pervasive and desktop technologies, including the technologies used by people with disabilities. The working group is open to everyone and includes web developers and disability access specialists. The working group meets once a week to discuss and update the best practices and define the rules that will be used by automated evaluation tools like FAE and the Firefox Accessibility Extension to estimate the implementation of IITAA requirements.

3   Testing Tools

At the heart of the best practices are two testing tools that have been designed to estimate the use of the iCITA HTML Best Practices [11]. The Illinois Functional Accessibility Evaluator [13] is a web based tool for evaluating web resources and the Illinois Firefox Accessibility Extension [14] extends the capabilities of the Firefox browser to support accessibility testing and enhanced features for people with disabilities.

3.1   Illinois Functional Accessibility Evaluator

The Illinois Functional Accessibility Evaluator (FAE) is design to provide both high level and detailed reports on the use of the iCITA Web Accessibility Best Practices to implement accessibility standards. FAE estimates the use of the of the best practices coding patterns allowing it to provide more extensive automatic validation of the web accessibility features of a web resource than traditional evaluation tools. One of the major features of the tool is the reduction in the amount of time consuming and inefficient manual accessibility checks required by other accessibility evaluation tools. FAE evaluates markup to identify coding patterns required for implementation of the navigation, text equivalents, scripting, styling and standards best practices. The reporting system of FAE provides three levels of reporting: summary report, site wide report and page level reports. The summary report (shown in Figure 2) provides an overview of a web site's accessibility features and is designed to give managers and less technical people an overall evaluation of the accessibility features of a website. The summary report can also be used for planning purposes to determine how accessibility resources will be allocated to have the biggest impact on accessibility. The site wide report provides information on the results of specific rules for all the web pages analyzed and the page level report looks at the accessibility results of an individual web page. These views are designed for web developers to identify and fix accessibility problems. One of the major features that developers like about FAE reports is the more explicit feedback on what they need to fix on their web pages to improve accessibility. Other testing tools only report known or potential accessibility problems and this forces web developers to first identify if there is an accessibility problem. If they do identify accessibility problems then they need to try to find effective techniques to fix them. Since the majority of accessibility warnings in conventional evaluation tools are manual checks, developers are easily overwhelmed and often ignore many of the manual check warnings. The ability to provide more explicit feedback on problems and repair was only possible through the use of the best practices which defined the coding practices that lead to functional accessibility. This does not mean that FAE detects every possible accessibility problem or that pages that pass FAE rules don't still have accessibility problems. But it is does mean developers using coding strategies that pass FAE rules have the basic accessibility coding patterns in place for functional accessibility and the limited resources available for manual testing (especially from people with disabilities) can focus on usability improvements and not basic accessibility coding tests. FAE is a free web service and there are currently over 2200 registered users.

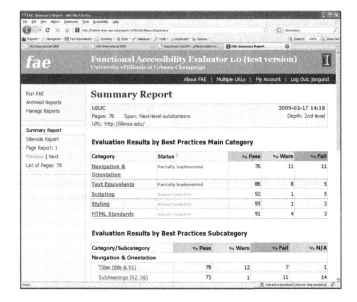

Fig. 2. Screen shot of FAE Summary Report

3.2 Illinois Firefox Accessibility Extension

The Illinois Firefox Accessibility Extension [14] provides a means for developers to test the accessibility of dynamically generated web resources and add additional features for people with disabilities to interact and view web content. The ability to test dynamically generated web pages or web pages that update automatically is very important as web applications become more popular and displace desktop applications as the way people use computer and internet technologies. The ability to test dynamic web content is based on the use of the Document Object Model (DOM) which represents the content of a web resource and is used by Javascript to update content on the web page. A new featured added this past year was the ability to send a copy of the dynamically generated web page to FAE to create an FAE accessibility report.

4 Conclusion and Next Steps

Best practices for dynamic HTML are the next step for the best practices. With the introduction and implementation of the W3C Accessible Rich Internet Applications [15] there are new technologies to make Dynamic HTML applications accessible to people with disabilities. The most telling statement on the nest practices cam from a web developer who said "I learned these practices because of accessibility, but I use them because they are better web design."

References

1. Chisholm, W., Vanderheiden, G., Jacobs, I.: W3C Web Content Accessibility Guidelines 1.0 (1999), http://www.w3.org/TR/WCAG10/
2. Section 508: Electronic and Information Technology Accessibility Standards (2000), http://www.access-board.gov/sec508/standards.htm
3. Dave Raggett, D., Le Hors, A., Jacobs, I.: HTML 4.01 Specification (1999), http://www.w3.org/TR/html4/
4. Bert Bos, B., Çelik, T., Hickson, I., Wium Lie, H.: Cascading Style Sheets Level 2 Revision 1 (CSS 2.1) Specification (2007), http://www.w3.org/TR/CSS21/
5. Cederholm, D.: Web Standards Soultions: The Markup and Style Handbook. Springer, New York (2004)
6. Caldwell, B., Cooper, M., Guarino Reid, L., Vanderheiden, G.: W3C Web Content Accessibility Guidelines 2.0 (2008), http://www.w3.org/TR/WCAG20/
7. Titling Requirements of the iCITA HTML Accessibility Best Practices, http://html.cita.uiuc.edu/nav/title/
8. Opera web browser keyboard shortcuts for document navigation, http://www.opera.com/browser/tutorials/nomouse/
9. How to Meet WCAG 2.0, http://www.w3.org/WAI/WCAG20/quickref/#qr-navigation-mechanisms-skip
10. Form labeling requirements of the iCITA HTML Accessibility Best Practices, http://html.cita.uiuc.edu/nav/form/
11. iCITA HTML Accessibility Best Practices, http://html.cita.uiuc.edu/
12. iCITA Web Best Practices Working Group, http://html.cita.uiuc.edu/group.php
13. Illinois Functional Accessibility Evaluator, http://fae.cita.uiuc.edu
14. Illinois Firefox Accessibility Extension, http://firefox.cita.uiuc.edu
15. Craig, J., Cooper, M., Pappas, L., Schwerdtfeger, R., Seeman, L.: Accessible Rich Internet Applications (WAI-ARIA) 1.0 (2009), http://www.w3.org/TR/wai-aria

Web User Interface Design Strategy: Designing for Device Independence

Panagiotis Karampelas[1], Ioannis Basdekis[2], and Constantine Stephanidis[2,3]

[1] Hellenic American University, Athens, Greece
[2] Institute of Computer Science,
Foundation for Research and Technology – Hellas (FORTH), Greece
[3] Computer Science Department, University of Crete, Greece
`pkarampelas@gmail.com, {johnbas,cs}@ics.forth.gr`

Abstract. Until recently, Web services were available only through a desktop web browser. Nowadays, methods of access move beyond the desktop computer towards ubiquitous access through portable devices. As a consequence, users have the chance to interact with a growing diversity of computing devices such as PDAs, smart phones, etc., with diverse characteristics that tend to replace conventional laptop and desktop computers. User interface designers, on the other hand, strive to design usable interfaces to cater for the diverse requirements of these devices. The design strategy proposed in this paper aims at assisting user interface designers in designing for diverse devices recommending a specific line of activities in the process of design. A case study of application of the proposed design strategy is presented, outlining its advantages.

Keywords: User interface design, Device independence, Web accessibility, Prototyping.

1 Introduction

Users nowadays confront with a growing diversity of computing devices that strive for substituting the conventional laptop or desktop computers in any form of everyday electronic activity. Manufacturers, correspondingly, struggle to attract more users for their novel and unique computing devices, often sacrificing design standards for increasing innovation. In such a controversial environment, user interface designers address the challenge of developing user interfaces that comply with the technical requirements of the devices and the desires of the manufacturers, and still remain usable and accessible for all potential users.

In the Human Computer Interaction (HCI) field several techniques have been proposed for producing user interfaces for multiple devices [1]. The existence of such a large number of techniques denotes that none of them is sufficient to address all the emerging design problems. Depending on the diversity of the devices, the business-specific requirements of the application, the user interface designer's experience, and the project limitations in terms of cost and/or time, the most appropriate or the least problematic technique is usually adopted.

C. Stephanidis (Ed.): Universal Access in HCI, Part I, HCII 2009, LNCS 5614, pp. 515–524, 2009.

This article proposes a user interface design strategy for addressing the above issues, based on the experience gained in the context of a research project which aimed at the development of a set of electronic services (eServices) for people with disability. The eServices are accessible via the Internet with the use of alternative computing devices such as laptops and mobile devices.

2 Related Work

As mentioned previously, designing for multiple devices is a problem that has engaged researchers' interest several years ago, when actually the first mobile devices were introduced [1, 2]. The need for different design techniques and approaches from the existing ones, addressing the design of conventional computers, stems from the diverse characteristics of new mobile devices such as smaller displays, limited or absent input devices, slower processors, less memory capabilities and limited power [3]. In addition to the aforementioned limitations, the context of use of such devices comes to add more constraints. The mobility of the user, the lighting of the environment and the attention span the user can devote to the device are some examples of such constraints [4, 5].

To address these limitations and constraints, several researchers have proposed a considerable number of different design approaches in order to create user interfaces for multiple computing devices. Moreover, different classifications for the aforementioned methods have been proposed using diverse criteria such as design stage, authoring approach, etc. One such categorization proposed by W3C[1] identifies three categories of techniques: multiple authoring, single authoring and flexible authoring. According to Simon et al. [6], the multiple authoring technique requires the user interface designer to produce a separate user interface which complies with each device's specific limitations. The single authoring technique, on the other hand, demands one single implementation of the user interface which is automatically adjusted when displayed on a specific device. This can be achieved either by using a device independent toolkit to produce the user interface, or using a markup language to describe the interface and a presentation mechanism to display it, or using model-based user interface design methods. The third category, flexible authoring, is a hybrid methodology combining multiple and single authoring techniques at the designer's will.

Another classification by Nilsson et al. [7] categorizes user interface design techniques using the model-based methodology again in three classes based on the different design stages. Thus, the first category comprises methods that produce at the design time a user interface for each device, while the second includes the methods that are used to transform the user interface of the application to fit one platform or the other. The third category, according to that classification, allows the user interface to decide automatically when it is necessary to adapt itself and how, based on the device displayed and the context of use.

Discussing the advantages and limitations of the different categories of the aforementioned methods, one can see that no method can be applied universally with the

---

[1] W3C Authoring Techniques for Device Independence, http://www.w3.org/TR/2004/NOTE-di-atdi-20040218/

same results. The multiple authoring technique, for example, while providing very well adapted user interfaces, requires the production of as many interfaces as are the devices, with the danger to defeat consistency [6]. Single authoring techniques, on the other hand, offer consistency and uniformity of the generated user interface [1], defeating though simplicity of creation and predictability of the final design, since the design process is most of the times administered by a software component. As will be discussed in the following sections, flexible authoring techniques have the potential to avoid some of the aforementioned limitations, since they combine methods from both other categories.

3 Design Strategy for Device Independence

The proposed approach is built upon the flexible authoring methodology. The method suggests the preparation of different designs for the diverse devices early in the user interface design life-cycle and the implementation of an automatic transformation process that is able to adjust the basic interface components of the user interface designs according to the limitations of each device. The objectives of the developed methodology are to address the most common requirements for a user interface (e.g., easy to learn and remember, efficient, powerful, and flexible [8] as well as accessible).

The proposed methodology includes the following steps:

1. *Identify device-specific constraints or capabilities.* In this phase the different limitations or features of the computing devices should be identified. The identified characteristics can be organized according to their type. Thus, a typical classification contain:

   - Output interaction capabilities such as the screen size of the device, screen resolution, number of colors, speech synthesizer, etc.
   - Supported input interaction modes, such as physical or virtual keyboard, size of keys, touch screen, stylus, speech recognition, etc.
   - Processing capability, e.g., processor power, memory size, etc.
   - Connectivity, e.g., support for different networking protocols such as GPRS, WCDMA, Bluetooth, WiFi (802.11b or g), WiMax (802.16)
   - Power supply, e.g., power connectivity, consumption and duration, etc.

2. *Identify the context of use for each device.* This phase comprises the analysis of the contexts of use for each device. In most cases, the devices are neither used in the same context nor interchangeably. However, there are cases where a user will continue using the same device even if there is the opportunity to use an alternative device with more capabilities. For example, the user comes home from outside and carries a PDA device using a specific application. Even though inside the house there is a computing device with fewer limitations (i.e., larger screen), the user continues working with the PDA device. Thus, in this phase the following issues need to be identified:

   - Potential use locations, e.g., outdoor/indoor environment, factory or office environment, etc.
   - Condition of use in terms of lighting, noise, etc. (usually related to the use location).

- Parallel activities, e.g., the device is used while working/walking, etc.

3. *Select the 'worst case' device.* The computing device that appears to have the highest number of important limitations against all the diverse contexts of use should be selected in this phase. If in a specific context of use just one device appears to have the most limitations, then the user interface design should be started based on these limitations and context of use. If more than one device appears to have similar limitations but in different contexts of use, then any device can be selected.
4. *Design the first user interface prototype according to the device-specific limitations.* Using well-established prototyping techniques [11], such as paper and pencil, mock ups, etc., proceed with the development of the first prototype for the selected device.
5. *Infer a generic set of requirements based on the first UI design.* Specific design requirements can emerge from the first prototype regarding, e.g., navigation, content structure, presentation, accessibility, etc.
6. *Design the user interface prototypes for the other devices applying the set of generic requirements.* Proceed with the user interface prototype development for the remaining devices taking into consideration the design requirements elaborated in the previous step. Additional design specific requirements may emerge for the alternative devices. These design artifacts can be incorporated and extend the set of the generic requirements.
7. *Decide which user interface components can be automatically transformed between the diverse computing devices.* Upon completion of the user interface prototypes, common components shared among the diverse devices can be identified. The appropriate transformation or adaptation strategy can also be inferred based on the prototypes of the different devices. E.g., if the user interface designs for all the devices are the same, then an automatic transformation should be adopted.
8. *Evaluate the user interface prototypes for all the different devices.* An appropriate usability evaluation methodology should be selected to identify potential usability problems in the user interface prototypes. The selection of the evaluation method depends upon several factors such as available resources, evaluators with expertise, time to complete the project, etc.
9. *Revisit the set of requirements and the prototypes according to the findings.* This stage requires an analytical review of the design requirements based on the evaluation findings, as well as a review of the user interface prototypes in order to amend potential usability problem or inconsistencies between the diverse computing devices.

4 Applying the Design Strategy for Device Independence

4.1 Project Description

The proposed design strategy was applied in the context of a project that aims at the development of a set of accessible electronic services for the Greek community of people with disability, and in particular the members of the Greek Association of the Blind. The web application is addressed to registered members and offers a variety of services including short messaging, blogs, news, web email, support for virtual communities and various other useful electronic tools. Most specifically, virtual community support is provided through services such as discussion boards, chat rooms, document areas, members' management and web links catalogues.

The aforementioned services are targeted to be available over the Internet and optimized for a specific Personal Digital Assistant Mobile Phone, HTC TyTN II, and for any web browser of a conventional desktop or laptop computer. Accessibility is one of the key requirements for the project, since the majority of the target end users are people with disability. Other requirements include the provision of advanced functions for the service administrators (e.g., members' management).

4.2 Implementation of the Design Strategy for Device Independence

In the performed case study, the design team, comprised of two experienced user interface designers, followed the steps proposed in section 3. The team started collectively working on the individual steps of the strategy as described below:

Step 1: Identification of the device-specific constraints or capabilities
In this step a comparison table with the identified features was created and the features were characterized as constraints or not (Table 1).

Step 2: Identification of context of use
The conventional PC was assumed to be used in a well-illuminated home/office environment, with average noise. It was also assumed that the user will be concentrated on a specific interaction task during the use of the system. Regarding the mobile device, the design team considered that it can be used outdoors in diverse light and noise conditions and in parallel with other activities, e.g., commuting, walking, etc.

Step 3: Identification of the 'worst case' device
Based on the previous steps, it was decided that the limited screen size and resolution as well as the limited memory and processing capabilities characterize the mobile device as the one with the most limitations. Taking also into consideration the diverse context of use of the mobile device, it was confirmed that this was the 'worst case' device in the specific project.

Table 1. Device-specific features. The features in bold denote device constraints

	HTC TyTN II	Conventional PC
Screen max resolution	**240x320**	1280x1024
Screen size	**2.8"**	19"
Interaction modes	**Small QWERTY Keyboard Touch screen Jog wheel**	QWERTY Keyboard Pointing device (mouse)
Processor power	**Qualcomm MSM7200, 400MHz**	Pentium Compatible Processor >2.0 GHz
Memory	**128 Mb**	1 or 2 Gbs
Connectivity	HSDPA / UMTS / GSM / GPRS / EDGE / Wi-Fi 802.11b/g / Bluetooth 2.0	ETHERNET / Wi-Fi 802.11b/g / Bluetooth 2.0
Power Supply	365 Hours	Continuous / 3 Hours

Step 4: Design of the User Interface for the mobile device
The design of the user interface started using the storyboarding technique for the e-mail service and continued for all the other services (Figure 1).

Fig. 1. Mockup of the main menu and the e-mail services for the mobile device. The identified generic guidelines/requirements have been appended to the mockup.

Step 5: Inference of the set of the generic guidelines
In the user interface prototyping step, several design considerations were generalized and drafted as a set of generic requirements. More specifically, the following generic requirements/guidelines were adopted to rule the overall design of the various user interfaces. The requirements/guidelines are listed below as they were generated, without taking into account priority considerations:

- Respect G. A. Miller's magical number [9]. List of objects, options, etc. should be limited to 7±2.
- The Return (back) button is of top priority and should be consistently placed throughout the UIs. Because of the limitations (small screen size and limited input modes) of the specific mobile device, users should be able to recover from wrong choices easily. Placing the Return button as the first option in all the screens can help users recover from their errors.
- The content should have higher priority than the menu options. Since the majority of the users are people with disability and use assistive technology in order to navigate through the application, the content of the page should be placed closer to the top of the page in order to have fast access and avoid information overloading (e.g., reading the menu again and again).

- Current navigation path (breadcrumb trail) should be available on request. The user should be able to reveal the full navigation path in order to get oriented inside the website if necessary but without overloading user's memory.
- Skip option should be available for all the group of links. To make navigation faster a skip link will be available for non-visual interaction.
- The icons used should be embedded into the application's cascade stylesheet. To avoid information overload, e.g., listening the alt image of the icons for people that use assistive technology, all the icons used should be defined in the stylesheets.
- Color coding should be used for all the available services. Since the application comprises different services, for enhancing user orientation, different colors will be used.
- The tasks/options displayed in each page should be content specific. To avoid user confusion, in each page should be allowed only options related to the content.
- The title of each page should be content related. Instead of repeating in each page the title of the application and other information that is irrelevant for completing the tasks presented in each page, only a short descriptive title about the actual content is allowed.
- No conventional options menu should be provided. The application should not have a conventional menu that runs at the top or side of the page. The menu options should appear only on the first page of the application. When a user selects a specific service it is considered that s/he should focus on the available tasks in this service and not be distracted by the other available services.
- A shortcuts mechanism should be available. A user defined list of favorites' options or shortcuts should be available as the first option for the users to prepare a personalized menu of options. In that way the users will be able to minimize the selections in order to use the most preferable services.

Step 6: Design of the User Interface for the conventional PCs
Using the set of the generic requirements/guidelines produced, the design team proceeded with the design of the user interface for the conventional PCs (Figure 2).

Step 7: Decision upon the common components between the different devices
In the mobile device, the content specific actions in most of the cases can be more than three. Together with the content, this may lead to the violation of the 7±2 rule. To address this issue, it was decided to gather all the content specific actions in a separate screen and to insert a link in the related content to display these actions. For example, the available options when viewing an e-mail are Reply, Reply to all, Forward, Move and Delete. In the case of the mobile device, instead of displaying all the options along with the text, only an option titled E-mail options will be displayed. When this option is clicked, the list of the aforementioned actions will be displayed.

Another decision that was reached through this phase was the extensive use of pagination in order to fit the content in the small screen of the mobile device.

Step 8: Evaluation of the alternative user interfaces
The evaluation process started when all the alternative user interfaces were designed. The cognitive walkthrough evaluation method [10] was selected and two expert investigators analyzed representative tasks for each service. Based on the feedback of the investigators, several minor corrections to both designs were applied, such as ordering of user defined shortcuts, login procedure, etc.

Fig. 2. Mockup of the E-mail service for the desktop

Step 9: Refinement of the requirements/guidelines and user interface designs
The user interface designs were revisited and the changes suggested were incorporated. There was no need to revise the set of guidelines at this stage. By completing this step, the design strategy for device independence was concluded and the prototypes were delivered to the development team for implementation.

5 Discussion and Future Work

The case study reported in the previous section was a first experimental application of the proposed Design Strategy for Device Independence, providing a test-bed for the usefulness and validity of the overall approach. Since the entire process was completed successfully in less than a month, the conclusion can be drawn that this design strategy can be very cost effective in terms of time devoted to the alternative user interface designs. The method allows for easy inclusion of an unlimited number of different devices, since the user interfaces developed for the computing device with the most constraints can easily be adapted to other devices with more or less constraints. Another advantage of the method is that it allows the designer to fully exploit the device characteristics, defining each time the functionality that cannot be supported in the 'worst case' devices. The method can easily be implemented, since the user interface design of the basic components remains unchanged in all devices, and only some limited functionality is rendered in a different way. The components defined while designing the electronic services can easily be reused in other projects with different objectives.

However, some limitations were also revealed through the implementation of the design strategy. First, there may be the risk that a designer limits the functionality of a component in order to achieve the best design for the 'worst case' device, For example, in the message board component the hierarchy of the replies was flattened for simplicity. However, this type of trade-offs can sometimes improve the overall usability. For example, the hierarchy of replies in a message can be considered as by design complicated even for desktop computers, let alone mobile devices with small screen. Thus, the design decision to simplify the replies structure also constitutes a better design decision for the desktop user interface.

In the case study presented, the designers had to deal with the design constraints imposed by one device. In case there are more devices with similar limitations, the design strategy seems to perform very well, since designing for the second 'worst case' device entails only some additional decisions regarding the transformation of the common components in Step 7 if necessary. All the other design decisions would have been consolidated in the process of defining the design requirements while designing for the 'worst case' device. Thus, the user interface design process for the second 'worst case' device seems to be more effective and efficient than designing the user interface from the beginning.

The planned usability evaluation of the system under development will contribute to further validate the proposed strategy. If the usability evaluation with real users reveals limited usability problems, then the method will be proved to be very effective. The authors plan to apply the same design strategy in other similar projects with a higher number of devices in order to test its effectiveness and efficiency and to better assess the outcomes.

Acknowledgments. The authors would like to thank Panhellenic Association of the Blind, as the coordinator of the project "Universally Accessible eServices for Disabled People" for their valuable support. The project is funded by the Greek Government under the 3rd Community Support Framework and the work done will be available at http://www.ameanet.gr

References

1. Schilit, B.N., Trevor, J., Hilbert, D.M., Koh, T.K.: Web interaction using very small Internet devices. Computer 35(10), 37–45 (2002)
2. Karampelas, P., Akoumianakis, D., Stephanidis, C.: User interface design for PDAs: Lessons and experience with the WARD-IN-HAND prototype. In: Carbonell, N., Stephanidis, C. (eds.) UI4ALL 2002. LNCS, vol. 2615, pp. 474–485. Springer, Heidelberg (2003)
3. Ye, J.-H., Herbert, J.: Framework for User Interface Adaptation. In: Stary, C., Stephanidis, C. (eds.) UI4ALL 2004. LNCS, vol. 3196, pp. 167–174. Springer, Heidelberg (2004)
4. Lemmela, S., Vetek, A., Makela, K., Trendafilov, D.: Designing and evaluating multimodal interaction for mobile contexts. In: 10th International Conference on Multimodal Interfaces, pp. 265–272. ACM, New York (2008)
5. Pascoe, J., Ryan, N., Morse, D.: Using while moving: HCI issues in fieldwork environments. ACM Transactions on Computer-Human Interaction 7(3), 417–437 (2000)

6. Simon, R., Wegscheider, F., Tolar, K.: Tool-supported single authoring for device independence and multimodality. In: 7th International Conference on Human Computer Interaction with Mobile Devices & Services, pp. 91–98. ACM, New York (2005)
7. Nilsson, E.G., Floch, J., Hallsteinsen, S., Stav, E.: Model-based user interface adaptation. Computer & Graphics 30(5), 692–701 (2006)
8. Mayhew, D.J.: Requirements Specifications within the Usability Engineering Lifecycle. In: Sears, A., Jacko, J. (eds.) The Human-Computer Interaction Handbook, 2nd edn., pp. 917–926. Lawrence Erlbaum Associates, Mahwah (2006)
9. Proctor, R.W., Vu, K.-P.: Human Information Processing: an Overview for Human-Computer Interaction. In: Sears, A., Jacko, J. (eds.) The Human-Computer Interaction Handbook, 2nd edn., pp. 43–62. Lawrence Erlbaum Associates, Mahwah (2006)
10. Jordan, P.W.: An introduction to usability. Taylor & Francis Ltd. London (1998)
11. Bailey, B.P., Biehl, J.T., Cook, D.J., Metcalf, H.E.: Adapting paper prototyping for designing user interfaces for multiple display environments. In: Personal and Ubiquitous Computing, vol. 2(3), pp. 269–277. Springer, London (2008)

Inclusive Design for Ordinary Users in Extraordinary Circumstances

Simeon Keates

IT University of Copenhagen
Rued Langgaards Vej 7, DK-2300 Copenhagen S
skea@itu.dk

Abstract. Universal access is commonly interpreted as focusing on designing for users with atypical requirements – specifically users with disabilities or older adults. However, universal access is also about providing access to users in all situations and circumstances, including those that place extraordinary burdens on the users. This paper examines the design of a user interface (UI) for use in an airport environment and explains how the lessons learned from designing for users with disabilities in particular have been applied in this new context. The paper further describes a series of experiments that were performed to demonstrate the usability of the new interface and also compare the efficacy of three different input strategies developed for the new UI. The most efficient method of input was a strategy of combined keyboard shortcuts offering access to the full functionality of the UI.

1 Introduction

A quick look through the technical programmes of many conferences addressing the thematic area of universal access shows that historically the overwhelming majority of papers address design for disabled users or design for older adults [4]. However, it has long been claimed that the techniques developed to design for such extraordinary users in ordinary circumstances could also be applied to ordinary users in extraordinary circumstances [3]. Indeed, many funding applications often feature this very claim.

Recently, more research has been performed on examining the role of innovative circumstances, or contexts, of use. For example, designing for ambient intelligence is one such area that has received much attention in the past few years [1].

This paper describes the development of a new user interface (UI) for use in an airport environment. The specific application was a Departure Control System (DCS).

Airports are very challenging environments in which to use computers, especially since many computers there are often old and, most importantly, do not have mice. While many UIs exist for use without mice, such as traditional command-line interfaces, the DCS UI was developed as part of an overall suite of applications that required a coherent branded appearance. Many of the other applications were to be used in a more typical office environment and needed to support typical mouse and keyboard input and resemble a traditional graphical user interface (GUI).

C. Stephanidis (Ed.): Universal Access in HCI, Part I, HCII 2009, LNCS 5614, pp. 525–534, 2009.
© Springer-Verlag Berlin Heidelberg 2009

Thus the DCS UI needed to have the look and feel of a typical GUI application and support mouse input, but actually be optimized for keyboard-only access. These design requirements represented an interesting challenge for the design team; a challenge that was resolved by examining design techniques used for users who cannot use a mouse, specifically blind users and those with severe motor impairments. In other words, methods developed for designing for "extraordinary" users were applied to a UI for "ordinary" users in "extraordinary" circumstances [3].

1.1 The Airport Environment

The airport environment itself is a very demanding one. Airports are often very noisy places, crowded and with unequal and often poor lighting. Airline staff are under constant time pressure to process passengers as swiftly as possible. In the event of a last minute cancellation or other service disruption, the members of airline staff need to have accurate and reliable information made available to them in a timely fashion to keep passengers informed and defuse any potential confrontation.

Airlines often do not have any control over the computer equipment available to them. While most airlines may invest in purchasing their own equipment for their major hubs, smaller airports will almost certainly use common use platforms. These are computer facilities that are provided by a subcontractor through the airport to the airlines.

The common use platform machines are typically Linux or Windows NT based and often support only 1024×768 CRT displays. Some are equipped with hand-scanners for processing 1-D and 2-D barcodes, but those scanners are notoriously unreliable.

Most crucially, they often are not equipped with mice.

1.2 The Departure Control System

Airline operations within an airport are very complex and diverse. The most obvious features to most people are those that they interact with as passengers – specifically check-in and boarding. While these are, in themselves, large design spaces, they represent only a fraction of what is often going on. A complete Departure Control System (DCS) needs to include the following functionality:

- Check in – identify passengers and whether they are travelling as part of a group, ensure that the passengers are correctly ticketed and have the necessary documentation to be eligible to travel, assign the passengers to seats or to the standby list, process their baggage (see below), collect any outstanding payments and issue boarding passes
- Boarding – prepare the flight for departure, perform all necessary security checks, ensure that all passengers that are eligible to fly board the aircraft and that all ticketed passengers that are denied boarding (for a variety of possible reasons) are found seats on alternative flights
- Baggage handling and tracking – ensure that all bags are correctly entered into the system, have tags issued and are tracked correctly, especially for lost luggage claims

- Catering – ensure that the correct number and type of special meals are onboard each aircraft
- Irregular operations – facilitate a smooth transfer of passengers from flights that have experienced sudden difficulties (e.g. cancelled because of adverse weather conditions) to other available flights
- Standbys and denied boardings – add or remove passengers from a particular flight prior to boarding
- Special services – ensure that passengers with particular special service requirements, such as wheelchair, are correctly identified and that the appropriate service is made available
- Flight manifests – ensure that the passenger and baggage manifests are complete for customs and immigration clearance

1.3 Summary

In summary, the airline personnel have to use machines running old technology that can be temperamental at times. They are under significant time constraints and need to have a high productivity rate (throughput). These are issues that can be addressed by traditional user-centred / usability design practices. The specific issue of interest for this paper is the absence of computer mice. The hypothesis to be examined here is that by drawing on the experiences of designing for users who cannot use a mouse because of severe motor impairments, a better design for nominally able-bodied users who do not have access to a mouse can be created.

2 The DCS Design Approach

As a whole, the DCS deign approach has followed an agile methodology. Rather than developing a complete detailed design specification prior to the coding of the application, the design and coding were both tackled at the same time. Thus, fast design creation and iteration was required to ensure a mature enough design was available to the coders in a just-in-time fashion.

To achieve the necessary design speed, it was important to establish a close working relationship with the client's subject matter experts. Weekly brainstorming sessions were set-up, supplemented by daily telephone conversations. Wireframe prototypes were developed in PowerPoint as a rapid prototyping tool – the ability to add "Action settings" to on-screen elements (hyperlinking to other slides in the deck) allowed a good simulation of actual use of the interface in a very short development time, without having to wait for the code-base to be fully developed and implemented.

The design of the UI had three principal goals within this overall approach:

1. To ensure that all of the necessary functionality was made available to the users
2. To ensure that the users could accomplish their daily tasks as time-efficiently as possible
3. To minimise training requirements for airport employees (specifically less than one day of training)

To achieve these goals, and the implicit sub-goals, within the development timeframe required a clear design vision.

2.1 The Design Vision

The other applications in the overall product suite were developed very much as Web 2.0 applications, using typical Web 2.0 metaphors and features. These were appropriate given the nature of the tasks.

The design of DCS was fundamentally different. For instance, forward and back buttons are meaningless in a DCS context. When a user performs an action, for example changing a passenger's seat allocation, that action is committed immediately, fundamentally changing the state of the DCS system. While it may be possible to back out that action, it is not guaranteed. For example, the passenger's original seat may have been allocated to another passenger in the time taken for the check in agent to undo the seat exchange. Close to the close of check-in for flight, this type of situation becomes increasingly common as the aeroplane is becoming full.

Consequently, the design had to support two correlated properties:

- Fast throughput for the users
- Minimised risk of user errors

An effective method for achieving both of these properties is to ensure that the users feel confident in how the application will respond to their input commands. Before they press a button, they should be sure what the outcome of that button press would be.

Thus, rather than considering the design of DCS as a typical Web application, the metaphor used was that of an ATM. The analogy of an ATM was chosen because, for example, not all actions offered by an ATM are easily countermanded and mice are not typically used. The user has to feel totally in control of how the system is operating – otherwise they would not trust their money to it. Even the visual appearance would be somewhat similar, with the need to keep pages lightweight (in size) and thus comparatively simple.

Further, the process of interaction in DCS was modelled as a series of flows – the check-in flow, the boarding flow, etc. – with self-contained, discrete modules of additional information (such as advanced passenger information, special service requests or limited release baggage) added orthogonally to the main basic flows. Each flow was modelled with its own progress bar / breadcrumb trail, clearly indicating the current stage in the overall task flow.

Finally, the design needed to visually resemble a typical GUI application, but be optimised for keyboard-only access.

3 Designing for Keyboard-Only Access

The standard approach to designing keyboard-accessible web pages is to follow the Web Content Authoring Guidelines 1.0 (WCAG 1.0) from the Web Accessibility Initiative (WAI) of the World-Wide Web Consortium (W3C) [5] - specifically Guideline 9 – "Design for device-independence" has the following checkpoints:

"9.4 Create a logical tab order through links, form controls, and objects. [Priority 3] For example, in HTML, specify tab order via the "tabindex" attribute or ensure a logical page design.

...

9.5 Provide keyboard shortcuts to important links (including those in client-side image maps), form controls, and groups of form controls."

Further, WCAG 1.0 is due to be superseded by WCAG 2.0 [6], which states:

"Guideline 2.1 Keyboard Accessible: Make all functionality available from a keyboard.

2.1.1 Keyboard: All functionality of the content is operable through a keyboard interface without requiring specific timings for individual keystrokes, except where the underlying function requires input that depends on the path of the user's movement and not just the endpoints. (Level A)

...

Note 2: This does not forbid and should not discourage providing mouse input or other input methods in addition to keyboard operation.

2.1.2 No Keyboard Trap: If keyboard focus can be moved to a component of the page using a keyboard interface, then focus can be moved away from that component using only a keyboard interface, and, if it requires more than unmodified arrow or tab keys or other standard exit methods, the user is advised of the method for moving focus away. (Level A)"

Fig. 1. The check-in search page from DCS

Taking these as a starting point, it can be seen that TAB key navigation between page elements should be supported wherever possible and keyboard shortcuts implemented for commonly used features.

The first design approach for DCS was to consider that the TAB key could be used to navigate between fields and keyboard shortcuts added to the buttons. This was the approach adopted for the other applications in the overall software suite. However, while such an approach yields a design that is accessible without the use of a mouse, it would still not provide the levels of keyboard optimisation required in the airports. More innovative thinking was required.

Looking at the initial search page for the DCS check-in application for finding a passenger who wishes to check-in to a flight (Figure 1) there are 6 possible search fields, some of which have multiple text entry fields. Using the TAB key, it would take 11 TAB key presses to reach the first text entry field for a phone number search. A faster method of navigation was required for the levels of throughput demanded in an airport.

3.1   Optimising for Keyboard-Only Input – The DCS Solution

Clearly to obtain sufficiently high levels of throughput, more radical changes to the keyboard input paradigm were required. A range of additions and changes were made to the typical "keyboard-isation" of Web pages [2]. These included:

- **Supporting the use of arrow keys between text entry boxes.** In the case of Figure 2, using the down arrow key would require 7 keystrokes to reach the telephone search fields, rather than the 11 for the TAB key (a 36% reduction in keystrokes). In DCS, all screens allowed the use of arrow keys to move between text entry fields.

- **Supporting the use of ALT+[number] to move to text entry boxes.** Looking closely at Figure 2, it can be seen that each main search field has been assigned a number and that number is underlined – the standard labelling technique for ALT-enabled keyboard shortcuts. In this case, pressing "ALT+6" jumps the focus from the first text entry field to the country code entry field for telephone searches. Thus the 11 TAB keystrokes required to reach this field can be accomplished by 1 compound keystroke (a 91% reduction).

- **Enabling direct selection of list items.** On many pages within DCS, a list is presented from which items have to be selected. Common examples include a list of passengers on the same booking, checked (i.e. hold) baggage and fees to be paid. Using the TAB key would require the addition of check-boxes next to each list item. The user would have to TAB to the check box and press either SPACE or ENTER to change the check box state. In DCS, all items in such lists are either numbered or lettered. Pressing the appropriate key (when keyboard focus is not in a text entry field) toggles the selection/de-selection of the respective item. Thus pressing "2" twice will select and then de-select the second item in an on-screen list.

- **Constraining the TAB key.** If coded like a typical Web page, once the TAB key has been used to move the keyboard focus to the "Number" text entry box in the Telephone Number search field in Figure 2, then pressing the TAB key again will move the focus to the buttons at the bottom of the screen. Continuing to press TAB will move the focus to the menus at the top of the screen and through the different tabs, adding approximately 11 TAB keystrokes to return to the first text entry box.

Since all of those other elements have their own keyboard shortcuts, the TAB order can be constrained to just the text entry boxes, meaning just a single TAB key-stroke will move the focus from the last text entry box on the page to the first.

- **Using INS to toggle between direct selection mode and text entry mode.** The direct selection mode works only if the keyboard focus is not on a text entry box – otherwise pressing a number puts that number into a text entry field rather than se-lecting/de-selecting an item from a list. Moving into and out of a text entry field can be achieved by simply TAB-ing. However, to streamline the process, DCS supported the use of the INS key to jump immediately to the first text entry box on the page, irrespective of where the TAB may be on the page.
- **Adding function keys to the "flow" (breadcrumb trail).** Typically breadcrumb trails have to be traversed in full to reach a particular link. In DCS, each stage of the "flow" (the specialised version of a standard breadcrumb trail) is associated to a function key. Thus pressing the appropriate function key jumps straight to the stage of the flow.
- **Adding a default button to each page.** While each button in DCS includes its own ALT+[underlined_letter] shortcut, the button most likely to be used on that page (most commonly the "Continue"-type button) is shaded in green and can be operated by pressing ENTER, as well as ALT+C (in the "Continue" case). This is very similar operation to Mac OSX button behaviour. This may look like a negligi-ble performance improvement (a single keystroke instead of a compound one), but proved to be very popular with users.

4   Evaluating the DCS Check in UI

The DCS check in user interface was the first component to be coded and evaluated. A 2-stage evaluation process was adopted:

1. Ensure the functional completeness of the UI and its learnability
2. Evaluate the efficiency of the keyboard input paradigm.

4.1   Validating the Functionality of DCS

The DCS user interface was assessed through a series of user trials over 4 days with 10 experienced airport personnel. Each user was asked to perform 12 typical and atypical check-ins. These ranged from domestic passengers with no bags, to a family of four where one passenger gets called away on an emergency and even a passenger that arrives at the airport for an international flight, only to discover that he cannot find his passport. All of the users were given 20 minutes of training – consisting of:

- A brief overview of DCS and the keyboard navigation paradigm;
- A screen-by-screen overview of the UI; and,
- A sample check-in to perform.

All of the users were able to complete the tasks that they attempted (not all had enough time to attempt all tasks) and found the keyboard navigation to be intuitive and easy to learn and use. The only exception was the use of the INS key, which was effective, but unpopular. While all of the users understood its use, they felt that it did not feel quite right. The use of INS was removed and now TAB is used to move into and out of text entry boxes.

The user comments were strongly favourable, with a unanimous acceptance that the required functionality had been included and also that the taskflows implemented were appropriate and complete.

4.2 Validating the Keyboard Input Paradigm

The second stage of DCS evaluation involved comparing the efficacy of the keyboard input paradigm, specifically the time to complete typical check in tasks. Two tasks were selected:

1. Search for a booking using the phone number associated with the booking
2. Complete a domestic check in for 2 passengers with 3 bags
   Additionally, 3 input methods were chosen for comparison:
1. TAB key only (no mouse use)
2. Mouse (and keyboard for data entry)
3. All keyboard shortcuts (no mouse use)
4. Arrow keys (search task only)

All users performed the search task 4 times per input method. The domestic check in was completed once per interaction method. 4 users, all familiar with the new DCS UI, participated in the evaluation and the interaction methods were randomly presented to avoid any order effects. However, all users performed the search task first and then the complete domestic check in task.

4.3 Search Task Results

The results for the search task are shown in Table 1.

Table 1. The mean times taken to complete the search task for the 4 different input methods. Also shown is the % difference from the mouse time. Positive % means slower input, negative % means faster.

Input method	Mean time to complete (s)	% difference from Mouse
TAB key	11.0	+8.8%
Arrow keys	11.5	+12.7%
Mouse	10.2	(-)
Shortcuts	8.3	-18.0%

It can be seen that using the TAB key only for navigation is 8.8% slower than using the mouse. Using the arrow keys is slower still, 12.7% slower than using the mouse. This is somewhat surprising since the critical path (i.e. the shortest possible route to complete the task) is 4 key presses fewer for the arrow keys than for the TAB key (11 arrow key presses instead of 15 TAB key presses), since the two right hand text entry boxes can be skipped using the down arrow key (see Figure 1). The most likely explanation for this difference is that use of the arrow keys for this type of navigation is no longer common and is much more unfamiliar now to GUI users than the use of the TAB key.

The fastest method of input was the full use of the shortcuts. The critical path here was:

```
ALT+6, [country code], TAB or RIGHT ARROW, [area code],
TAB or RIGHT ARROW, [phone number], ENTER
```

This gives a total of 4 key presses that are non-data entry (cf. 13 and 11 respectively for the TAB and ARROW keys). Here the unfamiliarity of the ALT key shortcut is more than offset by the reduction in total number of key presses required.

4.4 Domestic Check in Results

Table 2 shows the results for the domestic check in results for the 3 different input methods compared.

Table 2. The mean times taken to complete the domestic check in task for the 3 different input methods. Also shown is the % difference from the mouse time. Positive % means slower input, negative % means faster.

Input method	Mean time to complete (s)	% difference from Mouse
TAB key	111.8	+29.7%
Mouse	86.2	(-)
Shortcuts	58.2	-32.5%

Table 2 shows that using the TAB key is almost 30% slower that using the mouse, whereas the use of the full range of keyboard shortcuts is over 30% faster. The difference between the TAB key input method and the full range of shortcuts is even larger – with the TAB key taking almost twice as long to complete the task.

5 Conclusions

The results shown in Tables 1 and 2 clearly demonstrate that relying only on the TAB key to provide principal keyboard-only navigation leads to interaction times that are between 9 and 30% slower than using a mouse and keyboard combination. This result is not unexpected, but shows that if designers take the easy route of only supporting this and think that the final UI is "accessible" then they are not doing all that they can for the users.

The benefits of taking a thorough user-centered, information architecture approach to the design process can be seen from the overall time savings for the full range of keyboard shortcuts. By supporting all the keyboard input techniques described in this paper, it has been shown that keyboard only entry can be up to 32.5% faster than using a mouse and keyboard combination. This is a significant improvement in performance, allowing each check in agent to process almost 3 groups of passengers in the time it would take to process 2 groups using the mouse. Such an improvement is of great financial value to an airline.

The overall design approach of looking at techniques developed for designing for accessibility (specifically designing for users with vision or motor impairments) was effective in suggesting methods of enabling keyboard-only access. This case study demonstrates that those methods can be applied when designing for ordinary users in extraordinary circumstances.

References

1. Adams, R., Granic, A., Keates, S.: Are ambient intelligent applications universally accessible? In: Karwowski, W., Salvendy, G. (eds.) Proceedings of AHFE International, Las Vegas, NV, July 14-17 (2008)
2. Keates, S.: Designing for accessibility: Extending to ordinary users in extraordinary circumstances. In: Karwowski, W., Salvendy, G. (eds.) Proceedings of AHFE International, Las Vegas, NV, July 14-17 (2008)
3. Newell, A.F.: Extra-ordinary Human Computer Operation. In: Edwards, A.D.N. (ed.) Extraordinary Human-Computer Interactions. Cambridge University Press, Cambridge (1995)
4. Stephanidis, C. (ed.) Proceedings of 4th International Conference on Universal Access and Human computer Interaction, Beijing China, July 22-27 (2007)
5. W3C. Web Content Accessibility Guidelines 1.0 (1999),
   http://www.w3.org/TR/WCAG10/ (accessed: February 20, 2009)
6. W3C. Web Content Accessibility Guidelines (WCAG) 2.0 (2009),
   http://www.w3.org/TR/WCAG20/ (accessed: February 20, 2009)

Towards Open Access Accessibility Everywhere: The ÆGIS Concept

Peter Korn[1], Evangelos Bekiaris[2], and Maria Gemou[2]

[1] Sun Microsystems, Mailstop UMPK17-101, 17 Network Circle, Menlo Park, CA 94025
Peter.Korn@Sun.com
[2] Centre for Research and Technology Hellas Hellenic Institute of Transport,
17, Poseidonos Av., 17455 Alimos, Greece
{abek,mgemou}@certh.gr

Abstract. The current paper presents the concept of ÆGIS Integrating Project (Grant Agreement: 224348), which aims to embed support for accessibility into every aspect of ICT-including the pre-built user-interface components, developer's tools, software applications and the run-time environment, and via embeddable assistive technologies. ÆGIS is a 3,5 years project, aiming to constitute a breakthrough in the eInclusion area, through the development of an Open Accessibility Framework, upon which open source accessibility interfaces and applications for the users as well as accessibility toolkits for the developers will be built. Three mainstream markets are targeted, namely the desktop, rich Internet applications and mobile devices/applications market segments.

Keywords: accessibility, open source, mainstream ICT, Open Accessibility Framework, design, development, assessment, desktop, rich web applications, Java-based mobile devices.

1 Introduction

With the recent emergence of a 3rd generation accessibility approach[1], mainstream (Information and Communication Technologies) ICT companies and the regulatory bodies that address ICT accessibility have now begun to recognize the importance of a formal division of responsibilities in ICT accessibility: tasks done by the ICT "platform", tasks done by ICT "applications", and tasks done by AT. This 3rd generation approach is also in service of a shift towards Universal Design. Still, this early emergence fails short from this goal, due to the lack of appropriate developer toolkits and methodologies/tools for embedding accessibility within mainstream products in a cost effective way. ÆGIS is an Integrating Project that comes to bridge this gap, by developing an Open Accessibility Framework (OAF) and open

---

[1] The first generation of ICT accessibility emerged in the 1960s with access to character-based systems to people with vision impairments. The second generation emerged in the 1980s with access to the graphical desktop via complex, reverse-engineering on the part of AT. This third generation began to emerge at the end of the 20th century, and is now actively being pursued in the desktop realm but not yet at all in rich Internet applications or for mobile devices.

C. Stephanidis (Ed.): Universal Access in HCI, Part I, HCII 2009, LNCS 5614, pp. 535–543, 2009.
© Springer-Verlag Berlin Heidelberg 2009

source accessible interfaces and applications for the users and accessibility toolkits for the developers. This is performed in three interconnected and high value mainstream markets, those of the:

- desktop,
- rich Internet applications, and
- mobile devices / applications, also taking into account the recent Information Technology (IT) convergence trend bringing together / combining these sectors into common applications (i.e. web applications on the desktop, cell phones that are browsers and play videos, etc.).

Therefore, ÆGIS does not seek to develop yet another accessible application(s) for the people with disabilities and/or elderly. It targets the very "heart of the problem", i.e. the "building blocks" of all applications offered through mainstream ICT to all people (whether with impairments or not). The project will produce major new open source results (and expand upon existing open source efforts) that are expected to:

- Bring key contribution to a collective mindset change towards placing users and their needs, such as utility, accessibility, simplicity and learnability, at the centre of all ICT developments.
- Focus on providing new solutions for embedding accessibility in current and future mass-market ICT-based products and services. ÆGIS solutions shall be open, plug & play, personalized & configurable, realistic and applicable in various contexts.
- Offer significant support to ICT developers, in order to encourage and empower them to contribute towards the inclusive ICT vision. The heart of this support is in the open source developer tools and user-interface building blocks into which accessibility support will be built. This support also support includes, but is not limited to, the delivery of standards and design guidance, know-how transfer through training and other means, in order to enable developers to verify and optimize the accessibility of their prototypes at all development stages.
- Facilitate the development of simple, cost-effective, useful, accessible, usable, and ultimately, adoptable ICT. Particular attention is paid to solutions and approaches that will extend the current population of ICT beneficiaries representing, nowadays, roughly 30% of the European population (a production force, and concurrently a market share, highly unexploited today). Thus, ÆGIS aims at mainstreaming and radically improving the user experience with ICT, by advancing the current paradigms of accessibility and usability for people with functional limitations, people lacking digital competence, and marginalized young and elder people [1].

2   What Is ÆGIS?

The ÆGIS project (Open Accessibility Everywhere: Groundwork, Infrastructure, Standards ; http://www.aegis-project.eu) seeks to determine whether 3rd generation access techniques will provide a more accessible, more exploitable and deeply embeddable approach in mainstream ICT (desktop, rich Internet and mobile applications). This approach is developed and explored with the Open Accessibility Framework (OAF) through which aspects of the design, development and deployment of accessible mainstream ICT are addressed. The OAF provides embedded and built-in accessibility solutions, as well as toolkits for developers, for "engraving" accessibility in existing and emerging mass-market ICT-based products, thus making accessibility open, plug & play, personalized & configurable, realistic & applicable in various contexts; ÆGIS is placing users and their needs at the centre of all ICT developments. Based on a holistic UCD, ÆGIS identifies user needs and interaction models for several user groups, (users with visual, hearing, motion, speech and cognitive impairments as well as application developers) and develops open source based generalized accessibility support into mainstream ICT devices/applications:

- desktop,
- rich web applications, and,
- Java-based mobile devices.

All developments will be iteratively tested with a significant number of end users, developers and experts in 3 phases and 4 Pilot sites Europe wide (in Belgium, Spain, Sweden and the UK).

The project includes strong industrial and end user participation (the participating industries are among the market leaders in the corresponding mainstream ICT markets). The project results' uptake is promoted by strong standardization activities, as well as the fact that much of the technology results will be either new open source applications or will be built into existing and already widely adopted open source ICT.

3   ÆGIS Users, Stakeholders and Domains

ÆGIS efforts occur in the following important domains:

- Desktop and mobile user agents and web browsers
- "Web 2.0" applications - rich Internet applications built with technologies like AJAX, DHTML, JavaScript, and JavaFX
- Mobile applications and devices (e.g. smart phones, PDAs, etc.)
- Developer's tools
- Document authoring applications
- Communications products
- In this context, ÆGIS addresses 2 main categories of end users:
- Developers of ICT infrastructure, applications and services –referred to hereinafter as "developers"
- People with disabilities –referred to hereinafter as "end users"– who experience one or more of the following mild to severe impairments:

    o   Blind and low-vision users
    o   Motor impairment users
    o   Cognitive impairment users
    o   Hearing impairment users
    o   Speech impairment users

It is worth noting that the target end user groups include also the elderly, given that the vast majority of elderly people experiences one or more of the above impairments.

These people have the competence, in most cases, to lead independent and active lives, but, are at risk of exclusion due to the impairment(s) that they are experiencing, as well as the complexity and lack of utility, accessibility and usability of ICT. It is worth noting that people with disabilities represent at least 16% of the overall EU working age population, but only 40% of persons with disabilities are employed compared to 64.2% of non disabled persons. This gap often exists because of a lack of properly adapted working environments (both in terms of hardware or software).

People with disabilities included in the main ÆGIS end user group are supported through a multitude of stakeholders that are duly considered and supported by the ÆGIS Open Accessibility Framework, such as:

- ICT providers (industrial players and SMEs)
- National, local and regional authorities
- Teachers / tutors / trainers/ formal informal care-givers
- Disability groups, forums and Associations
- Family members
- Mobile service providers
- Public / private Social security service providers and insurance companies
- Web service providers
- Health care and emergency support service providers
- Policy makers / standardization bodies

Individual end users (people with disabilities), who will actively participate in the project's User Centered Approach and iterative evaluations will be recruited through Partner networks and contacts of the end user representatives in the Consortium (RNIB, FONCE, EPR, ACE, SUDART) and key individual specialists working with people with disabilities.

Based on the ÆGIS User Centered Approach, the above end users will be involved throughout the project in all of its phases, as well as various other stakeholders such as accessibility assessors and developers, service providers, and where applicable relevant accessibility units within public bodies. In addition, ÆGIS addresses indirectly all stakeholders who are engaged with the well being of people with disabilities, such as formal / informal care-givers, teachers / tutors/ trainers, family members, public / private social security service providers, insurance companies, health care and emergency support service providers, etc. Their views are represented in the ÆGIS Consortium either directly (e.g. FONCE incorporates FIAPAS, the Spanish Federation of Associations of Parents and Friends of the Deaf), or indirectly (through partners' contacts).

4   ÆGIS Concept and Objectives

4.1   The ÆGIS Concept

ÆGIS aims, through user research and prototype development with current and next-generation ICT, to develop and validate the necessary infrastructure and accessibility frameworks needed for deeply embedding accessibility into the desktop, for mobile devices, and rich Internet applications; with a focus on the needs of users with mild, severe or complex disabilities served via assistive technologies; and, where appropriate, to propose these results to the appropriate standards organizations for review and potential adoption, as well as to make them available through open source as much as possible. In realizing this aim, the following cornerstones of the approach are highlighted:

- ÆGIS is addressing the entire "accessibility value delivery chain" in this new, 3rd generation ("built-in") approach to accessibility and support for assistive technologies - where programmatic accessibility mechanisms are defined, built into the building blocks of software applications, supported by developer tools, and exposed on the user's platform and web browser - thus creating a welcoming environment for AT on those platforms.
- As the participating industries and especially the Technical Coordinator (Sun Microsystems) have key technology in all aspects of this "value delivery chain", ÆGIS is in an ideal position to develop ÆGIS support "everywhere" (the "E" in ÆGIS). Furthermore, the Partners' technology is itself deeply embedded in the mobile space (80% of cell phones sold have Java-based technology in them) and for rich Internet applications, thus ÆGIS Consortium is the best positioned organization to bring "built-in accessibility" to these devices.
- The vast majority of work undertaken by ÆGIS will be on open source technologies, available for all to use under open source (and royalty-free) licenses, so there will be (for example) 5 assistive technology prototypes that will be all open source, and built-in DAISY and Braille support in a major office suite that is open source, etc.

The software development that will be undertaken in this respect follows a predictable path as illustrated in the figure below. Using user interface elements from a component set, (1) the software developer composes them in a developer's tool (2) in order to build a rich Internet application (3), or a desktop application (4), or a mobile application (5) for a PDA or cell phone. The rich Internet application requires a web browser (6) that knows how to expose it to an assistive technology running on the desktop (7). Likewise, the more typical desktop application is accessible because of an assistive technology running on the desktop. Mobile applications are accessible because of the work done by an assistive technology (8) on the cell phone or PDA.

4.2 ÆGIS Objectives

The big ÆGIS innovation lies in the fact that, while there have been limited and rather isolated attempts at addressing a few specific pieces of this ICT development process, never has such a comprehensive and holistic approach been taken, and never on so large a scale (encompassing rich Internet applications and mobile devices, in addition to the desktop). The fundamental scientific objectives of the ÆGIS Open Accessibility Framework, towards the achievement of which the project will steer the Consortium's research are:

1. to demonstrate and prove that use of 3rd generation access techniques results in equal or better end-user access experiences as compared to the existing, 2nd generation approaches;

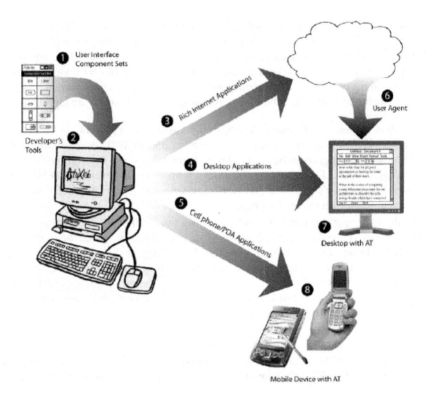

Fig. 1. The ÆGIS software development path

2. to identify and develop the right combination of developer's tools aiding in creating accessible applications which leverage sets of pre-built and accessibility enabled user interface components for desktop, mobile, and rich Internet applications; which together allow developers to comfortably and easily create accessible applications;
3. to develop a set of embeddable assistive technologies for mobile devices that fit into this framework and deliver a satisfying experience to people with disabilities;
4. to develop a set of user agents for desktop and mobile devices which leverage and translate a cross-platform accessibility API from the 3rd generation access techniques of the web, to the desktop and mobile accessibility APIs – in such a fashion as to give users with disabilities the same utility and accessibility with rich Internet applications as they have with accessible desktop applications.

In addition to this overarching, framework approach to providing generalised access to mainstream ICT, ÆGIS will also address two of the key purposes for which people use ICT – for creating accessible documents and information, and for communicating with other people in an accessible manner. For document and information creation, the project will bring the latest research into assistance for people with cognitive impairments into use with a popular, open source office suite. Further, ÆGIS addresses the issues of accessibility document creation by building direct support for DAISY digital talking books and Braille and large print to that office suite – so that ÆGIS aids not just developers, but also document authors – in the ÆGIS project. To aid the deaf and hard of hearing community in communicating with one another and with people outside of that community – and also with emergency services – the project will build into mainstream ICT communication software the ability to communicate using real-time-text. Our objective is to demonstrate how mainstream ICT communication applications can utilize these techniques to integrate and support real-time-text within their existing communication product. For people with speech impairments, ÆGIS will develop and demonstrate affordable – and open source – AAC applications that can be embedded into future mobile devices and desktop systems.

The final, core objective of ÆGIS is to address the major economic barriers to e-Inclusion. The project takes the traditional approach of involving key industrial partners in the consortium, and then goes a step further by developing all of infrastructure, developer's tools, our prototypes assistive technologies under an open source software license. This will allow mobile device manufacturers to extend, complete, and embed these assistive technologies into their products cost effectively. It will also allow desktop systems to include real-time-text communications systems – that interoperate with those on cell phones and PDAs – cost effectively. It will enable developers to obtain the developer's tools and user interface component sets to create accessible applications at no cost. And it will allow the translation and customization of these access solutions to the languages and needs of every EU Member State.

5   ÆGIS Overall Strategy and Innovation

In the holistic approach to accessibility that is taken within ÆGIS, the project directly supports developers, to dramatically reduce their burden on making applications

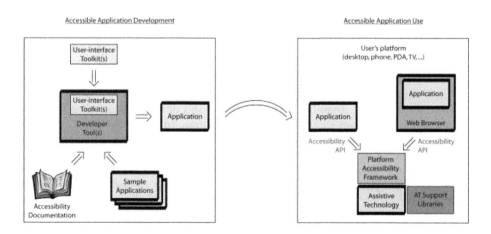

Fig. 2. The ÆGIS approach

accessible. While a number of the ideas and techniques used aren't new (the basic concept of UI component sets is well established, and the project technical coordinator Sun was one of the first to apply this in service of accessibility), nobody before ÆGIS has woven them into a complete, holistic approach to accessibility, called the "Open Accessibility Framework" of ÆGIS.

ÆGIS will establish a set of user interface components supporting accessibility one step further – by making it a cross-platform set of components designed for rich Internet applications. To fully prove the technique, the project will implement the emerging WAI ARIA specification on several different user interface component sets, and on several particular complex user interface components. In this fashion, the project may discover some limitations of the WAI ARIA specification and engage with the W3C Standardization effort to change and improve the standard based on our discoveries. ÆGIS will also transfer the Java Accessibility API to the more complex world of highly visual/animated web user interfaces – these are user interfaces created not with typical user interface component sets, but rather with animated bitmap and vector graphics drawing primitives.

Further, ÆGIS will apply these cross-platform accessibility APIs to a pair of cross platform user agents – a web browser and a Java run-time environment. These user agents, in turn, translate the cross-platform accessibility APIs into their native platform accessibility APIs, so that assistive technologies need not support both the platform accessibility API and the rich Internet accessibility API; the user agent mediates that information for the AT.

While parts of the ÆGIS approach – third generation access and user interface components implementing accessibility support – have been realized by some of ÆGIS consortium participants on desktop systems, they have never been attempted on mobile devices, like cell phones and PDAs. Access on those devices is still mired in the second generation approach to accessibility. ÆGIS will take the holistic approach in building out on the desktop and web, and apply it to mobile devices. This means ÆGIS will define accessibility APIs for the mobile space, define user interface component sets and prototype built-in support for the accessibility APIs on those component sets, create developer tool support to help developers create accessible mobile applications, prototype the necessary platform accessibility services to support assistive technologies (including text-to-speech services), and then go on to develop a set of prototype assistive technologies as well. While this is a large undertaking that breaks new ground in many areas, the history the ÆGIS partners have in developing many of these components for the desktop provides confidence it can be accomplished.

All of this implementation work is for nothing if it doesn't result in a satisfying experience for users with disabilities. For that reason this project is undertaken in close collaboration with expert disability user organizations, with a strong focus on User Centered Design. These user organizations bring a strong mixture of experienced technology users (expert in the use of second generation access solutions) and novice users, for whom much of this technology will be brand new. This combination will allow us to build prototype solutions that are proven to meet a broad range of new as well as experienced technology users. Such a thorough and comprehensive design approach is novel in the field of assistive technology development.

Particularly innovative is the development, hand-in-hand, of the mainstream consumer products and the assistive technology solutions for them, all with the close consultation and collaboration of disability organizations and users.

Finally, ÆGIS brings critical innovation to the problem of the major economic burden access solutions can impose – especially on the high percentage of unemployed among people with disabilities, and among those in the less wealthy EU Member states who lack government programs that provide expensive access solutions. ÆGIS addresses this issue through the use of open source solutions throughout all aspects of the accessibility value delivery chain. First, ÆGIS will develop most of the user interface component sets under open source licenses, so that they may be used free of license or royalty charge in applications. Second, ÆGIS will build accessibility support into existing and newly created open source developer's tools, so that developers need not make a single software purchase in order to develop an accessible application. Next, to the greatest extent possible, the project will choose open source end user platforms to make accessible – including open source UNIX and GNU/Linux desktops, open source user agents and web browsers, and open source mobile device platforms – in addition to working with the major existing commercial desktop and mobile platforms. This greatly lowers the purchase price of these platforms (for example, all schools in Extremadura and Andalusia in Spain use open source GNU/Linux desktops in all classrooms, because they are much more affordable that commercial alternatives, like Windows). Finally, ÆGIS will prototype five open source assistive technology prototypes that will run on these platforms. Assistive technologies are often the most expensive piece of an accessible solution. By developing these under an open source license, the project dramatically lowers the cost of accessible technology – a cost that the significantly unemployed set of Europeans with disabilities can little afford.

Open source is also key to the ÆGIS plan for dissemination and exploitation. Today, desktop solutions cost several thousand Euros, and in addition supporting assistive technologies such as screen readers and screen embossers would need to be acquired as they are default not built in, again costing at least thousand Euros. The total package is obviously out of reach of people with disabilities who often lack financial means. But if the desktop solutions and the supporting assistive technology solutions were open source and free, ÆGIS will have removed the single greatest barrier to their inclusion, and their subsequent adoption by users who need them.

The final benefit of note to the innovation of an open source accessibility framework, across the overall delivery value chain – and that also significantly aids in exploitation – is the fact that every link in the chain can be directly modified by a company that wishes to exploit it – directly tailored to suit the specific needs of the environment it will be used and exploited in. This ability to modify open source technologies – and to use them free of charge – is a key reason for the widespread adoption of GNU/Linux in mobile devices. ÆGIS' innovation is to apply that same technique to accessibility.

Reference

1. Annex, I.: Description of Work, Open Accessibility Everywhere: Groundwork, Infrastructure, Standards (ÆGIS). In: 7th FW, ICT-2007.7.1, ICT & Ageing (September 11, 2008)

On the Privacy-Preserving HCI Issues*
(Extended Abstract)

Taekyoung Kwon[1], JongHyup Lee[2], and JooSeok Song[2]

[1] Dept. of Computer Engineering, Sejong University, Seoul, 143-747, Korea
[2] Dept. of Computer Science, Yonsei University, Seoul, 120-749, Korea
tkwon@sejong.ac.kr,
{jhlee,jssong}@emerald.yonsei.ac.kr

Abstract. Actual interactions between human users and computers occur at the user interface, which includes both hardware and software. When users attempt to input sensitive information to computers, a kind of *shoulder surfing* that might use direct observation techniques, such as looking over someone's shoulder, to get the information could be a great concern at the user interface. In this paper, we observe privacy-related issues at the user interface and then present an abstract model for privacy-preserving human-computer interactions. In such an abstract model, we also present two prototype methods which could work with traditional input devices.

1   Introduction

Human-Computer Interaction (HCI) is recently one of the most significant research topics in computer science. Since actual interactions between human users and computers occur at the user interface, which includes both hardware and software, privacy concerns should remain on that user interface unless all sort of possible intrusions and observations are eradicated. Needless to say, it is not trivial to remove them. When users attempt to input sensitive information to computers using a keyboard, keypad, mouse or touch screen, a kind of *shoulder surfing* that might use direct observation techniques, such as looking over someone's shoulder, to get the information could be a great concern at the user interface [7].

In this paper, we observe privacy concerns at the user interface and present an abstract model for the consideration of privacy-preserving HCI. In such an abstract model, we also present two prototype methods which could work with traditional input devices. One is a method with a single user interface, while the other is with more user interfaces, implying out-of-channels. More details of our study will be presented in the full paper version, with regard to the observation, model, and method.

---

* This research is made by the support of industry, university and research cooperation business of Seoul Metropolitan city (subject No. 10557).

C. Stephanidis (Ed.): Universal Access in HCI, Part I, HCII 2009, LNCS 5614, pp. 544–549, 2009.

The rest of this paper is organized as follows. In Section 2, we observe privacy concerns at the user interface. In Section 3, we present an abstract model for privacy-preserving HCI, and then two prototype methods in Section 4. This paper is concluded in Section 5.

2   Privacy Concerns at the User Interface

The user interface - also known as Human Computer Interface or Man-Machine Interface (MMI) - is the aggregate of means of input and output (I/O) between human users and computer (or electronic/mechanical) systems, for allowing the users to manipulate systems and the systems to indicate the effects of the users' manipulation. In computer science, a common understanding of the user interface is that it is a kind of general purpose I/O device along with its corresponding software. Thus, it is trivially considered to input sensitive as well as non-sensitive information at the same user interface, such as a keyboard, keypad, mouse or touch screen. Here the sensitive information implies user-private information including a password, Personal Identification Number (PIN), Social Security Number (SSN), and so on. When users attempt to input such information at Automated Teller Machines (ATMs), public pay phones, kiosks, or any traditional computer systems, the so-called shoulder surfing attack is a big concern. Note that the shoulder surfing attack is neither a kind of technical attack, for example, based on malicious software, nor a social engineering attack. It is done by direct observation techniques, such as looking over someone's shoulder, and also can be done at a distance using binoculars, Closed-Circuit TeleVision (CCTV) cameras or other vision-augmenting devices.

There have been a number of technical proposals to prevent shoulder surfing, for example, by a physical shield at the user interface, sophisticated display which grows darker beyond a certain viewing angle, keypad which alters the physical location of keys at each input trial, graphical password which is less trivial to guess, and eye-tracking technique which is less traceable by simple observations [1,2,4,5,6]. Also, there have been the policy-based or legal enforcement such that security cameras are not allowed to be placed directly above the user interface or other users are not allowed to get close to the active user at the user interface [7].

However, those schemes are eventually vulnerable to the overall attacks of an accurate shoulder surfer who also breaks the policy-based or legal enforcement. If the shoulder surfer is equipped with sufficient monitoring devices placed around the user interface and allowed to record the user's input transactions more accurately, the shoulder surfer can succeed in obtaining the user's sensitive information at the user interface.

3   Abstract Model for Privacy-Preserving HCI

The basic assumption of our approach is that the user interface is under the observation of a shoulder surfer, as like that the network is under the control

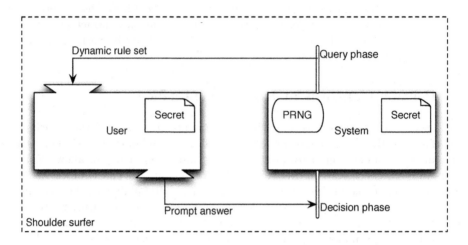

Fig. 1. Abstract model for privacy-preserving HCI

of an attacker in the famous Dolev-Yao model. Thus, both user and system are considered as black boxes but the user interface between them are not from the perspectives of the shoulder surfer. That means, the shoulder surfer can observe and log every conversation between the user and the server at the user interface, while (s)he cannot break into the memory of both user and server, in our model. Fig. 1 illustrates this model in very abstract levels. The user who memorizes a secret may be queried by the system which stores the same secret and is equipped with a Pseudo-Random Number Generator (PRNG), with regard to a set of dynamic rules or puzzles, in a *query phase*. The user prepares a prompt answer from the secret and the given dynamic rule set in a cognitive sense, and then inputs the answer at the user interface, which is followed by a decision of the system, in a *decision phase*. Those phases may be repeated for a sufficient amount of time, so that the system can make a correct decision with overwhelming probability. For achieving the goal of privacy-preserving, the followings should be attained in the query and decision phases at the user interface.

- The probability that the shoulder surfer gets the information about the secret from dynamic rule sets and prompt answers, should be negligible.
- The probability that an active attacker succeeds in forging prompt answers correctly on the given dynamic rule sets, should be negligible.
- The dynamic rule sets should be sufficiently random to prevent replay attacks.

In this abstract model, we could consider both singe and multiple user interface models between the user and the system. The single interface model means a trivial case that the user is given a I/O device within the same flow of control, while the multiple interface implies a out-of-band channel which means that the user is given another I/O device out of the flow above, saying, beyond the control of the shoulder surfer. In the following section, we will present two prototype methods in those respective models.

4   Prototype Methods for Privacy-Preserving HCI

In the sense of aforementioned privacy-preserving model using human recognition, we present prototype methods in our abstract model, to secure authentication based on PINs against the shoulder-surfing attack. Usually customers using ATMs are required to enter their PINs at the user interface provided by the ATMs. However, the customers' input actions at the user interface could disclose the secret PINs to the shoulder surfer. Thus, we devise prototype systems, in which users enter perturbed numbers (as prompt answers) instead of the secret PINs themselves. Given a set of dynamic queries from ATM, users should be able to produce a correctly perturbed number, by a simple and intuitive method in a cognitive sense, using their knowledge of respective PINs.

In the proposed prototype methods, we assume the system has a keypad implemented on a touch screen, which is already wide-spread in modern ATMs. Fig. 2(a) shows the initial configuration of keypad in the prototype method. Like a normal ATM, ten digit keys (0 ~ 9) and two special keys (* and ♯) are shown but with modification of the shape of digit keys from 1 to 9 to contain nine sub-blocks in each key. For more flexible constructions, we color each key distinctly according to the digit. The assigned digit of the key appears at the

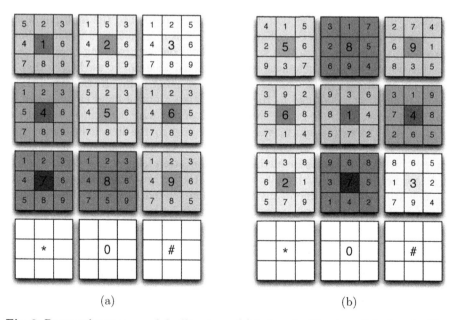

(a)   (b)

Fig. 2. Proposed prototype of shuffling keys. (a) before shuffling keys (b) after shuffling keys.

center block with thicker and larger font, and the other digits except zero and the assigned digit are shown in the surrounding sub-blocks, which indicate eight directions from the key. Then, in each query phase, both keys and surrounding sub-blocks are shuffled[1] randomly as shown in Fig. 2(b). In other words, the randomly shuffled keypad corresponds to the dynamic query set.

There are two options regarding the starting point. One is to start from the first digit of user's PIN. Otherwise, we could start from a color or number possibly indicated in each query. (See below for more flexible constructions.) Then, from the starting point (i.e., key) on a keypad, a user moves to the next key according to the direction indicated by subsequent digit of the secret PIN, *without* touching the keys actually. The user may only stare at the keypad and follow the direction on it. If a digit of user's PIN is 0, the user stays with the current digit key.

The user may stop following directions if (s)he finishes following all digits in the PIN or there is no way to move on the keypad. Then, finally the user enters the last digit key (s)he has followed on the keypad, into the system. The whole processes from the random shuffling above are repeated to ensure the possession of the secret PIN with overwhelming probability. For example, using the configuration of Fig. 2(b), if the PIN is 46013 and the first option of starting point is considered, then the user may start at the digit key '4' and move to '3', '7' and then reaches '2' as a final destination. Thus '2' is entered by the user. In the same case but with a different PIN such as 57852, the user may proceed with '5', '1' and '6' according to 5785, but there is no more digit key in the left side of key '6'. Thus, '6' is entered by the user in this case.

In the prototype system above, basically we assume the single interface model discussed in the previous section, but it can be extended to the multiple interface model, in which attackers hardly observe all interfaces at the same time. For example, we can consider a small handheld device providing another user interface for out-of-band channels, so that such a device can be used for notifying the color or number of keypad as a random starting point. In this case, since the starting point is notified to the user through a out-of-band channel and is more difficult to trace or guess, the shoulder surfer may have more difficulties in obtaining the secret information. With regard to the handheld device and the out-of-band channel, we con consider a PDA or cell phone such as i-phone, equipped with a bluetooth or further communication facility.

As for security, the probability that an attacker guesses a right answer in a single attempt is $\frac{1}{9}$ without any information related to the PIN itself. Since the authentication process is repeated, the probability that the attacker finally succeeds in authentication is reduced to $(\frac{1}{9})^t$ simply, where t is the number of iterations very related to the length of PIN. In addition, the attacker cannot succeed in guessing a right digit at a specific position of the PIN because each query-answer phase can be stopped at any digit of the PIN, feeding nonlinearity

---

[1] More specifically, we can consider two levels of random shuffling of those keys and sub-blocks. That is, firstly we shuffle the nine digit keys, and then respective surrounding keys.

to the prototype system. Hence, the only meaningful attack is that the attacker guesses all possible cases of digits based on the entered number from the observation and repeats this guessing through a huge number of shoulder-surfings on a specific target user. Then, the attacker tests all possible sequences using the statistics for candidate digits but such an attack is impractical.

To sum up, the prototype system is secure against shoulder-surfing attacks in the sense of practicality since even accurate surfing may not work.

5   Conclusion

In this paper, we observe privacy concerns at the user interface, with regard to more powerful (or less restrictive) shoulder surfers who may break the rules assumed in the previous schemes, and then we present a simple model in abstract levels, along with prototype methods for privacy-preserving HCI. The prototype methods do not require any arithmetic computation to the user [3] in a practical sense, but provide relatively stronger security against accurate shoulder surfers than the related schemes [1,2,4,5,6]. In the full paper version, we provide experimental results and analyses, along with more details of our study.

References

1. Hoanca, B., Mock, K.: Screen Oriented Technique for Reducing the Incidence of Shoulder Surfing. In: International Conference on Security and Management (SAM) (2005)
2. Hoanca, B., Mock, K.: Secure Graphical Password System for High Traffic Public Areas. In: ETRA - Eye Tracking Research and Applications Symposium (2006)
3. Hopper, N., Blum, M.: Secure human identification protocols. In: Boyd, C. (ed.) ASIACRYPT 2001. LNCS, vol. 2248, pp. 52–66. Springer, Heidelberg (2001)
4. Kumar, M., Garfinkel, T., Boneh, D., Winograd, T.: Reducing Shoulder-surfing by Using Gaze-based Password Entry. In: Symposium on Usable Privacy and Security (SOUPS) (2007)
5. Roth, V., Richter, K., Freidinger, R.: A PIN-Entry Method Resilient Against Shoulder Surfing. In: Conference on Computer and Communications Security (CCS) (2004)
6. Tan, D., Keyani, P., Czerwinski, M.: Spy-Resistant Keyboard: Towards More Secure Password Entry on Publicly Observable Touch Screens. In: Computer-Human Interaction Special Interest Group (CHISIG) of Australia (2005)
7. "Shoulder Surfing" in Wikipedia, the free encyclopedia, http://www.wikipedia.org

E-Inclusiveness and Digital Television in Europe – A Holistic Model

Peter Olaf Looms

Danish Broadcasting Corporation, DR,
DR-Byen
Emil Holms Kanal 20
DK-0999 Copenhagen C
polooms@gmail.com

Abstract. This paper reviews the nature and size of the accessibility challenge and identifies pitfalls in the current strategies to promote e-inclusiveness. Using examples such as the DTV4ALL project which focuses on free-to-air broadcasting, the paper argues the case for working systematically with stakeholders associated with the entire access service supply chain to draw up and implement a continent-wide strategy to promote e-inclusiveness and digital television.

1 Introduction

For most people around the world, watching television is a simple matter: find the remote control, press the "power" button and then zap to the channel you want to see. By 2012, most industrialised countries will switch to digital terrestrial television (DTT) transmission and switch off analogue transmissions. But switching from analogue to digital offers benefits that come at a price. Experience from the first 12 years of digital television shows that analogue switch-off may create problems and require corrective action. Free-to-air television aims to be socially inclusive and usually has obligations to make television accessible for all. Who are likely to encounter problems during the transition to DTT? How can digital television become more inclusive? What are the access options DTT can adopt in the short and medium term to promote inclusiveness? What are the prerequisites for widespread take-up of these services? These are four of the questions I would like to address in this article.

2 Who Are Likely to Encounter Problems during the Transition to DTT?

2.1 Setting Up the Digital Television Receiver

Watching DTT requires the viewer either to purchase an integrated digital television receiver or to buy a digital set-top box and connect it to an existing television set. The viewer may have to change the aerial or buy a new one. On the face of it, setting up should not be a big problem, but Clarkson and Keates [2] indicate that the design of

C. Stephanidis (Ed.): Universal Access in HCI, Part I, HCII 2009, LNCS 5614, pp. 550–558, 2009.

digital television interfaces and services can exclude various groups of the population. In a report on a DTT technical trial [3] notes that "a minority needed support - most issues were resolved over the telephone by the Trial Helpline. A small minority needed a lot of support – mostly the very elderly and the disabled." The elderly needed help for a number of reasons: difficulties in installing their own equipment, difficulty in re-scanning, lack of confidence (extra advice and re-assurance were needed in using the equipment), remote control issues, the use of subtitles because of hearing difficulties, and difficulty in bending down.

In a related trial, [4] reports that "Not all 'vulnerable' people need help. In Bolton, where installation help was made available only as a 'fallback', family and friends successfully installed the equipment for 69% of the elderly participants. Only 31% needed help from Trial engineers."

2.2 Watching Digital Television

Having set up the receiver, the next challenge is whether the viewer can find and watch the programmes he or she wants. Do people really have problems watching programmes on digital television? If so, what are the problems, causes and options for taking corrective action?

The nature and size of the problem can be difficult to gauge. In Hong Kong, according to Census and Statistics Department from 2001, about 4% of the population is reported to have some kind of physical, sensory or mental impairment. Disability Status (2000) in the USA reports that "approximately 1 in 5 Americans has some form of disability, and 1 in 10 has a severe disability". In Great Britain, the studies referred to by [9] indicated that some 17.3% of the adult population (persons 16 or more) have one or more disability.

The differences between the Hong Kong figures on the one hand and the US and UK figures on the other could reflect genuine differences. A closer examination reveals that the smaller figures for Hong Kong could also be ascribed to differences in terminology and definitions. Mellors [16] identified similar issues when analysing levels of hearing impairment in various European countries, with a range of 4.7% (the UK) to 1.7% (Italy) that could be accounted for by differences in the threshold used to assess hearing impairment (35 dB in the UK and 55 dB in Italy).

There are various schools of thought about the metrics for exclusion and inclusiveness. Mellors [16] makes use of hearing measurements. Other major studies such as [9] base their figures on capability problems reported by subjects themselves. The advantage of self-reporting is that it covers a wider range of problems than can be covered by formal assessments of impairment.

While there seem to be national differences in quantifying the inclusiveness challenge, the studies mentioned above all demonstrate a causal link between capability problems and age. Stallard [20] notes that "today there are more than 70 million people aged 60 and above in the EU, representing just under one in five of the population.... Many of these citizens will experience dexterity, cognitive, hearing and sight problems in later life."

2.3 Accessing Digital Television

The rationale for action across Europe was outlined in a European Commission policy document [8] from 2005: "People with disabilities constitute about 15% of the European population and many of them encounter barriers when using ICT products and services"…"18% of the European population was aged over 60 in 1990, while this is expected to rise to 30% by 2030." … "The implications are clear: making the benefits of ICT available to the widest possible number of people is a social, ethical and political imperative."

Digital television is one of the most widely used ICT products and services. The European Commission argues that the transition from analogue to digital terrestrial transmission in Europe by 2012 represents a unique opportunity to provide better access to TV and other services. Written evidence [10] given to the House of Commons Select Committee on the Television without Frontiers Directive (2006-7) indicates that the overwhelming majority of those with perception, cognition or motion impairments would like to be able to watch television like everyone else.

Assessing the size and nature of the demand for access services is far from easy as there is no direct relation between impairment and demand. OFCOM [18] notes that "the demand for access services such as audio description and subtitling is very significant."…"7.5 million (equivalent to 12.3% of the population) said that they had used subtitles to watch television, of whom about 6 million (10%) did not have a hearing impairment."

It seems that subtitling in particular is used not only by those with hearing impairments but also by those who find it difficult to understand young people speaking quickly or using slang (intra-lingual communication), by those in countries with two or more official languages (inter-lingual communication to facilitate the understanding of all of these languages by offering opt-in subtitles) and in countries with significant immigrant groups for whom subtitling in their mother tongue may promote integration and social cohesion.

A report by Klein et al [12] on usable and accessible design for the UK's Digital Television Project estimated that 4.4% of those currently able to access analogue television could be excluded from simply viewing when using digital terrestrial television set top boxes at switchover. A further 1.6% currently able to access analogue television could be excluded from using advanced features such as digital text and interactive services.

As part of work on the European Commission project DTV4ALL, we have listed a number of access problems and used UK data from Grundy et al. (op. cit.) available online to make some rough estimates of the number of people who could be excluded from accessing digital television. A summary is included in table 1.

We can conclude that the elderly and those with various capability problems may well have difficulties getting started with DTT, unless they have help from family and friends or a support programme. The DTT platform, however, does have the potential to make television more inclusive by offering a range of access services.

Table 1. Proportion of the adult population in Europe expected to have problems accessing digital television (DTV4ALL estimates based on Grundy et al (1999))

Access issues with digital television	estimate (% of population)
1. Finds it difficult/impossible to hear the audio of TV programmes	1,8%
2. Finds it difficult/impossible to hear/understand speech in mother tongue	2,3%
3. Sometimes finds it difficult to hear/understand speech in mother tongue	2,3%
4. Finds it difficult/impossible to understand speech in a foreign language	n.a.
5. Finds it difficult/impossible to see the visual component of TV	0,7%
6. Unfamiliar with remote controls and interface conventions on DTT	10,9%
7. Finds it difficult/ impossible to use services such as Subtitles (SDH)	9,4%
8. Finds it difficult to switch gaze from screen to remote control device	3,4%
9. Finds it difficult to read subtitles, On Screen Displays including EPGs	3,4%
10. Finds it difficult/impossible to use the television remote control device	10,9%
11. Finds it difficult/impossible to set up and configure TV set or Set Top Box	10,9%

3   How Can Digital Television Channels and Programmes become More Inclusive?

In many parts of the world, some access services such as subtitles and signing have been available for some time on analogue television using Teletext and simultaneous interpreters signing in a corner of the screen. Offering access services usually lies between the following two extremes: the Individual, or Medical, Model that focuses on impairments and the Social Model of Disability first coined by [19], where "disability" is used to refer to the restrictions caused by society when it does not give equivalent attention and accommodation to the needs of individuals with impairments.

In the first model, those with impairments would have to buy specialised DTT set-top boxes themselves or get them as part of public health provisions in social welfare states. Critics of this model claim that it often ignores the self-esteem of those involved and tends to be ad-hoc, parochial and expensive.

In the second model, however, society at large assumes a collective responsibility for being inclusive. Here the technology required for access services by and large is built into all DTT receivers. Dewsbury [5] suggests a shift of focus, focusing on what the individual wants to do and making a sensible mix of both models.

Enabling audiences with impairments to get what they want out of television will often require access services that can be merely assistive or truly inclusive. Analysis of current access provisions shows three main scenarios:

1. At the one extreme, the service is provided for all content genres both during the day and at peak viewing hours so that viewers of all ages and abilities can derive benefit

from watching the same television programmes. Subtitles for the deaf and hard of hearing at the BBC is an example of a service that is both assistive and inclusive.

2. In the middle we have an access service provided for all content genres but the scheduling of the programme is such that it does not lead to reactions from those who do not want or need the service. An example is visual signing for programming that is offered on channels with more limited audience share and scheduled in connection with repeats aired late at night, well away from peak viewing. This approach is assistive and inclusive outside key viewing hours.

3. At the other extreme, the access service is not provided for general output, but there are schedule slots designed for audiences with special needs. An example is again visual signing where a policy decision has been taken to offer programmes made specifically for those requiring signing, rather than providing visual signing for "normal" content genres such as news programmes. As with (B), these programmes are scheduled away from peak viewing hours. This approach is exclusive, and is only assistive outside key viewing hours.

In an ideal world, it should be possible to offer both scenario A and C. Feedback from call centres from broadcasters and operators indicates that offering "open" solutions such as signing that have to be viewed by all on major channels and/or in prime time can lead to adverse reactions from viewers without impairments. Offering easy-to-use, opt-in access services would thus seem to be the approach that leads to the fewest objections from general audiences.

4   What Are the Solutions DTT Can Adopt in the Short Term and Medium Term?

DTT based on MPEG-2 technology already has a range of mature access services solutions that broadcasters and platform operators can offer. The nature and extent of access services depend in the first instance on the regulatory climate governing DTT and then the application of three general criteria suggested by ISTAG [11]: Is the service to be offered acceptable and have a demonstrable benefit to its intended audience? Is there a technology that can be integrated into existing work flows and that is scaleable? And is there a sustainable business model for the service in question?

For an access service to be viable, all three criteria have to be met. Unlike Pay-TV which is dominated by the operator, the decision-making process for free-to-air broadcasting on DTT is not driven by one stakeholder. The introduction of an access service requires a high degree of consensus among all of the stakeholders involved before improved access services can be implemented. For compromise to take place and consensus reached, a key prerequisite is that each stakeholder understands the interests and resources of everyone else in the value chain. Unless the solutions chosen constitute a win-win for all concerned, coercion in the form of national legislation, public service contracts or standards for digital television receivers and remote control devices will only lead to obfuscation, passive or active resistance on the part of one or more stakeholders, or worst of all to services that cannot be sustained.

The problem facing DTT in particular is that in the course of the coming five years, new production and distribution technologies using encoding and decoding standards such as MPEG-4 and displayed on flat panels in high definition will take over. Access services that work well today may come under threat for various reasons. Wood [22] notes that the challenge of such transitions is exacerbated by timing differences. Not only is the transition from analogue to digital television taking place at different times, so too is the transition from first generation, MPEG-2 based solutions to second-generation MPEG-4 based solutions delivered via broadcast or even IPTV networks. While some countries such as the UK choose to wait for the finalisation of DVB2 standards before migrating to high definition on DTT, others such as France have been obliged to find a solution pre-empting DVB2. Instead of marching in step, the transition from one generation of digital television to another is more like leap-frogging. Whereas in the past we had standards and stable solutions for several decades, the effective lifetime of a transmission platform is now measured in years rather than decades.

All services have a lifecycle: new technologies emerge, become "sunrise solutions" and some become widespread. After some time – years or decades – the solution shows sign of age, of not being viable. These "sunset technologies" then have to be phased out and replaced by a new sunrise solution. The challenge is to find the optimum switch-over point.

Two examples of sunset solutions highlight the issues: the use of Teletext to offer subtitles for the deaf and hard of hearing, and Audio Description delivered as a second pair of stereo channels (the so-called broadcast mix). EBU [7] describes the two main standards for subtitle delivery for the DVB digital television standard, DVB Teletext (EN 300 472) and DVB Subtitling (EN 300 743). Subtitles via Teletext have been with us for decades, whereas DVB subtitling has only gained ground in the last decade. Whether and when to switch to DVB subtitling depends on which stakeholder one asks. Viewers may not be aware of the existence of the two delivery mechanisms. When shown both on a high definition television receiver, however, most prefer DVB subtitling for its flexibility, attractiveness and usability, especially since DVB subtitles can be recorded and viewed on PVRs, which is not necessarily the case for Teletext subtitles. Consumer electronics manufacturers would like to see pan-European agreement on such services, ideally agreement not to have to support both standards in order to keep down costs. Where the regulator, standardisation body or DTT platform operator does not mandate the use of Teletext, this is likely to be dropped. Broadcasters who have offered Teletext subtitling services can continue to use their existing production set-ups but will need to change the contribution and transmission set-ups for their services.

Laven [13] discusses the options for Audio Description on DTT and explains the rationale for moving from the so-called broadcaster mix to a receiver mix, where the mono audio track with AD is mixed with the conventional stereo tracks in the receiver. The transition from standard to high definition will exert additional pressure on bandwidth allocation for access services. As some HD programming offers multi-channel audio, the broadcaster mix solution will become unacceptable for DTT. Even the receiver mix method will be demanding if AD services are scaled up and two television channels with AD are present in the same multiplex. Ultimately the solution could be a kind of AD based on audio subtitles in which a speech synthesis chip in the receiver converts text into speech with male and female voices as required. Assuming that the method can deliver speech at an acceptable quality, the bandwidth requirements can be reduced from 256 kbits/s to less than 30 kbit/s if the audio subtitles that form the basis of this synthetic speech service are delivered using DVB-subtitling.

These two examples highlight the need for holistic access service strategies that take into consideration all the stakeholders involved in that service. They also show that a given service goes through a maturity cycle during which the metrics of success may change as the service level is ramped up.

5 What Are the Prerequisites for Widespread Take-Up of These Services?

E-inclusiveness is thus more than just access services. It is also about television programming in general, about making it easier for anyone to benefit from television regardless of age or possible disabilities.

Access services for digital television are already available in many countries. To improve the e-inclusiveness of television, action is required on three fronts:

1. In the short term, facilitating the take-up of mature access services on what we have termed first generation digital television (1997-2012, broadcast systems based on MPEG-2).
2. Preparing for the next generations of digital television by assessing whether mature services are still viable on these emerging digital television platforms.
3. Identifying and validating emerging solutions that will either replace mature access services or extend the scope of access provisions on emerging digital television platforms.

In our work on the DTV4ALL project, we are carrying out a Pilot of mature services. We have asked ourselves the question: *Who needs to know what in order to be able to plan, produce, deliver, promote and successfully use mature access services by 2010?* As regards the "*who*" part of the statement, our existing plans focus on those with access problems, primarily those with impaired sight and hearing. Mention is also made of consumer electronics manufacturers. We suggest the use of the complete supply chain as our starting point for scoping. It is necessary to keep in mind the needs of the viewers, the stakeholders in the supply chain itself and those who influence it such as regulators and legislators. Data from the pilot will be used in a maturity model that encourages decision-makers to revisit their strategies at regular intervals in order to make adjustments in the light of political, social, economic and technological change. Proof of Concept work on emerging solutions will help identify promising candidates for future access services.

Unlike Pay TV which makes use of proprietary solutions and where the service provider can call the shots, DTT requires consensus all down the value chain because no one stakeholder can decide anything – compromise and consensus is a fact of life. As a result, selling DTT receivers over the counter requires a greater degree of agreement on standards and interoperability than for Pay TV solutions, especially if there is no compliance mechanism in place. Agreeing on new solutions for DTT takes a lot of discussion and time that ultimately pays for itself, if there really is consensus

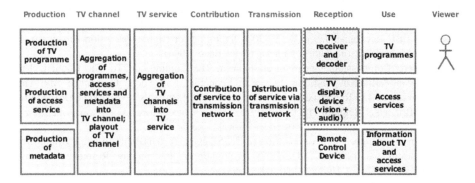

Fig. 1. Generic supply chain for digital television. Source: Looms et al. [14].

on access services. This is why in Europe we are seeing special-interest groups, broadcasters, hardware manufacturers and embarking on national, regional or even European endeavours to discuss options and come up with scaleable solutions that hopefully will ensure that digital television is accessible to all. We hope to identify both solutions and strategies that can be generalised and applied more widely as part of our work on DTV4ALL.

Standardisation bodies are also at work on accessibility. W3C [21] has come far in its work on standardisation and is currently working on both speech synthesis and speech recognition for the Web. Mpatwa [15] describes a recent ITU project potentially with global ramifications. It aims to complete a strategy toolkit for promoting e-inclusiveness on a wide range of information technology platforms.

As can be seen from this paper, standards in themselves are no guarantee that the market will work towards e-inclusiveness unless there are relevant incentives and sanctions to facilitate compromise and consensus.

Acknowledgement. This paper is based on work funded by grant agreement no. 224994 under the European Commission programme ICT PSP/2007/1. The opinions expressed by the author of this paper are not necessarily endorsed by either the European Commission or DR.

References

1. Census and Statistics Department, Persons with disabilities and chronic diseases, Special Topics Report (STR) Number 28, Hong Kong SAR (2001)
2. Clarkson, J., Keates, S.: Digital Television For All. A Report on Usability And Accessible Design Appendix E – Investigating The Inclusivity of Digital Television Set-Top Box Receivers. DTI, UK (September 18, 2003)
3. DCMS. Report of a Digital Switchover Technical Trial at Ferryside And Llansteffan, Department for Culture, Media and Sport, UK (July 2005) (2005a)
4. DCMS. Report of Bolton Digital Television Trial. Department for Culture, Media and Sport, UK (May 26, 2006) (2005b)
5. Dewsbury, G., et al.: The anti-social model of disability. Disability & Society 19(2) (March 2004)

6. Disability Status (2000 U.S). Census 2000, C2KBR17, U.S. Census Bureau. March 2003 and Disabilities and Age (October 1994-January 1995)

7. EBU. EBU Recommendation R-110-2004 Subtitling for Digital Television Broadcasting. European Broadcasting Union, Geneva, Switzerland (2004)

8. European Commission, Communication From The Commission To The Council, The European Parliament And The European Economic And Social Committee And The Committee of The Regions eAccessibility [SEC, 1095] Brussels, 13.9. 2005 COM, 425 final. Brussels, Belgium (2005), http://eur-lex.europa.eu/LexUriServ/site/en/com/2005/com2005_0425en01.pdf

9. Grundy, E., Ahlberg, D., Ali, M., Breeze, E., Sloggett, A.: Disability in Great Britain: results from the 1996/1997 Disability Follow-up to the Family Resources Survey. Charlesworth Group, Huddersfield, UK (1999)

10. House of Commons Select Committee on European Union - Written Evidence. Page 162, http://www.parliament.uk/documents/upload/Final%20TVWF%20HL27.pdf

11. ISTAG. New Business Sectors in Information and Communication Technologies. The Content Sector as a case study. Final Version (instigated by Ms. Vivian Reding). The European Commission, Brussels, Belgium (September 2007)

12. Klein, Dr Jeremy A., Karger, Simon A. and Sinclair, Kay A. Digital Television For All. A report on usability and accessible design. Prepared for the Digital Television Project (Department of Trade and Industry) by The Generics Group, Harston, Cambridge, UK 18 September (2003)

13. Laven, P.: Broadcasting for all. EBU Technical Review No. 296, European Broadcasting Union, Geneva, Switzerland (October 2003)

14. Looms, P.O.: D2.2. Evaluation Methodology. Public Report from the DTV4ALL Project. ICT PSP/2007/1. ICT Policy Support Programme (ICT PSP). Accessible digital Audiovisual (AV) system (Pilot B). p. 6. European Commission, Brussels, Belgium (2009)

15. Mpatwa, A.: Toolkit on e-Accessibility & Service Needs for People with Disabilities (PwD) ITU, Geneva, Switzerland (2009), http://www.itu.int/ITU-D/projects/proj_call-partners_GP.asp

16. Mellors, W.J.: WGHI - Working Group on Hearing Impairment Statistics on age and disability and in relation to Telecommunications - A significant market (2006), http://www.tiresias.org/phoneability/wghi/stats.htm#ECfigures

17. OFCOM. Guidelines on the provision of television access services. Selection and scheduling of programmes section 3.3. Published, London, UK (September 22, 2006) (2006a)

18. OFCOM. Television access services. Summary, London, UK(2006), http://www.ofcom.org.uk/consult/condocs/accessservs/summary/

19. Oliver, M.: The Individual And Social Models of Disability. Paper Presented At Joint Workshop of The Living Options Group And The Research Unit of The Royal College of Physicians on People With Established Locomotor Disabilities In Hospitals, London, UK, Monday 23 July (1990)

20. Stallard, G.: Standardisation Requirements for Access to Digital TV and Interactive Services by Disabled People. Final Report to CENELEC on TV for All. Chandlers Ford, Hants, UK (2003)

21. W3C. Web Accessibility Initiative (WAI) (2008), http://www.w3.org/WAI/

22. Wood, D.: General Overview of Production and Delivery Trends from an EBU perspective. Seminar on Multimedia Production and Delivery Services. Arab States Broadcasting Union / International Telecommunications Union, Tunis, Tunisia, 31 October-1 November (2008)

Modelling Product-User Interaction for Inclusive Design

Anna Mieczakowski, Patrick Langdon, and P. John Clarkson

Engineering Design Centre, Department of Engineering, University of Cambridge
Trumpington Street, Cambridge, CB2 1PZ, United Kingdom
{akm51,pml24,pjc10}@eng.cam.ac.uk

Abstract. Despite continuing technological advances, there are still many daily living products that are unusable for broad sections of the population, including older and impaired users. Therefore, in order to design more accessible and usable products, designers need better models that can predict how people with varying levels of capability interpret and use different features on product interfaces. The aim of this paper is to survey the background of modelling product-user interaction, discuss strengths and weaknesses of various approaches and focus on appropriate methodology to investigate inclusive interaction with everyday products. This paper concludes that a model of product-user interaction should include three representations of specific information: (1) what people want to do when operating a product (goals); (2) what people actually do while operating a product (actions); and (3) what happens to the functional parts of the product during the operation (objects). Further research is necessary in order to identify methods for combining goal, action and object approaches and developing a usable and inclusive model of product-user interaction.

Keywords: Inclusive Design, Product-User Interaction, Mental Models, Cognitive Representations, Prior Experience.

1 Introduction

One of the long-standing issues in product design is that many people are not able to access and use products that are necessary for leading an independent daily living. It has been shown that the lack of understanding of users' capabilities in product design leads to complex product features, user frustration, human error and accidents, and in extreme cases even total user exclusion [21]. In recent years, the Inclusive Design movement has been encouraging designers to better understand users' capabilities and design products that address the needs of as many people as possible [31]. Inclusive design is a user-centred design that embraces the principles of universal design, which is popular in the United States and Japan. However, it is widely accepted in the inclusive design discourse that designing 'one product for all' is implausible because people of different ages, capabilities and social and cultural backgrounds prefer different products [1]. It has been shown that inclusively designed products not only minimise the exclusion of less capable users, but they are also easier for everyone else to use [32].

C. Stephanidis (Ed.): Universal Access in HCI, Part I, HCII 2009, LNCS 5614, pp. 559–567, 2009.
© Springer-Verlag Berlin Heidelberg 2009

1.1 Motivation

Creating products that are easier to learn and use by everyone, irrespective of age or ability, has become the primary concern of product designers. In response to designers' brief to design more accessible and usable products; Persad et al. [11] emphasise the importance of understanding the interaction between product interface features and the diversity of user sensory, cognitive and motor capabilities. However, the implementation of this principle in the real design situations is far from satisfactory as, firstly, there is no easy-to-access and usable guidance on the product-user interaction in the context of inclusive design; and secondly, designers of everyday products often design their products without clearly specified users, goals, or context of use [7]. It can also be said that in order to design accessible and usable products, it is essential to get appropriate, representative information of target users at the right stage in the design cycle. Unfortunately, the reality is that many designers either do not include the users in the product design process due to lack of knowledge, experience, time and financial constraints, or involve them "too little" or "too late" [29]. Currently, the design community suffers from the lack of a unified source of information on the interaction between product features and human capabilities that could be used to assess the usability and accessibility of design concepts early in the design process. Bellerby and Davis [28], having performed a study with product developers and marketing specialists, argue that the use of inclusive design standards and guidelines could be very beneficial to the design community, but they would have to be presented in a very quick-to-use and understandable format in order to combat the time and cost constraints.

1.2 Product-User Interaction

During the interaction between a product and a user, there is a cyclic process of perceiving the features of a product, thinking about these features and associating them with images of features stored in the long term memory, thinking about the effects of using these features, and acting, followed by the evaluation of the effects of action with regards to user goals [30]. Monk [10] suggests that interaction between a product and the user's information processing system is a cyclic process, which includes the connections between user intention, action and the environment. Throughout this cyclic process, people's actions make changes to the state of the environment. Subsequently, all actions are evaluated in line with users' current goals, which in turn leads to the reformulation of goals and further action that changes the state of the environment and so the cycle repeats again. Freudenthal [19] adds that the fundamental characteristics of product-user interaction are: human, product, environmental aspects and the period of time in which the interaction occurs. According to Freudenthal's [19] framework, the interaction process begins when a user performs some type of action, for example pressing a button on the product interface, or a product initiates it by attracting a user. When a user initiates the interaction with a product, the cognitive processes and actions trigger the product to react, closely followed by new sensory activities of the user.

Winograd and Flores [26] believe that a model of product-user interaction could lead to enhancing the designers' understanding of how users may interact with products and, therefore, such model should contain information about:

- the cognitive domain, in which user's goals are important; and
- the structure of a product, where user's actions and product's objects are the key.

The following section is dedicated to investigating the cognitive processes of users in order to identify how they set their goals when interacting with product features. Whereas, section 3 reviews five product modelling methods in order to find out which one of them is the most efficient at capturing users' goals, actions and functional parts of products (objects).

2 Cognitive Processes

The tasks users perform during the interaction with domestic products involve certain cognitive processes. Thus, in order to design more intuitive and usable products, designers need to have a better understanding of the fundamental functions in cognition. The simplified model of cognition, shown in Figure 1, provides an understanding of how four main elements of cognition (perception, attention, memory and recognition) interact with one another and in the wider context of cognitive processing [8, 16]. The sensory organs perceive an object from the real world. Perception is then responsible for analysing and processing the incoming sensory information and modifying knowledge based on that information [23]. Working memory stores the modal information currently under consideration. The executive function manages working memory in retrieving long term memories, directing attention, initiating actions and reasoning. The executive function decides to act on the selected stimuli by referring to memory and it uses attention to focus on the most informative parts of the stimuli. Working memory has a limited capacity for holding seven plus or minus two temporary items of information at a time [9] and it has to refer to long term memory in order to match the selected stimuli. Once the object has been recognised, it can be grouped with objects of similar physical properties and functional attributes into categories in memory and named [20]. If the stimuli have been experienced before, then the information about this is likely to affect the speed and efficiency of acting upon the interface features. It has been shown that ageing has profound effects on working memory, long term memory, perception, attention and reasoning. In addition, older users interact more slowly with unfamiliar products, make more errors and a higher cognitive burden is reported to slow down their reaction time [8].

2.1 Mental Models

Every user has a cognitive representation or construction with which they "approach, explore, or interact with what designers consider a form" [6]. Consequently, it has been suggested that designers need to understand the ways in which people build and use cognitive representations of products in order to see how users' goals and actions are formulated and to design more accessible and usable product features [14]. In this paper, the cognitive representations of users are referred to as mental models [22].

When interacting with a product, it is thought that a user constructs a mental model about operation of that particular product and the structural relationships between its components. A mental model is "a dynamic representation created in working

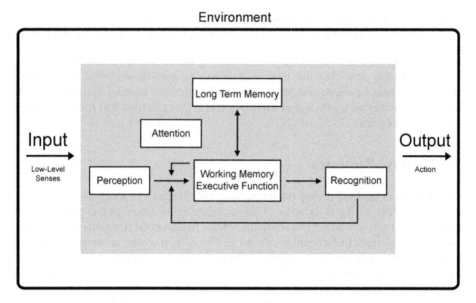

Fig. 1. A simplified model of cognition incorporating perception, attention, working memory, executive function, long term memory and recognition

memory by combing the knowledge stored in long term memory and the information extracted from the task characteristics" [2]. For example, in order to use a product previous knowledge about the features of that particular product together with the knowledge of how that product works are handled in the working memory and certain episodes of knowledge of a product have to be retrieved from the long term memory [30]. Rouse and Morris [12] suggest that the concept of a mental model can be thought of as a 'black box'. During the interaction with products, users tend to perceive an input, a product form and an output. Somehow the input is converted to the output through the medium of the product (a 'black box') and the users' internal explanation of what takes place inside that 'black box' can be referred to as a mental model.

Mental models are constructed through observations and feedback and they change as people gain more experience in interacting with products and, as a result, it is very difficult to capture them due to their evolving nature. Mental models are, moreover, believed to be very difficult to infer as they can be incomplete, limited, unstable, unscientific and parsimonious and vary in complexity depending on the degree of previous experience [13]. Norman [22] claims that an accessible and easy-to-use product can be designed by a means of matching the designer's conceptual model with the user's mental model. The elicitation of user mental models can be used by designers for predicting the device responses, explaining why the device reacted the way it did and deriving appropriate design properties that would contribute to the design of more accessible and usable products [19]. According to Persad et al. [30], a good representation of users' mental models should include information on different product features and how they work, as well as a representation of the sequences of action between an initial state and the goal state.

2.2 Prior Experience

People learn how to use new products by making use of their experiences with previously encountered products [3]. Therefore, designers should exploit what people already know and new product interfaces should be designed to look familiar based on previous knowledge and experience [25]. Blackler [15] suggests that prior experience leads to intuitive interaction with products to complete tasks more easily and that people prefer to rely on the previously-learnt knowledge rather than learn new knowledge. The results of the study by Langdon et al. [8] showed that the absence of prior experience with a product interface led the users of all age groups to adopt the 'trial and error' method during the interaction with a product. The 'trial and error' method has been described as slow, repetitive and error prone; and it has been suggested that this method is generally used as a copying strategy when a user has not yet developed stored long-term automatic processes and chunked procedures in working memory. Accordingly, Langdon et al. [8] advise that designers should pay particular attention to facilitating learning in new products by "the use of previously well-learnt and transferable functional features; clearly identifying key visual features associated with function; and avoidance of product states and unrecognisable error states that are not accompanied by clear, visible feedback of the results of actions". Overall, it can be said that prior experience positively affects users' interaction with products as users can carry out tasks on a product interface in a more intuitive, faster and less error prone manner.

3 Review of Product Modelling Methods

An extensive literature review has been conducted in order to identify different modelling methods that are currently used by designers to enhance the product design processes. Subsequently, each method was evaluated in terms of its appropriateness for capturing three representations of specific information: (1) what people want to do when operating a product (goals); (2) what people actually do while operating a product (actions); and (3) what happens to the functional parts of the product during the operation (objects). In due course, five representations with the highest overall score were selected in order to determine which one of them is the most effective at modelling goals, actions and objects. The usefulness of these models was then analysed on the example of a washing machine and the results of this review are described in the following sections. The five selected modelling methods include:

- State Transition Diagram (STD);
- Statechart;
- Object-Oriented Analysis (OOA);
- Thimbleby-type State Diagram; and
- Conceptual Graph Analysis (CGA).

3.1 State Transition Diagram

The state transition diagram (STD) is generally used for modelling the states of a given product, the conditions that cause a transition from one state to another, and the actions that result from the change of state [27]. During the review, the STD was found to be very effective at modelling the behaviour of the functional parts of products (objects). In addition, this model can be very useful at modelling the sequences of actions that a user needs to take to accomplish their goal with a product. However, the STD appears not to be flexible enough to model users' goals and, therefore, this model may not be a good support for designers of products for heterogeneous users for whom the understanding of what drives users during the interaction with products is the key.

3.2 Statechart

The statechart was devised by Harel [5] and it describes the behaviour of a given product through the hierarchy of diagrams and states, though, it does not provide a detailed description of the actions that occur. Additionally, the statechart can model parallel transitions that are independent of each other, as well as a product that can be in two or more states concurrently [17]. The analysis of the statechart on the example of a washing machine showed that, similarly to the STD, the statechart is more suited for modelling the functional behaviour of products (objects) and the sequences of actions rather than users' goals. In particular, the structure of this model does not allow for coherent display of how users' goals affect the sequences of actions taken on the product interface.

3.3 Object-Oriented Analysis

The OOA method organises a product as a collection of discrete objects that incorporate data structure and behaviour, and events that trigger operations and change the state of objects [18]. The OOA model is organised around data and allows for data within one object to be used by other objects [17]. The review has shown that the OOA representation is the most suitable for capturing the functional parts of products and how they work. Furthermore, this model is organised around data rather than actions and, therefore, it does not provide good enough basis for modelling and matching the sequences of actions that a user needs to take to accomplish their goal with the functional parts of products (objects). In addition, the OOA method is very weak at modelling how users' goals influence the operation of product objects.

3.4 Thimbleby-Type State Diagram

In contrast with Yourdon [27] and Harel [5], Thimbleby [24] proposes a new use for state diagrams. In particular, he suggests, and our review also confirms, that a state diagram can be used not only for describing the functional behaviour of products, but it can also be used to model users' actions. In addition, Persad et al. [11], having conducted an analysis of a toaster using the Thimbleby-type state diagram, argue that this diagram is very useful at evaluating the user feedback on each state of the product. However, our analysis found that this model is not suitable for modelling the goals that the users have before taking any action on the product interface and, therefore, it would not provide designers with a lot of support during the creation of inclusive products.

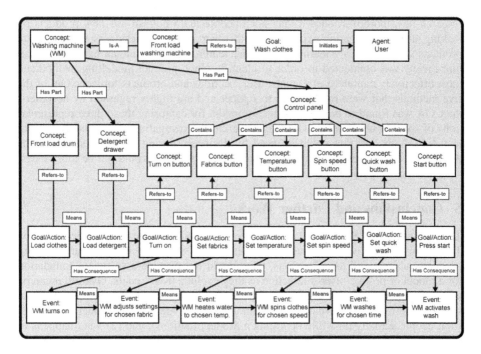

Fig. 2. A conceptual graph analysis (CGA) of a washing machine with a linear interface

3.5 Conceptual Graph Analysis

The CGA method is commonly used for developing functional models of products, as well as databases for expert systems and decision support systems [4]. Conceptual graphs contain information in the form of a concept or a statement that falls into one of five categories, including: state, event, style, goal or goal/action. The CGA model provides a well-organised framework for developing a detailed model of a product. It has also the capacity to show more relationships between different parts of a product and in a more structured manner than any of the other reviewed models. In comparison with the other four models, the CGA is the only representation discussed in this paper that captures three representations of specific information, specifically, users' goals, users' actions and products' objects. An example of a CGA model of a washing machine with a linear interface is shown in Figure 2.

4   Discussion

In this paper, we highlighted the cognitive processes that occur while users perform tasks on product interfaces and aid in the formulation of users' goals. We have also emphasised that in order to design more accessible, usable and intuitive products, designers need to have a better understanding of users' mental models as they play an essential part in establishing what people want to do when operating products. Our research has, moreover, shown that since people learn how to use new products by making use of their prior experience with other products; designers should create products with previously-learnt and familiar features. In addition, an extensive literature review was conducted in order to identify which product modelling method can most effectively capture users' goals, users' actions and products' objects. Out of the five methods that were reviewed in this paper and are highly regarded by designers, the CGA was found to be the most useful model for capturing these three representations of specific information. Ongoing research is investigating other models (similar to the CGA model) that could be used by designers during the early stages of the design process in order to determine what product features would be the most accessible and usable for users.

5   Conclusions and Further Work

The analysis of the STD, the statechart, the OOA and the state diagram described by Thimbleby [24] showed that, although these models are very effective at capturing products' objects and users' actions, they would not provide a sufficient foundation for a model of product-user interaction as they exclude users' goals. Overall, it can be said that a model of product-user interaction should describe three representations of specific information: (1) what people want to do when operating a product (goals); (2) what people actually do while operating a product (actions); and (3) what happens to the functional parts of the product during the operation (objects). Insofar, the only of the analysed representations that captures these three elements is the CGA. However, the CGA is not without its limitations because the actions and objects captured by this method might not be as detailed and well-structured as objects described by other four methods. Therefore, further research is necessary in order to identify appropriate methods for combining goal, action and object elements and developing a usable and inclusive model of product-user interaction.

References

1. Bichard, J.A., Coleman, R., Langdon, P.: Does My Stigma Look Big in This? Considering Acceptability and Desirability in the Inclusive Design of Technology Products. Universal Access in HCI 1, 622–631 (2007)
2. Cañas, J.J., Antolí, A., Quesada, J.F.: The Role of Working Memory on Measuring Mental Models of Physical Systems. Psicologica 22, 25–42 (2001)
3. Carroll, J.M., Thomas, J.C.: Metaphor and the Cognitive Representation of Computing Systems. IEEE Transactions on Systems, Man, and Cybernetics 12, 107–116 (1982)
4. Gordon, S.E., Schmierer, K.A., Gill, R.T.: Conceptual Graph Analysis: Knowledge Acquisition for Instructional System Design. Human Factors 35, 459–481 (1993)
5. Harel, D.: Statecharts: A Visual Formalism for Complex Systems. Science of Computer Programming 8, 231–274 (1987)
6. Krippendorff, K.: On the Essential Contexts of Artifacts or On the Proposition that Design is Making Sense (of Things). Design Issues 5, 9–39 (1989)
7. Kwahk, J., Han, S.H.: A Methodology for Evaluating the Usability of Audiovisual Consumer Electronic Products. Applied Ergonomics 33, 419–431 (2002)
8. Langdon, P.M., Lewis, T., Clarkson, P.J.: The Effects of Prior Experience on the Use of Consumer Products. Universal Access in the Information Society, Special Issue on Designing Accessible Technology (Ibid) (2007)

9. Miller, G.A.: The Magical Number Seven, Plus or Minus Two: Some Limits on Our Capacity for Processing Information. The Psychological Review 63, 81–97 (1956)
10. Monk, A.: Cyclic Interaction: A Unitary Approach to Intention, Action and the Environment. Cognition 68, 95–110 (1998)
11. Persad, U., Langdon, P., Clarkson, J.: Characterising User Capabilities to Support Inclusive Design Evaluation. Universal Access in the Information Society, Special Issue on Designing Accessible Technology (Ibid) (2007)
12. Rouse, W.B., Morris, N.M.: On Looking into the Black Box: Prospects and Limits in the Search for Mental Models. Psychological Bulletin 100, 349–363 (1986)
13. Norman, D.A.: Some Observations on Mental Models. In: Gentner, D., Stevens, A. (eds.) Mental Models, ch. 1. Lawrence Erlbaum Associates Publishers, London (1983)
14. Rutherford, A., Wilson, J.R.: Models of Mental Models: An Ergonomist-Psychologist Dialogue. In: Trauber, M.J., Ackermann, D. (eds.) Mental Models and Human-Computer Interaction. Elsevier Science Publishers B.V., North Holland (1991)
15. Blackler, A.: Intuitive Interaction with Complex Artefacts. PhD Thesis. School of Design, Queensland University of Technology (2006)
16. Braisby, N., Gellatly, A.: Cognitive Psychology. Oxford University Press, Oxford (2005)
17. Budgen, D.: Software Design. Pearson Addison Wesley, London (2003)
18. Coad, P., Yourdon, E.: Object-Oriented Analysis. Prentice Hall, Englewood Cliffs (1990)
19. Freudenthal, A.: The Design of Home Appliances for Young and Old Consumers. PhD Thesis. Delft University Press, The Netherlands (1999)
20. Humphreys, G.W., Bruce, V.: Visual Cognition: Computational, Experimental and Neuropsychological Perspectives. Lawrence Erlbaum Associates Ltd., Hove (1989)
21. Keates, S., Clarkson, J.: Countering Design Exclusion: An Introduction to Inclusive Design. Springer, London (2003)
22. Norman, D.A.: The Design of Everyday Things. Basic Books, London (2002)
23. Sloman, A.: The Computer Revolution in Philosophy: Philosophy, Science and Models of Mind. The Harvester Press (1978)
24. Thimbleby, H.: Press On: Principles of Interaction Programming. MIT Press, Cambridge (2007)
25. Wickens, C.D., Gordon, S.E., Liu, Y.: An Introduction to Human Factors Engineering. Addison-Wesley Educational Publishers Inc., New York (1998)
26. Winograd, T., Flores, F.: Understanding Computers and Cognition: A New Foundation for Design. ABLEX Publishing Company Co., Norwood (1985)
27. Yourdon, E.: Modern Structured Analysis. Prentice Hall, New York (1989)
28. Bellerby, F., Davis, G.: Defining the Limits of Inclusive Design. In: Proceedings of Include, pp. 1:00–1:17. Royal College of Art, London (2003)
29. Dray, S.M.: Structured Observation: Techniques for Gathering Information about Users in Their Own World. In: CHI, April 13-18, pp. 334–335 (1996)
30. Persad, U., Langdon, P., Clarkson, P.J., Brown, D.: Cognitive Scales and Mental Models for Inclusive Design. In: Proceedings of HCI International 2007, 12th International Conference, HCI International 2007, Beijing, China (2007)
31. British Standards Institute, British Standard 7000-6:2005: Design Management Systems: Managing Inclusive Design. Guide (2005),
    http://www.bsi-global.com/en/Shop/
    Publication-Detail/?pid=000000000030142267
32. Ricability: Easier Living: A Guide for Older and Disabled People Living in London (2001),
    http://www.ricability.org.uk/reports/pdfs/easierliving.pdf

Culture, Politeness and Directive Compliance

Christopher A. Miller, Peggy Wu, Vanessa Vakili, Tammy Ott, and Kip Smith

Smart Information Flow Technologies, 211 First St. N., Suite 300 Minneapolis MN 55401
{cmiller,pwu,vvakili,tott,ksmith}@sift.info

Abstract. We argue that traditional cultural factors models (from Hofstede, Nisbett, etc.) are too abstract to provide good predictions of important human performance behaviors such as directive compliance. Instead, we focus on culture-specific social interaction behaviors (i.e., "etiquette") as a bridge between abstract cultural factors and human performance. We describe a computational model of etiquette and politeness perception, called CECAEDA (Computational Effects of Cultural Attributes and Etiquette on Directive Adherence). CECAEDA consists of four parts: (1) a culturally universal model of politeness perceptions, their causes and effects, (2) a culturally universal cognitive model compliance decision making and behaviors, (3) a set of hypotheses about how politeness perceptions alter directive compliance, and (4) a set of hypotheses about how cultural factors (specifically, those proposed by Hofstede [1]) affect etiquette perceptions and, thus, directive compliance in culture-specific ways. Each component is discussed in detail, followed by a brief presentation of our research test bed and paradigm for evaluating CECAEDA.

Keywords: culture, politeness, etiquette, directive compliance.

1 Introduction

The need to examine cultural factors that affect human performance has perhaps never been greater. As business, government, charitable and military activities all become more international and diversified, as organizations themselves becomes more culturally diversified, and as training needs necessarily change, we need to know (and, ideally, to be able to develop predictive models of) what cultural factors have an impact on why one human performs differently than another.

Substantial research exists on identifying cultural patterns (e.g., [1,2]) and on how cultural factors affect cognitive processes [3], but none provides a direct link from these factors to human performance. There is little doubt that cultural factors do affect performance. For example, Nisbett has found that North Americans and South East Asians see different objects in the same picture due to what he calls field dependence [3], implying differences in pattern recognition, problem solving, and decision making skills among cultures. But it has proven difficult to trace the chain of causality from these differences to actual, valuable behavioral differences. This is particularly true of the highly concrete, contextually-dependent and individualized interactions that represent a huge proportion of work interactions: directives—where one offers an instruction, command, request, etc. to elicit a specific response.

C. Stephanidis (Ed.): Universal Access in HCI, Part I, HCII 2009, LNCS 5614, pp. 568–577, 2009.

We suggest that to develop models of the interaction of cultural factors and human performance, we need to find a "bridge"—a quantifiable, explicit, culture-specific and critically, modelable phenomenon that can be related to abstract cultural factors and to human performance. We claim human interaction "etiquette" is such a phenomenon.

2   Etiquette, Culture and Directive Compliance

The terms etiquette and politeness are likely to evoke notions of formal courtesies and which dinner fork to use. But *politeness* in anthropology, sociology and linguistics has to do with the processes by which we signal, interpret, maintain and alter power and familiarity relationships, interpretations of urgency, indebtedness, etc. We use *etiquette* in the sense of protocol—a usually unwritten social "code" by which we signal and interpret meanings. Emily Post's etiquette about place settings is just one of many "etiquettes" with which we are familiar—other more common ones include who gets to speak first in an interaction, what sorts of address are suitable to a stranger vs. an old friend, and what it means when a colleague stops greeting you.

Politeness is therefore a different type or level of "cultural factor" than the more abstract categories proposed by Nisbett, Hofstede, etc. Their factors represent deep-seated, abstract attributes. For example, Hofstede's [1] Power Distance Index (PDI) refers to the degree a society sees equality or inequality among its members as natural. This only very indirectly describes attitudes, much less responses, that a specific individual might exhibit. If we try to use such abstract attributes to predict individual behavior to a request, we might find correlations, but these are undoubtedly more powerfully (and more predictably) influenced by more immediate attributes of the interaction—such as the degree of deference included in the request, the specific relationships between the interactants, the perceived degree of imposition, etc.

In our work, we refer to this chain of influence as our **CECAEDA model**—for *Computable Effects of Cultural Attributes and Etiquette on Directive Adherence*. This chain refers to hypothesized links between deep-rooted cultural factors which influence the cognitive and affective patterns of members of a culture. These then impact perceptions of the attributes and relationships expressed by etiquette, which in turn impact decisions and subsequent actions in response to those directives.

A simple example may clarify: Hofstede's PDI factor is a description of a culture but individuals will detect and exhibit specific power relationships in specific contexts via the etiquette framework that is available in that culture. The way I determine that another individual does, in fact, have power over me, (which will likely affect how I choose to behave) is at least partly a function of the etiquette (verbal and non-verbal) the individual uses—and of my knowledge and interpretation of it.

In recent work funded by the U.S. Air Force, we have focused on behaviors associated with *directives*. Directives are statements about what one should or must do—a statement "directing" the hearer to perform in some way (e.g., commands, requests, instructions, advice). Cultural factors likely to have the most immediate impact on response to a directive are not (or not directly) abstract psychological attributes, but rather the specific, culturally-determined manifestation of the etiquette in the directive's delivery. This is not to say that abstract cultural factors are irrelevant—far from it. We suspect that cultural factors determine sensitivity to, weighting of, and even perhaps the range of etiquette markers available in a culture.

We will describe CECAEDA in more detail below, including specific hypotheses derived from it, and then describe experimental tests of some of these hypotheses. CECAEDA consists of four basic components discussed separately below:

1. A culturally universal model of the perception of etiquette and politeness.
2. A model of the process of decision making and directive compliance—that is, of the mechanism by which perception of contextual elements (including etiquette) affect an individual's willingness to comply.
3. Hypothesized relationships between etiquette perception and compliance decisions.
4. Hypothesized relationships about the effects of abstract culture-specific factors on the perception of etiquette (from step 1) and, therefore, a resulting hypothesized correlation between cultural factors and compliance behaviors (in steps 2 and 3).

3   Components of the CECAEDA Model

3.1   A Culturally-Universal Model of Social Interaction Etiquette

To understand etiquette effects on directive compliance, we need a model of etiquette itself and its role. Brown and Levinson [4] provide such a model. They collected a large database of instances of politeness in communication across three major cultural/linguistic groups (English, Tamil and Tzetzal) and, from this data, developed a qualitative model which proposed a culturally universal model of politeness in use.

Their explanation for politeness usage stems from the fact that humans have the potential to have their will, intentions, and sense of self-worth or -regard (that is, their "face" [5]) threatened. My simple act of speaking to you places a demand on your attention that threatens your ability to autonomously direct it wherever you want. This, then, is the reason for saying "please" in many requests. If I state my desire bluntly (e.g., "Give me the salt") I am ambiguous about whether I have the power or right to compel you to give it and you might take offense. "Please" (as for all politeness behaviors) is thus a *redressive strategy* which mitigates threat. Furthermore, the *expectation* that redress be used is an example of etiquette that enables interpretations.

Our interpretation of Brown and Levinson's qualitative model (see Figure 1) declares that an interaction between two individuals will be perceived as balanced or "nominally polite" if the face threat in it is balanced by the value of the polite redressive behaviors used. If more politeness is used than threat, the interaction will be seen as "over polite"; if less, then it will be seen as rude. Face threat itself is a function of the observer's perception of three additional parameters:

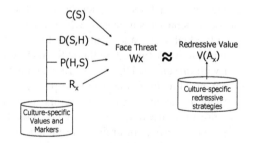

Fig. 1. Our interpretation of Brown and Levinson's politeness model

- P(H,S) is the *relative power* that the hearer (H) has over the speaker (S).
- D(S,H) is the *social distance* between S and H—roughly the inverse of familiarity.
- R is the *ranked imposition* of the raw act itself. Some acts and topics are simply more threatening than others.

With regard to polite, redressive strategies, Brown and Levinson identify some 40 types they observed across multiple cultures in their corpus. If I ask a stranger: "I'm sorry, sir, but I'm in real trouble, I'd very much appreciate it if you could possibly give me a quick ride to the airport" I've used several of the strategies:

- *Apology*—"I'm sorry…" Acknowledges the threat and shows contriteness
- *Give deference*—"… sir…" Explicitly builds up H's face by using an honorific.
- *Give Reasons*—"… but I'm in real trouble…" Accounts for the face threat as stemming from other sources than my explicit intentions
- *Incur Indebtedness*—"… I'd very much appreciate it…" Acknowledges debt
- *Be pessimistic*—"…if…possibly…" Leaves the compliance decision with H
- *Minimize imposition*—"…quick ride…" Implies magnitude of imposition is small.

Note that the general dynamics of this model are intended to be *culturally universal*: all cultures are believed to determine politeness in context based on whether their perception of the face threat is balanced by their perception of redress, to reckon face threat as a function of P, D and R, and to use redressive behaviors from the categories described above. That said, what counts as a face threat, what counts as P,D and R, and what counts as a specific instance of a redressive behavior, as well as the value of these parameters, all differ from culture to culture. This is so obvious as to be almost missable in language: I say "sir" in English vs. "saheb" in Pashto—two different sound patterns each of which is an instance of the general category "honorific" (and each of which may have a different redressive values in their respective cultures).

We have been developing a quantitative, computational implementation of Brown and Levinson's qualitative model. We have developed methods for representing and quantifying P,D and R and redressive value. Detailed descriptions of our representation and its applications may be found in [6-8]. We have now completed several partial validation exercises involving this model, and can claim that it shows promising accuracy at least for American cultural interpretations [9].

There are several core benefits of a computational representation of politeness perceptions. We have now demonstrated the ability for the same core algorithm to both recognize politeness behaviors directed at it in a game-like setting, and to select politeness behaviors to be used in generating utterances in response [7]. Representing verbal versus nonverbal politeness behaviors is no challenge (if they can first be recognized); both are simply instances of redressive behaviors and can be scored and combined similarly. We have demonstrated that our core algorithm can be populated with culture-specific knowledge bases containing values for P, SD and R scores as well as a culture-specific lexicon of politeness behaviors and their values. Such "cultural modules", once built (an important caveat, of course), enable us to change the cultural sensitivities of a simulated character from, say, an Iraqi imam to an American private with the "flick" of a software switch. While the development of such knowledge bases is still a non-trivial effort, we are exploring ways our model streamlines knowledge capture and representation.

3.2 A Cognitive Model of Directive Compliance

While the above model explains how a given directive will be perceived in a cultural context, it says nothing about actions in response to it. To understand etiquette variations on directive compliance we need a model of the decision and action process. One such model can

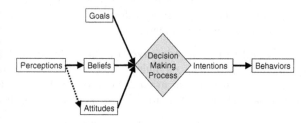

Fig. 2. Conceptual behavior chain (after [10])

be adapted from the work of Lee and See [10]. Figure 2 shows our modification of this model to define a chain of cognitive and affective responses resulting in overt behaviors. Definitions of the steps are provided below.

- *Perceptions* are direct observations of the world. Interpretations come later and are more influenced by culture (though some attention focusing is culture-specific [3]).
- *Beliefs* are interpretations based on perceptions and incorporating additional knowledge. The interpretation of a perceived event as a directive, and the force, urgency, imposition, etc. associated with it, are likely to be affected by the presence and variety of cultural and linguistic knowledge H possesses.
- *Attitudes* are "an affective evaluation of beliefs that guides people to adopt a particular intention." ([10], p. 53). Attitudes exist prior to belief construction and color the intentions that result. Many of Hofstede's factors can be viewed as attitudes—e.g., the relative weight a culture assigns to power differences will affect how a member views directives from, say, a general vs. a private.
- *Goals* are the objectives an individual has prior to perceiving a directive. Different cultures may have different general goals, or different weightings of goals. The tradeoff between fitting in as an acceptable group member vs. being self-determined (cf., [3]) seems to be a variance in the valuing of alternate goals.
- *Intentions* to perform a behavior are formed by a decision making process represented by the diamond in Figure 2. Various decision making processes (rational choice, recognition-primed decision making, stimulus-response, etc.) may all be involved in various contexts. Intentions are not always realized in overt behavior.
- *Behaviors* are overt, observable, volitional and conscious actions (including inaction). Complying or not complying with a directive are behaviors.

Figure 2 represents the process of perceiving a directive, interpreting it, deciding whether and how to comply, and then executing that compliance. It is intended as a single pass through what is, normally, an ongoing and iterative process. This model is necessarily highly simplified. For example, feedback loops are not shown, though clearly some feedback exists and is highly relevant: intention and behavior will undoubtedly affect subsequent events (and, therefore, subsequent beliefs and attitudes). We are using this model to develop a research program to test the directive compliance effects of etiquette and cultural factors by identifying variables which can be manipulated or selected for or observed or inferred in accordance with each step.

3.3 Hypothesized Effects of Etiquette on Directive Compliance

Etiquette may affect the directive compliance process at many points. The etiquette with which a directive is delivered must be perceived and interpreted via existing beliefs, though it may well alter perceptions and beliefs pertinent to the decision itself. For example, if I speak loudly and quickly, and if you perceive those cues and believe them to signal urgency, you may be inclined to respond to my request more quickly— and/or you may decide adjust your attitude toward me and my future directives.

When an observer hears politeness near what was expected, there is no need to re-examine assumptions. When substantially more or less redress is used, however, then re-examination is warranted. For example, if you use less politeness in asking me to prepare a report than I expect given my beliefs about our relationship and the imposition of the report, I may assume that you think you have (or want to claim) more power over me, that you think we are (or would like us to be) more friendly, that you don't view this as as large an imposition as I did, or simply that you are less sensitive to my feelings than I thought. Which of these I conclude may well depend on your specific wording. What I do about it will depend on my interpretation, plus my goals and available behaviors: do I accord you more power and obey (perhaps more quickly) or resist your power by delaying or answering rudely?

We speculate that redressive utterances with very large deviations from expectations will have detrimental effects on performance. When such behavior provokes an "unbelievable" response, the resulting cognitive dissonance may increase workload and interrupt ongoing tasks, thus harming all other performance metrics. However, such occurrences are generally rare, whereas smaller deviations occur frequently and provoke reinterpretations as outlined

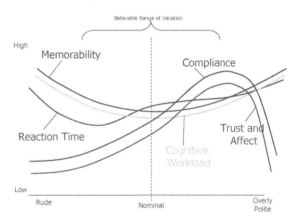

Fig. 3. Hypothesized relationship between Etiquette and Performance Dimensions

above. Figure 3 describes our hypotheses about how small deviations in politeness will affect performance dimensions. Note that we are referring to *perceived* politeness. We are attempting (as Brown and Levinson) to abstract away from specific culture and instead to describe universal phenomena. While the contextual conditions and polite redress might be interpreted very differently by different cultures, our hypothesis is that *whatever* produces a perception of believable politeness in context for a given observer will have the behavioral effects illustrated toward the right hand side of Figure 3, while whatever is perceived as rude will push an observer toward the left hand side. The hypothesized effects are:

- Behavior perceived as polite will tend to increase compliance whereas slightly rude behavior will tend to decrease it. The presumed increase in compliance is driven by a likely increase in trust and positive affect that comes with expected, pleasing and/or adequately polite interactions. Relevant results for this claim are summarized by [10] and some specific experimental data are provided in [11] with regards to trust and affect, and by [12] with regards to pleasure and affect and [13] with regards to the relationship between flattery and affect. Thus, the curves for trust and affect are unified in Figure 3 and both parallel the curve for compliance.

- For subjective (and, perhaps, objective) cognitive workload, either slightly rude or slightly overly polite behavior will cause cognitive dissonance and, therefore, additional workload with the H trying to decipher any possible "hidden messages".

- Perceived "rudeness" may result in shorter reaction times because it suggests urgency (precisely because it offers less redress for Imposition than expected). This may be highly sensitive, though: as more rudeness is used, net reaction times increase as H spends more time considering why the Speaker is behaving so rudely.

- "Memorability" refers to memory for the interaction and social context in which it occurs. Whenever unexpected levels of redress are used, H attempts to compensate by reevaluating initial assumptions. This additional attention and processing of situation information may produce better awareness of and memory for it.

Figure 3 does convey strict mathematical relationships between performance dimensions--e.g., cognitive workload and compliance do not have the same "performance value" at nominal politeness. Curves illustrate general relationships only.

3.4 Hypothesized Effects of Cultural Factors on Directive Compliance

As outlined above, we believe the politeness perceived in a directive will have detectable affects on compliance behaviors. What a specific individual perceives as rude or polite, however, will certainly be influenced by culture. Hence, there will be *cultural effects on etiquette perception* which will, in turn, produce *etiquette effects on directive performance*. This relationship is depicted in Figure 4. Next, we offer hypotheses about how some of Hofstede's cultural factors might affect perception of etiquette dimensions in Brown and Levinson's model and therefore, ultimately, performance.

Hypothesis. Power Distance Index (PDI) Enhances Power (P(H,S)) Effects

Factor Description: PDI refers to the degree of tolerance that a society has for large differences in power between individuals. High PDI cultures tend to tolerate large power differences, while low PDI cultures will strive to minimize or reduce them.

Hypotheses— This implies an enhancing effect on the power in our etiquette model. A high PDI culture will regard P as "mattering more" toward face threat. Powerful Hs from a high PDI culture will expect more deference from low powered Ss, but powerful Ss will feel even less need to offer polite redress. We hypothesize that PDI and weighting for P will be correlated. If P has greater weight in a high PDI culture, then a given amount of redress will not "go as far" in offsetting the P factor in face threat. This perceived rudeness will push toward the "rude" end of the behaviors in Figure 3. That is, individuals from high PDI cultures will generally exhibit reduced

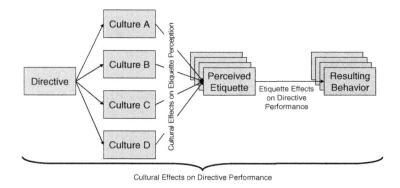

Fig. 4. Relationship of cultural factors, etiquette perception and performance

compliance, trust and affect, and quicker reaction time, but increased workload and memorability for a given value of redressive behavior compared to a low PDI culture. The relationship should be similar to that depicted in Figure 5.

Hypothesis. Individualism (IDV) Diminishes Social Distance (D) Effects

Factor Description--High IDV cultures are where individualism is more highly prized and loose relationships are the norm, whereas low IDV cultures place more weight on familial and social relations ("collectivism").

Hypotheses-- IDV seems to have a diminishing effect on Brown and Levinson's Social Distance term D in high IDV cultures; D "matters less" in the calculation of face threat. Conversely, in low IDV societies, there may be increased motivation to attend to D. Reducing the importance of D in an interaction means a net reduction in the resulting face threat. If the threat is perceived to be lower, then less redress will be needed to offset it. This relationship is identical to that depicted in Figure 5 with Social Distance (D) substituted for Power on the x-axis and IDV substituted for PDI on the various culture lines. This, in turn, means that directives will seem less rude when coming from a high D (that is, unfamiliar) individual in a high IDV culture than in a low IDV one—and this reduction in perceived rudeness will allow a given utterance to be perceived as more polite. Thus, individuals from high IDV cultures will generally exhibit increased compliance, trust and affect, and slower reaction time, but decreased workload and memorability for an utterance with a given value of redress.

Masculinity (MAS). Affects Power (P(H,S)) given Speaker Gender

Factor Description—High Masculinity/Femininity cultures are those where high value is placed on sex differentiation in roles and relationships and, generally, this translates to more power accorded to males than females. Low MAS cultures are those in which gender makes comparatively little difference in authority or power.

Hypotheses—We hypothesize that the higher the MAS of an H, the more power will be afforded to a male S by default, and the less to a female S. Individuals from low MAS cultures will show less differentiation based on gender. Since Face Threat is dependent on the P of H over S, and since male Ss will generally be perceived as higher P in high MAS cultures, being given a directive by a female will enhance the P(H,S) factor and, thus, increase the face threat. If the same redress is used, a directive will seem more rude coming from a female than from a male by those from high MAS cultures. Thus, a directive given by a male will

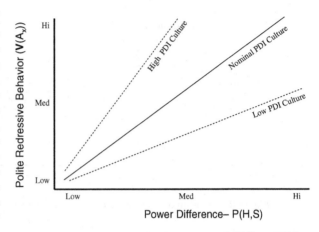

Fig. 5. Hypothesized relationship between P(H,S) and PDI

evoke increased compliance, trust and affect, and slower reaction time, but will decrease workload and memorability relative to the same directive from a female for those in high MAS cultures.

4 Summary and Future Work

We have implemented a test bed (Figure 6) for conducting research to evaluate the hypotheses and models described above. Participant play the role of a dispatcher in a park service fire fighting scenario who receives requests for information from field operators via a chat channel and responds with that information. We can manipulate the level of polite redress in requests, as well as "who" they come from. Via an initial scenario description and the use of naming conventions and iconography for the various directive givers, we can control their power levels, social distance and gender. For example, for an experiment examining power levels, we have developed a scenario in which directive givers come from various levels within the park service hierarchy. This hierarchy is reinforced by icons containing a number of stars indicating a person's level. Similarly, we have manipulated icons and scenario details to convey social distance (via membership in the same or different organization as the participant) and gender of directive givers in other experiments.

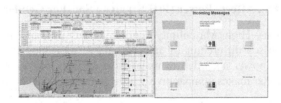

Fig. 5. Vehicle monitoring and chat interface screens from our test bed

While not an optimal test of members of different cultures, participants have been selected primarily from a U.S. university community for ease of access. All speak English, and the test was conducted in English, but we emphasized the selection of international students with relatively short time in the U.S. Pre-test questionnaires assessed participants' scores on PDI, IDV and MAS dimensions via standard [14]. These scores are being used in correlation analyses with dependent variables (performance metrics and subjective ratings) collected from interaction with the test bed itself. These data are not yet fully analyzed and ready for public release.

While this work will only begin to examine the complex relationships between the etiquette, human performance and the cultural factors which color both, we have provided a rich conceptual framework for structuring such work. Our results will represent a step forward toward developing better understanding and, ultimately, predictive models of such relationships and, furthermore, will do so via directly observable aspects of great relevance to work domains.

Acknowledgements. This work was supported by a SBIR grant (Contract # FA8650-06-C-6635) from the Air Force Research Laboratory. We thank Ms. Kellie Plummer and Dr. Rik Warren, our Technical Contract Monitors. We also acknowledge Dr. Curtis Hammond, Ms. Marie Kirsch, Dr. Michael Wade, and Mr. Harry Funk for their contributions.

References

1. Hofstede, G.: Culture's Consequences, 2nd edn. Sage, London (2001)
2. Klein, H.: Cognition in Natural Settings: The Cultural Lens model. In: Kaplan, M. (ed.) Cultural Ergonomics, Advances in Human Performance and Cognitive Engineering Research, vol. 4, pp. 249–280. Elsevier JAI, Boston (2004)
3. Nisbett, R.: The Geography of Thought. Free Press, New York (2003)
4. Brown, P., Levinson, S.: Politeness. Cambridge University Press, Cambridge (1987)
5. Goffman, E.: Interactional Ritual. Aldine, Chicago (1967)
6. Miller, C., Chapman, M., Wu, P., Johnson, L.: The Etiquette Quotient. In: Proc. 14th BRIMS Conference, Paper 35. SISO, Orlando (2005)
7. Miller, C., Wu, P., Funk, H., Wilson, P.: Computational Approach to Etiquette and Politeness. In: Proc. 15th BRIMS Conference, Paper 51. SISO, Orlando (2006)
8. Miller, C., Wu, P., Funk, H., Johnson, L., Viljalmsson, H.: An Etiquette Engine for Cultural Interaction Training. In: Proc. 16th BRIMS Conference, Paper 45. SISO, Orlando (2007)
9. Miller, C., Wu, P., Funk, H.: A Computational Approach to Etiquette and Politeness: Validation Experiments. IEEE Intelligent Systems 23(4), 28–35 (2008)
10. Lee, J., See, K.: Trust in Computer Technology. Human Factors 46(1), 50–80 (2004)
11. Parasuraman, R., Miller, C.: Trust and Etiquette in High-Criticality Automated Systems. Communications of the ACM 47(4), 51–55 (2004)
12. Norman, D.A.: Emotional design. Basic Books, New York (2004)
13. Cialdini, R.: Influence: Science and Practice. Harper-Collins, New York (1993)
14. Dorfman, P., Howell, J.: Dimensions of National Culture and Effective Leadership Patterns. Advances in International Comparative Management 3, 127–150 (1988)

A Harmonised Methodology towards Measuring Accessibility

Alexandros Mourouzis[1], Grammati-Eirini Kastori[2], Kostantinos Votis[2], Evangelos Bekiaris[1], and Dimitrios Tzovaras[2]

[1] Centre for Research and Technology Hellas (CERTH)
Hellenic Institute of Transport
Thermi, Thessaloniki, GR-57001, Greece
[2] Centre for Research and Technology Hellas (CERTH)
Informatics & Telematics Institute
Thermi, Thessaloniki, GR-57001, Greece
{mourouzi,abek}@certh.gr, {gkastori,kvotis,tzovaras}@iti.gr

Abstract. This paper introduces the *harmonized accessibility methodology (HAM)* that has been defined and deployed in the context of the ACCESSIBLE project. HAM is aimed to harmonize existing collections of related design knowledge, such as heuristics, guidelines, standards, etc., and thereby provide the grounds for defining ontology-based rules and, and thereby implementing, within ACCESSIBLE and beyond, automated accessibility assessment of ICT designs and developments. Ultimately, ordinary developers will be enabled to conduct rapid, yet specialized, accessibility assessments focused on any relevant disability types, assistive technologies, platforms, and contextual conditions.

Keywords: Accessibility, Disability, Evaluation, Assessment tools.

1 Introduction

Accessibility and ease of use for the elderly and the disabled has attracted a lot of attention during the last few years. This is strongly supported by the fact that an increasing number of governments are legislating towards promoting and enforcing equality of opportunity and of access for everyone within the economy and society (*Inclusion*), including in terms of access to ICT and the evolving Information Society (*eAccessibility*). Soon after the appearance and early developments of assistive technology, such as screen readers, special interaction devices, etc., researchers and practitioners realised that access to a computer-based system is often denied to large numbers of potential users as a result of the system's design. In the old days, it was widely believed that the interaction ability of an individual is simply subject to his/her functional characteristics. Yet, we now understand that it is the design of system in combination with the functional characteristics of the user that renders the person able or unable to interact with it.

However, the development of software requires specialised expertise and a strong effort from developers. With the additional encumbrance of taking into account different kinds of accessibility requirements, guidelines and best practices, and different

C. Stephanidis (Ed.): Universal Access in HCI, Part I, HCII 2009, LNCS 5614, pp. 578–587, 2009.

implementation technologies (which by themselves might pose severe problems of delivering accessible applications), developers are faced with a daunting task. To this end, numerous sets of guidelines to help developers produce systems that are accessible and usable by elderly and disabled people have been recently proposed and put in practice. These range from very general guidelines to the very specific guidelines for Web user agents, authoring tools, and content developers. However, it is questionable whether providing guidelines is an effective method for ensuring usable and accessible designs, since their usage alone requires specialised skills and since the provided guidance might be differently interpreted among developers and designers. Moreover, designers and developers are often required to select among a number of similar guidelines sets without clear understanding of which set is more suitable for their specific task at hand. Ultimately, the highly specialised skills required for developing accessible software sets aside most developers. To mitigate such problems, developers should be guided in their development process about accessibility concerns within ICT development. Thus, developers need a conceptual framework in which to situate disability-related guidelines, which they often do not have due to lack of experience with disabled population and their technologies.

2 The ACCESSIBLE Project: Objectives and Rationale

Under the light of the above, and in response to the invitation to submit a proposal for 7th EU Framework Programme for Research and Technological Development (FP7), the ACCESSIBLE STREP Project[1] "Accessibility Assessment Simulation Environment for New Applications Design and Development" aims to define an overall European Assessment Simulation Environment making extensive use of the latest available IT technologies and concepts. This will constitute the base for a future generalised European Assessment Environment that will allow producers of ICT to assess the effectiveness of the various ICT tools, understand their caveats, and where to enhance their design to ensure full accessibility. The outcome will reflect a quality mark for users of assistive ICT, who will be assured that the acquired ICT will fully meet their needs. More specifically, the ACCESSIBLE project will implement specific methodologies and tools for ensuring accessibility for designers and software developers. To contribute for better accessibility for all citizens, to increase the use of standards, and to develop an assessment simulation environment (including a suite of accessibility analysing tools for Web services and applications, JavaFX Script applications as well as developer-aid tools) to access efficiently, easily and rapidly the accessibility and viability of software applications for all end user groups (with disabilities or not). Figure 1 depicts the rationale of ACCESSIBLE.

This paper presents the methodological approach (the ACCESSIBLE *harmonized accessibility methodology* - HAM) that has been determined for the structured assessment of software developments and the definition of accessibility assessment metrics for people with disability. The framework aims to formalize conceptual information about: (a) the characteristics of users with disabilities, assisted devices,

---

[1] Official Project website: http://www.accessible-eu.org/

applications, and other aspects that should be taken into account when describing an audience with disability; (b) accessibility standards and associated checkpoints and guidelines; and (c) semantic verification rules to help describing requirements and constraints of users, and associating them to accessibility checkpoints.

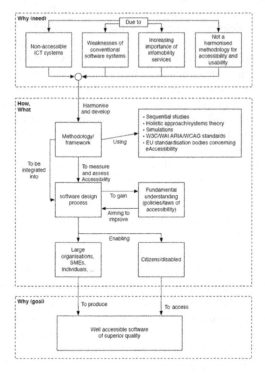

Fig. 1. Overview of the ACCESSIBLE project's rational and objectives

One of the many challenges of ACCESSIBLE is the integration of combinations of many possible disabilities, rather than on an individual basis. How do we design or assess for a person with both a hearing and sight loss, or a blind person with only one hand? This is particularly important as with ageing, everyone is likely to acquire multiple weaknesses, and although each one might be relatively minor their combined effects are often major. The proposed HAM is aimed to harmonize existing collections of related knowledge, such as heuristics, guidelines, standards, etc. and provide thereby the grounds for describing ontology-based rules and implementing, within ACCESSIBLE, automated assessment of ICT designs and developments (see [1]). Ultimately, designers, programmers, evaluators, etc. will be enabled to conduct specialized accessibility assessments focused on specific disability types, assistive technologies, platforms, and / or contextual conditions. Section 3 below serves as an introduction to the rationale of the HAM methodology described in the sections after.

3 Design and Accessibility Engineering: In Retrospect

Both practitioners and researchers have a strong interest in understanding why people may resist using computers, in order to develop better methods for designing technology, evaluating systems and predicting how users will respond to new technology. Previous research has identified a number of reasons why 'customers' use, or do not use, a computer-based system (see [4]). Utility and usability, for instance, have long been considered by the scientific community and practitioners as salient system adoption factors. The term usability (as ease of use), for example, was first introduced, and its importance recognised, long time before the appearance of computer systems and digital technologies. Back in 1842, De Quincey argued that "it is not the utility, but the usability of a thing which is in question". Nevertheless, it is nowadays commonly admitted that optimising utility and usability alone, although certainly a high priority, does not necessarily mean that take-up rates of a system will reach their full potential. Admittedly, the design and development of contemporary ICT applications and services that meet the needs and requirements of as many diverse users as possible is a difficult and demanding task. Computers, further enhanced by the Internet, serve nowadays as an unprecedented resource for knowledge, communication, and data and services acquisition, and play a key role in an increasing number of aspects of everyday life, including commerce, information, education and training, job searching and remote collaboration, entertainment, social participation, and interaction with public administrations. Information systems, thanks to their potential universality and the evolving usefulness (if not necessity) of the content, hold an unprecedented potential of reaching an enormous number of individuals; a population of potential users significantly characterised by diverse interaction skills, abilities, preferences, and access equipment (personal computers, mobile phones and other small display devices, kiosks, assistive technology, etc.).

Yet, the vast majority of developers today, by "tradition" (if not as a compromise), insist on designing their artefacts for the typical or so-called "average" users, trusting this as the best solution to cater the needs of the broadest possible population. These are most probably the leftovers of last century's anthropometry and the important role it played in industrial design, clothing design, ergonomics, and architecture, where statistical data about the distribution of body dimensions in the population were used to optimize products. Unfortunately, this approach when ported into the design of ICT, it eliminates our chances offered by the new medium (digital) to provide more flexible optimisations. In fact, this approach, typically employed in user interface design for quite some years, leads into excluding numerous "outliers", such as non-expert IT users, the very young or the elderly, people with disability, etc. [2]. As computers started to penetrate all aspects of our everyday lives, and becoming a critical asset for social inclusion, developers are eventually pushed by social or market needs towards broadening their user base, are often required to further "improve" their artefacts so that these adhere to generalised (i.e., average - again) usability and accessibility principles.

Over the years, accessibility has been addressed through various collaborative efforts. These fall into three main categories, which are distinctively characterised by their underlying focus and normative perspectives [1]:

- The first, which is also referred as reactive approach (or retrofit approach), aims to adapt products so as to build the required accessibility features. The qualification of this approach as reactive results precisely from the a posteriori adaptations that are delivered.
- The second and more recent approach aims to proactively account for accessibility by taking appropriate actions during the early phases of a product's life cycle. Proactively accounting for accessibility implies Design for All.
- Finally, the third perspective is that accessibility can be addressed by means of policy measures, such as legislation and standardisation.

As a result, there are now several on-going efforts to promote accessibility in national and international standardisation bodies and industrial consortia (e.g., the World Wide Web Consortium - W3C). The majority of these efforts aim to formulate accessibility guidelines, either general (e.g., HFES/ ANSI Draft, Section 5), platform specific (e.g., for Graphical User Interfaces or the Web), or domain-specific guidelines (e.g., for text editing, graphic manipulation). Such guidelines are typically documented on paper, and reflect previous experience gained and best practice available for designing accessible interactive software (also including content). The systematic collection, consolidation and interpretation of these guidelines is currently pursued in the context of international collaborative initiatives (e.g., W3C-WAI Initiative[2], ISO TC 159 / SC 4 / WG 5), as well as R&D projects, and international scientific fora. In this context, it is worth pointing out the efforts carried out in the area of Web accessibility guidelines by the W3C-WAI Initiative and by the US government in Section 508.

Clearly, there is now a vast amount of knowledge now available in the international literature concerning inclusive user interface design. Knowledge that is incarnated in guideline sets, standards, corporate guides, etc. Knowledge that is generic or specific, for example for the elderly, or for web or mobile interfaces, etc. As a result, developers are finding it difficult to locate and deploy effectively such knowledge in their development process. For instance, a web developer with no prior experience in web accessibility engineering would find it extremely difficult to identify the differences between the WCAG 1.0 and the Section 508 guidelines, would be uncertain about the actual types of users affected by each particular guideline, and would be confused, the least to say, by most of the checkpoints entailed. What happens if the developer would like to provide two alternative designs for the same task in order to cope with conflicting needs of two user types (e.g., see [3])? Not to mention that contemporary users increasingly desire and expect the delivery of interfaces that are highly tailored to their own needs, and hardly compromise on rigid designs for some imaginary "average" users. In such cases, how can an inexperienced developer identify which guidelines are most appropriate for each one of the alternative design? All these questions make clear the need for the envisioned methodology for harmonising design knowledge and rendering it easy to understand and apply for modern ICT designers and developers.

---

[2] World Wide Web Consortium - Web Accessibility Initiative (http://www.w3c.org/WAI/)

4 ICF: A Starting Point towards Harmonisation

As mentioned above, the main objective of this work is to provide a methodology for harmonising existing design knowledge and structuring it into a way (following an ontological approach) that will allow its automated exploitation. But, where can we start from to achieve this? Design knowledge is in numerous forms and often consolidated / generalized, thus difficult to directly relate items to specific disability types, assistive technology, or other contextual parameters. For instance, the generic W3C instruction "Ensure user control of time-sensitive content changes" cannot easily related to specific user types.

To this end, we decided to place the International Classification of Functioning, Disability and Health (ICF) approach at the core of our methodology. ICF is WHO's framework for health and disability[3]. It is the conceptual basis for the definition, measurement and policy formulations for health and disability. The list of domains in ICF becomes a classification when qualifiers are used. Qualifiers record the presence and severity of a problem in functioning at the body, person and societal levels. For the classifications of body function and structure, the primary qualifier indicates the presence of an impairment and, on a five point scale, the degree of the impairment of function or structure (no impairment, mild, moderate, severe and complete). In other words, ICF classifies *body functions* (see Table 1), as the physiological functions of body systems (including psychological functions) and thereupon, *impairments*, as problems in body function as a significant deviation or loss.

What is interesting about the ICF classification for our work in ACCESSIBLE is that the ICF *body structures* (BS) are not overlapping and are directly related to impairments and, thus can be directly linked to (a) disability / user types, (b) human-computer interaction limitations, (c) specialized design guidance (guidelines, standards, etc.), assistive technologies, etc. This is explained in section 5 below.

Table 1. Excerpt of the ICF List of Body Functions (some examples)

❑ *MENTAL FUNCTIONS*
❑   *Consciousness*
❑   *Intellectual (incl. Retardation, dementia)*
❑   *Attention*
❑   *Perceptual functions*
❑   *...*
❑ *SENSORY FUNCTIONS AND PAIN*
❑   *Seeing*
❑   *Hearing*
❑ *Touch function*
❑ *VOICE AND SPEECH FUNCTIONS*
❑ *NEUROMUSCULOSKELETAL AND MOVEMENT RELATED FUNCTIONS*
❑ *...*

---

[3] International Classification of Functioning, Disability and Health (ICF), ISBN 92 4 154542 9 – see http://www.who.int/en/

5 The ACCESSIBLE Harmonised Methodology

As mentioned above, ICF provides a concrete classification of impairments of the body structures, which ensures no overlaps. In this way, experts in ACCESSIBLE can work on linking user types (e.g., disability types) to certain ICF body structures and their related impairments (e.g., see Figure 2).

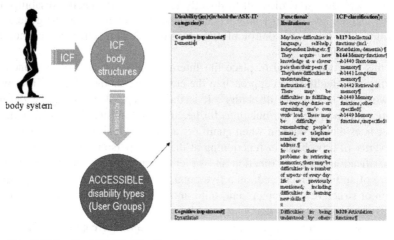

Fig. 2. Using the ICF classification as a base for harmonizing multiple user types

Then, experts in ACCESSIBLE have worked on deriving a classification of "interaction limitations" based on ICF. These are, in essence, a subset of the ICF functional limitations; we simply disregard body structures and functions that are not related to human-computer interaction, so that we can, for example, harmonise (i.e., link) assistive technologies indirectly to specific body structures (see Figure 3).

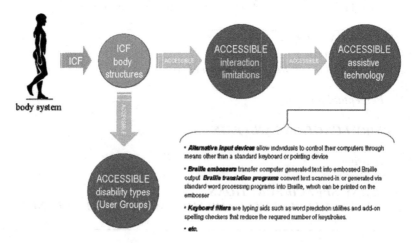

Fig. 3. Towards translating ICF body structures into interactions limitations and there upon relating individual assistive technologies to specific body structures and / or to disability types

In addition, the "translation" of the ICF body structure impairments into interaction limitations further facilities the linking of existing guidelines and heuristics from the literature to specific body structures and thereby to user types (see Figure 4). Although, it is often somehow hard to understand what type of user benefit the most from a given guideline (because it hard for inexperienced developers to understand a disability or it's the effects) it is much easier to correlate a guideline to an explicitly described interaction limitation. Such as the guideline for using specific colors ranges can be easily related to an interaction limitation "cannot see yellow, red or green' on a screen but to the user type with a certain color deficiency such as protanopia.

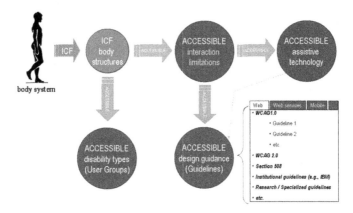

Fig. 4. Towards harmonizing design guidance with assistive technology and user types

At last, but not least, the above workplan, allows us to implement assessment rules that are derived from one ore more guidelines, and use the above classification (organised into an ontology) in order not to loose track of which user types do benefit and which assistive technologies are affected (see figure 5). Ultimately, in this way, a developer will be in the position to initiate an assessment by defining (alone) any one of the following: User Group(s), Guidelines collection(s), Assistive technology(ies), Assessment rule(s), or any other classification that can be integrated into this schema.

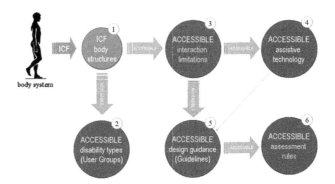

Fig. 4. Overview of the ACCESSIBLE harmonised methodology for measuring accessibility

Table 2 below shows an example (excerpt) of the relations established in the AC-CESSIBLE ontology as part of the proposed harmonised methodology for measuring accessibility. The selection of the ICF categories was relevant to those that were directly linked to disabilities that will be addressed in ACCESSIBLE. Topics such as sleep functions, temperament and personality functions were considered as out of scope of the project.

Table 2. Excerpt of the ACCESSIBLE harmonised methodology for measuring accessibility

Disability(ies)	Interaction limitations	ICF classification	Checkpoints W3C/WCAG 1.0	Checkpoints W3C/WCAG 2.0	Section 508
Vision impairments Blindness	A total lack of vision represents the extreme end of the scale of a condition that we call blindness; Difficulties in reading, identifying symbols, identifying people, identifying graphics or reading signage; Difficulties in crossing streets, in seeing approaching traffic, in communicating with large groups of people difficulties in walking around, etc. It is difficult to perceive facial features and expressions, difficulties to recognise the edge of the pavement and the stairs, it may also cause difficulties in reading;	b156 Perceptual functions b1561 Visual perception b210 Seeing functions	1, 2, 3.3, 5.1, 5.3, 5.5, 6.1, 9.4, 12.1, 12.2, 14.2	1.1, 1.2, 1.3, 1.4 2.4, 3.1	1194.22 (a), (c) (d), (e), (i)

6   Current Status and Future Steps

At this stage most common user types / disability types (see #2 in Fig. 4) and the "ACCESSIBLE interaction limitations" (see #3) have been collected and inserted in the ACCESSIBLE ontology. A number of "assistive technology" (see #4) products have also been recorded along with their correlation to the "ACCESSIBLE interaction limitations". Regarding "design guidance" (see #5), most of the work has been done for WCAG 1.0, WCAG 2.0 and Section 508 guidelines, yet the processing of independent guidelines collections (including for platforms other than the Web) is still undergoing. Thereupon, a number of "assessment rules" (see #6) have been implemented and used in testing (see [1]) verifying the whole concept of the proposed harmonized approach. Within the following periods, our consortium focuses on making widely available the ACCESSIBLE taxonomy seeking feedback from external expert groups, for instance regarding the proposed correlation of interaction limitations to specific guidelines and assistive devices, while test are conducted in parallel with the ongoing development of the assessment rules and the assessment simulation modules of ACCESSIBLE.

7   Conclusions

Facing the background presented earlier, a holistic approach to accessibility is still missing. The work presented here goes beyond state of the art (see section 3) and provides the grounds for developing the ACCESSIBLE assessment simulation system for developers and designers; a type of adaptive environment that will enable them, on one side, to design accessible software applications and, on the other side, to understand about their problems, and analyse and test its accessibility. The ACCESSIBLE project integrates both new ICT driven concepts and disabled user oriented approaches with methodologies and tools regarding accessibility. Within this context, and by exploiting HAM, the ACCESSIBLE project aims at developing a new scalable, interoperable and integrated assessment simulation system as an accessible-driven solution with a user-centred approach. Partly as a consequence of the problems of relying only on guidelines to drive design for disabled people, and partly due to the need to develop practical methodologies that instantiate the universal design philosophy, ACCESSIBLE allows designers / developers to make an initial assessment of how usable a design might be for people with particular disabilities before conducting end user evaluations. By promoting accessibility and usability, the ACCESSIBLE project can act as a paradigm shifter. First, in the way it provides developers and designers a framework for gaining insight into the accessible software development process - the right disability and accessibility information, standard, tool or methodology. Instead of a simple developer and designer-aid framework, the designers/developers will have a user-centred interface to get access to the different piece of methodological approaches they need. At last but not least, it provides a "harmonised methodology" between different standard developing organisations, end user groups, expert groups, decision makers and policy makers.

References

1. Votis, K., Lopes, R., Tzovaras, D., Carrico, L., Likothanassis, S.: A Semantic Accessibility Assessment Environment for Design and Development for the Web. In: Stephanidis, C. (ed.) Proc. of 13th International Conference on Human-Computer Interaction (HCI International 2009), San Diego, USA, July 19-24. Springer, Berlin (2009)
2. Stephanidis, C., Salvendy, G., Akoumianakis, D., Bevan, N., Brewer, J., Emiliani, P.L., Galetsas, A., Haataja, S., Iakovidis, I., Jacko, J., Jenkins, P., Karshmer, A., Korn, P., Marcus, A., Murphy, H., Stary, C., Vanderheiden, G., Weber, G., Ziegler, J.: Toward an Information Society for All: An International RD Agenda. International Journal of Human-Computer Interaction 10(2), 107–134 (1998)
3. Doulgeraki, C., et al.: Adaptable Web-based user interfaces: methodology and practice. eMinds International Journal of Human Computer Interaction I(5), 1887–3022 (2009) ISSN: 1697-9613 (print) (online)
4. Antona, M., Mourouzis, A., Stephanidis, C.: Towards a Walkthrough Method for Universal Access Evaluation. In: Stephanidis, C. (ed.) HCI 2007. LNCS, vol. 4554, pp. 325–334. Springer, Heidelberg (2007)

Interactive System to Assist Rehabilitation of Children

Shuto Murai[1], Kenta Sugai[1], Michiko Ohkura[1], Mizuma Masazumi[2],
and Amimoto Satuki[2]

[1] Shibaura Institute of Technology
[2] Shouwa University Rehabilitation Hospital
{105118,105061}@shibaura-it.ac.jp,
ohkura@sic.shibaura-it.ac.jp,
mizuma@med.showa-u.ac.jp, r6108@sufrh.com

Abstract. We developed a new interactive system to support a child with physical disorders to continue appropriate rehabilitation pleasurably at home. We selected a ten-years-old boy suffering from "Spina Bifida Aperta" as the target
patient and constructed an interactive system that employed the step motion, an
effective rehabilitation method for him. Experiments were performed to evaluate the system.

Keywords: rehabilitation, children, system.

1 Introduction

Ambulation difficulty and paralysis are the examples of symptoms caused by congenital diseases such as Down syndrome and brain paralysis. For such symptoms,
symptomatic recovery is remarkable by early rehabilitation from childhood. However,
rehabilitation is operative and monotonous. If the patient is a child, the continuation
of long-term rehabilitation is even more difficult.

For domestic rehabilitation without the support of physical therapists, another
problem exists: it is almost impossible to judge whether the rehabilitation is appropriate. Thus, this study constructed an interactive system for children with physical disorders to appropriately assist continuous rehabilitation pleasurably in the home.

Since the symptoms caused by congenital diseases vary among patients, we
constructed an interactive system for a particular patient. Then, we will expand our
system for other patients. Such trials are very useful to assist the rehabilitation of children with congenital diseases. However, few researches exist, probably because
bringing them to commercially-based development is difficult. Therefore, we consider
our trial unique and important.

2 Method

2.1 Determination of the Target Patient

As the target patient, we selected a ten-years-old boy suffering from "Spina Bifida
Aperta," which causes muscle force degradation and sensory disturbance in the pe-
riphery of the lower limbs as an after effect of myelomeningocele.

C. Stephanidis (Ed.): Universal Access in HCI, Part I, HCII 2009, LNCS 5614, pp. 588–593, 2009.
© Springer-Verlag Berlin Heidelberg 2009

2.2 System Design

Due to patient's inability to put pressure on his tiptoes, he walks with too much pressure on his heels. For his rehabilitation, step motion was considered effective, in which he continues to put pressure on his tiptoes for a while. We built an interactive system using step motion for the system operation (Fig. 1).

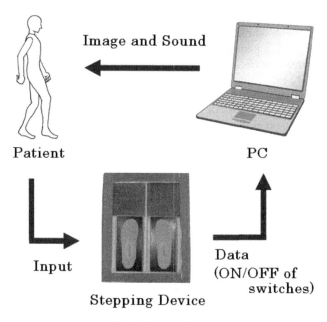

Fig. 1. System diagram

2.3 Stepping Device

We made an input device for step motion called a "Stepping Device" (Fig. 2). Two switches for the tiptoes and one switch for the heel were set under each foot's position

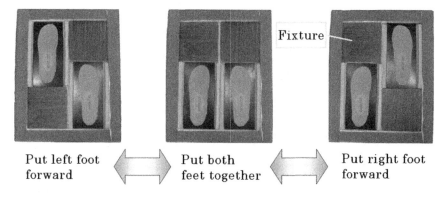

Fig. 2. Stepping Device

on the Stepping Device. In addition, each switch was adjusted to avoid being activated by the patient's body weight.

2.4 Content

The patient likes creatures, especially insects and reptiles. Thus, we made a game system in which the patient captures such creatures as a "Hercules beetle" and a "King cobra" by maintaining the step motion for a certain period of time. During the game, the patient looks at the conditions of the switches on a game screen (Fig. 3). In addition, we prepared a parameter to control the degree of difficulty to maintain his interest. The degree of difficulty fluctuates based on the number of creatures captured the day before. By increasing the degree of difficulty, the score for each capture and the necessary time increased to maintain step motion. The dates, the degrees of difficulty, the total scores, the times of the moments of capture, the times of the switches being turned on, and other data were acquired as log data. Fig. 4 shows an example of a screenshot just after a successful capture.

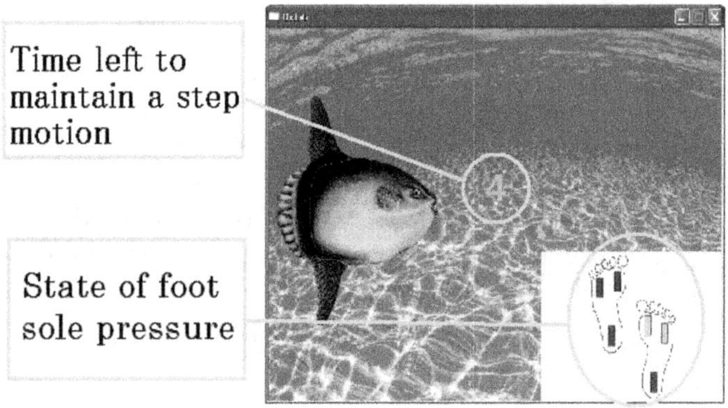

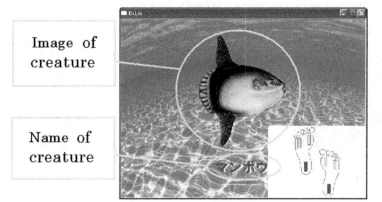

Fig. 3. Screenshot (1)

Fig. 4. Screenshot (2)

3 Assessment Experiment

3.1 Examination of Assessment Indexes

Game scores and foot pressure data were used to evaluate the rehabilitative effect. As for the foot pressure, strength distributions for clinging to the sole were calculated. The sole is divided into five parts; heel, toe, first toe, big toe tip, and middle. In addition, analysis of the data of the game's records and simple questionnaire answers were used to evaluate its continuity.

3.2 Experimental Procedure

1. Foot pressure was measured about one month before using the system.
2. Foot pressure was measured immediately before using of the system.
3. The game system was used daily for about one month.
4. Foot pressure was measured daily just after using of the system.
5. Foot pressure was measured about one month after using the system. During this period, the system wasn't used.

Fig. 5 shows the flow of the assessment experiment.

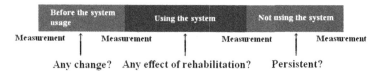

Fig. 5. Flow of the assessment experiment

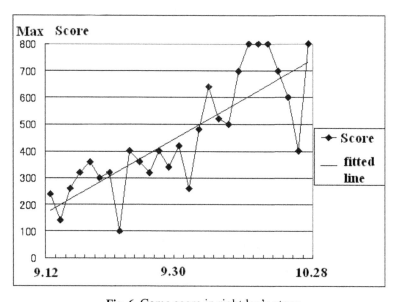

Fig. 6. Game score in right leg's steps

3.3 Experimental Results and Consideration

Figure 6 shows the time series of the game scores of the right leg's step. The score advanced well day by day, and became full marks. Moreover, the frequency at which he failed to continue pushing the switch decreased from 33 at the beginning to 12 at the end. This confirms that playing the game improved his step motion.

Figure 7 shows the ratio of the right leg's foot pressure in its steps, and Fig. 8 shows their standard deviation. Comparing the foot pressure data before and after system usage, the heel strength increased after system usage. On the other hand, tiptoe strength decreased. This result was contrary to our expectations. However, the standard deviation value decreased(Fig. 8).His balancing ability increased, although that was not our intended result.

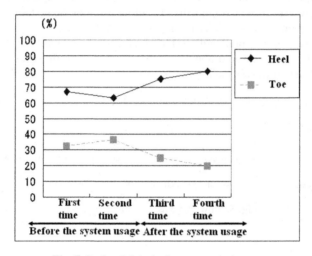

Fig. 7. Ratio of right leg's pressure in its steps

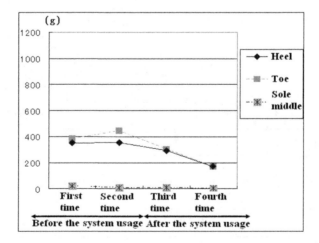

Fig. 8. Standard deviation

4 Discussion

Before the evaluation we expected that the increase of foot pressure to the toes would be the effect of rehabilitation. However, after the system usage, we noticed an improvement of the child's ability to keep his balance. Therefore, examining how to evaluate the effect of rehabilitation is necessary in the future.

5 Conclusion

We developed a new interactive system to support a child with a physical disorder to continue his rehabilitation appropriately and pleasurably at home. We built an interactive system using step motion for its operation and continued rehabilitation from the experiment outcomes. Before the evaluation, we expected that increased foot pressure to the toes would be the effect of rehabilitation. However, after system usage, we noticed improvement in the ability to keep balance. Therefore, examining how to evaluate the effect of rehabilitation is necessary in the future.

A Framework for Remote User Evaluation of Accessibility and Usability of Websites

Christopher Power, Helen Petrie, and Richard Mitchell

Department of Computer Science
University of York
York, YO10 5DD, UK
{cpower,petrie,mitchell}@cs.york.ac.uk

Abstract. The inclusion of participants that are representative of the diverse populations of users is essential for meaningful and useful evaluations of usability and accessibility on the web. This paper proposes the requirements and architecture for an automated tool suite to help manage the design and deployment of evaluations to these participants. A prototype implementation of this architecture that is being prepared is also discussed.

1 Introduction

There is a need to evaluate designs and prototypes much earlier than is currently common practice. Indeed, there has been an ongoing call in the usability and accessibility communities to increase user testing for web applications; a call that, after a decade of experience with web systems, has not been realized. The current lack of user engagement often stems from the inability to collect large enough samples of representative users to get meaningful results from the evaluations. This problem is magnified when evaluating web applications with people with disabilities due to the variety of user agents and assistive technologies that must be accounted for during the evaluation process. In this case, the combination of technologies and user preferences further divides participants into smaller and smaller subgroups, from each of which data must be collected.

One solution to the challenge of collecting enough evaluation results, particularly about web applications, is to engage users in remote evaluations. These evaluations provide valid data [2, 8] without the logistical problems associated with having users visit a laboratory [3]. Further, it allows users to conduct ecologically valid evaluations in their own homes and places of business. This gives designers a view of how their applications will be used in real environments after deployment and most importantly, an understanding of the impacts that different technologies will have on the web application after deployment.

Currently, many of these remote evaluations are conducted through bespoke implementations designed for testing a single web application, and as a result a great deal time and effort are committed to creating a test environment specifically tailored to that single application. This type of extraneous development contributes to the low adoption of remote evaluations in practice due to the time and resources that designers and developers are reluctant to commit.

C. Stephanidis (Ed.): Universal Access in HCI, Part I, HCII 2009, LNCS 5614, pp. 594–601, 2009.
© Springer-Verlag Berlin Heidelberg 2009

In order to reduce the resources required for remote user evaluations the evaluators require a robust, usable environment for constructing the evaluation trials for their web application. This paper discusses the design and architecture of an online application intended to meet the requirements of these web practitioners. The paper begins by discussing some of the challenges associated with conducting user evaluations and what is required of a suite of tools or applications to address these challenges. Following this, the authors discuss the architecture and implementation of a prototype of such a suite of tools, named Klingsor, to assist evaluators in managing evaluations and delivering them to targeted user groups. The paper will conclude with a discussion of future work, included pilot tests of the evaluation application scheduled for the autumn of 2009.

2 Related Research

Remote evaluation has been used for over a decade, with researchers and practitioners moving the evaluation of interactive technology beyond the walls of the laboratory setting. Barriers to user involvement such as distance of travel for participants, evaluator time and overall cost of evaluation become lessened through the application of remote evaluation methods. Indeed, remote evaluation, particularly task-based asynchronous remote evaluation, also provides for the engagement of a broader range of users in evaluation activities due to the ability of users to administer the trials themselves without being dependent on the presence of an evaluator. As such, web applications can be evaluated with a wide variety of people, technology configurations and environments [11]. This is particularly attractive for purposes of testing interactive systems with people with disabilities, where the wide variety of personal preferences, assistive technology and user agents lead designers, developers and researchers to claim that it is impossible to get a representative sample of users [8].

Due to the potential benefits that can be gained from remote evaluations, a great deal of work has been undertaken in the last decade examining how to exploit the networking and mobility aspects of personal computing to conduct remote evaluations. Hartson, Castillo *et al.* [4,5] identified several different methods for conducting remote evaluations. These remote evaluations were classified in the following subcategories:

- *Portable evaluations* where an evaluation unit conducts evaluations in the users' own work/home environments.
- *Local evaluation at a remote site* where external equipment is installed at a remote site and evaluations are conducted at that remote site.
- *Remote questionnaires/surveys* where the display of the survey to the participant is triggered by actions in the interface.
- *Remote control evaluation* where the users' environments are equipped with recording equipment for synchronous or asynchronous recording of data.
- *Video conferencing as an extension of the usability laboratory*, a technique that involves the users undertaking particular tasks while engaging in synchronous communication with an evaluator at a remote site.

- *Instrumented remote evaluation* where user applications are augmented with components that record information about user workflows.
- *Semi-instrumented remote evaluation* where the users are trained to identify critical incidents and record the positive of negative aspects of their use of the application.

A decade later, Petrie *et al.* identified several other dimensions that can be used to further categorize the remote evaluation activities [8]. Whether or not the participant is independent in evaluations or dependent on the presence of an evaluator, if communication is synchronous or asynchronous and whether the participant requires training in the tasks before conducting them are all aspects that need to be considered when planning remote evaluations.

Further to this, Andraesen *et al.* [1] indexed existing work on remote evaluation by the methodology followed, by the type of data collected and on the dimension of synchronicity. Within this analysis, there are examples of traditional asynchronous studies, such as diary studies [4], self-administered questionnaires and workflow logging [9] among others. These methods are often supported by often general-purpose tools that are specialized for purposes of the evaluation or through bespoke implementations. While these bespoke tools are very useful, the specialization of the tool to the evaluation makes it potentially difficult to reuse components from these implementations in future remote evaluation protocols.

Due to the wide variety of techniques available, and the different types of information that can be collected, it is perhaps unsurprising that no unified framework or tool support has emerged to support the evaluator in the tasks of designing, deploying and conducting remote evaluations with users. In the following sections the architecture and prototype implementation of such a tool suite for conducting evaluations on websites are presented.

3   Requirements for Managing Evaluations

The phases of remote accessibility or usability evaluation are similar to those in standard co-operative evaluation techniques [7]. Evaluators must recruit a representative group of participants and record their demographic information for use in later analysis. They must design experimental tasks that are representative of what the users will do in the application. They must deploy the evaluation to the users, usually with some instruction of how to perform the task. Finally, the data must be analyzed through a variety of qualitative and quantitative methods. Currently, only the final step of this process is supported through automated tools statistical for quantitative analysis or qualitative analysis tools.

For the first three stages of the process, the authors analyzed existing literature and examined five investigations for requirements regarding what evaluators and participants would require from a suite of tools supporting remote evaluation. These five investigations were conducted under the auspices of the Benchmarking Tools and Methods for the Web (BenToWeb) project[1]. This project had the goal of producing tools and methods that aided in the validation and evaluation of websites for accessibility. Within that project there were several development efforts in which data was

---

[1] www.bentoweb.org retrieved 03/2009

required to inform the design of new tools. Among the investigations conducted by the project were: language simplification, navigational consistency, perception of colour contrast and colour confusion zones for people with colour vision deficiencies. Each of these investigations used a combination of remote tools, such as surveys/questionnaires and bespoke applications, to collect information from users throughout Europe. In addition to these investigations, there was an initiative to create a test suite for checking new accessibility tools as they come on the market for correctness and completeness. This initiative also collected information from remote users with disabilities about the success or failure of web implementations [10].[2] After an analysis of the functionality that was used in all of these remote data collection activities, the following sets of functional requirements were defined for a general online testing framework.

For the recruitment and registration of users, the test suite must have the following available:

- Participants must be able to record their demographic information such as age, sex, functional disability information and nationality for analysis purposes.
- Private aspects of participants' information, such as their names, addresses or billing information must not be associated with their evaluation result data.
- Participants must be able to specify technology configurations and their experience with different types of technology. This record must include: general operating systems, user agents and assistive technology to form a personal profile under which they will conduct trials.
- Many such technology profiles may be required for each participant to account for different contexts of use (e.g. home versus work).
- Participants must be able to select which and how many trials they would like to participate in from the overall set of remote trials available.
- Participants must be able to specify whether they would like to have their direct actions recorded for analysis, as opposed to reporting critical incidents or completing surveys. Some users may be uncomfortable with such monitoring components, or the components may conflict with aspects of their technology.
- A record of the trials completed by participants must be kept accurately so that participants can be appropriately reimbursed for their activities.

For the evaluator, the key user requirements come from the need for flexibility in specifying the applications that will be tested as well as the types of information that will be requested from the participants. These requirements include:

- Evaluators must be able to specify both custom built websites and websites in "the wild" for purposes of evaluation.
- Evaluators must be able to specify tasks on a website that are to be completed by a subgroup of users. These tasks are referred to as trials hereafter.
- Evaluators must be able to specify an arbitrarily large set of questions to ask the user before or after a trial, or set of trials, has been completed.

---

[2] This work resulted in two tools, Parsifal and Amfortas, that have provided inspiration for the test suite discussed in this paper. Thus the name of the test suite, Klingsor is drawn from the same source as those, the opera *Parsifal* by Wagner.

- Evaluators must be able to specify alternate choice, multiple choice, Lickert scale or open answer questions for each trial.
- Evaluators must be able to specify subgroups of the user population for engagement in remote trials. This can include grouping people by user characteristics such as technology experience, or through specification of the availability of technology to a participant (e.g. trials intended for screen reader users).
- User group profiles may be reused between remote evaluations. As such, evaluators must be able to save profiles about subgroups.
- Evaluators must be able to provide instructions and training documents through the test suite for each trial or set of trials.
- Evaluators must be able to specify an external tool that can be used for remote monitoring of user activities.
- Evaluators must be able to retrieve extracts of collected data from the system at any time in order to perform analyses on the data.

The system itself has the core requirement that it must perform correct profile matching between the trials specified by the evaluator and the participants. When complete, different users will be presented with different subsets of trials that are appropriate to their personal preferences, their technology and their experience.

4   Klingsor: A Remote Evaluation Tool Suite

With the above requirements in place, the authors proceeded to design and implement a prototype tool suite to manage remote evaluations of websites. In this section the architecture and implementation of these prototypes are discussed.

4.1   Architecture

The overall architecture of Klingsor is presented in Figure 1. The evaluation suite has two distinct tools, one for the evaluator and one for the participants, each of which have interface components connected to processing components that read and store different types of data regarding trials and participant respectively. A third processing component performs matching between the data models for the trials and profiles of participants.

In the evaluator interface, the evaluator is able to edit information regarding the evaluation or individual evaluation trials. For the evaluation, briefing and debriefing information can be presented to the participants at appropriate times, and instructions about the website/web application being used in the evaluation can be included to aid in training them. For each trial, the evaluator can specify the following pieces of information:

- *Target users*: this includes functional disability information and other information about the desired participants.
- *Target technology*: a description of the types of technology that are needed in the trial. For example, a screen reader or other assistive technology may be required for a particular trial. When this information is entered, the target user information can be updated with user experience on that particular technology.

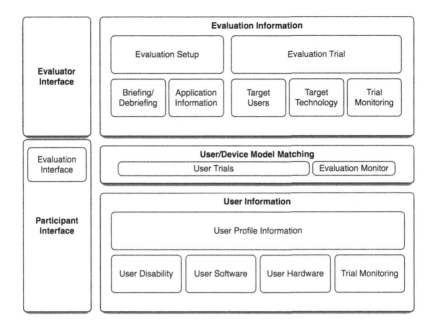

Fig. 1. The architecture for the Klingsor evaluation suite

- *Trial monitoring*: an indication as to whether a trial requires that the user be monitored by an external application or augmentation to the browser. This can include a reference to the monitoring software for installation on the participants' computers.

In the participants' interface, each participant can enter his or her own personal information as well as several technology profiles under which they will undertake the trials. Only one profile can be marked as active at any given time. This active profile will be the one used for matching with specific trials.

When a user logs into the participant interface, the model-matching component will compare the active profile of the user with the information regarding the trials. When there are trials available that match the participant's profile, he/she will be presented with a list of evaluation trials he/she may undertake. If the user undertakes any of the displayed trials, he/she will be credited with the completion for purposes of recompense.

4.2 Implementation

The Klingsor prototype evaluation suite has been implemented to be a cross-platform Java servlet application with Java Server Pages (JSP) serving as the web interface for the user. The JSP code has been engineered to produce static code that is rendered in the users' web browsers (either evaluators or participants) to avoid accessibility issues that may arise from dynamic content (such as enriched internet applications implemented in AJAX). As a result, the web application relies on heavy use of form fill-in interactions with the user, leading them through the process of specifying evaluations (for the evaluator) or accessing currently available trials (for the participant).

For data storage, the components are implemented on a mySQL database that has been decoupled from the application code. The intention is that the data aspect of the application can be replaced with a Resource Description Framework (RDF) data repository or other data modeling language should the need arise.

5 Future work

The prototype implementation of the Klingsor suite is in the final stages of verification and validation. When complete, the tool will be deployed for use by student evaluators at both the University of York and the Technical Universität Dresden for an initial pilot. This work is scheduled for autumn 2009.

6 Conclusions

This paper has presented the requirements and architecture for a suite of tools for evaluators to manage and deploy evaluation protocols to remote users. Such a tool suite must be flexible enough to account for the variety of users that an evaluator may wish to engage, as well as in what types of information will be collected from participants.

This architecture collects information regarding the preferences and technology configurations of the participants and uses it to match them with evaluation trials specified by an evaluator.

A prototype implementation is being prepared for a large-scale deployment in the coming months in which evaluators will test the functionality for its usability, its accessibility and how fit-to-purpose the tool suite is for their needs. When complete, this tool will provide a new, innovative way to manage and conduct remote evaluations in both research and practice communities.

References

1. Andreasen, M.S., Nielsen, H.V., Schrøder, S.O., Stage, J.: What happened to remote usability testing?: an empirical study of three methods. In: Proceedings of the SIGCHI Conference on Human factors in Computing Systems (2007)
2. Castillo, J.C., Hartson, H.R., Hix, D.: Remote usability evaluation: can users report their own critical incidents. In: CHI 1998: Proceedings of the SIGCHI Conference on Human factors in Computing Systems, pp. 253–254 (1998)
3. Dray, S., Siegel, D.: Remote possibilities?: International usability testing at a distance. Interactions 11(2), 10–17 (2004)
4. Hartson, H.R., Castillo, J.C.: Remote evaluation for post-deployment usability improvement. In: AVI 1998: Proceedings of the working conference on Advanced visual interfaces, pp. 22–29. ACM, New York (1998)

5. Hartson, H.R., Castillo, J.C., Kelso, J., Neale, W.C.: Remote evaluation: the network as an extension of the usability laboratory. In: CHI 1996: Proceedings of the SIGCHI conference on Human factors in computing systems, pp. 228–235. ACM, New York (1996)
6. Hill, W.C., Terveen, L.G.: Involving remote users in continuous design of web content. In: Proceedings of the conference on Designing interactive systems: processes, practices, methods, and techniques, pp. 137–145 (1997)
7. Monk, A., Wright, P., Haber, J., Davenport, L.: Improving your human-computer interface: A practical technique. Prentice Hall International (UK) Ltd., Englewood Cliffs (1993)
8. Petrie, H., Hamilton, F., King, N., Pavan, P.: Remote usability evaluations with disabled people. In: Proceedings of the SIGCHI conference on Human Factors in computing systems (2006)
9. Siochi, A.C., Ehrich, R.W.: Computer analysis of user interfaces based on repetition in transcripts of user sessions. ACM Trans. Inf. Syst. 9(4), 309–335 (1991)
10. Strobbe, C., Koch, J., Vlachogiannis, E., Ruemer, R., Velasco, C.A., Engelen, J.: The Ben-ToWeb test case suites for the web content accessibility guidelines (WCAG) 2.0. In: Miesenberger, K., Klaus, J., Zagler, W.L., Karshmer, A.I. (eds.) ICCHP 2008. LNCS, vol. 5105, pp. 402–409. Springer, Heidelberg (2008)
11. Winckler, M.A.A., Freitas, C.M.D.S., de Lima, J.V.: Usability remote evaluation for www. In: CHI 2000: CHI 2000 extended abstracts on Human factors in computing systems, pp. 131–132. ACM, New York (2000)

Ergonomic Issues in the Material Re-use Process

Maciej Skowronski and Jerzy Charytonowicz

Wroclaw University of Technology,
Faculty of Architecture,
ul. B. Prusa 53/55, 50 – 317 Wroclaw, Poland
{maciej.skowronski,jerzy.charytonowicz}@pwr.wroc.pl

Abstract. The major purposes of ergonomic design in architecture are as follows: creating comfortable space and environment around the human- body and mind, the optimization of working and living spaces, and preservation of the natural environment. One of the most important aspects of the design process is proper building materials selection. In accordance with extraction and manufacturing processes, building materials are divided into the following groups: natural materials, synthetics, and composite materials. In the second half of twentieth century, mainly due to natural resource depletion, people began to focus their attention on re-use and recycling strategies. Nowadays it seems, that thanks to material recovery and recycling, we are able to limit the destructive impact of human activity on the natural environment. However it needs to be pointed out, that today's re-use technology needs to be adjusted and improved regarding modern environmental and ergonomic issues.

Keywords: architecture, ecology, energy saving, recycling, reuse, alternative technology.

1 Background

The beginning of the twenty-first century can be characterized by a high level of urbanization, high index of energy consumption and intensified flow of various materials. Natural resources, similarly to the second half of the twentieth century, are intensively drawn out from the environment, processed into materials and used in different industrial branches. The process would not raise any controversy if it had not been for the fact that the majority of the finished products mentioned above, after their term of exploitation go to the dumping ground. The resources that were originally natural in the environment after being processed, at different stages of their life cycle, finally contribute to the pollution and degradation of the natural environment. At the beginning, those problems that undoubtedly result from Industrial Revolution were not noticed. Decades had to pass until people became convinced about the negative consequences of this revolution and about the large scale of its influence on natural environment.

The pace of change happening in the modern world is significantly connected with the rapid growth of population. In 1950 there were two-and-a-half billion people living in the world. Until 2002, the population of our planet grew to 6.2 billion, which

C. Stephanidis (Ed.): Universal Access in HCI, Part I, HCII 2009, LNCS 5614, pp. 602–608, 2009.

means the growth as big as 1.2 percent yearly. The United Nations Organization estimates that by 2050 the population may grow up to 8.9 billion [1]. A high gross world product (GWP) is a natural consequence of the population growth and the concurrent industrial expansion. During the second half of the last century the gross product value grew from 6.7 up to 48 trillion dollars [2]. A yearly increase on the level of 3.9 percent should also be understood as the fact that the world population, day by day, keeps consuming more and more goods and natural resources, which highly contributes to pollution and, consequently, rubbish growing very fast, so soon there will be no place to dump it. The pessimistic forecasts from the beginning of the twenty-first century predict the growth of energy consumption and the flow of different materials nearly three times larger only until 2050. Treating the nature as inexhaustible, never-ending source of raw materials, as well as unlimited dumping ground will inevitably and significantly influence the quality of life and this will provoke the growth of civilization diseases. Ecologists warn that at the current way of exploitation, the resources will be quickly exhausted, which will start a new era – the era of shortage or deficit. This situation demands from people that they introduce a new, rational way of exploiting raw materials.

The description of society from the turn of the twentieth and twenty-first centuries presented above, as well as the influence of man's activity on the surrounding world makes a good background for reflections on modern architecture, which– as the statistics say– has a large contribution to a high level of exploiting resources and generating a lot of waste. At the moment, in highly-developed countries the building sector swallows one-third of all energy produced. An important reason for limiting the usage of energy is the degradation of natural environment, which is progressing very fast, and the amount of fossil fuels, such as crude oil, gas, uranium and coal, drastically decreasing. With the continuous development of energetics based on traditional raw materials it is estimated that the resources will last merely for the nearest few decades, except for coal that will last a little longer. Besides, we should not forget about the problem of waste and a lack of places for a dumping ground. Currently, only within the European Union 1.3 billion tons of waste is produced, and the tendency is still growing [3]. Every year there is by 10 percent more waste, which highly exceeds the average pace of economic growth. This upsetting situation is now approached by a new direction or style in architecture, which is called the architecture of re-consumption. As the current conditions show, the proper selection and the usage of recycled materials makes it possible to achieve the designing aims assumed, with the possibility to consider a wide spectrum of ecological and ergonomic aspects. The process of using the recycled materials that are generally treated as disposable ones makes it possible to save resources which are now in short supply, and may be understood as one of basic principles of sustainable design.

2   Re-consumption in Modern Architecture

While in many technologically complicated products the race in the search for energy-saving solutions has taken place for a long time now, the application of those solutions in the building sector still seems to be quite new. The slowdown has been mainly caused by high prices of energy-saving materials and techniques as well as by too traditional approach to the product called a „building object". However, the last decades of the previous century brought about a rapid change in order to make the rules of natural environment protection much stricter than before. This enhanced wider considering of ecological and ergonomic aspects in designing, including architectural projects. Modern buildings ought to save energy, be ecological and planned according to the rules of ergonomic designing, i.e. they should protect a healthy environment and comfortable surrounding conditions for the people inhabiting them, and they should not be a nuisance to the natural environment at all stages of their existence. Nowadays, the main designing guidelines and assumptions of eco-architecture are the following:

- smaller scale of buildings designed
- careful selection of building materials preceded by a detailed analysis of their life cycle
- using harvested lumber in the building process
- systems of regaining and collecting rain water
- saving energy and renewable energy sources
- proper location of buildings in the area
- general accessibility to public transport
- minimal using of chemicals, which badly influence the ozone layer
- protection of green places and existing plants
- re-consumption.

The re-use and recycling architecture is subconsciously rooted in so-called Green Design. Plenty of objects of this kind were created as early as in the 60's of the last century. However, in those days the reasons for creating them were completely different, rather ideological than ecological. This does not underestimate the fact that nowadays, in the first years of twenty-first century the idea of re-consumption is one of the main foundations of eco-architecture and energy saving building industry. It gives modern engineers a variety of possibilities to use new solutions, especially when it comes to many aspects of the designing and investment process that were formerly neglected. The idea of re-consumption is quite sophisticated and can be understood in many ways. It includes such elements as: the second-use of materials without their earlier processing, recycling, use of existing building structures (renovation, adaptation, modernization), revitalization of urban areas, selection of materials, mobility of object functions, modern strategies of pulling down and engineer's designing. These are only some of the problems strongly connected with the terminology of re-consumption. All of them are equally important and only being considered together may result in the effect demanded, i.e. the state of the natural environment improved by limiting wasteful exploitation, reducing and hopefully eliminating the side effects of the industrial process and waste accumulation.

3   Influence of Recycling Process on Product Characteristics

In order to cope with the problem of the amount of waste growing, in the second half of the twentieth century a hierarchy of solutions was established, which is contained in the principle of three R's: reduction, re-use and recycling [4]. The biggest advantage for the environment results from limiting the excessive consumption and multiplied use of product that should be categorized as waste as late as possible. Finally, the rational processing helps to solve the problems caused both by obtaining a product from original raw materials and by the accumulation of waste mentioned above. While the rightness of this strategy is beyond doubt, its practical usage is still far from being perfect. It is often a consequence of a poor selection of re-used materials for the function planned, or not always proper approach to their processing. To illustrate that fact, it would be practical to analyze some aspects of the recycling process, which is regarded as one of complex principles applied to natural environment protection. At present the repeated processing of materials that were withdrawn from exploitation is quite often limited to so-called down-cycling. It leads to reducing the quality and parameters of the initial material due to its processing, modification and finally the connection with a new, different component. As a result of joint processing of materials that have different structures and chemical compositions but belong to the same ordinal group, an apparently ecological product is created which is ready for repeated industrial use. Yet, it is usually a highly complicated structure being difficult to reduce to its elements, which additionally has its durability, quality and visual characteristics much worse than the original materials.

The phenomenon of down-cycling refers mainly to re-processing metals and often involves an irreversible loss of copper, chromium and manganese that are valuable for industry. This situation takes place for example when some steel elements taken from scrapped cars are regained and adapted for the second-use. While being processed good quality steel is connected with other components, such as copper regained from electric wires, lacquer coatings, some plastics, etc. [5]. Their joint thermal treatment and putting them together in the production process significantly lowers the quality of the new product. This consequently makes it necessary to enrich the production by using more good quality materials, minerals or chemicals that would improve the features of the final hybrid.

The recycling of paper waste– so popular recently– cannot be fully approved either. Again the right idea of processing and repeated industrial use has not been fully completed by the production engineering process applied. The strategy of maximum use of waste paper instead of wood should be promoted undoubtedly. It makes it possible to reduce the amount of energy used, helps to save water and crude oil, alleviates the problem of uncontrolled cutting down trees and ubiquitous rubbish. However, both the production method and the final product have some faults, e.g. when it comes to the ergonomic point of view. For example, the method of whitening the paper pulp by means of chemicals with chlorine results in creating a lot of sewage containing significant amounts of toxic substances that cannot be easily decomposed. The process of recycling is then accompanied by preparing the mixture of unhealthy chemicals and paper pulp as well as toxic printing- ink that was not designed for the second-use. Thus the characteristics of paper processed are much lower than expected. The surface is not smooth and the fibers are shorter than in the original material. This causes the dangerous situation when chemically toxic particles contained in the new product can penetrate the air. Then they may get into the respiratory system of man causing its vexation [5].

Similarly, in the building process some of technical solutions presently used, which include using of recycled elements, may occasionally threaten the customer's health and lower their comfort. For instance, some of thermal insulation systems made of organic materials should be considered. The necessary adaptation of cellulose or sheep wool to fire- proof principles as well as impregnation against the activity of biologically destructive factors may frequently cause the situation in which the final product is just soaked in toxic chemicals. This consequently causes that the people staying in the room insulated in this way may suffer from allergies or respiratory system irritation. Anyway, the rightness of pro-ecological character of cellulose insulation is beyond question. It helps to reduce the amount of waste and save energy, both while exploiting the building and while the insulation material is being produced.

4 Modern Strategies of Engineer's Designing

The examples above prove that the process of recycling materials- although apparently friendly to the environment and the organisms living in it- may also cause negative side effects completely different from the assumed ones when it is used incompetently. They usually result from a wrong approach towards the process of manufacturing original materials, which were not designed for a later de-materialization, utilization or recycling. The fact of neglecting proper technical solutions at the production stage may lead to irreversible losing of those components that come from not renewable sources and are often in short supply. To solve this problem, it is necessary to improve the existing solutions so that the product in its life cycle would be used in accordance with the logic of its cycle in nature. The key factor of this strategy is the process of designing for recycling that would include the necessity of the later decomposition, utilization or dematerialization of the product withdrawn from exploitation. A solution of this kind comprises a lot of aspects neglected before, both ecological and ergonomic ones. The guidelines above should also be applied in the modern architectural designing which is understood as using properly selected materials as well as the designing for an easy decomposition afterwards. Considering the ergonomic aspects seems to be specially important because it is directly and immediately connected with ensuring comfort for the potential users.

One of such materials that were designed for the future exploitation as well as re-processing is "nylon 6". This is a synthetic polymer that in highly developed countries is now more and more frequently applied in the process of making carpets. This material makes it possible to gain good quality synthetic yarn that is resistant to abrasion. Its predominance over "nylon 6.6", which has been commonly used for many years, results from the possibility of the used product to undergo a simplified process of de-polymerization. Finally, the original monomers are regained, which can be repeatedly used in manufacturing new carpets that have the same utility features as the original product. Re-processing makes it possible to regain at least 99 percent of the original monomers [6]. Modern weaver's techniques additionally improve the material's esthetic value and resistance to unfavourable outside conditions. The variety of patterns and colors is practically unlimited.

Another example of de-polymerization applied in the recycling process is decomposition of poly(methyl methacrylate) (so called organic glass or Plexiglas) which results in regaining methyl methacrylate. Decomposition into original elements takes place in the temperature of 300 degrees of Celsius. The products of the condensation and distillation are pure monomers that are at the same time the initial substance used for repeated polymerization in the production process [7].

Also, the method of connecting various production branches gives measurable effects helping to solve the problem of growing amount of waste. In order to make this kind of engineer's solutions more popular, in early 70's of twentieth century the Heineken company worked out the system of building walls from specially designed beer bottles. The WOBO bottles of rectangular cross-section after having performed their package function could be used as a modular building element. The modern equivalent of the solution described above can be the concept system of raising buildings by means of using specially designed plastic bottles for mineral water, which was developed in 2006. The United Bottle, as this is the name of the product designed by a Swiss project study "Instant", after having performed the original function automatically becomes a modular building element. Insulation parameters of the external wall constructed in this way give the possibility of modification through filling in the air bricks used for its construction with the material of organic origin (soil, sand, feather). The final stage will be the recycling of single elements of the system. This complementary function, i.e. the building application, in this very case should be understood as the solution for the areas affected by disasters. The neutralization of negative effects after disasters is usually connected with the necessity of providing fresh water to the area affected, which is a necessary condition of survival, as well as building of temporary shelters for people who lost their homes. Both the WOBO bottle and the Unite Bottle systems should be treated as experiments illustrating the possibility of uniting different production branches, which in this case are the production of drinks and the building industry.

5 Conclusion

The turn of twentieth and twenty-first centuries is the time when the process of natural environment degradation seems to be highly advanced. One of the consequences of industrial revolution and the western lifestyle promoted is a ubiquitous problem of waste. It results from mechanisms and ideologies that accompanied rapid industrialization in the second half of twentieth century. The approach in those days was mainly aimed at the fastest and the cheapest mass production and the sale of ready for use products. This significantly determined the way of designing, the process of creating and utilization of the given product. The obvious consequence of such approach up till now has been a wasteful excavation of raw materials and their mass processing without paying attention to a high energy consumption and the pollution of natural environment. On different stages of the materials life cycle the natural environment has been gradually contaminated. Not long ago the ecological aspects of production, exploitation and utilization were still completely neglected in any specifications and analytical studies. Such state of social awareness was deprived completely of the logic considering the natural cycle.

For the well-being of future generations this attitude to nature which is regarded as a never-ending, inexhaustible source of raw materials and a dumping ground for used materials or waste must be changed as quickly as possible. The population growth and the exploitation of natural resources progressing along makes it necessary to pay attention to modern, ecological strategies of engineer's designing. Nowadays, both the building sector and other industrial branches ought to aim at perfecting the production techniques applied. One of the solutions available, which is intended to improve the conditions of life in modern world, is the idea of material re-consumption. The process of designing and production according to the logic of natural cycle seems to be one of major strategies to guarantee a balanced progress in twenty-first century.

References

1. Auroville Earth Institute, http://www.earth-auroville.com
2. Assadourian, E.: Economic Growth Inches Up. Vital Signs. Worldwatch Institute, Washington (2003)
3. Dubas, W.: Podstawy budownictwa energooszczędnego. In: Przeglad budowlany. AB Druk, Warsaw (2005)
4. Wikipedia, http://pl.wikipedia.org/wiki/Zasada_3R
5. McDonough, W., Braungart, M.: Cradle to cradle. Remaking the Way We Make Things. North Point Press, New York (2002)
6. McDonough, W., Braungart, M.: The Promise of Nylon 6. Green@Work (2002)
7. Wikipedia, http://pl.wikipedia.org/wiki/Depolimeryzacja

User Empowerment in Standardization

Mathijs Soede, Nienke Blijham, and Manon Verdonschot

VILANS, Centre of expertise for long during Care, P.O. box 8228,
3503 RE Utrecht, The Netherlands
{M.Soede,N.Blijham,M.Verdonschot}@vilans.nl

Abstract. With the Mandate 376 on Public Procurement, the European Union aims at supporting inclusion of persons with disabilities. It is felt necessary to prepare the End-Users, i.e. persons with disabilities for participation into the standards processes (especially standardization in ICT) themselves. The background, motivation behind this goal is discussed and a special course is developed for the End-Users and presented in this paper.

Keywords: Public Procurement, Inclusion for all, Design for All, Course development.

1 Introduction

Our society is becoming more and more focused on ICT supported activities. ICT supported activities are: communication between people and communities, ordering products, electronic payments, controlling identity cards, games, electronic reading and much more. More over, not just people are connected but "the Internet of Things" (Objects and environments are connected by internet) is growing and people must stay "connected" with the Internet of Things. Thus, it is increasingly important that all people can access and use the modern and new activities.

An approach to get and maintain accessibility is to make the organizations and people creating and installing ICT-systems aware of this issue and try to convince them to make solutions which are accessible and usable for everyone.

However, with no regulation, just a free option to choose, the world of accessibility will not change far enough or fast enough[1]. The USA showed that some level of regulation, starting with the governmental institutions can have a large effect.

A regulation alone cannot enhance accessibility, it is needed that the implementation of the regulation is supported by good standards for the services and the technology applied. The phrase "good standards" means that standards are developed with accessibility as a requirement and we believe that this can only be achieved by consulting those end-users, who may experience accessibility problems. They must directly be involved in developing the standards.

---

[1] One hundred institutions and companies in The Netherlands undersigned in 2005 the intention to make their websites accessible within a year. It turned out after a year that the situation was not improved but even worse then at the beginning of the year (www.accessibility.nl /Dutch).

C. Stephanidis (Ed.): Universal Access in HCI, Part I, HCII 2009, LNCS 5614, pp. 609–614, 2009.
© Springer-Verlag Berlin Heidelberg 2009

This paper describes the development and implementation of a course to educate persons with disabilities to take part in standardization projects.

1.1 A Short History

Good information can be obtained from the Internet [1,2]: "The U.S. **Rehabilitation Act of 1973** prohibits discrimination on the basis of disability in programs conducted by Federal agencies, in programs receiving Federal financial assistance, in Federal employment, and in the employment practices of Federal contractors". This act has four sections of which the fourth one addresses the ICT accessibility, section 508, which "establishes requirements for electronic and information technology developed, maintained, procured, or used by the Federal government". Section 508 requires Federal electronic and information technology to be accessible to people with disabilities, including employees and members of the public. The Federal government as a major client caused a change in policy in industry: If this large client, the Federal Government, requires accessible ICT why not delivering all ICT in an accessible form?

The European action in this field is to develop a solution for common requirements and conformance assessment. A mandate is given to the European Standard Organizations (2005/6) – Mandate 376. This mandate asks for:

- Phase I: Inventory

Technology products (ICT); Existing accessibility requirements & current gaps; Existing standards to comply with accessibility requirements Assessment: requirements as technical specifications/ award criteria ; Report on testing and certification schemes

- Phase II: Standardization

European standard (EN) Accessibility requirements for ICT domain, to be used as technical specifications ; Technical report (TR) listing existing technical standards ; Guidelines on award criteria ; Guidance and support material

- On line freely accessible toolkit

European Standards organizations (CEN and ETSI) have accepted the mandate and the Phase I has been accomplished. As now the standardization work will soon be started, it is of utmost importance that user involvement in this work is enhanced. This is the reason to issue a project on USer EMpowerment in standardization, USEM.

1.2 The Project USEM

Proactive user participation in standardization will be an asset to future standards in the field of ICT, assistive technology and design for all. Users and user organizations can provide a valuable knowledge platform concerning user characteristics and user needs. Direct input from user experts can be valuable for cooperation with technical and standardization experts. The European project "User Empowerment in standardization (USEM) intends, as a pilot, to unlock such resources by selecting and training user experts from Europe for participation in standardization.

The USEM project started in April 2007 and will end in December 2009. The project addresses three main objectives:

- To facilitate participation of user organizations in the standardization process of IST (Information Society Technologies).
- To qualify more users (who represent user organizations) with disabilities and elderly people for the participation in European standardization of IST.
- To improve European exchange of experiences by user information networking, to disseminate information and encourage the uptake of new IST standardization.

USEM is based on the Fortune concept. The Fortune concept, developed for inclusion of users with disabilities in the design process by the Fortune consortium (1999-2000), is based on seven principles:

1. Partnership as a basis
2. Users are members and/or representatives of user organizations
3. Users gets payment on an equal basis
4. Accessibility of all relevant materials and premises is guaranteed
5. Every partner guarantees qualified staff
6. Sound plan for the project including time and resource planning (for user participation)
7. Partnership is implemented from the beginning of the project. The two main results of the USEM project are: an USEM training and an USEM network of trained users [3].

1.3 The USEM Principles

In fact, the development of a standard is a matter of technical development taking into account all kind of environmental and situational requirements. The product is a standard which complies to the requirements once set. Although Fortune developed the recommendations for regular product development it is therefore very plausible to take the Fortune's project result as the starting point for the conceptual basis of the USEM training.

As a result of an analysis by user organizations and standardization bodies, it can be concluded that each FORTUNE principle , can be translated to the USEM project. The reality is, however, that some of the issues are not as effective easy to accomplish as one might hope for. For example the accessibility of the relevant material can technically be done but having, for example, a complex drawing or scheme (as a part of a standard) to be understood and used for a blind person, it turns out that in practice the blind person has difficulties in taking part in the discussions at the same level or speed as others. Also the partnership from the start of the project might be difficult when documents are not yet made accessible and the definition of the work is not yet complete.

2   The USEM Course

The USEM course has been developed in two phases. We learned from the first phase, the pilot course that the trainees needed time before entering the course, to get acquainted with the material to be used in the course: some of them would like to organize the material in their own computer/laptop for a fast search when needed, and some of them having a lower level of general education would like to be a little ahead in reading the material to be acquainted with terminology and the material itself.

It became also clear that the time together during the course meetings was very valuable for meeting each other and training the abilities needed in negotiating requirements in standards projects. In the second phase, the final training course is developed. The final training consisted of five parts:

1. Information on standardization
2. USEM concept
3. Users in standardization
4. Ongoing and future processes
5. Networking

These modules form together the USEM curriculum: Objectives and Learning outcomes.

2.1 Information on Standardization

Basic information on the European, national and international standards organizations is provided in this part of the training. The process of standardization and the different steps in this process is given . Finally the role of the user in the process is discussed, which is of course a critical issue in this module.

The learning outcome is:
a) Summarize the standardization process,
b) Acknowledge different standardization organizations,
c) Identify activities of different standardization organizations.

2.2 USEM Concept

Good user participation requires a good understanding of the USEM (Fortune based) concept. The seven recommendations are discussed. The recommendations seem to be simple but the real implementation can cause a lot of discussions.

The learning outcome is: a) Outline needs and possibilities for participation in standardization, b) Differentiate different tasks when participating in standardization. Some tasks are better then others to be accomplished with a particular impairment.

2.3 Users in Standardization

The use of basic knowledge about people's abilities, with and without impairments relies on how to collect experience: personal experience but foremost collective experience to be obtained via the person's own user organizations. This is why the second USEM principle, 'the person must be part of an user organization' is so important. In this module also an element to explain the different roles in the standardization: User, Developer of a product, Producer, Distributor, Maintenance, Finance. The learning outcome is: a) summarize the USEM concept, b) understand the principles and ideas behind the USEM concept, c) understand the added value of USEM in the standardization practice, and be able to communicate this to other partners.

2.4 Ongoing and Future Processes

Standardization is a relatively long procedure: thus entering a standardization activity is very much dependent on the phase and status of that activity. The course gives an overview of the various relevant lines of standardization. The most important one is the Mandate 376 activity. Also, for example the WAI/W3C activity is relevant. The trainees are expected to be active in one of those lines: therefore they were asked to choose a line of activity which suited them most: interest, required level of knowledge etc.. The learning outcome is: a) able to follow the status of ongoing standardization, and b) being informed about possible future actions.

2.5 Networking

Networking is important for the trainees for two reasons: first to know what is going on in the field of standardization, to know what the possibilities are and what the partners in standardization are heading for. Second it is important to consult their user organizations and members in those organizations: to get the answers needed and to know what the priorities are which have to be negotiated. The learning outcome is: a) use network tools (EDEAN-website – work environment), b) able to raise questions and collecting answers from their own user organizations.

3 Training Manual

While the group of trainees was just 30 persons large it is needed to repeat the course at regular intervals. The course book is two-fold: one is for (new) trainees and one is for the future trainers. Also it will be investigated which part of the course will be made available as an e-course version. Not the complete course can be done in distant course version: especially the parts where role-play is the important part needs face to face meetings.

4 Evaluation and Discussion

The course evaluation by the 30 participants has been very positive. The method used was using questionnaires after each module of the course. Comments were made on the need for early inspection and preparation of the material (pilot course), the accessibility of the material (main course concerning the material for blind persons has been rather much based on MS-Powerpoint translated material). A unanimous outcome was that the course was well balanced, contributed to the knowledge of the trainees and thus judged as very successful.

Further implementation of the course is still under consideration. The partners in the USEM project are making a proposal to maintain the course and seek for future possibilities in administering the course at several places [4].

The course fills a gap in the European Union to get more educated end-users working in standardization. A new opportunity for enhancing the inclusion of requirements of end-users in standardization is the Stand4All project which runs partly in parallel with the USEM project and is seamless going into education of the present experts in standards processes. The experts now involved in standardization are then learning to include the E-Inclusion methodology in their own work and discussions.

Acknowledgements. The USEM project is funded by the European Commission as a Special Support Action of the 6-th Framework program "Policy oriented Research – Scientific support to policies" (INFSO-IST unit e-Inclusion).
The partners in the project are Standards organizations:

NEN (Dutch organization for standardization, NL)
CEN (European Committee for Standardization, located in BE)

User organizations:

CG-Raad/the Dutch Council of the Chronically ill and the Disabled (NL)
BAG SELBSTHILFE (DE)/umbrella of German self-help organizations
COCEMFE (ES) Spanish user organization

Organizations in disability and technology research and development :

VILANS (NL, main contractor)
FTB (DE)
KUL-RD (BE)

References

1. http://www.access-board.gov/index.htm,
   http://www.ada.gov/cguide.htm
2. http://ec.europa.eu/information_society/activities/
   einclusion/index_en.htm
   http://ec.europa.eu/information_society/policy/accessibility/
   deploy/pubproc/eso-m376/index_en.htm
3. http://www.usem-net.eu
4. Please contact the authors

Emotion Detection: Application of the Valence Arousal Space for Rapid Biological Usability Testing to Enhance Universal Access

Christian Stickel[1], Martin Ebner[1], Silke Steinbach-Nordmann[2],
Gig Searle[3], and Andreas Holzinger[3]

[1] Social Learning/Computing and Information Services, Graz University of Technology,
Steyrergasse 30/I, A-8010 Graz, Austria
[2] Fraunhofer Institute for Experimental Software Engineering (IESE)
67663 Kaiserslautern, Germany
[3] Institute of Medical Informatics, Statistics and Documentation, Research Unit HCI4MED
Medical University Graz, Auenbruggerplatz 2/5, A-8036 Graz, Austria
martin.ebner@tugraz.at, stickel@tugraz.at,
Silke.Steinbach-Nordmann@iese.fraunhofer.de,
gig.searle@meduni-graz.at, andreas.holzinger@meduni-graz.at

Abstract. Emotion is an important mental and physiological state, influencing cognition, perception, learning, communication, decision making, etc. It is considered as a definitive important aspect of user experience (UX), although at least well developed and most of all lacking experimental evidence. This paper deals with an application for emotion detection in usability testing of software. It describes the approach to utilize the valence arousal space for emotion modeling in a formal experiment. Our study revealed correlations between low performance and negative emotional states. Reliable emotion detection in usability tests will help to prevent negative emotions and attitudes in the final products. This can be a great advantage to enhance Universal Access.

Keywords: Biological Rapid Usability Testing, Valence, Arousal, Emotion.

1 Introduction

The principle of Universal Access [1] extends the definition of users to include people who would otherwise be excluded from information society by rapidly changing technology, e.g. the elderly and ageing [2]. Barriers are mostly not only physical but also mental [3]. The skill of adaptation decreases with age and slowly every new perception, which cannot be solved, is likely to create negative emotions, which in turn hinder the learning process and the motivation to adjust/change. However, mental barriers are not only a problem of the elderly but also for every non-expert end user.

The adaptation of a systems action to enable response to, even influence of, human emotions is a valuable goal for universal access. Nevertheless, if emotion detection is used as a usability tool in the software engineering lifecycle, major stressful issues could be eliminated before they even occur. However, the successful detection of

C. Stephanidis (Ed.): Universal Access in HCI, Part I, HCII 2009, LNCS 5614, pp. 615–624, 2009.
© Springer-Verlag Berlin Heidelberg 2009

emotions is not trivial and the question arises how to implement this in existing methods of usability engineering and how to interpret the changing of emotional states during a test, with regard to all possible influencing factors. An example from experimental psychology [4] shows that an unnoticed word previously associated with shock produces a galvanic skin response, even while subjects fail to notice its occurrence. So far, the measurement of minimal psycho physiological parameters during a users' test is sufficient to show changes in the autonomic nervous system (ANS). The use of biometrics in a usability context has been demonstrated by several previous work, e.g. [5], [6], [7], [8]. To meet the pragmatic and hedonic goals, which are related to the overall experience and results of human–computer interaction, we speak about User Experience (UX). [1] define this term as "A consequence of a user's internal state (predispositions, expectations, needs, motivation, mood, etc.), the characteristics of the designed system (e.g. complexity, purpose, usability, functionality, etc.) and the specific context (and/or the environment) within which the interaction occurs (e.g. organizational/social setting, meaningfulness of the activity, voluntariness of use, etc.)." Fun, or enjoyment, is a significantly important aspect of user experience with influence on overall satisfaction [10], [11]. The subjective experience of "joy of use" is a crucial factor, which, in the end, determines the success of a product. A software interface might be efficient and easy to use and thereby fulfilling the basic functional needs of the user, however if it creates bad experiences users won't like it, which will create an emotional barrier. Emotions have also an impact on cognitive processing during every interaction a user performs with an interface; For instance, joy allows unusual associations and improves creative problem solving [12]; on the contrary anxiety or stress constrains attention to features of the environment concerned with safety, danger and basically survival [13]. Every experience with the product increases or decreases the value a user gives it, which in turn influences the expectations and motivations to use the product. Motivation itself is a factor that influences learning behavior and tolerance towards errors, or as Norman states "Attractive things work better" [14]. A positive attitude on the part of the user towards the product will almost certainly overcome many barriers and the successful detection of emotions during user tests in the development process is crucial to this goal. However, a straightforward application of biometric methods alone will not reveal the dimension of emotions, which might be crucial to its adaption in the development process.

This paper covers an approach to utilizing the valence arousal space, which is a 2D model for emotion modeling [15] in a Usability performance test to extend and support standard usability methods [16].

2   Theoretical Background

Emotions are created every time a perception of important changes in the environment or in the physical body appears. Basically an emotion is a psychological state or process that functions in the management of maintaining the balance of information processes in the brain and the relevant goals. Every time an event is evaluated as relevant to a goal, an emotion is elicited. Positive emotions occur when the goal is advanced; while negative emotions occur when the goal is impeded. The core of an emotion is the readiness to act in a certain way [4], so some goals and plans can be prioritized rather than others. An emotion can interrupt ongoing interactions; it tends to change the course of action, e.g. if the users' goal of browsing a certain website for information is continually impeded by the slow loading of the site and the relevance of this site to their goal is low, they will change their course of action and search for the information on another website. If they can only find the information on this site, then the relevance towards the goal is high, the frustration tolerance is higher and so the likelihood of leaving the site will be lower.

Knowing the process now, the emotions still need to be labeled. Throughout the last 150 years there have been several theories on basic emotions with changing "fundamental emotions", including anger, aversion, disgust, desire, happiness, interest, surprise sorrow, etc. The different theories also have different bases, such as facial expressions, hardwired, instinctive or tendencies in relation to action [17]. However, the present dominant theory of emotion in neuroscience research lists a discrete and limited set of basic emotions.

So far, the approach of Schlosberg [15] is still up-to-date; it categorizes all kind of emotions in a two-dimensional model, postulating that every emotion has two aspects: a cognitive and a physiological component. The two dimensions are called valence and arousal. There's also a broad agreement that at least one more dimension of emotion exists, however with unclear definitions. According to Huether [18] there are three basic emotions, namely: joy (valence), anxiety (arousal) and surprise. He states that all other emotions can be categorized in one of these dimensions. Hence, a third dimension could be surprise, however, it could also be time or intensity and was not used in the present study. The 2D model of emotion therefore is expedient, as it allows an a priori reduction of complexity and better application for usability testing.

2.1 Modeling and Classification of Emotions

Once the accordant data is gathered, it's quite straightforward to classify emotions in the 2D valence-arousal space. Arousal describes the physical activation and valence the pleasantness or hedonic value.

An emotion such as stress, for instance, is modeled as high arousal and low valence, while joy and elation would be high arousal and also high valence. The arousal component can be measured with psycho physiologic methods, such as Skin Conductance Level (SCL), Heart Rate Variability (HRV) or Electroencephalography (EEG). Changes in the sympathetic and parasympathetic nervous system allow conclusions on the physical activation to be drawn.

The valence component is more difficult, as it consists of cognitions. Valence can be determined by the right questions and questionnaires. There are, however, also approaches to measure and calculate the valence from physiologic data. Chanel [19] reports the successful use of pattern classification to distinguish between three specific areas of the valence-arousal from both peripheral and EEG signals. The original Schlosberg model was later enhanced by [20] (for a discussion see [21]) and called "circumplex model of affect" (fig. 1a): all affective states arise from two fundamental neurophysiologic systems related to valence and arousal. Specific emotions arise from activation patterns within these two systems, accompanied by cognitive interpretations and the labeling of the physiological experiences, e.g. in this model joy and happiness are conceptualized as a combination of strong activation in the neural systems associated with pleasure and moderate activation in the neural systems associated with arousal. These facile ways of modeling emotions in two dimensions [15], [20] can be mapped nicely to the dimensions of User Experience as shown in fig. 1b) and thus provide a measure for the overall UX.

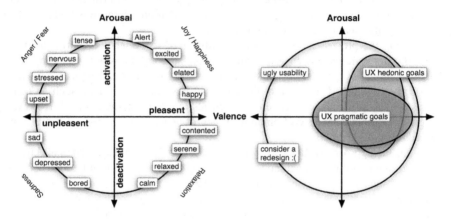

Fig. 1. a) The circumplex model of affect from Russel [20] b) applied to UX dimensions

Thereby the users' pragmatic and hedonic goals from UX correspond with certain areas of emotional states. Pragmatic goals concern functional metrics such as effectiveness and efficiency, whereby one can anticipate that some stress and unpleasantness will be accepted by the user in order to reach a goal. Hedonic goals, such as stimulation, identification, evocation, however, require a pleasant experience.

2.2 Measuring Emotions

Changes of physiological signals can be analyzed for stress arising during an interaction of a user with a product. These signals are regulated by the autonomous nervous system (ANS) and can be respiration, muscle tension, skin temperature or clamminess. More obvious signals are facial expressions, tone of voice, articulation, posture or gesture [22]. Each of these signals can be monitored or observed with some kind of sensor and method. The present study focuses on two these of these methods, which are measures of heart rate (HR) and skin conductance level (SCL). Skin conductivity depends on the activity of respiratory glands. This means the more sweat is produced the more electric current will be transported. SCL is generally a perfect indicator of the emotional state, as simple stress stimuli are followed by a rapid rise of skin conductivity within seconds. Muter et al. [23] found that especially SCL seems to be a good indicator for the overall usability of software, as they found a correlation between user-hostile systems and an increase of SCL. The heart rate (HR) is calculated as the number of contractions of the heart in a minute. It is therefore counted in "beats per minute" (bpm). The heart of an adult beats at about 70-75 bpm in resting state and 80-100 bpm during the day. However this is varies among people, depending on their physiology, age and stress levels, when the body is dealing with stress the heart rate increases. From the HR the heart rate variability (HRV) can be calculated. High performance mental task is usually accompanied by an increase of heart rate (HR), blood pressure (BP) and a decrease of heart rate variability (HRV) [24]. Thereby the task complexity is positive correlated to the changes of the parameters, as the decrease of task complexity will lead to opposite changes.

2.3 Aspects of Emotion Detection in Practice

As the levels of arousal are subjective, it is also necessary to collect basic data from the test person in a relaxed state, which can then be compared to the data collected during the test situation. Further, it must be noted that the levels fluctuate during the day, especially when EEG is applied, so constant time windows for testing have to be defined. In order to build the valence-arousal space, the valence dimension has to be determined continually. Therefore it is sufficient to ask the user. This can be done with a six-point scale from UNPLEASENT to PLEASANT after every task.

The skin conductance level (SCL) is a method of observing event related changes of the ANS, as this parameter responds very fast. The place of the sensor should be chosen carefully, because pressure and movement influence it. The placement of the sensors at the fingertips, as it was done in the present study, might therefore be reliable, however it restricts user input on the keyboard. Using the heart-rate variability (HRV) means taking a delay into account, as the heart-rate (HR) does not change as fast as the SCL. HRV in combination with HR is a reliable stress detector, however bigger time windows are needed.

3 Methods and Materials

We used a modified NPL Performance Measurement method [25] and tested a learning management system, which was developed at Graz University of Technology. The approach included the combination of two formal usability methods, additional psycho physiological measures and valence/difficulty rating after every task, in order to assess the users' emotions. Two different parts of the system were examined, whereby two user groups with 20 subjects each accomplished five fundamental tasks for every system part.

3.1 Research Questions

Our study was targeted to investigate connections of performance metrics and emotions. It was anticipated that the tested system would have a good learnability. The first hypothesis (**H1**) was that the stress level of all test users decreases during the test, as they rapidly become accustomed to the interface. The second hypothesis (**H2**) assumed a positive correlation between user efficiency and the hedonic quality of the classified emotions. This implicates that those users who performed badly showed negative emotions, while users that performed well showed positive emotions. As different psycho physiologic methods had been used, the secondary question was how the results of these methods would correlate. Another question was the correlation of the emotion dimensions with the task difficulty rating and overall SUS rating.

3.2 Experimental Design

The test was split in a control condition (K1), the performance test (L1) and a short thinking aloud test (L2). Right after test, the System Usability Scale (SUS) questionnaire from Brooke [26] was used to derive User Satisfaction. During the whole test psycho physiological measures of EEG, SCL and HR were recorded. In L1 and L2 additional videos and screen recordings were made (examples can be seen in [8]. In the control condition, the test persons were asked to relax in order to get some base data. The relaxation process was supported by a Brainlight system (http://www.brainlight.com). It was used as a stimulation unit to induce relief by Steady State Visual Evoked Potentials (SSVEP), changing in a frequency range between 8 and 12 Hz for the duration of 10 minutes. The EEG recordings were done with an IBVA 3 electrode headband EEG from Psychiclabs Inc. (http://www.psychiclabs.net) at a rate of 512 Hz. The headband uses only 3 electrodes, so it can record an EEG of the frontal lobe only. For SCL and HR recordings a Lightstone from the wild divine project (http://www.wilddivine.com) was used. The HRV was later on calculated from the raw HR data. All data was recorded and synchronized using apple script on an Apple powerbook.

3.3 Analysis Procedure

For the control condition and the main tasks, the averages of SCL and HRV were calculated, per user and task. This data was then normalized in order to be comparable to the other datasets. The normalized values of all psycho physiological metrics from all test persons were summarized in a single database and combined with the outcome of the valence/difficulty task ratings. The data was then split into two groups (best/worst) according to the metric of user efficiency. Then the intersection of the arousal data per task, as well as the valence rating, was calculated over all users per group and normalized (see fig. 2), providing the necessary data for building the overall valence-arousal space. The space was built twice, first using HRV as arousal measure and then SCL. In a further approach the running difference measure of the normalized SCL (scaled by the maximum range of the data) was used to get an approximation for the instantaneous change in slope of the original signal. This signal was then thresholded at different levels, in order to get a sense of the number of peaks of the original SCL signal. Thereby, small thresholds should catch smaller peaks, while larger thresholds should catch only few very large peaks, which are usually correlated to high stress events.

3.4 Results

The analysis revealed a positive correlation between the user efficiency (performance) and the emotional state, determined in the valence arousal space. As can be seen in figure 2., the task results for the "worst" group show negative emotions, here less valence and a bigger variance in arousal, while the "best" group is distributed in an area of positive valence with less variance in arousal. Every datapoint in fig. 2 represents the average data of one task (for each group). The data is normalized on a (-2 / 2) scale. Fig 1 shows how to label the results with actual emotions, respectively mapping them to UX dimensions.

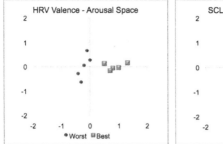
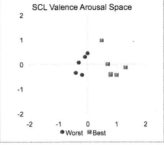

Fig. 2. a) Valence / Arousal (HRV)   b) Valence / Arousal (SCL)

The comparison of both groups' averaged changes of HRV and SCL (fig. 3) over all tasks shows that HRV changes (fig. 3a) of the "worst" group range from stress to relaxation, while the "best" group shows no significant changes during the tasks. SCL changes (fig. 3b) shows an increasing trend for the "worst" and a decreasing trend for the "best". The success in Task 2 was very low (> 0. 5) and there the overall HRV decreased rapidly, which is a clear sign for stress. Figure 3 b) shows that the overall SCL of the "worst" increased during the whole test, beginning at task 2, showing stress.

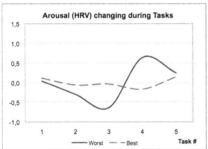
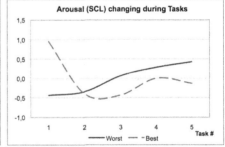

Fig. 3. a) HRV best vs. worst group   b) SCL best vs. worst group

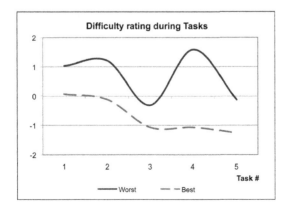

Fig. 4. Task Difficulty rating of best vs. worst group

The task difficulty rating displayed in fig. 4, shows that the "worst" group rated the overall difficulty higher and the variance of their rating is higher.

The user satisfaction metric, derived from the SUS, showed no significant difference between the two groups. The approach of counting large SCL peaks showed little, but no significant, differences between the groups.

4 Discussion

Hypothesis (H1) expected a decreasing stress level for all users, however this was only true for the successful group. Rather than the expected (H1) improvement in the worst group, a downward spiral was observed. Failure in a task appeared to increase the stress, which in turn appeared to increase the likelihood of failure in the following task. Hypothesis (H2) that expected a high user efficiency accompanied by positive emotions and vice versa low user efficiency with negative emotions was found to be true. The "Worst" group showed a high variance in the HRV values and a continuous increase of the SCL values, these are strong indicators for stress, as the valence-arousal space also shows. The high variance in the "worst" groups rating of the task difficulty in combination with the physiologic data is hard to explain. The 4th task was rated as very difficult although the HRV showed relaxation and the overall task success was moderate. The 2nd task was also rated as difficult and the HRV showed tension, however this task had an overall low task success. A hypothesis is that the relaxation reaction in task 4 was a counter reaction of the parasympathetic nervous system to the stress reaction, which can be seen in task 2 and 3 (low HRV Value). The valence-arousal space showed that this group tended to be frustrated. The "Best" group showed balanced values in HRV. The difficulty rating and SCL have a decreasing tendency. The balanced variance of the HRV might count for concentration. The decreasing SCL shows relief, which in combination with the valence can be seen as positive emotion. The approach of the peak extraction for SCL, for the overall test, showed no differences between the groups. So far, it is only reasonable to use this measure if the time of the task is invariant, particularly for small thresholds, because there will be more peaks in longer time windows. Further the number of peaks must be counted for every task in order to show any correlations between SCL peaks and task success or performance. So far, it can be concluded that the tested system elicited negative emotions for a group of users whose performance was low on the metric of user efficiency. These negative emotions are clues for a deeper analysis of the problems of this user group, as the ultimate goal should be a shaping of the user experience towards positive emotions. For users with a high efficiency positive emotions were detected. The area of the positive emotions can be mapped to the pragmatic goals of user experience, which means that the system fulfils the functional needs for these users. Emotions modulate almost all human interactions. If they are detected and synchronized to events or tasks the gained insight will help detecting causes of hidden irritation or frustration and provide a more complete picture of the overall user experience. Detecting issues when products are causing stress or aggravation will help developers to target areas for redesign.

Acknowledgements. This work has been partly funded by the European Commission under the project no. FP6-IST-2005-045056 EMERGE.

References

1. Stephanidis, C., Savidis, A.: Universal Access in the Information Society: Methods, Tools Interaction Technologies. Universal Access in the Information Society 1(1), 40–55 (2001)
2. Adams, R., Russell, C.: Lessons from ambient intelligence prototypes for universal access and the user experience. In: Stephanidis, C., Pieper, M. (eds.) ERCIM Ws UI4ALL 2006. LNCS, vol. 4397, pp. 229–243. Springer, Heidelberg (2007)
3. Holzinger, A., Searle, G., Nischelwitzer, A.: On some Aspects of Improving Mobile Applications for the Elderly. In: Stephanidis, C. (ed.) HCI 2007. LNCS, vol. 4554, pp. 923–932. Springer, Heidelberg (2007)
4. Frijda, N.H.: The emotions. Cambridge University Press, Cambridge (1986)
5. Riseberg, J., Klein, J., Fernandez, R., Picard, R.W.: Frustrating the user on purpose: using biosignals in a pilot study to detect the user's emotional state. In: Conference on Human Factors in Computing Systems, pp. 227–228 (1998)
6. Ward, R.D., Marsden, P.H.: Physiological responses to different Web page designs. International Journal of Human-Computer Studies 59(1-2), 199–212 (2003)
7. Stickel, C., Fink, J., Holzinger, A.: Enhancing Universal Access – EEG based Learnability Assessment. In: Stephanidis, C. (ed.) HCI 2007. LNCS, vol. 4556, pp. 813–822. Springer, Heidelberg (2007)
8. Stickel, C., Scerbakov, A., Kaufmann, T., Ebner, M.: Usability Metrics of Time and Stress - Biological Enhanced Performance Test of a University Wide Learning Management System. In: Holzinger, A. (ed.) 4th Symposium of the Workgroup Human-Computer Interaction and Usability Engineering of the Austrian-Computer-Society, pp. 173–184. Springer, Berlin (2008)
9. Hassenzahl, M., Tractinsky, N.: User experience - a research agenda. Behaviour & Information Technology 25(2), 91–97 (2006)
10. Cockton, G.: Putting Value into E-valu-ation. In: Law, E.L.-C., Hvannberg, E.T., Cockton, G. (eds.) Maturing Usability: Quality in Software, Interaction and Value, pp. 287–317. Springer, Heidelberg (2007)
11. Ebner, M., Holzinger, A.: Successful Implementation of User-Centered Game Based Learning in Higher Education – an Example from Civil Engineering. Computers & Education 49(3), 873–890 (2007)
12. Isen, A.M., Daubman, K.A., Nowicki, G.P.: Positive affect facilitates creative problem solving. Journal of Personality and Social Psychology 52, 1122–1131 (1987)
13. Adams, R.: Decision and stress: cognition and e-accessibility in the information workplace. Springer Universal Access in the Information Society 5(4), 363–379 (2007)
14. Norman, D.A.: Emotional Design: Why we love or hate everyday things. Basic Books, New York (2004)
15. Schlosberg, H.: 3-Dimensions of Emotions. Psychological Review 61(2), 81–88 (1954)
16. Holzinger, A.: Usability Engineering for Software Developers. Communications of the ACM 48(1), 71–74 (2005)
17. Ortony, A., Turner, T.J.: What's basic about basic Emotions. Psychological Review 97(3), 315–331 (1990)
18. Hüther, G.: Biology of fear. Vandenhoeck & Ruprecht, Göttingen (1997)

19. Chanel, G., Ansari-Asl, K., Pun, T.: Valence-arousal evaluation using physiological signals in an emotion recall paradigm. In: IEEE International Conference on Systems, Man and Cybernetics, pp. 375–380. IEEE, Los Alamitos (2007)
20. Russell, J.A.: A circumplex model of affect. Journal of Personality and Social Psychology 39, 1161–1178 (1980)
21. Remington, N.A., Fabrigar, L.R., Visser, P.S.: Reexamining the circumplex model of affect. Journal of Personality and Social Psychology 79(2), 286–300 (2000)
22. Picard, R.W., Vyzas, E., Healey, J.: Toward machine emotional intelligence: Analysis of affective physiological state. IEEE Transactions on Pattern Analysis and Machine Intelligence 23(10), 1175–1191 (2001)
23. Muter, P., Furedy, J.J., Vincent, A., Pelcowitz, T.: User-Hostile Systems and Patterns of Psychophysiological Activity. Computers in Human Behavior 9(1), 105–111 (1993)
24. Schapkin, S.A., Freude, G., Erdmann, U., Ruediger, H.: Stress and managers performance: Age-related changes in psychophysiological reactions to cognitive load. In: Harris, D. (ed.) HCII 2007 and EPCE 2007. LNCS, vol. 4562, pp. 417–425. Springer, Heidelberg (2007)
25. Rengger, R., Macleod, M., Bowden, R., Drynan, A., Blayney, M.: MUSiC Performance Measurement Handbook, V2. NPL, DITC, Teddington (UK) (1993)
26. Brooke, J.: SUS: A "quick and dirty" usability scale. In: Jordan, P.W., Thomas, B., Weerdmeester, B.A., McClelland, A.L. (eds.) Usability Evaluation in Industry. Taylor & Francis, Abington (1996)

Teaching and Learning HCI

Harold Thimbleby

Future Interaction Technology Lab
Swansea University, Wales
harold@thimbleby.net

Abstract. We consider how to teach effectively with particular reference to HCI. HCI can be taught to explicitly empower students to engage with their own learning. Further, HCI motivates because HCI empowers students to make a valuable and lasting contribution to the world.

Keywords: Teaching and learning, HCI (human-computer interaction).

"The main part of intellectual education is not the acquisition of facts but learning how to make facts live." *Oliver Wendell Holmes, Jr.*

1 Introduction

The world could be a better place, and of all the things that need improving, user interfaces should be near the top of the list, because bad design of user interfaces makes many other things and experiences worse. A bad user interface for a web site can cause users to make expensive errors; or a bad car radio design can distract a driver from attending to the road that they have an accident. A badly designed user interface for a hospital drug delivery system (an infusion pump) can induce nurses to make fatal drug overdoses. A badly designed web site can detrimentally influence millions of people: it has a huge and hidden social cost. Indeed many user interfaces are bad, and their faults are so obvious — at least to those who know HCI and have the background, inclination and education to *see* the faults — they clearly ought to be taken as a point of high leverage to invest in to improve quality of life. **The most effective way to improve user interfaces is by improving HCI education**, for each educated and motivated HCI student will go on to have many opportunities to continue to improve user interfaces far into the future, and improved user interfaces will leverage improved experiences for all their users. (If you do not believe user interfaces are bad, please read *Press On* [12].)

Many user interfaces are bad yet we have the processes and knowledge to do better, therefore HCI *education* must have failed the developers or marketing people or managers who create and distribute the current poor systems — it has certainly failed the users of these systems, the people affected detrimentally by them. At face value, then, the problems of HCI are symptoms of a lack of appropriate and effective education. The people who know HCI are somehow not in the right place to use it, or the people who need HCI are unaware of it, or the HCI that has been taught has not motivated students sufficiently to apply their knowledge. Perhaps we have only taught students to pass exams and not to use their knowledge in the world of work?

C. Stephanidis (Ed.): Universal Access in HCI, Part I, HCII 2009, LNCS 5614, pp. 625–635, 2009.
© Springer-Verlag Berlin Heidelberg 2009

Unfortunately, questions about education and understanding a subject are rarely addressed in the academic or research literature about that subject.

Consider the instructions for writing ACM papers, the ACM being the leading international computing organization. The ACM computing classification system gives an explicit list of topics, but these classifications do not expect articles that talk about how any subject is acquired, understood, used or taught; they expect topics like "human factors," not the topics of *thinking about or reflecting about* "human factors," whether teaching, communicating, or even using it. It is as if just stating facts are sufficient, as if nobody needs to think about how facts are presented or learnt, whether by researchers or by students, or even how such facts may be effectively communicated from author to readers, and how those ideas are then applied to change the world. Ironically, while computer science includes topics like communication (and HCI human-human and human-computer communication, *etc*) we ignore communication specifically to communicate human knowledge about our own areas of work! (This view will be encountered again, below, as an expression of Ramsden's Theory 1; and as the concept of interactional expertise.)

Kline [7] presents many ways that our academic culture undervalues pedagogy — pedagogy being one way of understanding and thinking about a subject. For example, while many organizations and industries have research arms, many universities have no research in-house into one of their core activities, specifically teaching. (Many universities research education, but they do so academically, not to enhance the university's own teaching processes.)

How then should we teach and think about teaching HCI? Teaching is the highest form of understanding; if we do not understand how to teach, we do not understand our subject. If we are not thinking about teaching, we are not thinking about communicating. Even the most hardened researchers must surely be concerned about the impact their research papers have; in fact, their research papers must surely aim to teach their readers new ideas and new ways of thinking about their subject. This isn't so different from wanting to teach students. Ironically, many researchers see prestige in reaching *fewer* researchers, rather than in being accessible to *more* students.

According to Ramsden's excellent survey [10], teachers (for instance, teachers of HCI) consider there are three approaches: **Theory 1** teaching is telling or transmitting facts; **Theory 2** teaching is organizing student activity; and, **Theory 3** teaching is about making learning possible.

That is, teachers adopt a tacit stance to teaching and learning, which can be put into one of these three classes depending on their approach. Moreover, students adopt a complementary approach, and subsequently the teacher's tacit views are reinforced as they teach better to meet the expectations they have created.

Many HCI textbooks are encyclopedias of knowledge about HCI techniques, as if their authors fall into a Theory 1 approach, into a style that supports an assumed Theory 1 style of teaching. The teacher's job, using such books, is to teach the students the facts of HCI, preferably as presented in the particular books chosen. The students know they will be examined on these facts, and they demand clearer teaching of those facts. Theory 1 encourages a style of thinking that every fact must be covered, and that it is the teacher in conjunction with the textbook author whose job it is to provide all facts that need teaching.

Different subjects and different stages of learning in those subjects call for different approaches. In an early anatomy or geography course there are indeed a lot of independent facts to learn, but these facts give way to deeper learning as the student progresses. Similarly in HCI, there are indeed many important facts to learn — what is affordance? what is contextual design? what is immersion? what are ethical experiments? — before one can build deeper knowledge and understanding.

There are of course many areas and stages of learning where Ramsden's Theory 1 may be entirely appropriate, most obviously in areas with many basic facts (e.g., anatomy) and at elementary levels when the student is not expected to need real understanding of the subject but needs to learn the definitions. This a student might be taught to "always end a sentence with a full stop." At school, there may be no room for debate on this fact. Yet when the student becomes a designer, they will discover that posters often have sentences without full stops, and that one can decide, not on rigid grammar, but on (for example) visual criteria, or on unrelated non-grammatical criteria such as whether your client will pay. Because language is necessarily first taught in elementary ways to young learners, many of us have grown up thinking that our use of language is rigidly constrained by what we were taught [3]. We've learnt (mostly in childhood) that it's *just* non-negotiable rules — unrelated facts. Perhaps this formative learning experience, learning language, has influenced our approach to other learning and teaching?

Theory 1 is necessary, but it is not always sufficient. We spent many of our formative years being taught elementary facts, and it is understandable how we end up ourselves being teachers who emphasize facts. If we are not careful, we end up with students who know some facts, namely, exactly the ones we teach them to pass their courses — but they don't know how to think for themselves about HCI, and are therefore unable to apply their knowledge to the work environment they later find themselves in. Ultimately, as students graduate and get jobs, we end up with interactive systems — web sites, ticket machines, voice menus, aircraft, medical equipment — that have bad user interfaces. Or as students graduate and become academics, their views influence how they participate in the academic community: they become referees (of research) and teachers (of students). The Theory 1 attitude affects referees for research papers and research proposals [11]: a common criticism in HCI refereeing is that some *facts* or references (pointers to facts) were missing (i.e., facts from a different subdomain of HCI that the referee wishes to emphasize), as opposed to some *reasoning* was flawed.

Collins and Evans [2] make a related distinction: there are two sorts of expertise as outcomes of teaching: *contributory expertise* and *interactional expertise*. Interactional expertise is the knowledge and ability to talk about a subject, perhaps passing off as real expertise, whereas contributory expertise also has the skills and know-how to work in or contribute to the field. Clearly, we want students with growing contributory expertise, rather than just the interactional expertise sufficient to pass assessments. In these terms, our failure is to teach students who pass off interactional expertise (which we assess) as contributory expertise (which they need to work, when they go on to design and evaluate user interfaces).

Ultimately, then, Theory 1 is not an effective form of teaching for HCI, at least if we want students to contribute to improving the world. Indeed, Ramsden makes it clear that Theory 3 is, for most things, better.

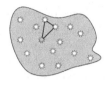

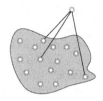

Fig 1. A visualization of all known HCI concepts, represented as stars

Fig 2. Forgotten facts (represented by a few missing stars) may be triangulated from known facts

Fig 3. New discoveries extending existing knowledge are made by triangulating from the known to the unknown

An example of Theory 3 teaching comes from Feynman [5], who is widely recognized as one of the most inspiring teachers of physics. Figure 1 shows an imaginary map of all HCI ideas and concepts within a region drawn as a grey blob; figure 2 shows how a student might be able to reconstruct a forgotten fact from several other remembered facts. Probably a student would use some remembered facts, some books, and some experiments: triangulation is somewhat of a simplification to the idea. (In reality, HCI is so complex that lots of facts would be needed to triangulate, and perhaps the idea might better be called interpolation.)

The purpose of teaching a student is so that they are eventually able to construct new knowledge — it would be a sorry state of affairs if they could only ever know less than their teacher! Figure 3 shows how the same triangulation idea works for a student discovering new knowledge. The point is, by teaching a student how to connect ideas together, they are empowered to learn new things, and even ideas they were not directly taught.

Feynman sees the blobs in these figures as knowledge, as potentially known by everyone. Instead the blobs might be used to represent the student's own knowledge. Then, that star in figure 3 might be some x a student missed. It is useful for a student to realize that x is missing and be able to work it out; this is far better than only knowing *at most* what they were taught from figure 1.

Perry's study of how students learn suggests that the least sophisticated students, students at early stages of learning (a point some students never progress beyond), want to learn *true* facts [9; 12]. Students at this level thus dovetail their expectations with a teacher's use of the Theory 1 approach to teaching. Unfortunately, both Theory 1 and Perry's low end of sophistication interact in a vicious circle: they support each other, and are ideal for teachers and students with little confidence in the subject. Neither enables the students to go beyond the teacher, so the students are limited to exactly what is taught. Students soon will only do work that leads to assessment. It is but a short step to automating the assessment, typically with multiple-choice questions, to see exactly what facts that the student has learned: once automated, the student is even denied any flexibility in interpreting the right answers.

Dweck identifies a personality dimension, performance—learning [4]. A performance- or outcome-oriented student wants to do well, and tends to avoid problems they find hard.. In contrast, a learning-oriented student prefers acquiring skills and understanding, and thus accepts making mistakes and under-performing in the short term.

The dimension is interesting because it correlates with many other personality factors, attitudes that reinforce each other. Thus performance orientation has also been called "fixed mindset" versus the "growth mindset" of the learning orientation. A performance-oriented student believes they have a fixed natural ability (or not) to achieve in particular areas (like sport, mathematics, HCI); they are endowed with specific abilities such as intelligence, and thus they are either born good at a subject or born bad at it. They believe they will never be much good at things they find "naturally" hard. In contrast, a learning-oriented student revels in challenges, and believes that abilities, such as intelligence, can be developed.

In formal education, students are generally assessed on performance rather than learning. It suits educators in many ways; performance is easier to assess than learning, and if students do badly, a teacher can hide behind a performance model: the students were bad anyway. In contrast, if a learning-oriented teacher has poor students, this is a challenge to try to help them find out how to learn better.

Dweck has shown that rewarding performance can make students worse when later work is more challenging and requires more effort; only praising good performance weakens a student's resolve to persevere through later failure. Learned helplessness is therefore a real problem for performance-oriented students: rather than risk not looking smart and risk the failure of poor performance (e.g., on an assessment) they sabotage themselves so their poor performance is due to some non-intellectual or less-personal factor, such as disorganization. If they put little effort in to a task, either they will do well (because they are naturally good), or they will do poorly (because they didn't try): it is thus safer for a performance-oriented student to learn helplessness in the face of anticipated weak performance or required effort.

Dweck's psychological model supports the descriptive views of Ramsden's Theory 3 and Feynman's triangulation. Performance-oriented students are threatened by the success of other students and they can therefore set out to drag a class down to their level. On the other hand, learning-oriented students are inspired by other people's success. It is important for a teacher to nurture learning and an *attitude* to embrace learning. Fortunately few real problems in HCI have known solutions — both teacher and students have to find out the answers by doing experiments. This puts the teacher on a level with students, develops learning-orientation, and encourages peer learning.

2   Teaching HCI as a Form of HCI

Teaching is about getting students to learn and engage with ideas, ultimately to own them. Correspondingly, we can consider that HCI is concerned with getting users to learn and engage with ideas about interactive systems. It's the same thing. Research in HCI, such as Carroll's classic work on "minimalism" [1], suggests that users are best helped when instruction or training follows four principles:

1   Choose an action-oriented approach; provide immediate opportunity to act;
2   Anchor the ideas in a task domain; select real tasks;
3   Support error recognition and recovery; prevent mistakes where possible;
4   Support reading to do, study and locate; be brief — don't spell out everything.

Of course Carroll elaborates these principles further, but even from this brief summary, it is interesting to note that Carroll's principle 4 manages to simultaneously contradict the "bad" Theory 1 teaching and support the "good" Theory 3 teaching. HCI itself suggests that HCI *teaching* should provide an immediate opportunity to act, based on real tasks, should prevent mistakes, and be brief. Indeed, a significant part of any HCI syllabus should be user learning, a topic that makes a useful counterpoint to students learning HCI, and is an opportunity for students to be taught learning and learning skills explicitly, something that, sadly, few have encountered in their higher education. Carroll is only one example; as HCI is concerned with the user experience, almost any HCI issue begs an analogy to teaching and learning. Dweck's notions of performance and learning orientation relate not just to students but also to users who have to decide whether to achieve results quickly or whether to learn more advanced features of a system so they can do even better, but by delaying immediate results.

Kline suggests that the worst sort of teaching presents unmotivated facts [7] (cf Ramsden's Theory 1); the facts may be motivated for the teacher, but to the student they seem pointless. Carroll's point 3, above, that suggests that students might learn by making mistakes and learning from them. It is fascinating to draw parallels between students' learning and mistakes with users' learning and mistakes: there are plenty of stories of aircraft accidents, clinical incidents ([6] is a highly-motivating resource, including Human Factors studies), and other disasters that illustrate HCI issues. Even my own fumbling with projectors and computers can be recruited to illustrate HCI issues, and certainly when students do presentations to the class their inevitable problems with equipment can very usefully be turned around to explore the latent errors in the design of the equipment they are trying to use under the real pressure of presenting to their peers.

Theory 1 does not do well from Carroll's perspective either. It is hard for a student to make a mistake when their teacher adopts Theory 1 and for them not to be simply wrong; there is no incentive to learn from mistakes. Worse, as Theory 1 approach leads to simple assessment, it's likely that the only feedback students get on their understanding is when they are formally assessed: a significant disincentive to make mistakes or even explore around the subject. Why would a learner experiment, possibly making mistakes, when doing so guarantees getting fewer marks?

Ong suggests [8] that ever since the invention of the alphabet (one of the earliest technologies) we have taken it for granted that knowledge can be written down. Further, if it can be written down, we can teach what is written. But that is Theory 1. Notice how it seems obvious we must do this, for how else (it seems) can the knowledge of writing be preserved?

Rather, ask why do we lecture when we have writing, and books in particular? The answer is that we should not teach facts, for that encourages shallow learning. Instead, we need to motivate, make accessible, *enthuse*. As Carroll's work suggests, we need to get students engaged with real tasks as quickly as possible. Why do students go to lectures when they could read books or read off the web? Somehow the interaction and excitement of the lecturer is supposed to rub off in a way that the textualized book or web page does not permit. Teaching is performance (in the theatrical sense), not just instilling facts.

Most universities have adopted computerized teaching systems. These provide ideal HCI hunting grounds, and in exploring them students not only learn to think about HCI in a domain that affects them, but they also learn more about learning.

3 Personal Values

We, whether students or teachers, are all different and we all have different perspectives to bring to the teaching and learning forum. As teachers, we have had formative experiences as students ourselves, and sometimes we tacitly emphasize personal values rather than ones supported by good pedagogy. I am no exception.

Here are some values I consider very important. My experience, as is obvious, influences the experience of my students and even the students who choose to come on my courses. This biased sampling reinforces my prejudices! You do not need to agree with me, but I think you need to work out your own framework.

Teaching and learning is fun. If people are not enjoying what they are doing, this in itself is demotivating. If students enjoy their work, they will do it better, they will be more committed to working on it, working hard, and thinking deeply about it. And work that a student has done that they have enjoyed will be more enjoyable to mark.

Teaching and learning is fire. It's not just fun, it's serious fun: fire in our hearts, fire that spreads, fire that lights the imagination. It's about things we feel strongly about — nothing luke warm. By teaching we light up students and are more effective than in ordinary jobs where we would have no such leverage. In each class we want to inspire especially those students who are sparked by the subject and are going to carry the flames forward.

Teaching and learning is exploration. I know the terrain, but I want students to find things out for themselves, and especially find out things I don't know. Because my lectures are interactive, students like leading me down garden paths. The students think they are distracting me; but I know we are exploring the HCI issues of what they are interested in. In HCI we are lucky, for there are so many unknowns, and so many new questions that can be answered by student exploration.

Teaching and learning are interactive. I do not go into lectures to tell students what I know; I go in to enthuse them, and that means finding our what they want to know, and apprenticing them with me to have deeper understanding, as I take what they know into areas they do not yet know they need to know. I am very reluctant to provide handouts, because the handouts are not the lectures; I have very few facts on slides used in lectures — mostly they are pictures that create discussion, and help organize my lecture so I cover planned topics. But a student who fails to come to a lecture and wants "the notes" won't be able to tell whether the slides are examples, say, of good or bad practice!

There is too much in HCI to teach in any single course. I do not presume that what I like in HCI is what will engage my students, and the early parts of my courses involves negotiating with the students what they will learn and engage with. I hope they want to learn about my preferred topics, of course, but if they want to learn about (say) CSCW, I'd rather help them learn that and get involved with the subject than just go through the motions of teaching them my agenda but they never properly engage again with it in the rest of their lives. Because my courses not assessed by exams, I do not need to teach to a prior syllabus; and if I have to use exams, then I want to set the exams *after* this period of negotiation.

Because I take this approach, my lectures potentially do not teach enough facts. I repeatedly emphasize that students have to take responsibility for learning facts: there are plenty of good books. Part of my teaching therefore covers reviewing the strengths and weaknesses of relevant books, including my own [12].

Teaching and learning is research. The students can find out things, test ideas, and find out things none of us knew to start with. The problem with this style of teaching is that it is hard to predetermine outcomes; it is certainly nearly impossible to provide notes beforehand. (But notes fall into Ramsden's Theory 1 view.) This stance makes it particularly difficult to support students with special needs who benefit from polished material and material presented in different media. Nevertheless, any special needs are a problem for the *whole* class (and any helpers), not just the teacher, and — most especially in HCI — initial homework for students can be to search for solutions and work out how to implement them in the session.

Teaching and learning encourages mistakes. Educational environments are a safe place to learn about recognizing and managing errors: if you are not dropping the balls, in juggling, you aren't learning anything. This short paper has said little about syllabus/curriculum, but a very important area that needs emphasizing (especially in HCI) is testing, user testing and debugging — iterative design and design discovery. Most HCI problems would have been avoided if their designers/developers had learned that systems are *always* inadequate and need further testing.

Teaching and learning is formative. The students want feedback about their achievements; I want feedback from them about my teaching — and both of us want it formatively, not at the end of the course. I believe I can do better, and I encourage students to give me feedback, to point out mistakes or things they like. Indeed, as Carroll [1] wanted with user training, if students can recognize my mistakes, I am lifting them from passive learning to active participation. By discussing mistakes in lectures, they are learning much more useful attitudes and skills.

Teaching and learning is open. There are many horrible arguments, real and imagined, for being secretive about teaching and learning. Failure is private. Success causes envy. People may steal my good ideas. It surprises me how rarely teachers share insights into each other's work — even if they know about it. I feel I am *intruding* when I go to other lecturer's classes! (And no colleague has been to one of my own classes for a long time.)

I am increasingly assessing students in open ways: for example, asking them to do coursework as posters, not essays. Then an afternoon's poster conference can both have me marking the coursework (and interacting helpfully with the students at the same time), as the system requires, but more importantly each student sees the quality of each other student's work. They learn by my creating open processes.

Teaching and learning is reflective. In addition to the obvious HCI content, I also teach how I teach and why I choose particular approaches, and I teach how students may learn better, and I do this within the course. We all then engage consciously with the teaching and learning process, and renegotiate changes each time I teach. I encourage students to think explicitly about how they want to be successful. I ask them to review and analyze which courses and styles they find helpful.

This approach to teaching is analogous to putting iterative design into practice, except I apply the benefits of formative evaluation for teaching. The analogy works powerfully when combined with actually teaching iterative design or evaluation, for instance as part of a lecture on ISO13047.

Teaching and learning are paradoxical. Over my life, I have learnt many complex things, like speaking and walking, without anybody really trying to teach me; and I'm glad I learnt these things before school. School "taught" me lots of things I have not, in the end, learnt, and it put me off many other things, like dance. Conversely, I have taught many complex things by not trying to teach at all. My children know how to solder, but I didn't teach them in any way a university would recognize, with notes, assessments or planned learning outcomes; it was a lot easier than that, and they never said they'd only do it if I assessed them!

Teaching and learning don't stop. I want my students to learn more than I know, and certainly more than I can teach. One consequence of this view is that, where possible, I use coursework rather than examinations. With exams, there is a fixed syllabus represented by the questions, and at some stage you have to start playing games with the students: in a revision class, for instance, you can't *really* tell them the answers to the questions you've set. You get into complex political games, made worse by "marking schemes" and other processes for fair marking. With coursework (portfolios and other techniques) you as a teacher always want the students to do as well as possible, and there is no need to hold back on telling the answers — you want the students to know, so they can go beyond them. Conversely, the students don't ask, "do we need to learn this for the exams?" as anything and everything you teach can help in their coursework (and, later, in their real world work) — there are virtually no exams in the real world, so why train students to perform to them?

Less is more. I could extend this list indefinitely, but less is more. You, the reader, must surely have started to have your own (and better) ideas about teaching and learning, and if I carry on with my ideas you will lose your own ideas. Similarly, if we put more effort in to teaching, say, writing detailed notes, the less we leave for the students, and the less space we leave for our lecturing to unfold in the dynamic relationship we create with the students. Then, the less the students own of what we teach, and the less they learn the gift to do things we didn't teach them explicitly.

4   Conclusions

A proper concern of *any* subject is how people learn that subject, for if they do not learn it successfully, then the subject fails — certainly the academic community fails. If the subject is too obfuscated, uninteresting, dead, then it becomes at best the isolated thinking of the few. HCI subject needs to be successful in the world: it needs practitioners who understand and apply and contribute to the subject. We therefore have to focus on pedagogy as a proper part of the discipline. To make the world better we want our students to engage and become contributory experts [2] who *actually* contribute; this coincides with Kline's, Feynman's, Ramsden's and Dweck's views.

HCI is concerned with how people learn to use complex systems effectively. A lot of HCI is fun, but a lot of it is crucial, both for manufacturers to stay competitive, and for users to stay safe. Many issues in HCI can also be presented as reflections on how HCI itself is taught; HCI is a complex system, and students are users of it. Am I teaching HCI in a way that is compatible with what I am teaching about good HCI practice? There is debate to be had, and students can get into it and start thinking, doing experiments, and triangulating new ideas from what they are learning. It is easy to show students that they are starting to learn important, life and death things that the world needs to know and to apply.

How do we teach HCI? My answer is to enthuse students with the enormous impact HCI can make to the quality of life around them *and* to teach them about learning. HCI itself is well-suited to this "metateaching," as one of its core concerns is user learning. HCI is a subject that is everywhere, even in the classroom. Even when the projector doesn't work, perhaps *especially* when the teacher despairs with the projector's terrible HCI, then HCI becomes relevant and alive to the students.

HCI is a subject with a crucial role in quality of life so we should take it seriously. It amazes me that taking things seriously, particularly in higher education, often leads to us making things private and unexciting. On the contrary, HCI begs to be public and exciting. Why do we hide academic results (and get bored) but get excited over football games, where success and failure are public? People strive to get better when they get excited, and frankly most students fail to work out how to get excited over anything that is as private and secretive as conventional education has become. As teachers we have a pleasurable duty to work out with our students what is exciting. Making HCI public is the best way to improve the world.

Acknowledgements. Harold Thimbleby is a Royal Society-Leverhulme Trust Senior Research Fellow, and gratefully acknowledges this generous support. This paper is a revised version of [13], "Teaching HCI to make it come alive," by permission of the author. Greg Abowd (Geogia Tech), Alan Blackwell (Cambridge University), Paul Cairns (University of York), and Tony Hoare (Microsoft) made extremely valuable comments, for which I am very grateful.

References

1. Carroll, J.M. (ed.): Minimalism: Beyond the Nurnberg Funnel. MIT Press, Cambridge (1998)
2. Collins, H., Evans, R.: Rethinking expertise. University of Chicago Press, Chicago (2007)
3. Crystal, D.: The fight for English. Oxford University Press, Oxford (2006)
4. Dweck, C.S.: Self-theories: Their role in motivation, personality, and development. Psychology Press (2000)
5. Feynman, R.P., Gottlieb, M.A., Leighton, R.: Feynman's tips on physics. Addison-Wesley, Reading (2006)

6. ISMP, Institute for Safe Medication Practice. Fluorouracil Incident Root Cause Analysis, Canada (2007), http://www.ismp-canada.org
7. Kline, M.: Why the professor can't teach. St. Martin's Press (1977)
8. Ong, W.: Orality and literacy: The technologizing of the word, Methuen (1982)
9. Perry, W.G.: Forms of ethical and intellectual development in the college years. Jossey-Bass (1999)
10. Ramsden, P.: Learning to teach in higher education, 2nd edn. Routledge Farmer (2003)
11. Thimbleby, H.: Supporting diverse HCI research. In: Dearden, A., Watts, L. (eds.) Proceedings BCS HCI Conference, vol. 2, pp. 125–128. Research Press International (2000)
12. Thimbleby, H.: Press on: Principles of interaction programming. MIT Press, Cambridge (2007)
13. Thimbleby, H.: Teaching HCI to make it come alive. In: Giovannella, C., Kotze, P., Wong, W. (eds.) HCIed 2008 Conference, Interaction Design and Architecture, 3–4, pp. 9–16 (2008)

Quantification of Accessibility: Guidance for More Objective Access Guidelines

Gregg C Vanderheiden

Trace R&D Center
University of Wisconsin-Madison
Madison, Wi USA 53706
gv@trace.wisc.edu

Abstract. Accessibility guidelines first began as recommendations or advice to designers interested in creating products that were more accessible to users with disabilities. Over the past two decades, societies have found that relying on voluntary efforts by industry was insufficient and began creating laws and regulations regarding accessibility. However these new regulations were based on the earlier voluntary recommendations, which were often qualitative in nature. For those guidelines where there were no clear objective criteria, it has created problems both for companies trying to conform and by those trying to evaluate conformance. Described here are several efforts to create more useful and objective measures to replace previous general recommendations in the areas of photosensitive seizure disorders, contrast, and provisions relating to low vision.

Keywords: Standards, quantification, regulations, accessibility.

1 Introduction

As technology has become more and more essential to daily living, including education, employment, recreation, and even self-care, the ability of people to access and use information and communication technologies has gone from important to essential. Recognizing this, societies have moved to ensure that these technologies are accessible to those who were experiencing disabilities, including older adults.

As it became clear that commercial competitive pressures prevented companies from voluntarily making products accessible in any systematic way, societies have begun creating laws and regulations to ensure accessibility by people with disabilities. For example, in the United States, laws requiring hearing aid compatibility on phones [1], were followed by regulations for public system accessibility in the Americans with Disabilities Act [2]. These were then followed with more general accessibility regulations for telecommunication, with Section 255 of the Telecommunication Act [3], and finally, access for all electronic and information technologies purchased by the federal government, including websites, in Section 508 of the Rehabilitation Act [4].

In all of these efforts, the access guidelines were drawn from earlier work on voluntary accessibility guidelines such as "Guidelines for the Design of Consumer Products to Increase Their Accessibility to People with Disabilities or Who Are Aging" [5], Transgenerational Design [6], "Design of HTML (Mosaic) Pages to Increase their

C. Stephanidis (Ed.): Universal Access in HCI, Part I, HCII 2009, LNCS 5614, pp. 636–643, 2009.

Accessibility to Users with Disabilities Strategies for Today and Tomorrow" [7], and EIA guidelines [8]. Unfortunately, many of these earlier guidelines, because they were advisory in nature, had more general statements in them, such as "use sufficient contrast," without clearly defining what "sufficient" was. The early accessibility regulations, therefore, were a mixture of both objective, testable access criteria and some subjective criteria.

This paper describes several efforts led by the Trace Center at the University of Wisconsin to create objective and testable measures.

2 Photosensitive Epilepsy

Early accessibility guidelines included a provision to help avoid photosensitive seizures by requiring that designers avoid any light sources that would flash between about 3 and 50 cycles per second. This prohibition was based upon a recommendation found in Vanderheiden and Vanderheiden 1992 [9] to avoid flashes in this range because they were found to be particularly provocative for people with photosensitive seizure disorders such as epilepsy (Figure 1). This recommendation was in turn based upon research by Jeavons and Harding [10].

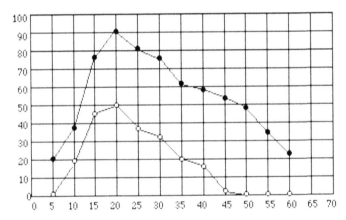

Fig. 1. Percent of photosensitive patients in whom a photoconvulsive response was elicited by a 2 second train of flashes with eyes open and closed. The greatest sensitivity is at 20 Hz with a steep drop off at higher and lower frequencies. (Jeavons & Harding, 1975).

These were in fact objective and measureable criteria. However, as a prohibition it was overly strict. For example, companies began worrying about the tiny LEDs which flickered indicating disc activity. Similarly, there were small LEDs next to Ethernet cables. In both cases the flickering fell within the prohibitive flash range. However the LEDs were small and dim enough that they provided no significant risk for causing photosensitive seizures.

In order to create measures that would prevent stimuli which *were* dangerous, yet permit design features were not dangerous, but fell into this flash range, the Trace

Center worked with Dr. Graham Harding and Cambridge Research Systems to develop a more precise measure that included both flicker frequency and the size of the stimulus (as a percentage of visual field) and brightness. Cambridge Research Systems had developed an automated instrument for use with television. However, it presumed that the television was at a distance where the screen would be approximately 10% of the field of view. Modern computer screens, however, are much closer – more in the range of 30% field of view. As a result, stimuli that would not be dangerous at typical television viewing distances would be problematic for computer displays immediately in front of the individual. In addition, the $20-30,000 cost for the analysis tool developed for the television broadcast industry was prohibitive for most individuals who were creating Web content.

Working with Dr. Harding and Cambridge Research Systems, a new algorithm was developed that would analyze every possible 10 degree region of the screen. The 10-degree region corresponds to .024 steradians, which represents the area of central vision in the eye, which is the area most sensitive to light. The exact criteria developed [11] were:

> [Content does] not contain anything that flashes more than three times in any one second period, or the flash is below the *general flash and red flash thresholds*.

General flash and red flash thresholds were defined as

- a flash or rapidly changing image sequence is below the threshold (i.e., content passes) if any of the following are true:
1. there are no more than three general flashes and / or no more than three red flashes within any one-second period; or
2. the combined area of flashes occurring concurrently occupies no more than a total of .006 steradians within any 10 degree visual field on the screen (25% of any 10 degree visual field on the screen) at typical viewing distance

     where:

- A *general flash* is defined as a pair of opposing changes in relative luminance of 10% or more of the maximum relative luminance where the relative luminance of the darker image is below 0.80; and where "a pair of opposing changes" is an increase followed by a decrease, or a decrease followed by an increase, and
- A *red flash* is defined as any pair of opposing transitions involving a saturated red.

> *Exception*: Flashing that is a fine, balanced, pattern such as white noise or an alternating checkerboard pattern with "squares" smaller than 0.1 degree (of visual field at typical viewing distance) on a side does not violate the thresholds.

These criteria provided objective measures that both addressed the stimuli that were most dangerous for people having photosensitive seizure disorders, while permitting flashing that was not dangerous to occur. Note that the three flashes within any one-second period provision is still part of the formulation. Therefore a simple test of "does it flash more than three times within any one-second period" can still be used as a test for conformance. However, if a product is found to have more than three flashes per second, a more complicated analysis can be conducted to determine whether or not the material was safe. To facilitate the process, the Trace Center worked with Dr. Harding and Cambridge Research Systems to develop a free tool that can be used for evaluation of most common Web and software content. Broadcast and commercial games are excluded. Figure 2 shows a typical screen from the Trace Center's Photosensitive Epilepsy Analysis Tool (PEAT) [12].

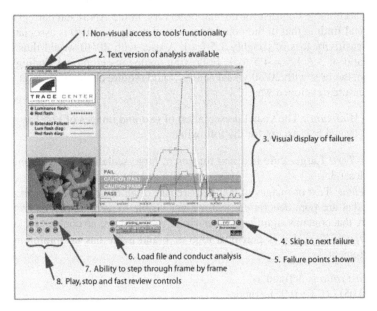

Fig. 2. Screenshot of the Trace Center's Photosensitive Epilepsy Analysis Tool (PEAT) showing a small (and therefore safe) version of the content under evaluation along with a chart diagramming failure points and a slider and controls that allow playing the video or rapidly moving to failure points to examine the material frame by frame.

The above measure has been adopted in the W3C's international Web Content Accessibility Guidelines 2.0, and it has also been recommended by the Telecommunications and Electronic & Information Technology Advisory Committee of the U.S. Access Board for use in the Section 508 refresh [13]. The Photosensitive Epilepsy Analysis Tool (PEAT) is available for download from http://trace.wisc.edu/peat/.

3 Contrast

The second area of effort was focused on contrast measurement. In the previous version of the Web Content Accessibility Guidelines (1.0) [14] the requirement was simply that "sufficient contrast" be provided.   In 508 it required "a range of contrast levels" with no specification of the range.   In order to address this problem, the Trace Center worked with Lighthouse International on the development of a quantitative measure.

The process of developing a quantitative measure was complicated by the fact that contrast is a problem both for individuals with low vision and also for individuals who have color vision deficits. Further, individuals with different types of color vision will see different contrasts for the same material. In order to address this problem, a contrast measure was developed which was color insensitive. That is, it controls for contrast regardless of an individual's color vision.

The measure also used research from Arditi and Faye to compensate for contrast due to low vision. The rationale is based on a) adoption of the 3:1 contrast ratio for minimum acceptable contrast for normal observers, in the ANSI standard [15], and b) the empirical finding that in the population, visual acuity of 20/40 is associated with a contrast sensitivity loss of roughly 1.5 [16]. A user with 20/40 would thus require a contrast ratio of 3 * 1.5 = 4.5 to 1. Following analogous empirical findings and the same logic, the user with 20/80 visual acuity would require contrast of about 7:1. [17]

The measure developed was:

Contrast (Minimum): The visual presentation of text and images of text has a *contrast ratio* of at least 4.5:1, except for the following:

- *Large Text:* Large-scale text and images of large-scale text have a contrast ratio of at least 3:1;
- *Incidental:* Text or images of text that are part of an inactive user interface component, that are pure decoration, that are not visible to anyone, or that are part of a picture that contains significant other visual content, have no contrast requirement.
- *Logotypes:* Text that is part of a logo or brand name has no minimum contrast requirement.

  contrast ratio is defined as
  (L1 + 0.05) / (L2 + 0.05), where

- L1 is the relative luminance of the lighter of the colors, and
- L2 is the relative luminance of the darker of the colors.

  [For enhanced contrast 7:1 would be used]

Several free tools are now available on the Web for carrying out this analysis.

4   20/70 Vision

Another area of difficulty came from guidelines which required researchers to make their products usable by people with 20/70 vision such as was done in both the Section 255 and Section 508 guidelines. Although this sounds quantitative, in fact this is a metric for measuring vision of individuals, but does not provide any guidance to designers as to how this would exactly impact their designs. How big should the letters be? If a cursor is supposed to be visible to this individual, how does the size, shape, stroke width, contrast, etc. affect its visibility to an individual with this type of vision?

The problem is exacerbated by the fact that a given font size may or may not be visible, depending upon all of the above factors. And since any combination of them could occur in a design, how does the difference in stroke width trade off against contrast or font size, etc. And when one considers things such as keyboard focus indicators (outlines appearing around buttons), etc., it is more complicated.

In order to address this, we again worked with researchers at Lighthouse International and explored the idea of using individuals with 20/20 vision (natural or corrected), who would view an object at 3.5 times the normal viewing distance. This should give the same ratio as 20/20 to 20/70 vision.

This does not take into effect close-vision, which is often used by individuals with low vision. However, these individuals are viewing the content using vision (natural or corrected) that is designed to operate at that focal length. Having anyone else whose vision is not in this range try to use close-vision would not provide any meaningful information.

Although the "3.5 times the viewing distance" measure does not provide an exact equivalent to 20/70 vision, there's nothing else that really does. In addition, individuals with low vision are not simply individuals with a different visual acuity. Low vision takes a wide variety of forms. After thought and analysis, it was determined that 3.5 times normal viewing distance was as good a criterion as one could come up with for ensuring that products would be usable by individuals who would generally be classified with vision in the 20/70 range. Viewing an object at 3.5 times the normal viewing distance would provide a simple test which could be carried out by any product design team. It automatically provides a way to balance the various visual factors that make something more or less visible. Although not as computationally precise as the above measures, it does provide something which is much more objective than "usable by somebody with 20/70 vision." It also provides a measure which is easier for designers to both relate to and to test their products against.

This approach was used both in the HFES 200 standards for software and the ISO 9241-171 software accessibility guidelines. The form of this test was in ISO 9241-171 was:

9.2.2 Provide high visibility keyboard focus and text cursors
Software shall provide at least one mode where keyboard focus cursors and text cursors shall be visually locatable by people with unimpaired vision at a distance of 2,5 m when software is displayed on a 38 cm (15 inch) diagonal screen at 1024 × 768 pixel resolution, without moving the cursor.

In the TEITAC report to the Access Board a more general approach was used to account for the fact that it would also be used on hand-held devices.

3-T - Focus Indicator: Any KEYBOARD operable user interface must support a mode of operation where the indication of KEYBOARD focus has a high degree of visibility.
Note 1: The presence of a highly visible text insertion point is sufficient for a text area.
Note 2: A focus cursor that is visually locatable at 3.5 times the typical viewing distance without moving the cursor by people who have unimpaired vision and are familiar with what the focus cursor looks like is sufficient. For example, when software is displayed on a 38 cm (15 inch) diagonal screen at 1024 x 768

pixels resolution, a focus cursor that is visually locatable at 2.5 meters without moving the cursor by people who are familiar with what the cursor looks like and have unimpaired vision is sufficient.

5 Conclusion

The development of accessibility guidelines is an extremely difficult process, due to the wide variety of visual, hearing, physical, and cognitive disabilities, and the wide variation within any disability subtype. However, unless clear and objective guidelines are created, developers of ICT will not be able to determine when they have a problem, or when they have designed their product in a way which is sufficient to meet accessibility guidelines or regulations. It is therefore important that objective measures be established, even if it is known that such measures are not perfect. No product can be designed so that it is accessible and usable by all people. Accessibility standards therefore do not make a product accessible, but ensure that a product meets some minimum level of accessibility.

The goal in creating these minimum accessibility thresholds is to create thresholds which are objective and which best approximate the needs of people with disabilities. Important to this ongoing process is the development of metrics which are increasingly objective, easy to administer, and best match the needs of people with disabilities. This paper described three advances that represent the best measures identified by standards working groups and that were substantial improvements over previous qualitative guidelines, and provide designers with much clearer and more usable targets for making their products more accessible to individuals with disabilities.

Acknowledgement. The contents of this paper were developed under grants from the U.S. Department of Education, NIDRR grant numbers H133E030012, H133E040013, and H133E080022. However, those contents to not necessarily represent the policy of the Department of Education, and you should not assume endorsement by the Federal Government.

References

1. Hearing Aid Compatibility Act of 1988 (1988)
2. Americans With Disabilities Act of 1990 (1990)
3. Telecommunications Act of 1996, 47 U.S.C. §§ 153, 255 (1996)
4. Section 508 of the Rehabilitation Act of 1973, as amended 29 U.S.C. § 794 (d) (1973)
5. Vanderheiden, G.C., Vanderheiden, K.R.: Accessibility Design Guide I: Guidelines for the Design of Consumer Products to Increase Their Accessibility to Persons with Disabilities or Who Are Aging (1991),
   http://trace.wisc.edu/docs/consumer_product_guidelines/consumer.htm
6. Pirkl, J.J.: Transgenerational Design: Products for an Aging Population (Design & Graphic Design). Van Nostrand Reinhold, New York (1994)

7. Vanderheiden, G.C.: Design of HTML (Mosaic) Pages to Increase their Accessibility to Users with Disabilities Strategies for Today and Tomorrow (1995), `http://trace.wisc.edu/archive/html_guidelines/version1.html`

8. Electronic Industries Foundation. Resource Guide for Accessible Design of Consumer Electronics (1996), `http://www.empowermentzone.com/products.txt`

9. Vanderheiden & Vanderheiden (1991)

10. Jeavons, P.M., Harding, G.F.A.: Photosensitive Epilepsy. London: Heinemann Medical (1975)

11. Web Content Accessibility Guidelines 2.0, W3C World Wide Web Consortium Recommendation, `http://www.w3.org/TR/WCAG20/`

12. Trace Center Photosensitive Epilepsy Analysis Tool (PEAT), Trace R&D Center, `http://trace.wisc.edu/peat/`

13. Telecommunications and Electronic and Information Technology Advisory Committee. Report to the Access Board: Refreshed Accessibility Standards and Guidelines in Telecommunications and Electronic and Information Technology (2008), `http://www.access-board.gov/sec508/refresh/report/`

14. Web Content Accessibility Guidelines 1.0, W3C World Wide Web Consortium Recommendation (1999), `http://www.w3.org/TR/1999/WAI-WEBCONTENT-19990505` (latest version: `http://www.w3.org/TR/WCAG10/`)

15. ISO 9241-3, Ergonomic Requirements for Office Work with Visual Display Terminals (VDTs) - Part 3: Visual Display Requirements. Amendment 1

16. Arditi, A., Faye, E.: Monocular and Binocular Letter Contrast Sensitivity and Letter Acuity in a Diverse Ophthalmologic Practice. Supplement to Optometry and Vision Science, 81 (12S), 287 (2004)

17. Web Content Accessibility Guidelines 2.0, W3C World Wide Web Consortium Recommendation (2008), `http://www.w3.org/TR/200X/REC-WCAG20-20081211/` (latest version at: `http://www.w3.org/TR/WCAG20/`)

Visualizing Design Exclusion Predicted by Disability Data: A Mobile Phone Case Study

Sam Waller, Pat Langdon, and P. John Clarkson

University of Cambridge, Engineering Design Centre, Department
of Engineering Trumpington Street, Cambridge, CB2 1PZ
{sdw32,pml24,pjc10}@cam.ac.uk

Abstract. Disability data can help to predict the number of people that will be unable to use a particular product. The greatest benefits of this prediction are the design insights that help to reduce exclusion and thereby improve the product experience for a broad range of people. This paper uses a mobile phone case study to demonstrate how a set of visualization outputs from an exclusion audit can generate prioritized design insights to reduce exclusion, particularly when multiple tasks place demands on multiple capabilities.

Keywords: Inclusive design, calculating exclusion.

1 Introduction

The Cambridge Engineering Design Centre is unique in developing analytical tools that can quantitatively assess the inclusive merit of different design decisions or products, according to the number of potential users that would be excluded: such tools have the potential to greatly assist the implementation of inclusive design in businesses [5]. In addition to those excluded from using a product, many more people will experience difficulty or frustration, so reducing the number of people excluded can improve the experience for a wide range of users [8].

Performing tasks with products typically involves a perception-cognition-action cycle, where the user perceives and interprets information from the product, that further thinking processes use, together with reference to long-term memory, to choose an intended action. All of these processes are affected by the context of use, and the user's ability to successfully perform this cycle impacts on whether they will find the product easy, difficult or impossible to use [11]. The tools that comprise an exclusion audit therefore intend to present population data about users' context dependent abilities to perceive, think and act, so that designers choosing the interface attributes of mainstream products and services can make better informed decisions to reduce the number of people who find the usage difficult or impossible [7].

Exclusion auditing is intended to complement other tools for evaluating inclusive merit, such as expert opinion [9], user trials [1] and impairment simulators [10]. In combination, these tools provide a holistic approach to discover the causes of design exclusion, and identify appropriate design improvements. An ideal data source for evaluating design exclusion would:

C. Stephanidis (Ed.): Universal Access in HCI, Part I, HCII 2009, LNCS 5614, pp. 644–653, 2009.
© Springer-Verlag Berlin Heidelberg 2009

- Be representative of a national population, and be customizable towards specific markets of interest.
- Contain data that covers users' abilities to perceive, think and act in real-world contexts.
- Be simple to apply and directly relevant to product interaction.
- Have sufficient scope to incorporate the variation of capability typically found within developed societies, yet sufficient granularity to predict the difference in exclusion between alternative mainstream products.

Surveys that are nationally representative are usually carried out to collect data about one specific aspect of perceiving, thinking or acting. However, product usage engages these abilities in combination, and it is not possible to combine several separate surveys together, so data that is suitable for estimating design exclusion is hard to find. Indeed no UK dataset exists that satisfies all of the criteria required to evaluate design exclusion [2]. The latest i~design research program [6] aims to address this shortcoming directly, by designing and undertaking a national survey specifically for this purpose. Until the results from this survey become available, the Office of National Statistics 1996/97 Disability Follow-up Survey (DFS) [4] remains the best available data source for estimating UK design exclusion [11].

This paper first examines the DFS in more detail, and then presents several ways of visualizing the results when this survey is used to predict design exclusion for one or more tasks. The objectives are to understand how many people are excluded, why those people are excluded, and to provide design insights for how they could be included. The exclusion audits presented here-in are based on the DFS, but the techniques are intended to apply to alternative data sources that could predict design exclusion, perhaps for different countries or for future data collected.

2 The Disability Follow-Up Survey

The survey was conducted in 1996/97 in order to plan welfare support for people with disabilities. The survey contained questions that were grouped together in 13 ability categories, 7 of which are most relevant for product interaction, namely seeing, hearing, intellectual function, communication, locomotion, reach & stretch, and dexterity (for the sake of clarity, seeing and intellectual function will be referred to in this paper as vision and thinking). Within each category, the questions were intended to cover the full range of severity of quality of life impairment.

Table 1. Extract from the ONS dataset, where the 4th row represents a person with full ability, according to the definition used in the survey

ID	Multi-plier	Age	Sex	Vision	Hear-ing	Think-ing	Comm-unication	Loco-motion	Reach & stretch	Dex-terity
1	1894	24	M	V9	H8	T9	C6	L14	R11	D9
2	1312	61	M	V10	H6	T12	C6	L9	R11	D12
3	1865	49	F	V10	H9	T12	C6	L8	R7	D12
4	1267	35	F	V10	H9	T12	C6	L14	R11	D12

For example, the dexterity questions range from disabilities with mild effect on quality of life, such as "can you tie a bow in laces or string without difficulty?" to disabilities with severe effect on quality of life, such as "can you pick up and hold a mug of coffee with either hand?". The complete set of ability levels can be found online [3].

The collection of self-reported ability levels for each of the 7200 survey participants in each of the seven categories forms the DFS capability database, the structure of which is illustrated in Table 1. Each person surveyed has a unique identifier, and statistical measures were used to calculate the number of people in the country represented by that person (labeled multiplier).

3 Estimating Exclusion from the DFS

The number of people excluded from using a product or service will depend on the demands that it makes on their capabilities, which depends on the goal the user wants to achieve with the product, and the tasks needed to perform that goal. The tasks that are actually required, and the level of ability required to perform those tasks will depend on the context of use, which includes both the current environment and the current state of all items involved in achieving the goal. An exclusion analysis is typically based on a single set of assumptions for the context of use, and the results would change for a different set of assumptions.

This paper focuses on visualizing the exclusion results for various different tasks that are associated with using a product. The visualizations are intended to help practical decision makers generate prioritized design insights to reduce exclusion. However, even with a single task, understanding the breakdown of design exclusion will likely require a numerate background, and the complexity of the breakdown rises exponentially with the number of tasks assessed, so specific training may be needed to understand how to best interpret the results when multiple tasks are involved.

To estimate the exclusion associated with a task, the demands placed on each DFS capability must first be assessed in a manner that is directly compatible with the DFS database, then the demand assessment can be used to evaluate exclusion. This assessment procedure is described in detail elsewhere [11], and summarized here.

The assessor must first break down the task in question and examine the demands it places on each of the seven DFS ability categories. For each category in turn, the assessor should examine all the statements in all the ability levels of that category, and judge whether that capability is required to perform the task. A demand of zero indicates that capability is not required.

If some level of that capability is required, the assessor should then consider the lowest ability level within the capability of interest, and judge whether a person with that ability level would be able to perform the task. In most cases, a person with such low ability would be unable to perform the task, in which case the judgment should be repeated for each higher ability level, until the threshold is identified where the task first becomes possible. The demand on that capability is now defined as the ability level that is one lower than the threshold just identified.

This procedure is repeated to identify the demand on each of the seven DFS ability categories. For example, charging a typical mobile phone may result in the demands

[V9;H0;T1;C0;L8;R5;D6], where each letter represents one of the seven DFS ability categories, each number indicates how much demand is placed on that category, higher numbers refer to products that are more difficult to use, and the meaning of each demand is explained in more detail later on. The DFS capability database can then be used to predict the proportion of the UK population who would be excluded from the task, taking due account of the people who may be excluded because the demands are too high in several ability categories.

4   Visualizing the Excluded Population for One Task

The task of charging a typical mobile phone is now examined in more detail, assuming that the user is holding the phone in his or her hand, and the charger jack is lying on the floor. Recall that the demand summary for charging a typical mobile phone is [V9;H0;T1;C0;L8;R5;D6], where the vision demand reflects identifying a small, black, poorly labeled charger socket from the rest of the chassis of the phone, the thinking demand reflects performing a simple task, the locomotion demand reflects bending down to pick up the charger jack, the reach & stretch demand reflects briefly holding both hands out a short distance from the body, and the dexterity demand reflects holding the phone in one hand, then aligning and inserting the charger jack with the other.

The DFS capability database predicts that 5.0 million UK adults will be excluded from attaching the charger to this typical phone. Of the excluded adults, some of them are excluded because only one demand exceeded their capabilities; others are excluded because several demands exceeded their capabilities, shown in Fig. 1(a).   In order to help understand which demands are causing the most difficulty for the most people, Figs 1(b) and 1(c) show exclusion predictions for two alternative scenarios. Firstly, supposing it was possible to redesign the task to eliminate the demand on one particular capability, Fig. 1(b) indicates how much the overall exclusion would reduce as a result. Secondly, supposing the task was redesigned to eliminate the demand on every capability except one, Fig. 1(c) shows how many people would be excluded by the one remaining demand.

In general, Fig. 1(b) represents a more realistic scenario; however its usefulness depends on how many of the excluded adults were unable to achieve the task because of a demand on just one capability. This number inevitably drops when more capabilities are involved, in which case the bars presented in Fig. 1(b) would tend to zero length, and Fig. 1(c) becomes the more useful predictor of which capability demand(s) are causing the most difficulty for the most people.

In this particular case, Fig. 1(a) shows that of the excluded adults, about half of them were excluded because of a demand on just one capability, and Figs 1(b) and (c) both suggest that reducing the locomotion demand has the greatest potential to reduce the number of people who are unable to attach the charger. The locomotion demand occurs because the user typically has to bend down to pick up the charger jack, so one way to achieve this reduction might be to supply the phone with a freestanding desk charger, or ensure that such an accessory is readily available with a mainstream price point.

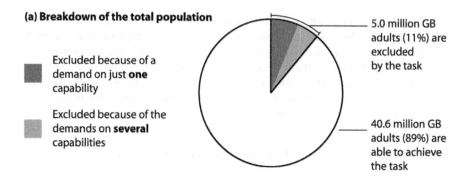

(a) Breakdown of the total population

■ Excluded because of a demand on just **one** capability

▨ Excluded because of the demands on **several** capabilities

5.0 million GB adults (11%) are excluded by the task

40.6 million GB adults (89%) are able to achieve the task

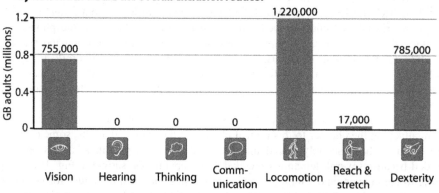

(b) If the task could be redesigned to eliminate the demand on just one capability, by how much would the overall exclusion reduce?

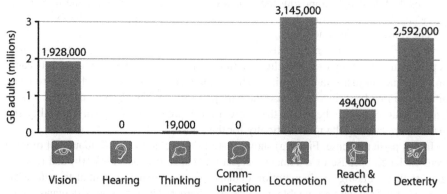

(c) If the task could be redesigned to eliminate the demand on every capability except one, how many people would be excluded because of the one remaining demand?

Fig. 1. Visualising the results from an exclusion analysis for charging a typical mobile phone. (a) shows the total number excluded, while (b) and (c) show exclusion figures for two alternative scenarios. Additionally, (b) is equivalent to a further breakdown of the people in (a) who were excluded because of a demand on just one capability.

5 Visualizing the Excluded Population for Multiple Tasks

Using a product will typically involve many tasks, and the previous example for charging a mobile phone is now extended to consider inserting the SIM card, turning the phone on, and receiving a call. For all of these tasks it is assumed that the user is sitting at a desk, with typical indoor lighting and no background noise. These tasks are now examined in further detail, and the demand summaries for each task are shown graphically in Fig. 2.

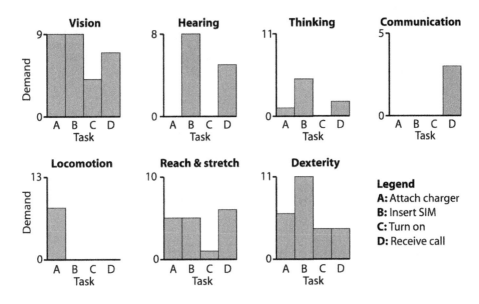

Fig. 2. The demands made by each task on each capability. Although the different scales have different numbers of levels within them, each graph has been drawn with the same vertical height, to reflect the original survey's intended equivalence for the full range of each scale.

For inserting the SIM card, it is additionally assumed that the user is familiar with the general concept of inserting a SIM card, but will use the instruction book to guide them through the task for this particular phone. The demand summary is therefore [V9;H8;T5;C0;L0;R5;D11], where the vision demand reflects reading the instruction manual, and identifying the small parts of the hatch that encloses the SIM card, the hearing demand reflects hearing the hatch click back into place (this confirmation is difficult to achieve by vision or touch), the thinking demand reflects reading short passages of text, then planning and executing a structured series of activities, the reach & stretch demand is the same as for attaching the charger, but the dexterity demand is higher because of the need to manipulate and align small parts with both hands. For turning the phone on the demand summary is [V4;H0;T0;C0;L0;R1;D4], where the vision demand reflects identifying a silver power button on the top of the phone, the reach & stretch demand reflects briefly holding one hand out a short distance from the body, and the dexterity demand reflects pushing the power button.

For answering a call, it is additionally assumed that the phone's loudspeaker is enabled, so the phone does not have to be held up to the head. The demand summary is therefore [V7;H5;T2;C3;L0;R1;D4], where the vision demand reflects identifying the button to answer the call, the hearing demand reflects hearing speech from the phone's earpiece, the thinking and communication demands reflect maintaining a conversation, the reach & stretch demand reflects holding one hand out a short distance from the body, and the dexterity demand reflects pushing the button to answer the call.

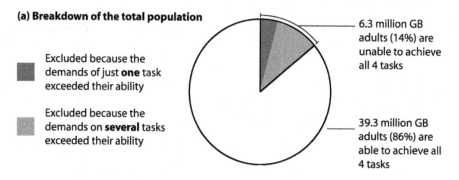

(a) Breakdown of the total population

Excluded because the demands of just **one** task exceeded their ability

Excluded because the demands on **several** tasks exceeded their ability

6.3 million GB adults (14%) are unable to achieve all 4 tasks

39.3 million GB adults (86%) are able to achieve all 4 tasks

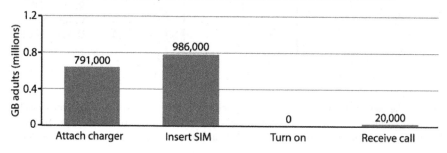

(b) If the product could be redesigned so that the user is no longer required to perform one of the tasks, by how much would the overall exclusion reduce?

791,000 — Attach charger
986,000 — Insert SIM
0 — Turn on
20,000 — Receive call

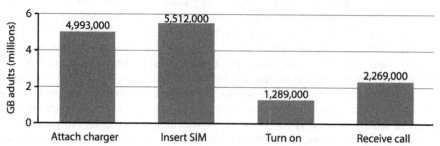

(c) If each task is considered separately, how many people are excluded?

4,993,000 — Attach charger
5,512,000 — Insert SIM
1,289,000 — Turn on
2,269,000 — Receive call

Fig. 3. Visualizing the results from an exclusion analysis for four different tasks with a typical mobile phone. (a) shows the total number excluded, while (b) and (c) show exclusion figures for two alternative scenarios. Additionally, (b) is equivalent to a further breakdown of the people in (a) who were excluded because of the demands of just one of the tasks.

Assuming that performing any of the tasks doesn't make any of the others more difficult (i.e. no fatigue effects), the DFS capability database predicts that 6.3 million adults will be unable to perform the set of four tasks. Of the excluded adults, some are excluded because the demands of just one task exceeded their ability; others are excluded because the demands of several tasks exceeded the ability, shown in Fig. 3(a). Similar to the visualizations presented in Fig. 1, Figs 3(b) and (c) show the results from two alternative scenarios that help to understand which task(s) are causing the most difficulty for the most people. The usefulness of Fig. 3(b) also similarly decreases as the number of adults who were excluded because of just one task decreases, which will inevitably occur as the number of tasks increases.

In order to fully understand the reasons leading to exclusion it may be useful to split the people unable to perform the set of tasks into 15 different categories, according to whether they are able or unable to achieve all the different combinations of the 4 tasks being considered, as shown in Fig. 4.

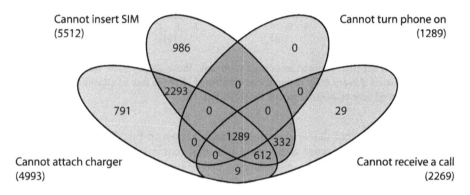

Fig. 4. Breakdown of the 6.3 million adults who are unable to perform four tasks with a typical mobile phone. All values are '000s GB adults, and numbers may not sum exactly due to rounding. The numbers within the areas that "stick out" from all the others are also shown in Fig. 3(b), while the number beside each seperate task is also shown in Fig. 3(c).

In this particular case, Fig. 3(a) indicates that of the excluded adults, only a small proportion of them were excluded because of just one of the tasks, which limits the insights available from Fig. 3(b), and also means that reducing the demands of just one task on its own will not make much difference to the overall exclusion. Figure 3(c) shows that considered independently, the tasks of attaching the charger and inserting the SIM are the most significant causes of exclusion, however the best insight comes from Fig. 4, which shows that of 15 different possible combinations, a clear majority (2.3 million adults) can turn the phone on and can make a call, but cannot insert the SIM and cannot attach the charger. Reducing the demands of both attaching the charger and inserting the SIM is therefore the most effective way to reduce the overall exclusion.

To further prioritize which aspects of attaching the charger and inserting the SIM card require the greatest attention, it may also be helpful to take each separate demand associated with each separate task in turn, and consider how many adults would be

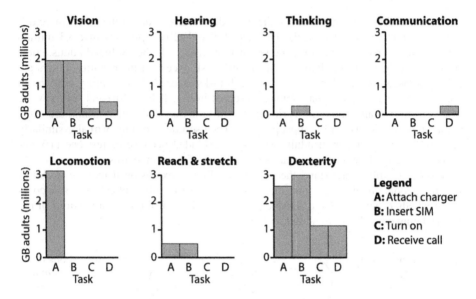

Fig. 5. For each separate demand associated each task, these graphs show how many people would be excluded if every other demand was eliminated. For the task of attaching the charger, the data presented here is identical to that shown in Fig. 1(c).

excluded if every other demand was eliminated, shown in Fig. 5. From Fig. 3, and Fig. 5, attaching the charger is the only task that requires locomotion ability, and inserting the SIM card requires more hearing and dexterity ability than any other task, so reducing these particular demands could be the most effective way to reduce the overall design exclusion. However, further iterative analyses would typically be recommended to refine the initial assumptions and check the true benefit of any proposed design solutions that would reduce these demands.

Additionally, comparing the relative magnitudes of the demands in Fig. 2 and the numbers of people excluded in Fig. 5 indicates the relative prevalence of capability loss within each category, according to the intended equivalence of each scale within the underlying survey. For this particular example the DFS considers the demand of bending down as roughly equivalent to communicating with a friend, yet the corresponding exclusion is nearly 10 times higher for bending down.

6   Conclusions and Further Work

An exclusion audit uses an assessor's judgment to compare a particular task against generic capability data, and the authors are currently planning research to investigate the reliability and validity of such judgments, and investigate how training an assessor with different tools and techniques could support this process. Although the best available accuracy in estimating exclusion from the DFS data is limited, the relative magnitudes of the different causes of exclusion and the design solutions they inspire are expected to retain some validity.

The hypothetical example presented here showed how visualizing the breakdown of exclusion can lead to real and prioritized design insights. Considering design changes in terms of the number of potential customers who might benefit provides a compelling business case for inclusive design.

References

1. Aldersey-Williams, H., Bound, J., Coleman, R.: The methods lab: User research for design. Design for Ageing Network (1999), http://www.education.edean.org (accessed February 2009)
2. Bajekal, M., Harries, T., Breman, R., Woodfield, K.: Review of Disability Estimates and Definitions. Department for Work and Pensions, London (2004)
3. Clarkson, P.J., Coleman, R., Hosking, I., Waller, S.: Inclusive design toolkit. EDC, Cambridge, UK (2007), http://www.inclusivedesigntoolkit.com (accessed February 2009)
4. Department of Social Security Social Research Branch, Disability Follow-up to the 1996/97 Family Resources Survey [computer file]. Colchester, Essex, UK Data Archive [distributor], 3. SN: 4090 (March 2000)
5. Dong, H., Keates, S., Clarkson, P.J.: UK and US industrial perspectives on inclusive design. In: Proceedings of Include, Helen Hamlyn Centre, London, UK (March 2003)
6. i design project website, http://www-edc.eng.cam.ac.uk/idesign3/ (accessed February 2009)
7. Persad, U., Langdon, P.M., Clarkson, P.J.: Characterising user capabilities to support inclusive design evaluation. Int. J. Universal Access Information Society 6(2), 119–135 (2007)
8. The Philips Index: Calibrating the Convergence of Health care, Lifestyle and Technology, http://www.philipsindex.ca (accessed February 2009)
9. Poulson, D., Ashby, M., Richardson, S.: USERfit: A practical handbook on user-centred design for rehabilitation and assistive technology. HUSAT Research Institute for the European Commission (1996)
10. Steinfeld, A., Steinfeld, E.: Universal design in automobile design. In: Preiser, W., Ostroff, E. (eds.) Universal design handbook, pp. 50.1–50.13. McGraw-Hill, New York (2001)
11. Waller, S., Langdon, P.M., Clarkson, P.J.: Using disability data to estimate design exclusion. Int. J. Universal Access Information Society (in press)

Investigating Prior Experience and Product Learning through Novel Interface Interaction: A Pilot Study

Christopher Wilkinson, Patrick Langdon, and P. John Clarkson

Inclusive Design Group
Engineering Design Centre, The University of Cambridge,
Department of Engineering, Trumpington Street,
Cambridge, CB2 1PZ, United Kingdom
{crw42,pml24,pjc10}@eng.cam.ac.uk

Abstract. In keeping with the ethos of Inclusive Design, this paper outlines a pilot study investigating how individuals perceive, process and respond to stimuli during interaction with products, and aims to reveal what occurs during novel product interaction whereupon users may posses limited, or non-existent, internal representations. Other areas of interest included the generational effect and the effects of ageing, upon interaction. A novel product is presented to a small number of participants who are recorded interacting with it whilst providing concurrent protocol and information elicited regarding the development of internal representations. The expectation was that prior experience with similar products would affect users' ability to interact with the product, and that this might be age-related. Whilst this was confirmed to a limited extent in the pilot study, experimentation provided clear evidence of internalised concept development that would, in itself, validate full-scale examination.

Keywords: Inclusive Design, Prior Experience, Interaction Learning.

1 Introduction

Inclusive Design has been referred to as an approach to design that considers those with and without specific needs, particularly of a cognitive and physical nature, the intention being to create interfaces, artifacts and products that are applicable, appropriate and accessible to as many users as possible within the constraints of the design specification [1].

Individuals and members of society whom possess specific dysfunction such as reduced functional capability, physical or cognitive impairment can be obstructed in their day to day lives by technological developments and designs that alienate them [2]. The ethos of Inclusive Design however, is not to create designs specifically for these obstructed groups [3], but to focus on optimizing design for maximum accessibility in conjunction with minimizing the user effort required for interface or artifact interaction [4]. Thus, inclusive design has the potential to increase long-term profits, enhance the competitive edge of companies and can assist in the production of better products for all end users [5]. One approach to achieve this is to examine how

C. Stephanidis (Ed.): Universal Access in HCI, Part I, HCII 2009, LNCS 5614, pp. 654–664, 2009.
© Springer-Verlag Berlin Heidelberg 2009

humans learn and interact with interfaces and designs, and by understanding more about how learning occurs, use this knowledge to influence future design in terms of ease of learning, use and access to all [6].

2 Background

According to the Office for National Statistics [7] the number of people in the United Kingdom aged over 60 has recently overtaken the number of those under 18 years of age, thus a product design that caters for both older people and younger users, with or without impairment will appeal to an ever-increasing commercial market. Distinct differences can be made between user groups, purely on the basis of age. A study by Langdon [8] reported how symbols, identifying features of an interface, across product families were recognised by different generations. Older generations of participants failed to recognise some of the modern symbols. According to Docampo-Rama [9] this is a factor of exposure to technology at a particular stage in life – modern symbols and layered computer interfaces being more familiar and most suited to the interactional processes of those 25 years and younger. Such factors may account for the difficulty experienced by older generations interacting with a variety of current products and designs.

It has been argued designers have failed to engage with users in the physical sense or in design terms, preferring to design products and artefacts from their own knowledge-base and under the presumption that product or design users will possess similar cognitive and physical abilities to the designers themselves [10]. Failing to understand or connect with users and their requirements may risk alienating or excluding a significant proportion of the population which makes poor and short-sighted commercial business sense [11]. Catering for diversity within the target market should not be a unique approach. It should be prerequisite for all design and a natural component within requirements specification. Design should consider the user as an individual, possessing individual aptitudes, experiences and other human characteristics [12].

3 Current Research and Models of Perceptual Processing

An area of current research adopts the premise that all interactions individuals have with their environment are effectively learning processes; perceived information being compared with that held in memory to aid understanding and facilitate the execution of appropriate responses [13].

There are numerous theories proposed to explain the form and way in which information is perceived and encoded, and the extent to which such processing is a conscious activity. The connectionist approach considers that knowledge gained through experience is encoded and stored in memory in elements or nodes that form neural networks. When information in the environment is perceived nodes of the network associated with previous experience of this perception, or potentially similar perceptions, are activated and this activation spreads to other nodes.

Johnson [14] proposed the theory of experientialism. Experiences of the world consisting of sensory-motor, emotional and social elements, refined into Image

Schemata: internalised structures of human experience that guide and facilitate subsequent understanding. These schemata are considered, not to be fixed, but flexible abstract patterns that are modified through further interaction with the world, in accordance with Norman's [15] views on mental models. Norman proposes that models are created by the accurate perception of a devices function and likely behaviour through its design. Thus, design may have a significant effect upon individuals' ability to perceive likely action or function, and thereby inhibit effective learning and interaction. A familiar interface will reduce the level of cognitive loading, attention and consciousness required. Rasmussen [16] proposed a model that accounted for fluctuations in the level of consciousness required during interaction based on the assumption that individuals operated at a level appropriate to the familiarity of the situation, and an individual's previous experience of it or something similar. Wickens [17] expanded this model to account for the type of processing that occurs (Fig.1).

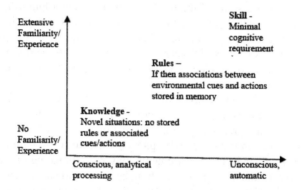

Fig. 1. Wickens' expanded version of Rasmussen's Skill, Rule and Knowledge-Based processing model

4 Pilot Study Rationale

It is the intention to investigate these issues, capturing further information regarding what occurs during interaction with products, particularly those of a novel nature, about which, users may posses limited, or non-existent mental models, memory traces or image schemata. The other significant area of interest to this research is the generational effect and the effects of ageing, upon interaction. As we age, our cognitive capabilities decrease [18]. Although older individuals may have larger 'memory banks of interface and interaction knowledge' they may possess issues retrieving useful chunks of memory that help them interact with familiar or non-familiar interfaces, and this may be linked to the knowledge that older individuals are required to exert greater effort in learning new tasks [19]. Decampo-Rama [9] refers to such differences in age and experience as the 'Generational Effect', identifying particular stages in life during which individuals are optimally receptive to adopting and interacting effectively with new technology.

Inclusive design attempts to address these issues in its quest to assist designers design products, artefacts and systems for maximum accessibility, regardless of age and impairment. Literature indicates prior experience of products is important to their usability, and the transfer of previous experience depends on the nature of prior and subsequent experience of similar tasks [20]. Familiarity of the interface design, its interactional style or the metaphor it conforms to if it possesses one, appear to be key features for successful and intuitive interaction [21]. Lewis et al. [22] investigated user interaction with an everyday device – a microwave. Two interface designs were examined – one dial controlled, the other button controlled. Both the younger and older generation performed more effectively and efficiently with the dial interface than the button interface, and differences occurred according to age.

5 Pilot Study

The objective is to examine how products can be improved or enhanced through their design to cater more effectively for those with and without impairment of any age. This will be achieved by gaining knowledge upon how humans and users perceive, process and respond to stimuli during interaction with products. By understanding of the role these factors play it is hoped information will be revealed about the development of internal representations, memory structures or mental models that users create of the product in question.

The aims of research are to identify:

- What effect does the level of prior experience with the same or similar products have upon users' ability to interact with products?
- Is there an effect upon interactional ability caused by age of the user and their membership of a corresponding technology generation?
- Is there evidence of an ageing effect – a declination of learning or cognitive ability due to increasing age – that affects product understanding and interaction?

To minimise the use of existing knowledge or model of interaction, users were recorded interacting with a potentially novel product (Figure 2). Further investigation involved:

- Assessment of participants' level of prior experience with technology via administration of a Technology Familiarity (TF) Questionnaire [23].
- Assessment of participants' level of cognitive processing/learning ability via administration of Cantabeclipse™ Cognitive Assessment Tool software,
- The allocation of participants to specific groups according to age, thus affording post experimentation analysis of differences between age groups.

Experimental Procedure. Administer pre-test Cognitive Assessment using Cantabeclipse™.

- Video-record participant exposure to the product and ask them to complete six tasks with it whilst providing a verbal commentary or concurrent protocol. The tasks were:
    o Find the lowest wattage reading for the device attached to the product.
    o Find the current reading for the device attached to the product.

    o Set Unit Cost Price to 99.50 £/kWh.
    o Find the frequency reading for the device attached to the product.
    o Find out how much the device attached to this product has consumed.
    o Find the highest wattage reading for the device attached to the product.

- Record participant reaction to the product at initial exposure, mid-way through the completion of tasks and after the task completion phase.
- Administer the Technology Familiarity (TF) Questionnaire.
- Participant Debrief

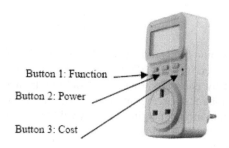

Fig. 2. Plug-in Electricity Cost & Usage Calculator, manufactured by Nikkai Power

Participants were initially presented with the product and asked their views upon it to gauge any pre-experimentation conceptions they possessed about it. At mid-way and end points this was repeated in an attempt to ascertain if their conception of the product had been developed or modified through interaction, and potentially to determine if their conception was accurate and therefore assistive toward task completion. The testing phase also presented the opportunity to investigate participants' perceptions of the task and its complexity, and seek to determine if a correlation existed between perceptions of task complexity and actual task completion times. Age may also be correlated to increased perceptions of task difficulty. Further discussion in this phase centred upon participants' recognition of any familiar features observed in the product and at what stage (if at all) the participants felt they understood the product and interaction. Participants were allocated to one of three age groups: 16-25, 26-59, 60-80 and a Between-subjects design adopted with one participant per group (this will be increased in the intended full-scale study). The dependent variables under investigation included overall individual task completion time and number of button presses and error rates (the minimum number of button presses required subtracted from the amount taken). Baseline data of individuals skilled in interacting with the product will be construed for comparison in future studies.

Data Analysis. Upon completion of the testing phase, the recorded video-data was analysed and segmented to verify how the concurrent protocol corresponded to the users' actions, assessment of task completion times, and rates of error. Analysis would also indicate if participants took longer to achieve task completion, according to age-group. The interview-phase material was intended to yield qualitative data upon user perception of interaction to confirm their overall level of product understanding. This would potentially elicit useful information about how individuals internalise understanding or representations of products and their interaction, and how in conjunction with their perceptions, interaction is influenced.

The Task Familiarity questionnaire administered asked two questions regarding a list of contemporary products; "How often do you use the following products?" and "When using the products, how many features of the product are you familiar with and do you use?". Answers were then rated to provide an overall Technology Familiarity score.

6 Results

Concurrent Protocol Summary. All participants referred to the Function button, particularly in the early stages. They rapidly learned the functionality it represented but all exhibited and voiced difficulty in attempting to complete task 3, as the functionality represented by the alternative buttons appears to have been less apparent. All participants were able to reference other products they felt held a degree of similarity with the novel product presented, and a consensus centred around watches in particular that often present multi-functionality through a single button clicked multiple times, as does the novel product (Button 1: Function) and the requirement to hold-down buttons in order to set the device (Buttons 1, 2 and 3). The outward aesthetic of the device was also mentioned, being referred to as reminiscent of an old mobile phone and the display appeared: "dated like an early seventies calculator". The response of the participants regarding their overall concept of the product was largely similar. Relevant and accurate inferences about the product were made from the beginning, all correctly assuming that the product was electrical in nature, and something into which an electrical device was inserted. By the mid-way questioning phase, the participant in the 16-25 age group correctly identified the purpose of the product, stating that: "...you're setting up the cost price – pound per kilowatt hour and then it records how much has been spent on electricity – it's basically just recording your usage". The remaining test and final discussion stage confirmed the development of participants' internal concepts of the device Table 3 indicates the level of familiarity with various forms of technology according to age group.

Table 1. Results Overview

	16-25	26-59	60-80
1. Mean number of button presses	24.6	44.5	40.5
2. Mean rates of error	19.6	39.5	35.5
3. Mean task completion times (seconds)	121.6	203.3	103.1
4. Mean times per button press	4.13	2.98	2.28

1: Total number of button presses divided by the number of tasks.
2: Error calculated by subtracting the theoretically-possible minimum number of button presses required to achieve the desired state, from the total number of button presses made.
3: Total task completion times divided by the number of tasks.
4: Total number of button presses divided by time taken.

Table 2. Specific Results of Task 3

Task 3		16-25	26-59	60-80
Minimum number of required button presses:	5	107	215	206
Error Rates		102	210	201
Completion times (seconds)		578	980	523
Average times per move		5.40	4.55	2.53

Table 3. Technological Familiarity (TF) Results

	16-25	26-59	60-80
Question 1	28	20	28
Question 2	13	16	18
Overall TF Score	41	36	46

Cantabeclipse^{TM} Cognitive Assessment Summary. The initial test (MOT) screening for vision, hearing, movement and comprehension impairment, highlighted no issues. The (SSP) test, designed to assess working memory capacity, indicated minimal differences between age groups, the 26-59 age group performing slightly better. The third test (IED), designed to assess visual discrimination and the maintenance and flexibility of attention, showed both the younger and older age groups performed good or better than 70-75% of the population, the 26-59 age group performing good or better than 90-95%. The RTI test measuring reaction time to a presented stimulus, and the RVP test, revealed participants in the younger age groups clearly performed better than the 60-80 age group.

7 Discussion

It is evident from Table 1 that the participant in the 16-25 age group had a lower average number of button responses than either of the other age groups. This age group also had a lower rate of error than either the 26-59 or 60-80 age groups. In both instances the 26-59 and 60-80 age groups were similarly matched for number of average button presses and rates of error. Task completion times were more variable, with the older generation age group completing tasks quicker than both the 16-25 and 26-59 age groups. This is surprising as in this instance it is counter to what literature would suggest. Evident in Table 2, Task 3 caused all age groups the greatest difficulty.

The administration of the Technological Familiarity Questionnaire, based on Blackler's [23] questionnaire, provided an opportunity for experimentation to establish the extent to which each participant interacted with technology on a regular basis, and the number of different products and interfaces they are familiar with. Although literature would suggest younger generations have greater familiarity with (new) technology than older generations, in this pilot study it is the older generation that yields the highest technological familiarity score, indicating they have a greater knowledge of different devices and interact with them more regularly.

The concurrent protocol yielded revealing information about the formation of internalised concepts regarding the product presented. Participants, although they referenced functionality or product design appearance that was sometimes familiar, did not reference specific devices in a way that would suggest they were using an internal representation or mental model of another device to facilitate understanding of, or interaction with, the novel product presented (Figure 3).

Pre-interaction	Mid-interaction	Post-interaction
All participants unfamiliar with the product and both its functionality and interaction. Reference made to product being electrical in nature – inferred from product design.	Understanding of key functionality – particularly effect of depressing specific buttons. Evidence of participants understanding the intended product use.	Understanding of intended product use further confirmed and expanded. Reference to similar but distinctly different products suggested models of interaction were not being used to facilitate novel product interaction.

Fig. 3. Summarised development of understanding over time, influencing product concept

Uniformity was noted with regard to the fact that although all participants were unfamiliar with the novel product, all were aware Button 1 (Function) would set the eventually adjusted cost setting; it was the sole button selected to achieve that specific goal. By the end of the testing phase participants belonging to the younger age groups had both accurately modified their concepts of, and identified, the actual products purpose. It is arguable that the concept described by the participant in the 60-80 age group had been modified, although perhaps not as accurately. The frequent admission by participants that they were adopting a random button press approach toward goal achievement, with little or no intention to think about a plausible solution to task achievement is acknowledged as a significant experimental problem. However, this is often the approach adopted by individuals in the real world, and so maintains ecological validity. Maintenance of a more rigorous concurrent protocol would be advocated and could have perhaps been facilitated by providing a better example of the level of information it was hoped participants would provide.

The Cantabeclipse^{TM} Cognitive Assessment results in general indicating that participants in the younger age groups clearly performed better than the 60-80 age group, concur with Lewis et al. [22] and Blackler's [23] findings regarding age and performance, although within the product interaction phase, this was not upheld.

8   Conclusions and Further Work

The older age groups' approach to task completion largely went against the expectation of literature, with the participant neither producing the largest number of button presses, or attempts, nor possessing the greatest rate of error. Indeed, task completion times for the 60-80 age group were the quickest within the study. In a larger-scale study it would be interesting to investigate if this effect correlated with technological familiarity as this age group possessed the highest technological familiarity score. There was largely insufficient evidence to confirm the existence of an ageing effect that affected product understanding or interaction, although the Cantabeclipse™ results for the older age group did indicate reduced performance and reaction time in comparison with the 16-25 and 26-59 age groups.

Observations in Relation to the SRK Model. In relation to interaction and learning, there is evidence of participants understanding a connection between both the affects of their interaction with the novel product and affects within their environment in accordance with Clark [24]. All participants were aware that the product either influenced or was influenced by the device connected to it, as a feature of their immediate environment. Learning undoubtedly occurred, as all participants performed fewer button presses in the latter stages of the test than at the beginning, and made fewer verbal references to not understanding how to proceed, nor admitted to random actions during this stage. In the latter stages the method of achieving task completion by repeatedly pressing the Function button was learnt in all conditions, and could perhaps be described as being performed automatically, verging on the Skilled level of processing according to Wickens [17] expanded model of Skill, Rule and Knowledge-based processing. There was certainly evidence of mental model development regarding the devices purpose throughout the study, although the exact form that this internal representation assumed was beyond the scope of this experimentation. This model development is however in accordance with Norman's [15] view that individuals develop models through experience, training and learning of devices, and that this model is based on the perception of the devices function and likely behaviour through its design.

Overall, the results facilitate the proposal that simple alterations to the design and the method of interaction would significantly enhance individuals' ability to learn and use this product. This is highlighted in the results of Task 3 in comparison with the other tasks: there is a dramatic increase in the level of difficulty experienced. The main interaction with the product comprises of single presses of Button 1 (Function) which results in the display cycling through the various readouts available. However, to set the Cost (Task 3) requires pressing Button 3 (Cost) twice, holding it down, then whilst held down, pressing and releasing button 1 (Function). This results in a flashing display (indicating arrival at the setting stage), at which point all button contact can be released, and the user can scroll up or down through the numbers displayed. To finally set the desired Cost requires a further single press and release of the Function button. Thus, simplification of this procedure and maintaining a similar level of complexity to the interaction of the other functions available would considerably ease the level and extent of learning required when initially exposed to the product.

Although specific information regarding effects of ageing upon interaction and the existence of generational effects were not ascertained during this experimentation, the observation of interaction with a novel product has yielded unique knowledge about the development of understanding through experience. In summary, we believe the results of this pilot study have validated the methodology proposed for intended full-scale study and contribute to the existing literature by providing a contextual and theoretical background for current and future research in the area.

References

1. Keates, S., Clarkson, J.: Countering design exclusion – an introduction to inclusive design. Springer, Heidelberg (2003)
2. Morris, J.: The effects of an introductory computer course on the attitudes of older adults towards computers. In: Proceedings of the 23rd SIGCSE technical symposium on Computer Science Education, Kansas City, Missouri, USA, March 5-6, pp. 72–75 (1992)
3. Haigh, R.: The ageing process: a challenge for design. Applied Ergonomics 24(1), 9–14 (1993)
4. Deisinger, I., Breining, R., Robler, A., Holfe, I., Ruckert, D.: Immersive ergonomics analyses of console elements in a tractor cabin. In: Proceedings Fourth Immersive Projection Technologies Workshop, Iowa: Ames, June 19-20 (2000)
5. Dong, H., Bobjer, O., McBride, P., Clarkson, J.: Inclusive product design: Industrial case studies from the UK and Sweden. In: Bust, P. (ed.) Contemporary Ergonomics, pp. 338–342. Taylor and Francis, Great Britain (2006)
6. Inclusive Design Group,
   http://www-edc.eng.cam.ac.uk/research/inclusivedesign/
   (last accessed October 2008)
7. Office for National Statistics,
   http://news.bbc.co.uk/1/hi/uk/7575869.stm (last accessed October 2008)
8. Langdon, P., Lewis, T., Clarkson, J.: The effects of prior experience on the use of consumer products. In: Universal Access in the Information Society, pp. 179–191. Springer, Heidelberg (2007)
9. Docampo-Rama, M.: Technology generations handling complex user interfaces. PhD Thesis. TU, Eindhoven (2001)
10. Nickerson, R.: How we know–and sometimes misjudge–what others know: Imputing one's own knowledge to others. Psychological Bulletin 125(6), 737–759 (1999)
11. Hollins, B.: 13 lessons in service design. The Design Council (2008),
    http://www.designcouncil.org.uk/en/About-Design/
    Design-Disciplines/Service-design-by-Bill-Hollins/
    13-lessons-in-service-design/ (last accessed October 2008)
12. Taish, M.A.: On documentation for the design of school buildings. Contemporary Ergonomics. Taylor & Francis, Chippenham (2006)
13. Edge, D., Blackwell, A., Dubuc, L.: The physical world as an abstract interface. In: Bust, P. (ed.) Contemporary Ergonomics, pp. 224–228. Taylor and Francis, Great Britain (2006)
14. Johnson, M.: The body in the mind. The bodily basis of meaning, imagination, and reason. The University of Chicago Press, Chicago (1987)
15. Norman, D.: The design of everyday things. Currency Doubleday, New York (1988)
16. Rasmussen, J.: Deciding and doing: Decision making in natural contexts. Ablex, Norwood (1993)
17. Wickens, C., Gordon, S., Liu, Y.: An introduction to human factors engineering. Addison-Wesley Educational Publishers Inc., New York (1998)
18. Rabbitt, P.: Does it all go together when it goes? The Nineteenth Bartlett Memorial Lecture. The Quarterly Journal of Experimental Psychology 46A(3), 385–434 (1993)
19. Howard, J., Howard, D.: Learning and memory. In: Rogers, A.F.W. (ed.) Handbook of human factors and the older adult, pp. 7–26. Academic Press, San Diego (1997)
20. Thomas, B., van Leeuwen, M.: The user interface design of the fizz and spark GSM telephones. Taylor & Francis, London (1999)

21. Okeye, H.: Metaphor mental model approach to intuitive graphical user interface design. PhD Thesis, Cleveland State University, Cleveland, USA (1998)
22. Lewis, T., Langon, P., Clarkson, P.: Prior experience of domestic microwave cooker interfaces: A user study. Springer, London (2008)
23. Blackler, A.: Intuitive interaction with complex artefacts. PhD Thesis. Queensland University of Technology, Australia (2006)
24. Clark, A.: Being there. Putting brain, body, and world together again. MIT Press, Cambridge (1997)

The Art of Cross-Cultural Design for Usability

Heike Winschiers-Theophilus

School of Information Technology
Polytechnic of Namibia
heikew@polytechnic.edu.na

Abstract. More and more HCI researchers and practitioners have realized the urgency of addressing culture as being more than just an interface tuning parameter. Recent publications, project initiatives and a growing number of globally dispersed collaborating workgroups explore cultural models for practical solutions. Yet many endeavors focus on singled out aspects thereby missing fundamental factors of cross-cultural design and evaluation such as contextual connotations, dynamics and integration. Thus a common research agenda should therefore be the de-construction of the entire process as a basis for a comprehensive integration of shared experiences, best practices and tested models to enhance cross-cultural design and evaluation.

1 Introduction

Designing usable information technology (IT) across cultures is an art, for it being highly creative and sensitive, situational unique, and contextually self-defined, ideally leading to a synergism of the created artifact with its environment. The designer must poses skills and master techniques required for the specific development context. However the understanding thereof has been lacking and the consequent challenges were underestimated in the past. Looking at the history of cross-cultural IT design and usability evaluation shows the originally naïve assumption that IT, being value neutral, only needs to be slightly adapted to its new environment. However Del Galdo and Nielson [3] at an early stage already discovered the necessity to add two more levels to software localization, namely the adaptation of usability methods to specific countries as well as the design of user interfaces in accordance with cultural models of how local people work and communicate. Many practitioners and a few researchers, rushing to find practical solutions, have overestimated available cultural models. Through a high abstraction specifics, unique to each development situation, are lost. Essential elements and relevant relations within the context are omitted of the process and product. Thus Young [17] argues "that the current state of research representing culture in the design of ICTs serves a limited scope of what culture can be in the design process". She requests designers to rethink the integration of culture in the design process while revealing their need for guidance in the form of frameworks and models.

In this paper, the author will illustrate that the manifold experiences and theories in cross-cultural design and evaluation are not comprehensive as yet. Only a full understanding of the cultural flow will facilitate a complete integration.

C. Stephanidis (Ed.): Universal Access in HCI, Part I, HCII 2009, LNCS 5614, pp. 665–671, 2009.
© Springer-Verlag Berlin Heidelberg 2009

2 The Forgotten Links

"Current approaches of using cultural models in software design and evaluation do not necessarily imply major usability improvement."

At first this statement seems rather provoking and absurd, as the obvious aim of using cultural models is to overwrite the IT intrinsic values by the users' values. However, looking at the means of penetration of intrinsic values in IT solutions shows the relative weakness of current approaches of integrating cultural models, to explicitly implant users' values.

2.1 IT Intrinsic Values

Commonly, as part of the development process a solution is modeled based on an abstraction of how the creator perceives a given reality [5]. Perception is based on the individual's cultural background. Thus IT creators model IT solutions according to their cultural background [13]. This is often explicitly expressed in statements such as this:

"As designers, we are naturally interested in facilitating these groups to use information technology in an effective, efficient, and sustainable way to further their goals" [9].

The propagation of western values in IT solutions is therefore established through the believed-to-be universally valid conceptualization of Software quality criteria, established methods and metrics [15]. For example the concept of usability, left unquestioned by the majority of researchers, is commonly considered equivalent to effectiveness, efficiency and satisfaction. It is therefore measured with methods such as GOMS and Think Aloud Task solving, in terms of number and time of task completion. However previous research by the author and colleagues has revealed that usability criteria such as task completion time are largely irrelevant in the Namibian context [14]. Further brainstorming sessions and focus group discussions with different Namibian user groups have evidenced a significant deviating understanding of usability from the commonly assumed one [15]. Thus all usability evaluations have, in the absence of a contextually redefined usability concept, examined human computer interaction qualities not necessarily applicable to the local user group. The twofold bias of usability evaluations, one through the underlying definition of usability and two through the application of specific methods has substantially contributed to the preservation of western values in deployed IT solutions [16].

2.2 Cultural Models -The Rescue-?

A number of cultural models have found their way into the HCI community, among the most cited are Hofstede's, Hall's, Victor's and Trompenaar's theories. These anthropologists have identified cultural dimensions, which explicitly differentiate cultural groups from each other in their way of thinking, feeling and acting. Hofstede [7], for example, differentiates the following dimensions: power-distance, collectivism vs. individualism, femininity vs. masculinity, uncertainty avoidance, long- vs.

short-term orientation. Such models are used to guide interface design as well as adapt usability methods.

Cultural Model as User interface Design Guidelines. The interest in cultural models by the HCI community has certainly increased since Marcus and Gould [8] have derived user interface guidelines directly from cultural dimensions. They suggest, for example that information structuring should directly correlate with the level of power distance, e.g. high power distance users require highly structured information presentation while low power distance users require less structured information presentation. These guidelines seemed like a welcome fast and cheap solution to develop applications for other cultural groups. However the linear mapping of single high abstraction level dimensions to specific user interface features has not proven its validity as yet [15]. Fitzgerald [4] concludes from his work on cross-cultural website design, that cultural models are rather culturally descriptive than interface directives. Remembering the intentions, context and authors of the cultural models raises doubts as to the adequacy and applicability for a different purpose namely the design of IT systems for specific groups. Many questions remain such as, why those specific cultural determinants? Are they relevant and complete in terms of what is pertinent for HCI? How can we derive user interface guidelines from the models at hand?

Problematic, furthermore is the currently limited integration of a cultural model into the whole process of IT design and evaluation. The restriction to user interface feature determination leaves the underlying usage values or quality criteria untouched thus in conflict. E.g. in Marcus and Gould's [8] early work the suggested correlation of power distance and information structuring, has an underlying assumption of striving towards effectiveness and efficiency of information access in any cultural context. However those values are not necessarily part of the target users' culture. Equally striking is the research presented by Ford and Gelderblom [6] in which no correlation could be established between South African user performance and cultural specific website characteristics using established usability evaluation methods. Such comparisons demonstrate the application of a cultural model to a singled out phase of design and evaluation only.

Cultural Models in Design and Evaluation Methods Adaptation. On the other hand, failures or successes reported about the application of common HCI methods in different cultural settings, can in most instances, retrospectively be linked to cultural theories. E.g. Trillo [11] reports on a lack of participation of females in a focus group in Tokyo. However would the facilitator have considered the Japanese gender determinant, which is one of the highest in the world (95) [8], would (s)he have adapted the method by not mixing genders and rather had separate sessions. We have had similar correlative experiences over the last decade evaluating the suitability and adaptation of methods in Namibia, a Southern African country. At first striking was the lack of criticism, no matter how "bad" a presented prototype was. However, understanding the cultural background with its immanent hierarchies, depicting a high power distance, explains the absence of expressed criticism to perceived respectful people such as teachers or developers [13]. Early user involvement in design and the usage of peers for evaluation increased the user feedback drastically. Similarly, having changed individual think aloud evaluations to group discussion evaluations, thereby considering the Namibian collectivistic[1] culture, has improved the quality and quantity of feedback [14]. In an attempt to identify "usability" connotations we have run a couple of successful term brainstorming sessions with different user groups. However in one of the sessions, where the user group consisted of only Hereros, one of the indigenous ethnical groups, the brainstorming approach was neither understood nor practicable. Instead the group elder filled the allocated time with narrating detailed stories on "usable" items in his life. Only a few inserts from other participants were recorded. Comparing this with experienced local communication customs does mirror the session behavior of the group; e.g. the eldest speaking first and most, leading the conversation, and communicating information through high context stories. The latter observation has for example been successfully used in Indian usability evaluation sessions where tasks are embedded in Bollywood stories to create an interesting context [1]. This demonstrates the importance of adopting indigenous communication strategies for the design and evaluation sessions. Furthermore do Shi and Clemmensen [10] argue, based on Nisbett[2] 's theory, that differences in thinking patterns influence the ability of think aloud evaluations; e.g. linear and analytical (western) thinking can be easier expressed during a task execution than circular and holistic (eastern) thinking. They therefore suggest the use of retrospective thinking aloud evaluation for eastern users. Those examples exhibit the vast experience in the usage of cultural models and theories to adapt methods to a specific cultural context.

However cultural models, describing one cultural group in isolation, exclude the situational dynamics originating from the interaction between the parties involved in the design and evaluation process. The influence of the interplay between designer/evaluator and user depending on their respective cultural backgrounds has been demonstrated in different studies. Vatrapu and Pĕrez-Quiñones [12] have evidenced the difference in usability evaluation outcomes depending on the evaluator-user pairing. The studies are based on structured interview techniques with different evaluator-user pairs from Europe and India. In Namibia the feedback depends on the perceived position of the evaluator by the user [13, 14]. Similar results have been obtained in studies conducted by Clemmensen and Plocher [2] in which users and evaluators from Europe and India were paired in all combination possibilities. A great variation in terms of outcomes depending on the pair was recorded. In these studies the local-local pairing prevail in identifying culturally specific problems. Shi and Clemmensen [10] remark, that "the appropriateness of a given cultural theory/knowledge depends on who the individual is together with. Sharing knowledge of usability problems and coordinating descriptions of usability problems depend on the mutual perception of group belongingness." They further explain that because Eastern societies are socio-emotional oriented their users may be more influenced when they are with foreign evaluators. In an attempt to capture this dynamic relationship Clemmensen and Plocher [2] introduce a cultural usability model, which distinguishes the user's

---

[1] Anecdote: Students who were asked to bring a user to the prototype evaluation session brought 20 users at the same time instead.

[2] Nisbett, R.E., The Geography of Thought. 2003, London: Nicholas Brealey Publishing (as referenced in Shi and Clemmenssen 2008).

internal cultural model of technology use, external artifacts and institutions. However, once more the model assumes that every individual strives for effectiveness, efficiency, and satisfaction of interacting with a product.

2.3 Understanding the Cultural Flow in a Cross-Cultural Process

Figure 1a depicts the previously discussed cultural influences of the developer, the users and the usage of cultural models within a cross-cultural design and evaluation process. The different colors represent the different value systems, e.g. red the western culture and blue any other culture. The IT experts who determines the design and evaluation process, usually adopts the common usage values, as set by western bodies, and chooses the methods, in some instances informed by cultural models. The later usually serves as guidelines for the design of the user interface only. In a later stage users are then involved for the evaluation. Thus depending on the intensity and interplay of user involvement, the usage of a cultural model to inform the choice of methods or the user interface only, the IT solution will carry a percentage of the developer's and user's cultural values. Striving for a synergy of users and deployed IT solution, the aim is to increase the users' cultural values and minimize the western developers' intrinsic values in the final solution. The current usage of cultural models and user involvement does not sufficiently take into account the strong influence of the developer's cultural background as well as the western values anchored in the assigned software quality criteria as well as the design and evaluation methods. Thus the inclusion of cultural models and users does have no major implication on the outcome. Only a full integration of an adequate cultural model and users in the cross-cultural design and evaluation process will drastically improve the final solution. Figure 1b depicts an integrated approach with a stronger users' cultural flow.

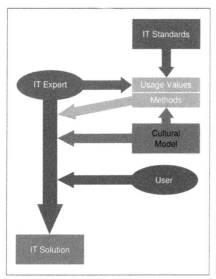 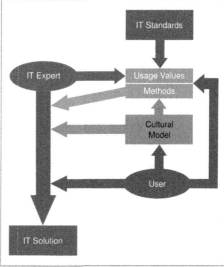

Fig. 1a. Cultural Flow in current process   **Fig. 1b.** Cultural Flow in integrated process

The cultural flow model clearly shows the delicacy of such a cross-cultural process, as well as the interplay between the people, techniques and standards involved. As each design evolves in its own specific context the developers' skills and understanding of the cross-cultural context determines the success of the outcome. Developers, in their role as cross-cultural process facilitators must be aware of their own cultural background as well as be able to anticipate the given cultural context. Developers have to accept that well-known practices might be inappropriate and that a cross-cultural design and evaluation process always is a mutual learning process. Thus the artful creation of a synergy requires high creativity and sensitivity within a unique situation of a cross-cultural context. A comprehensive cultural model should therefore address contextual connotations, the dynamics and its integration.

3   Outlook

Many valuable cross-cultural experiences have been reported, which contribute to guidelines and best practices in cross-cultural design and evaluation. However overestimating the strength of current cultural models and their lack of appropriate integration in the entire process does not result in, as intended, locally usable solution. We need to understand the complete cultural flow within the design and evaluation process as well as the requirements of a cultural model to be beneficial to this process. One common research agenda of the HCI community should be the establishment of relevant cultural models and their integration into the cross-cultural design and evaluation. In a first step HCI specific determinants should be identified. An analysis of in the literature reported causes of failures of application of common methods can substantially contribute towards the identification of pertinent cultural determinants. For example, most Namibian participants would not fill in a questionnaire truthfully but rather put the assumed expected answer [13]. Thus an indicator to consider for the HCI cultural model would be the expectation relevance factor. Furthermore mapping cultural dependent communication and thought patterns to the design of HCI interfaces means abandoning many familiar features.

As to the integration in the process a meticulous de-construction of cross-cultural design and evaluation should be on the agenda to facilitate a successful integration of best practices.

This paper has demonstrated the global variety of relevant research results, which yet are lacking consolidation. The author hopes to initiate such an endeavor within the HCI community to improve the cross-cultural design and evaluation process aiming for cultural usability.

Acknowledgments. I would like to thank Mr. J. Fendler for the numerous critical discussions and editing suggestions.

References

1. Chavan, A.: The Bollywood Method. In: Schaffer, E. (ed.) Institutionalization of Usability; a Step-by-Step Guide, pp. 129–130. Adisson Wesley, New York (2004)
2. Clemmensen, T., Plocher, T.: The Cultural Usability (CULTUSAB) Project: Studies of Cultural Models in psychological Usability Evaluation Methods (UEMs). In: Aykin, N. (ed.) HCII 2007. LNCS, vol. 4559, pp. 274–280. Springer, Heidelberg (2007)

3. Del Galdo, E., Nielsen, J.: International User Interfaces. John Wiley & Sons, New York (1996)
4. Fitzgerald, W.: Models for Cross-Cultural Communications for Cross-Cultural Website Design. Technical Report Published as NRC/ERB-1108. NRC-46563, National Research Council Canada (2004)
5. Floyd, C.: Autooperationale Form und situiertes Handeln. In: Cognito Humana - XVII. Deutscher Kongress fuer Philosophie, pp. 237–252. Akademie Verlag, Leipzig (1997)
6. Ford, G., Gelderblom, H.: The effects of Culture on Performance Achieved through the use of Human Computer Interaction. In: Proceedings of SAICSIT, pp. 218–230 (2003)
7. Hofstede, G.: Cultures and Organizations. Software of the Mind. McGraw-Hill, New York (1997)
8. Marcus, A., Gould, E.: Cultural Dimensions and Global Web User-Interface Design. What? So What? Now What? In: Proceedings of the 6th Conference on Human Factors and the Web, Austin (2000)
9. Merkel, C., Xiao, L., Farooq, U., Ganoe, C., Lee, R., Carroll, J., Rosson, M.: Participatory Design in Community Computing Contexts: Tales from the Field. In: Proceedings Participatory Design Conference 2004, Toronto, Canada (2004)
10. Shi, T., Clemmensen, T.: Communication Patterns and Usability Problem Finding in Cross-Cultural Thinking Aloud Usability Testing. In: Proceedings of CHI, Florence, Italy (2008)
11. Trillo, N.: The Cultural Component of Designing and Evaluating International User Interfaces. In: Proceedings of the 32nd Hawaii International Conference on System Sciences (1999)
12. Vatrapu, R., Pĕrez-Quiñones, M.A.: Culture and Usability Evaluation. The Effects of Culture in Structured Interviews. Journal of Usability Studies 1, 156–170 (2006)
13. Winschiers, H.: Dialogical System Design across Cultural Boundaries. PhD thesis, Fachbereich Informatik, Universitaet Hamburg (2001)
14. Winschiers, H., Paterson, B.: Sustainable Software Development. In: Proceedings of SAICSIT 2004, pp. 111–113. ACM Press, New York (2004)
15. Winschiers, H., Fendler, J.: Assumptions considered Harmful: The need to redefine usability. In: Aykin, N. (ed.) HCII 2007. LNCS, vol. 4559, pp. 452–461. Springer, Heidelberg (2007)
16. Winschiers-Theophilus, H.: Cultural Appropriation of Software Design and Evaluation. In: Whitworth, B., de Moor, A. (eds.) Handbook of Research on Socio-technical Design and Social Networking Systems (2009) ISBN: 978-1-60566-264-0
17. Young, P.: Integrating Culture in the Design of ICTs. British Journal of Educational Technology 39(1) (2008)

HCI Standards for Handicapped

Zbigniew Wisniewski and Aleksandra Polak-Sopinska

Department of Production Management, Technical University of Lodz,
ul. Wolczanska 215, 90-924 Lodz, Poland
{zwisniewski,olapolak}@p.lodz.pl

Abstract. The study presents conclusions from the project realization so far. The main aim of the project is to work out the rules of evaluation and validation of application interfaces on the basis of study of the process of man-computer communication. The target group for the benefit of which the research will be carried out are disabled persons and people over 55 years of age. The disabled and the elderly, are in the social stratum systematically ignored by software producers and internet service providers as a target group of computer users.

Keywords: HCI, elderly, disabled people, digital divide.

1 Introduction

The term digital divide refers to a rapidly extending gap between Internet users and non-users. According to research about 40% of Europeans does not use the Internet in their daily life. There are a variety of reasons, including lack of funds, limited availability of the network, insufficient computer literacy. Less than 12% of people over 65 use the Internet, which is associated with the fact that only 3% of the websites meets the accessibility standards. The issue of no accessibility in the first place refers to people with various dysfunctions of the organ of sight. In most cases website designers are not aware of the difficulties the blind and sand-blind people encounter when trying to use the Internet.

The ageing process has become so common in many countries that it is reflected in virtual world as well, since older people constitute an increasing number of Internet users. The popularity of life-long learning is growing, too. Many older people want to learn new things and acquire new skills, develop themselves and fully participate in everyday life at the same time fighting with weaknesses.

The above tendency results in implementation of Internet usage facilities aimed at older and disabled people. In European Union countries approximately 10-15 % of the whole population is disabled people with various types of dysfunctions. The report published by the United Nations Organizations shows that in 2050 almost two billion people will be over 60, whereas nowadays the number of people over 60 does not exceed 800 million. The Internet is a great opportunity for the disabled and the elderly, who cannot be fully active due to some limitations. Internet access facilitates independence, contact with other people, the ability to do some everyday activities unassisted.

C. Stephanidis (Ed.): Universal Access in HCI, Part I, HCII 2009, LNCS 5614, pp. 672–676, 2009.
© Springer-Verlag Berlin Heidelberg 2009

All efforts notwithstanding, older and disabled people still encounter a number of barriers. These are mainly due to some technical restrictions of designed websites and applications. In this case the significance of accessibility is undeniable. Applications and websites designed in accordance with accessibility principles enable their easy and friendly use by the disabled.

2 Standards

W3C (World Wide Web Consortium) – international consortium with more than 400 members representing some of the biggest and most renowned companies, institutions, organizations and universities from all over the world. The goal of W3C is to create Web standards. W3C recommendations are the guidance for the whole civilized world.

Since 1997 W3C has been running an activity called Web Accessibility Initiative (WAI), embracing a group of people and organizations engaged in development and promotion of Internet (mainly website) accessibility standards aimed at disabled people. Among the participants of this initiative there are such organizations as IBM, Microsoft, Bell Atlantic, Lotus Development Corporation, the government of Canada, National Institute on Disability and Rehabilitation Research at the American Department of Education and European Union representatives. WAI has created the following sets of guidelines.

Authoring Tool Accessibility Guidelines – a set of guidelines for authors designing Web content. In order to enable disabled people to use the Internet to its full potential it is essential to help them publish their own materials. Thus software for creating websites should provide facilities for the disabled. The updated version of the guidelines is currently being prepared.

- User Agent Accessibility Guidelines – guidelines on designing web browsers that satisfy the requirements of people with disabilities.
- XML Accessibility Guidelines. XML is a standard devised by W3C, which focuses on storage of all types of data. Due to its expansible nature it is necessary that authors of new languages based on XML do not impede accessibility.
- Web Content Accessibility Guidelines (WCAG) – guidelines on designing websites that satisfy the requirements of people with disabilities. Since 1999 WCAG 1.0 has been the official W3C recommendation. Currently the second updated version of this standard is being prepared. WCAG guidelines have become the basis for accessibility regulatory requirements for many European Union members and other countries. Given the above, it is worth taking a closer look at the guidelines. The main goals of WCAG include: providing access to Web content to users of various devices (text and graphic web browsers, voice browsers, portable devices), logic and readable content organization as well as clear and convenient navigation.

3 Research and Findings

The scope of research included identification of groups of users who have difficulties with the Internet due to the fact that the interfaces are not adjusted to their specific needs. These people are able to use peripheral devices (keyboard, mouse, and monitor):

- people with motor disabilities:

  - upper limb dysfunctions restricting the ability to use mouse and keyboard,
  - problems with long-term remaining in sitting position,

- people with ADHD,
- people with moderate mental disability,
- people with moderate impairment of the organ of sight,
- people with defective perception of colours,
- people with epilepsy,
- people with dyslexia,
- older people (55+),

The research on Web accessibility, functionality and usability is carried out by means of special applications. The first application is aimed at testing and identifying the needs of users with specific perceptual-motor dysfunctions. The application is based on the following pattern:

- generating a website with features required by the program in order to have composition tested by the users,
- gathering results in the data base,
- statistic processing,
- reporting.

The research is carried out among organizations grouping older people willing to use the Internet: universities of the Third Age, senior clubs, etc.

The second application is used for a wide-sample research and is made up of the following stages:

1. Gathering user information,
2. Gathering web browser information,
3. Gathering website content information:

   - HTML (controls and their parameters, other elements and their parameters - colour, typography),
   - Text statistics,
   - Picture analysis– colour, text contrast, text size, detection and analysis of composition of typical website elements),

4. Sending report to the data base.

This application has the form of a FireFox browser plug-in. It concentrates on gathering data on user activity and their opinion of visited websites. The data refer to how users deal with a website and what operations they perform. During these observations the ability to perform particular operations is being assessed (the number of repetitions, the number of failed operations, and the time spent on particular operations, etc.) Moreover, the users are occasionally asked to express their opinion and provide some information, including their disability, if applicable.

Both tools enable better identification of the special needs disabled people have when using the Internet. The first application helps recognize perceptual-motor abilities of the focus group. The second application is used to verify the results of the first one as well as to extent the scope of exploration. In the first case the application generates assigned patterns in the form of interfaces and the participants are aware of the test, whereas in the second case the research is carried out on real websites. Due to the fact that it is performed via a browser plug-in the participants are not 'tempted' to show off and behave more naturally and at ease than in the first case.

This last research provides some interesting findings on websites most frequently visited by people with dysfunctions. The users are able to select an area in the Net where they want to be active and simply perform typical activities. The findings provide some noteworthy information on Internet activity of various users and their perceptual-motor abilities. However, the final conclusions can be presented only after the research completion, bound next year.

For the time being the available conclusions seem to be in accordance with Web content creation guidelines published by the mentioned organizations. The guidelines are as follows:

1. sound and visual elements should have their alternative equivalents,
2. colour should not be the only means of distinguishing information,
3. technologies defining structure and presentation should be used,
4. language used in a website or its fragments should be constrained, which is absolutely necessary for proper functioning of screen readers,
5. tables describing website structure should be avoided, tables should only be used for comparisons or summaries, moreover they should be properly named so that screen readers are able to present their content to the users,
6. website content should be available to users not possessing the latest technology, e.g. script languages, plug-ins,
7. it should be possible to switch off or stop the animation (which is crucial for users suffering from epilepsy), animated elements should be avoided where possible,
8. objects located in the website structure (e.g. applets, scripts, etc.) should have interface available for a variety of manipulators (e.g. mouse, keyboard, etc.),
9. new technology implementation should be accompanied by temporary solutions to enable access to all users,
10. elements facilitating structure orientation (e.g. labels, summaries, etc.) should be used,
11. navigation should be consistent and clear, which assures good orientation in the website structure,
12. documents should be readable, clear and written in a simple language.

The most common errors of website designers include the tendency to use Flash and technology and DHTML elements much more than it is necessary. Obviously these technologies help create an attractive website; however, their excessive use leads to lowered accessibility for disabled people.

The most serious error of Web content authors is non conformity of the source code with the guidelines published by such organizations as World Wide Web Consortium or The Unicode Consortium.

The core principle of useful and accessible website designing is to follow the standards of competent organizations (e.g. W3C). Conforming to and following the standards maximizes accessibility of all websites for disabled people. This aspect of Web content design is particularly significant in case of e-learning platforms, websites of national organizations or banks.

References

1. Laurel, B.: The art of human-computer interface design. Addison-Wesley, Reading (1990)
2. Landauer, T.K.: The trouble with computers: Usefulness, usability, and productivity. MIT Press, Cambridge (1995)
3. Mullet, K., Sano, D.: Designing visual interfaces: Communication oriented techniques. Sunsoft Press/Prentice Hall, Englewood Cliffs (1995)
4. Raskin, J.: The humane interface: New directions for designing interactive systems. Addison-Wesley, Reading (2000)
5. Wiśniewski, Z.: Ergotronics – object, composition, message, transfer. In: Pacholski, L.M., Trzcieliński, S. (eds.) Ergonomics in contemporary enterprise. IEA Press Madison, Poznań (2007)

User Evaluation of Age-Centred Web Design Guidelines

Panayiotis Zaphiris[1], Ulrike Pfeil[2], and Dorian Xhixho[2]

[1] Department of Multimedia & Graphic Arts, Cyprus University of Technology
pzaphiri@gmail.com
[2] Centre for HCI Design, City University London
{zaphiri,U.Pfeil-1,d.xhixho}@soi.city.ac.uk

Abstract. We report an evaluation of a set of age-centred web design guidelines (SilverWeb guidelines) with older web users. We invited 24 older web users and used a cooperative evaluation to validate the guidelines and collect any additional problems. As a result of the experiment, 36 out of the original 37 guidelines were accepted, 1 guideline was disagreed with, and 5 new issues that were not covered by the guidelines were identified by users. Our findings show that input from users is a valuable contribution to the development process of web design guidelines and is essential in order to ensure a user-centred design approach.

Keywords: Ageing, guidelines, web, user evaluation.

1 Introduction

As the number of older internet users is increasing, it is important that web designers adopt age-centred guidelines in developing websites for universal access. Many guidelines are available for web developers to follow (e.g. [19]), but severe usability and accessibility problems are still commonly found on websites [3]. This shows that there is still much work to do, both in developing accessibility guidelines that capture the needs of the user population more accurately and in raising awareness for accessibility on the side of web developers.

There are many issues which designers should consider carefully when using web design guidelines. According to Nicolle and Abascal [10], using guidelines is fairly difficult and working with them is not an easy matter. They can be ambiguous, contradictory or only partially true. They are not always clear and can have many interpretations. Thus, there is a need for a systematic and careful process in developing and validating such web design guidelines.

Most of the existing sets of web design guidelines that address the needs of older people are derived from literature reviews or are rules of thumb based on experience. But are these age-centred web design guidelines in line with the preferences of the users? Do they cover all their needs and do users actually agree with them? How can we improve existing accessibility guidelines in a way that they capture more accurately the users' needs and preferences?

In order to address these questions, we evaluated the SilverWeb guidelines [20], a set of age-centred web design guidelines, with older web users. As reported elsewhere [20], the development process of the SilverWeb guidelines includes a review of gerontology and HCI literature, expert evaluations, and comparisons with other existing

C. Stephanidis (Ed.): Universal Access in HCI, Part I, HCII 2009, LNCS 5614, pp. 677–686, 2009.

age-centred web design guidelines. We believe that an evaluation of this set of guidelines with users will give us insight into the level of acceptance of the SilverWeb guidelines and will show whether the guidelines cover the needs and preferences of the users accurately and sufficiently. We break this aim down into the following objectives:

- For each guideline, evaluate whether it is accepted by the users.
- For each guideline, assess its importance as rated by the users.
- Investigate whether the set of guidelines is complete or whether there are important issues that are not yet covered by the guidelines.

Firstly, we will give some background information about the limitations that come with age and their impact on web usage. We will then give an overview over inclusive design guidelines, in which we will also elaborate on the development process of the SilverWeb guidelines so far. Furthermore, the methods section will describe the procedure that we followed in order to evaluate the SilverWeb guidelines with older people. The results will be stated in the results section and interpreted in the discussion section. We summarize our findings and give suggestions for practitioners and researchers in the conclusion section.

2   Background Information

2.1   Older People and the Web

According to the Office for National Statistics [14], the population aged 65 and older in the UK has increased from 7.4 (in 1971) to 9.5 million (in 2004) and is estimated to increase to 15.3 million in 2031. The statistics also reveal that the 'oldest old', people aged 85 and older are the fastest growing group in Britain, with their numbers increasing by 84 per cent between 1984 and 2004, to over 1.1 million [14]. Hayslip and Panek [8] state that more people will be reaching their seventies and eighties, because of an improved healthcare, better nutrition, lower mortality associated with serious illness, and perhaps an increased awareness of taking care of one's health.

In addition, more and more older people are accessing the internet. According to the Guardian [7], the Forrester Research's Consumer Technographics survey of 2004 indicated that there are 20.7 million internet users in Europe who are over 55, and 25% of European seniors go online. A 2004 Pew Internet and American Life Project study found that the percentage of American seniors who went online between 2000 and 2004 had increased by 47% [15].

There are many reasons why older people are drawn to the internet and persist in using it. SeniorNet surveyed 2,084 people in the US aged 50 and older and determined that 94 per cent of older people use the internet to communicate with friends and family, followed by browsing news, searching for health information, online shopping, playing games, etc [16]. Older people are also very interested in tracing back their family history. Over 55's are four times more likely to visit ancestry and genealogy sites than the average internet users [1].

The challenge of designing websites for the older population is in thinking about how to accommodate for limitations that older people are likely to experience.

Hayslip and Panek [8] highlight that vision, including sensitivity to glare, depth perception, and colour and flicker sensitivity, start to decline in the late 50's and early 60's. Tinker [18] shows evidence of greater incidence of both acute and chronic health conditions among older people. Dooghe [5] argues that at old age, the perceptual functions gradually regress, which is manifested in hearing impairments, visual effects and deterioration of speech.

Hayslip and Panek [8] argue that ageing is affected by many biological, psychological, social, and cultural factors. Hence, not all older people suffer from impairments or are necessarily disabled. For that reason, when it comes to older people interacting with the web, it is often not an individual functional impairment that leads to a noticeable difference in their user experience. However, if all limitations are taken together, they may have a cumulative effect that makes Web interaction more difficult for older people. In one of his studies, Nielsen [11] concluded that websites are twice as hard to use for seniors as they are for non-seniors.

It is very positive news that there has been a shift in attitude in recent years, away from treating older people as special cases requiring special solutions towards integrating them in the mainstream of everyday life through an inclusive design approach [4]. Nevertheless, unless the internet is designed for universal access, older people may struggle to keep up, or at worse they might give up using the internet and feel alienated.

Even from governments, there is still much to be desired when it comes to improving internet access for older people. A report released by UK EU presidency in 2005 pointed out that the vast majority of public service websites in Europe are failing to meet international e-accessibility standards. The report shows that only a mere 3 per cent of the EU public service websites comply with the minimum accessibility requirements of the World Wide Web Consortium (W3C) guidelines [19].

2.2 Inclusive Design Guidelines

Inclusive design, also known as universal design or design for all is about designing products or services to be accessible to as many people as possible. In order to be inclusive for most people, products, systems, and environments need to be accessible especially to older and disabled people. Colman [4] argues that the unprecedented growing number of older people is challenging common assumptions about the way products and services should be designed, if they are to meet the needs of the majority.

The mismatch between the designed world and the changed capabilities of older people has a significant impact on their independence. Nicolle and Abascal [10] supports this, by stressing that older people may lag behind the advances in information and communication technology, unless technologies are designed with their functional impairments and requirements in mind.

One of the cheap and effective ways that designers and developers use in order to match the design of their products with users' needs is through the use of design guidelines. In the context of HCI, Dumas and Redish [6] describe guidelines as specific goals that HCI specialists and designers distil from the design principles for different users, environments, and technologies. According to Nicolle and Abascal [10], inclusive design guidelines are simplifications that must be general enough to be applicable to a wide range of products and services, usually drawn from best available practice. Inclusive design guidelines are expected to make the design process easier and to help maintain coherence with previously taken decisions.

Nicolle and Abascal [10] further argue that the use of inclusive design guidelines contributes not only towards an inclusive design philosophy leading to more usable systems for all, but also facilitates the storage of knowledge and transmission of successful experiences among designers. In assessing the longevity of a 1986 usability report, Nielsen [13] concluded that its guidelines endured the time and the majority of them were still found to be valid, because they depend on human behaviour, which changes very slowly.

2.3 SilverWeb Guidelines

The SilverWeb guidelines were initially based on a literature review of over 100 peer-reviewed papers from the area of Human-Computer Interaction, web design and ageing. Out of the reviewed papers, an initial set of 52 guidelines was extracted, and the results of this process were reported in a CHI 2005 paper and an ASSETS 2005 paper [9], [21]. Card sorting was then applied in order to improve their categorisation, and a Focus Group with HCI experts reviewed the guidelines to further improve them. This process resulted in a new smaller set of 38 guidelines that were sorted into 11 categories. The results of this part of the work are reported in a UAIS Journal paper [20]. In order to validate the new smaller set of guidelines, a Heuristic Evaluation was performed with both sets of guidelines and the guidelines were then evaluated in a controlled experiment with 16 older web users.

The SilverWeb guidelines were then compared to seven other sets of web design guidelines for older and/or disabled people. Discrepancies between the set of guidelines were identified, and a Focus Group was conducted in order to discuss changes to the existing guidelines. This process resulted in a revised set of 37 SilverWeb guidelines.

The aim of the work reported in this paper was to further validate the success and acceptance of this final set of the SilverWeb design guidelines (also listed in Table 1) with older web users and to identify any remaining usability problems not surfaced so far. We believe that a complete and user-centred methodology in the development of the SilverWeb guidelines is necessary to ensure clarity and accuracy of the guidelines. After a literature review, expert evaluations, an experiment with users, and comparisons with other guidelines, we think that a final evaluation of the guidelines with older web users completes the development cycle of the SilverWeb guidelines. Furthermore, the inclusion of users in the guideline development might lead to an easier acceptance and increased use of them by web developers.

3 Methods

The study was conducted in the form of a cooperative evaluation with 24 older web users who helped us validate the acceptance of the SilverWeb guidelines and identify any additional problems. The result comprised the accepted guidelines, disagreed guidelines and new problems identified from user feedback. The following sections outline the procedure that we followed.

Before each session, we had an informal chat with the users, introducing them briefly to past research and the procedure we intended to follow. Right after the briefing, the users were asked to sign a consent form. The evaluation was run with one user at a time and lasted between one and two hours per user.

A simple and easy to use website was developed in HTML, where each guideline was allocated a page with a good and a bad example. The number of guidelines was 37, which meant that at least 74 examples had to be developed, a pair for each guideline. Some of the examples would point to a particular website, whereas some others were built onto the page itself.

A pre-evaluation questionnaire was designed to collect background information about the participants, concerning their age, information about any experienced impairments, and about their experience, training and skill level in using computers, and especially the internet. We were also interested in the activities of the participants on the internet: what they use the internet mostly for, their likes and dislikes about the internet, and how simple and easy to use the internet was considered by them.

The guidelines were evaluated with the help of the prepared examples, which were used to "visualise" each guideline and probe reactions from the participants.

The evaluator first read the description of each guideline, explained it briefly to the user and then presented the user with a good and a bad example, which best conveyed that guideline. The evaluation was a continuous dialogue between the evaluator and the user, as the guidelines were presented to the user one by one.

The user had the option to agree or disagree with the necessity of the guideline, give a rating from 1 to 5, where 1 meant "not at all important" and 5 meant "very important". Furthermore, the user was encouraged to comment on agreement or disagreement with each guideline and suggest any additional problems.

During the dialogue with the user, the evaluator prompted the user to elicit reasons for his/her judgements. Right after each evaluation, the evaluator went through the recorded protocol to check for any discrepancies with the notes taken. This was necessary to make sure that no comments were missed.

The post-evaluation questionnaire was filled out right after the evaluation. It was designed to collect information mainly about any additional problems or issues not mentioned during the evaluation. This information was useful during the analysis of results in identifying any additional guidelines, as that was one of the objectives of this study. The debriefing with users took place after they filled out of the post-evaluation questionnaire. It was not recorded. The interviewer gave participants the opportunity to speak out freely and "off the record" about their experience and gave the opportunity for the users to add any additional comments or problems that they encountered during the evaluation. The whole process was facilitated in a way to make sure that the users understood and felt that their contributions were highly valued and useful to us.

4 Results

The average age of participant was 66.3 years, with the youngest participant being 58 years old and the oldest one being 79 years old. Among the users, 42% (10 participants) were male and 58% (14 participants) were female. Only 12% of the participants said that they had problems using the web due to vision and/or hearing problems.

On average, participants were using the computers for 6.4 years (range between 1 month and 25 years) and were using the internet for 2.1 years (range 1 month to 10 years). Most people ranked themselves being either a novice or competent with using computers (38% novice, 42% competent), with only few of them reporting being advanced or even an expert. Concerning internet usage, less people ranked themselves as novice (25%) and more as competent (63%), but again, very few thought that their skills were advanced or expert. All participants reported using the computer and the internet at least once a week, with the average number of days being 2.7 for computer usage and 2.3 for internet usage. 71% of the participants stated that they were trained in using the internet, and their activities included searching the internet for information about their hobbies, writing emails, online shopping, and even designing their own website.

When asked about the perceived usability of websites, the majority of users (92%) found the Web to be fairly easy, easy, or very easy to use, only 8% finding it difficult. None of the users found using the internet very difficult. 33% reported that they come across websites that are not easy to use either often or very often. The majority of people said that this happened to them occasionally (34%), with 33% of the people reporting it to happen rarely or not at all.

When asked whether the Web should be more accessible to the elderly, all participants agreed that the internet should indeed be more accessible to older people. When asked to rate the importance of it being accessible, on a scale of 1 (not important) and 5 (very important), the average rating was 4.54. The last two questions of the pre-evaluation questionnaire were about users' experiences with the internet. Users were asked to list three things they least and most liked about the internet. After removing any duplicates, the following issues were mentioned:

What are three things you least like about the Web?: Small illegible text, pop up windows, animations, confusing navigation, outdated information, junk mail, complication, repetition, bad background, cluttered information, scrolling text, ambiguity, useless help, jargon, broken links.

What are three things you most like about the web?: Search engine, email, news, learning, online booking, lots of choice, information all in one place, research, convenience, blogging, access to music, socialising, freedom of speech, games, keeps company, publish information.

Overall, our evaluation showed that the SilverWeb guidelines were accepted and rated highly by older internet users. According to the findings, 36 of the original 37 guidelines were accepted by all our participants, 1 guideline was rejected by one participant and 5 new user problems were identified. The guidelines were rated from 1 to 5, the lowest rating being 4.50, the highest 5.00 and the average 4.84.

All participants reported that they found the evaluation interesting and the tasks and examples easy to understand. When asked if they could think of any other issues or problems not covered by the guidelines, 5 additional issues were mentioned:

- Websites should warn users to take breaks if staying in front of them for a prolonged time.
- Text input should be saved regularly to assist users with mistakes.
- Websites should all have a print button on each page.

- A sorting filter should exist in displaying results, when searching by keywords.
- Websites should all have an option of translating the content into English.

The last question of the post-evaluation questionnaire was whether users thought that the guidelines developed will help older people in the future to have better access to the Web. 96% thought it will definitely help, whereas 4% thought that that "might" be the case.

5 Discussion

The main objective of this report was to validate the SilverWeb guidelines with users. We investigated whether the developed guidelines were accepted by older internet users, and to what extent. Since the number of the developed guidelines was relatively large and many guidelines received equal ratings, we decided to examine in detail the guidelines that received the two highest and lowest ratings.

The guideline with the highest rating of 5.0 was guideline number 15 "Avoid information overload on the screen, e.g. introduction paragraphs should be relevant and short". Berners-Lee [2] and Nielsen [11] argue that people browse websites for their content. They wish to get to it quickly and easily. After users were shown the bad example of this guideline, their comments about it were that, when the information is literally "dumped" on the screen with no spaces or introduction paragraphs, it is difficult to understand and "decipher" it. The rating of this guideline indicates that it is important for older web users that the information is presented to them in a clear and organised manner with not too much information at once. Texts should be divided into paragraphs that make it easy for the user to get a first overview over the structure and content. As Brink et al. [3] advocate, non-functional graphics and other interface elements can skew a user's perception of usability.

The next second highest rating was 4.96, which was given to the guidelines: 7 "Clear navigation should be provided that matches the user's mental model", 14 "Language should be simple, clear and consistent, using the active voice", 17 "Information should be concentrated mainly in the centre", and 32 "Choose typefaces and fonts by their familiarity, advisably use san serif type font i.e. Helvetica, Arial of 12-14 point size. Drop shadows on text".

Guideline 7 "Clear navigation should be provided that matches the user's mental model": In order to get to the information, users have to go through the navigation of a website, which to users can either be a helping hand or a time wasting maze and strain. One of the users considered navigation as the main aspect of his web experience. He admitted that in several occasions, although he knew that particular websites held the information he was looking for, he could not access it, because of their confusing navigation. This finding shows that navigation is a key element in accessibility of websites for older people and should be taken seriously by web designers. As the high rating of this guideline shows, a confusing navigation structure can seriously restrain older internet users from accessing a website.

Guideline 14 "Language should be simple, clear and consistent, using the active voice": The language has to be inclusive, simple and clear to follow. The bad example of this guideline was commented from users to be confusing, irritating and unhelpful.

Again, users wanted the information and content of a website as easy and clear as possible. One of the users suggested an additional guideline, which was based on the language. She suggested that all websites should have an option of translating their content into English, so that it is accessible to a wider audience.

Guideline 17 "Information should be concentrated mainly in the centre": This guideline was rated to be very important and the information was commented to be easier to read and less time consuming to find if placed at the centre of the page. A lot of websites put the content in the centre of the page with the navigation and sometimes advertisements placed around it. This strengthens users' expectations that the main content is placed in the centre of the page. Content that is placed at the border of the page is therefore often overlooked.

Guideline 32 "Choose typefaces and fonts by their familiarity, advisably use san serif type font i.e. Helvetica, Arial of 12-14 point size. Drop shadows on text": As vision deteriorates with age, larger font is more visible and easier to read for older users. Furthermore, a clear font style adds to an effortless reading experience. All of the users found a large font size more readable. Even users who argued that their vision was fine, and they were able to read small fonts preferred a large font size as it made reading the text easier for them.

The lowest rated guideline was number 10 "Avoid pull down menus" (rating: 4.50). Many users did not mind the pull down menus. Some did not think that pull down menus made the navigation difficult, while others even enjoyed them. One user said that they help in grouping the information all in one place. The results showed that 20% of users rated this guideline 3 out of 5, 8% at 4 out of 5 and 72% at 5 out of 5. Users seemed to prefer alphabetic lists to drop down menus, since it helped them scan through menu options easily.

The second lowest rated guideline was number 19 "There should be differentiation between visited and unvisited links", at 4.67 out of 5. The majority of users rated this guideline relatively high and recognised that it was very helpful in distinguishing between visited and unvisited links. However, some users indicated that sometimes the change of colour was not clear enough to distinguish between the links. Although raised by a small number of users, these comments point out that web designers should be careful in colour selection of links.

A number of users had concerns regarding some of the guidelines. One user disagreed with guideline number 11 "Do not have a deep hierarchy; avoid this by grouping information into meaningful categories". He argued that information is easier to find in deep hierarchies, and believed that the more horizontally spread the information is, the less precise the categorisation is likely to be.

On the other hand, the deeper the hierarchy, the more difficult it is for an older internet user to select the information. 17% of users participating in the evaluation suffered from different disabilities, one of which was arthritis. A deep hierarchy would prove to be an unnecessary difficult challenge for this user group. Looking at the ratings of this guideline by the rest of our users, it can be seen that most of them rated this guideline as quite important. 8% of the participants rated it 4 out of 5 and 88% rated it at 5 out of 5. Although disagreed by one user, since the overwhelming majority agreed with this guideline, it can safely be considered as accepted.

6   Conclusions

Our study showed that the inclusion of older people in the development and evaluation of age-centred web design guidelines is crucial in order to ensure that the guidelines are in line with users' needs and preferences.

Although the SilverWeb guidelines were generally rated high by our evaluation participants, additional problematic issues that were not covered by the guidelines were identified. This shows that guidelines need to constantly be evaluated and revised according to current user needs.

The results of this study should be looked in combination with the previous stages of our systematic approach in developing the SilverWeb guidelines. Overall our previous papers [9], [20], [21] together with this reported study provide a complete approach and methodology for user-centred development of design guidelines for older people. We believe that such an approach achieves better accuracy and clarity of the guidelines and leads to an easier acceptance and use of them by web developers.

The SilverWeb guidelines and the results of our evaluation can serve as a basis for future research. Investigations need to be conducted in order to validate, improve, and refine the guidelines and to bring them in line with user needs and preferences. The additional guidelines generated from this study need to be analysed in more detail in order to generalise and validate them with a larger user population. Furthermore, the SilverWeb guidelines can be fed into analysis tools, which check the compliance of websites with accessibility guidelines.

We encourage researchers to apply our approach of guideline evaluations with the user population to accessibility guidelines that focus on other user populations. We believe that the inclusion of the user in the development and evaluation of web design guidelines is a crucial part to ensure the validity and usefulness of these guidelines.

References

1. BBC. Silver surfers taking to the net (2002),
   http://news.bbc.co.uk/1/hi/sci/tech/1899354.stm (accessed May 13, 2007)
2. BrainyQuote. Tim Berners-Lee quotes (2006),
   http://www.brainyquote.com/quotes/authors/t/
   tim_bernerslee.html (accessed May 13, 2007)
3. Brink, T., Gergle, D., Scott, W.: Usability for the web: designing websites that work. Morgan Kaufmann, San Fransisco (2006)
4. Coleman, R.: Inclusive design (2006),
   http://www.designcouncil.org.uk/inclusivedesign (accessed May 13, 2007)
5. Dooghe, G.: The ageing of the population in Europe: Socio-economic characteristics of the elderly population. Garant Publishers, Leuven (1992)
6. Dumas, J., Redish, J.: A practical guide to usability testing. Intellect. Exeter (1999)
7. Guardian Unlimited. On the crest of a wave (2004),
   http://technology.guardian.co.uk/online/story/
   0,3605,1353207,00.html (accessed May 13, 2007)

8. Hayslip, B., Panek, P.: Adult development and ageing. Harper & Row Publishers, New York (1989)
9. Kurniawan, S., Zaphiris, P.: Research-derived web design guidelines for older people. In: Proceedings of 7th International ACM SIGACCESS Conference on Computers and Accessibility (ASSETS 2005). ACM Press, Baltimore (2005)
10. Nicolle, C., Abascal, J.: Inclusive design guidelines for HCI. Taylor & Francis, London (2001)
11. Nielsen, J.: Designing Web Usability: The Practice of Simplicity. New Riders, Indianapolis (1999)
12. Nielsen, J.: Usability for Senior Citizens (2002),
http://www.useit.com/alertbox/20020428.html (accessed May 13, 2007)
13. Nielsen, J.: Durability of usability guidelines (2005),
http://www.useit.com/alertbox/20050117.html (accessed May 13, 2007)
14. ONS. Population trends 123 – Press release January 2006: Rise in proportion of over 85s living alone (2006),
http://www.statistics.gov.uk/pdfdir/pop0306.pdf (accessed May 13, 2007)
15. Pew. Older Americans and the Internet (2004),
http://www.pewinternet.org/pdfs/PIP_Seniors_Online_2004.pdf (accessed May 13, 2007)
16. Senior Journal. Seniors online increase (2003),
http://www.seniorjournal.com/NEWS/SeniorStats/ 3-02-04SnrsOnline.htm (accessed May 13, 2007)
17. The Register. Government Websites Fail to Meet Standards – Elderly, disabled, not being served (2005),
http://www.theregister.co.uk/2005/11/28/ electric_disabled/ (visited May 29, 2006)
18. Tinker, A.: Elderly people in modern society. Longman, New York (1992)
19. W3C. Web Content Accessibility Guidelines 1.0 (1999),
http://www.w3.org/TR/WAI-WEBCONTENT/ (accessed May 13, 2007)
20. Zaphiris, P., Kurniawan, S., Ghiawadwala, M.: A Systematic Approach to the Development of Research-Based Web Design Guidelines for Older People. Universal Access in the Information Society (2007)
21. Zaphiris, P., Ghiawadwala, M., Mughal, S.: Age-centered research-based web design guidelines. In: Proceedings of CHI 2005 Human Factors in Computing Systems. ACM Press, Portland (2005)

Author Index